THE ART OF

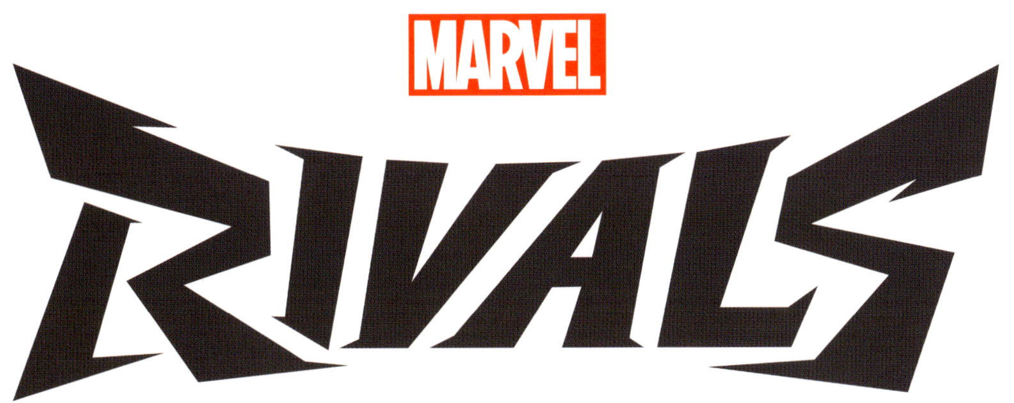

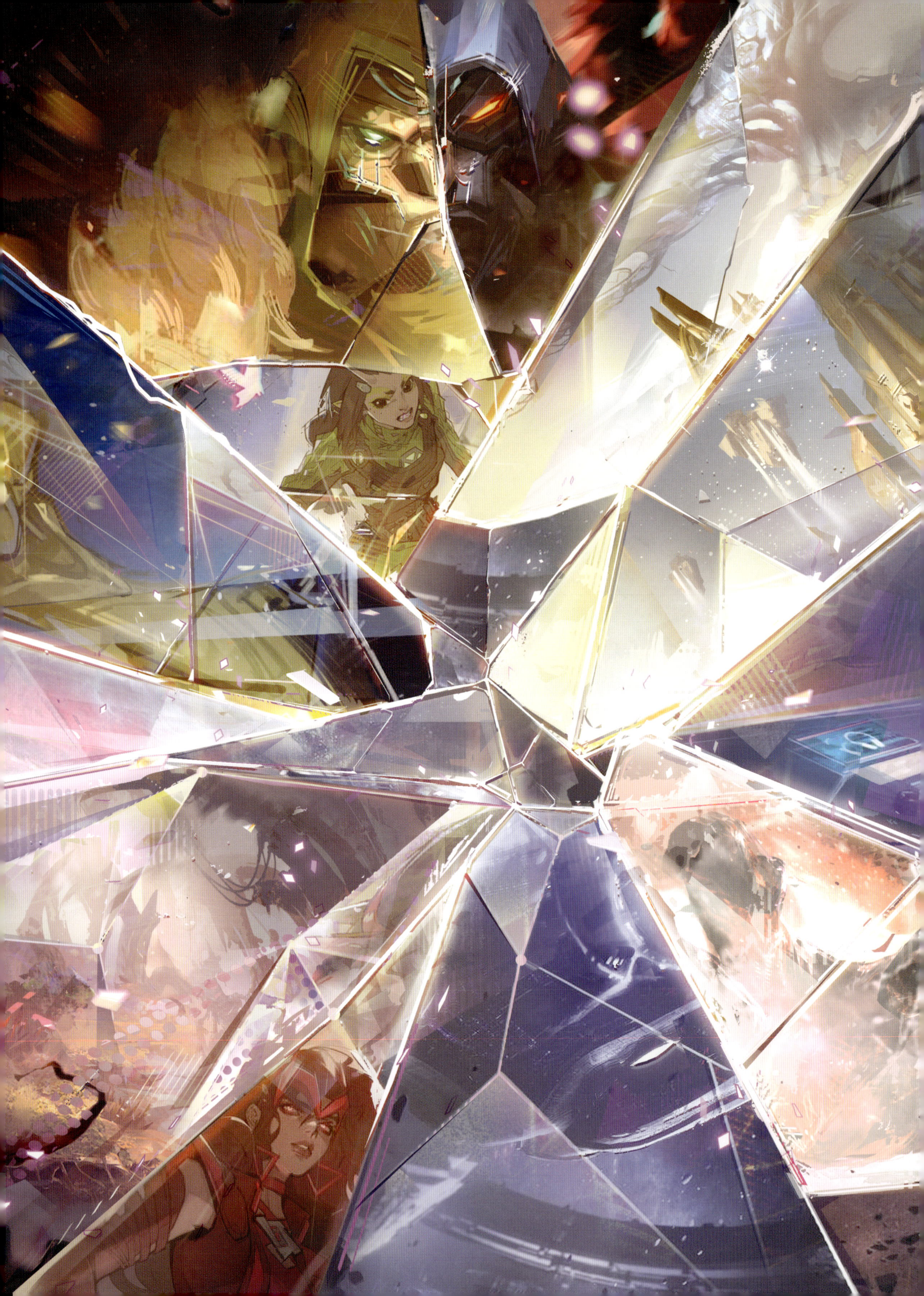

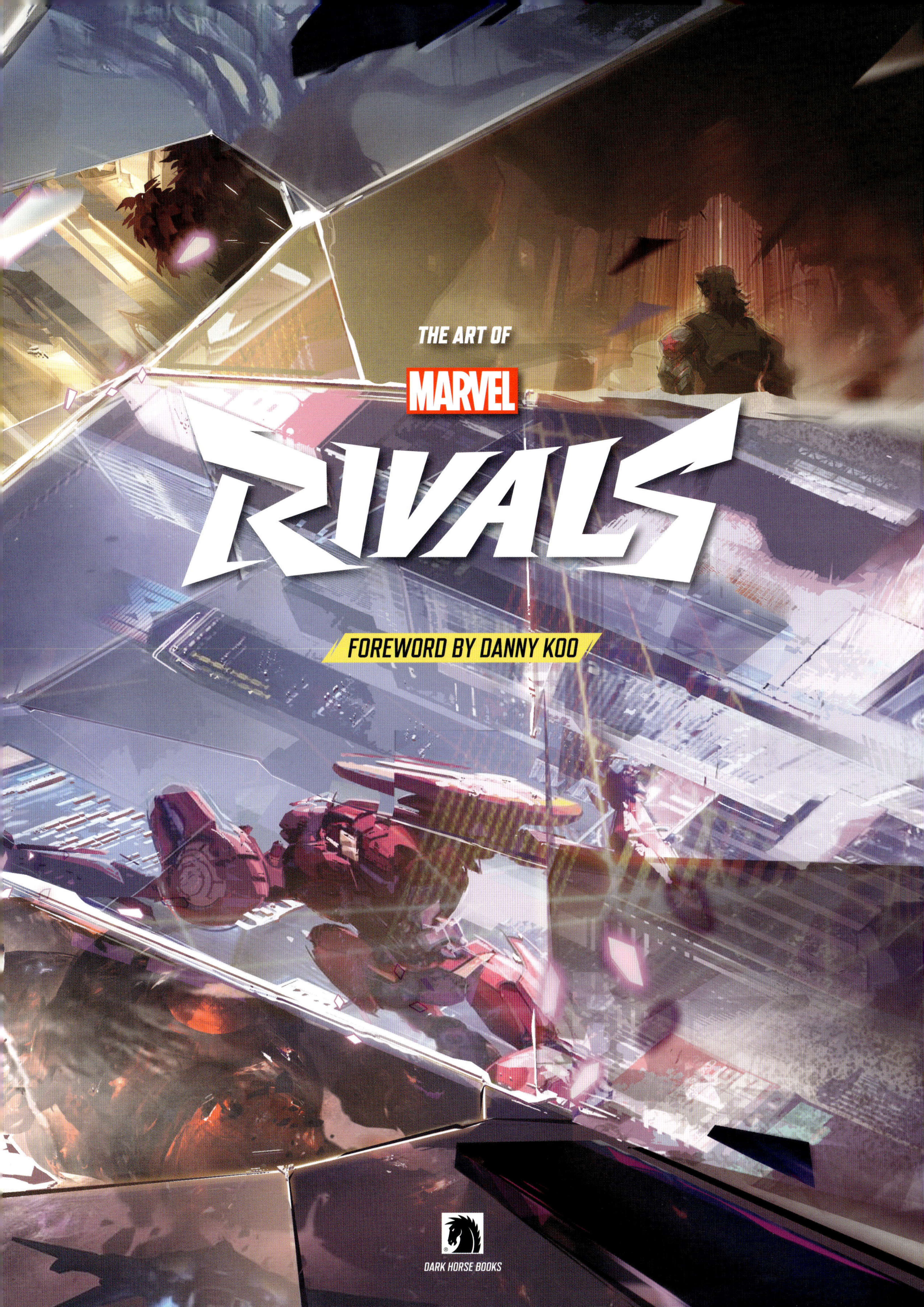
THE ART OF
MARVEL
RIVALS
FOREWORD BY DANNY KOO
DARK HORSE BOOKS

DARK HORSE BOOKS
President & Publisher
MIKE RICHARDSON
Editor
IAN TUCKER
Assistant Editor
JENNIFER WURTELE
Designers
SKYLER WEISSENFLUH
and **STEPHEN REICHERT**
Digital Art Technician
TYLER LI
Prepress Technician
RIKKI MIDNIGHT

MARVEL PUBLISHING
VP, Production and Special Projects
JEFF YOUNGQUIST
Editor, Special Projects
SARAH SINGER
Manager, Licensed Publishing
JEREMY WEST
VP, Licensed Publishing
SVEN LARSEN
VP, Print & Digital Publishing
DAVID GABRIEL
Editor in Chief
C. B. CEBULSKI

MARVEL GAMES
Head of Marvel Games
HALUK MENTEŞ
VP, Product & Creative
TIM HERNANDEZ
Executive Producer & Project Lead
DANNY KOO
Product Development Manager
DAMIAN PATRINOSTRO
Senior Art Director
DAN LaDUCA
Creative Development Manager
DAKOTA MAYSONET
Director of Business Development
CHRIS BAGGIO
Senior Manager, Portfolio Operations & Integrated Planning
AMANDA AVILA
Commercialization & Data Analytics Manager
DAVID BODINGER
VP & Creative Director
BILL ROSEMANN
Executive Director, Product & Creative
TIM TSANG

THE ART OF MARVEL RIVALS

Published by Dark Horse Books
A division of Dark Horse Comics LLC
10956 SE Main Street
Milwaukie, OR 97222
DarkHorse.com

Represented in the EU by
Authorised Rep Compliance Ltd.
Ground Floor, 71 Lower Baggot Street
Dublin, D02 P593, Ireland
ARCCompliance.com

First edition: September 2025
Ebook ISBN 978-1-50675-222-8
Hardcover ISBN 978-1-50674-657-9

10 9 8 7 6 5 4 3 2
Printed in China

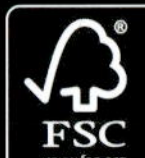

Names: Koo, Danny, author of foreword.
Title: The art of Marvel Rivals / foreword by Danny Koo.
Other titles: Marvel Rivals
Description: First edition. | Milwaukie, OR : Dark Horse Books, [2025]
Identifiers: LCCN 2024053357 (print) | LCCN 2024053358 (ebook) | ISBN 9781506746579 (hardcover) | ISBN 9781506752228 (ebook)
Subjects: LCSH: Marvel Rivals (Video game)--Pictorial works. | NetEase Games (Firm)--Pictorial works. | Video games--Design--Pictorial works. | Computer art--Pictorial works. | Computer drawing--Special effects--Pictorial works.
Classification: LCC GV1469.35.M365 A78 2025 (print) | LCC GV1469.35.M365 (ebook) | DDC 794.8/5--dc23/eng/20250208
LC record available at https://lccn.loc.gov/2024053357
LC ebook record available at https://lccn.loc.gov/2024053358

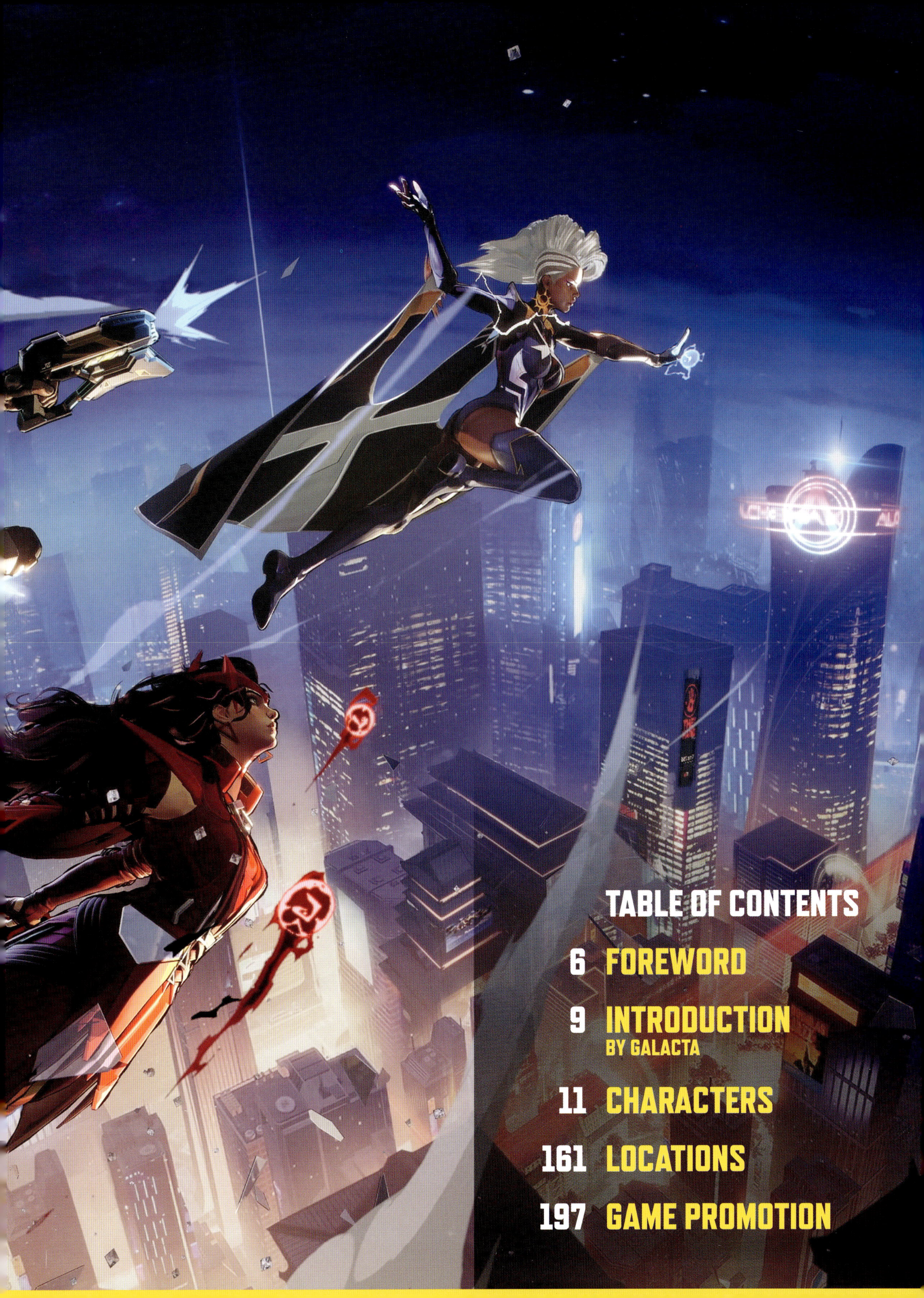

TABLE OF CONTENTS

FOREWORD

Hi Rivals,

First of all, I want to thank you for your interest in this art book! This book is a work of art in and of itself, featuring amazing pieces that we have carefully worked with Dark Horse to curate, highlighting the best artwork the *Marvel Rivals* team have to offer.

It has been a long journey for both the Marvel Games and the NetEase Games teams to finally deliver Marvel's first team-based 6v6 hero shooter game to the world. One of the many things that stood out in *Marvel Rivals* is the amazing art, and we are here to show you everything that went into this labor of love.

I would like to take this opportunity to thank Dino Ma (art director), Jinghua Duan (lead narrative designer), and the entire NetEase Games team for their unwavering push for artistic excellence. Through all these years of collaboration, they have continued to push the boundary in showcasing the best Marvel characters in the Marvel Universe. From the initial conception of the characters all the way to execution and seeing them animated and moving through environments that are living and breathing, this game signifies one of the biggest and most ambitious titles either of our teams has done to date. As you flip through the pages, you will see all the care and meticulous detail the team has put into the game. Narrative plays an important part in each aspect of the design, from storyboarding the trailers to key visuals of what the game is trying to communicate.

I would also like to thank our Marvel Games team, especially Dan LaDuca (senior art director) and Dakota Maysonet (creative development manager), my partners in crime, for ensuring that we put out the most amazing title possible. I also want to thank Damian Patrinostro (product development manager) for his constant behind-the-scenes coordination to allow the team to continue moving through the huge number of assets.

Both teams have great passion for the industry with amazing spirit to spare for the herculean effort of video game development. It is truly an honor to work side by side with everyone. The energetic, anime-inspired art adopts an "East meets West" design sensibility. Please enjoy this art book, and we look forward to creating more great *Marvel Rivals* content in the future.

Ignite the battle!

Danny Koo
Executive Producer
Marvel Games

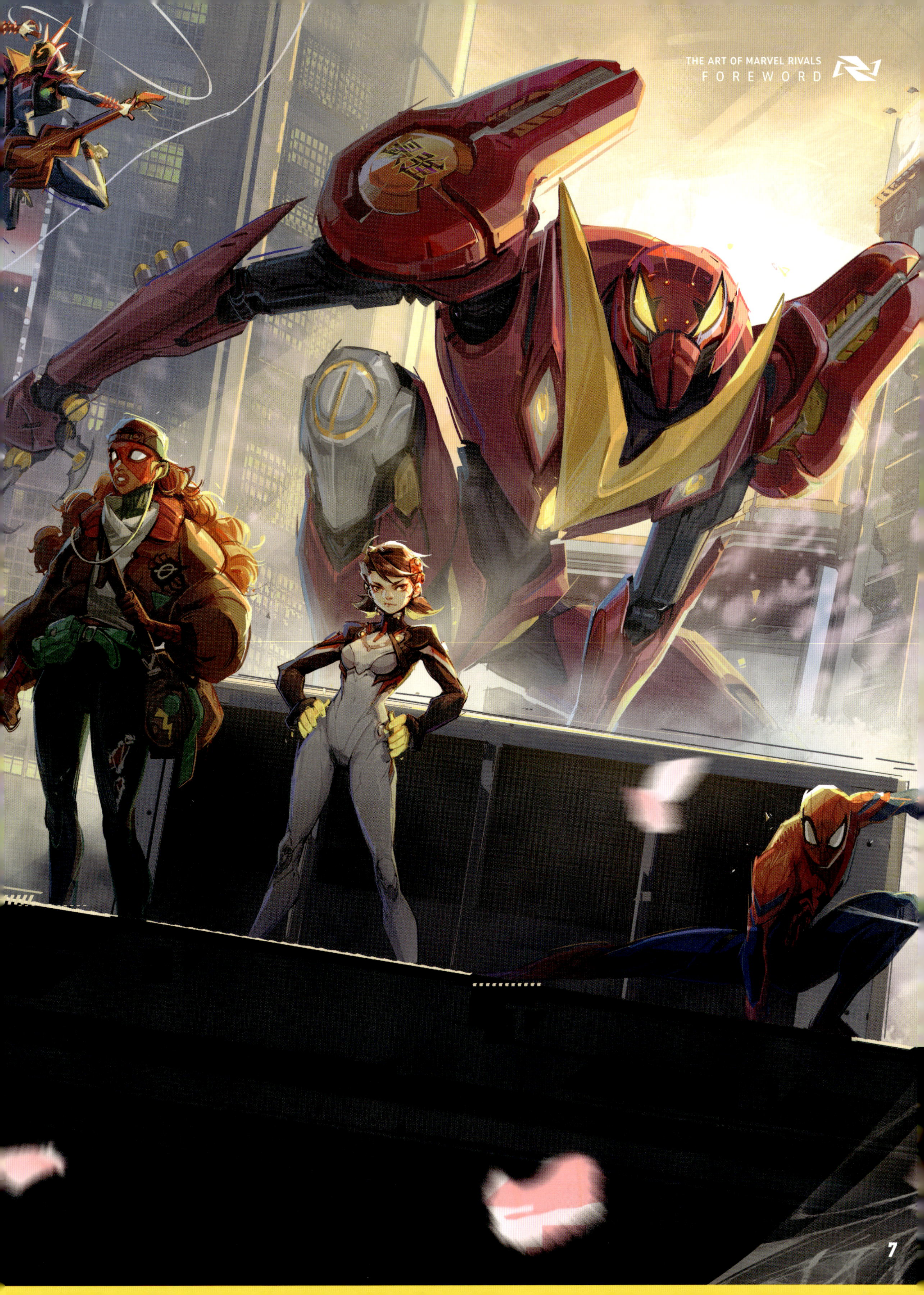

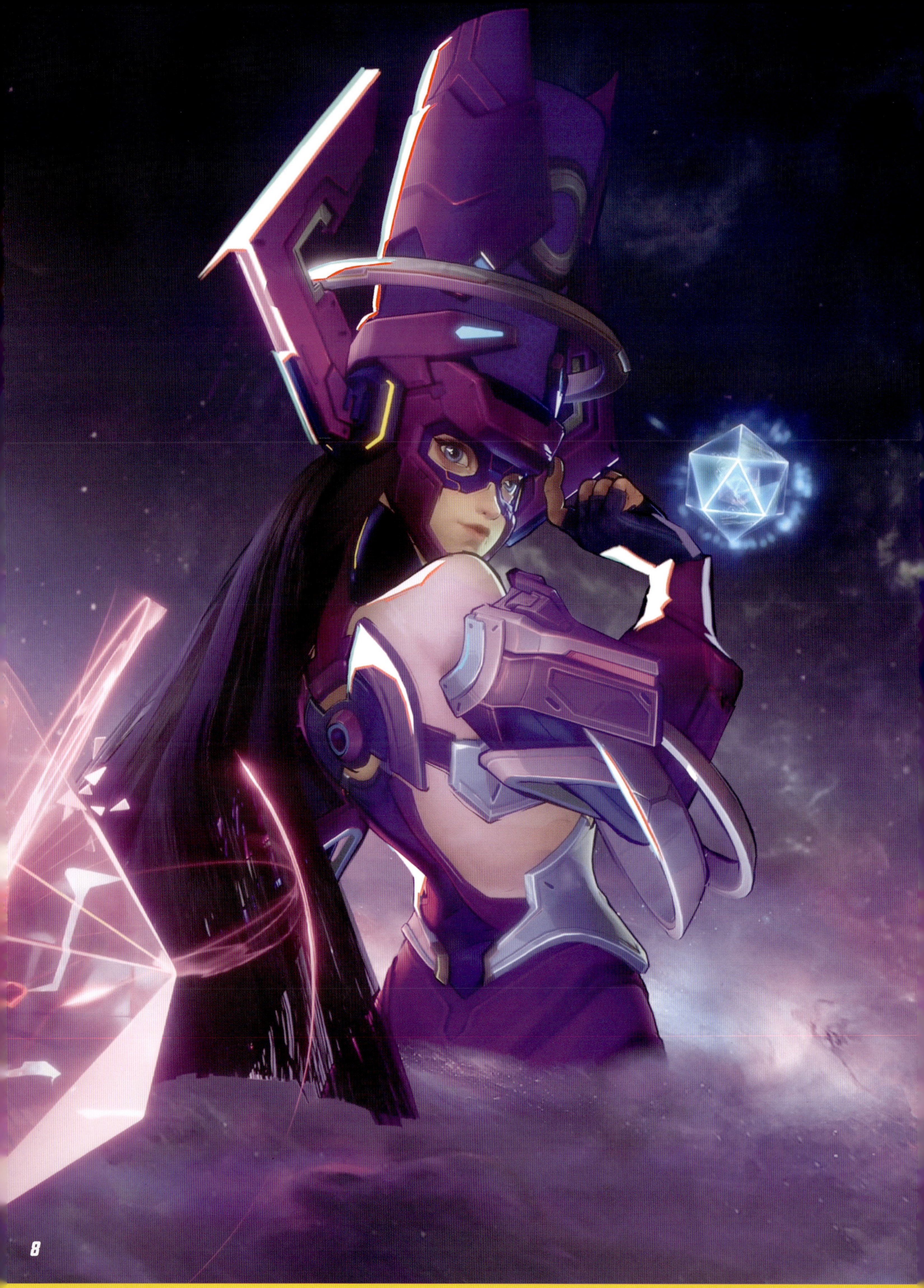

INTRODUCTION
BY GALACTA

Hey there! It's your girl, Galacta!

What you're about to dive into is way more than just a peek into the Chronoverses, full of unbridled wonder and limitless imagination—it's also the very foundation upon which these extraordinary realities have been built, brick by brick and stroke by stroke. The creators of these bold new worlds have poured their boundless passion and creativity into them, fueled by the hope of welcoming you into the single greatest reimagining of the Marvel Multiverse humanly possible. They truly believe that, together, we can all forge these shared dreams into reality! (Pretty cool, right?!)

In this unprecedented new frontier, you'll rediscover heroes you've known for years—classics like Iron Man, Star-Lord, and Storm—with appearances you'll recognize in an instant that somehow seem both familiar and fresh. And along the way, you'll also meet bold, unconventional heroes and promising rising stars, like new spins on Psylocke and Iron Fist, as well as K-pop sensation Luna Snow!

But that's just the start of your journey! You'll also be embarking to the farthest corners of the Chronoverses. Witness Wakanda rising anew in the heart of the galaxy, where Afrofuturism seamlessly melds with the grandeur of a space opera in their intergalactic empire! Roam the neon-drenched streets of Tokyo 2099, where traditional design and technology fuse like the strands of a spiderweb! Uncover Hydra's most closely guarded secrets in the icy Antarctic wilderness and explore the alien reaches of Klyntar, both packed to the brim with alien horrors that defy comprehension! A universe of endless possibilities awaits your eager eyes, kids!

And trust me, the shared vision of these creators didn't begin on the first page of this book. Neither will their pursuit of imagination and creativity end on the last page. They're already super busy bringing new heroes and new realities to life! In the meantime, I'll be here as your guide, accompanying you on this breathtaking journey through time and space—a visual and narrative odyssey like no other!

Okay, that's it from me for now. Time for you to get reading!

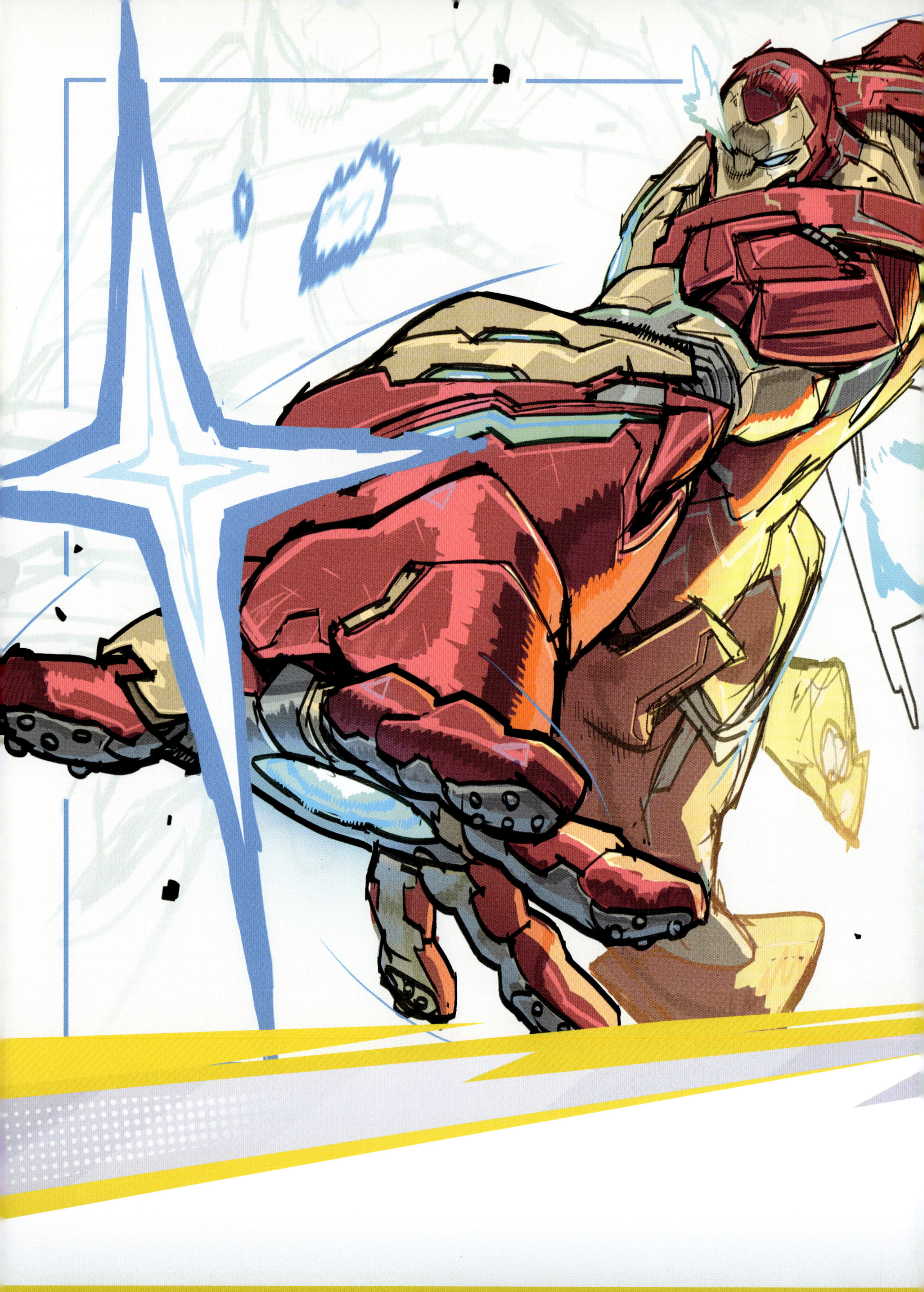

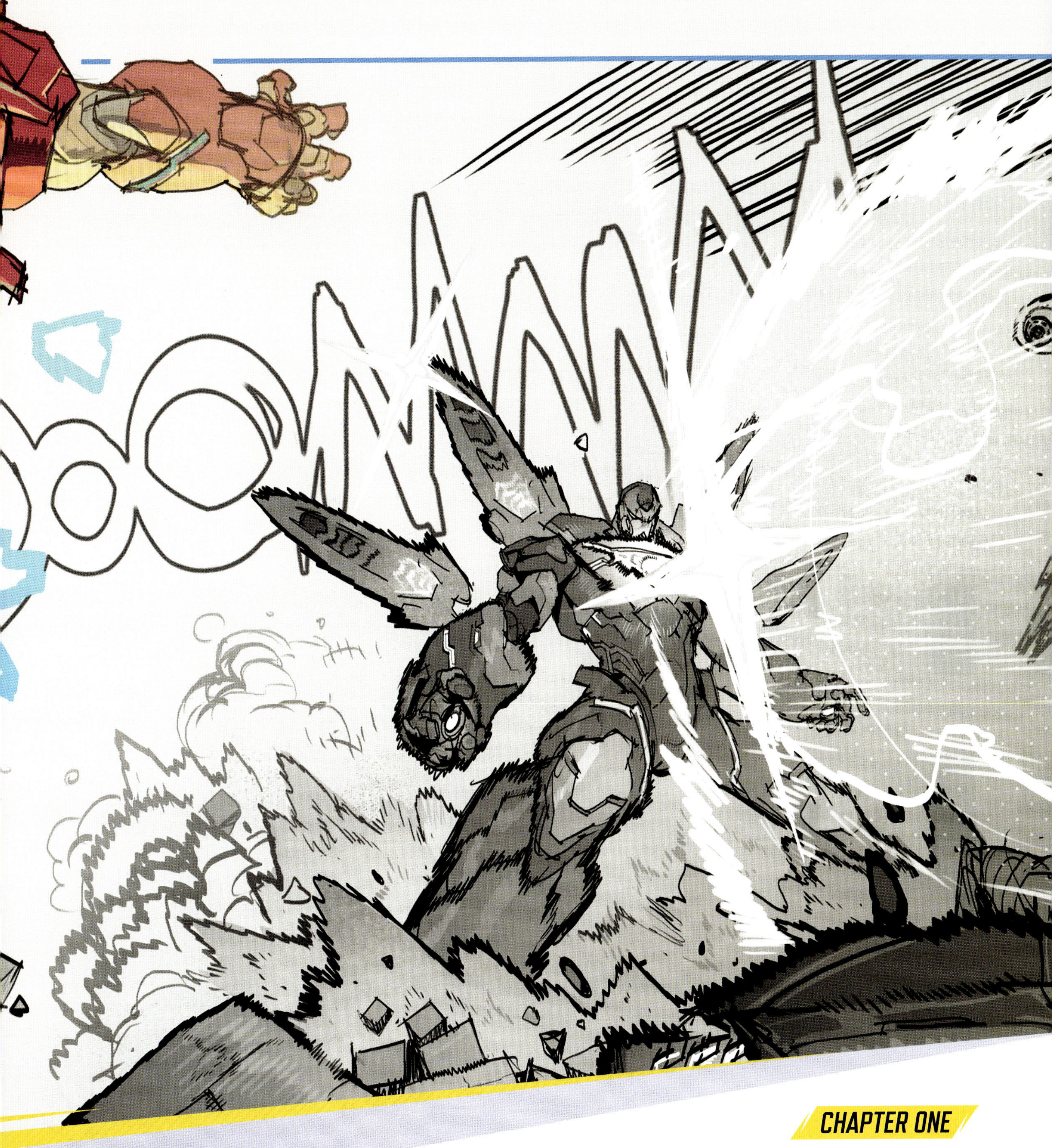

CHAPTER ONE

CHARACTERS

Every epic story is told with epic characters. Some of them are Astonishing and Fantastic, while others are Amazing and Spectacular. But all of them are super heroes rooted in fantasy, embodying the pursuit of beauty, strength, and nobility that is ingrained in our very genes. Marvel is storytelling, and *Marvel Rivals* has an all-new adventure to share.

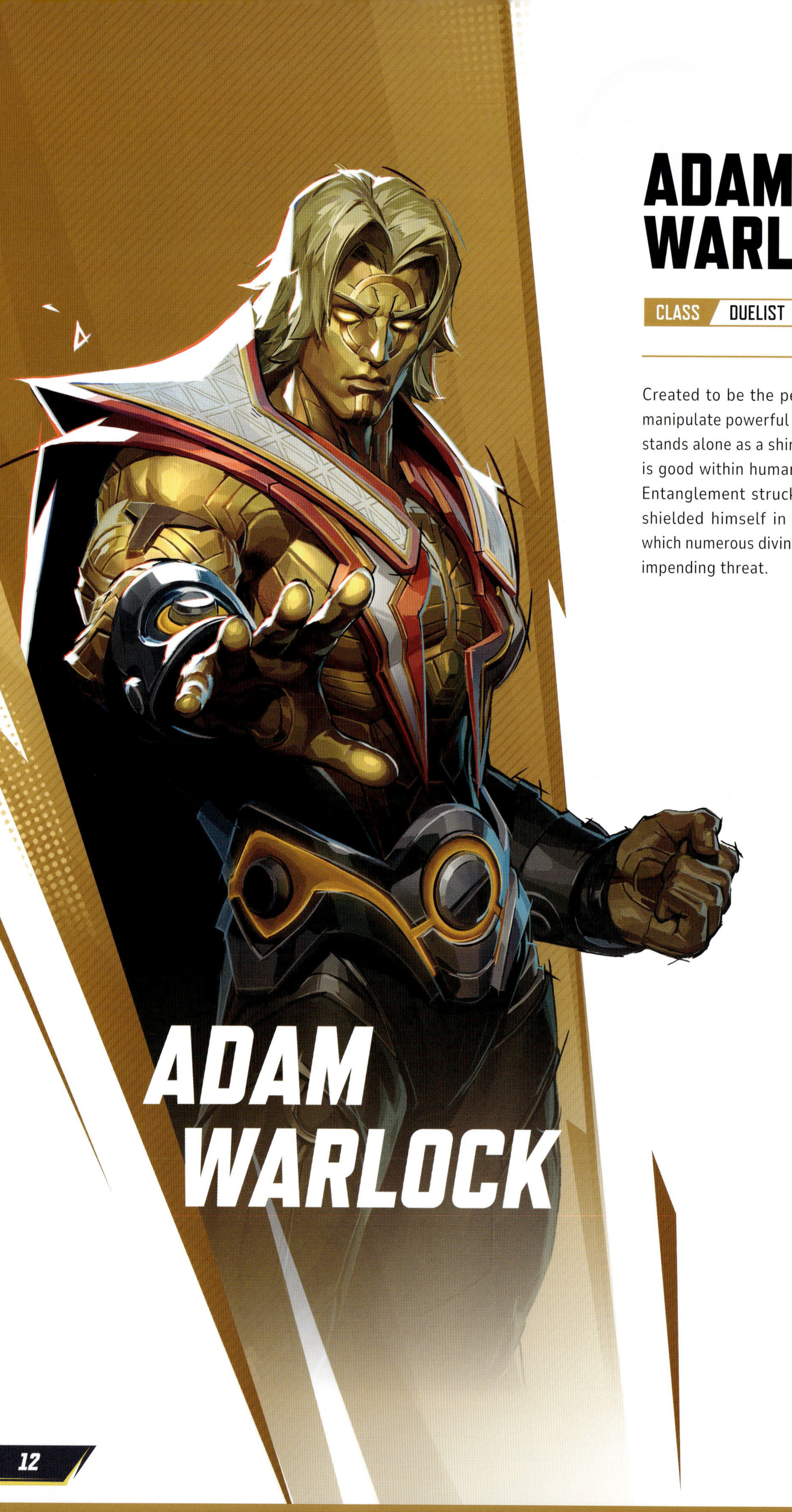

ADAM WARLOCK

CLASS / DUELIST

Created to be the perfect specimen and able to manipulate powerful cosmic forces, Adam Warlock stands alone as a shining golden beacon of all that is good within humankind. When the Timestream Entanglement struck, Adam Warlock reflexively shielded himself in a protective cocoon, within which numerous divine forces alerted him to Knull's impending threat.

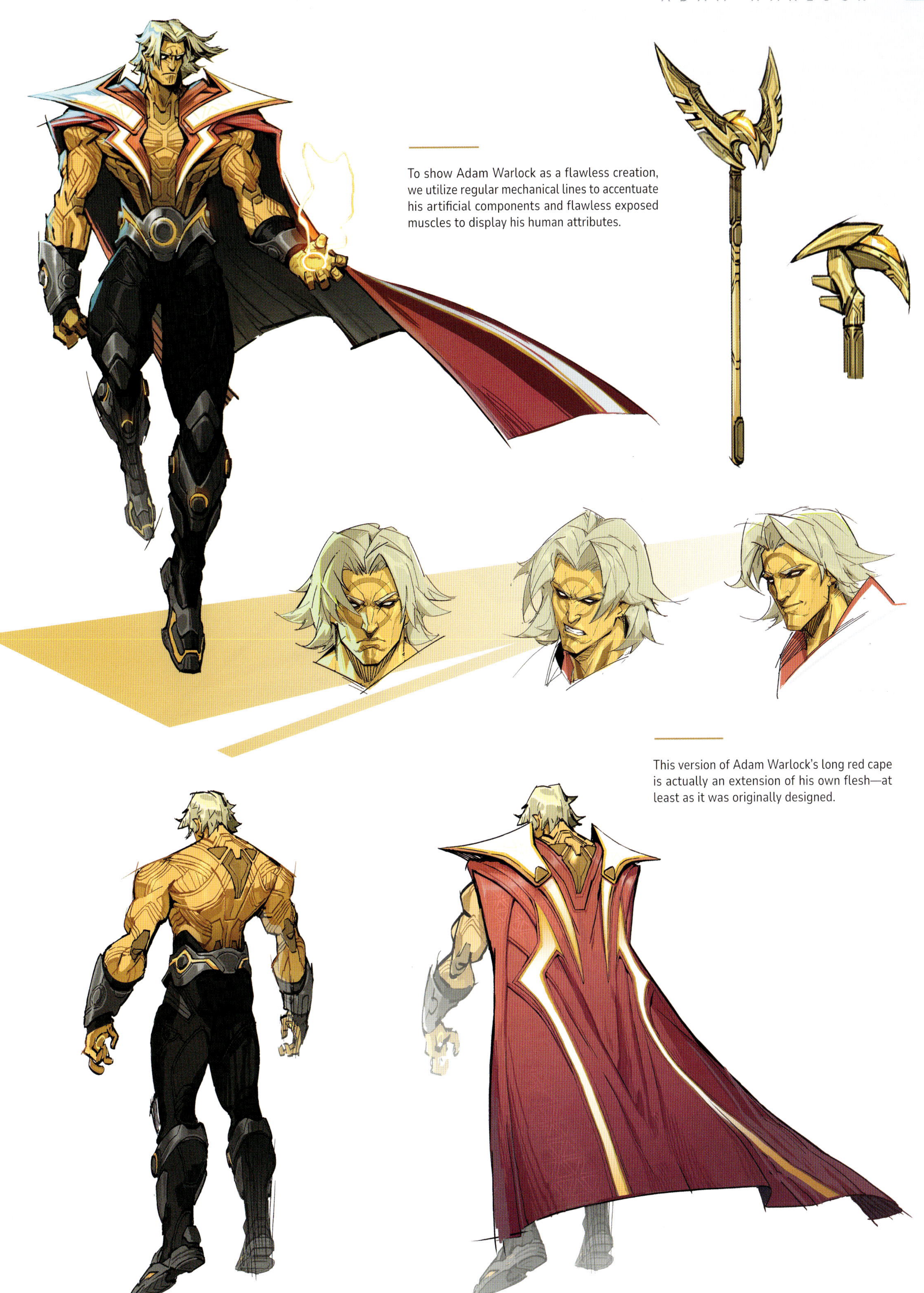

To show Adam Warlock as a flawless creation, we utilize regular mechanical lines to accentuate his artificial components and flawless exposed muscles to display his human attributes.

This version of Adam Warlock's long red cape is actually an extension of his own flesh—at least as it was originally designed.

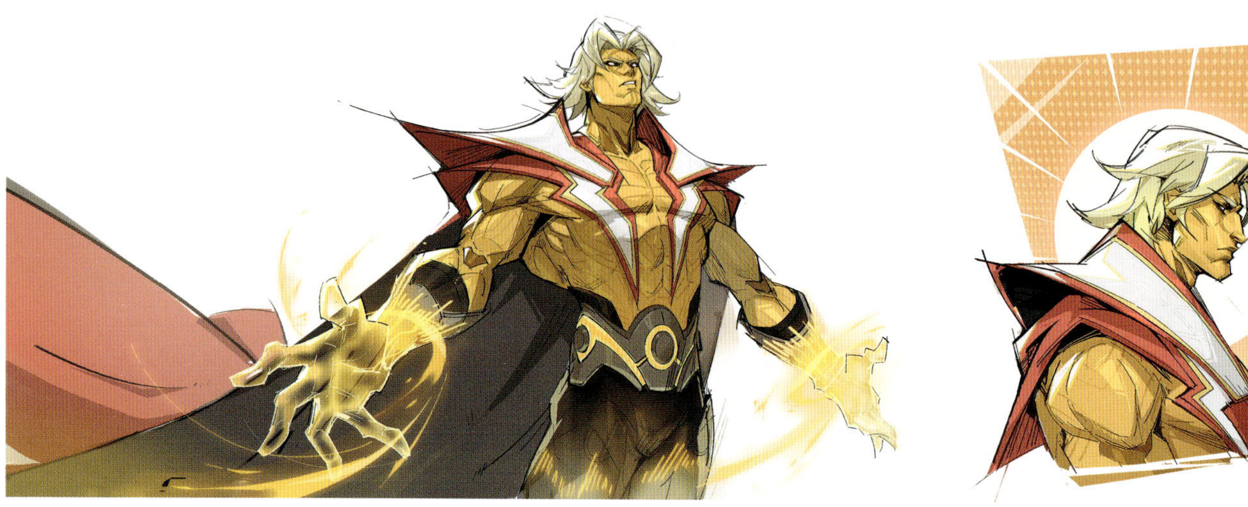

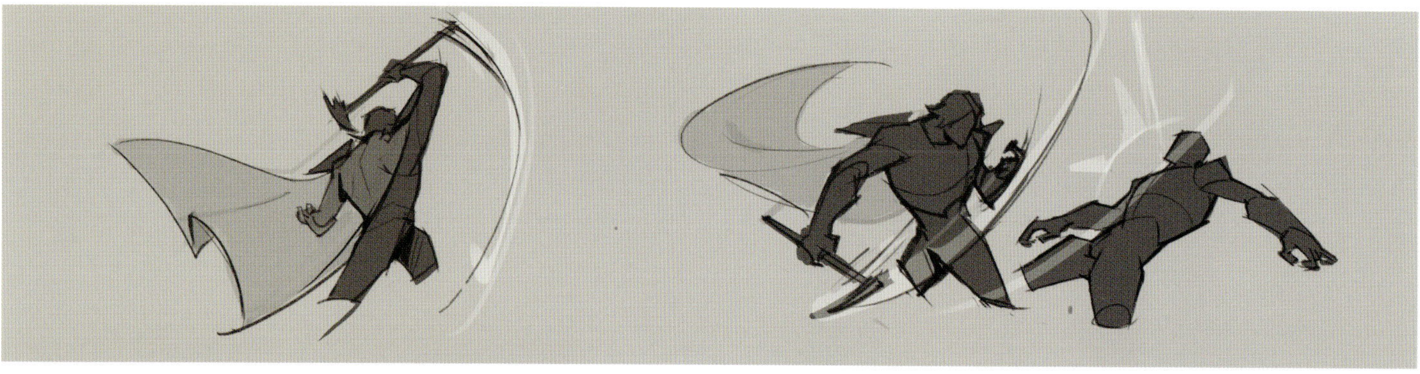

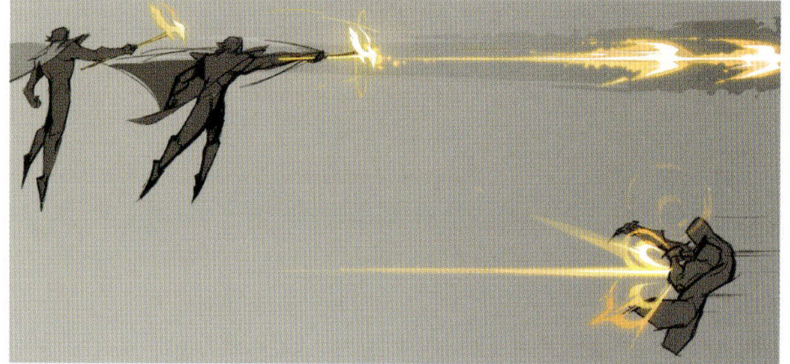

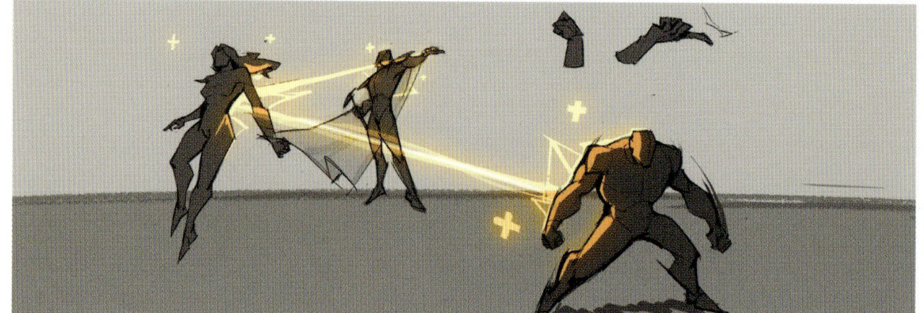

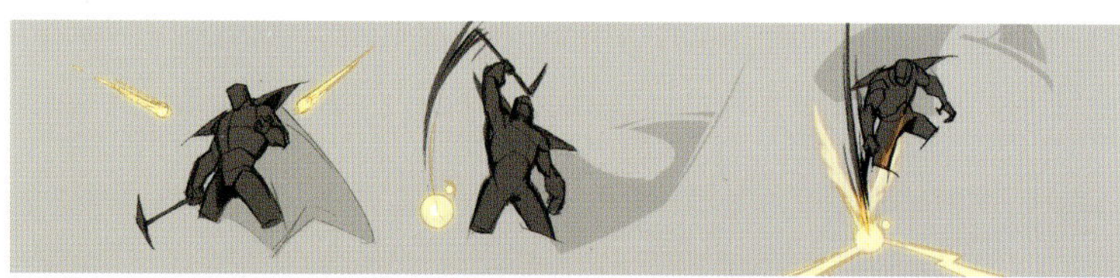

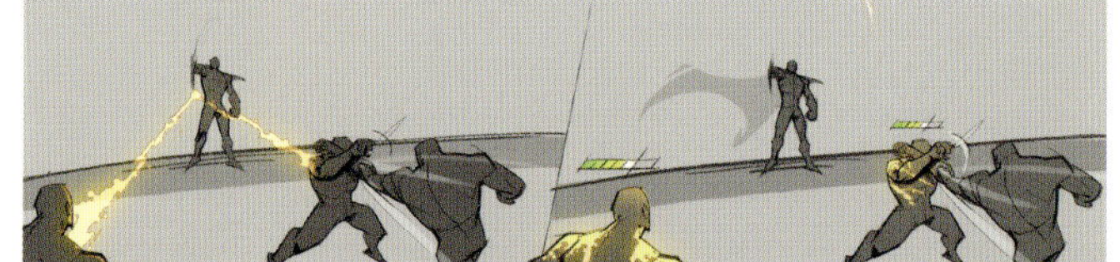

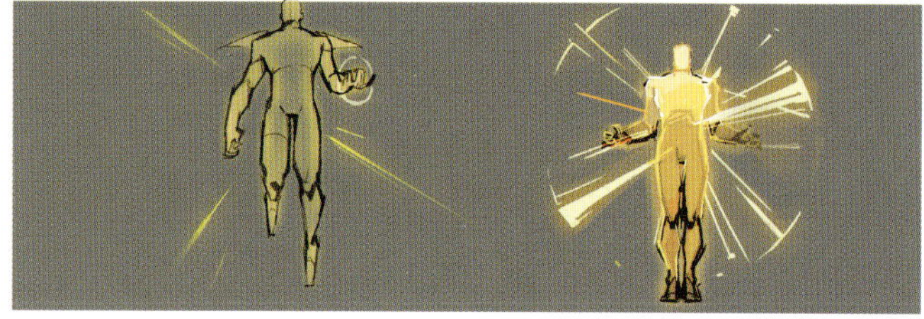

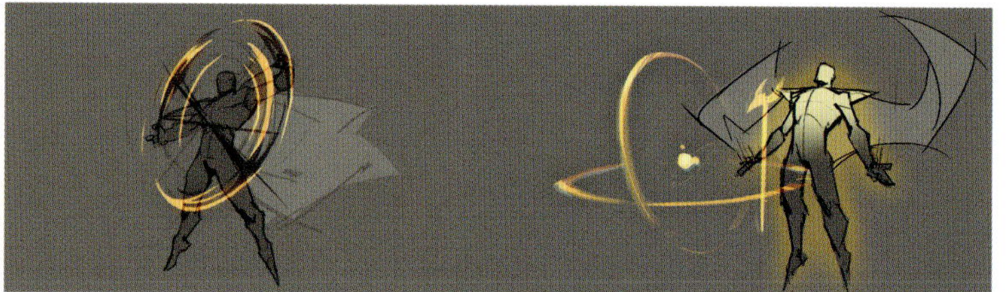

ADAM WARLOCK: ABILITIES

Adam Warlock can use quantum magic, is able to heal multiple teammates simultaneously, and has a potent resurrection ability, making him capable of reviving all enemies at once and reversing the situation.

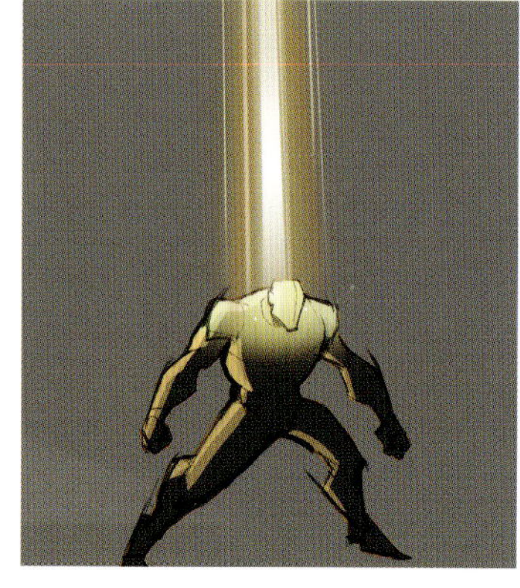

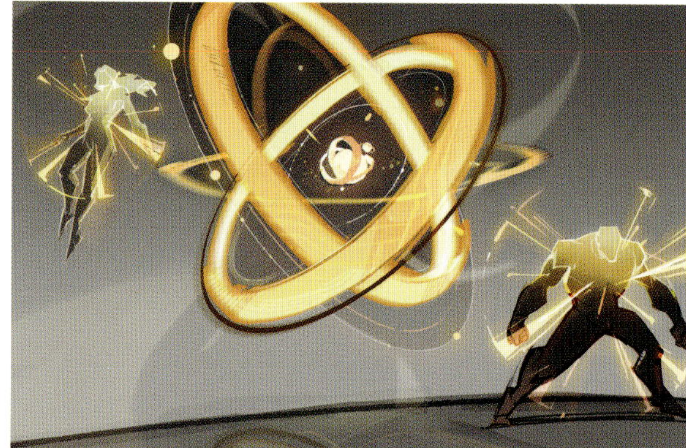

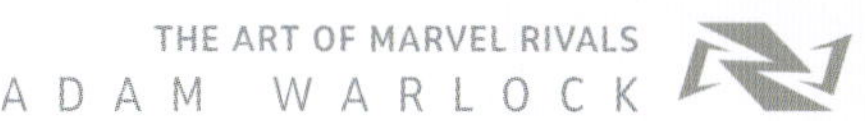

ADAM WARLOCK: COSMETIC VARIETY

The golden mask and red cloak, inspired by Victorian attire, evoke the feeling of a divine vampire hunter, creating a sharp distinction with the super hero himself by suggesting an antiquated holiness.

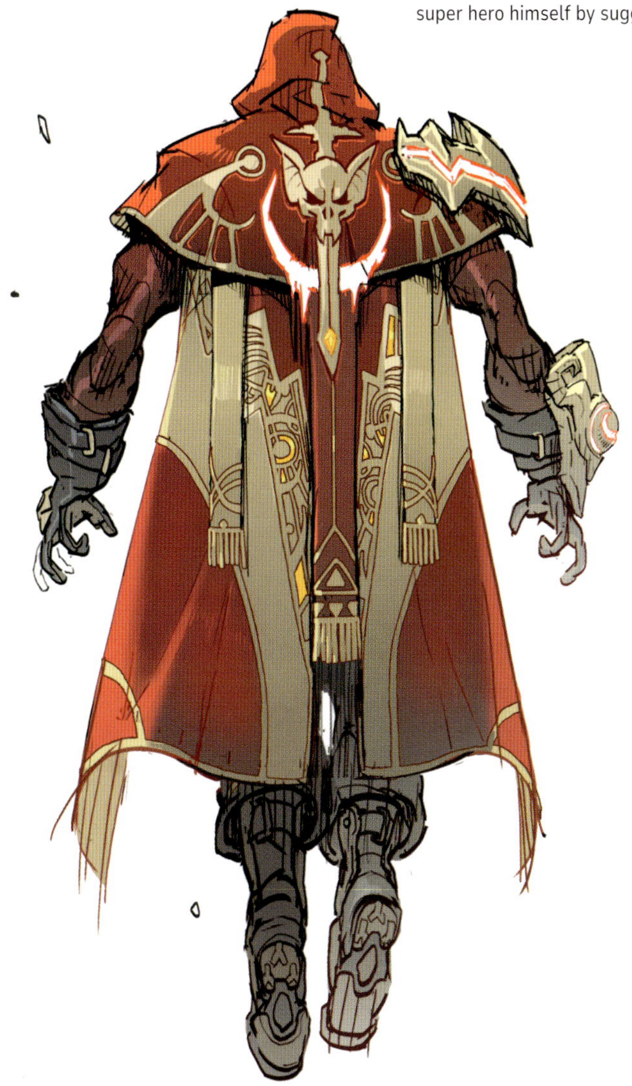

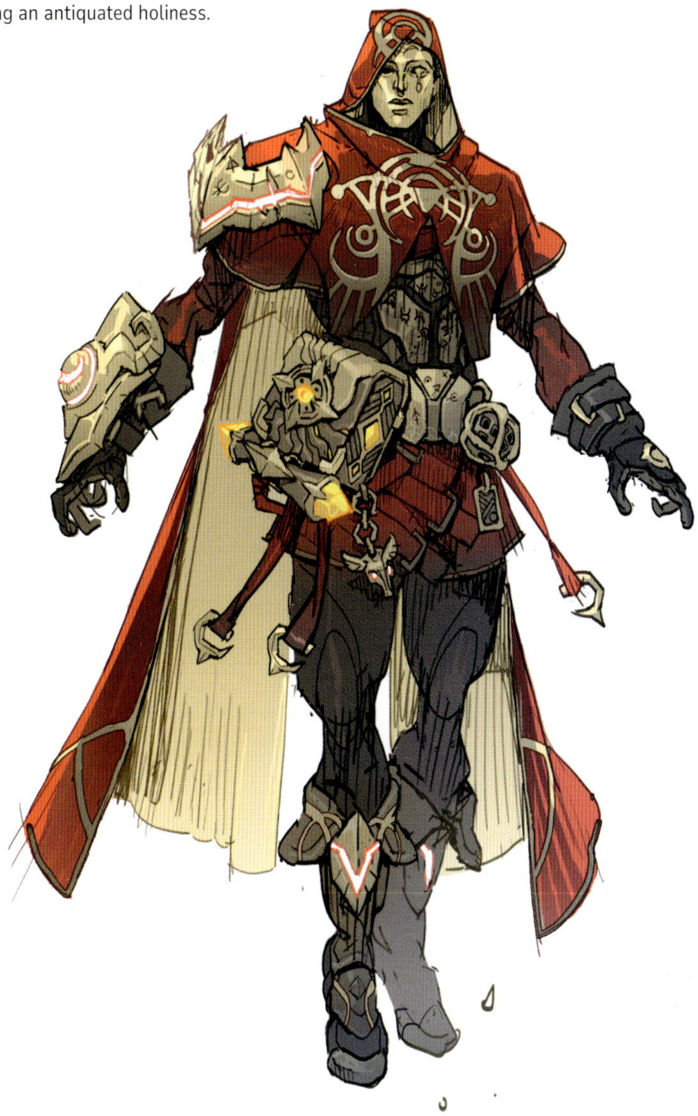

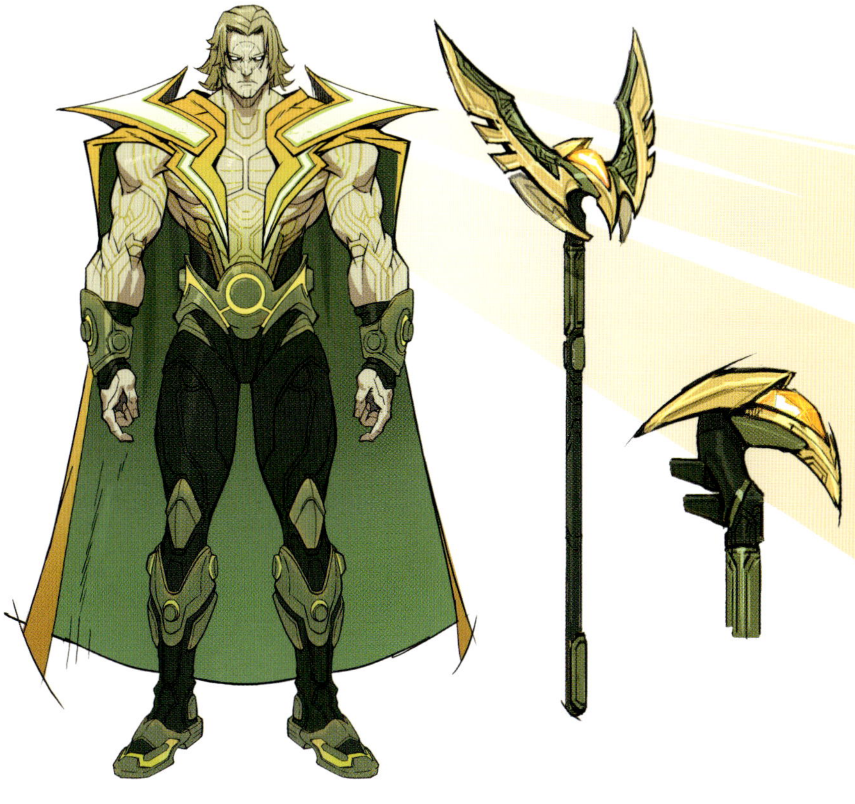

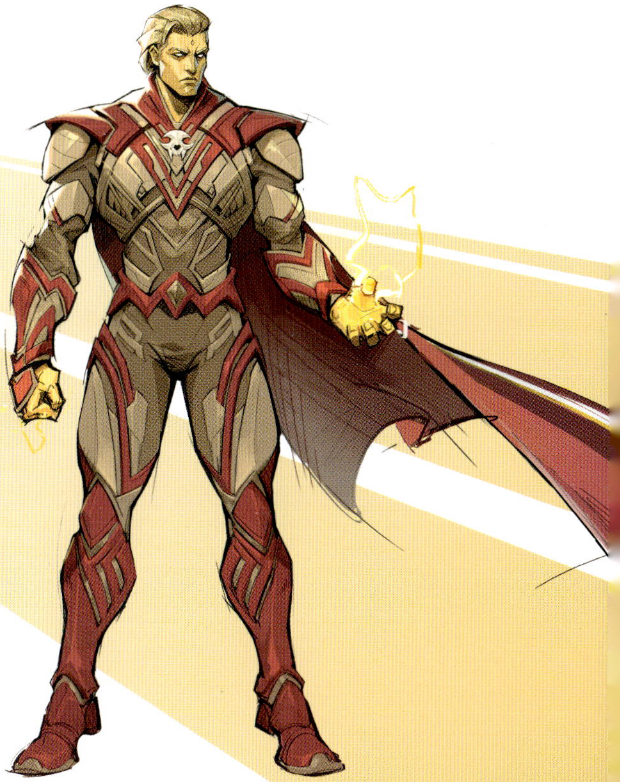

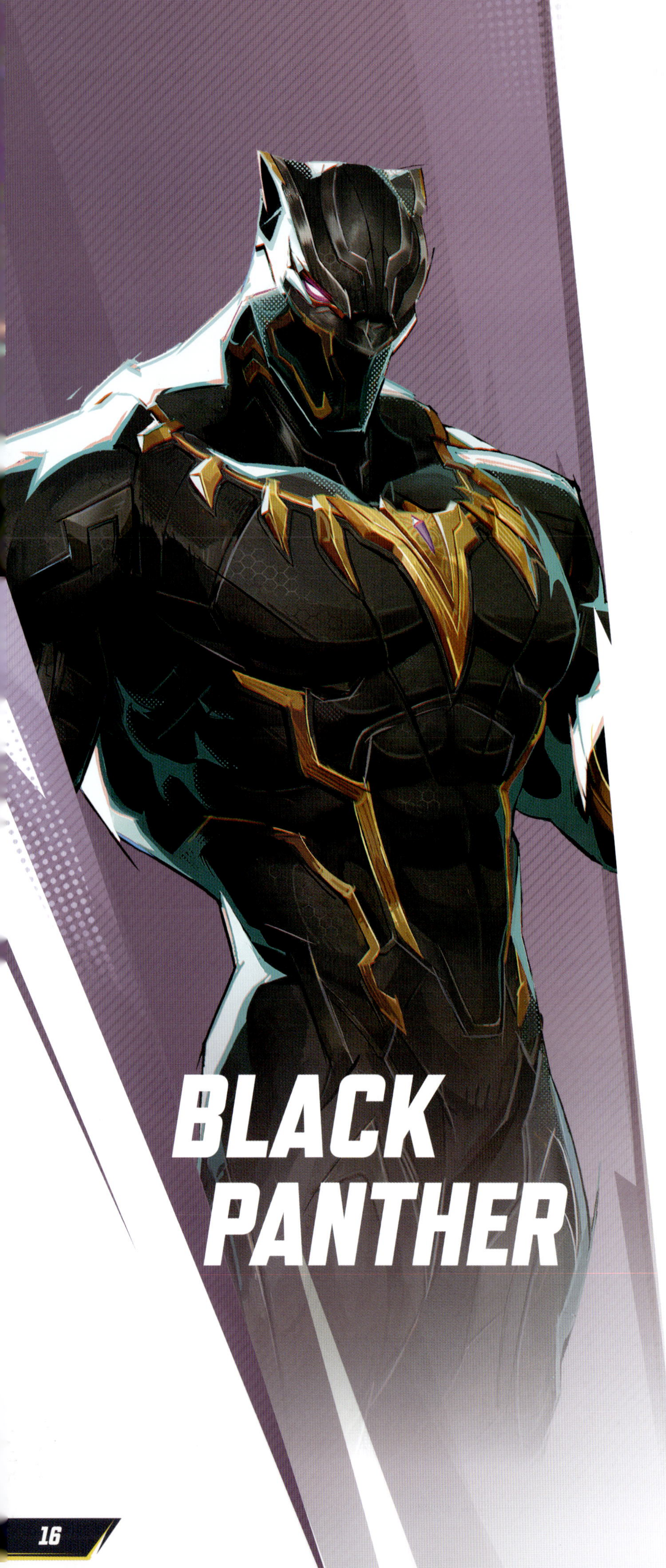

T'CHALLA

CLASS / DUELIST

King T'Challa is more than just the genius ruler of the Intergalactic Empire of Wakanda; he also wears the mantle of the Black Panther, the sacred protector of his people. Having expanded their reign into the cosmos, T'Challa and Shuri stand opposed on how to guide their empire: They can either share their technological secrets with new allies from across time or await signs from the Orisha on how to face the encroaching darkness.

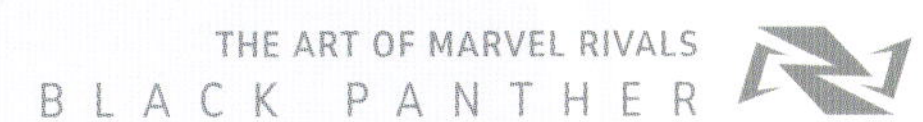

King T'Challa of Wakanda has incorporated advanced Vibranium technology with the power of Bast, the Panther God. The battlefield serves as Black Panther's hunting ground, where he patiently awaits the opportunity to take down his opponents.

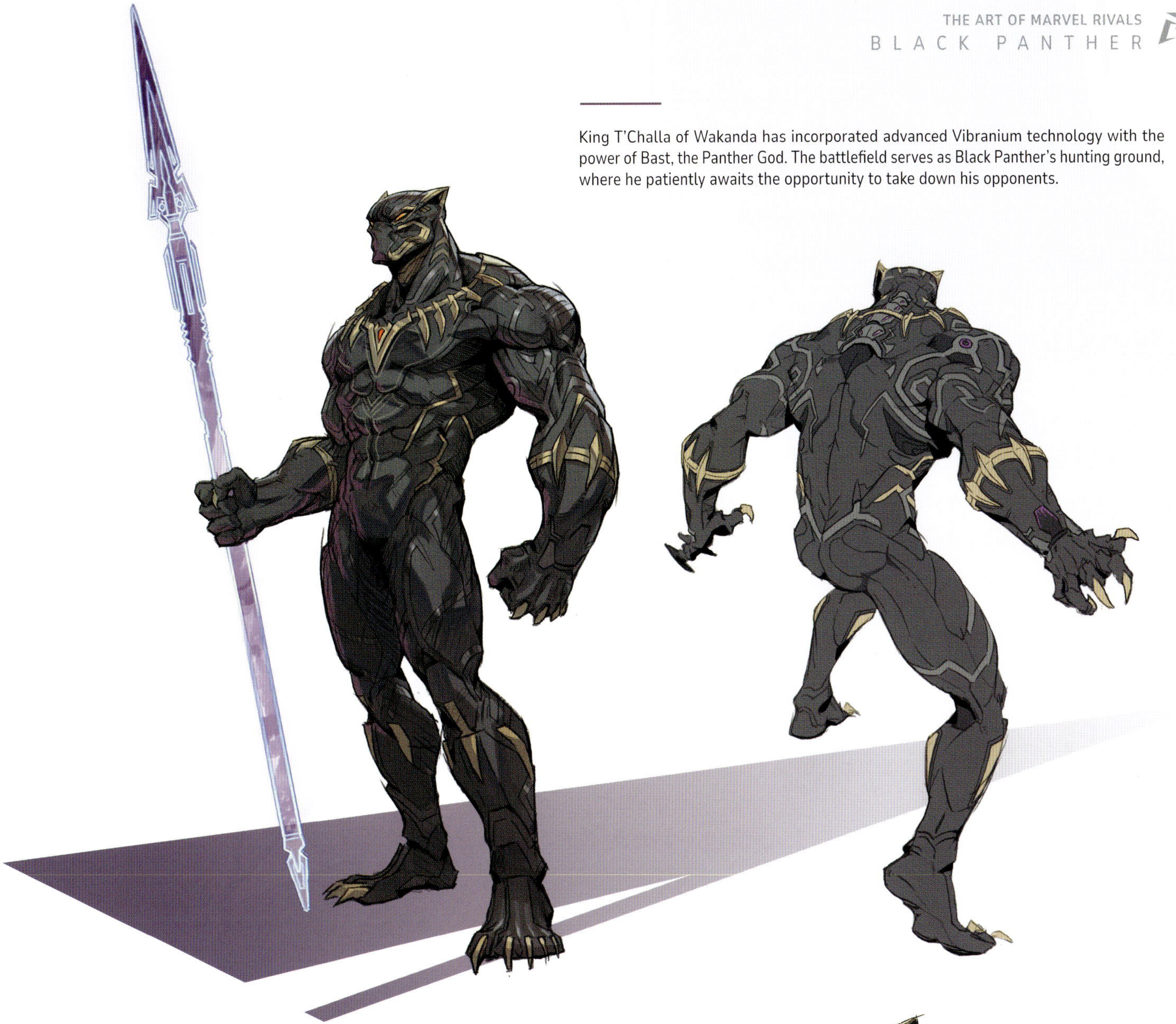

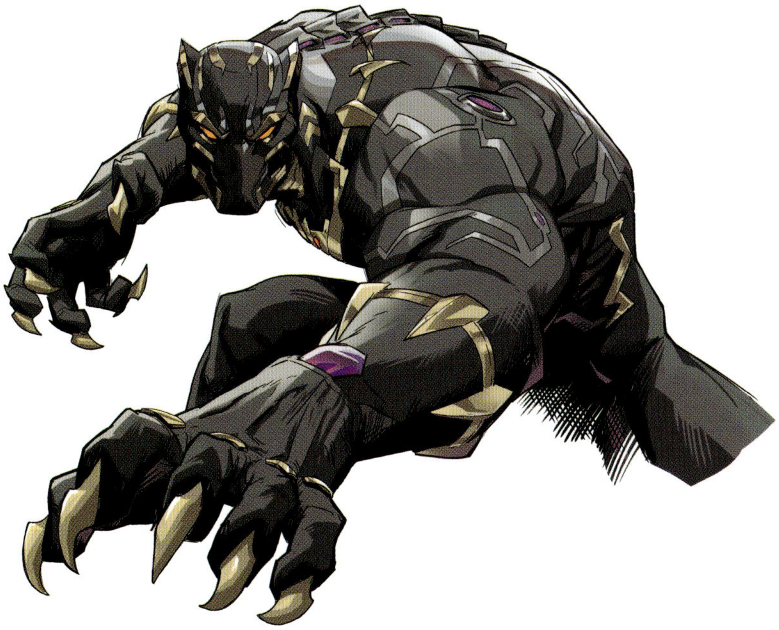

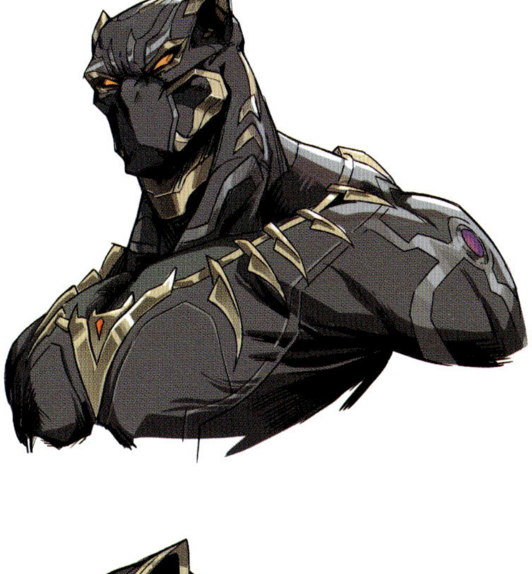

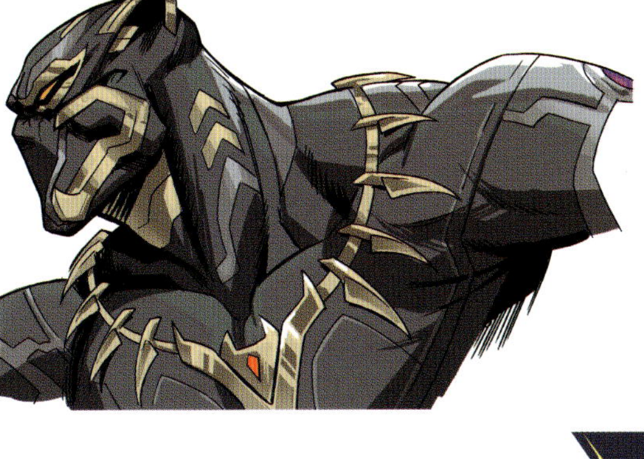

The armor integrates Wakanda's culture and technology, boasting explosive power and agility in its Vibranium weave. The Vibranium-constructed panther-tooth chain around the neck and various nodes on the body can exude the accumulated energy.

BLACK PANTHER: ABILITIES

Black Panther attacks with sharp claws, scales walls across various terrains, exhibits diverse displacement skills, and launches continuous attacks using the Vibranium Mark.

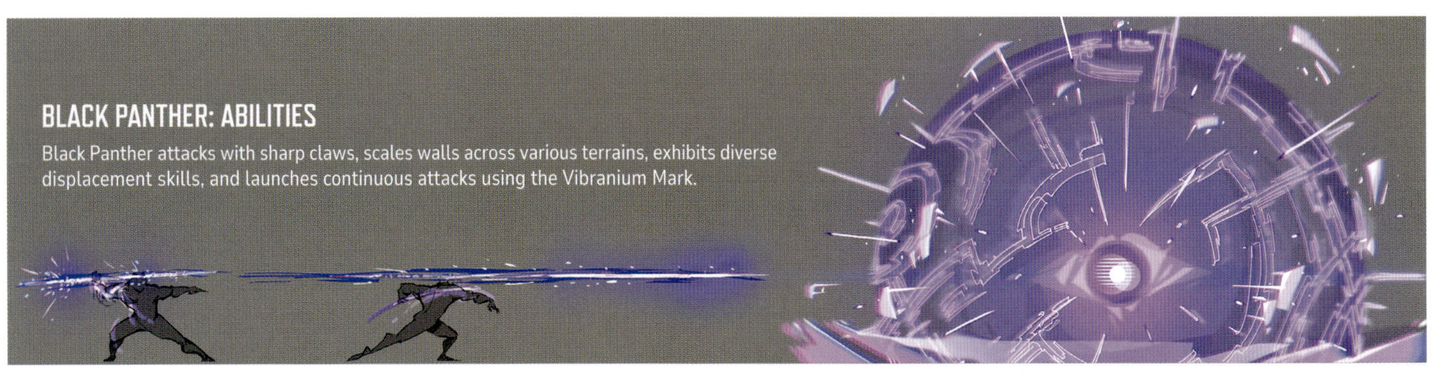

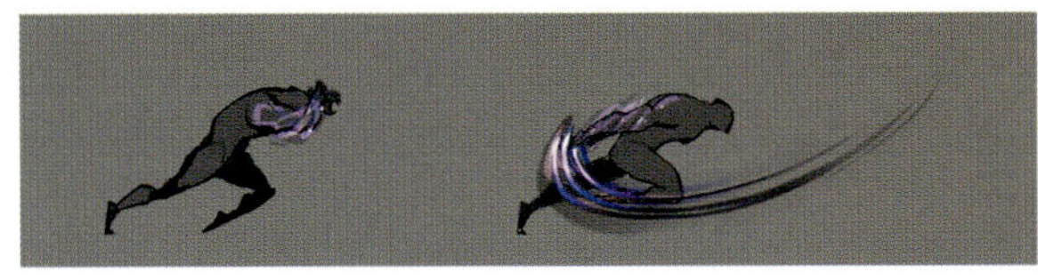

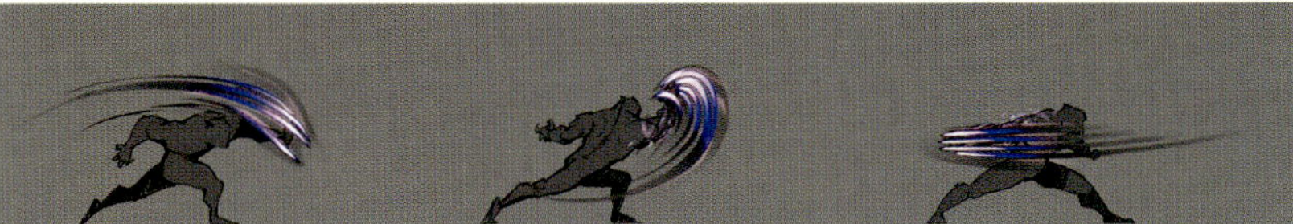

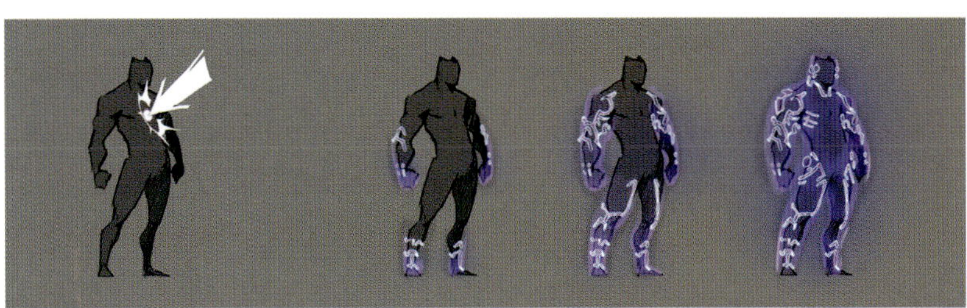

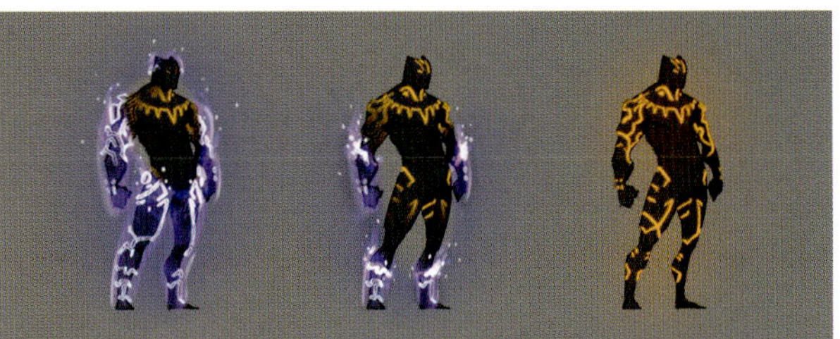

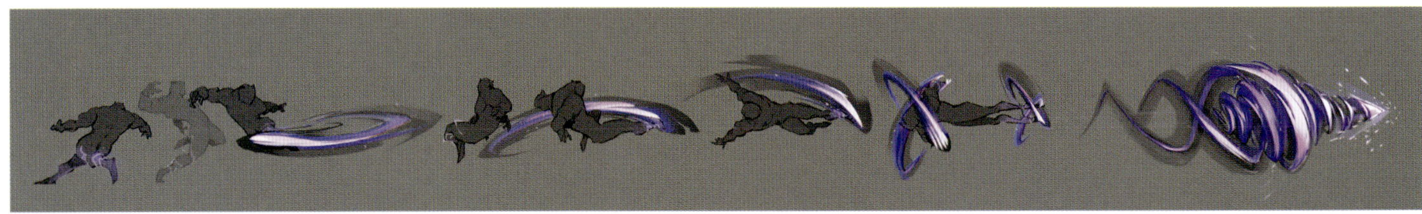

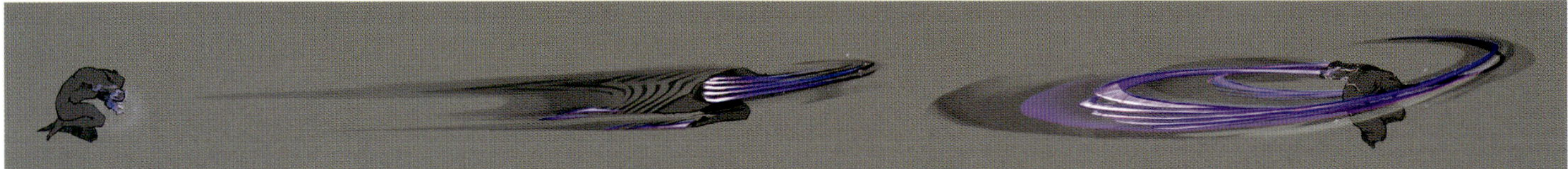

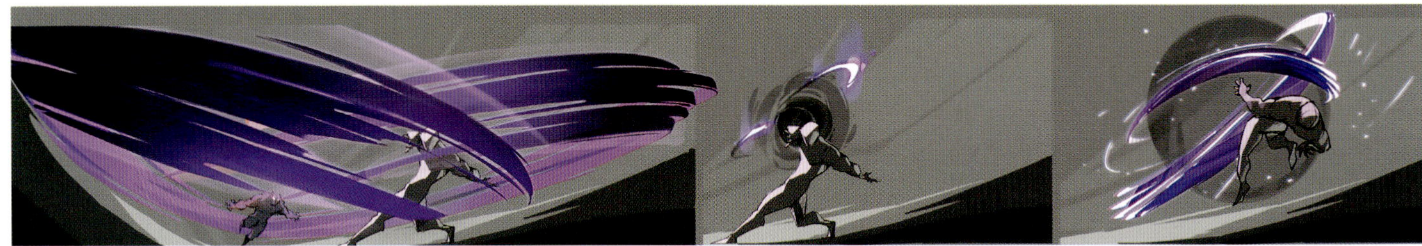

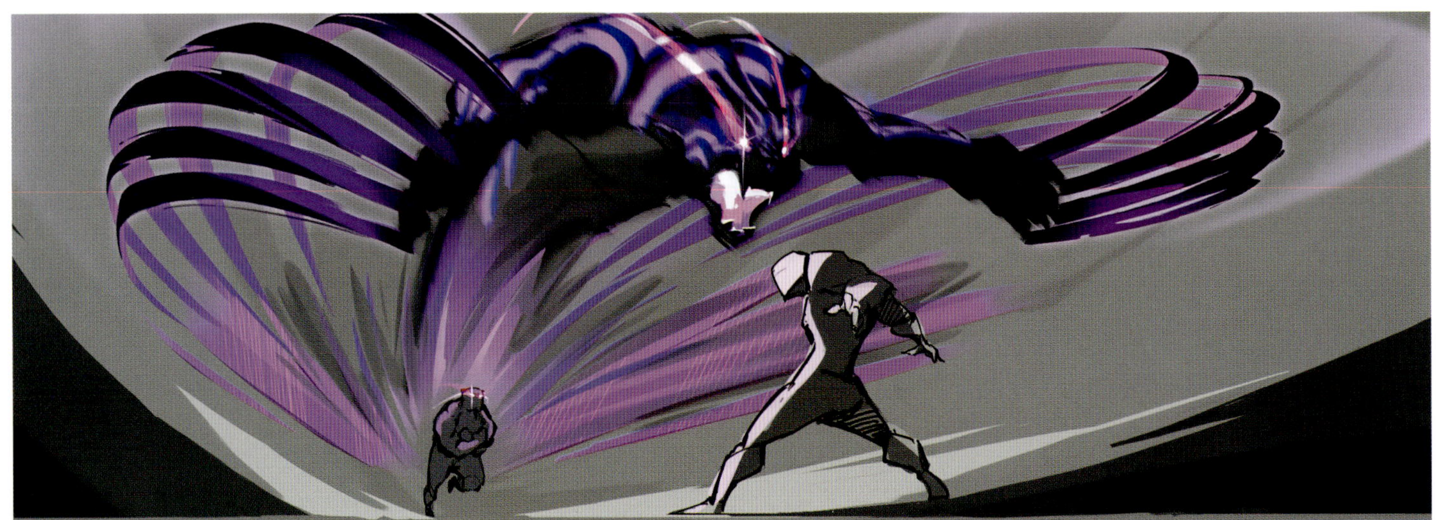

BLACK PANTHER: COSMETIC VARIETY

As a vampire king under Dracula's control, T'Challa dons silver armor with sculpted musculature, an inversion of one of his storied comic costumes. His duties for Wakanda persist despite becoming the Thrice-Cursed King.

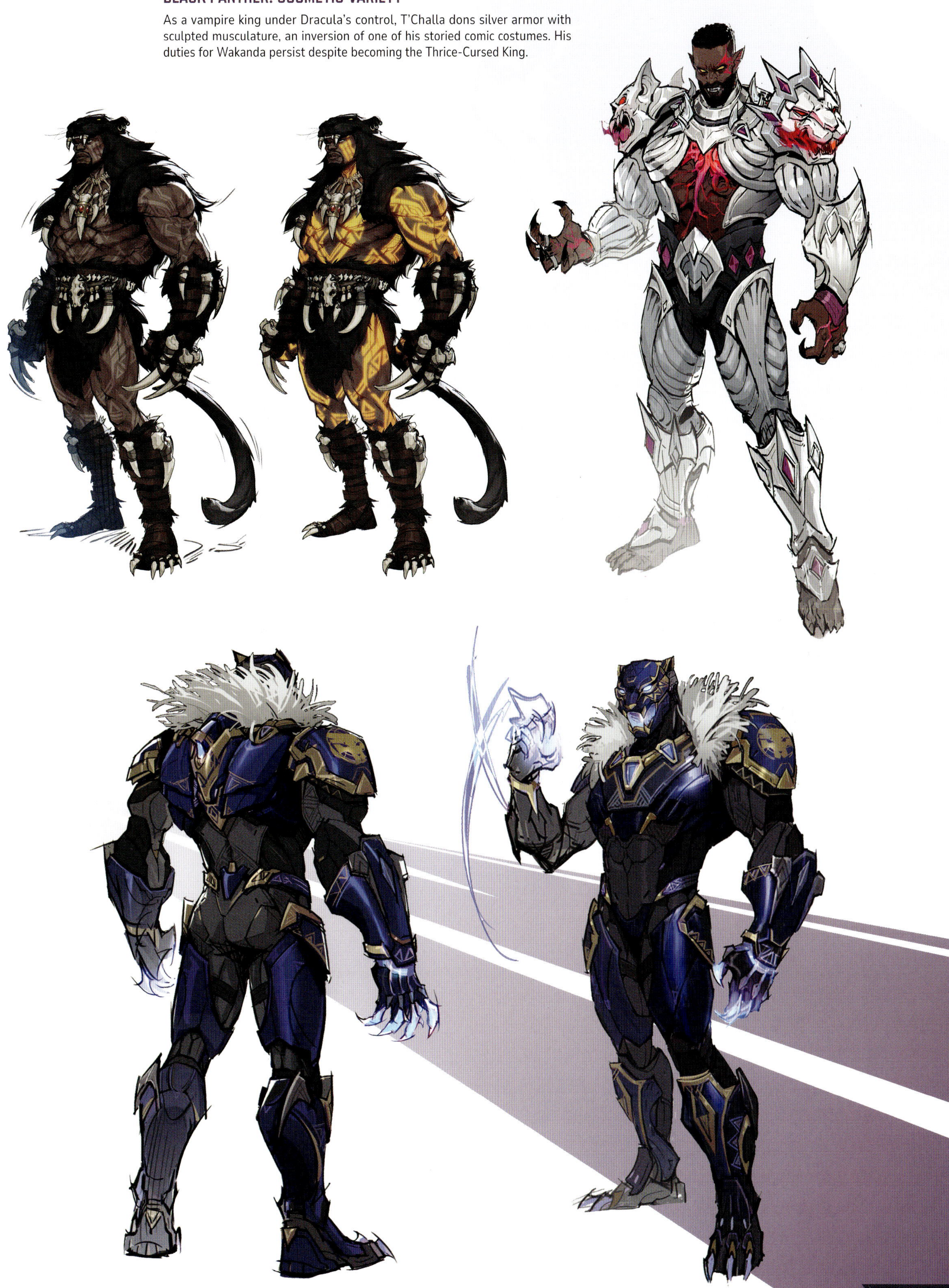

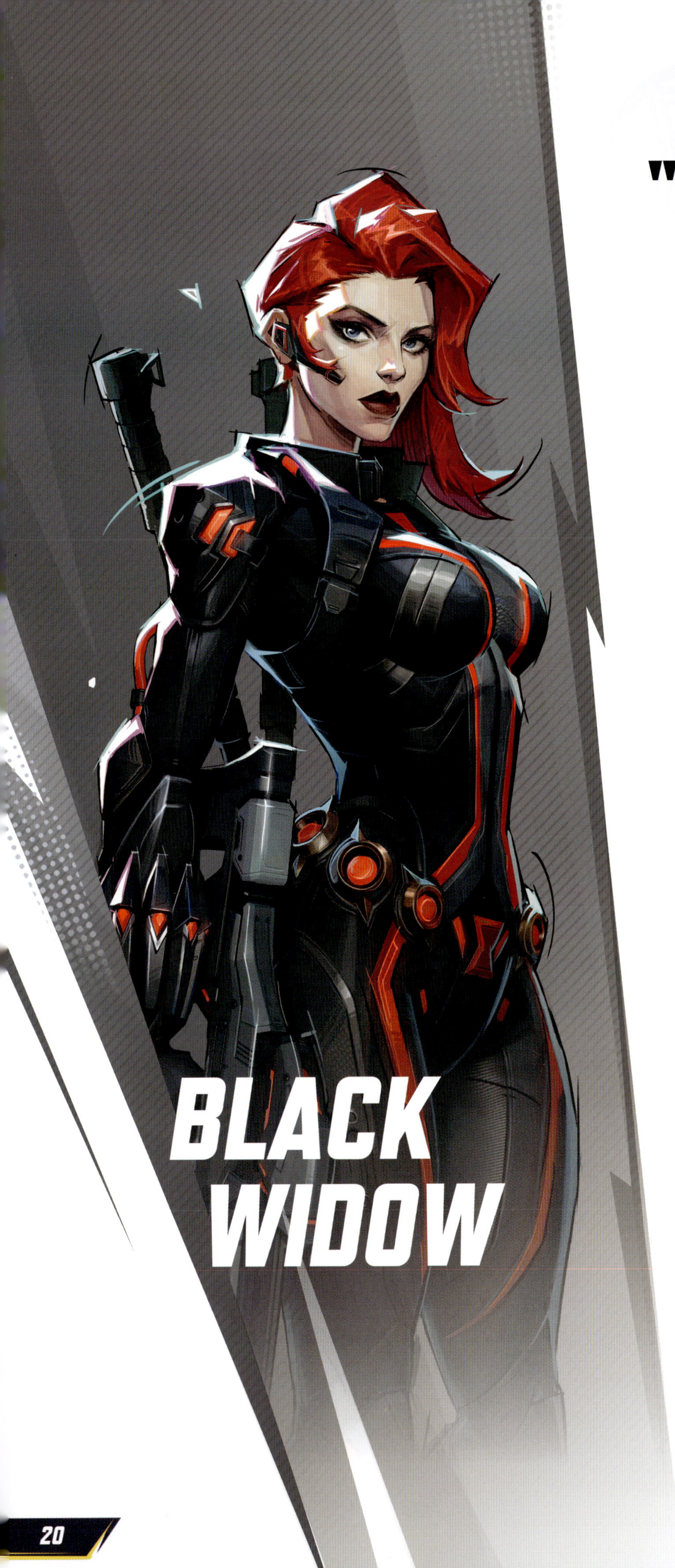

NATALIA "NATASHA" ROMANOVA

CLASS / DUELIST

Trained from childhood in the infamous Red Room, Natasha Romanova became one of the most feared spies and saboteurs in the world under the infamous Black Widow moniker. Imbued with a serum that vastly extended her lifespan, Black Widow sought its source within Alchemax's labs, only to uncover a frozen Captain America held captive for nefarious experimentation.

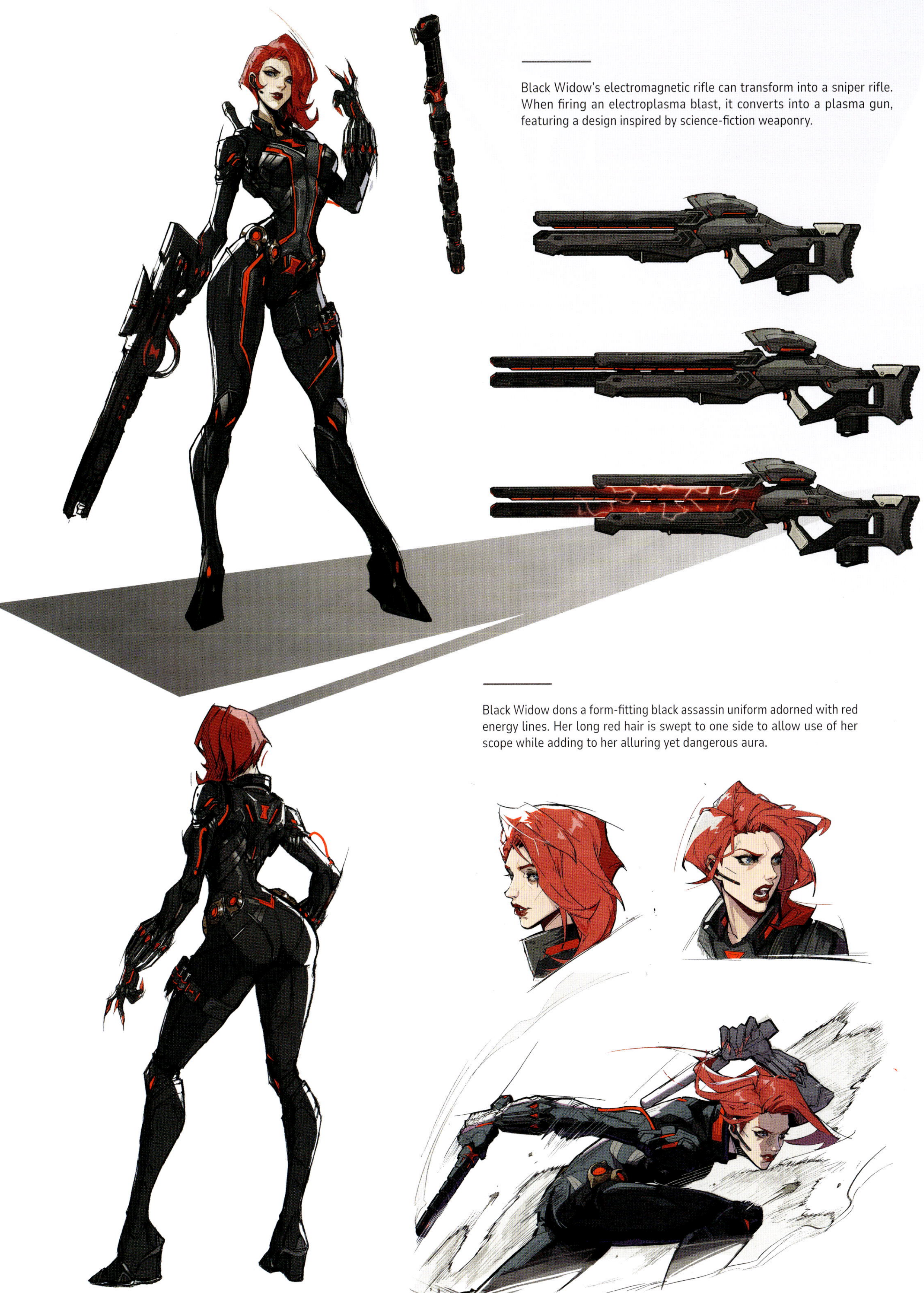

Black Widow's electromagnetic rifle can transform into a sniper rifle. When firing an electroplasma blast, it converts into a plasma gun, featuring a design inspired by science-fiction weaponry.

Black Widow dons a form-fitting black assassin uniform adorned with red energy lines. Her long red hair is swept to one side to allow use of her scope while adding to her alluring yet dangerous aura.

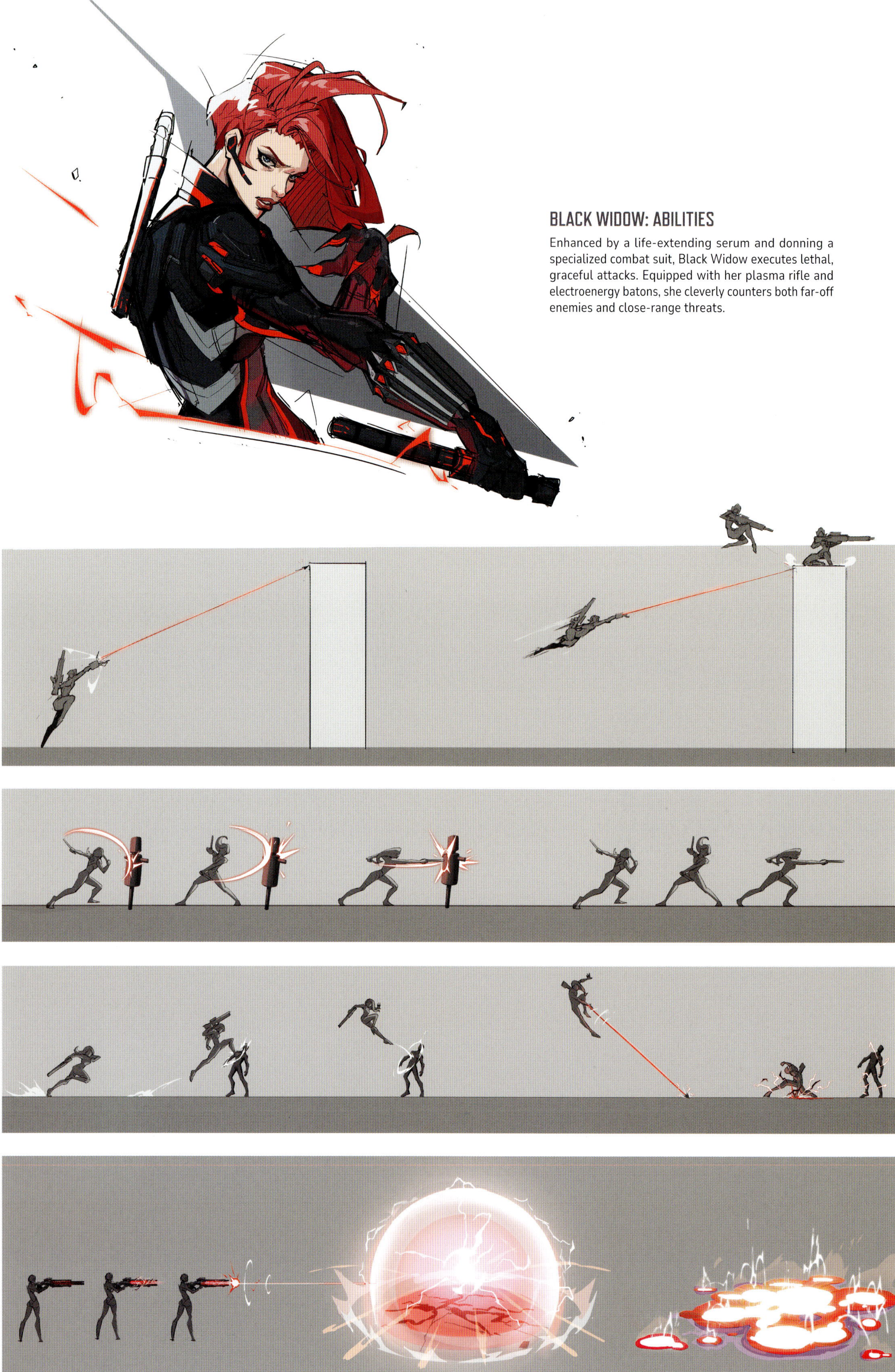

BLACK WIDOW: ABILITIES

Enhanced by a life-extending serum and donning a specialized combat suit, Black Widow executes lethal, graceful attacks. Equipped with her plasma rifle and electroenergy batons, she cleverly counters both far-off enemies and close-range threats.

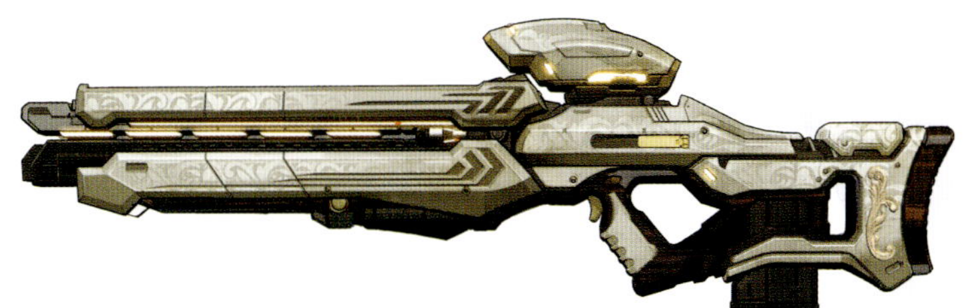

BLACK WIDOW: COSMETIC VARIETY

Black Widow is a feared assassin in the 1872 universe, wearing a sleek cowboy outfit and steampunk-style Widow Bite Gauntlets while disrupting the corrupt powers of the Wild West.

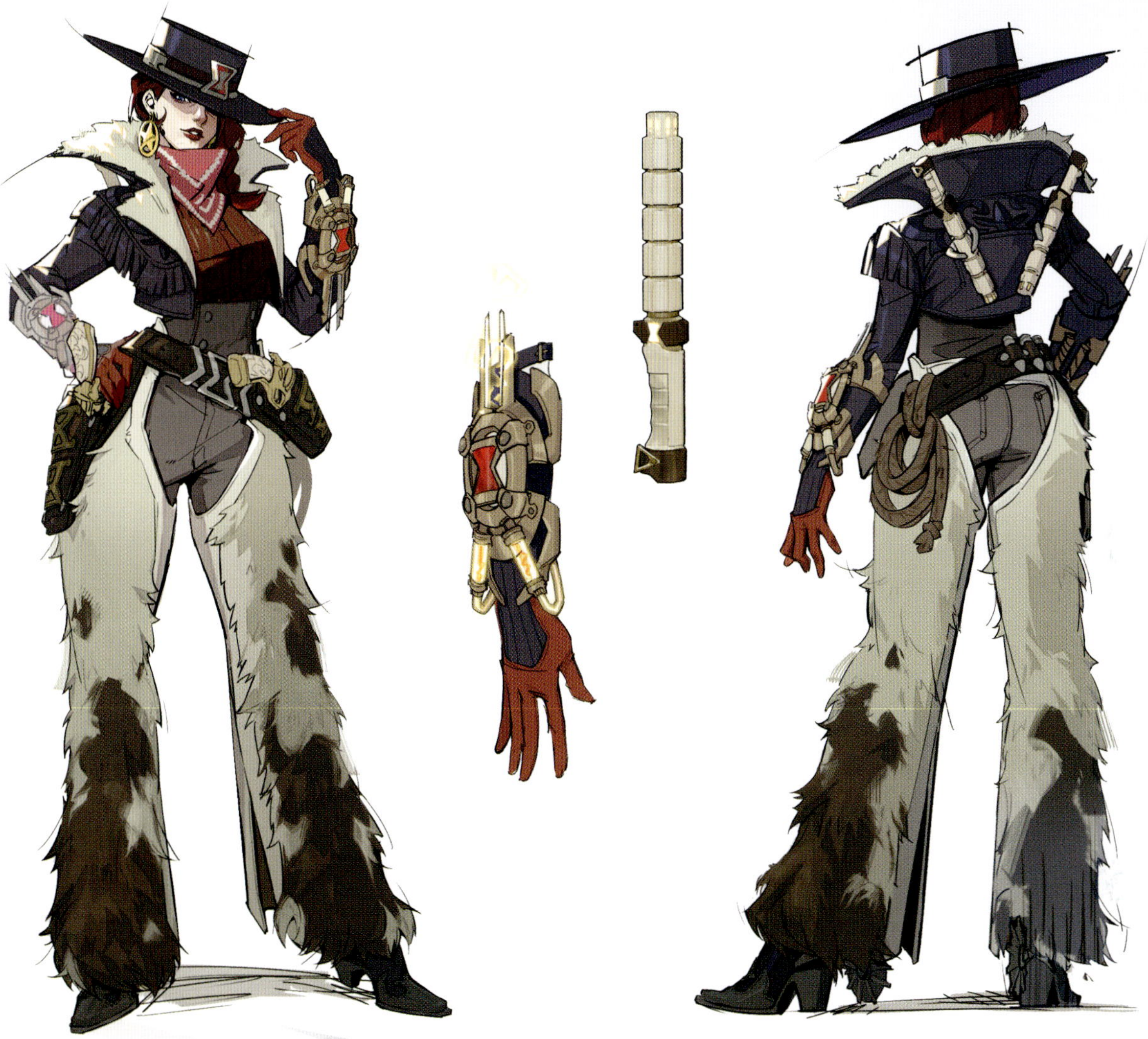

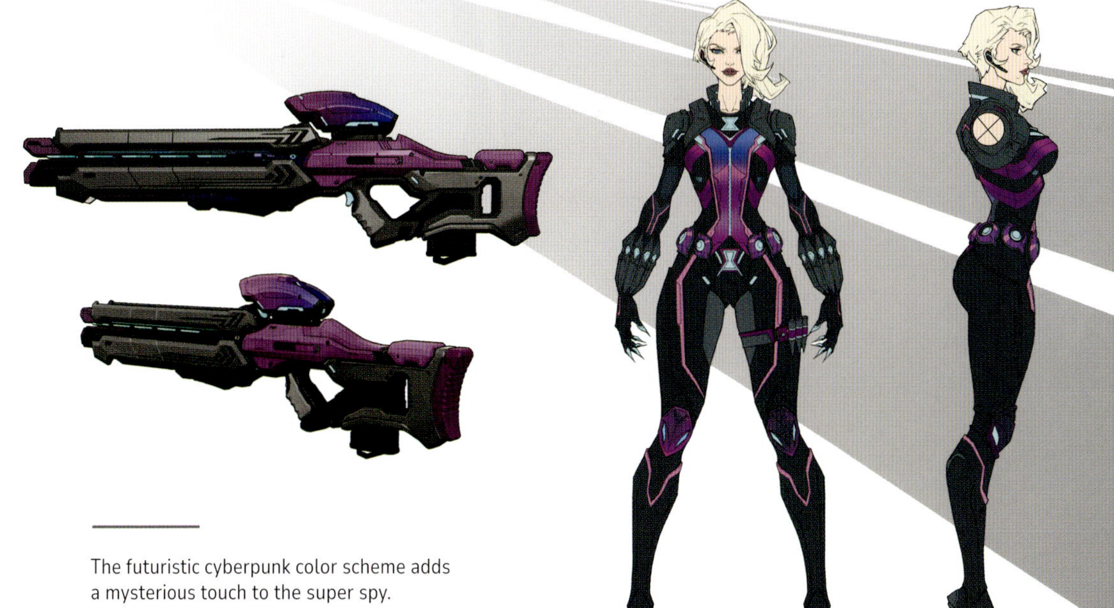

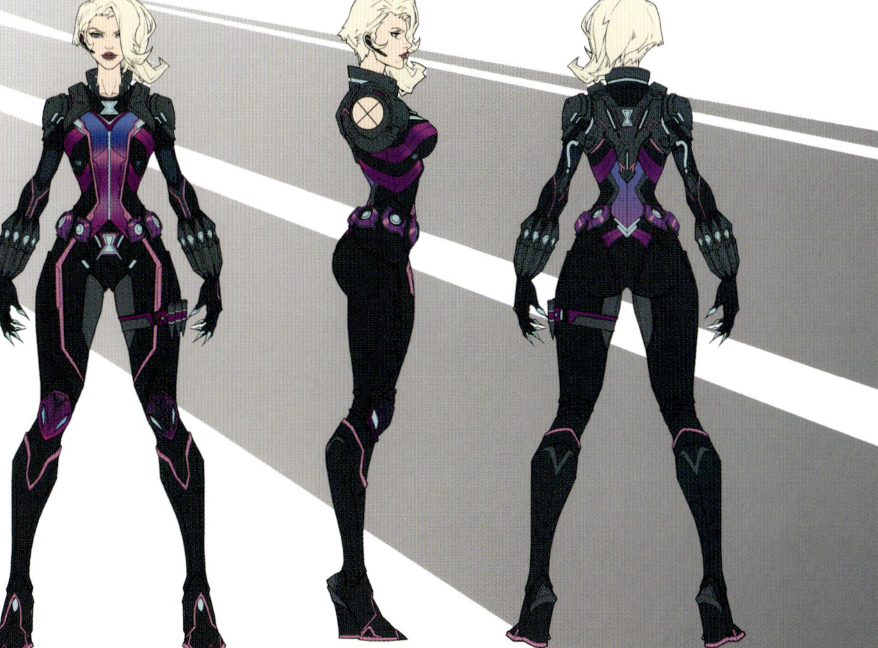

The futuristic cyberpunk color scheme adds a mysterious touch to the super spy.

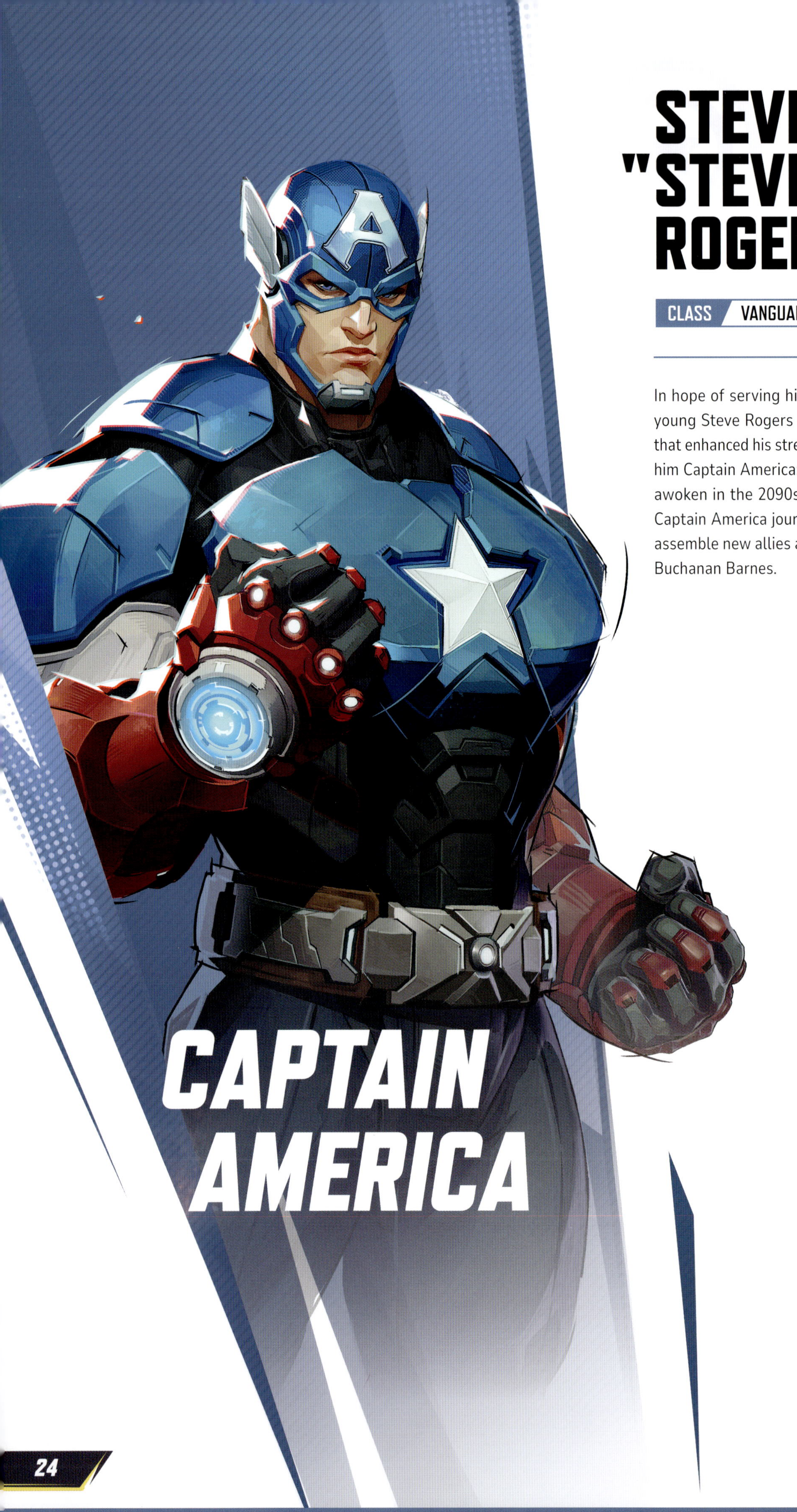

STEVEN "STEVE" ROGERS

CLASS / VANGUARD

In hope of serving his country during World War II, young Steve Rogers volunteered for an experiment that enhanced his strength, speed, and agility, making him Captain America: the first Super-Soldier. Having awoken in the 2090s with all of time under threat, Captain America journeyed across the spaceways to assemble new allies and find his oldest friend: James Buchanan Barnes.

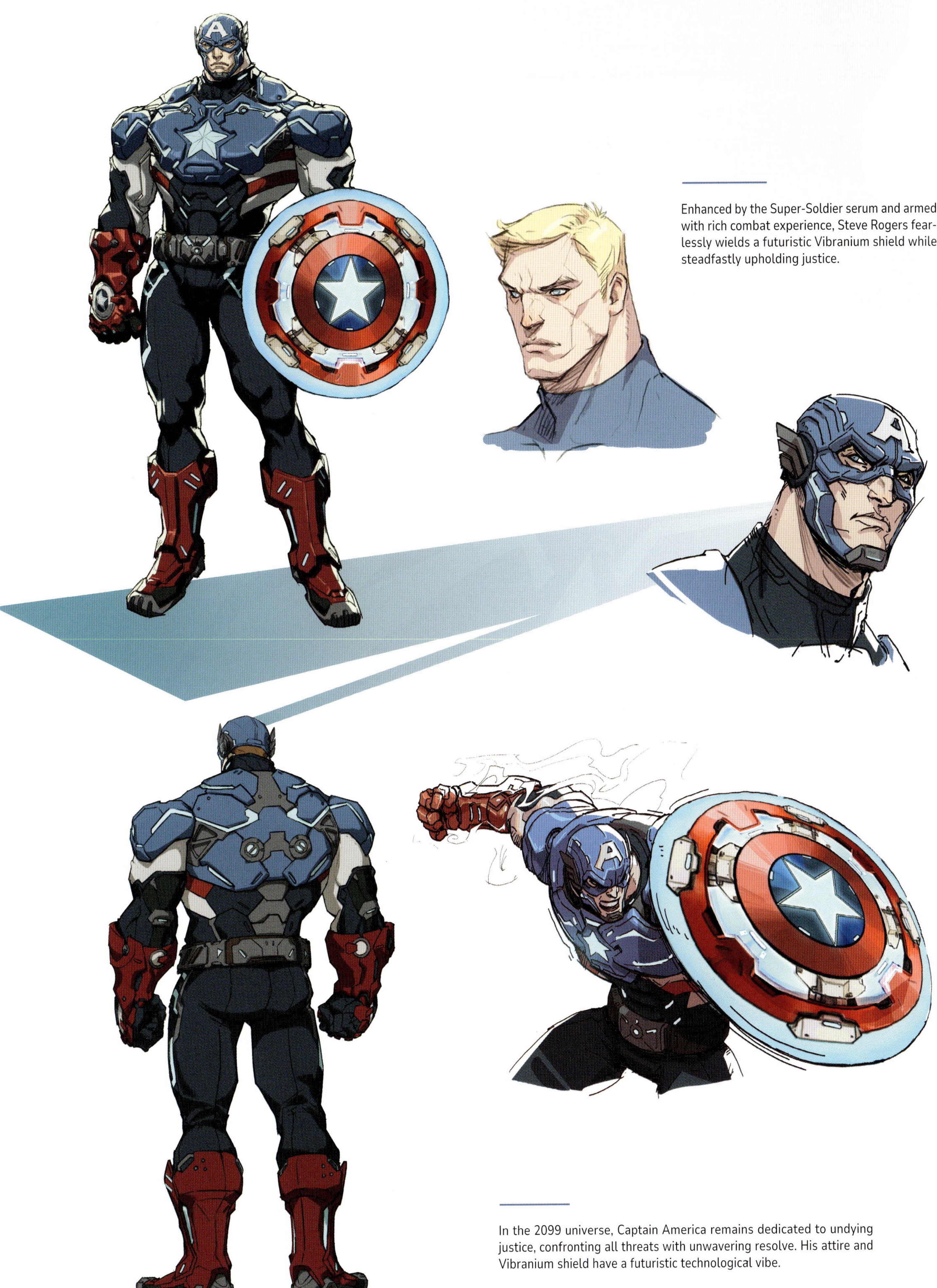

Enhanced by the Super-Soldier serum and armed with rich combat experience, Steve Rogers fearlessly wields a futuristic Vibranium shield while steadfastly upholding justice.

In the 2099 universe, Captain America remains dedicated to undying justice, confronting all threats with unwavering resolve. His attire and Vibranium shield have a futuristic technological vibe.

CAPTAIN AMERICA: ABILITIES

Captain America's abilities include high-speed mobility while using his shield for both offense and defense. He can block frontal damage and redirect it while also enhancing his team's combat capabilities.

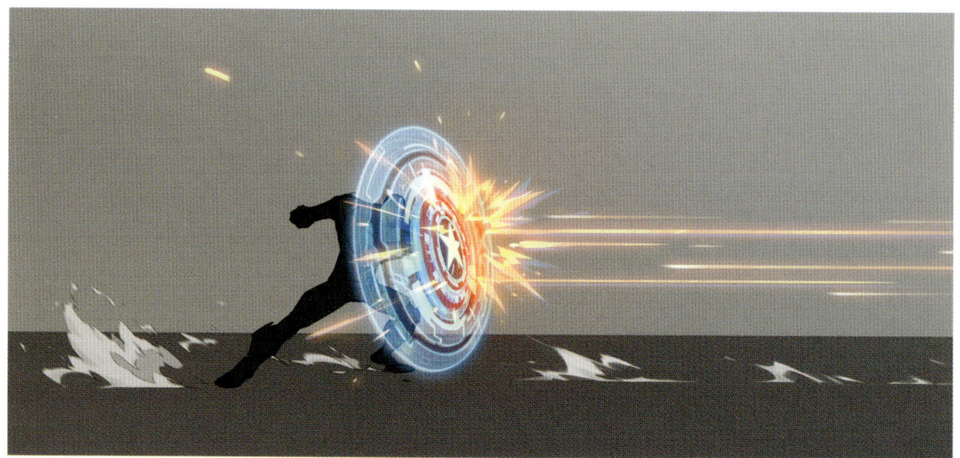

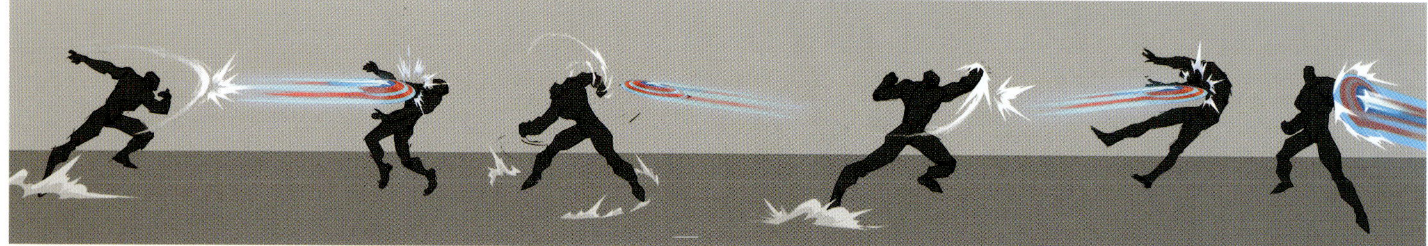

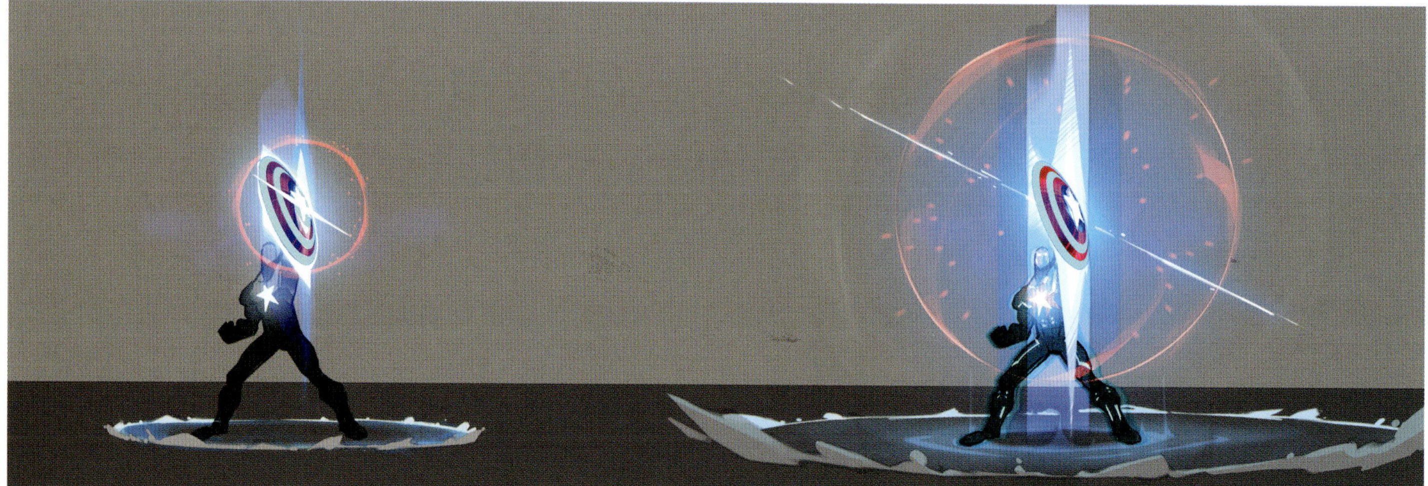

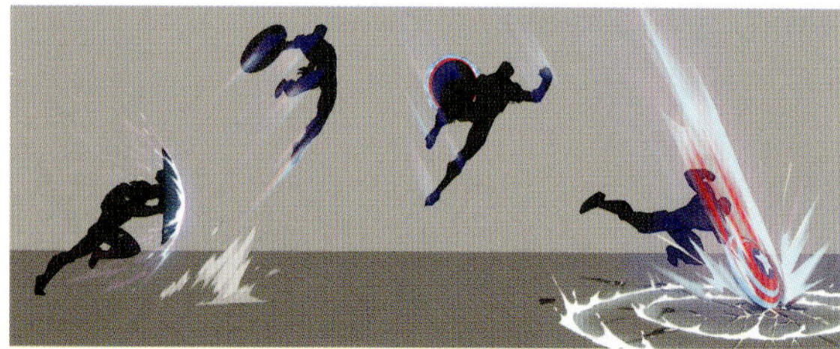

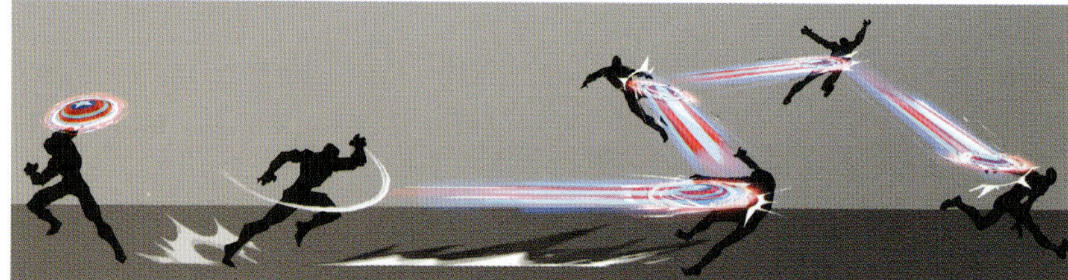

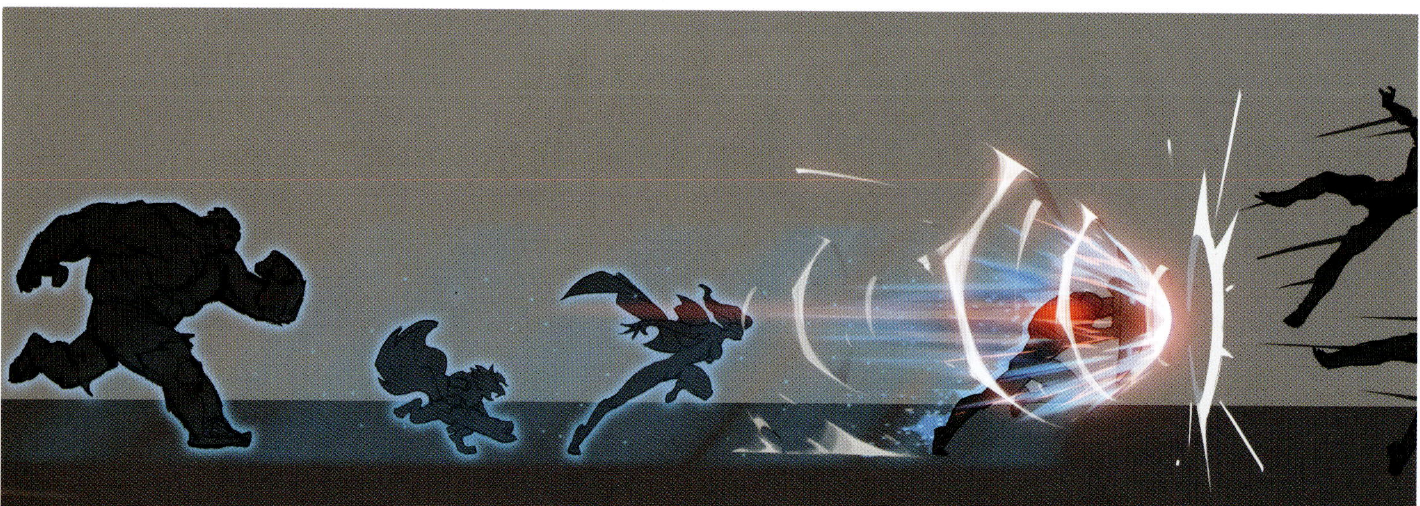

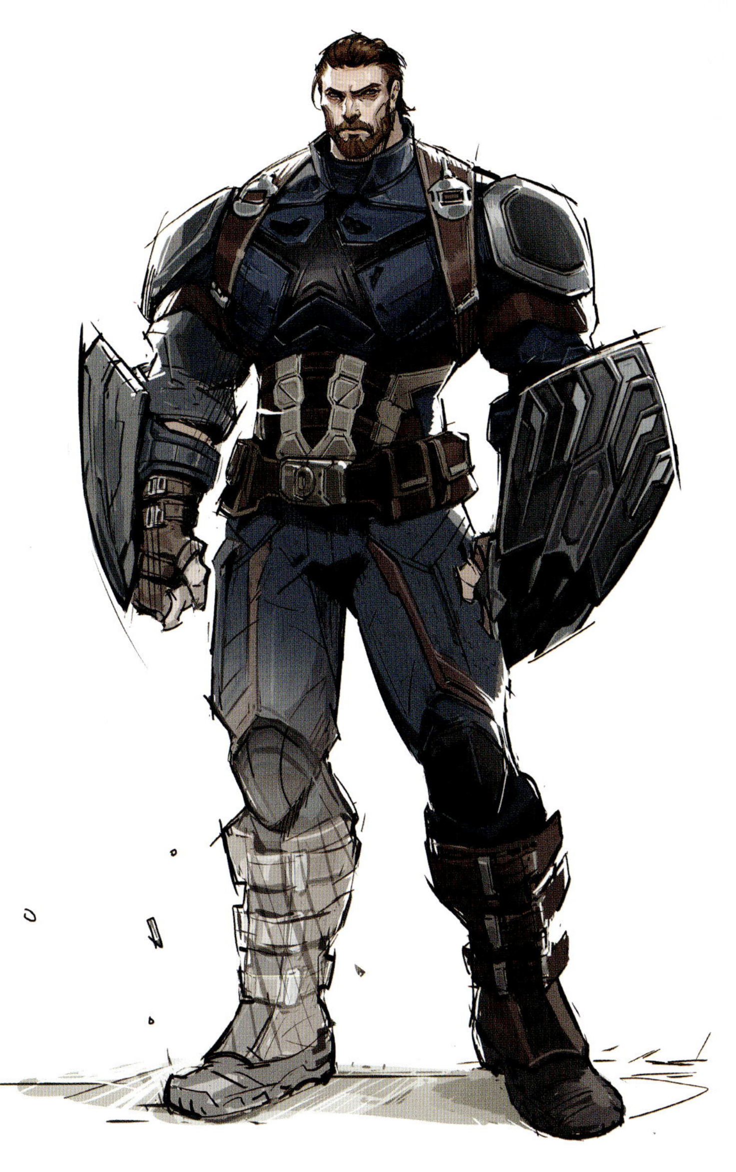

CAPTAIN AMERICA: COSMETIC VARIETY

Inspired by Wakanda's futuristic technology and the eagle symbol, the oversized armor with jet engine elements and sharp claws empowers him to charge fearlessly toward enemies.

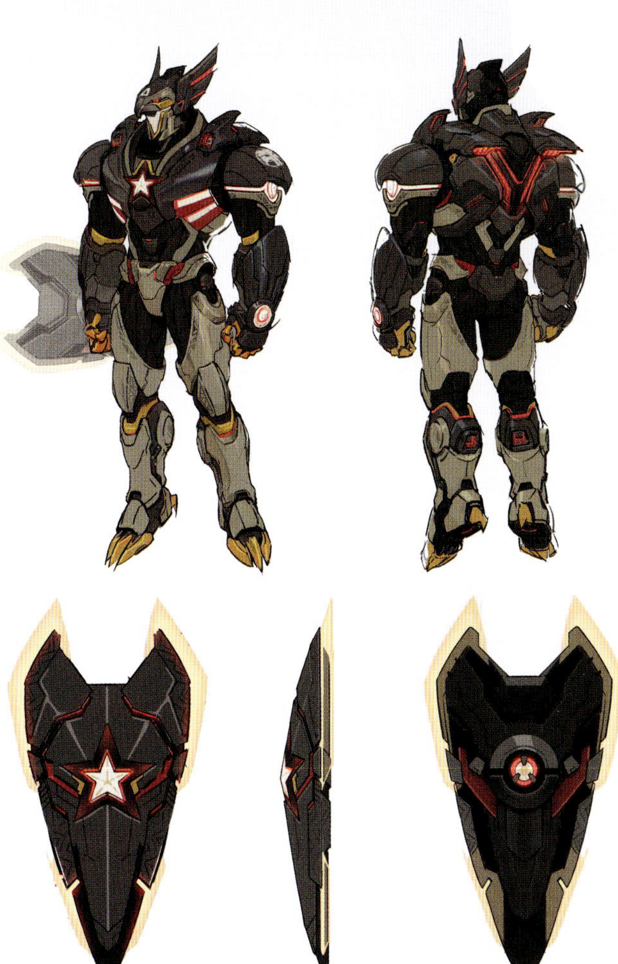

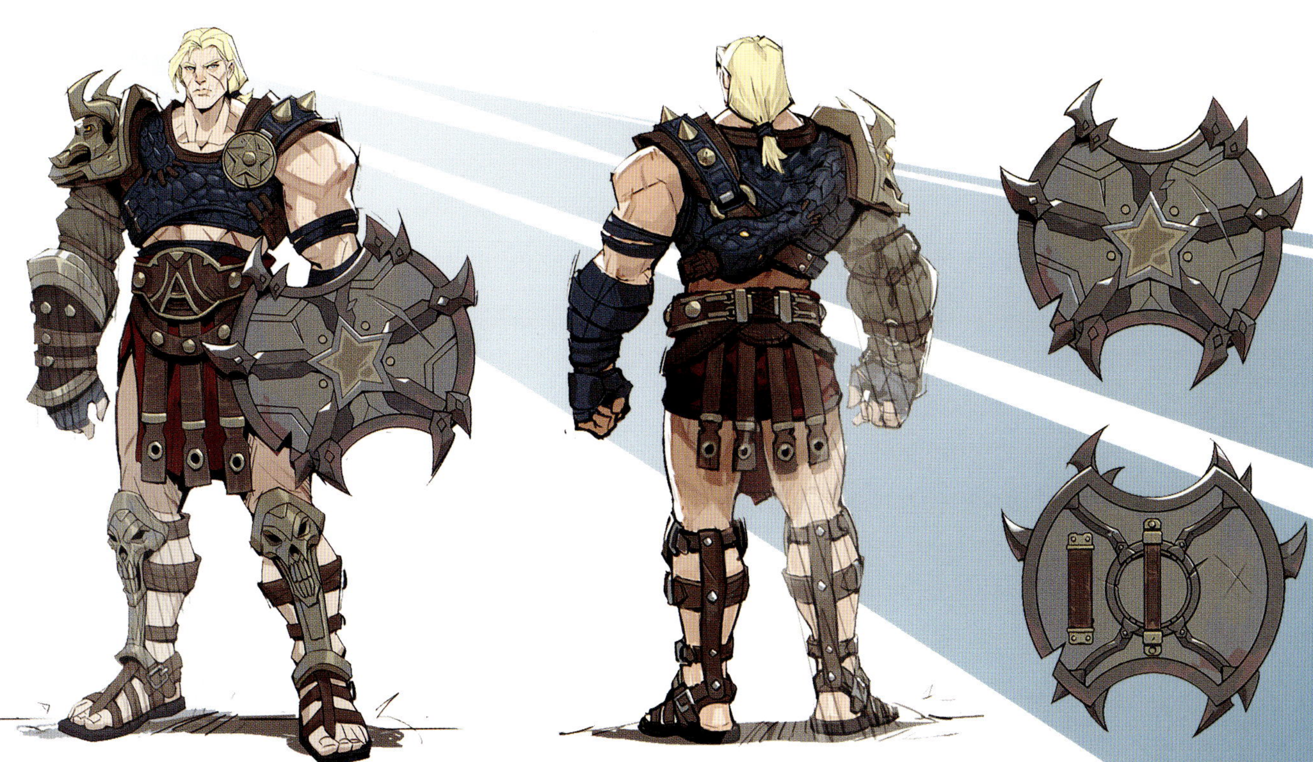

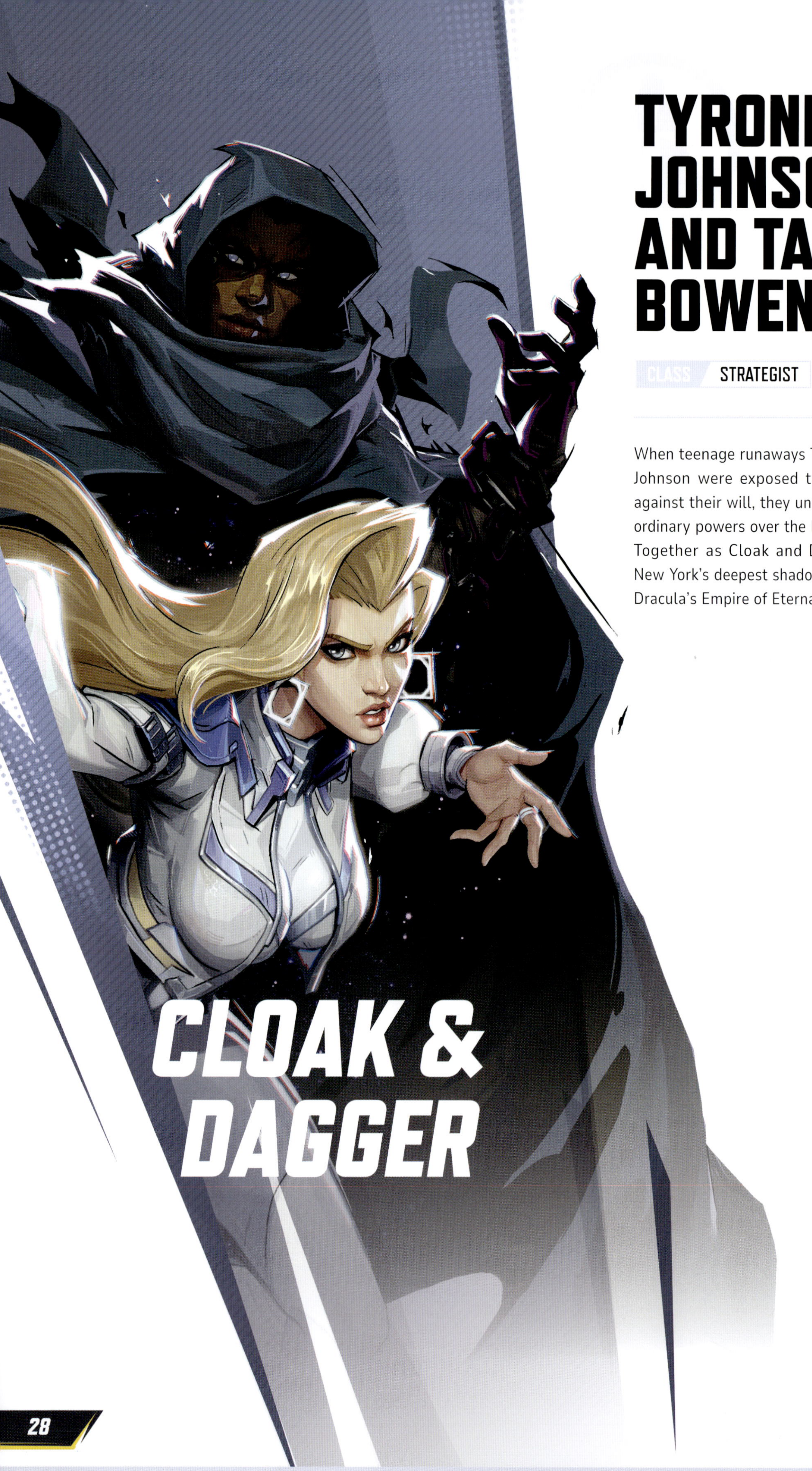

TYRONE JOHNSON AND TANDY BOWEN

CLASS STRATEGIST

When teenage runaways Tandy Bowen and Tyrone Johnson were exposed to an experimental drug against their will, they unexpectedly gained extraordinary powers over the Lightforce and Darkforce. Together as Cloak and Dagger, they illuminate New York's deepest shadows as they battle against Dracula's Empire of Eternal Night.

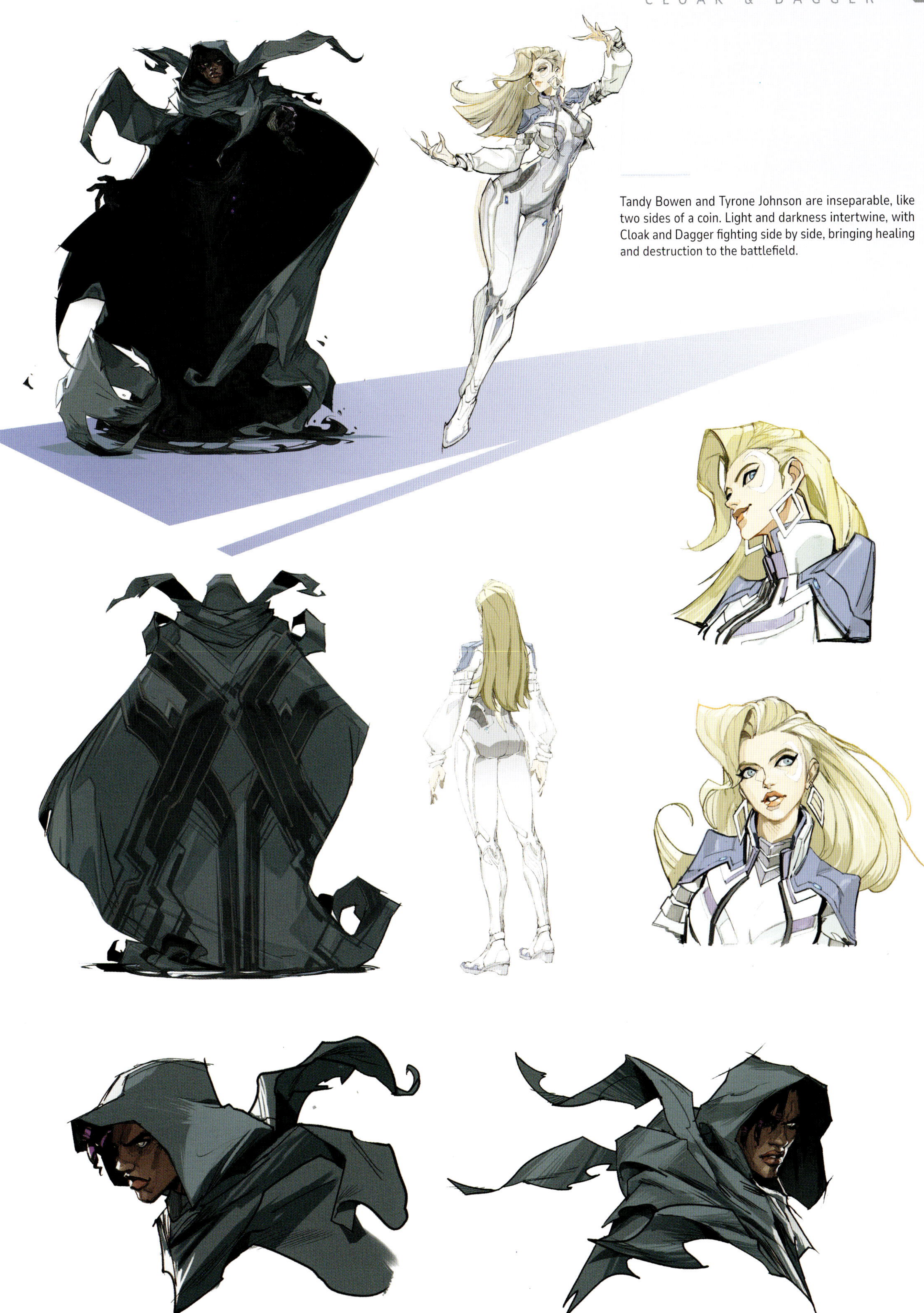

Tandy Bowen and Tyrone Johnson are inseparable, like two sides of a coin. Light and darkness intertwine, with Cloak and Dagger fighting side by side, bringing healing and destruction to the battlefield.

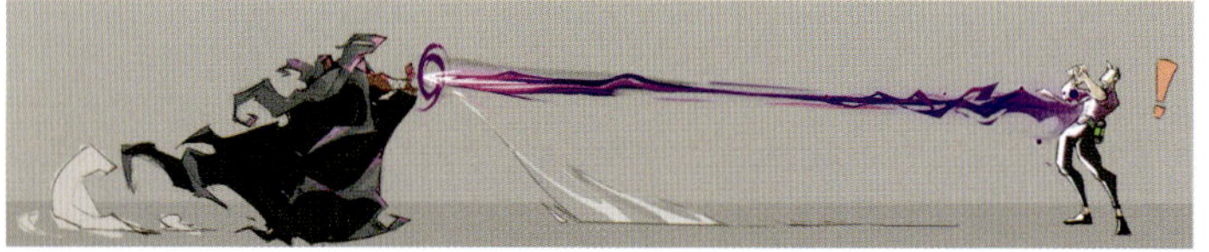
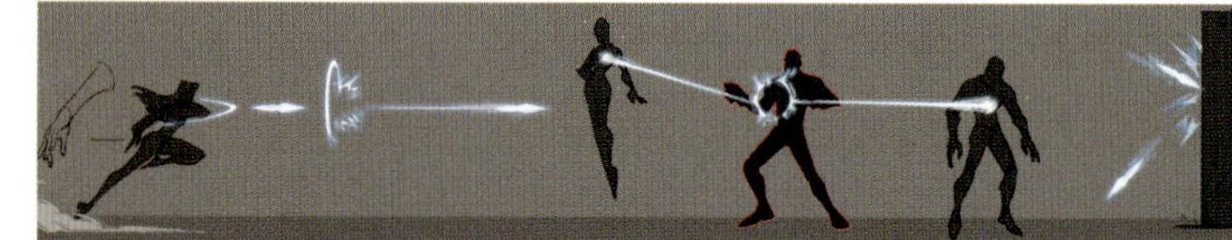
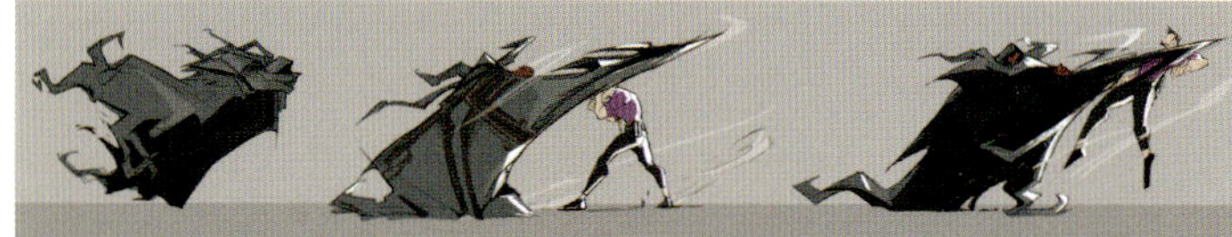
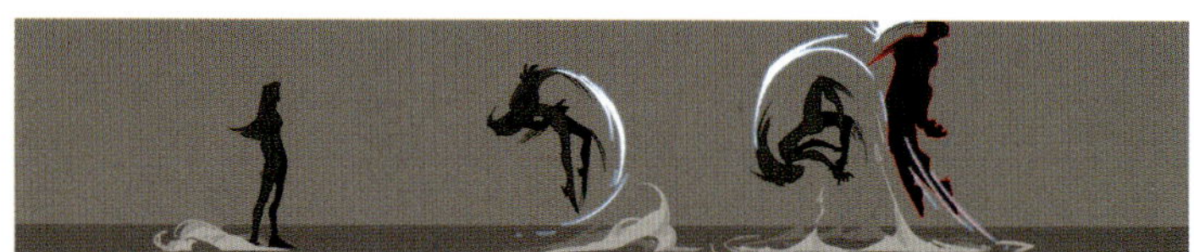
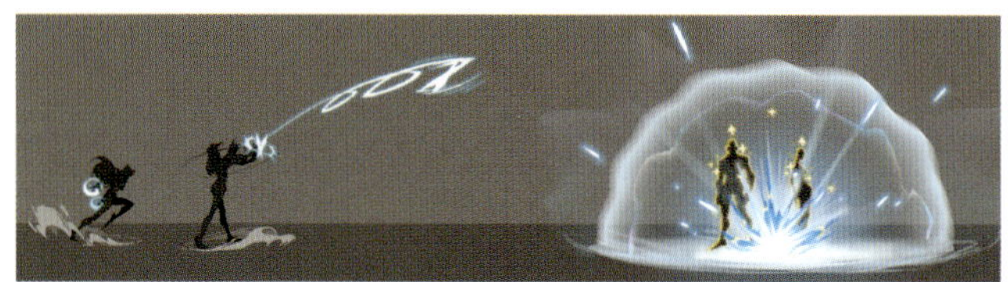
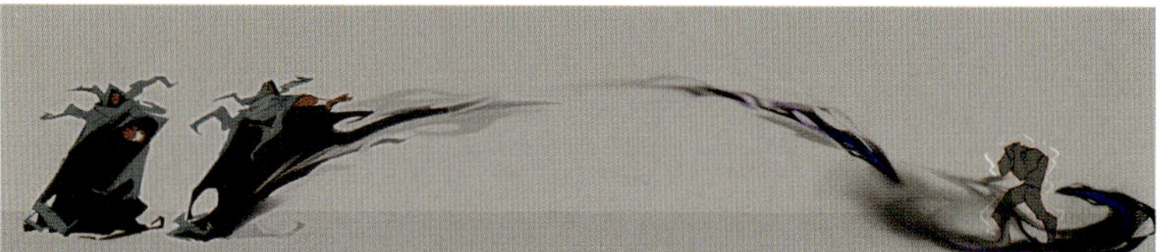
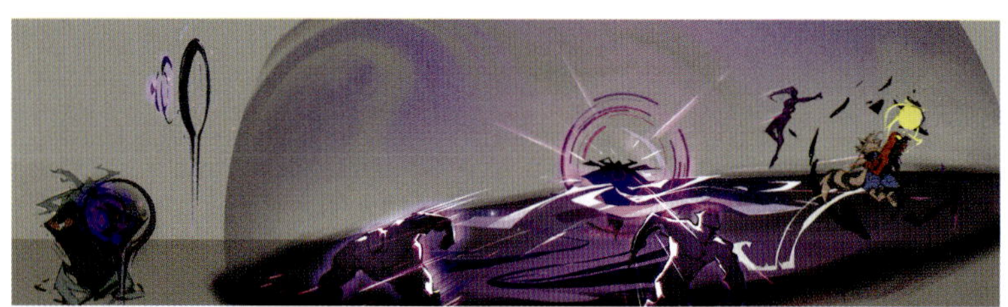
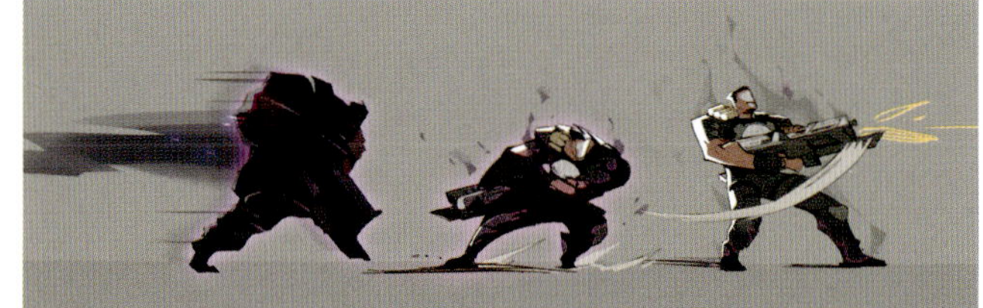
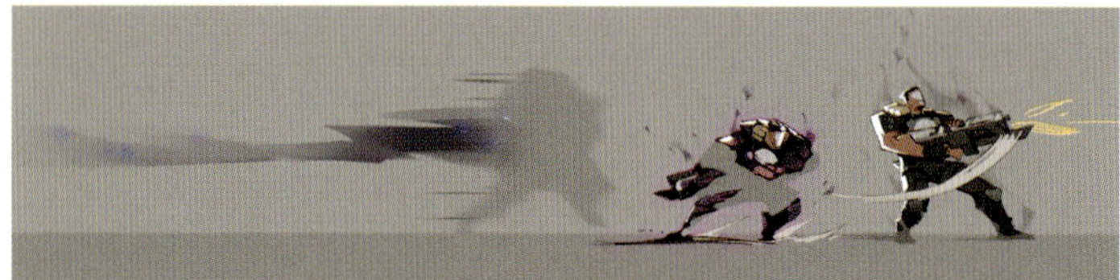
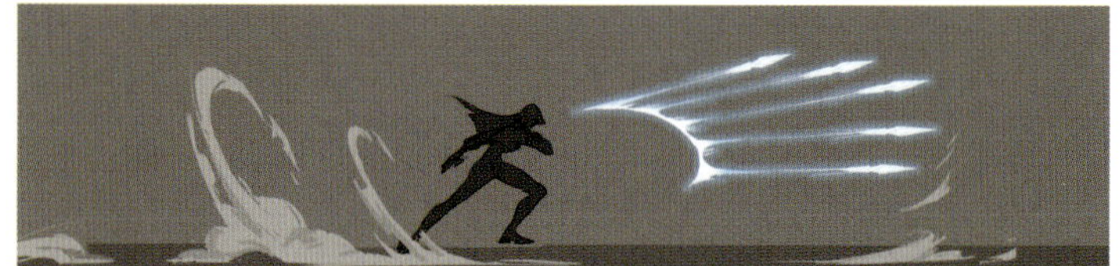
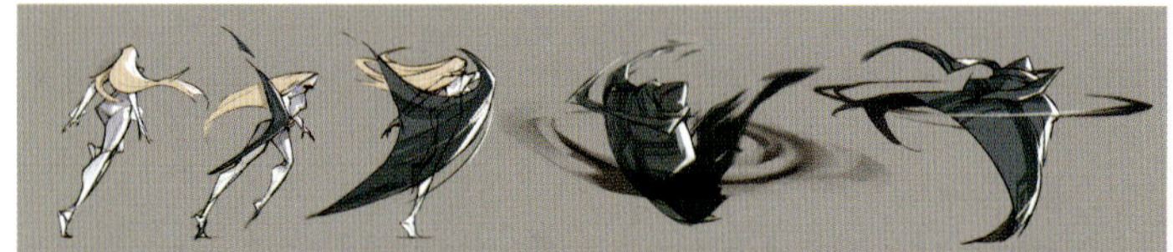
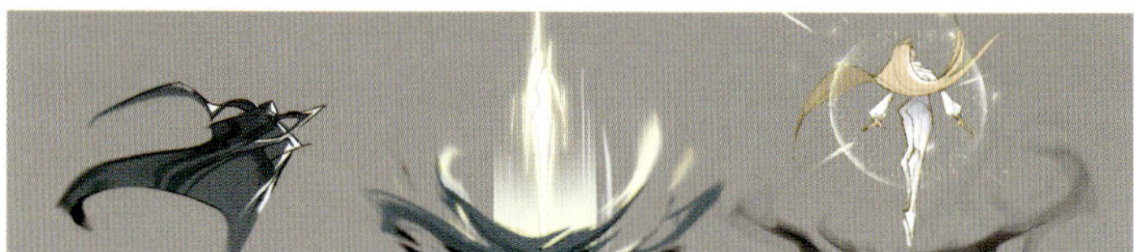
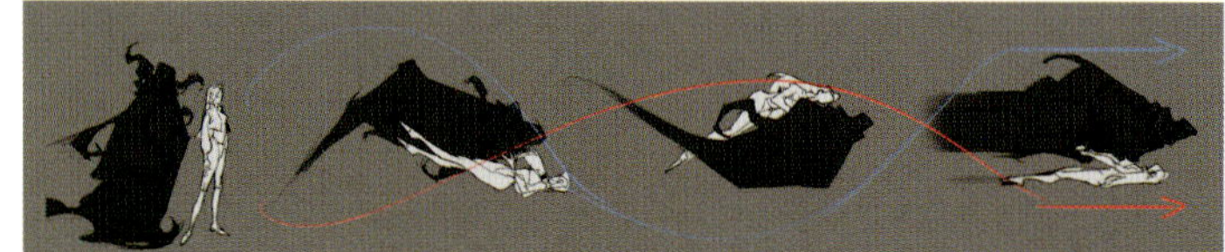
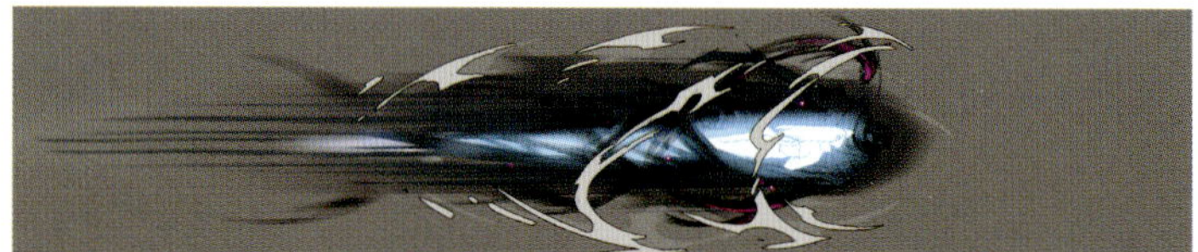

CLOAK & DAGGER: ABILITIES

Cloak and Dagger can be interchanged at any time. Dagger, as the light, can heal the team and provide buffs, while Cloak inflicts continuous damage and negative status on the enemy.

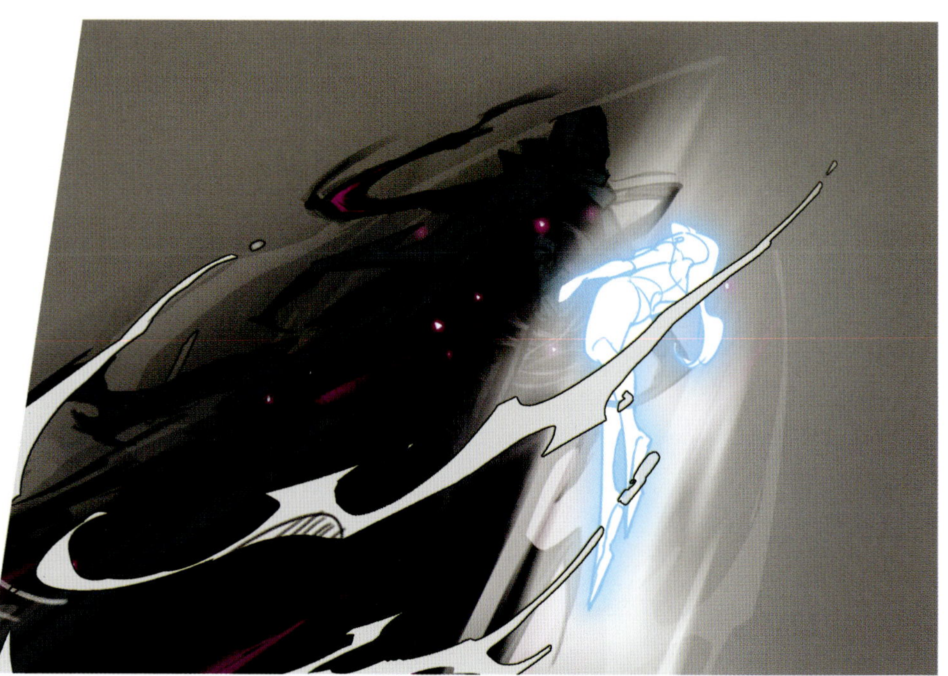

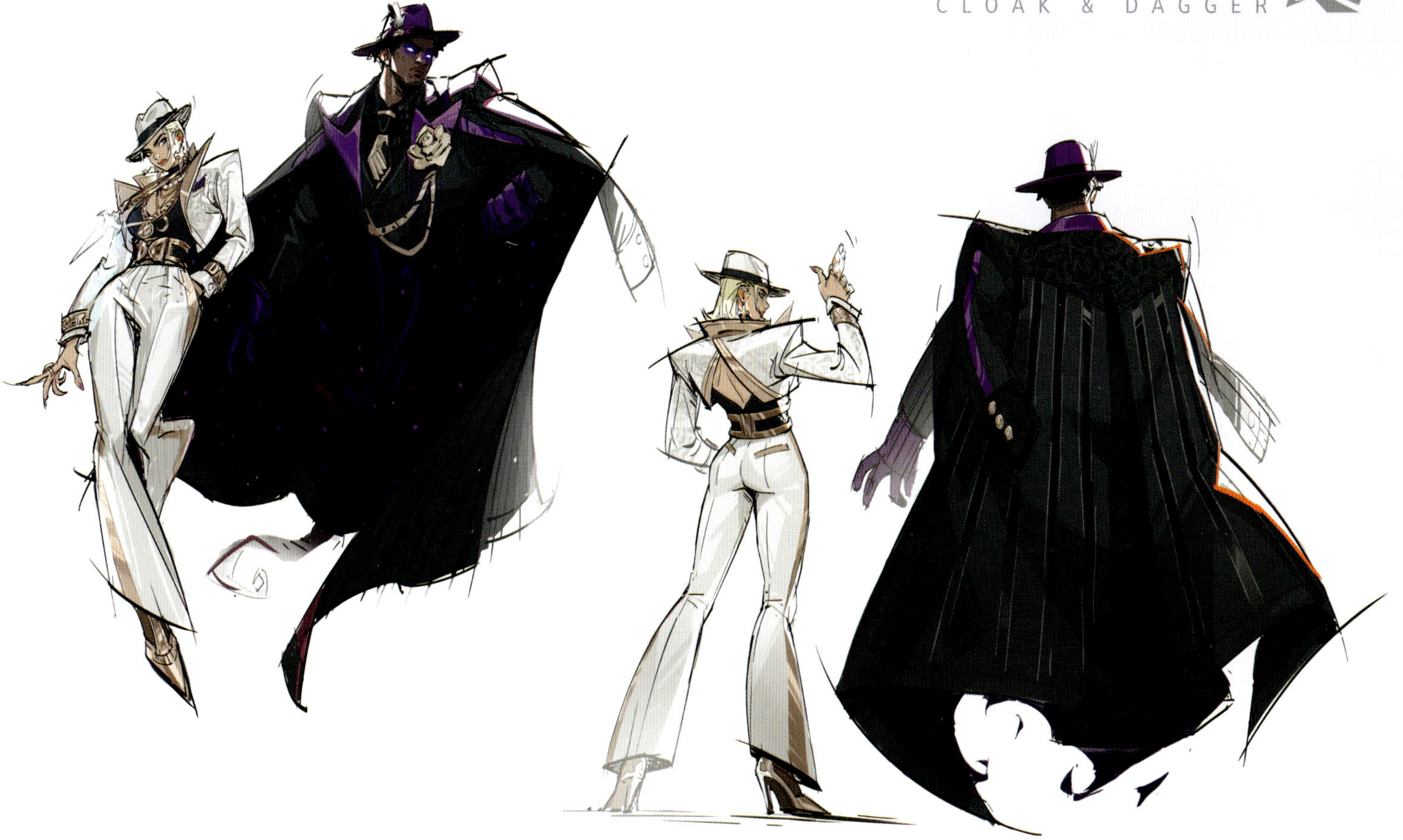

CLOAK & DAGGER: COSMETIC VARIETY

Petals, thorns, and old wood . . . Nature provides boundless inspiration. The spirits of light and darkness intertwine in spring, akin to a dormant branch springing back to life.

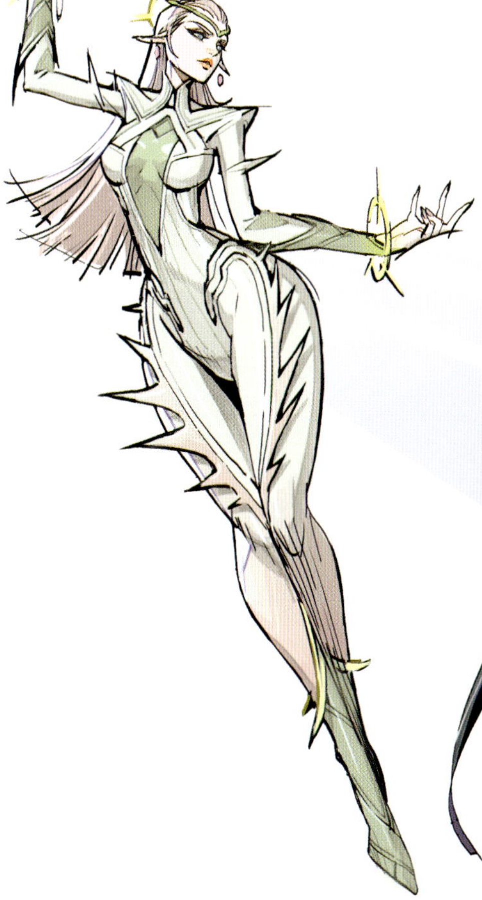

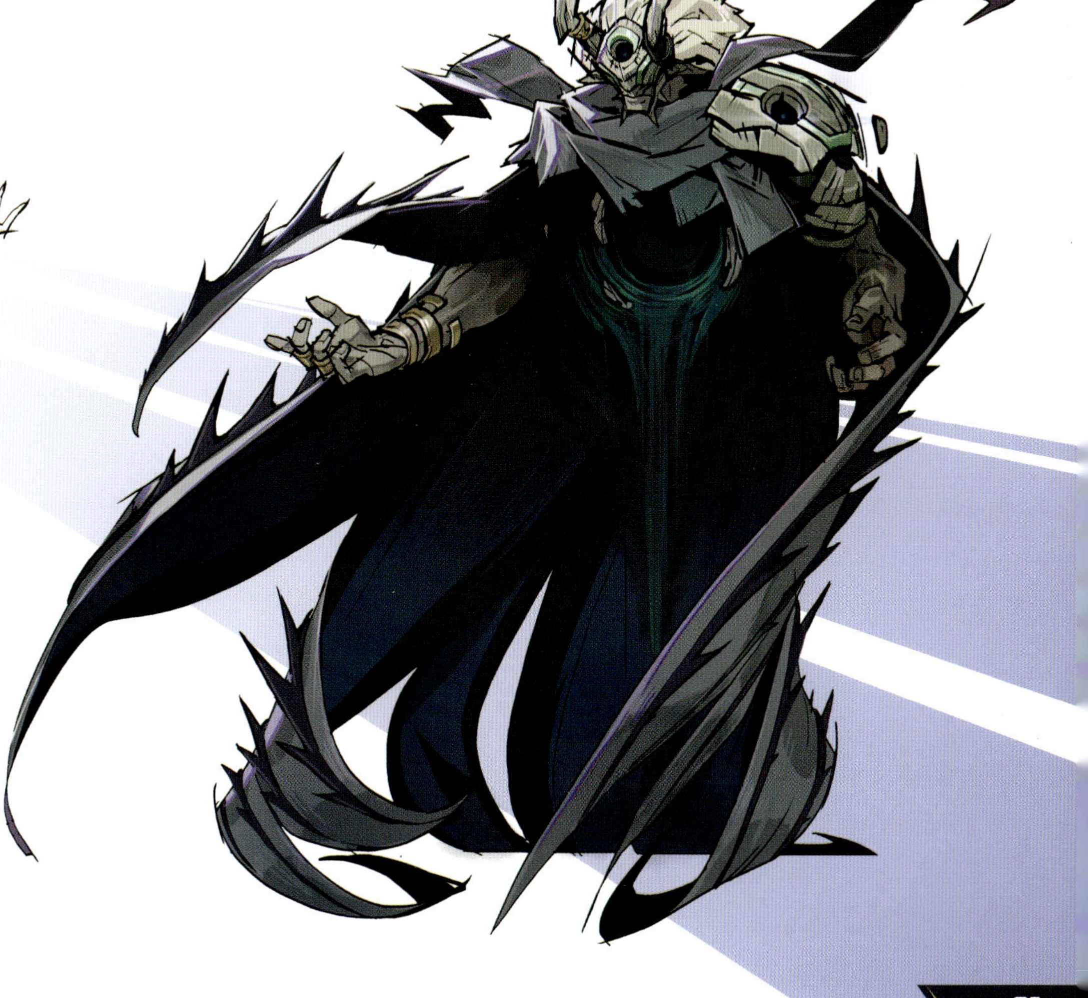

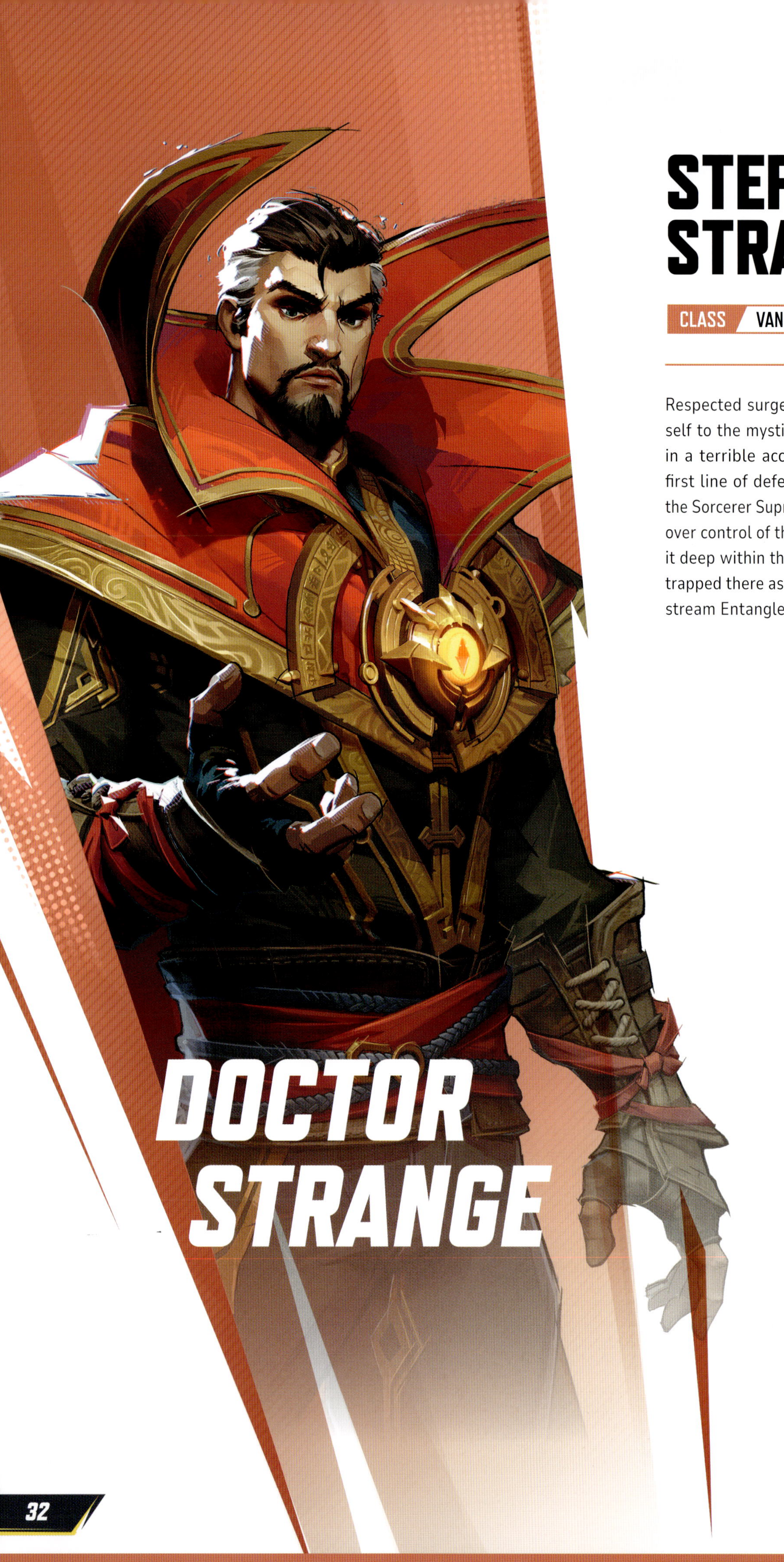

STEPHEN STRANGE

CLASS / VANGUARD

Respected surgeon Stephen Strange devoted himself to the mystic arts after his hands were injured in a terrible accident, becoming this dimension's first line of defense against supernatural threats: the Sorcerer Supreme. After combating Doctor Doom over control of the Darkhold, Doctor Strange buried it deep within the Astral Plane, only to find himself trapped there as well when caught within the Timestream Entanglement.

As Sorcerer Supreme, Doctor Strange elegantly uses spells to restore balance in battle. However, the use of magic comes with a cost, as each employment of arcane power slowly awakens the darkness within his heart.

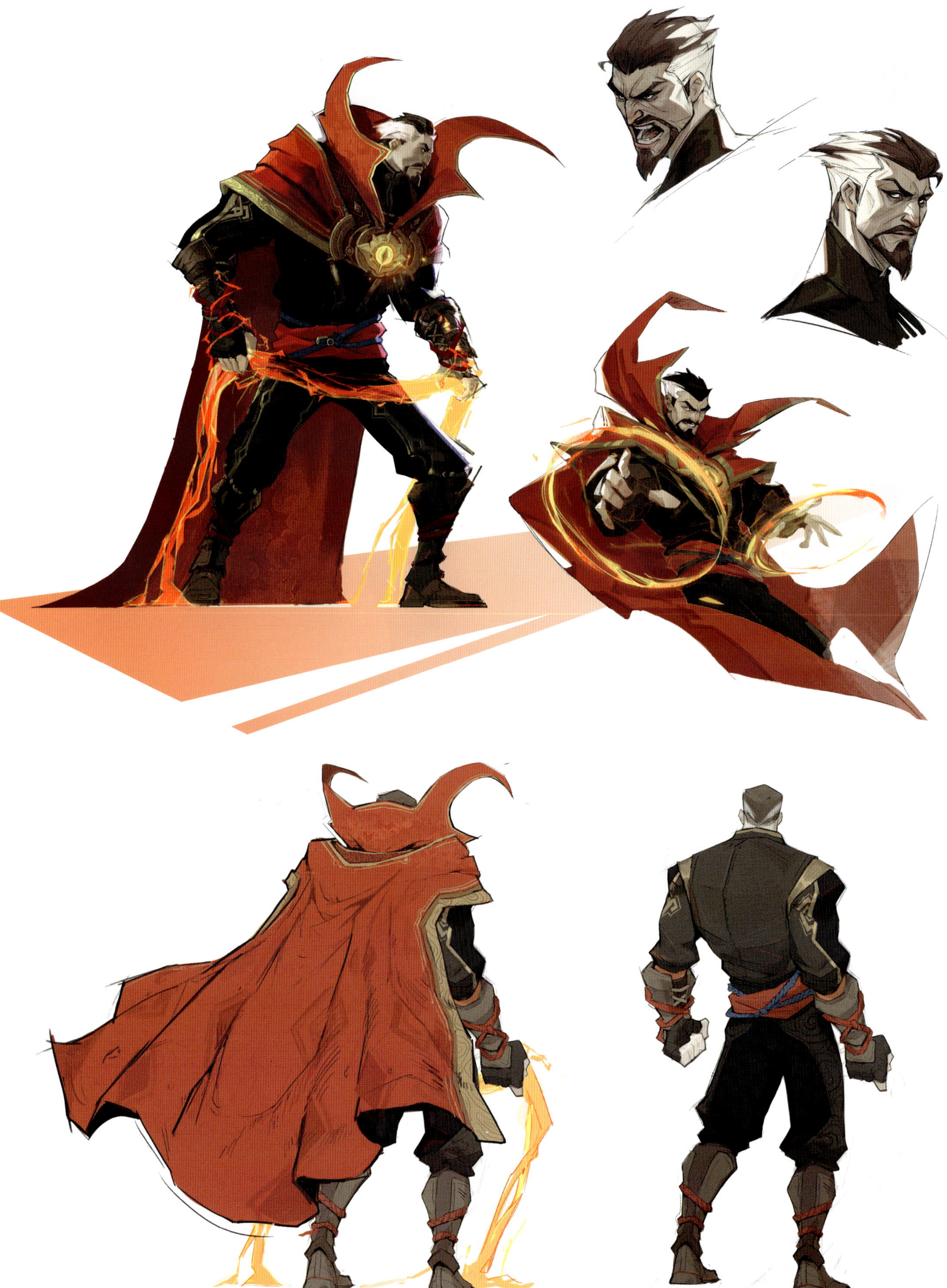

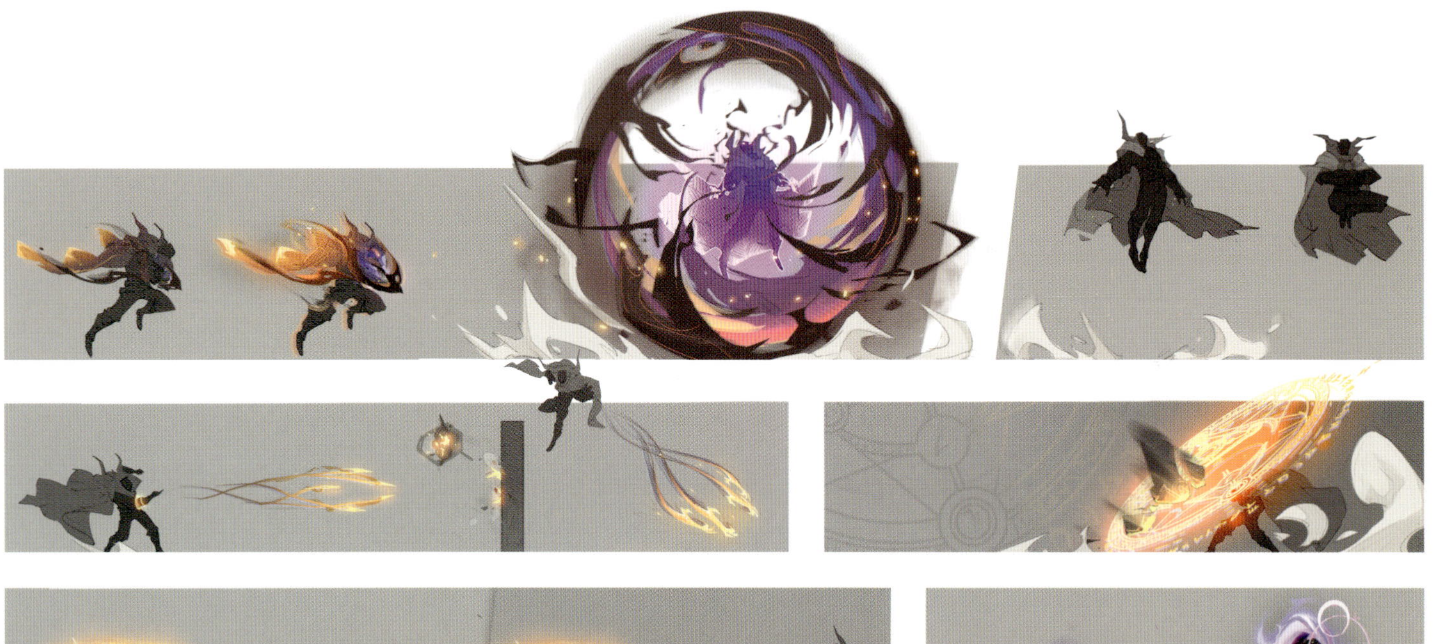

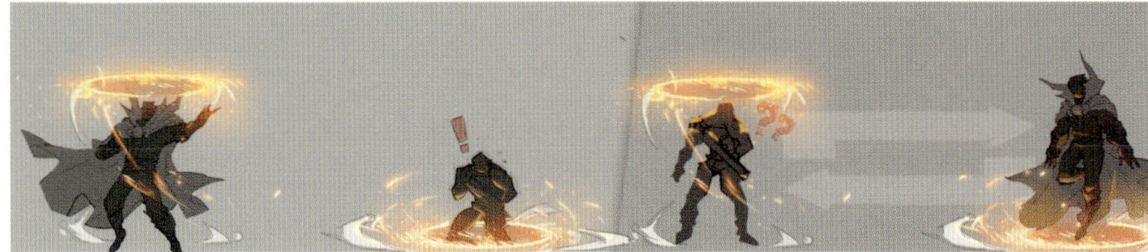

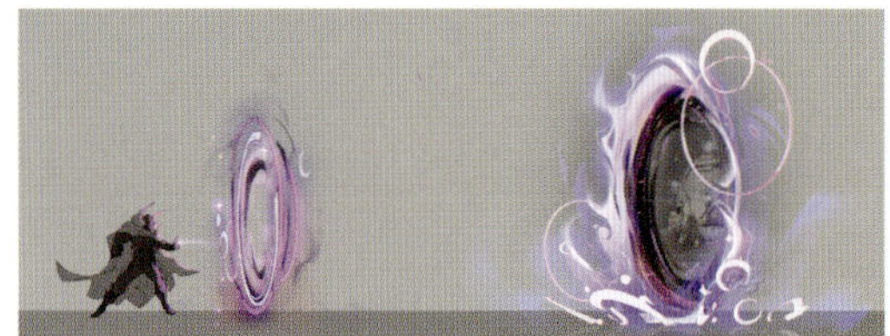

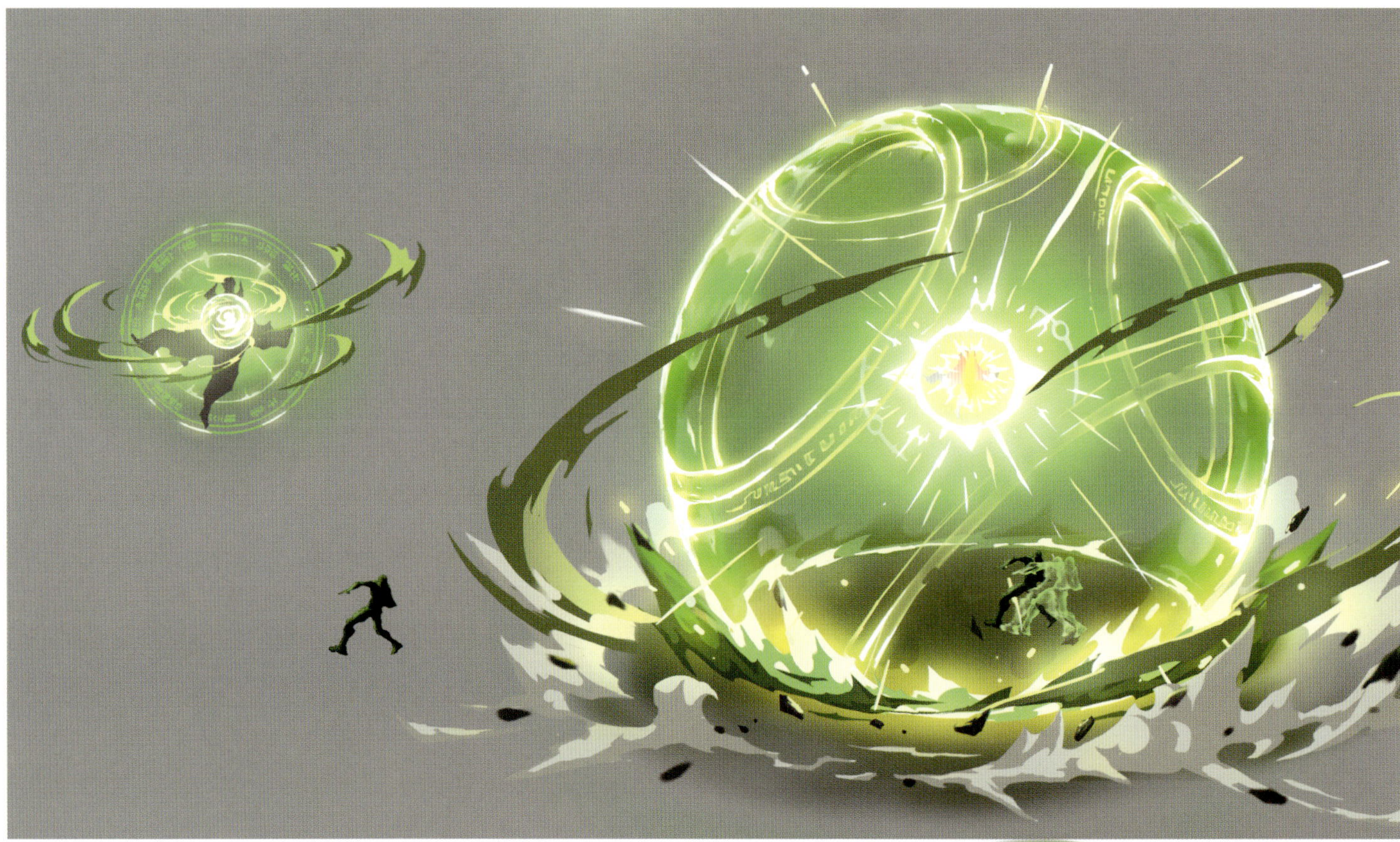

DOCTOR STRANGE: ABILITIES

Doctor Strange creates portals for swift movement through space, deploys a formidable shield to withstand enemy attacks, and utilizes the Eye of Agamotto to separate souls from bodies, thereby achieving widespread control of multiple people.

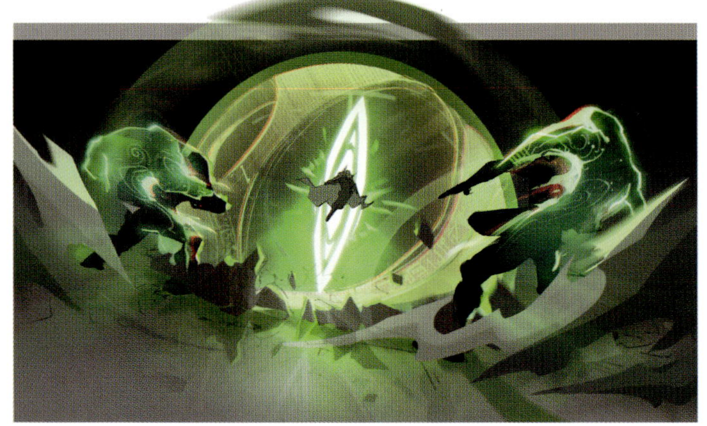

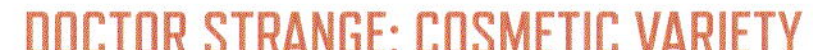

DOCTOR STRANGE: COSMETIC VARIETY

The God of Magic, adorned in a white robe with three eyes, wears clothing woven in a crossed pattern beneath, displaying a unique style reminiscent of Nordic mythology.

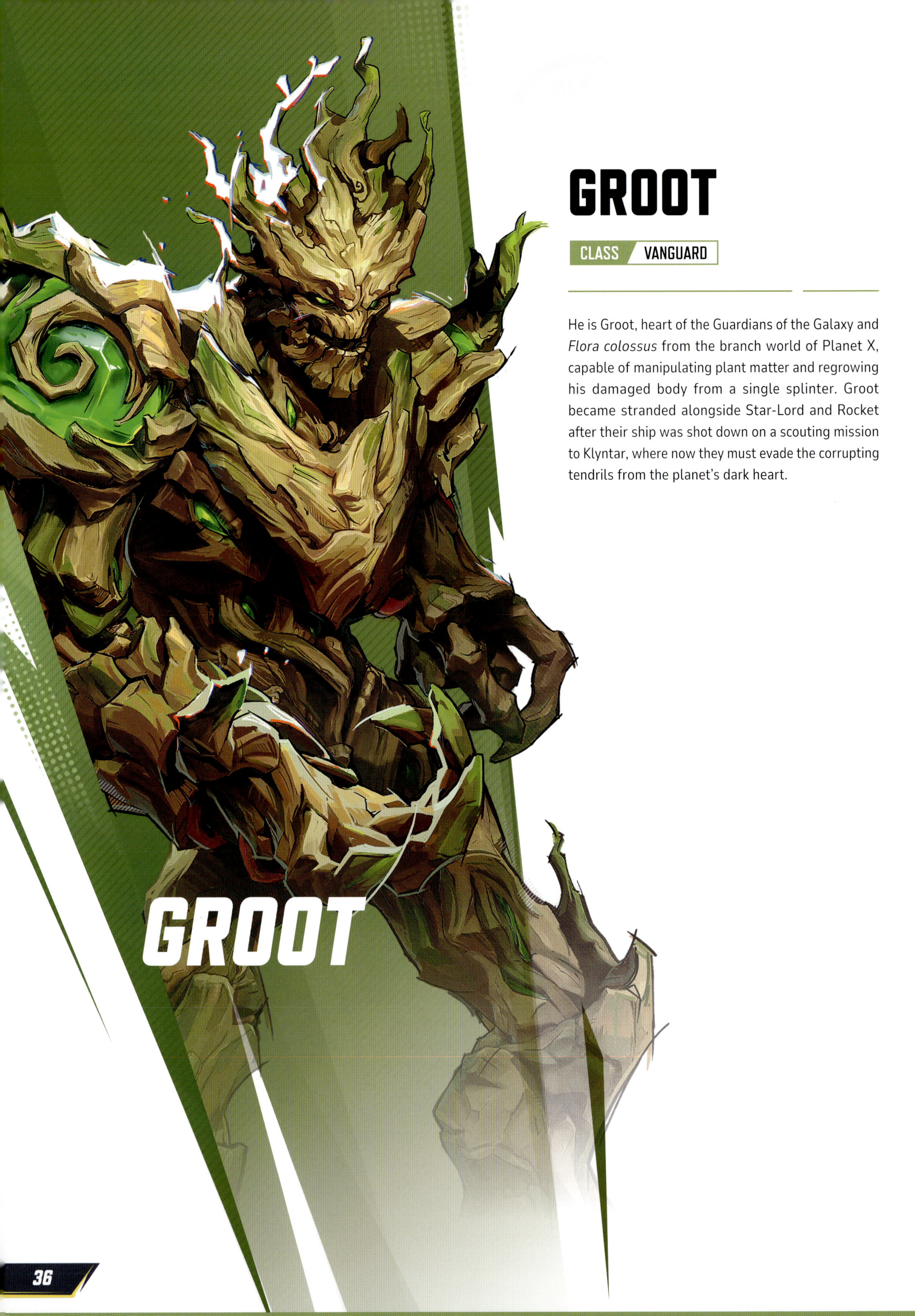

GROOT

CLASS / VANGUARD

He is Groot, heart of the Guardians of the Galaxy and *Flora colossus* from the branch world of Planet X, capable of manipulating plant matter and regrowing his damaged body from a single splinter. Groot became stranded alongside Star-Lord and Rocket after their ship was shot down on a scouting mission to Klyntar, where now they must evade the corrupting tendrils from the planet's dark heart.

Groo boasts exceptional vitality and plant manipulation abilities. Resilient and sturdy as a towering tree, he acts as the team's silent yet dependable pathfinder.

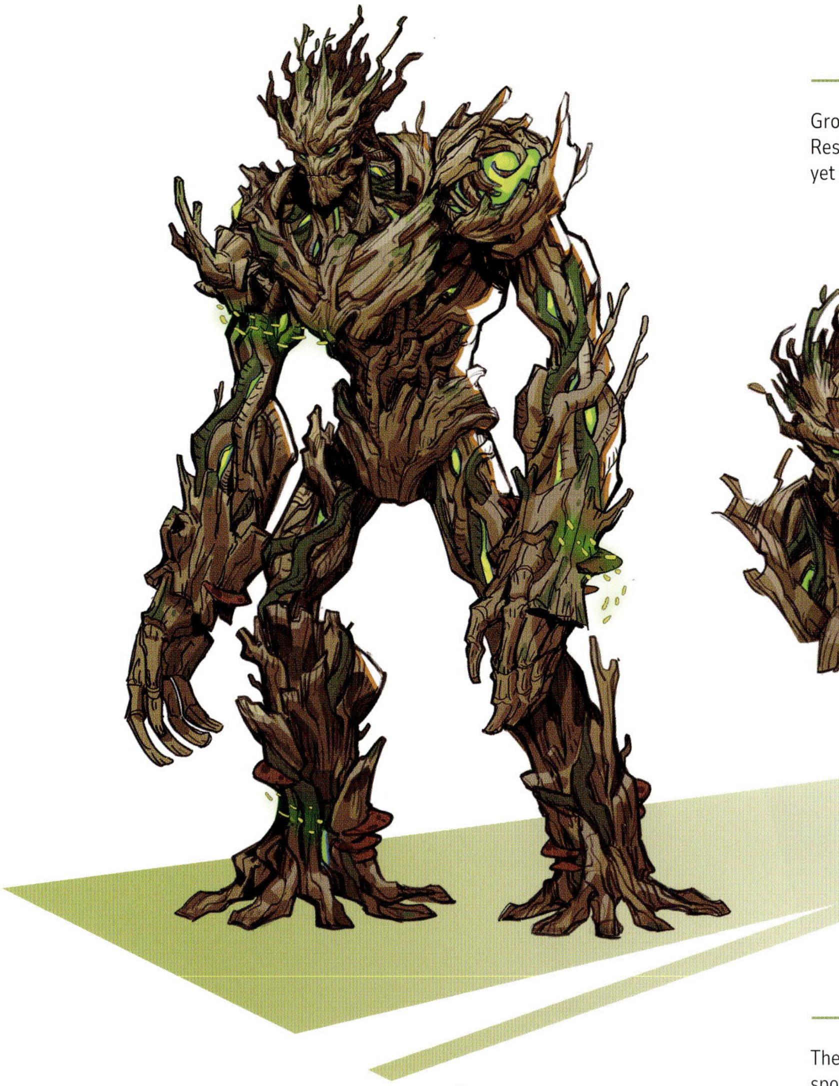

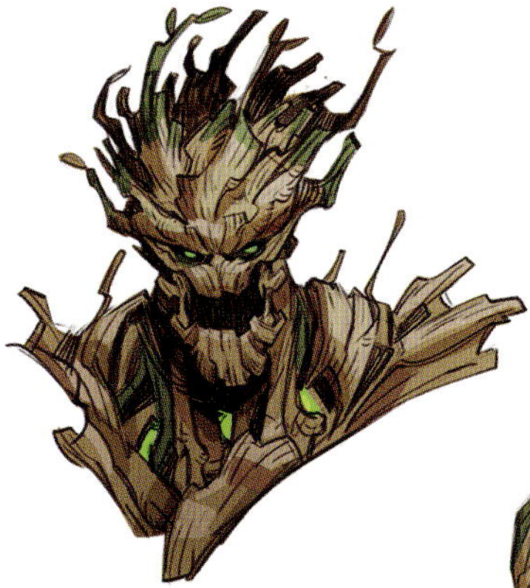

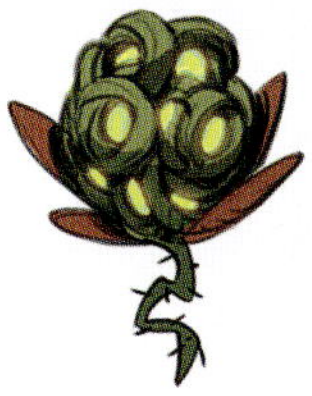

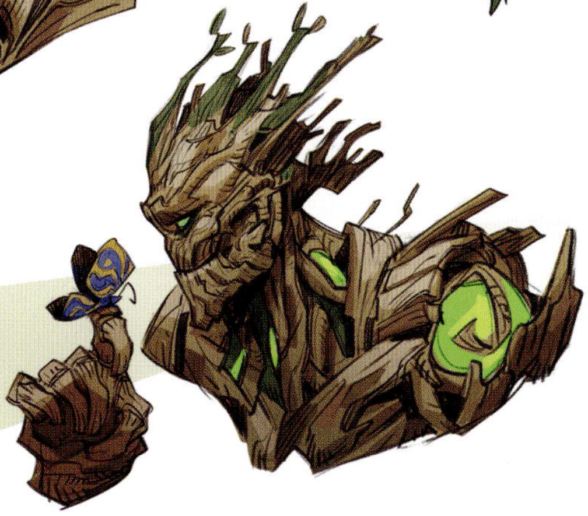

The body covered with entwined branches is adorned with luminous spores and budding growths, often drawing small radiant creatures to pause and encircle it, forming a miniature ecosystem.

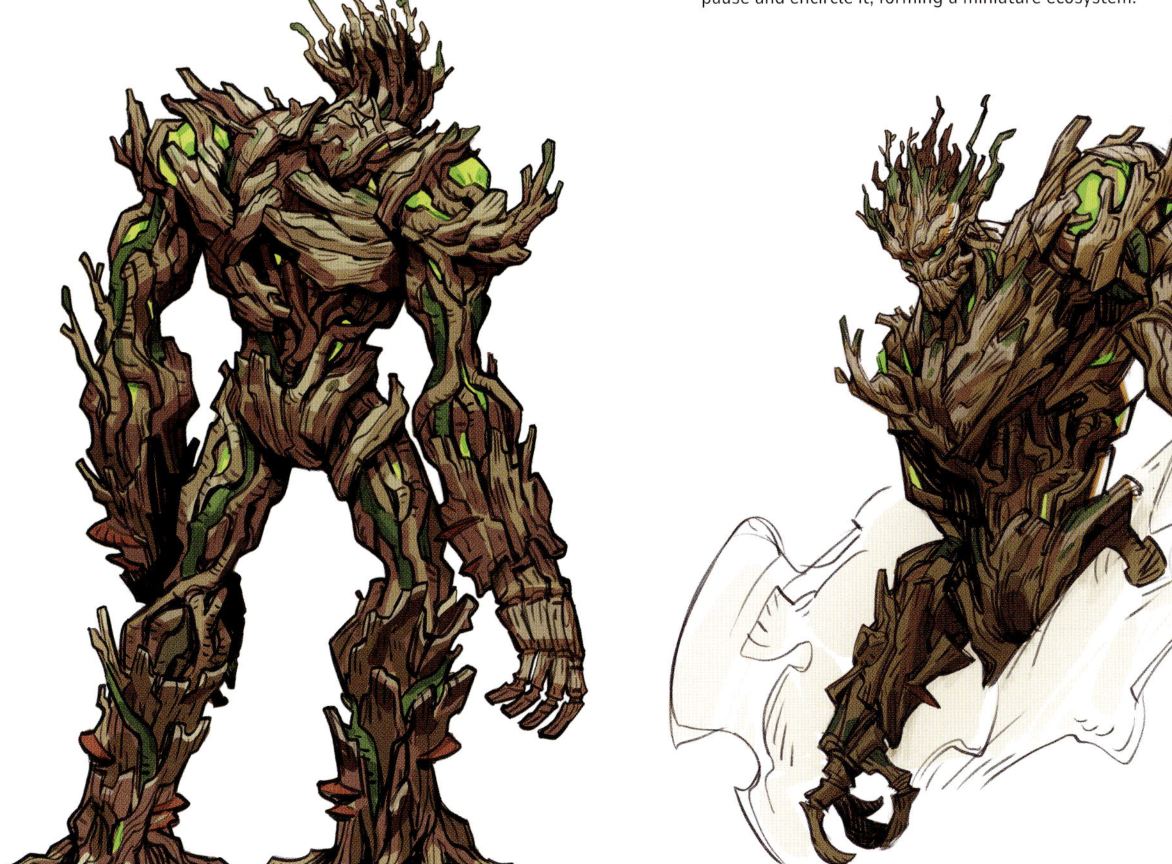

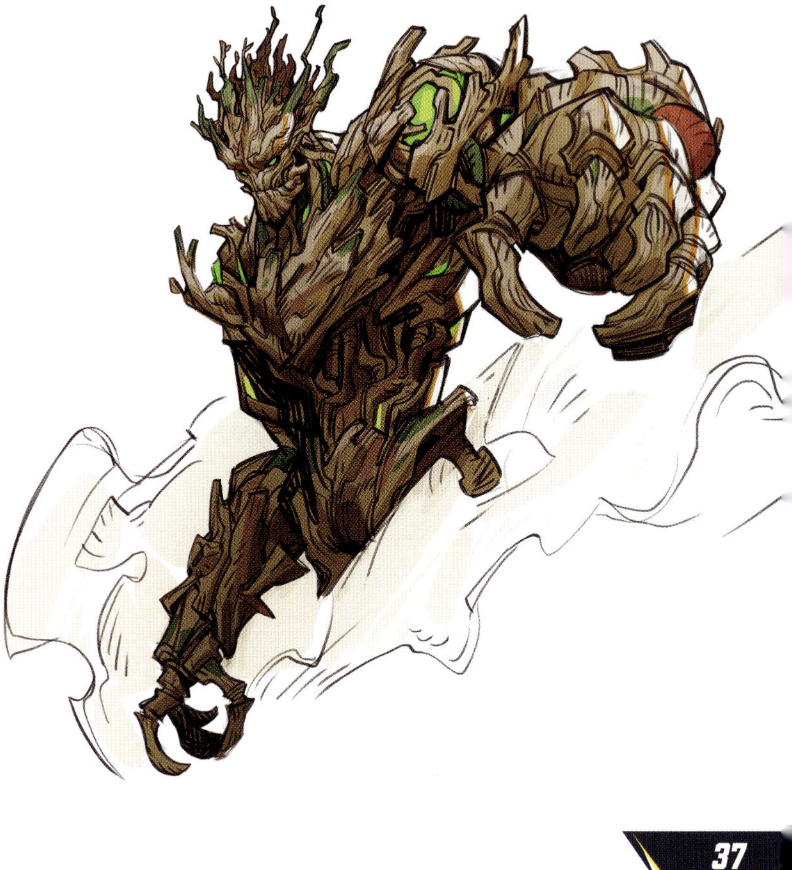

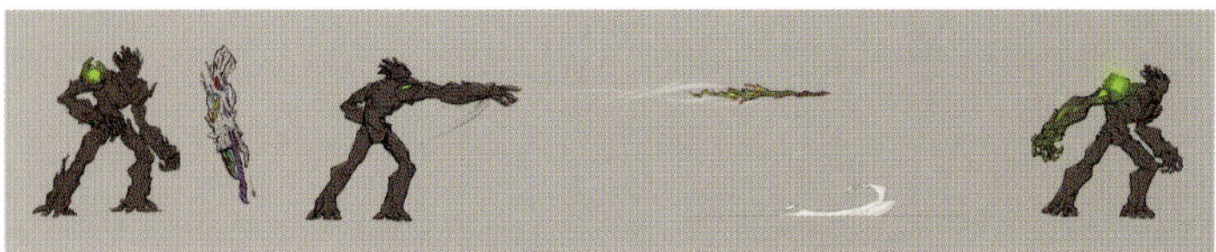
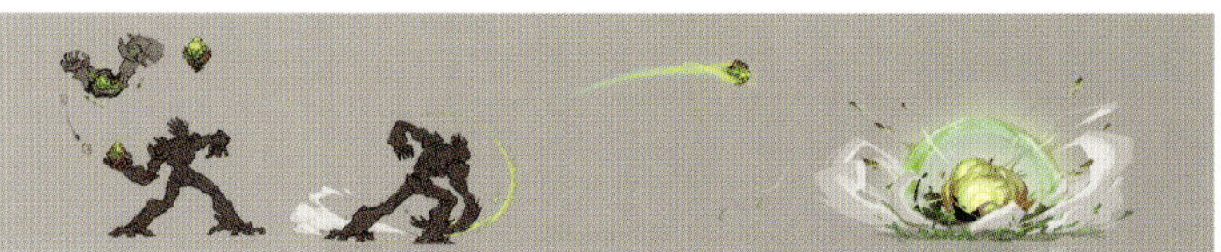
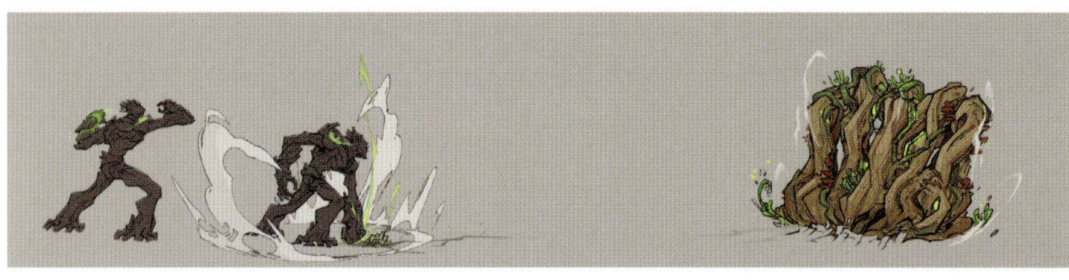
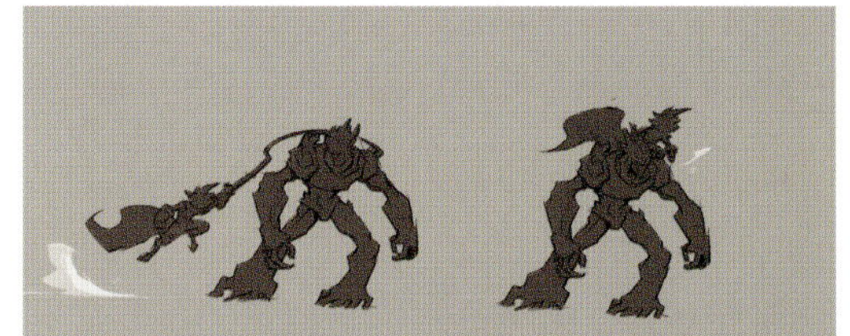
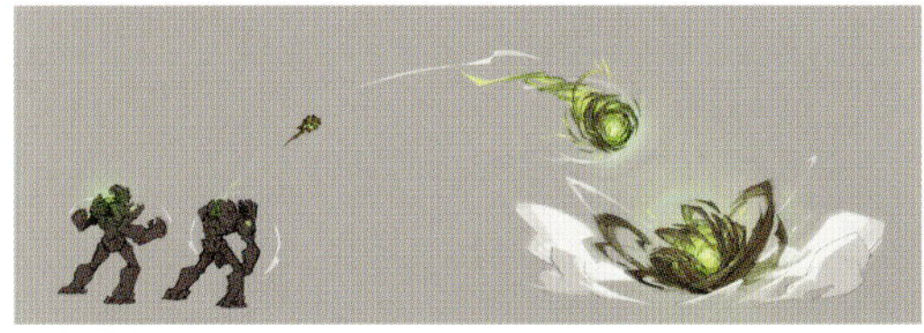
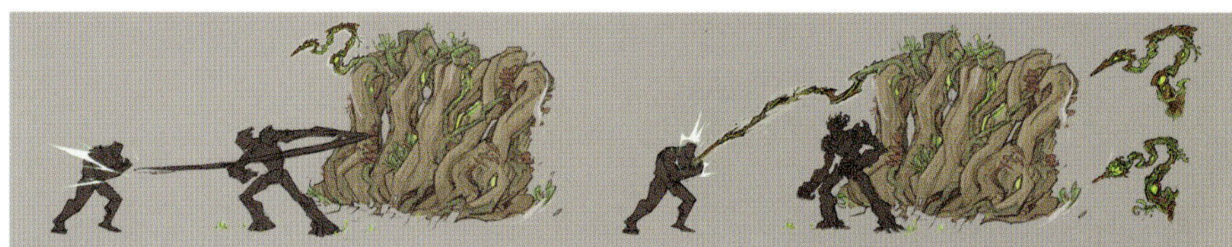
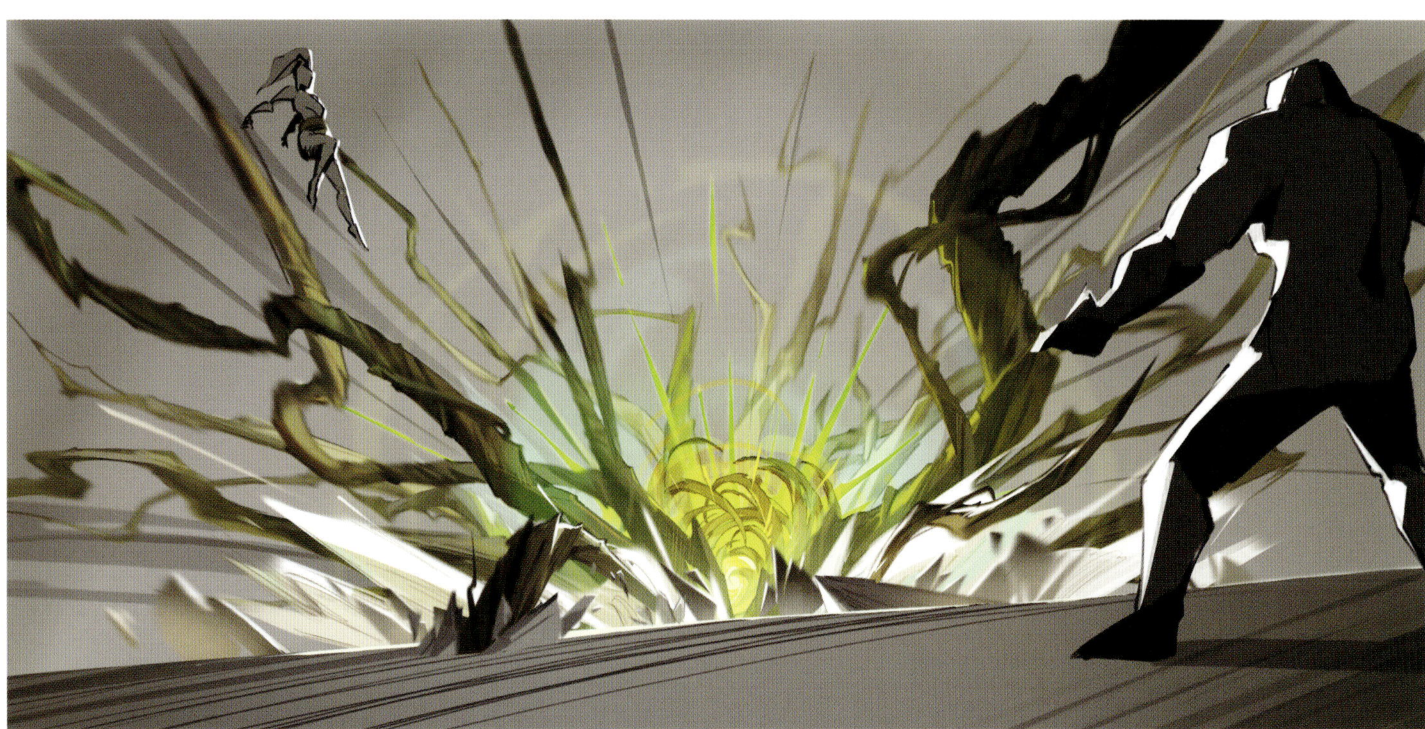
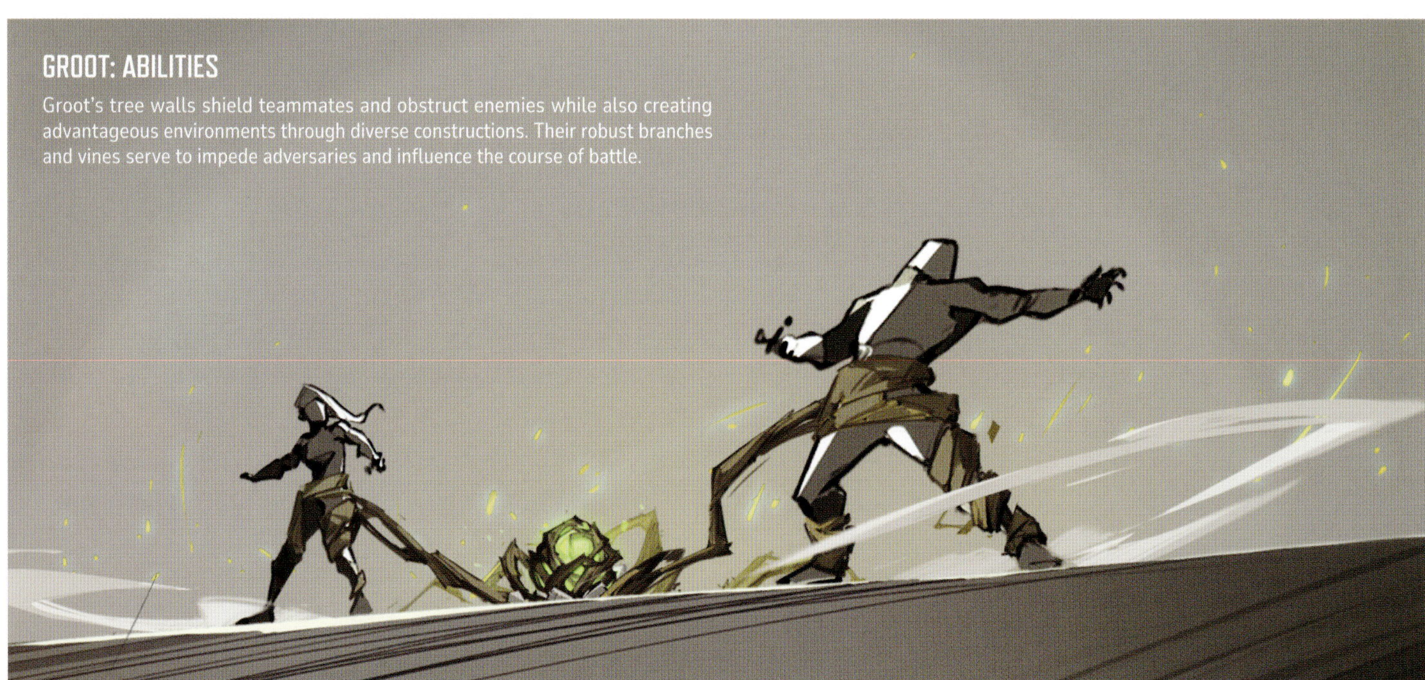

GROOT: ABILITIES

Groot's tree walls shield teammates and obstruct enemies while also creating advantageous environments through diverse constructions. Their robust branches and vines serve to impede adversaries and influence the course of battle.

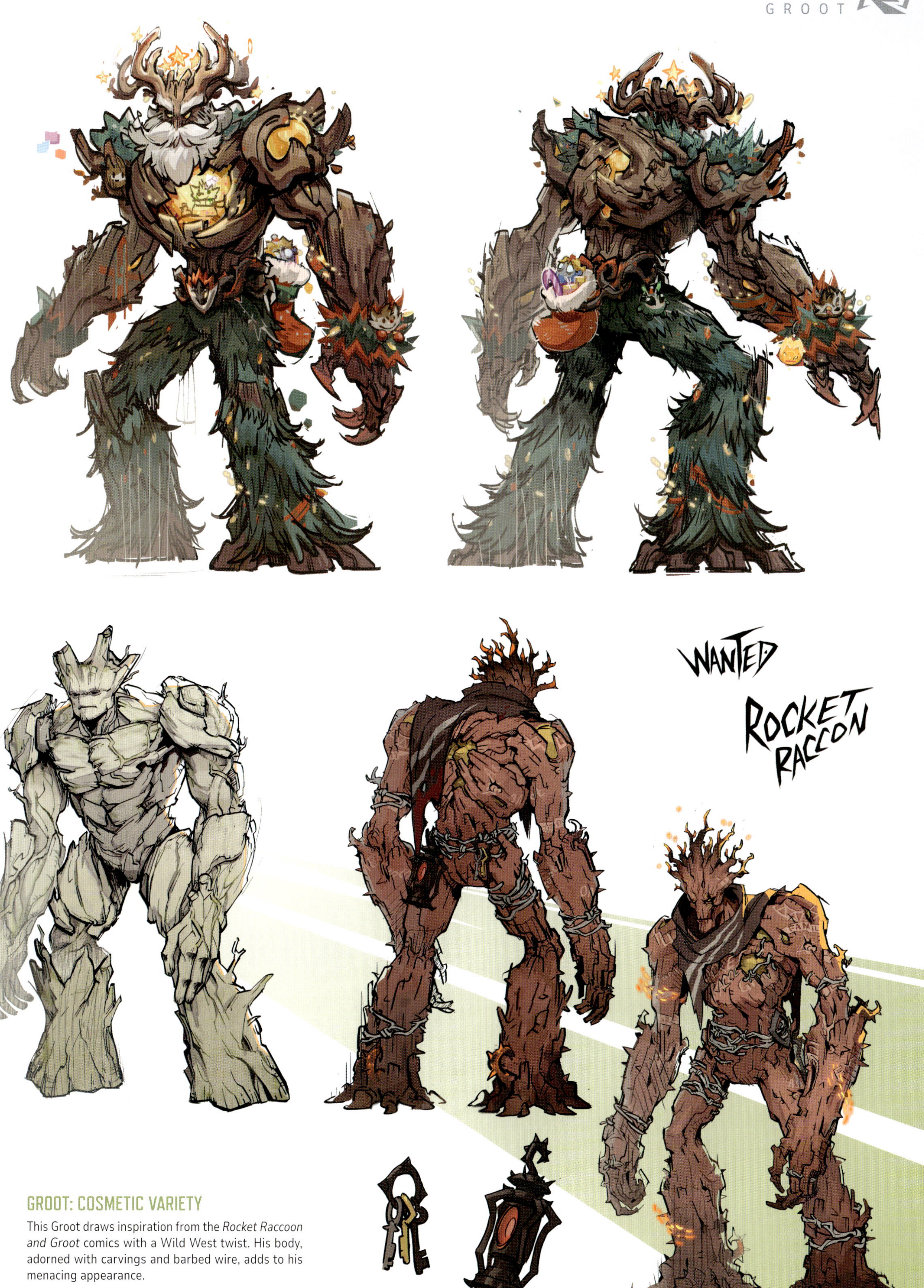

GROOT: COSMETIC VARIETY

This Groot draws inspiration from the *Rocket Raccoon and Groot* comics with a Wild West twist. His body, adorned with carvings and barbed wire, adds to his menacing appearance.

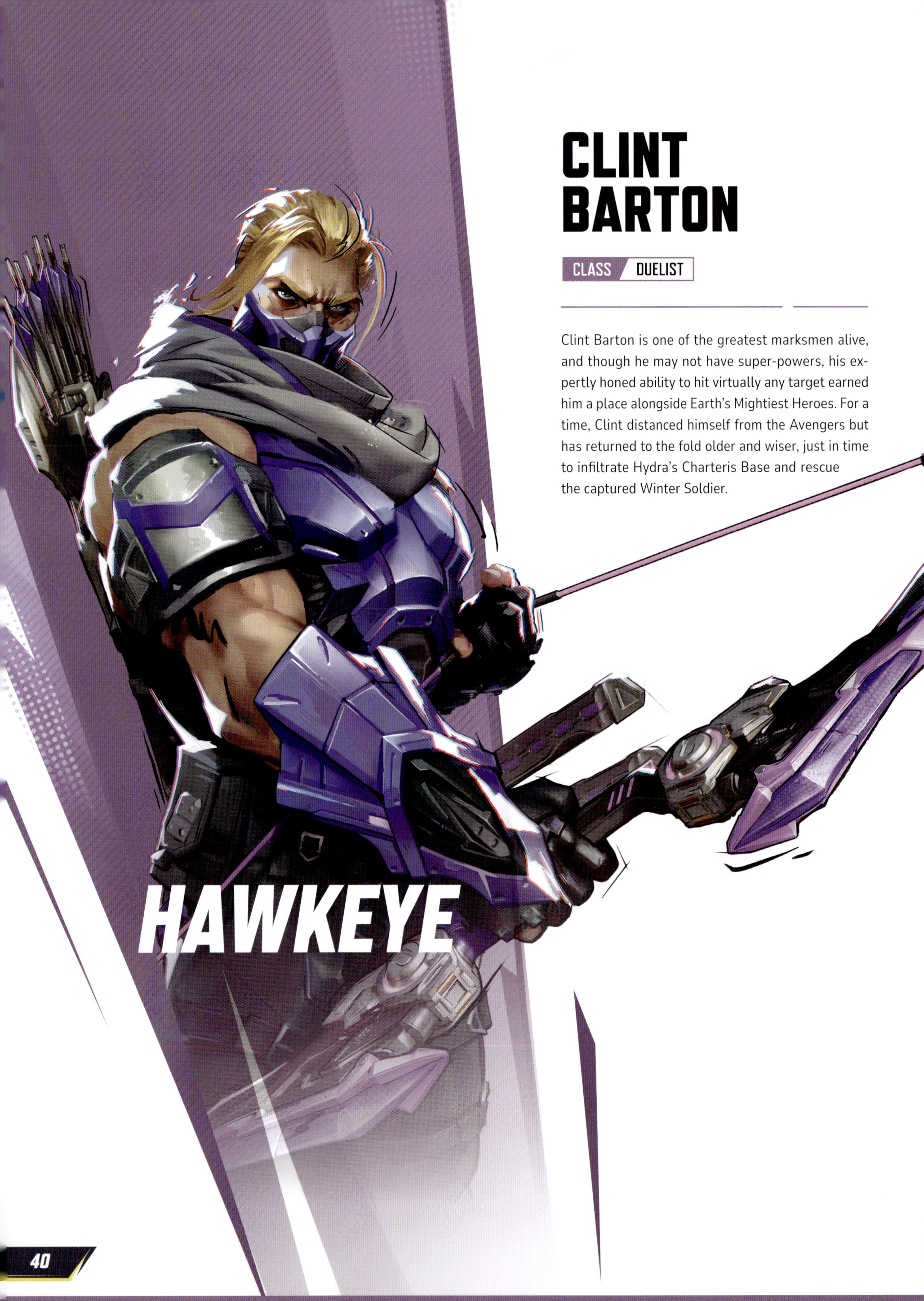

CLINT BARTON

CLASS / DUELIST

Clint Barton is one of the greatest marksmen alive, and though he may not have super-powers, his expertly honed ability to hit virtually any target earned him a place alongside Earth's Mightiest Heroes. For a time, Clint distanced himself from the Avengers but has returned to the fold older and wiser, just in time to infiltrate Hydra's Charteris Base and rescue the captured Winter Soldier.

A composed marksman with unmatched accuracy in archery, Hawkeye never misses his target, allowing no escape for those in his sights!

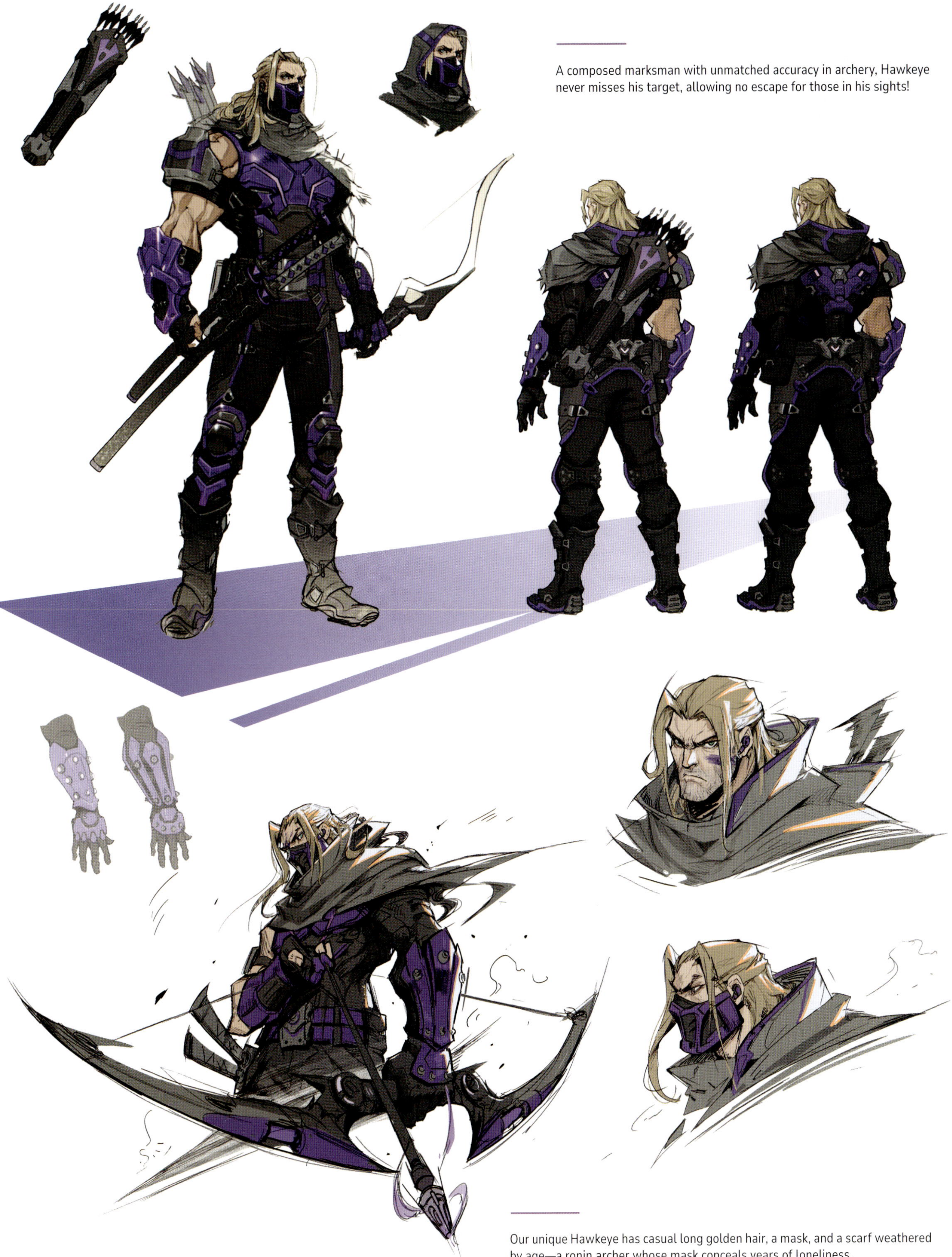

Our unique Hawkeye has casual long golden hair, a mask, and a scarf weathered by age—a ronin archer whose mask conceals years of loneliness.

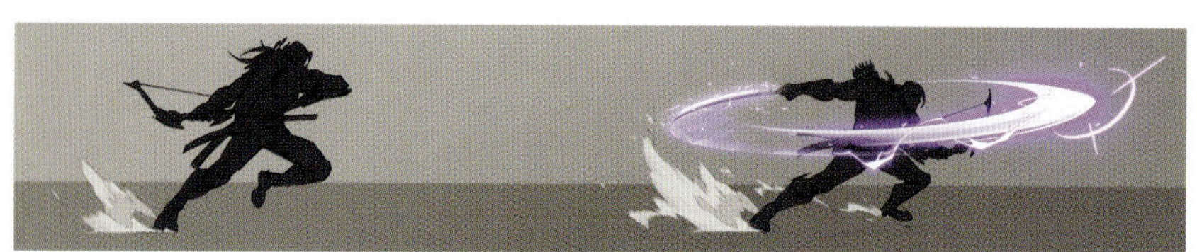
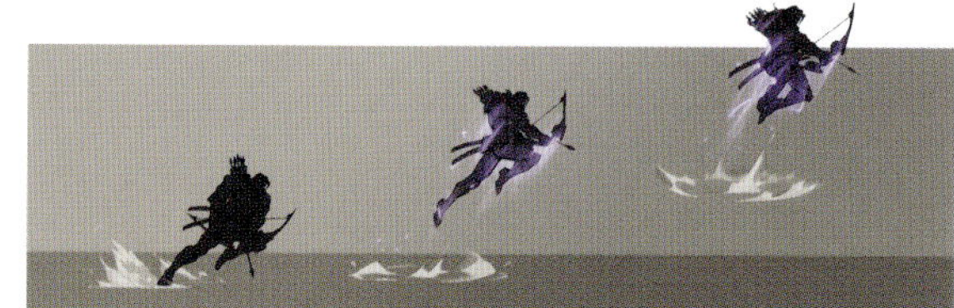
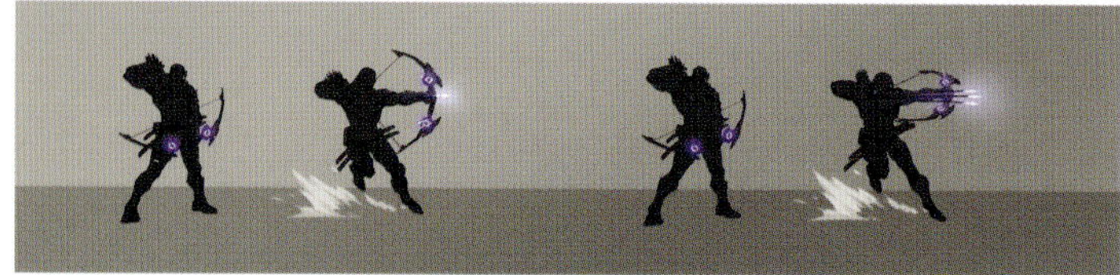
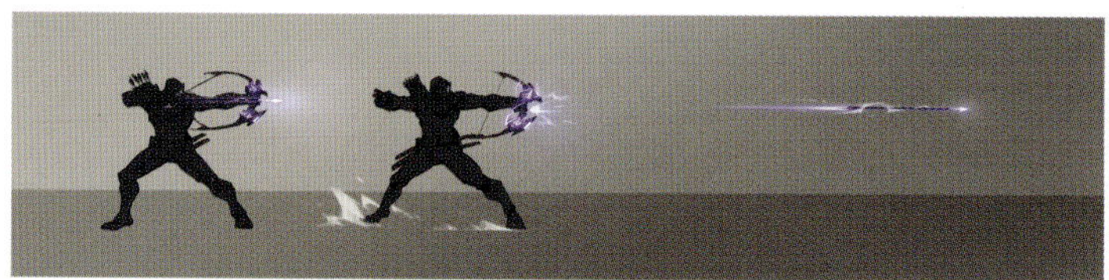

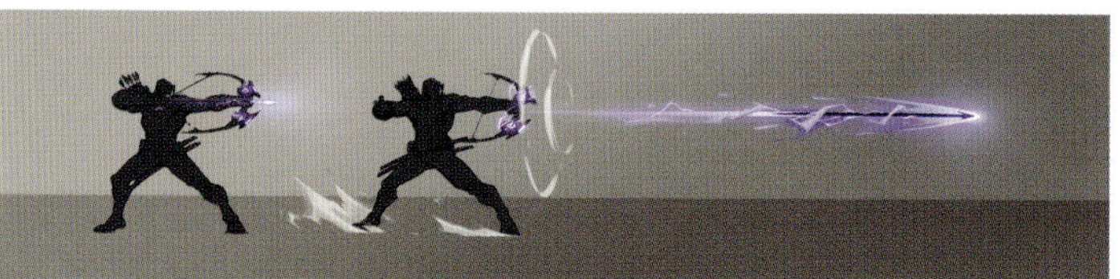
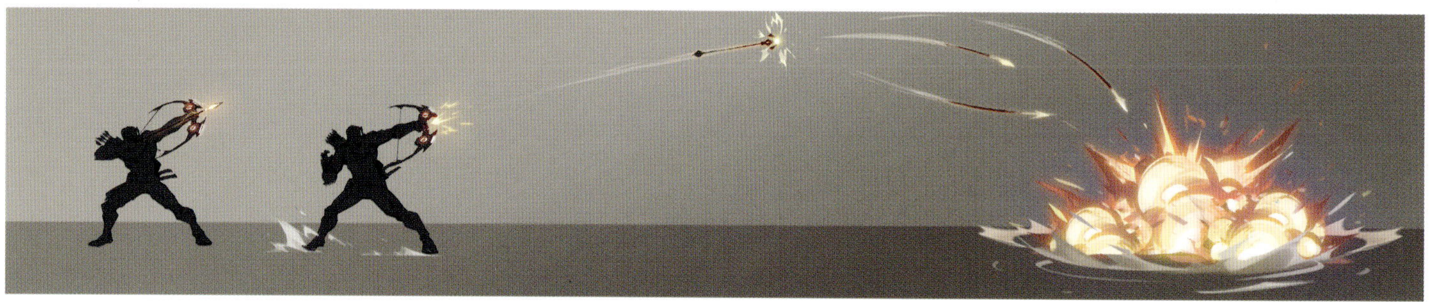
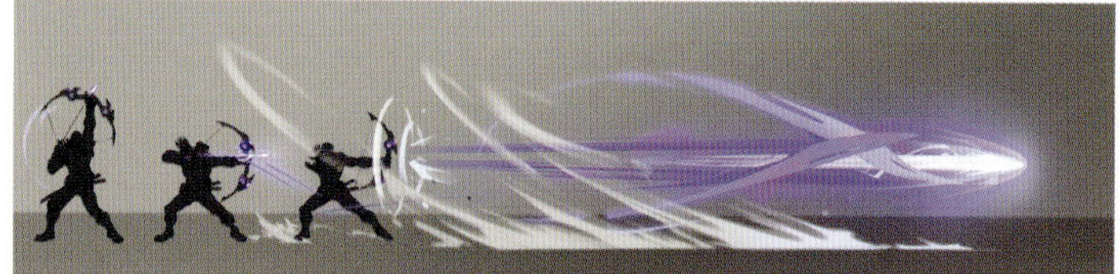
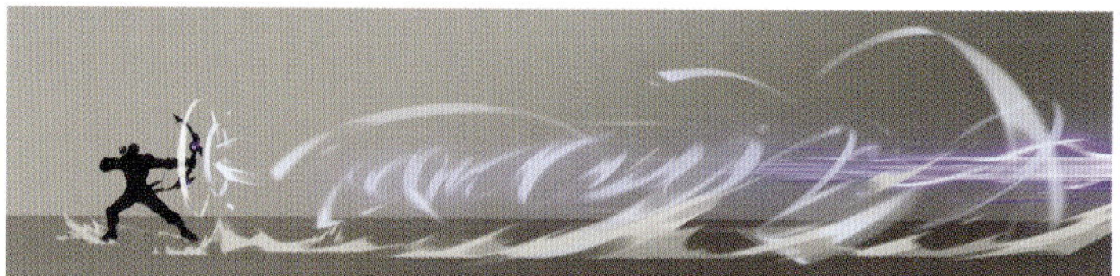
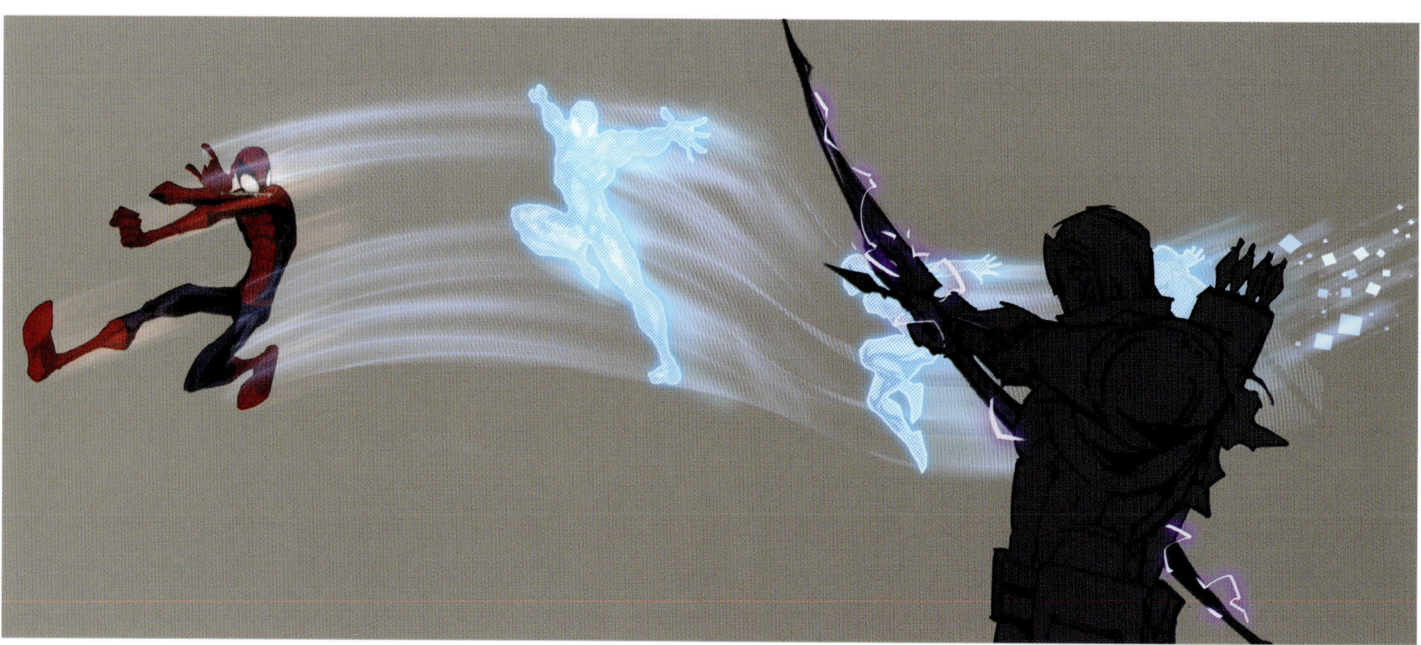

HAWKEYE: ABILITIES

Hawkeye employs various arrows for attack, his katana can deflect enemy bullets, and his super-dynamic vision allows him to anticipate enemy actions.

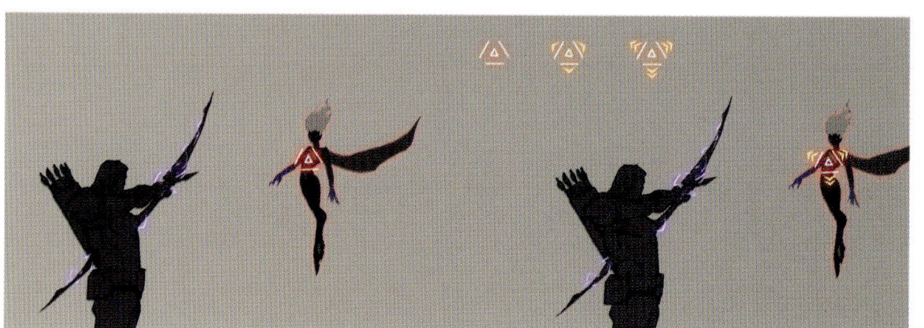

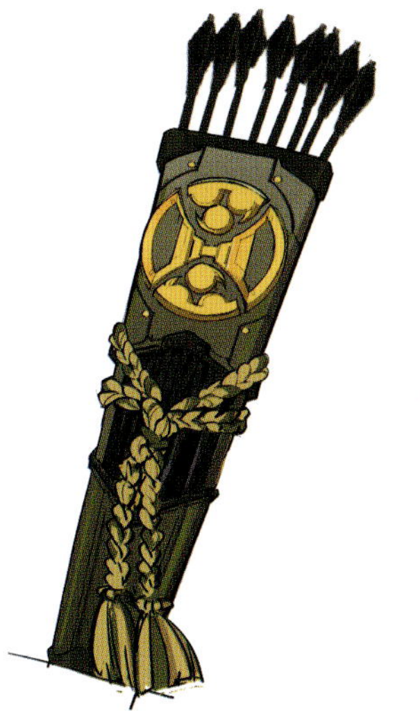

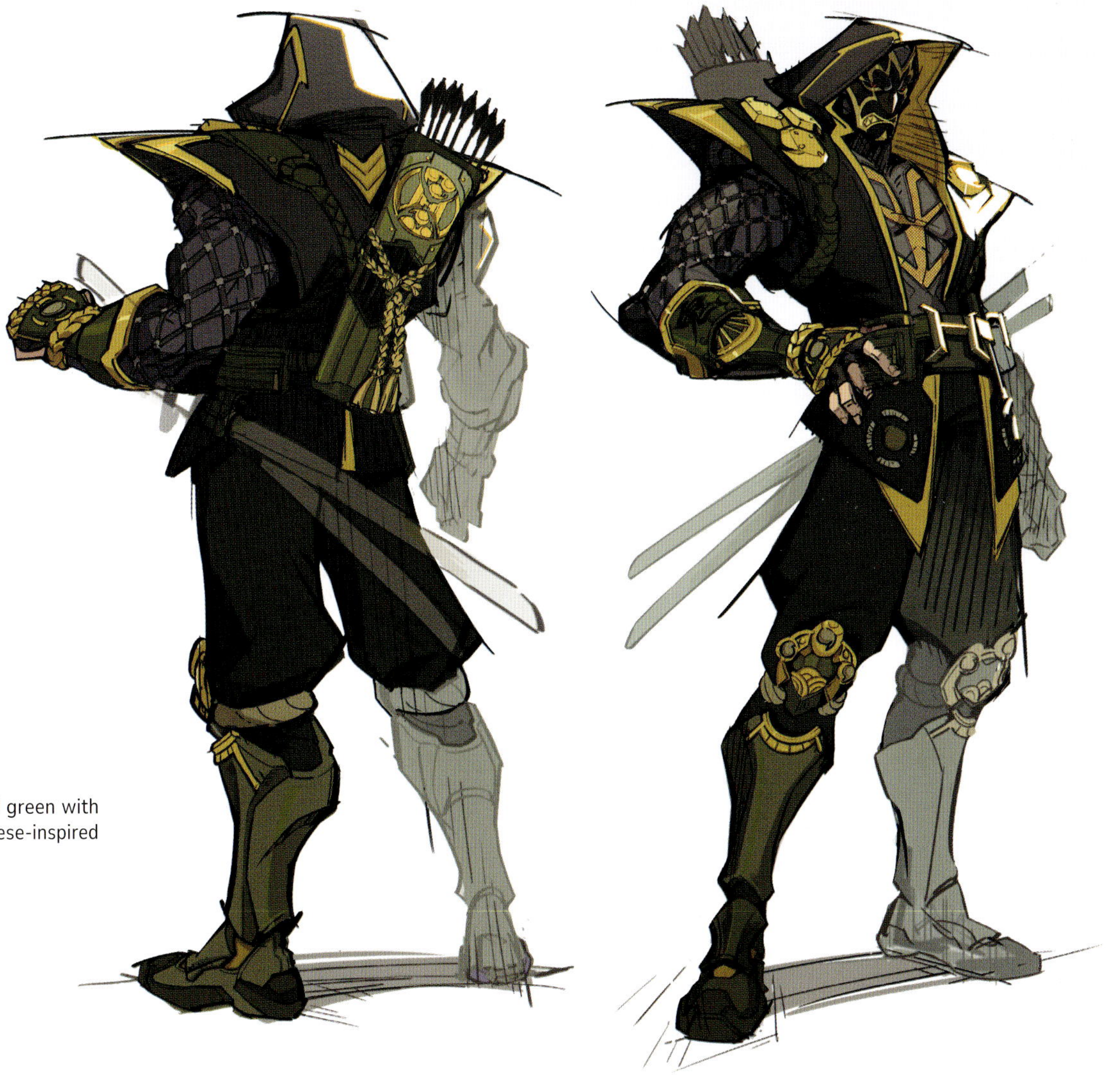

HAWKEYE: COSMETIC VARIETY

The uniform features black, yellow, and green with ronin elements, complemented by Japanese-inspired armor and a painted mask.

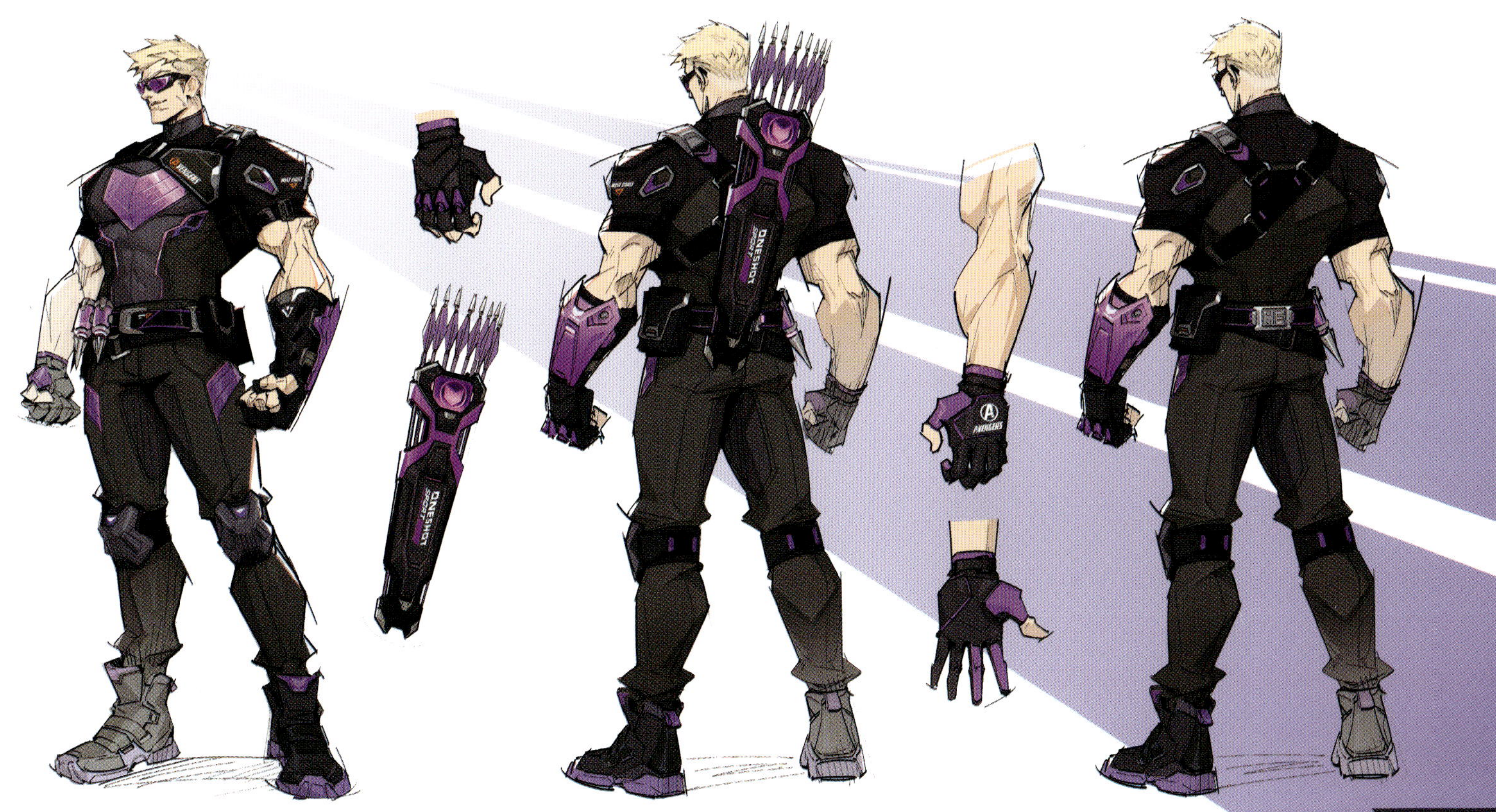

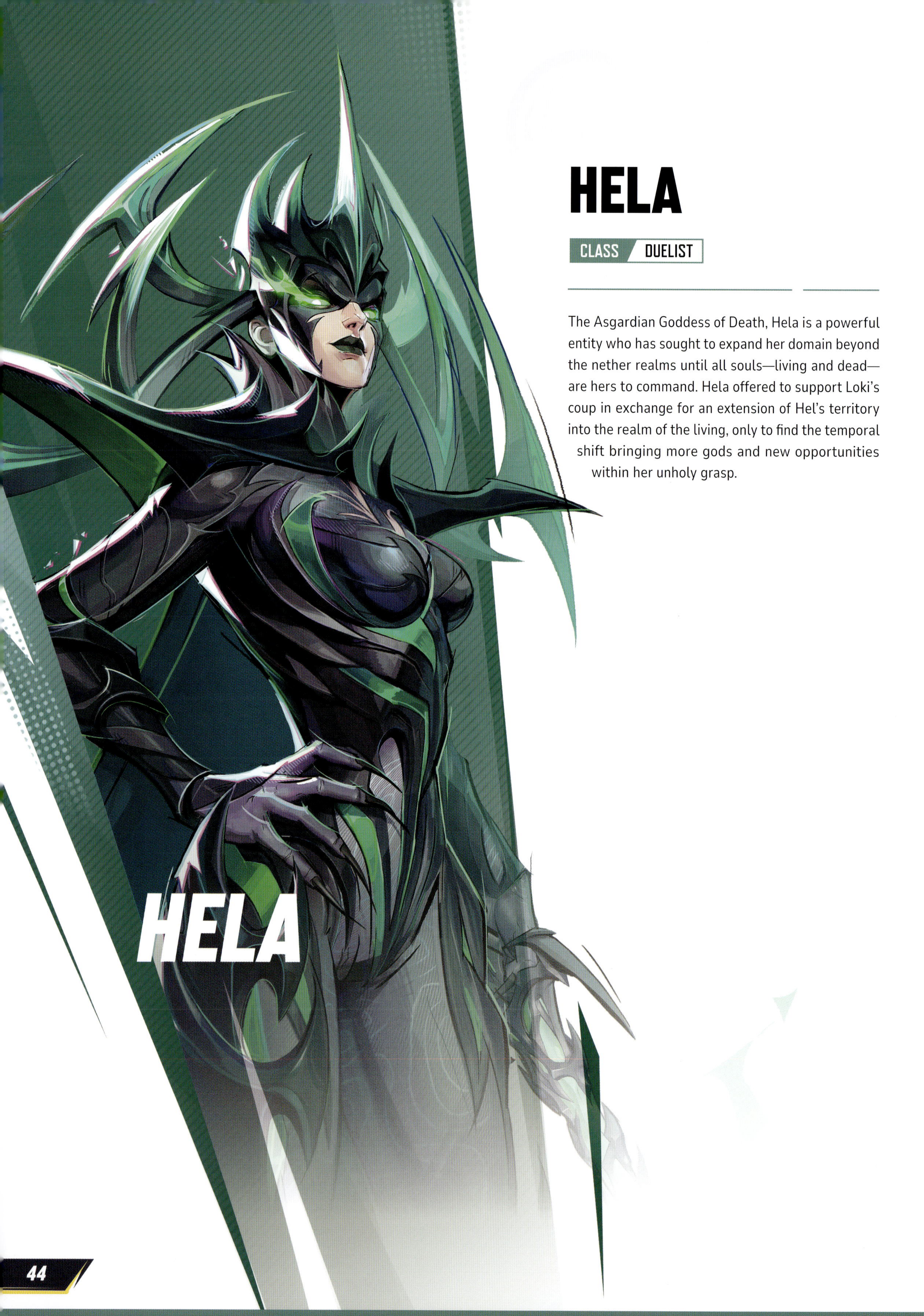

HELA

CLASS / DUELIST

The Asgardian Goddess of Death, Hela is a powerful entity who has sought to expand her domain beyond the nether realms until all souls—living and dead—are hers to command. Hela offered to support Loki's coup in exchange for an extension of Hel's territory into the realm of the living, only to find the temporal shift bringing more gods and new opportunities within her unholy grasp.

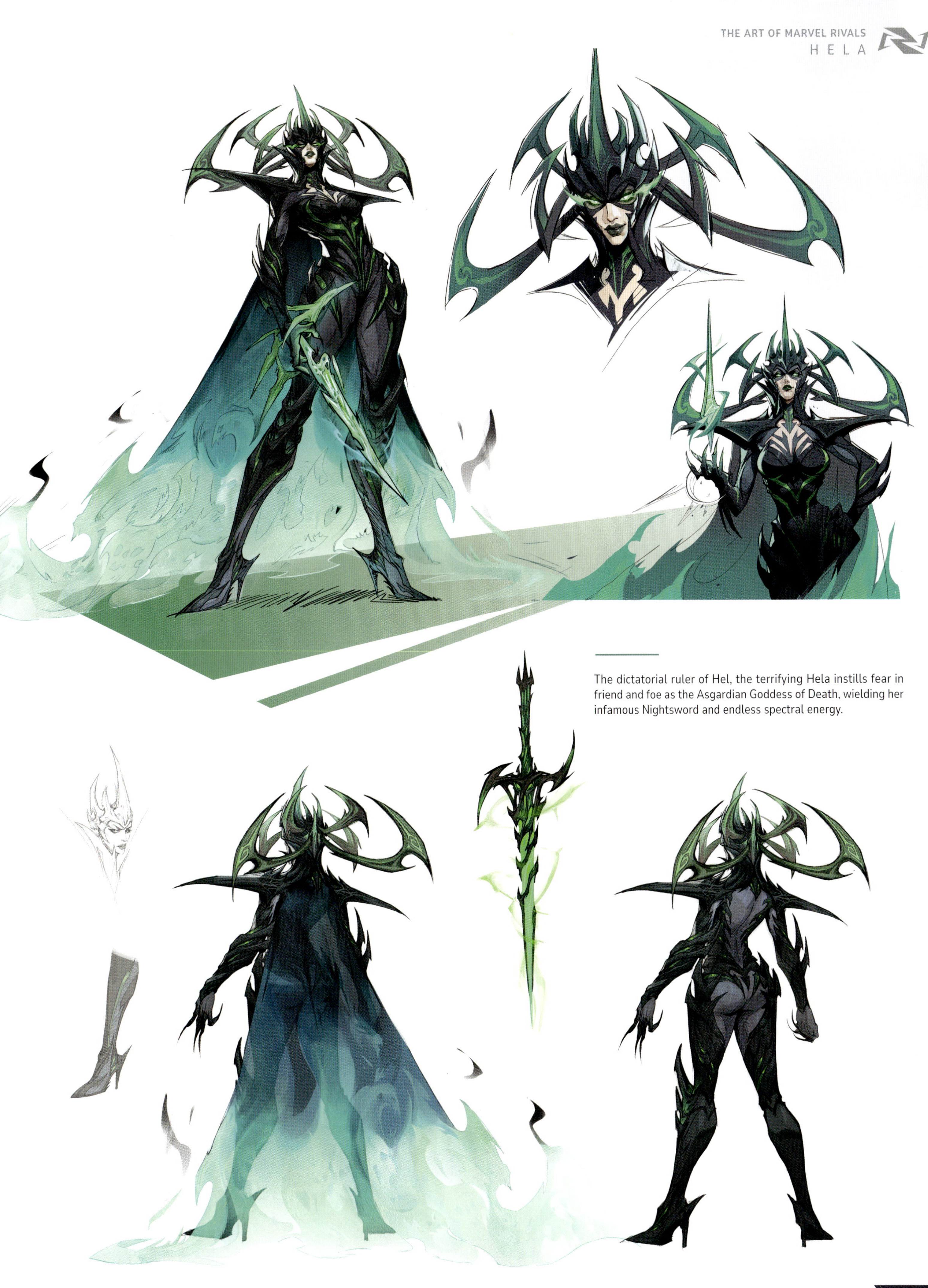

The dictatorial ruler of Hel, the terrifying Hela instills fear in friend and foe as the Asgardian Goddess of Death, wielding her infamous Nightsword and endless spectral energy.

HELA: ABILITIES

Hela wields powerful and terrifying soul energy. She transforms into crows and awakens her goddess form to ruthlessly bombard her enemies from the air.

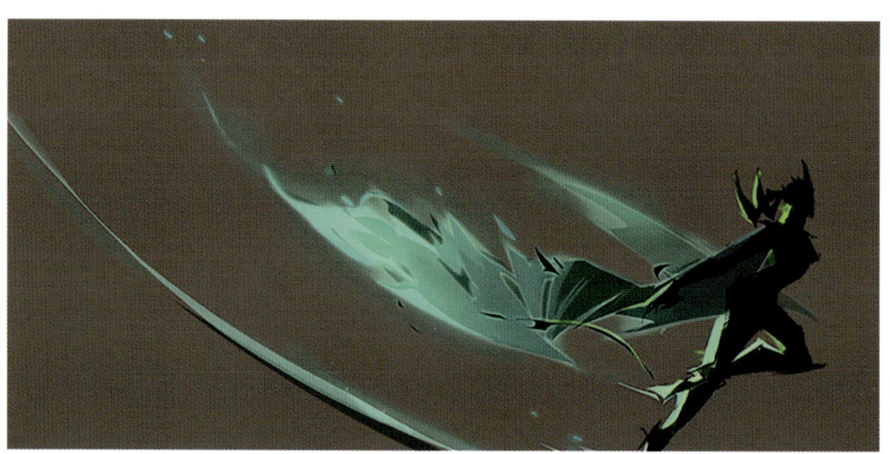

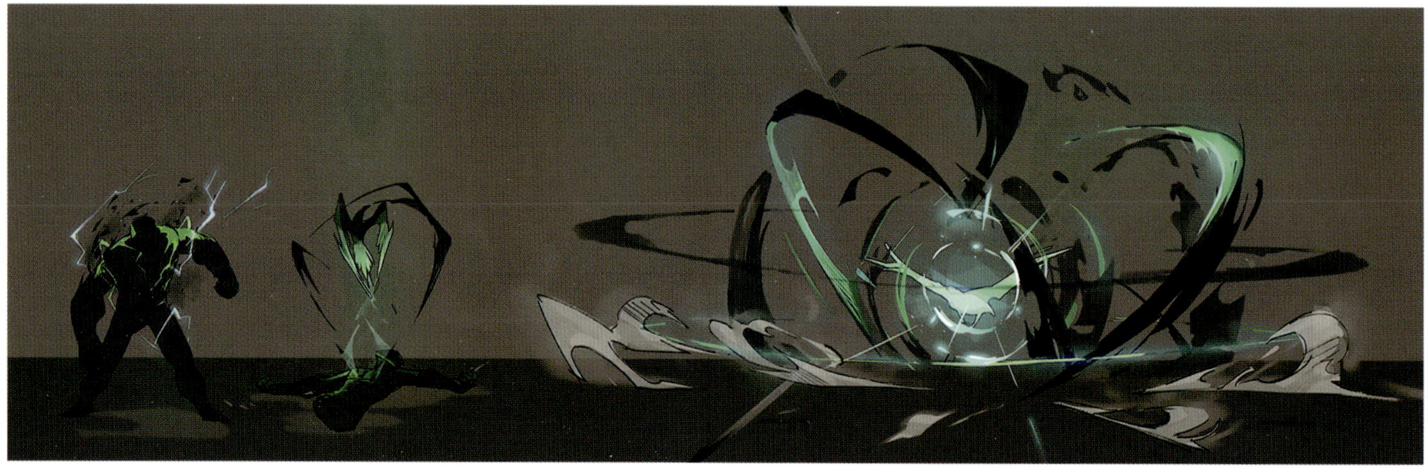

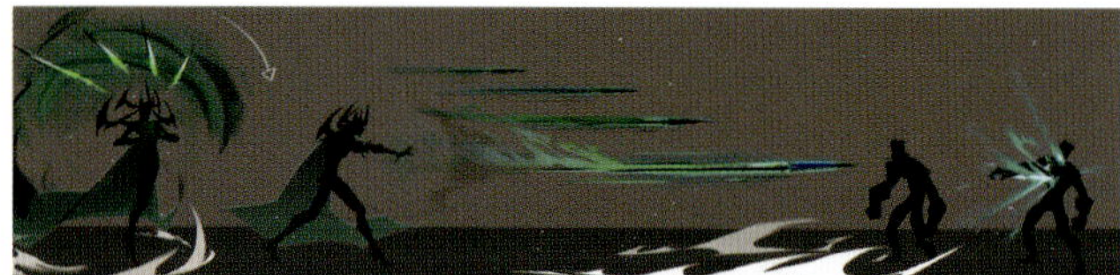

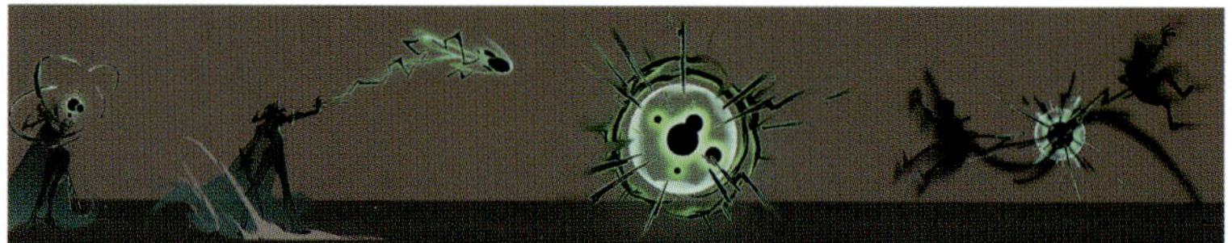

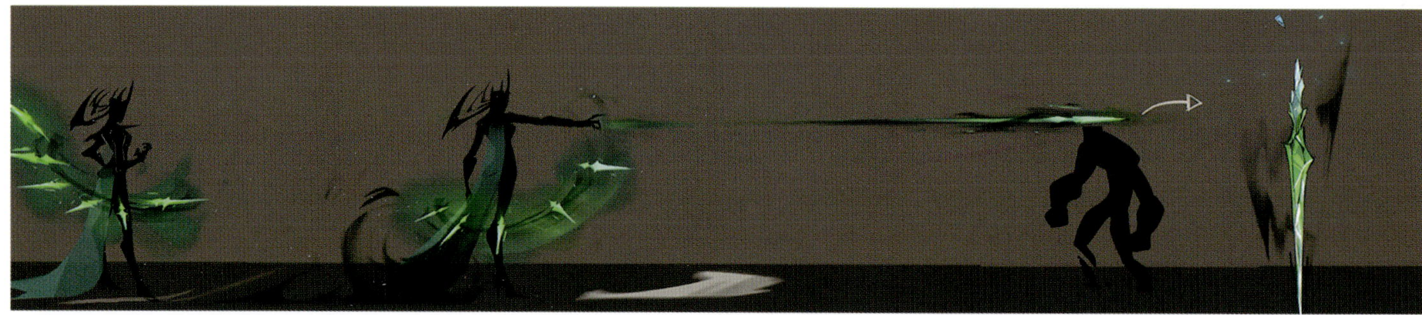

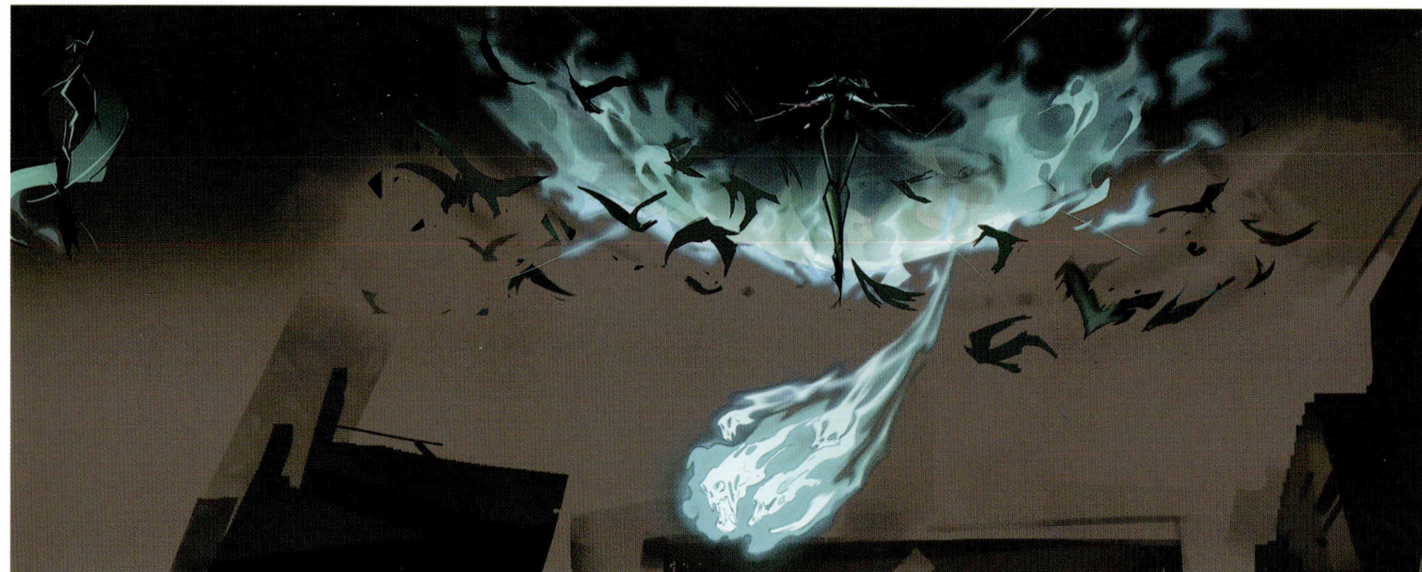

HELA: COSMETIC VARIETY

The Queen of the Stars blends Norse mythology with the aesthetic of the cosmos, her body resembling an ever-flowing universe where celestial bodies are conceived, born, and die in deep and boundless space.

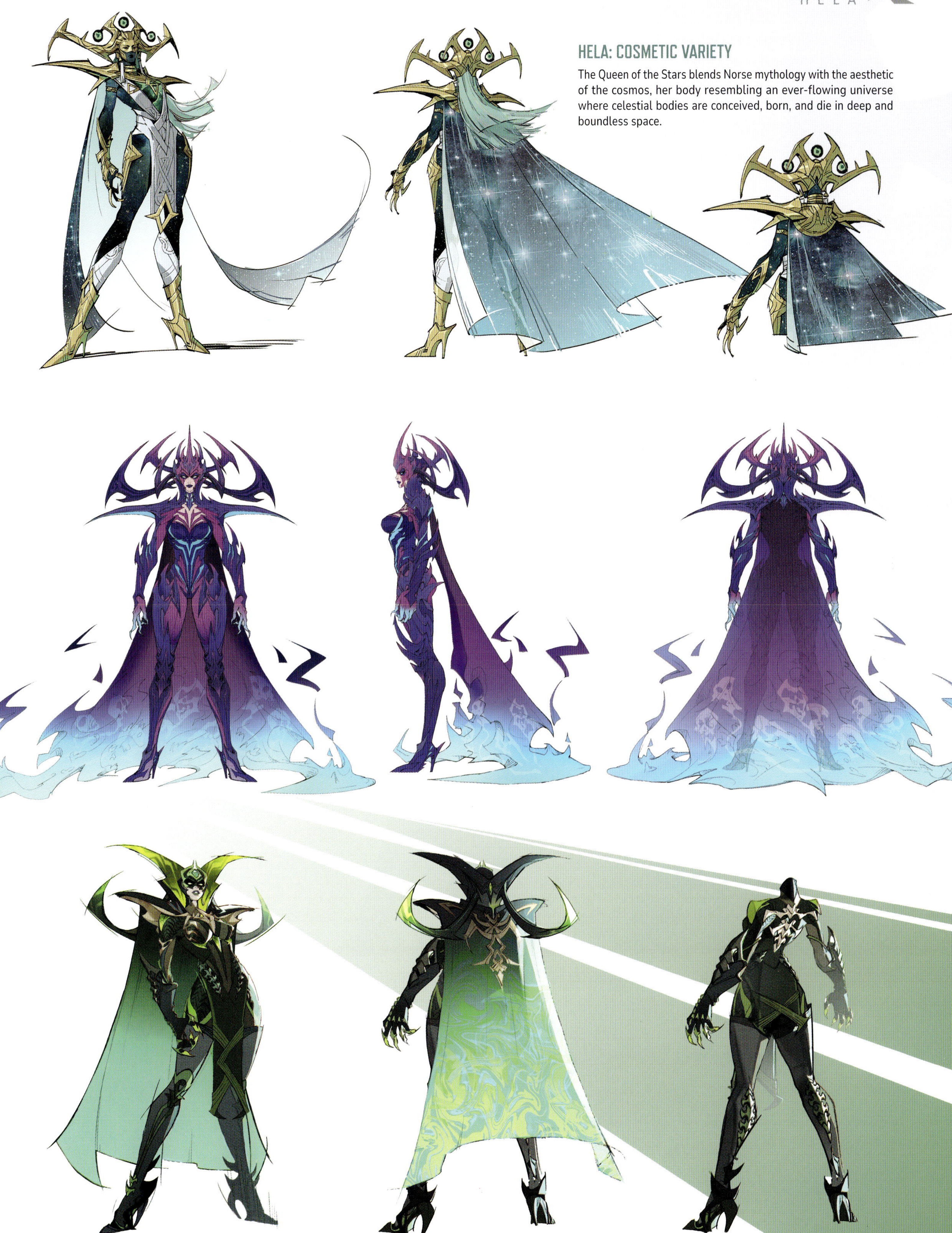

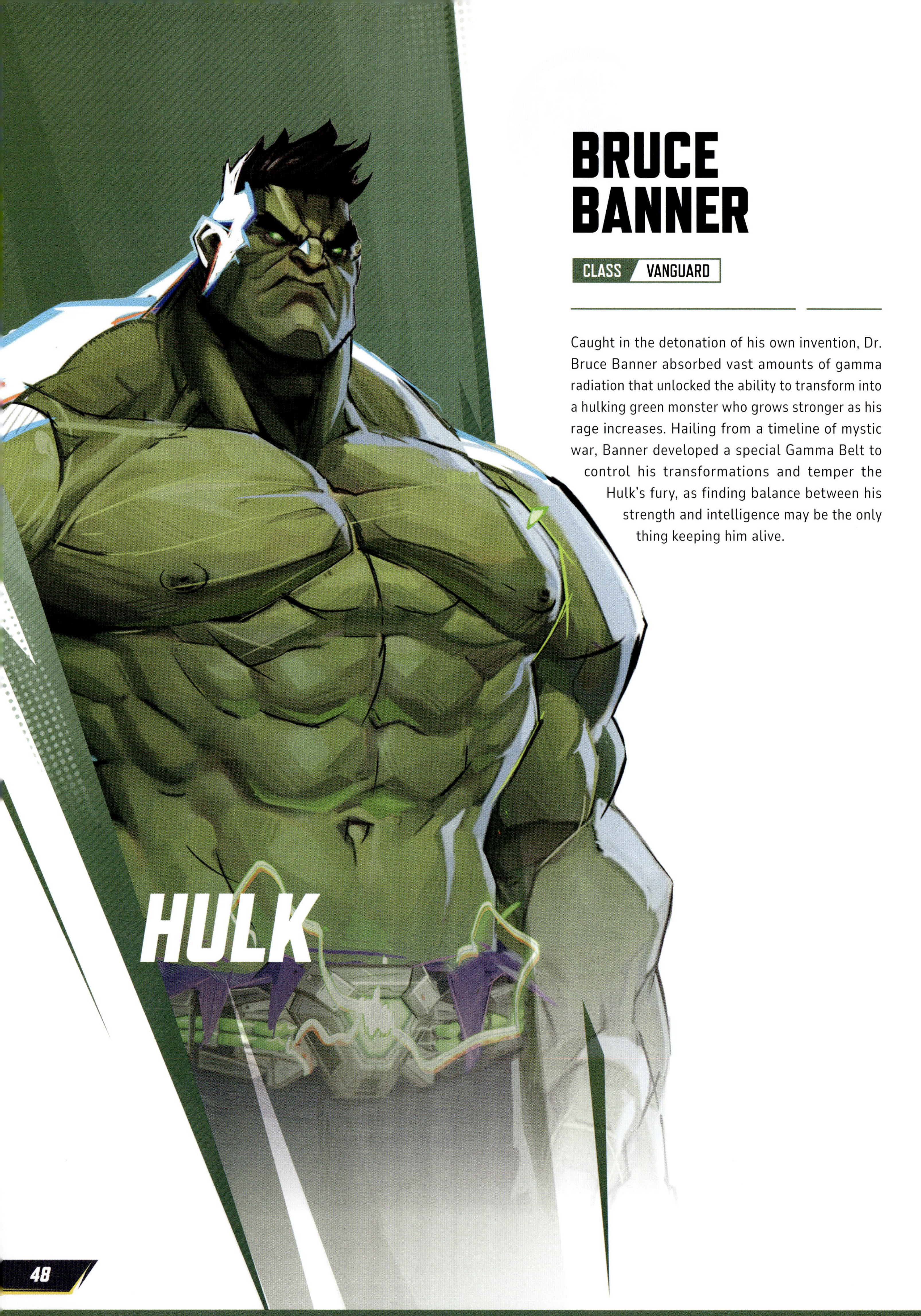

BRUCE BANNER

CLASS / VANGUARD

Caught in the detonation of his own invention, Dr. Bruce Banner absorbed vast amounts of gamma radiation that unlocked the ability to transform into a hulking green monster who grows stronger as his rage increases. Hailing from a timeline of mystic war, Banner developed a special Gamma Belt to control his transformations and temper the Hulk's fury, as finding balance between his strength and intelligence may be the only thing keeping him alive.

Dr. Bruce Banner can undergo multiple transformations by accumulating gamma energy. Hero Hulk possesses both wisdom and strength, while Monster Hulk represents sheer destruction, embodying the most violent presence on the battlefield.

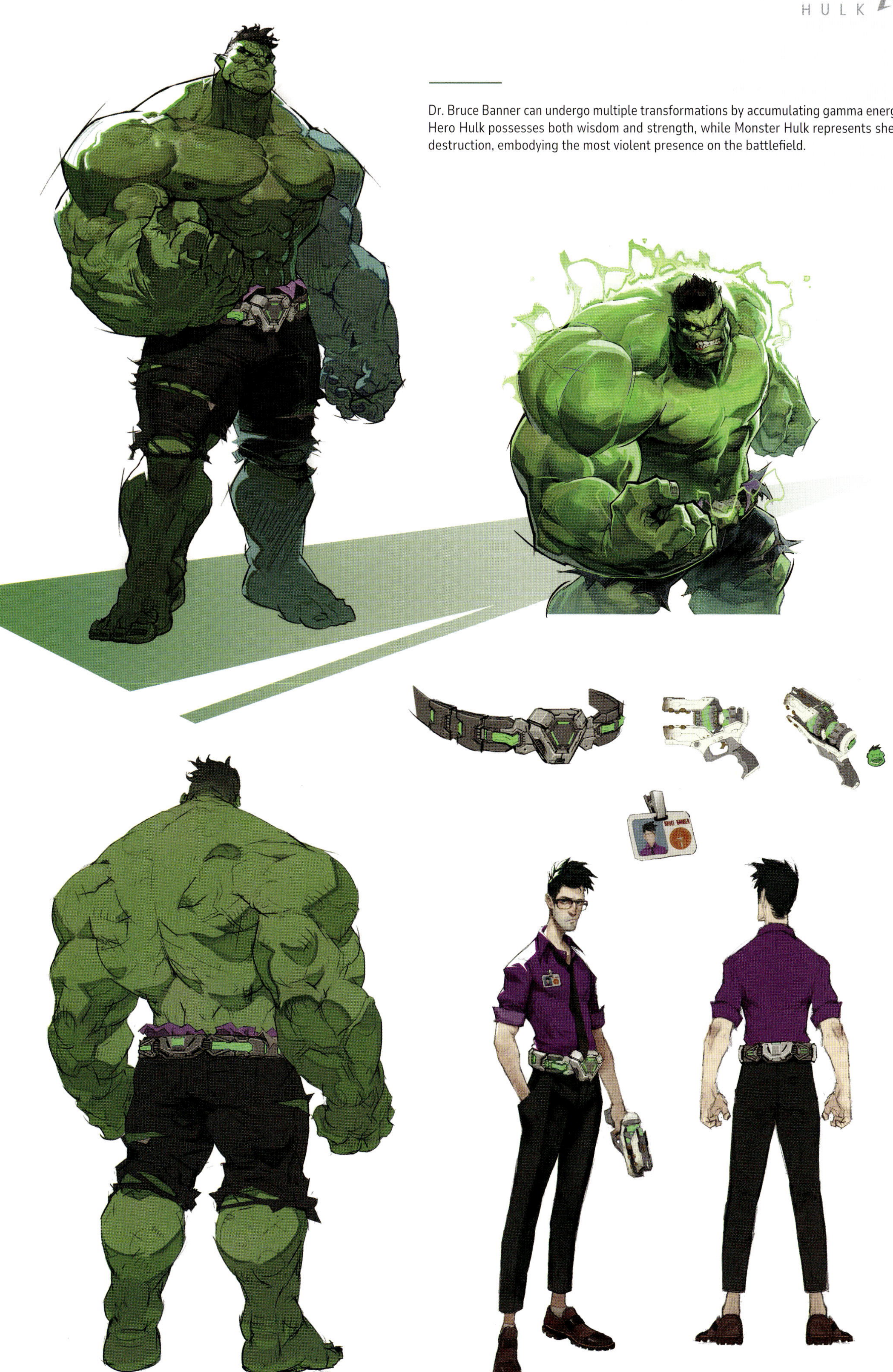

HULK: ABILITIES

Banner's two transformations, Hero Hulk and Monster Hulk, provide him with formidable survivability. His powerful jumps enable him to swiftly reposition himself, effectively protecting his teammates.

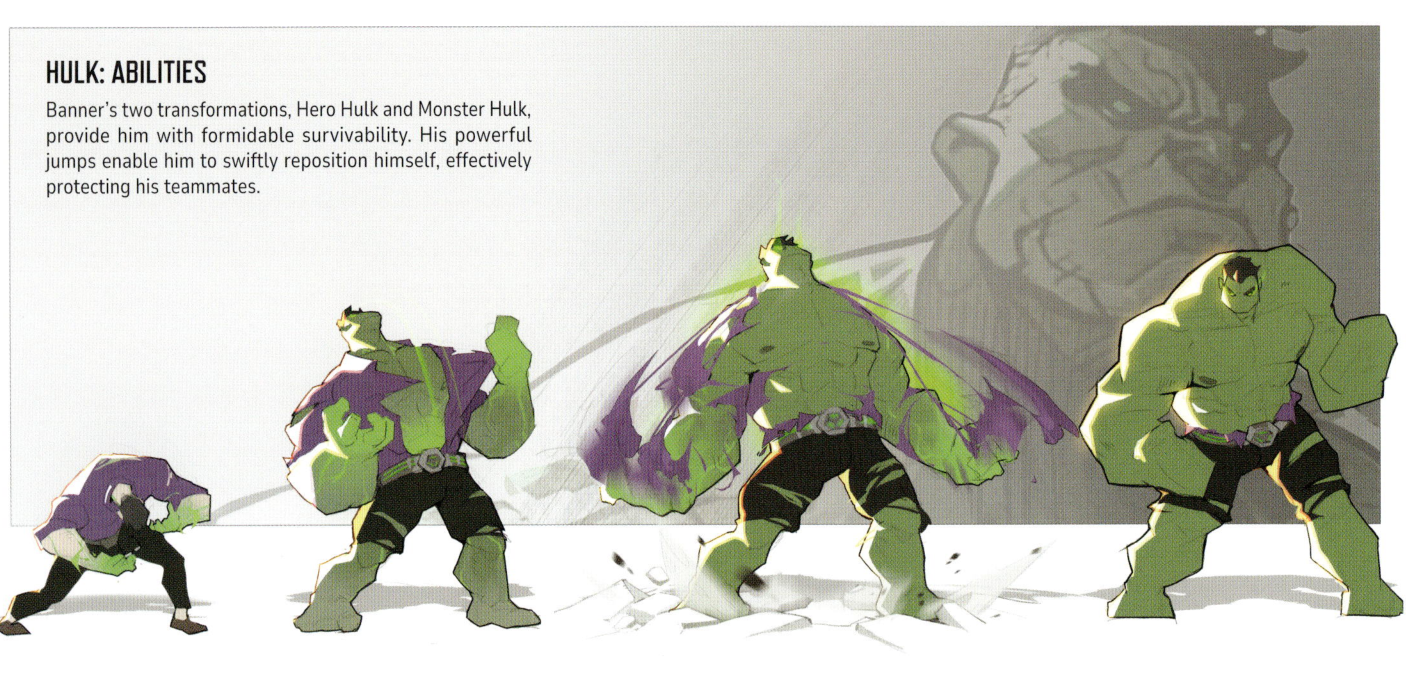

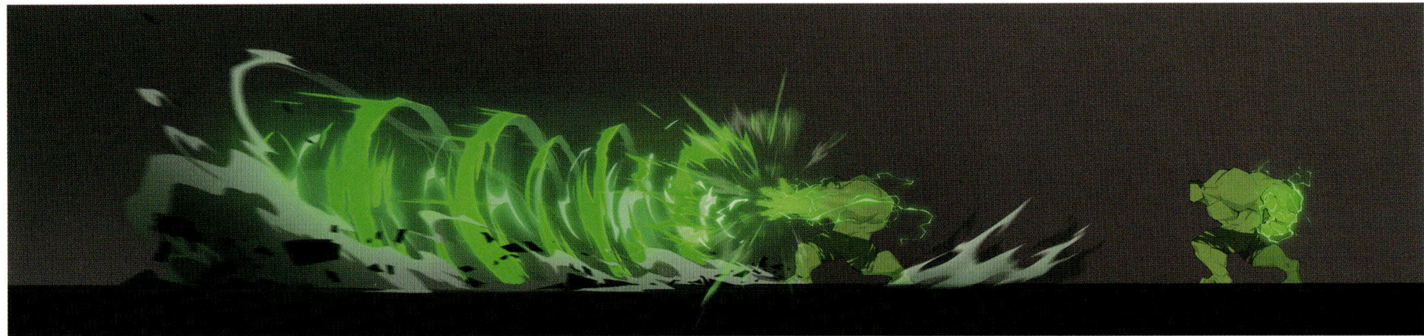

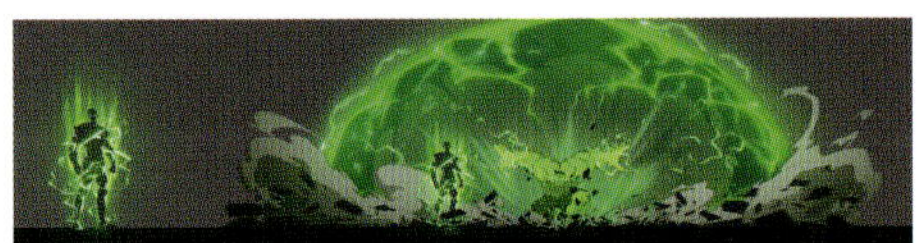

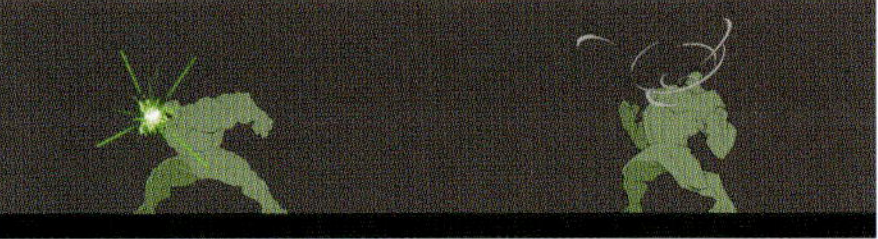

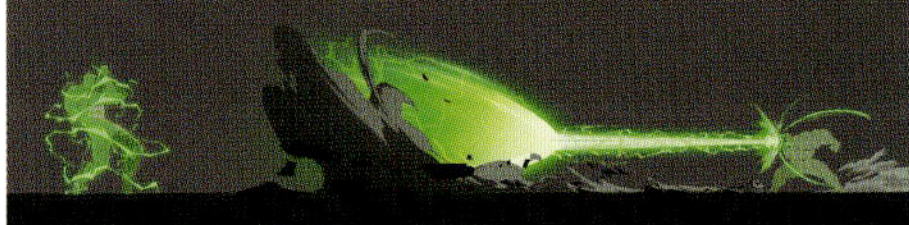

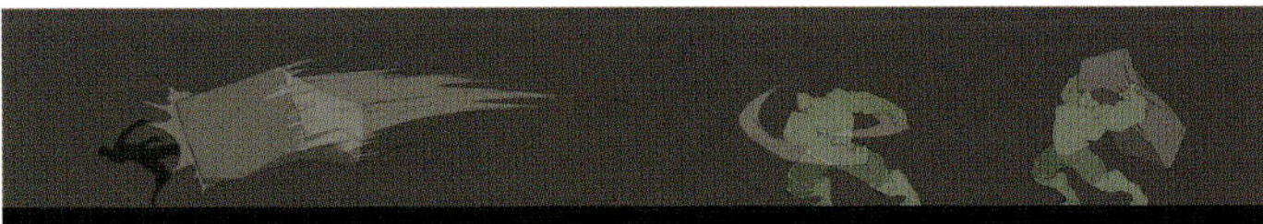

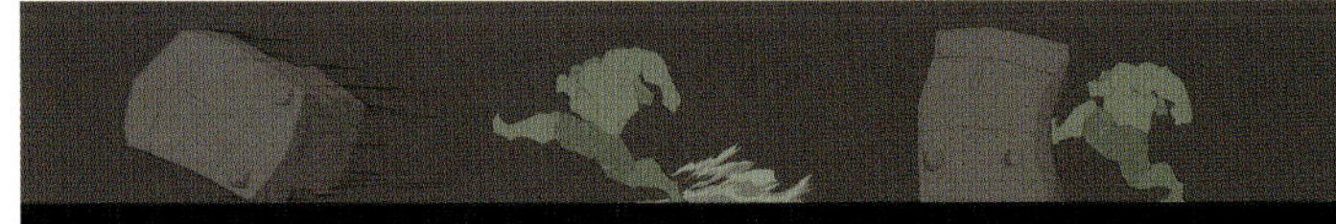

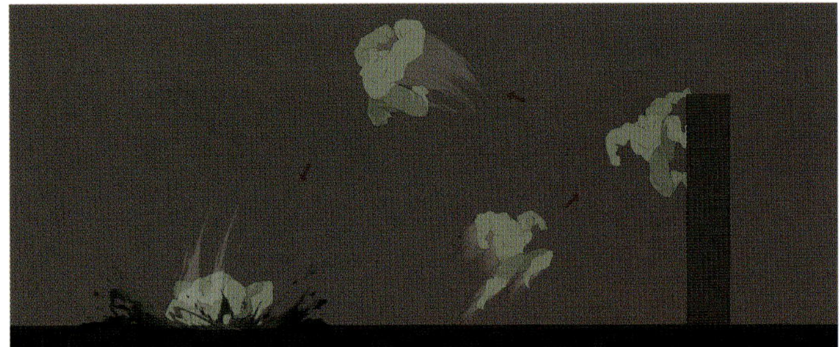

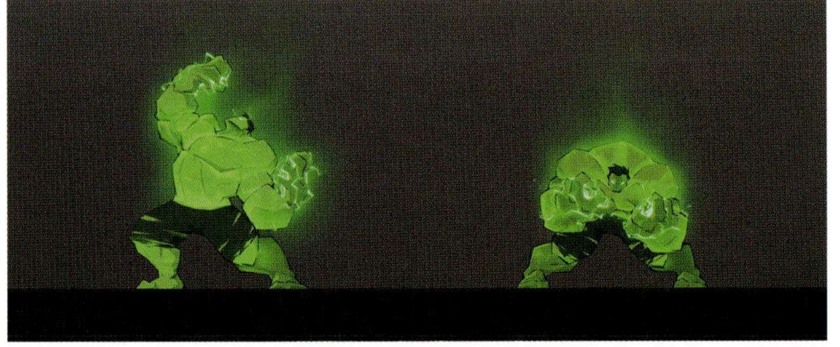

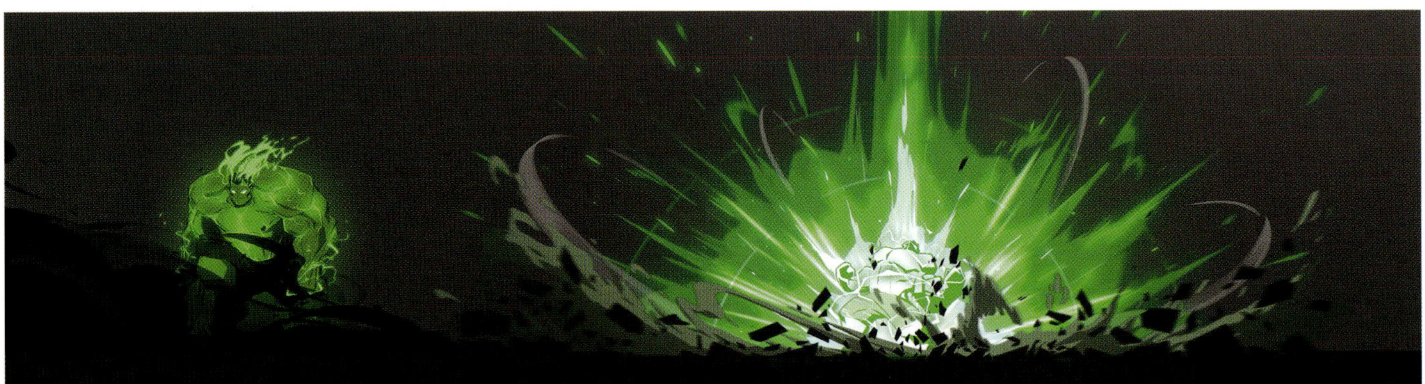

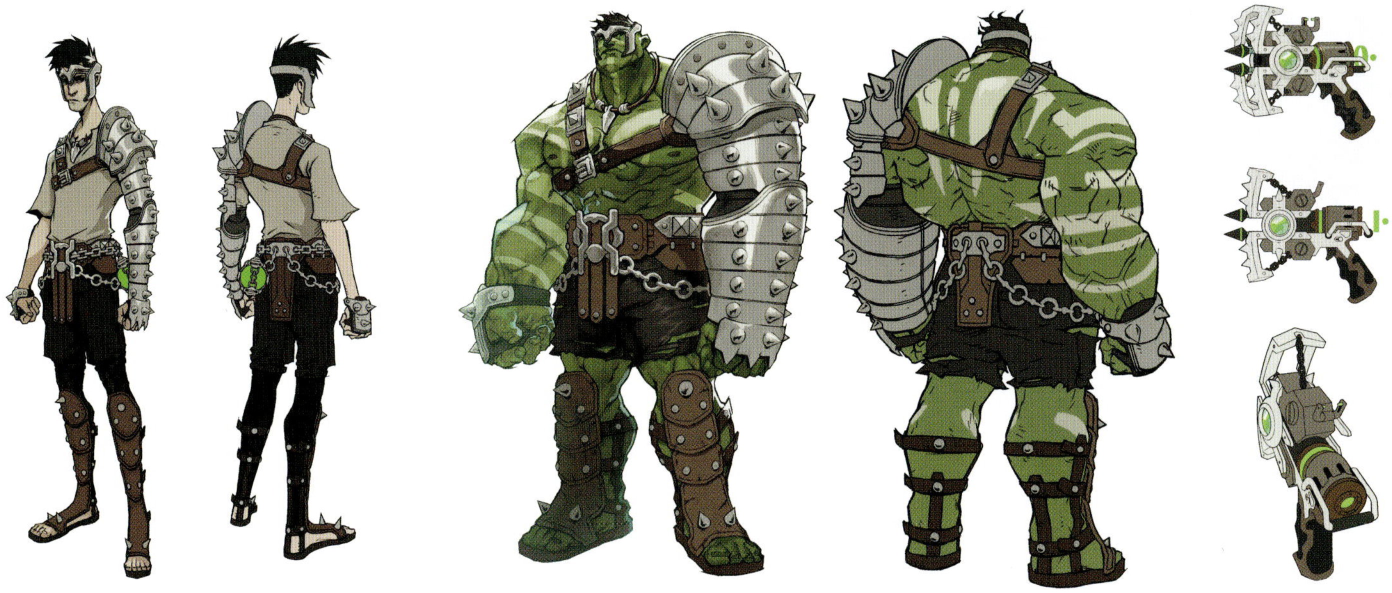

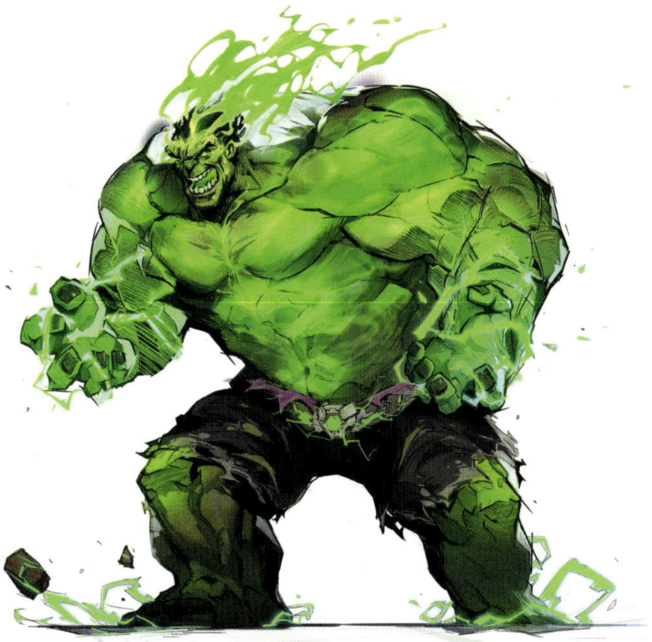

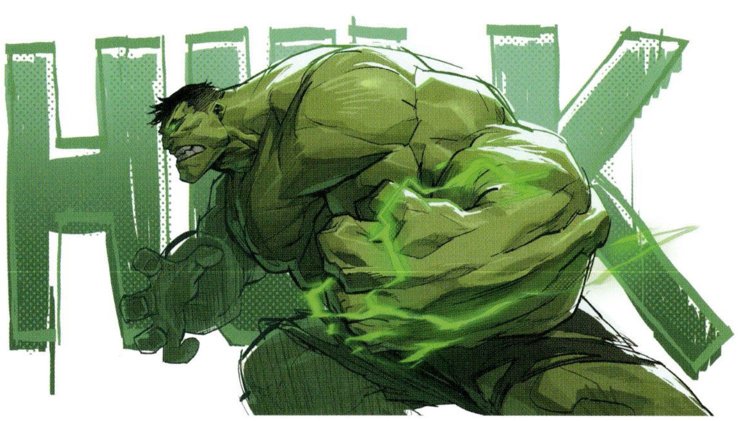

HULK: COSMETIC VARIETY

Hulk and Banner sport wild hairstyles and unique tattoos, embodying a punk spirit that endures in his anarchistic world. Long live punk, and may Hulk's anger remain as immortal as the music itself!

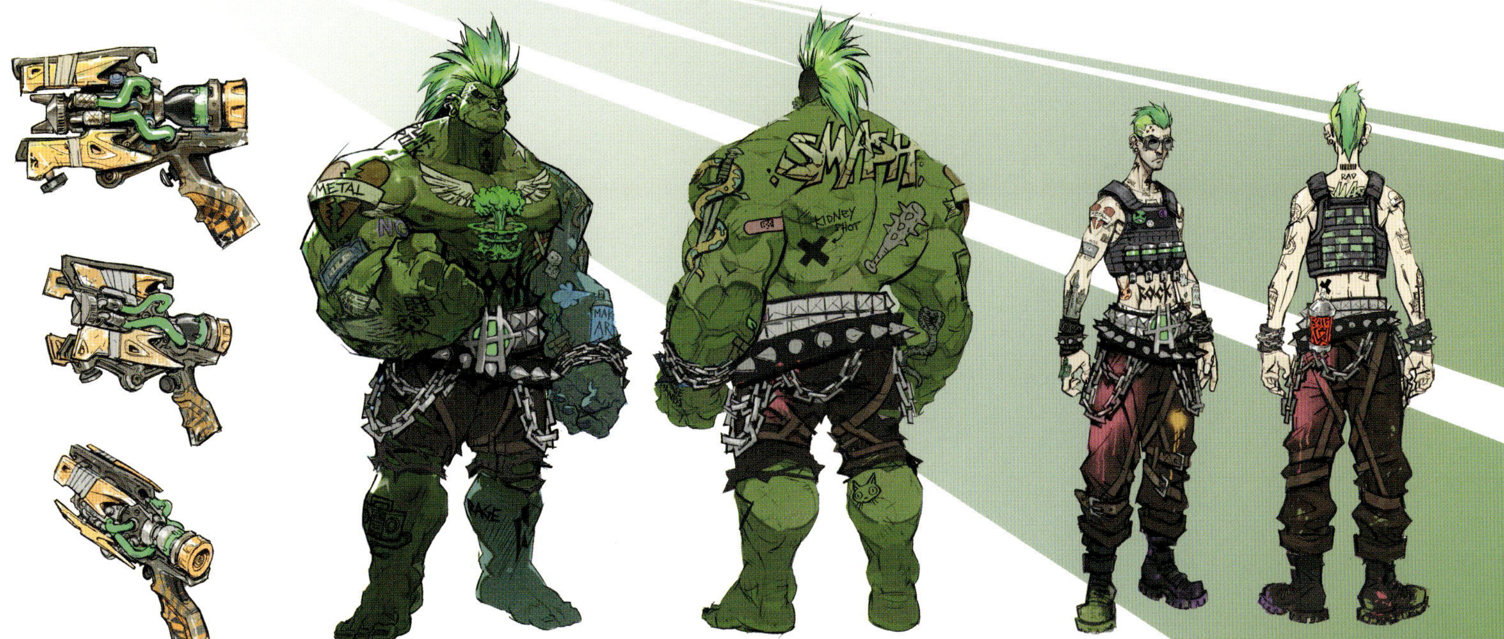

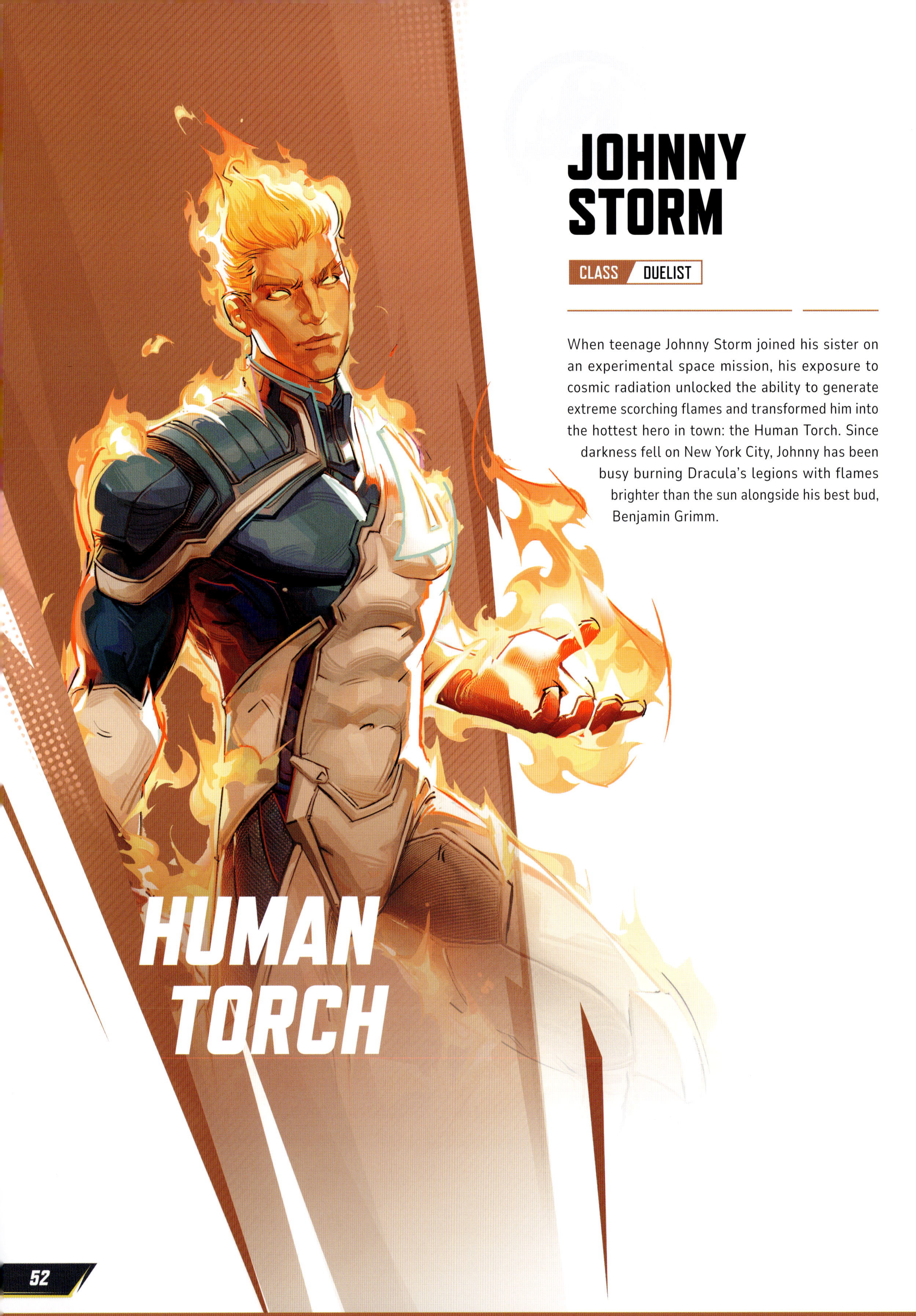

JOHNNY STORM

CLASS / DUELIST

When teenage Johnny Storm joined his sister on an experimental space mission, his exposure to cosmic radiation unlocked the ability to generate extreme scorching flames and transformed him into the hottest hero in town: the Human Torch. Since darkness fell on New York City, Johnny has been busy burning Dracula's legions with flames brighter than the sun alongside his best bud, Benjamin Grimm.

The Human Torch is the Fantastic Four's beloved heartthrob. He thrives on thrilling battles: With his body constantly enveloped in flames, he's ready to scorch his enemies at any moment!

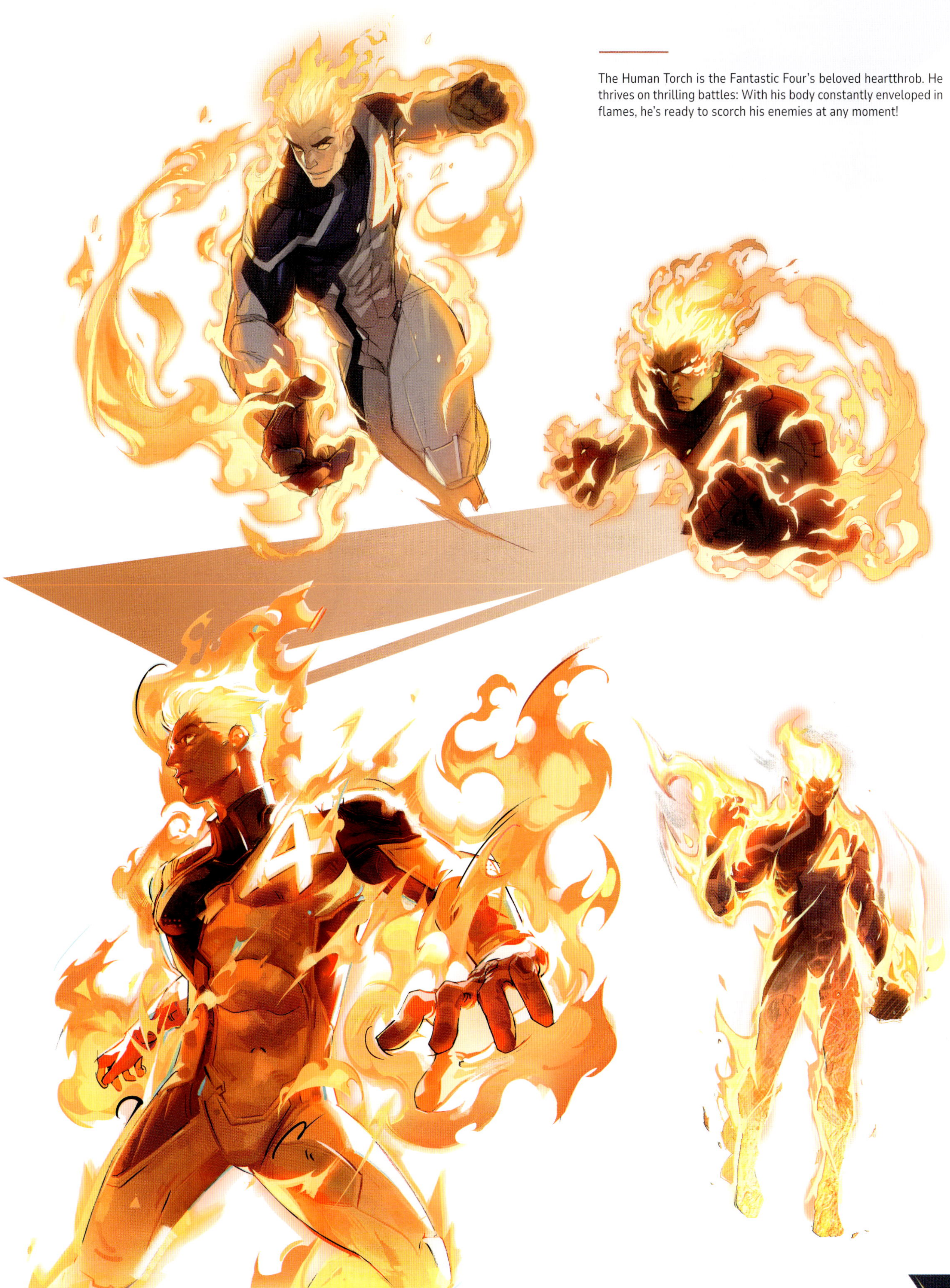

HUMAN TORCH: ABILITIES

The flaming Human Torch possesses the ability to fly, transforms into a burning meteor for up-close attacks, creates a prison of fire, and explodes into a supernova firestorm.

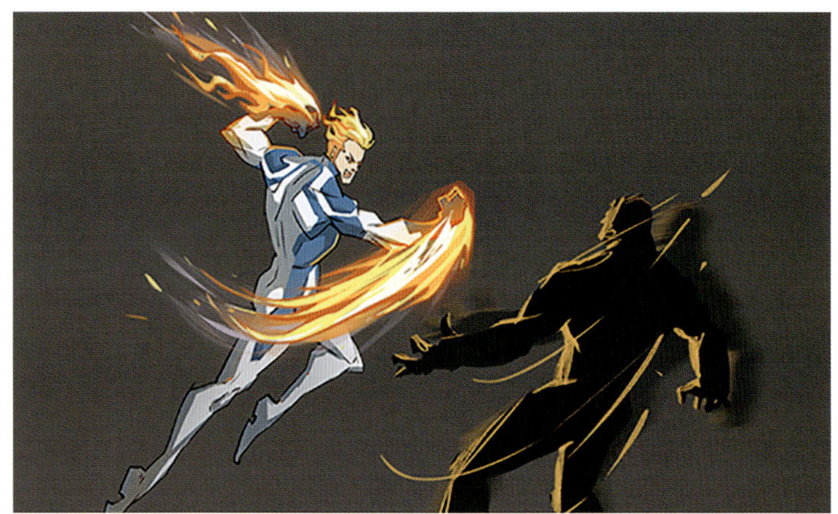

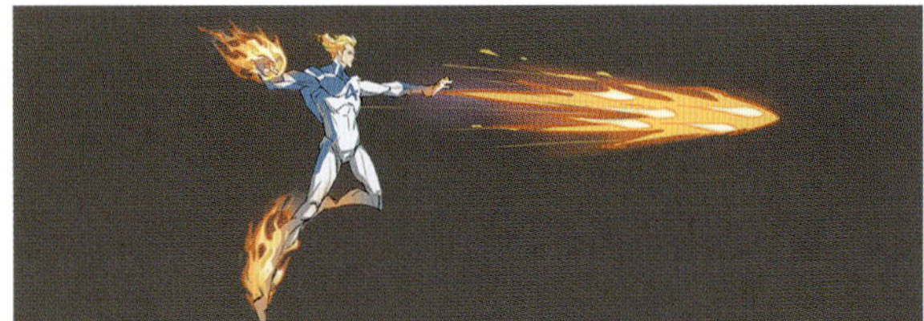

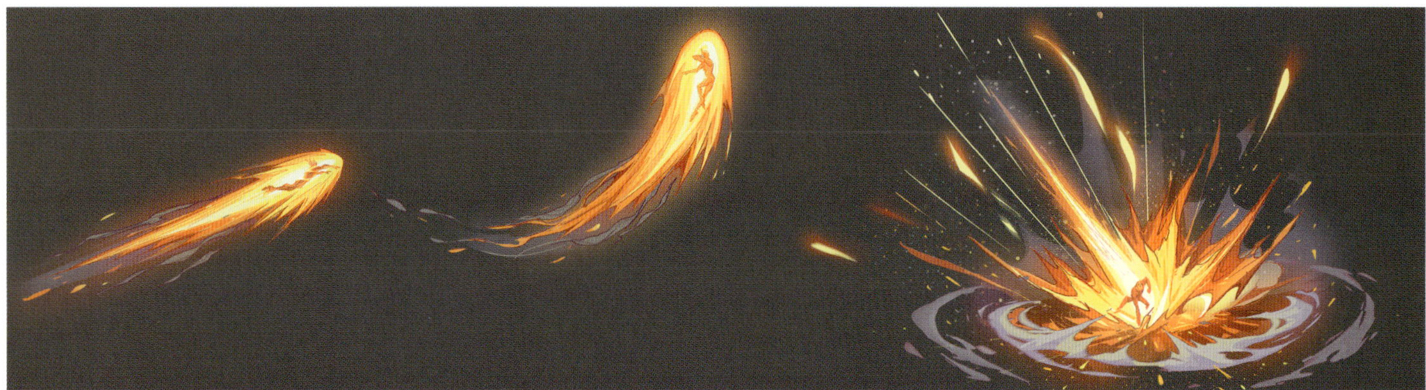

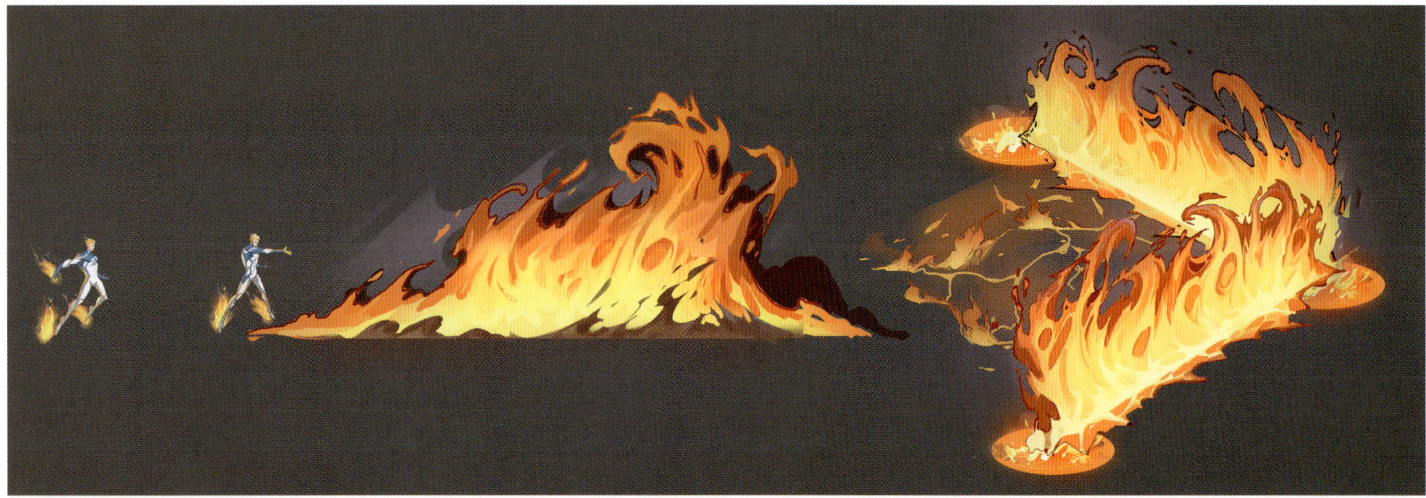

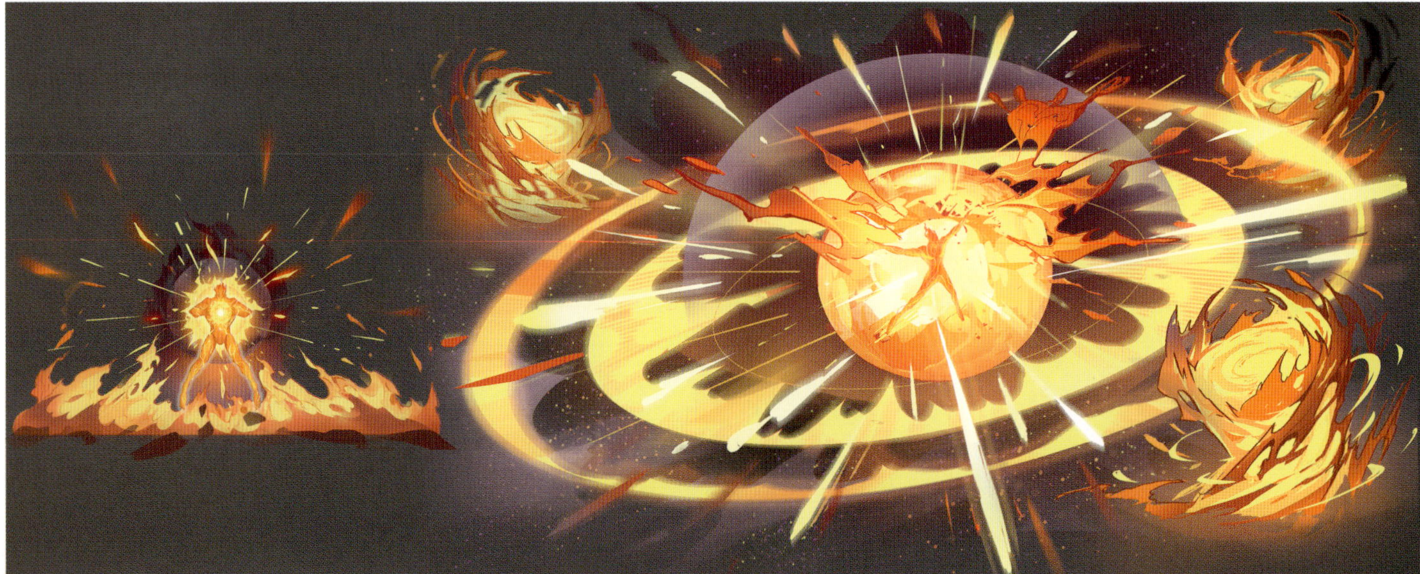

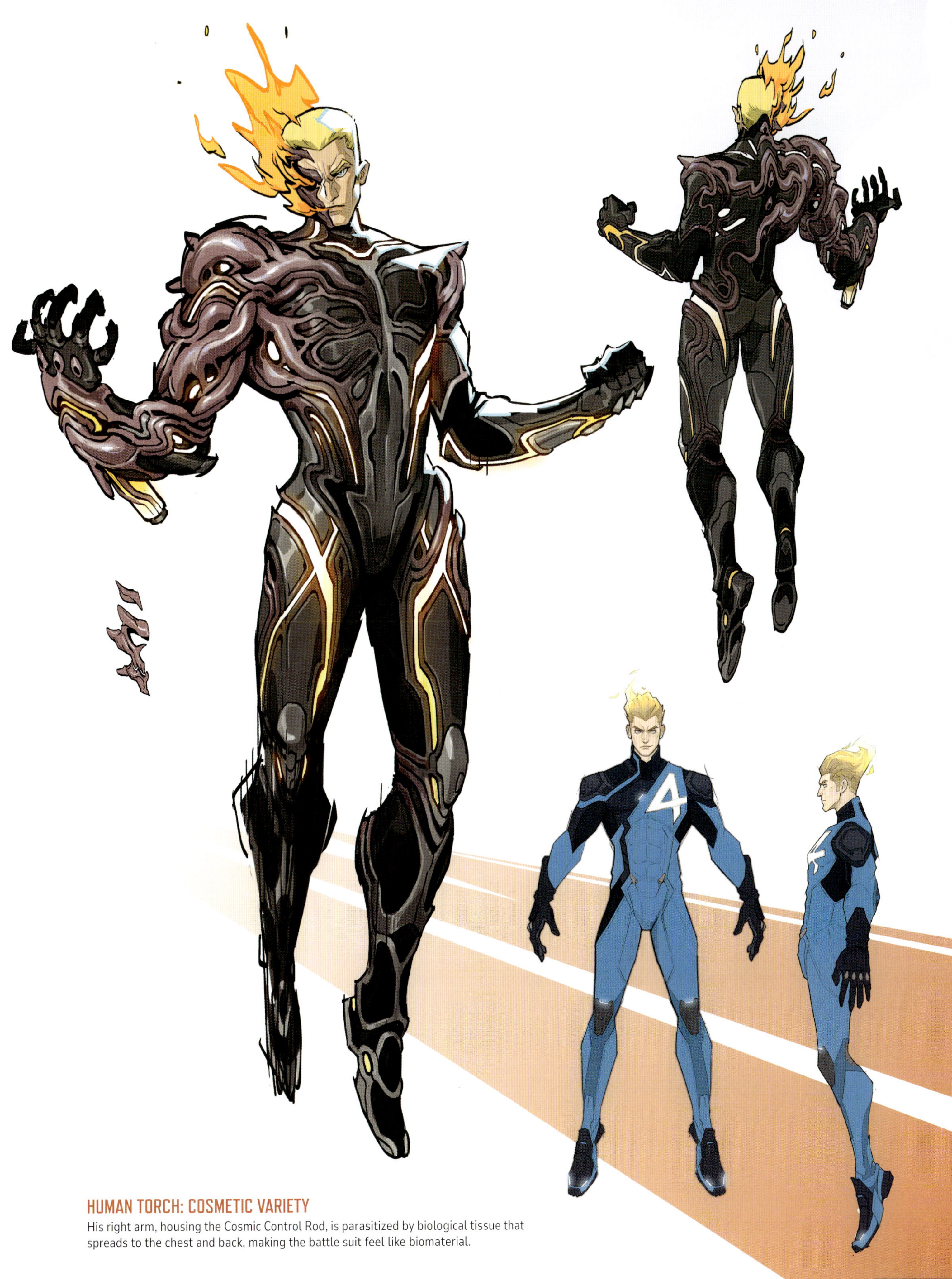

HUMAN TORCH: COSMETIC VARIETY

His right arm, housing the Cosmic Control Rod, is parasitized by biological tissue that spreads to the chest and back, making the battle suit feel like biomaterial.

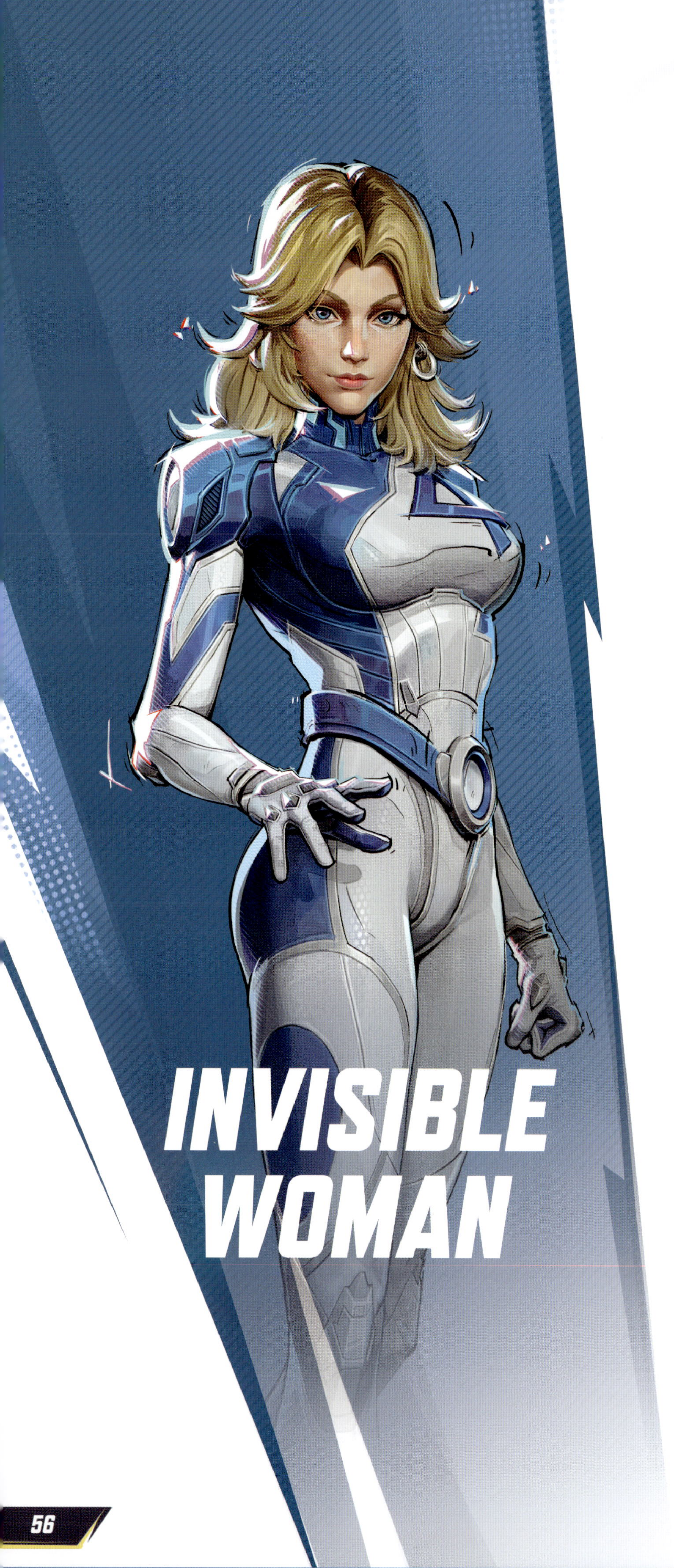

SUSAN RICHARDS

CLASS / STRATEGIST

Cosmic rays altered Susan Richards on a cellular level, granting her the ability to generate impenetrable force fields and to make herself fade from sight in an instant. Now, the Invisible Woman has taken full advantage of her powers, using stealth to explore locations too dangerous for her fellow heroes in the battle against the undying legions of Dracula.

As the Invisible Woman, Susan Richards can enter and leave any battle without a trace. She maintains composure during intense battles and provides powerful force field support for her teammates.

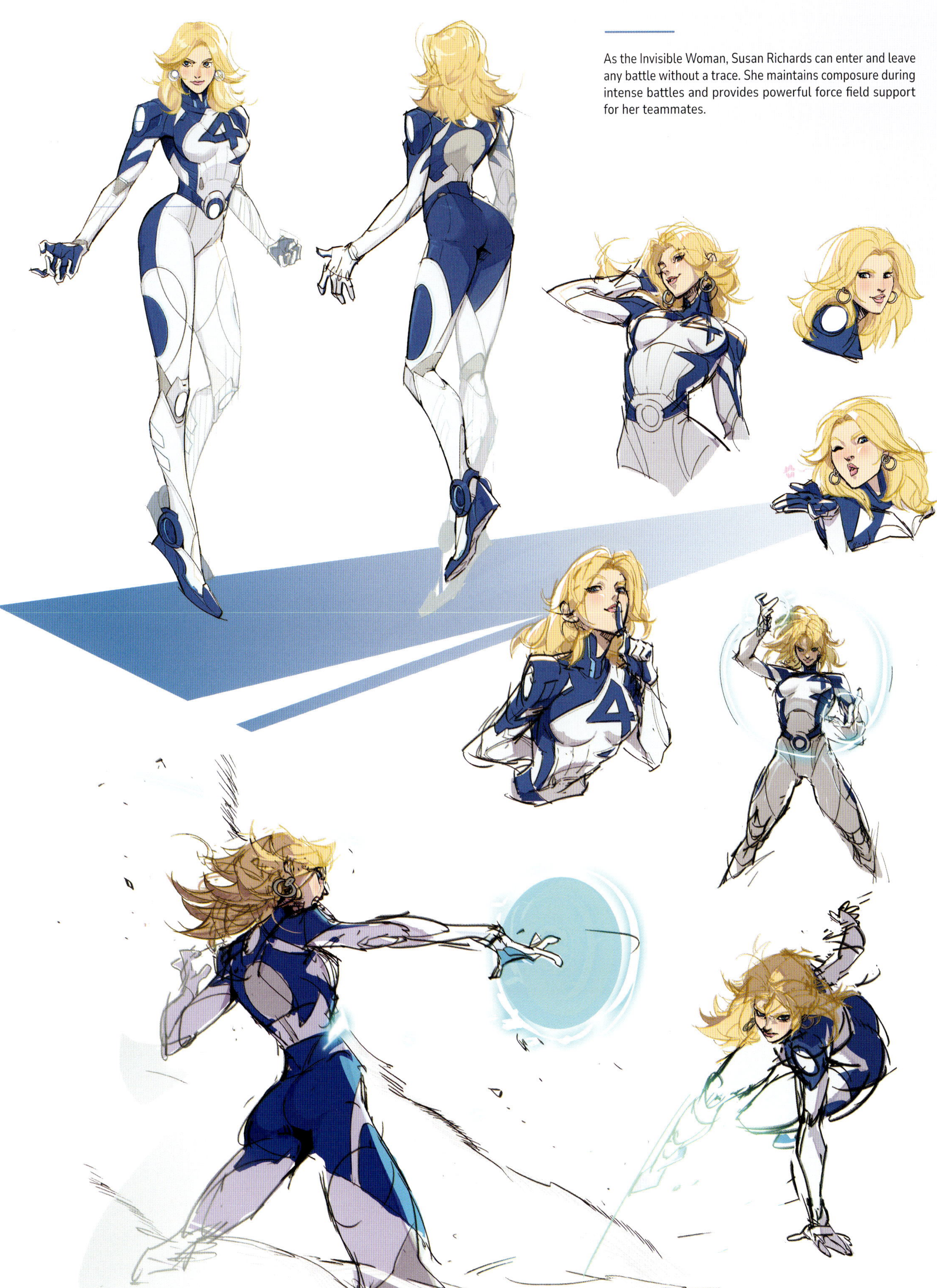

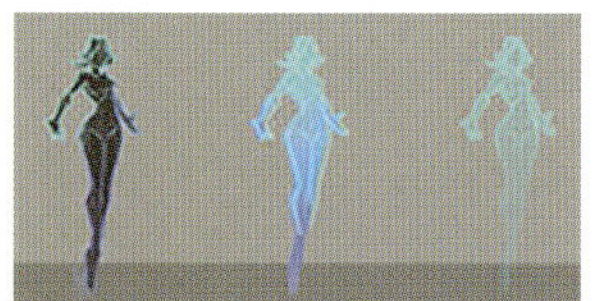

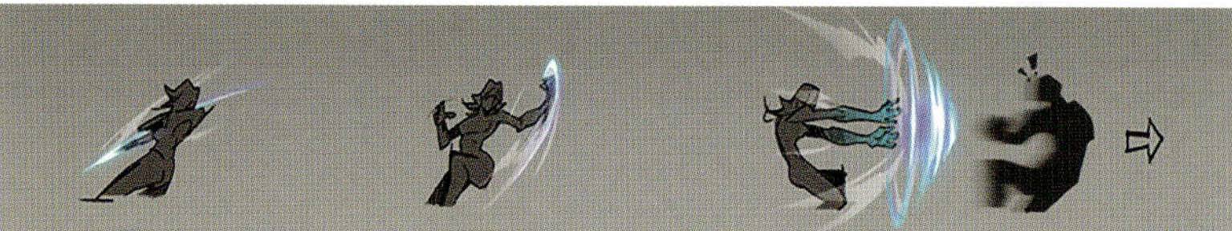
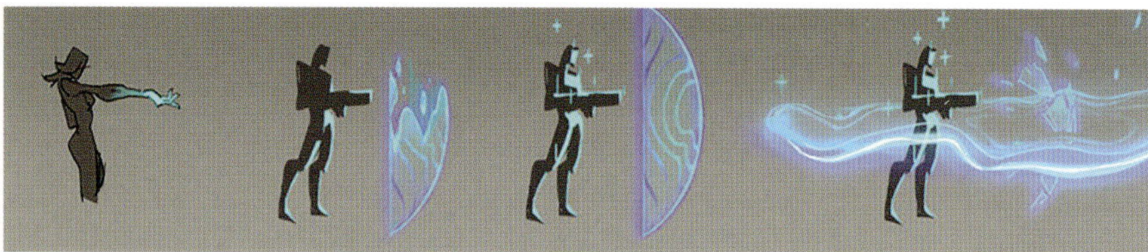
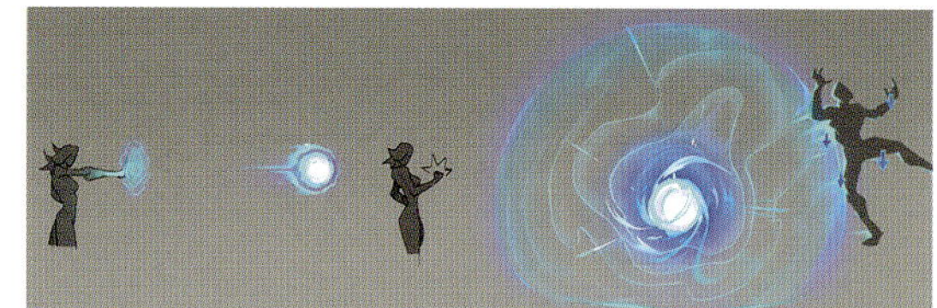
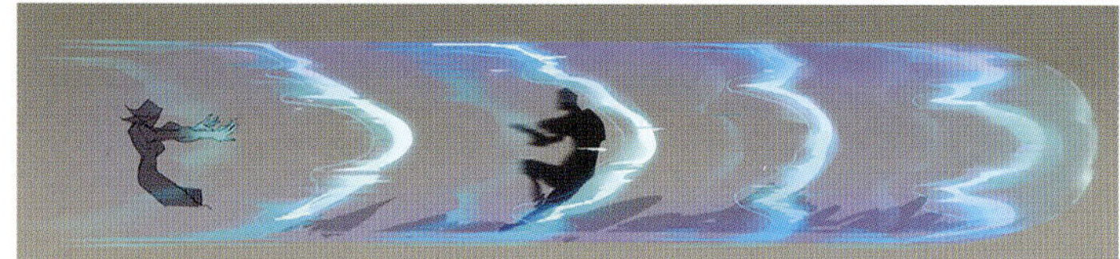
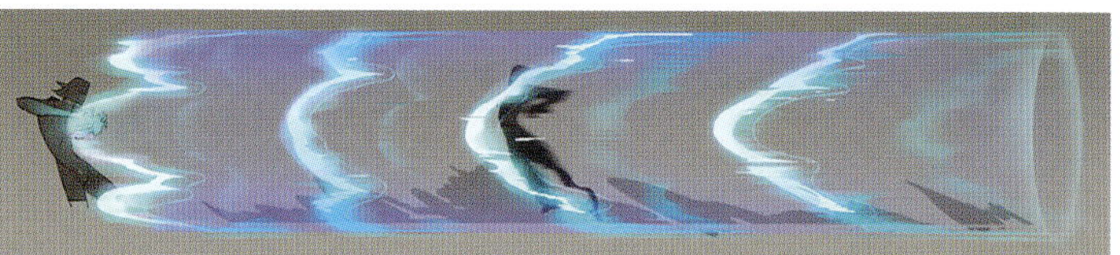
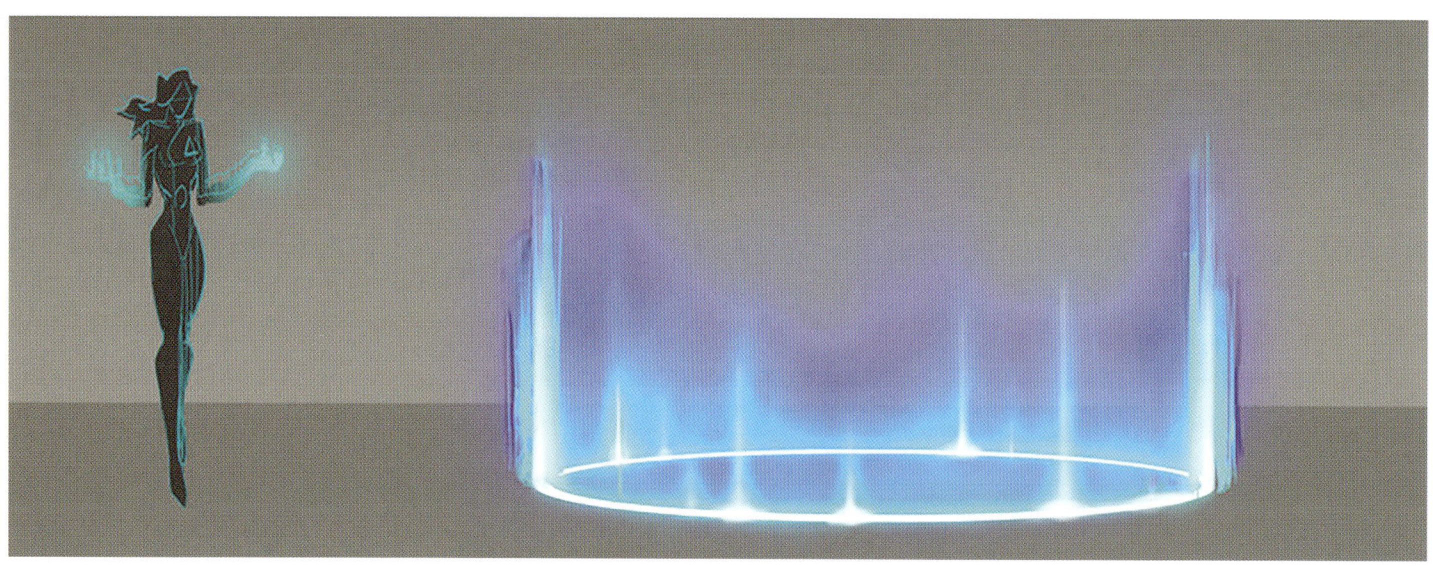
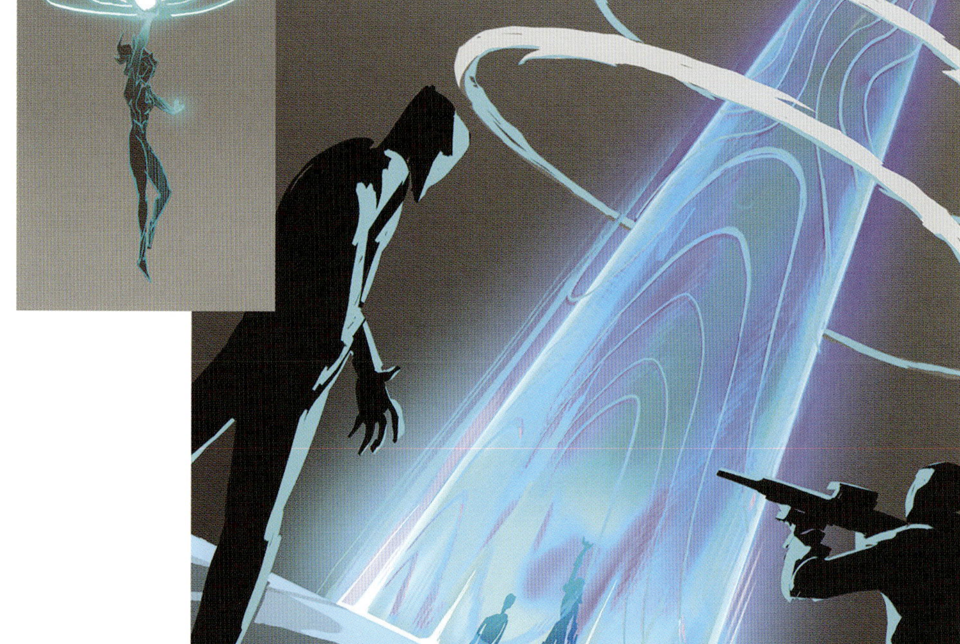

INVISIBLE WOMAN: ABILITIES

The Invisible Woman is capable of concealing herself on the battlefield, using protective barriers to shield and heal her team. Her potent psychic field can render all teammates invisible, creating strategic advantages.

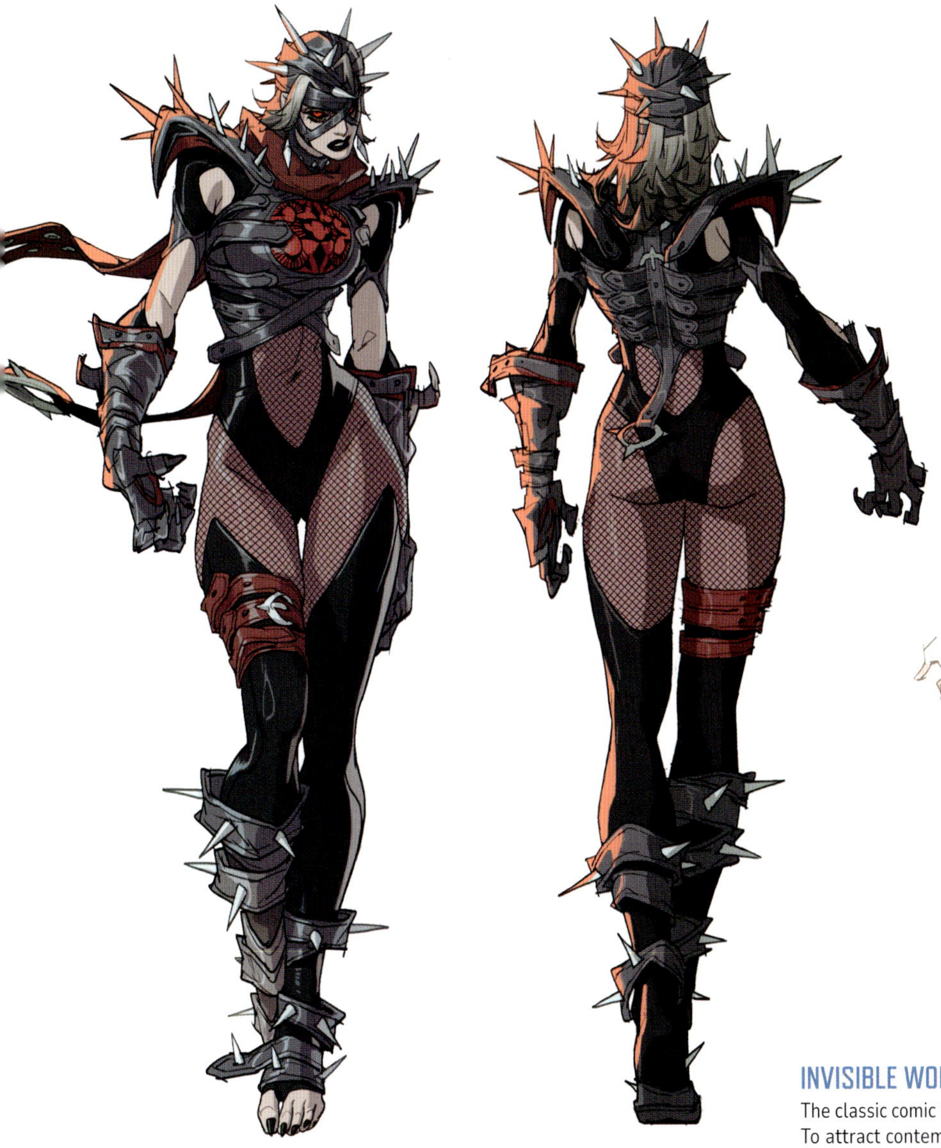

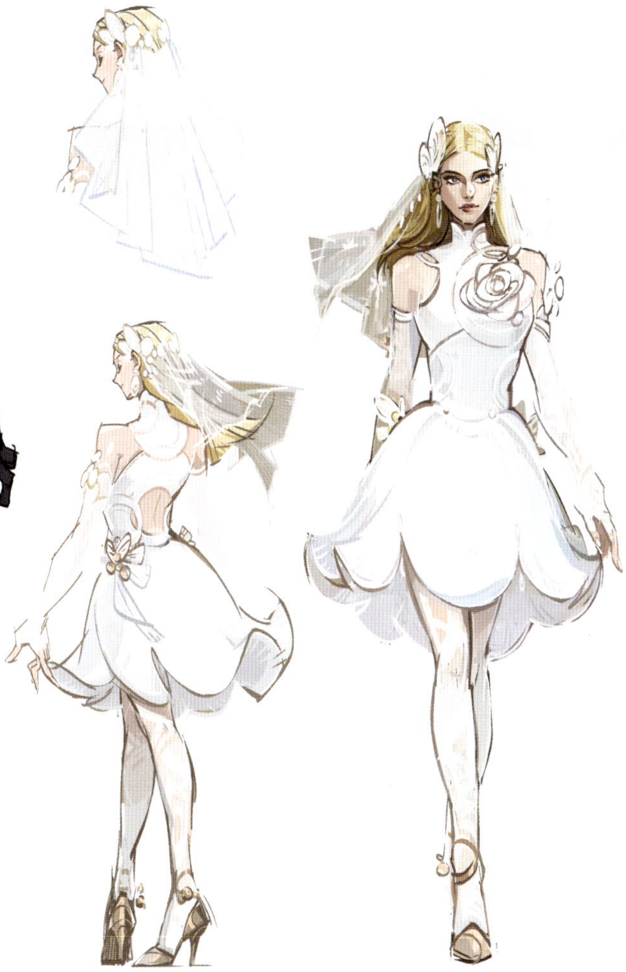

INVISIBLE WOMAN: COSMETIC VARIETY

The classic comic image of Malice may not be well known among today's younger audience. To attract contemporary players, designers needed to carefully consider her design and boldly innovate to make something that resonates with modern tastes.

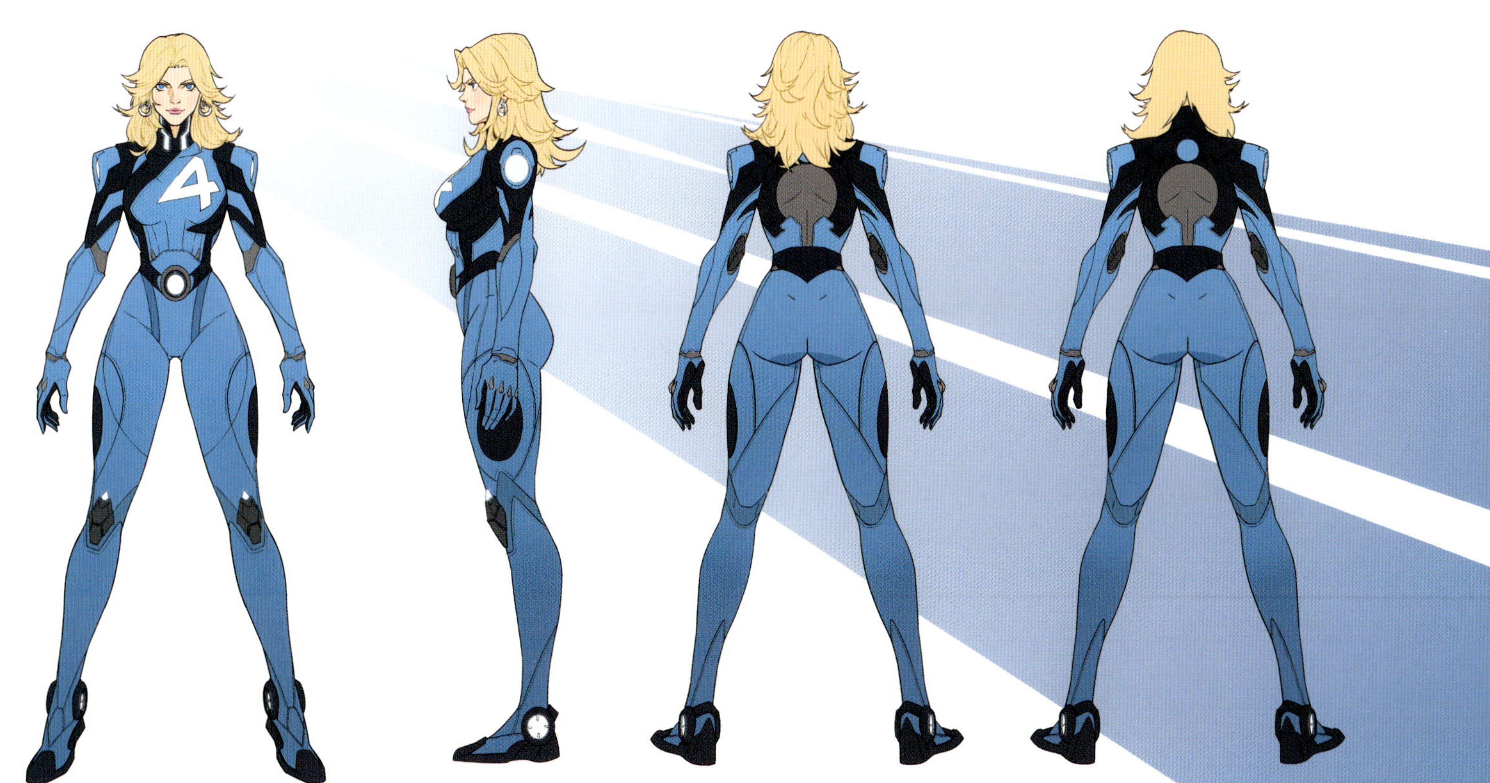

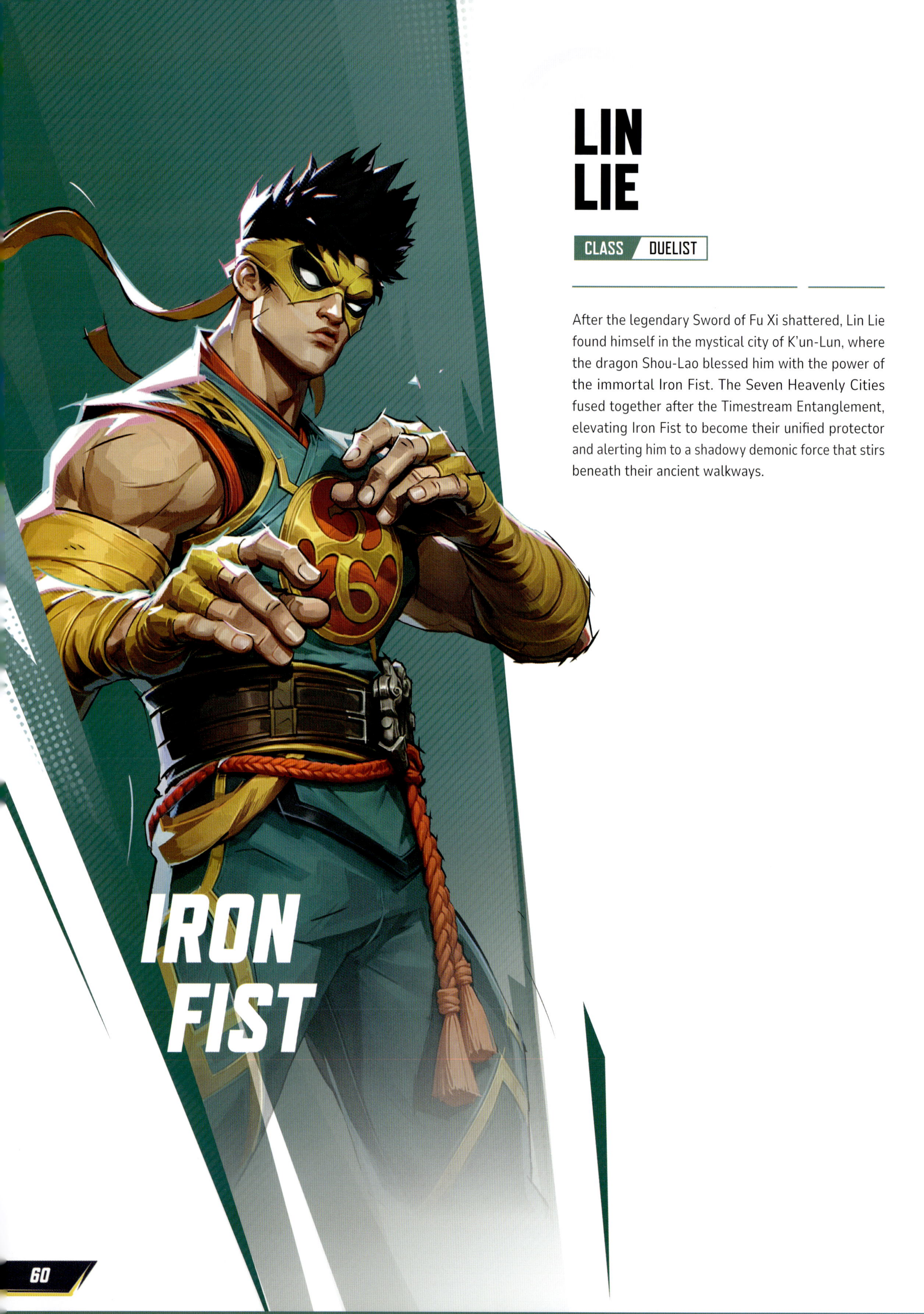

LIN LIE

CLASS / DUELIST

After the legendary Sword of Fu Xi shattered, Lin Lie found himself in the mystical city of K'un-Lun, where the dragon Shou-Lao blessed him with the power of the immortal Iron Fist. The Seven Heavenly Cities fused together after the Timestream Entanglement, elevating Iron Fist to become their unified protector and alerting him to a shadowy demonic force that stirs beneath their ancient walkways.

Lin Lie, now a Chinese kung fu master, once wielded the Sword of Fu Xi. After merging its shards with the chi of the dragon Shou-Lao, he now strikes with the power of K'un-Lun as the new Immortal Iron Fist.

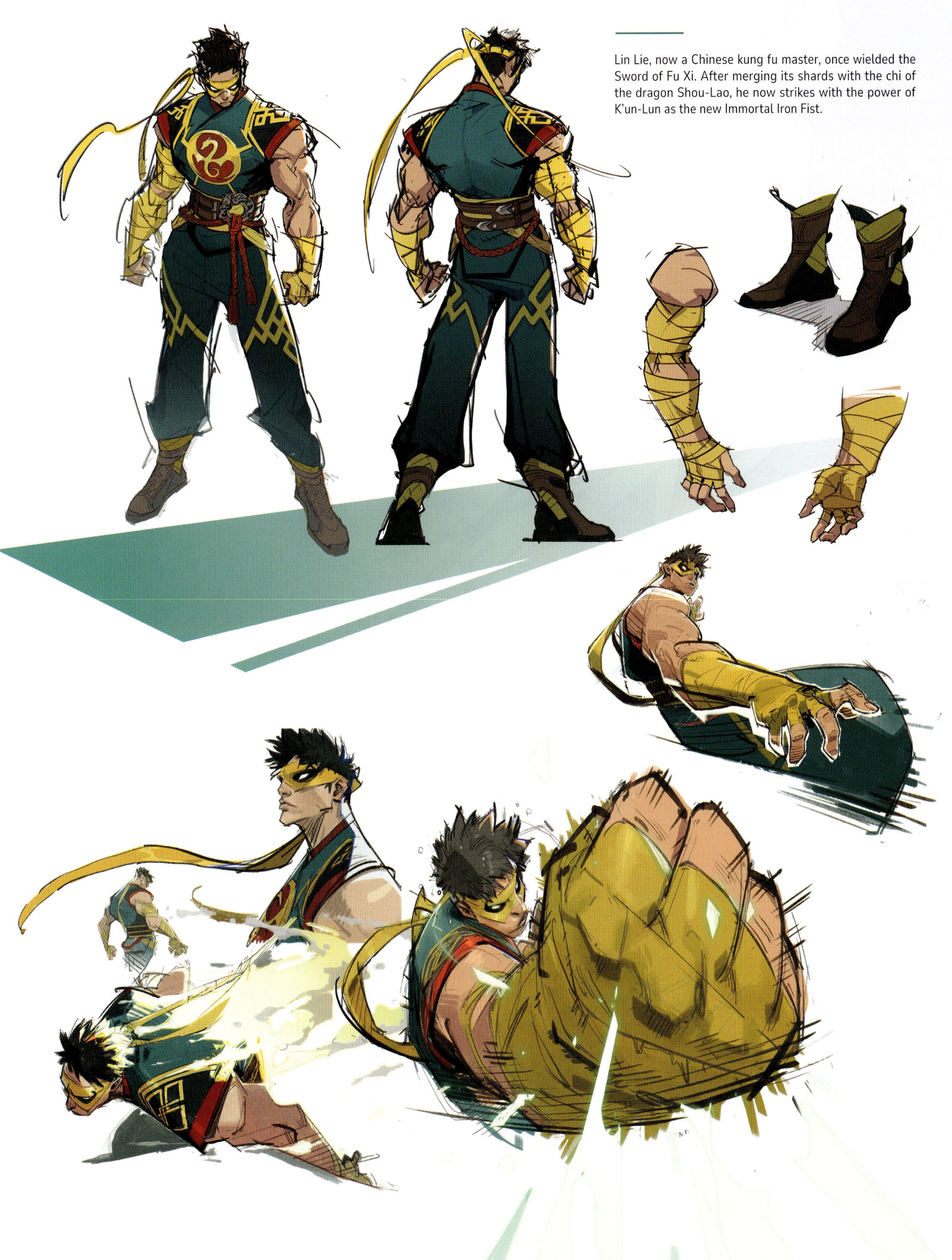

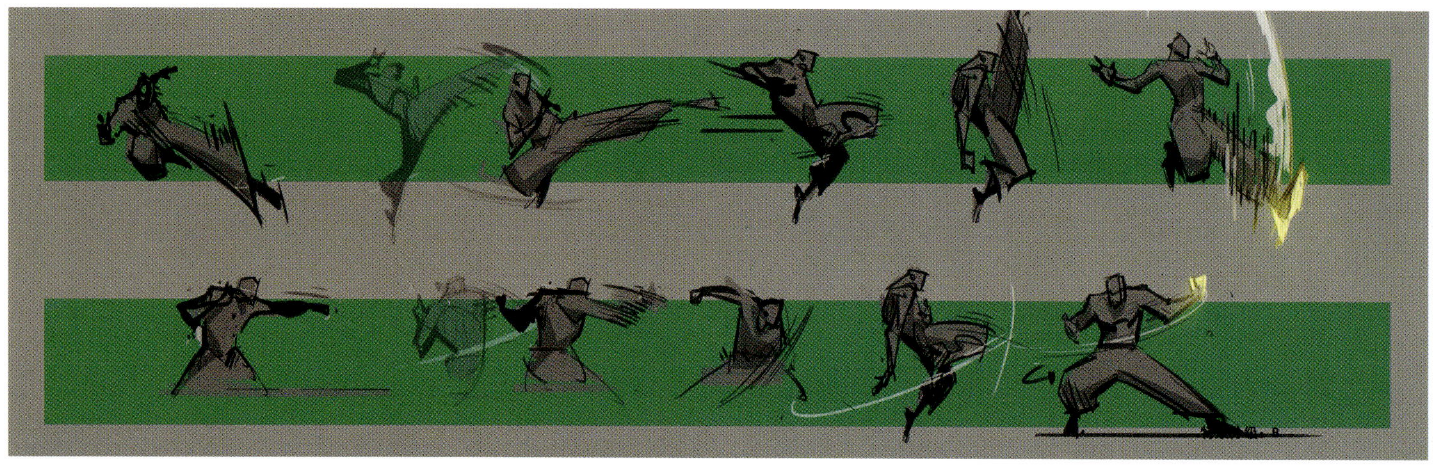

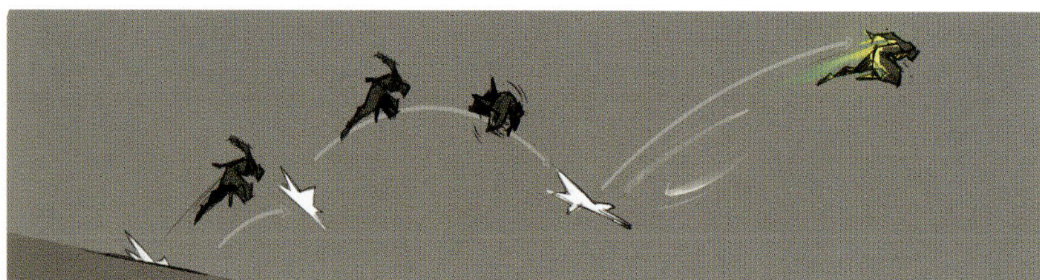

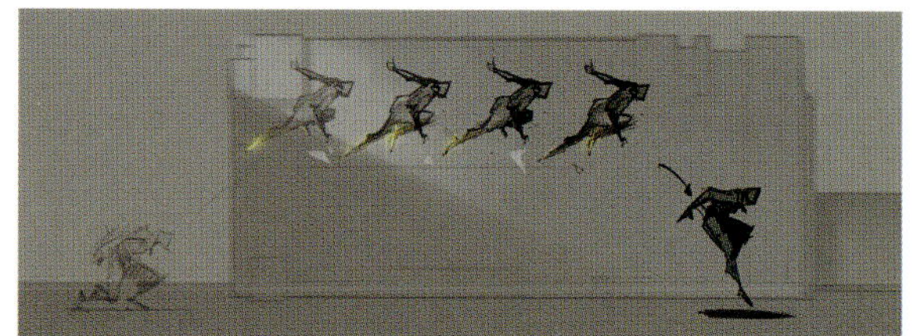

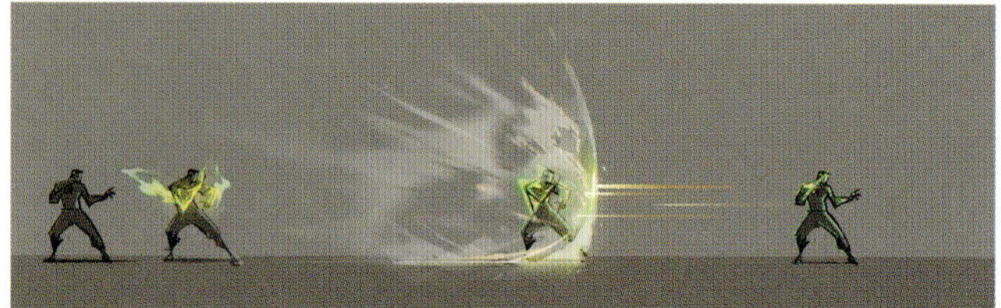

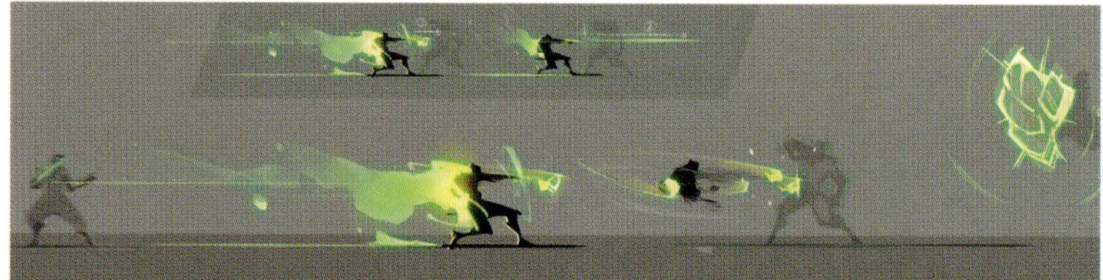

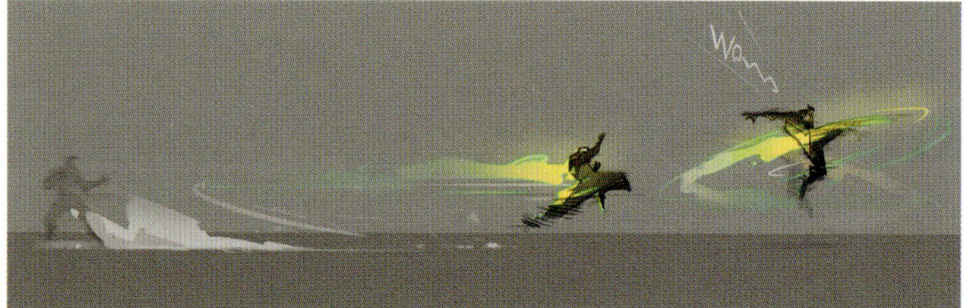

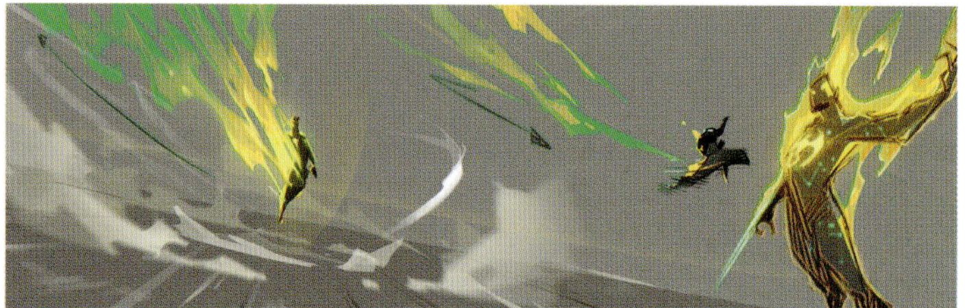

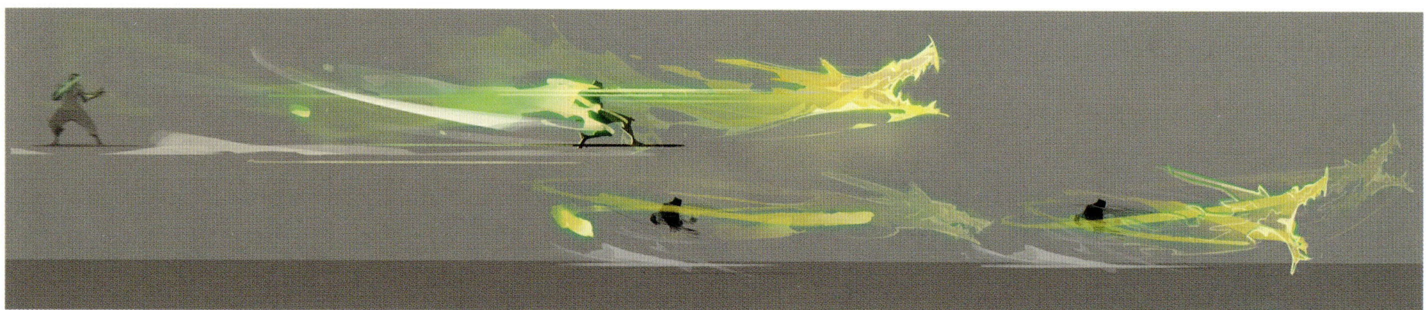

IRON FIST: ABILITIES

Iron Fist employs Chinese kung fu for health restoration and shields through the lotus position. He is also capable of making a series of flexible aerial jumps and can relentlessly pursue his enemies through a chi-infused flurry of punches.

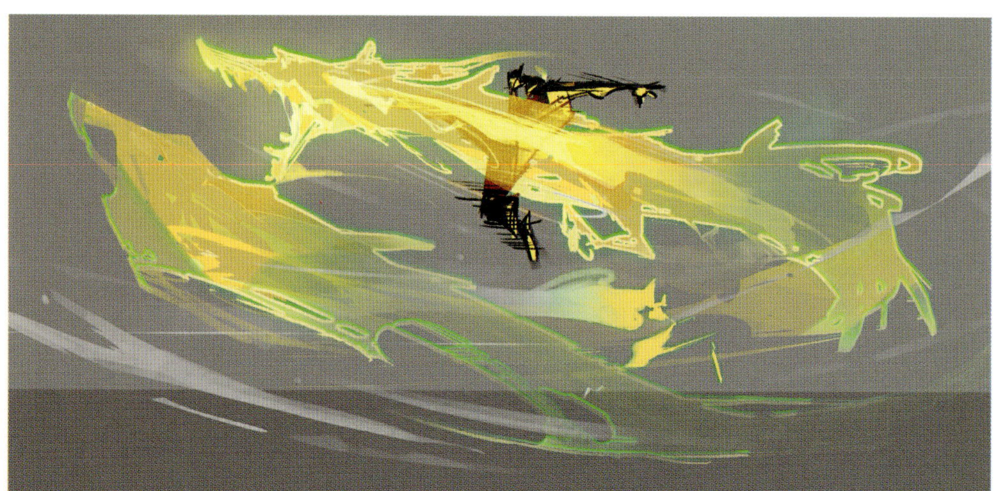

IRON FIST: COSMETIC VARIETY

The costume, inspired by Chinese lion dance culture, allows him to blend fashion sense with traditional costuming as he leaps into action!

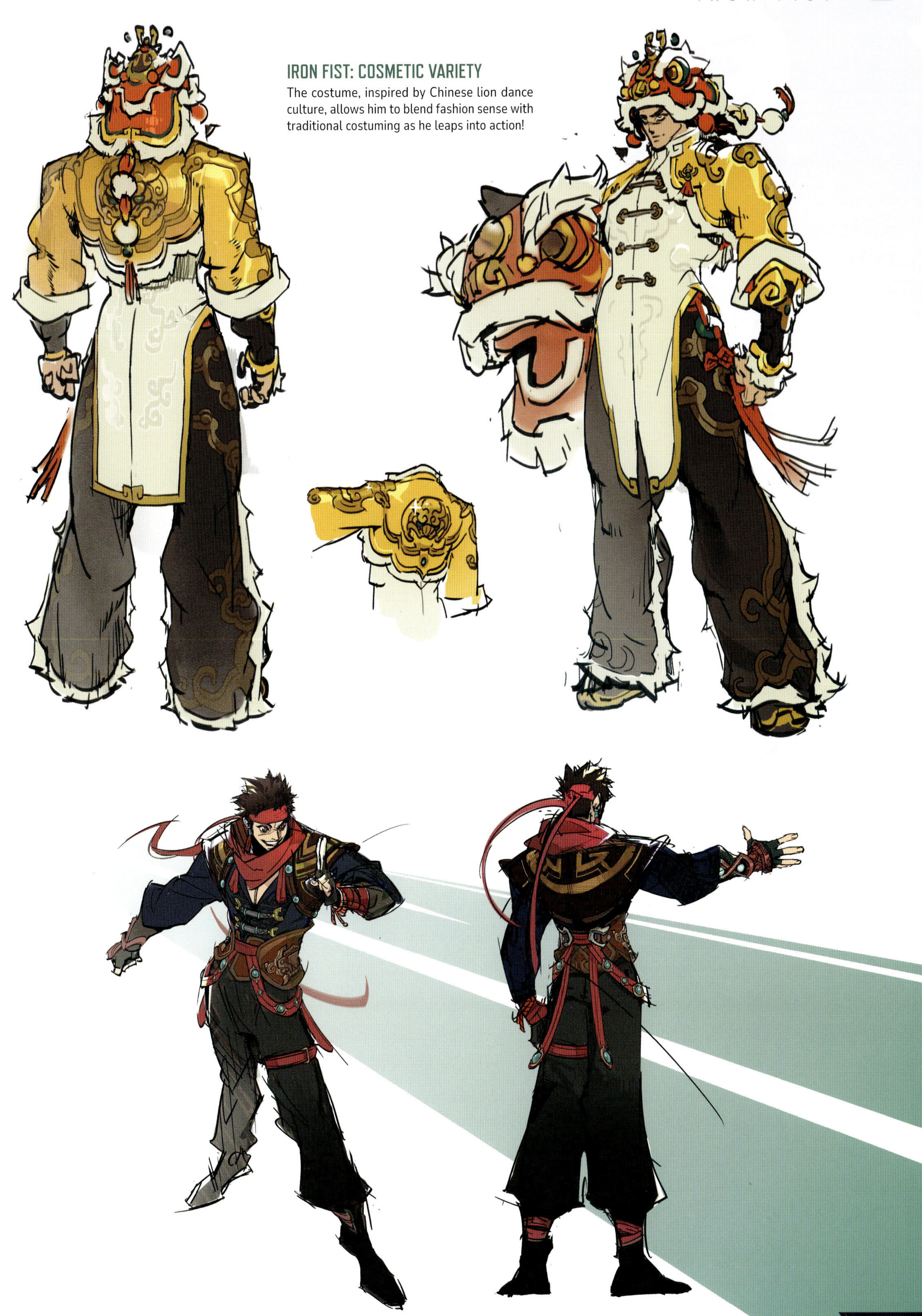

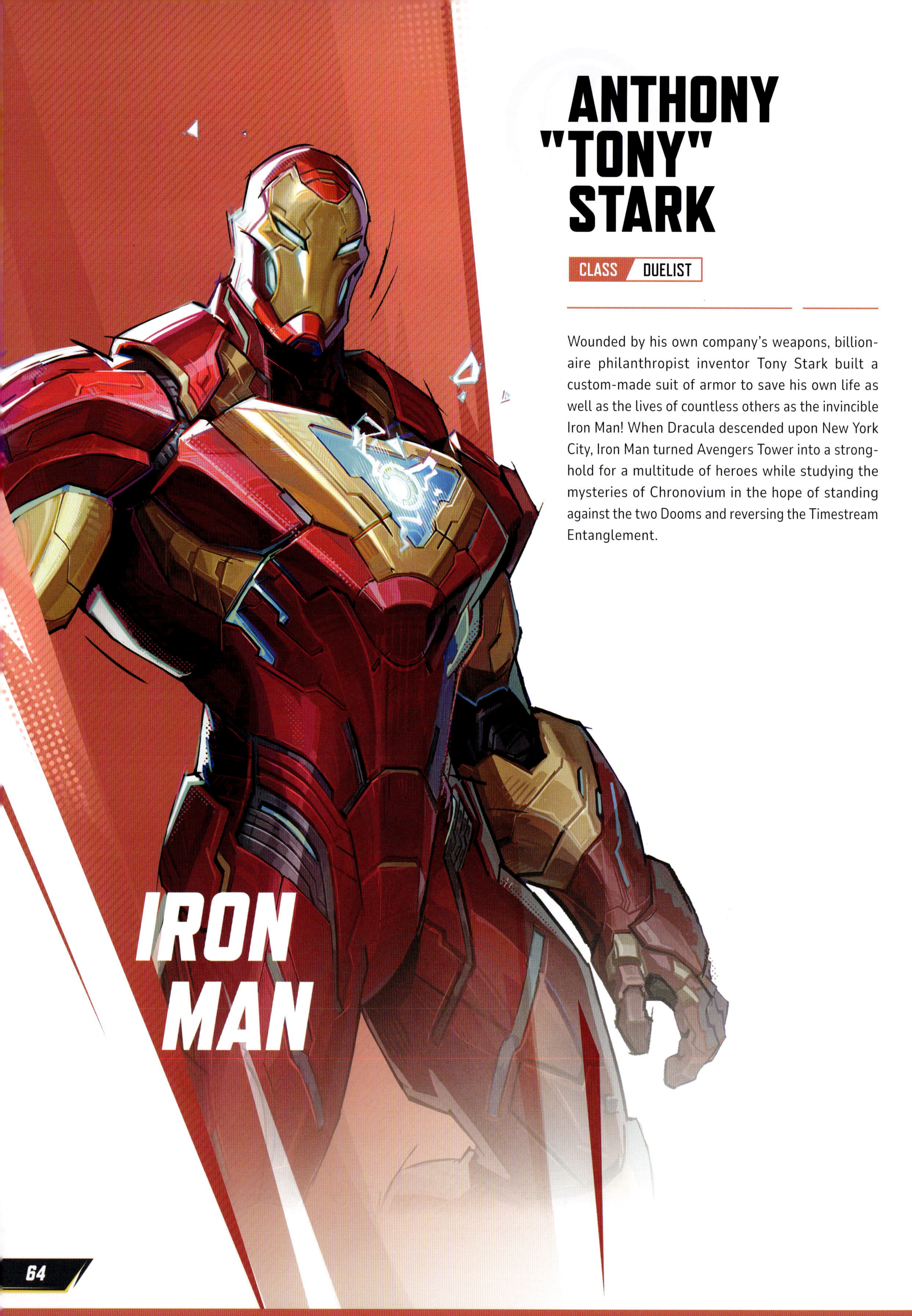

ANTHONY "TONY" STARK

CLASS / DUELIST

Wounded by his own company's weapons, billionaire philanthropist inventor Tony Stark built a custom-made suit of armor to save his own life as well as the lives of countless others as the invincible Iron Man! When Dracula descended upon New York City, Iron Man turned Avengers Tower into a stronghold for a multitude of heroes while studying the mysteries of Chronovium in the hope of standing against the two Dooms and reversing the Timestream Entanglement.

The genius billionaire philanthropist channels his rebellious nature in his armor with fiery red and dazzling gold. Naturally, Tony Stark makes it well known that Iron Man is taking care of business with style.

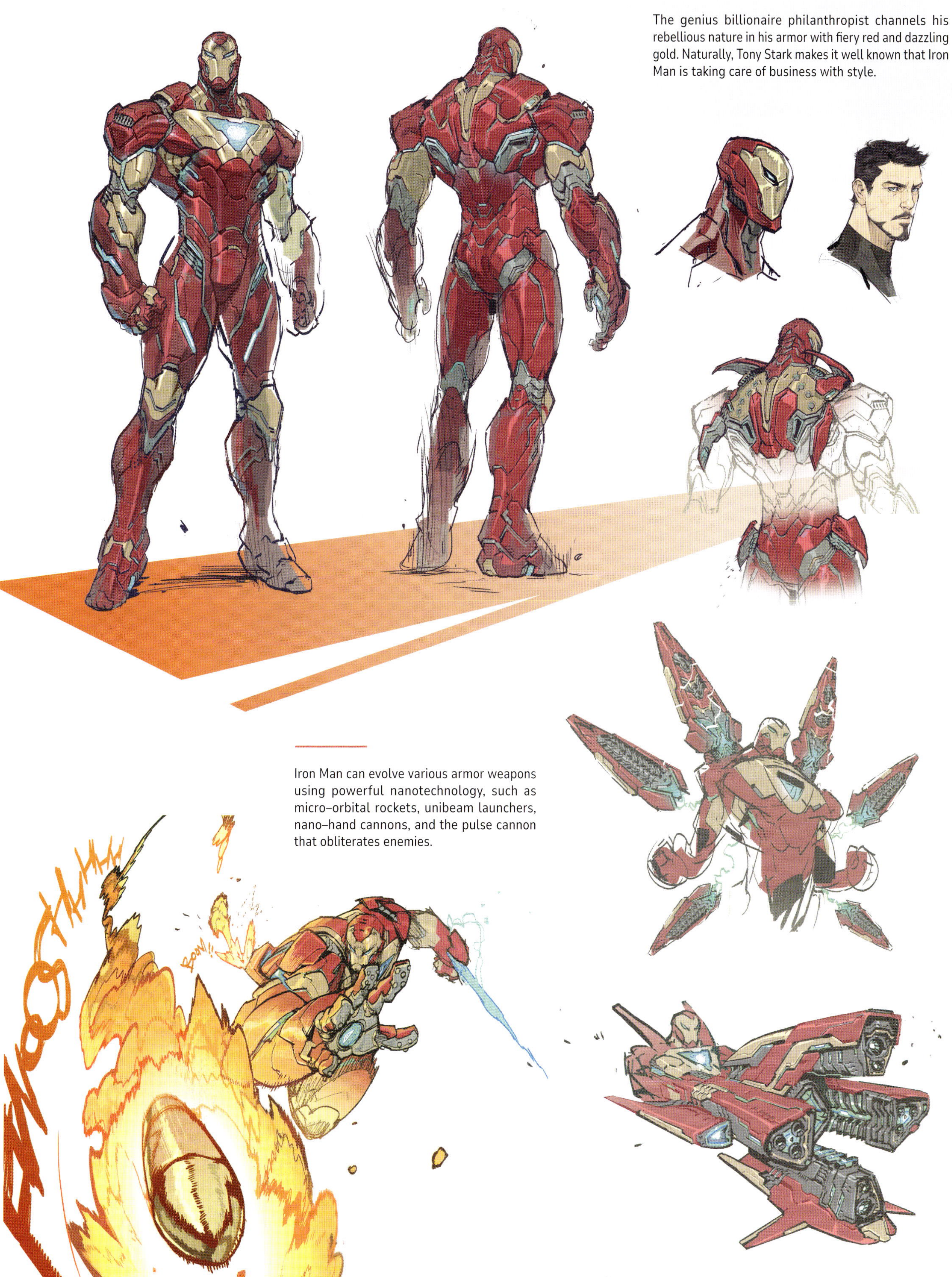

Iron Man can evolve various armor weapons using powerful nanotechnology, such as micro-orbital rockets, unibeam launchers, nano-hand cannons, and the pulse cannon that obliterates enemies.

IRON MAN: ABILITIES

Undoubtedly, Tony's brilliant performance involves utilizing the dazzling weapon system on his armor and his agile flight to assert complete air superiority in battle.

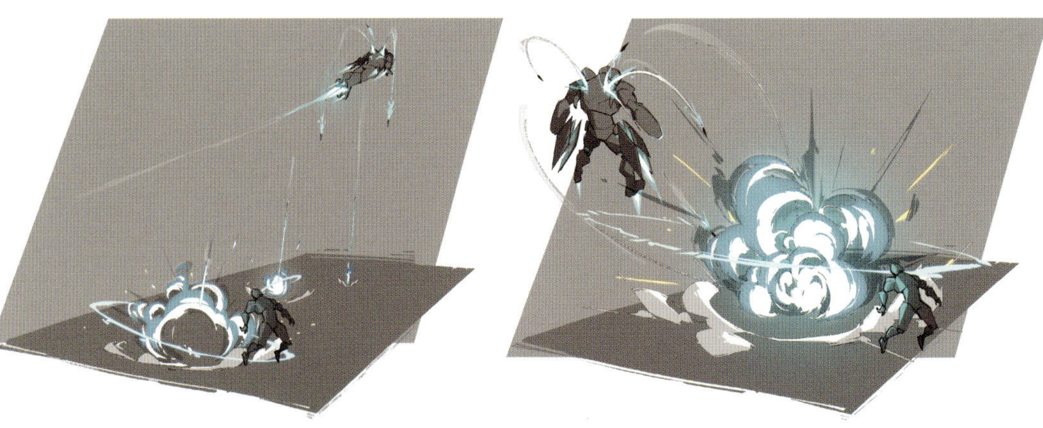

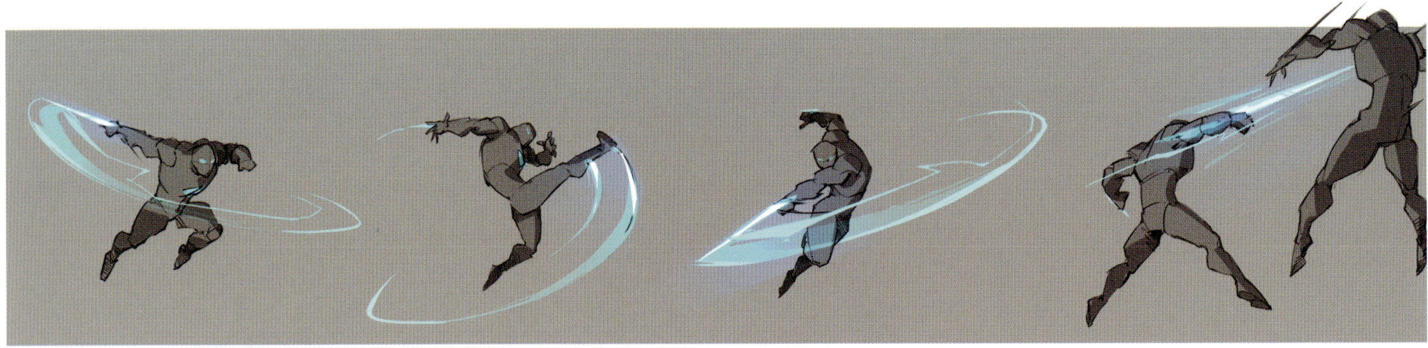

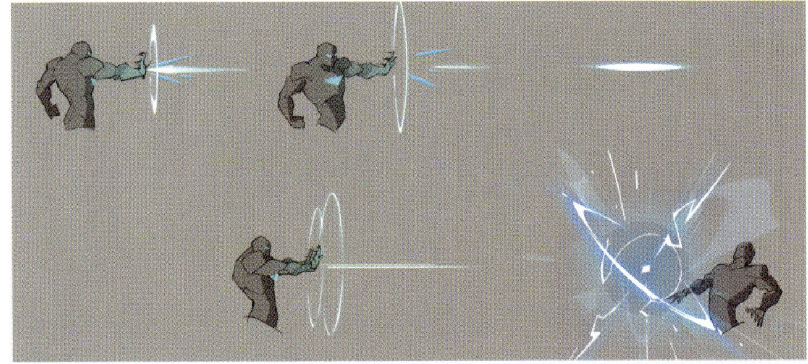

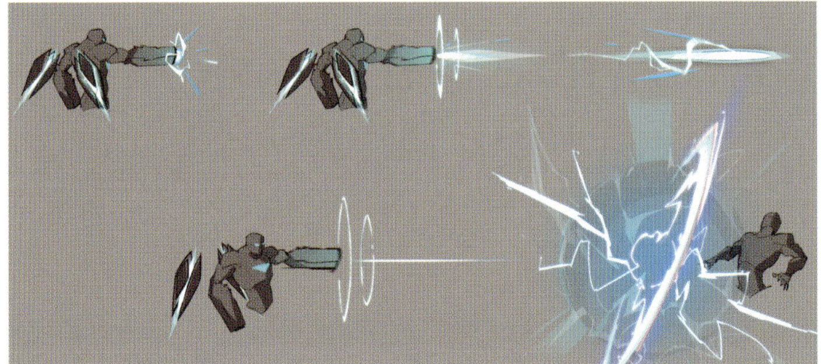

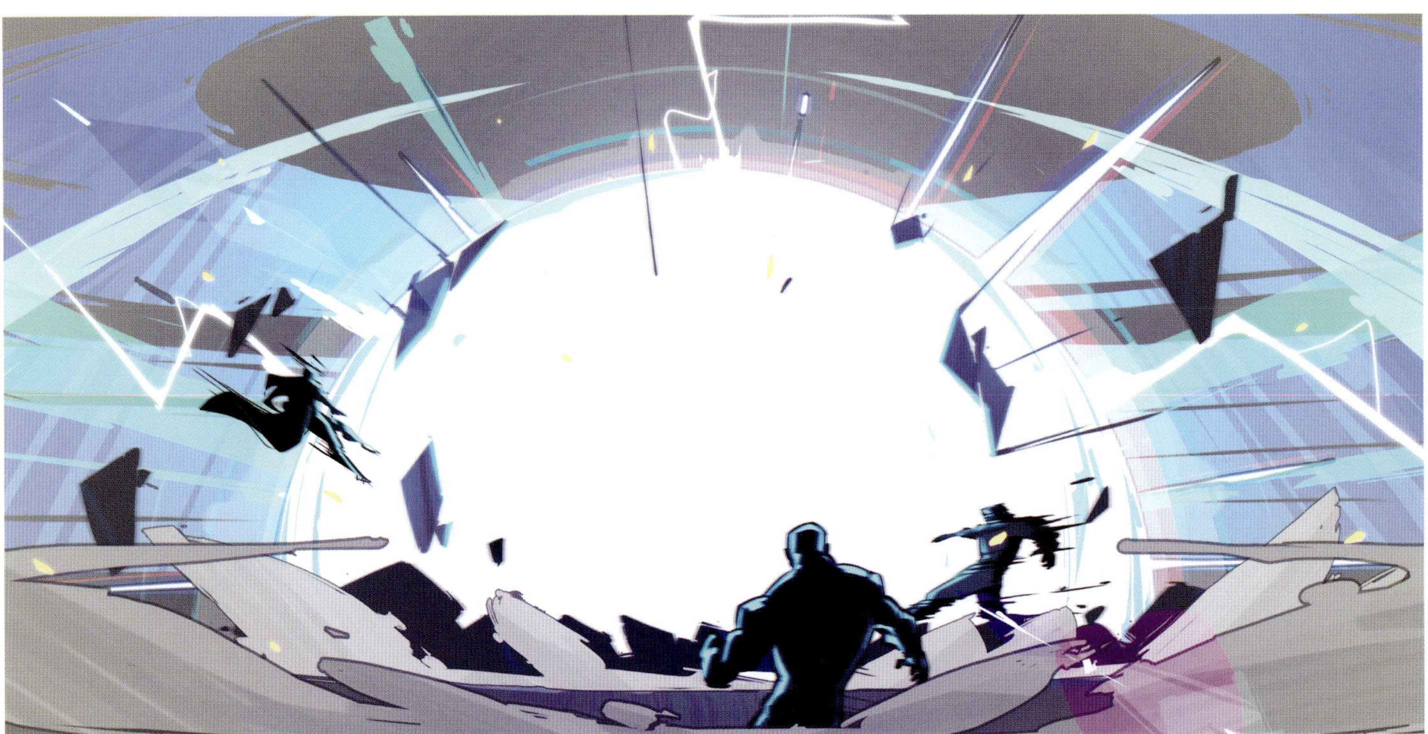

IRON MAN: COSMETIC VARIETY

The red-and-gold color scheme of the Marvel Studios' *Avengers: Endgame*–inspired armor makes Mark 85 shine. With each element we meticulously pay homage to, we hope players feel inspired to say: "I am Iron Man."

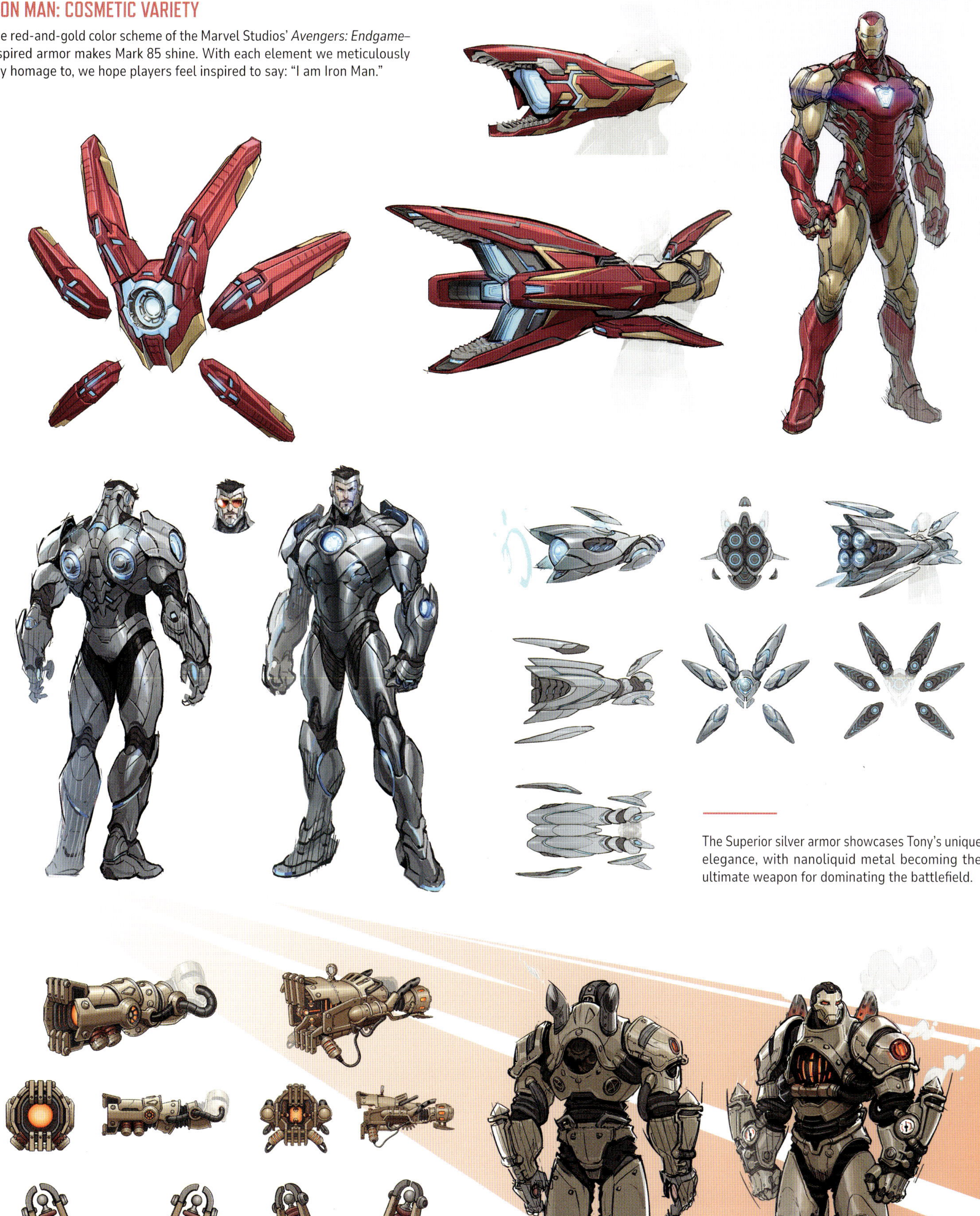

The Superior silver armor showcases Tony's unique elegance, with nanoliquid metal becoming the ultimate weapon for dominating the battlefield.

JEFF

CLASS / STRATEGIST

He's more huggable than a puppy and hungrier than a great white: It's Jeff! This baby land shark may be one of the most unusual and adorable creatures to ever waddle his way out of the ocean, but after escaping captivity within the Collector's theme park, Jeff now has his chance to prove he's a hero, one chomp at a time!

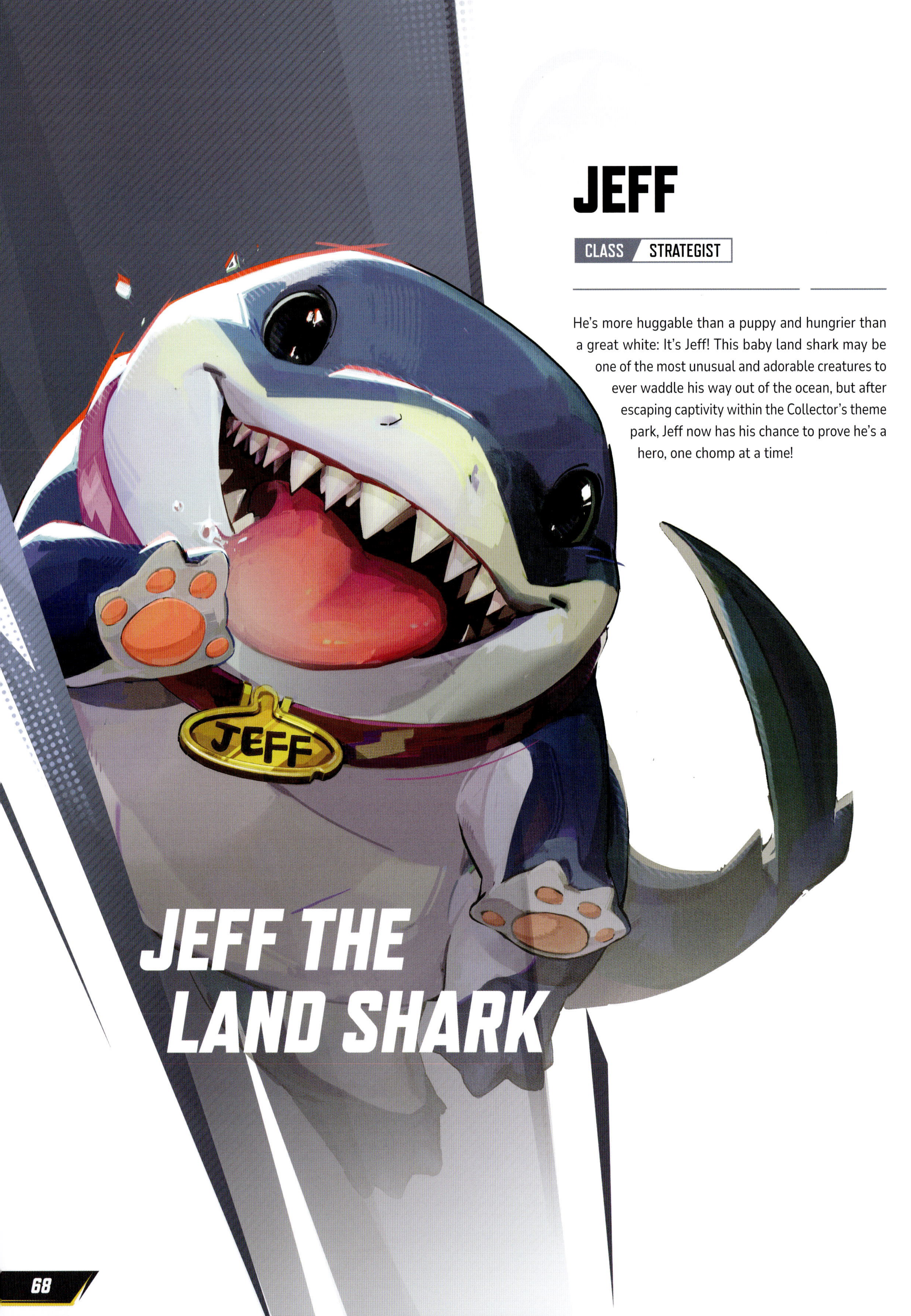

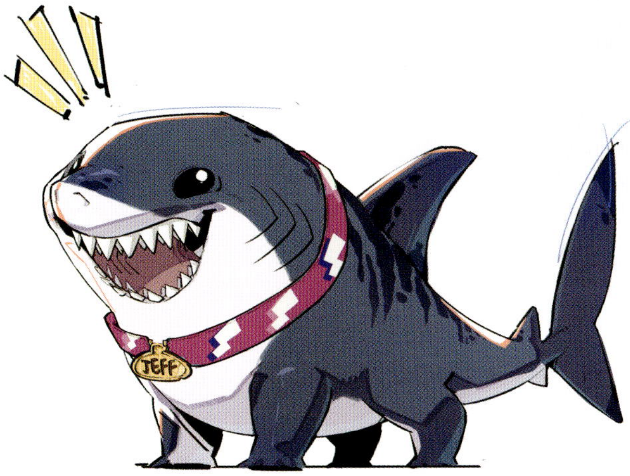

This mischievous cutie loves spreading joy and healing his friends! When needed most, the tiny land shark becomes a big eater, swallowing enemies whole in an adorable gulp!

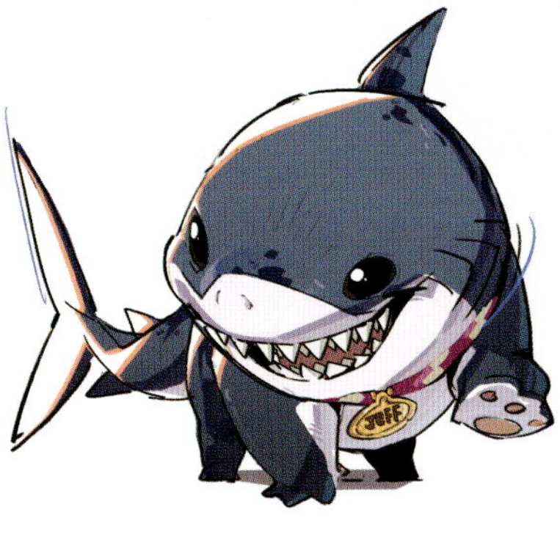

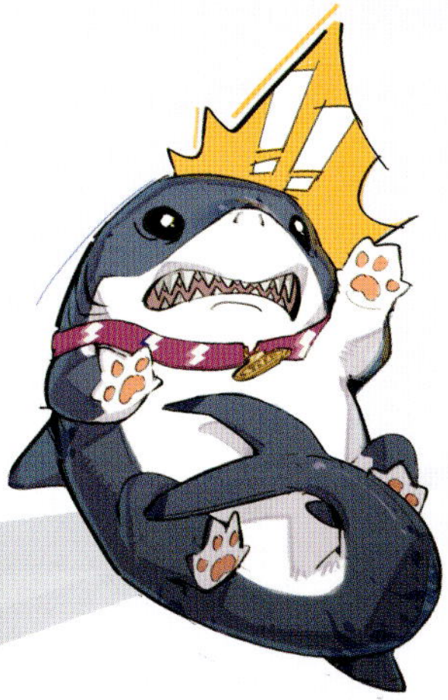

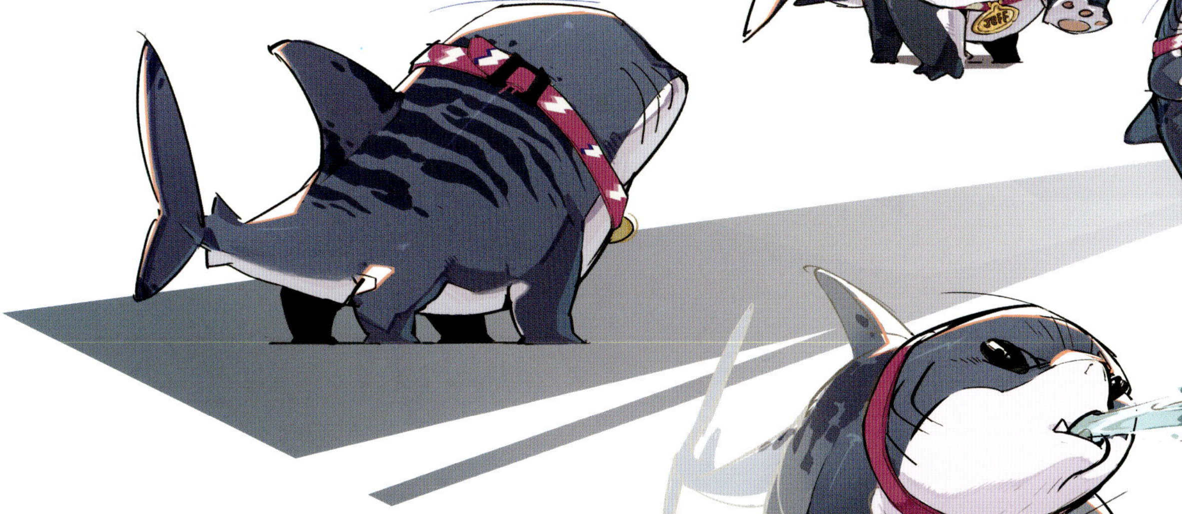

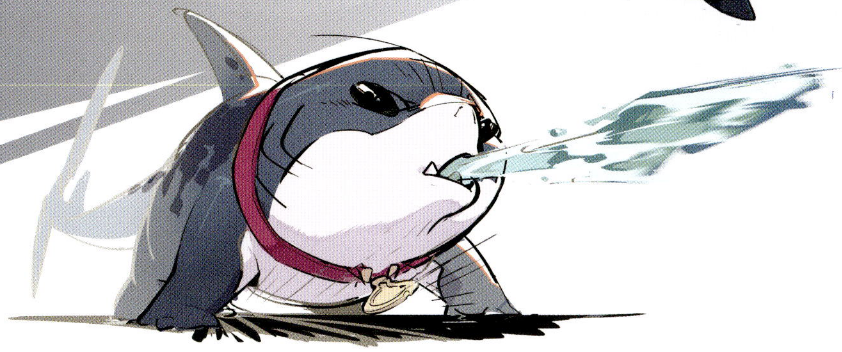

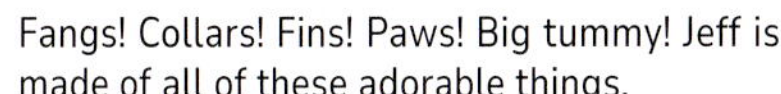

Fangs! Collars! Fins! Paws! Big tummy! Jeff is made of all of these adorable things.

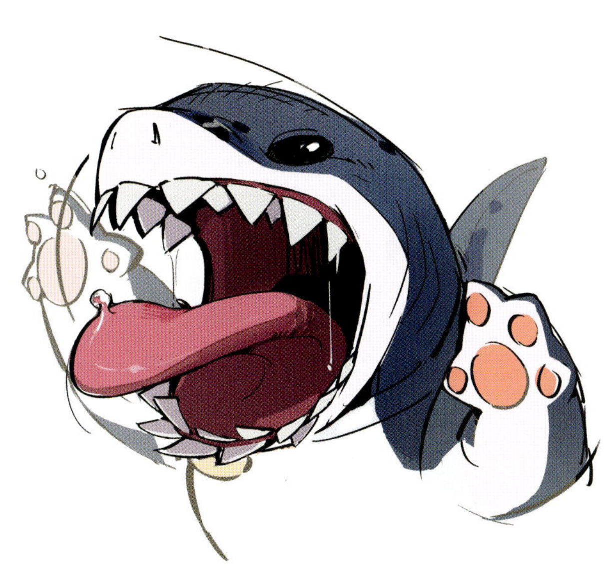

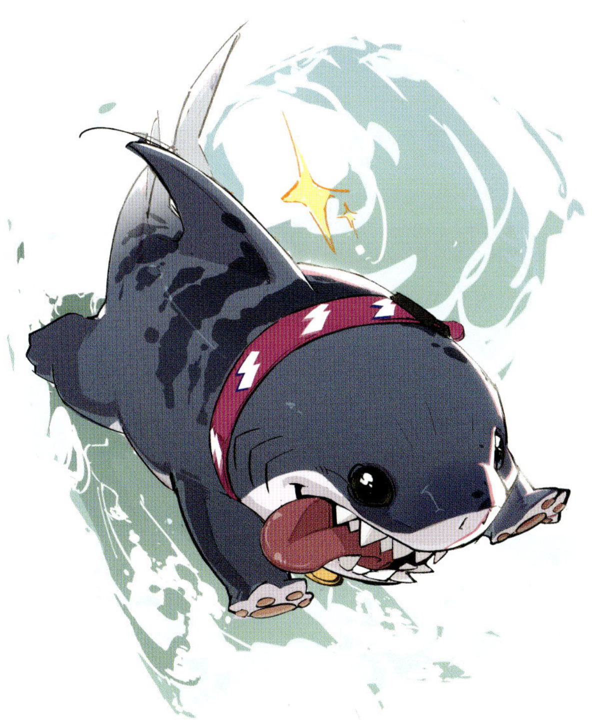

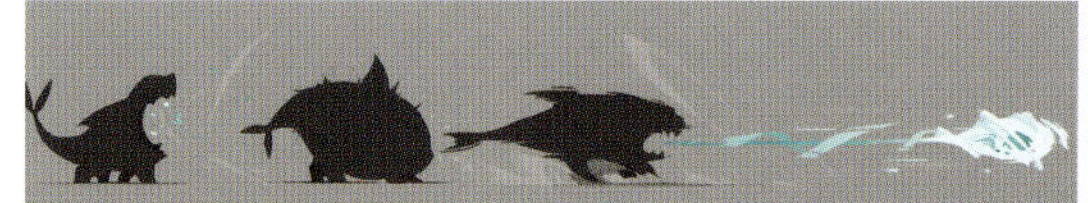

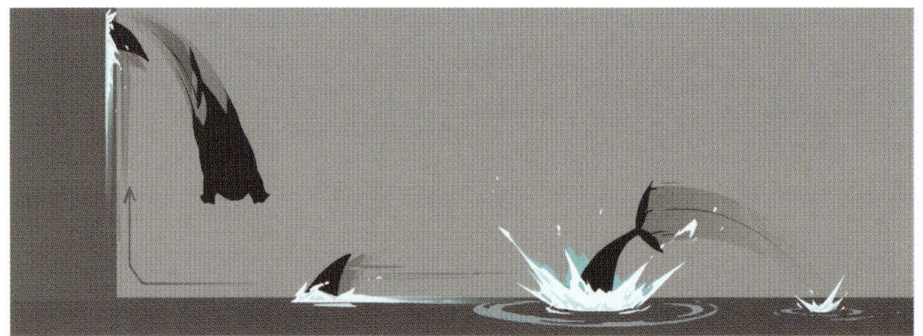

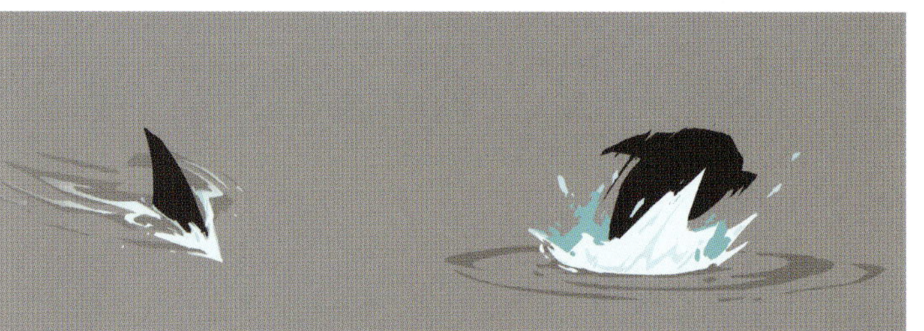

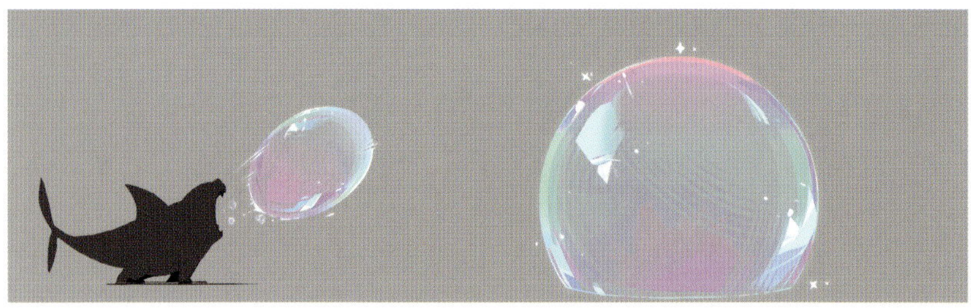

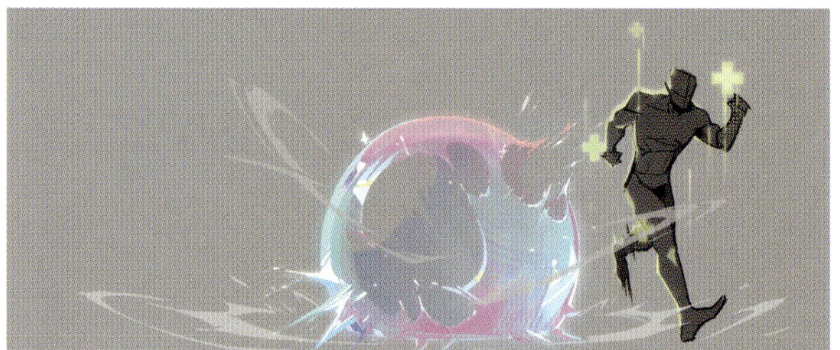

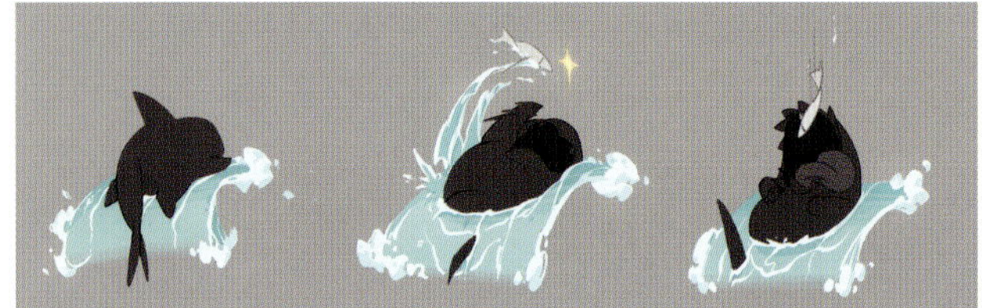

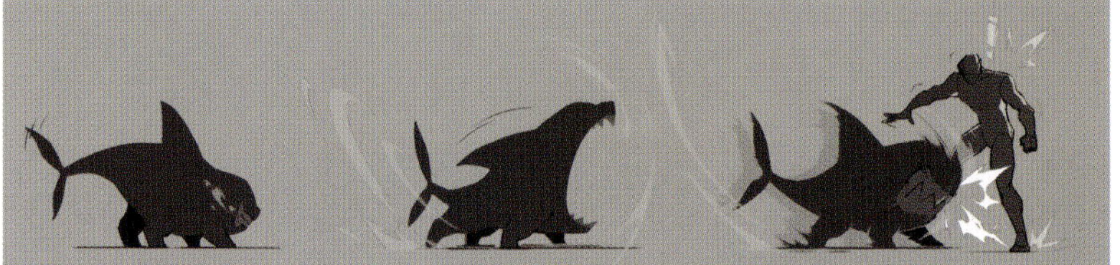

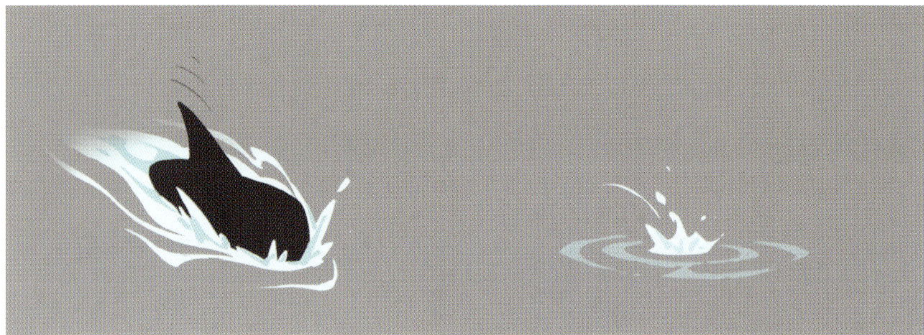

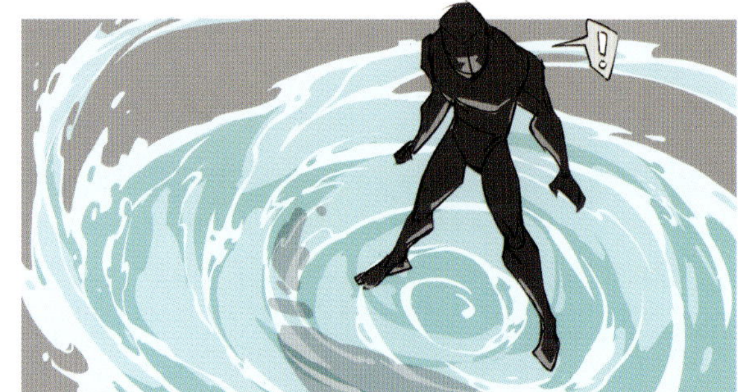

JEFF THE LAND SHARK: ABILITIES

Jeff moves quickly on both land and water. He loves using water in battles. While his bubbles and water can heal his teammates, he can dive into the ground to play hide-and-seek with those chasing him!

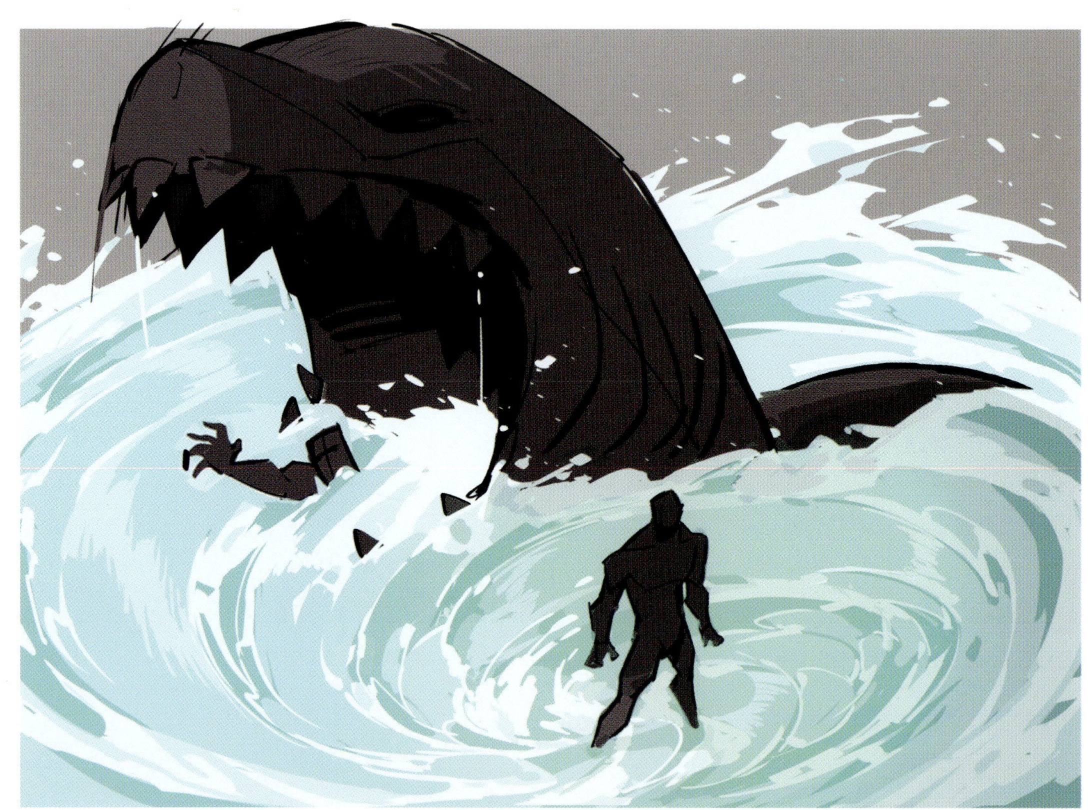

JEFF THE LAND SHARK: COSMETIC VARIETY

This fuzzy pink-and-white dolphin-doll attire is carefully curated by Jeff to not scare his friends at the beach!

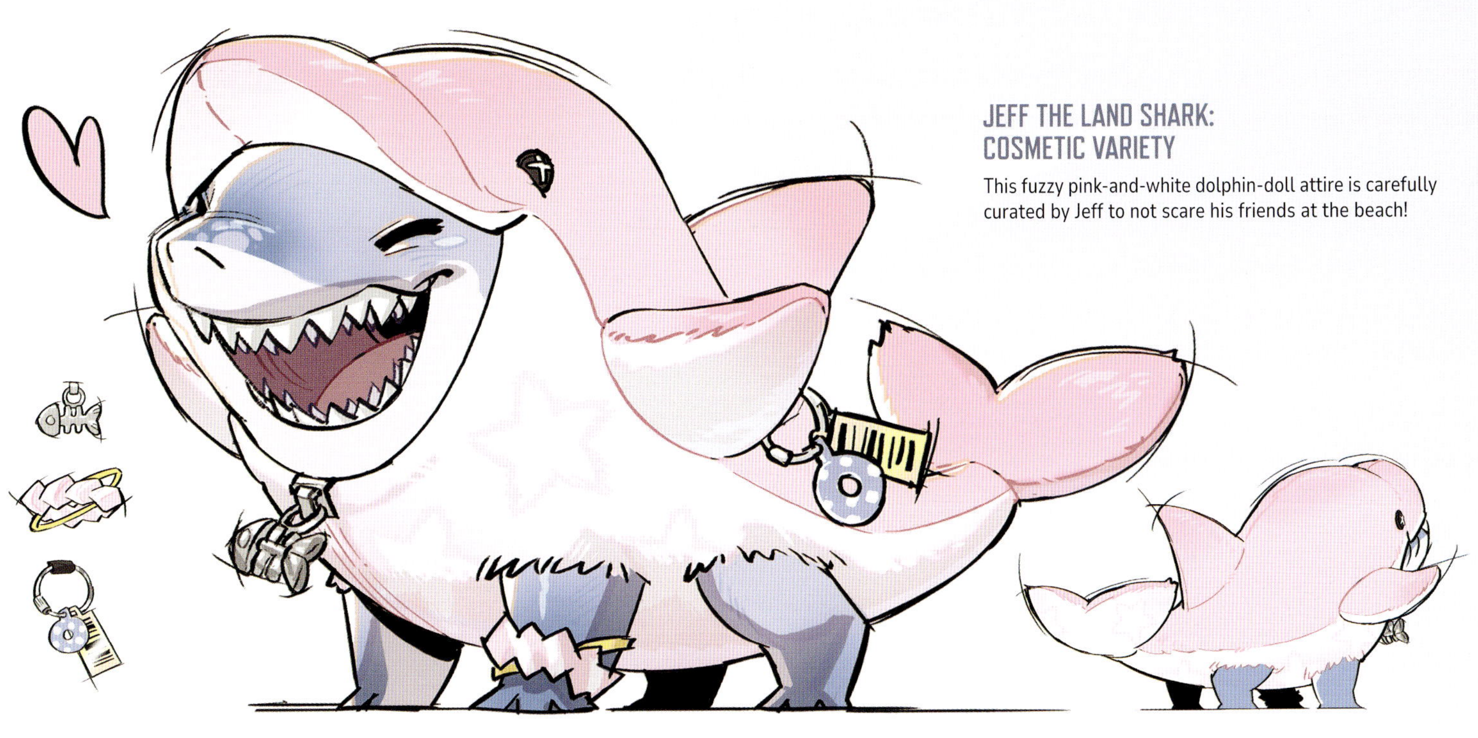

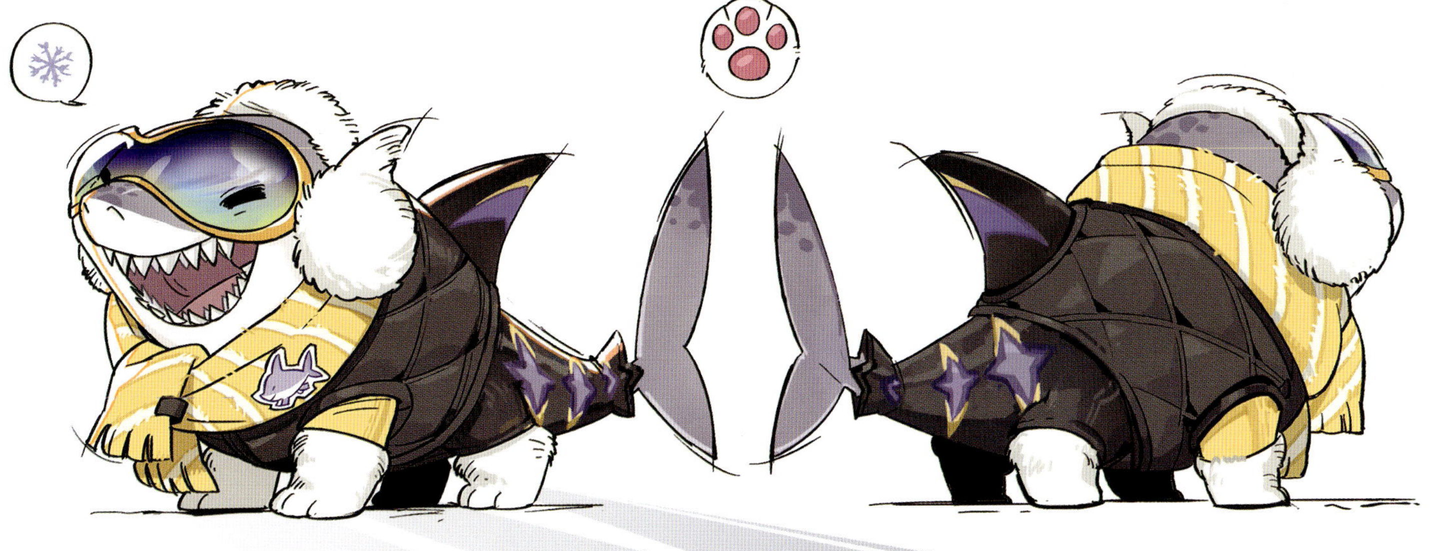

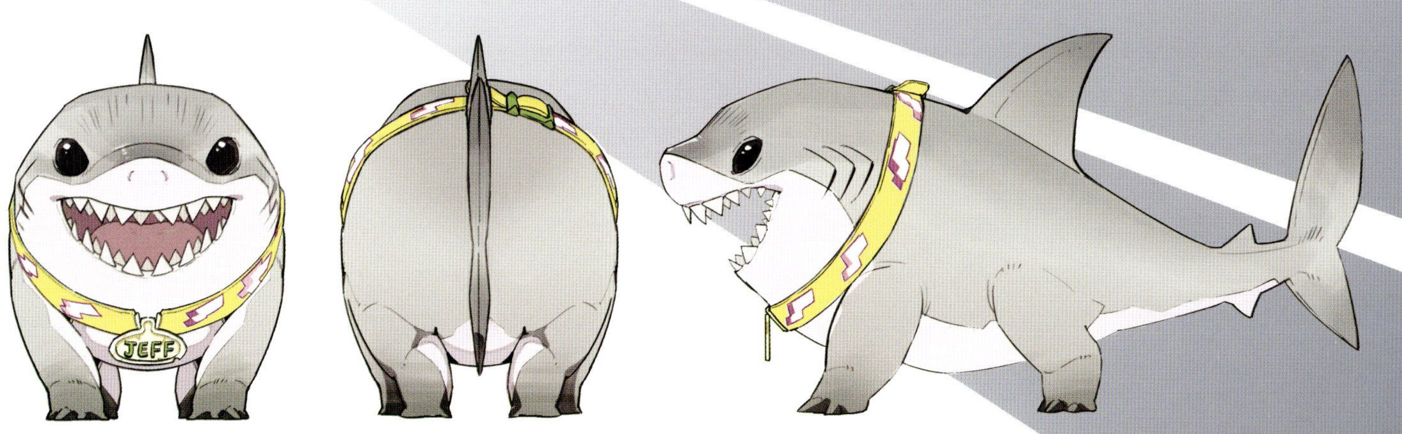

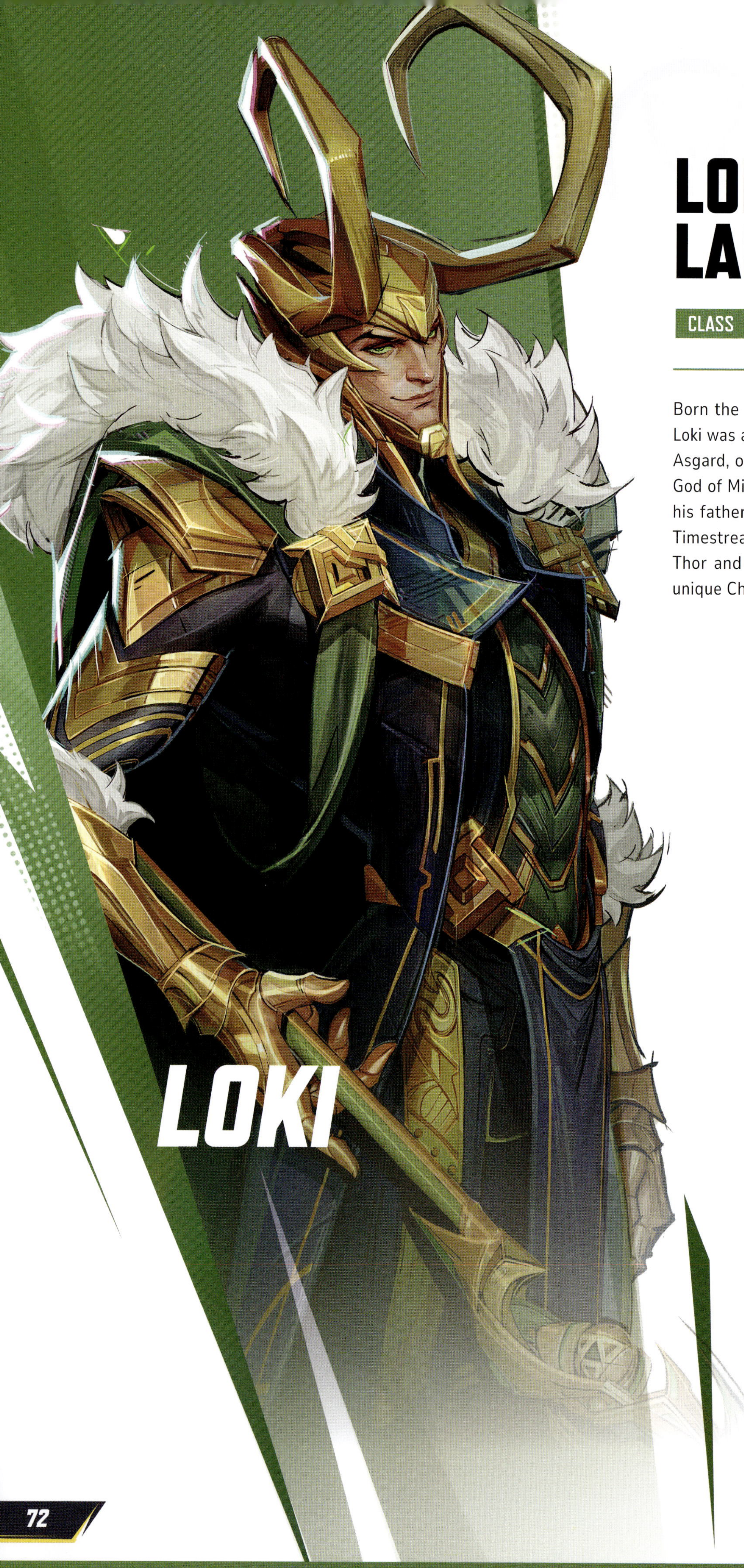

LOKI LAUFEYSON

CLASS STRATEGIST

Born the son of Laufey, king of the Frost Giants, Loki was adopted by Odin and raised as a prince of Asgard, only to later fully embrace his role as the God of Mischief. Loki would seize the throne after his father's descent into the Odinsleep after the Timestream Entanglement, banishing his brother Thor and seizing the power of the World Tree's unique Chronovium for himself.

What could be more satisfying to the God of Lies than to crush his enemies with deception? Loki, who relishes trickery, uses clones and shapeshifting to deftly navigate battlefields and whimsically toy with adversaries.

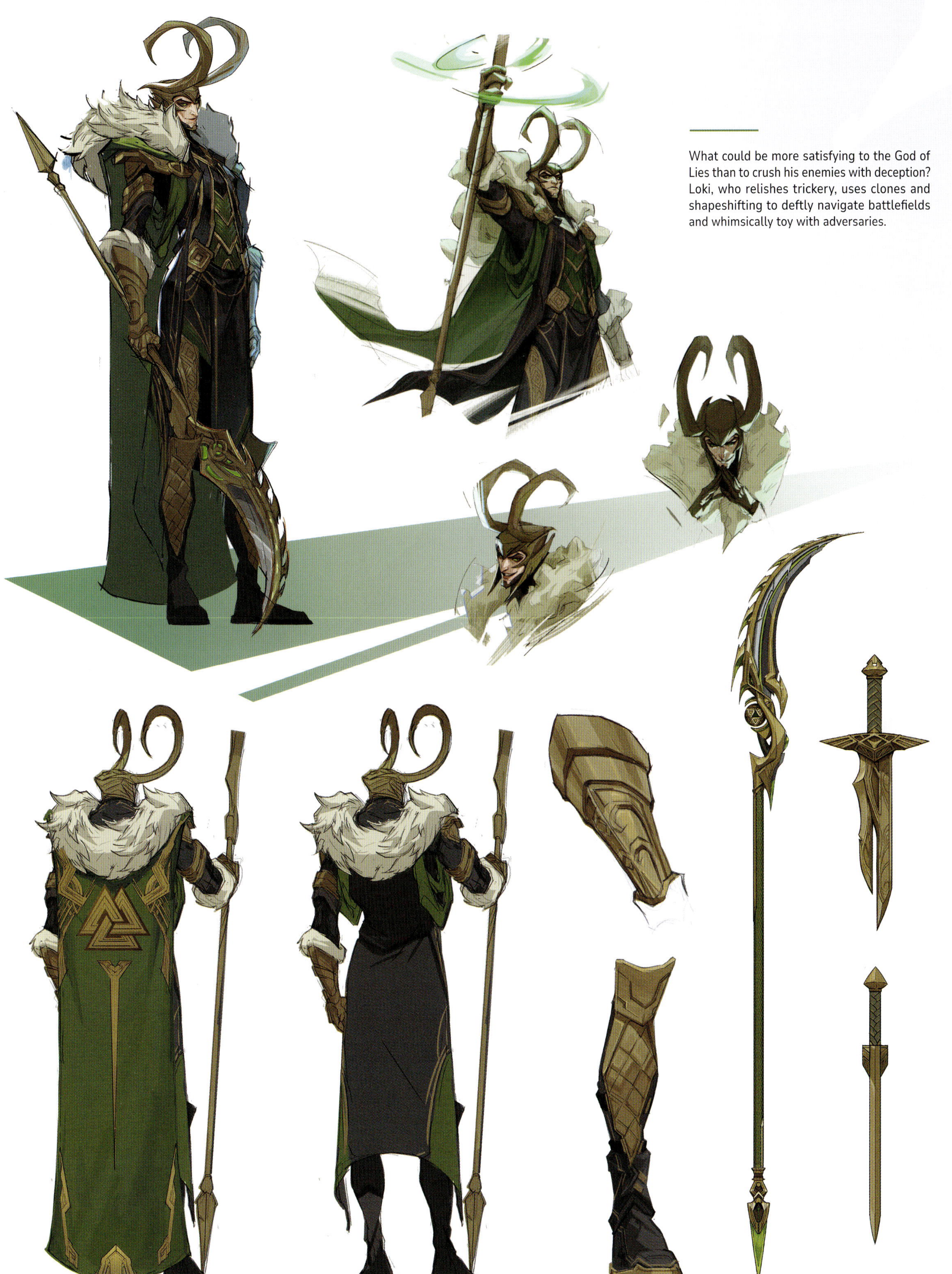

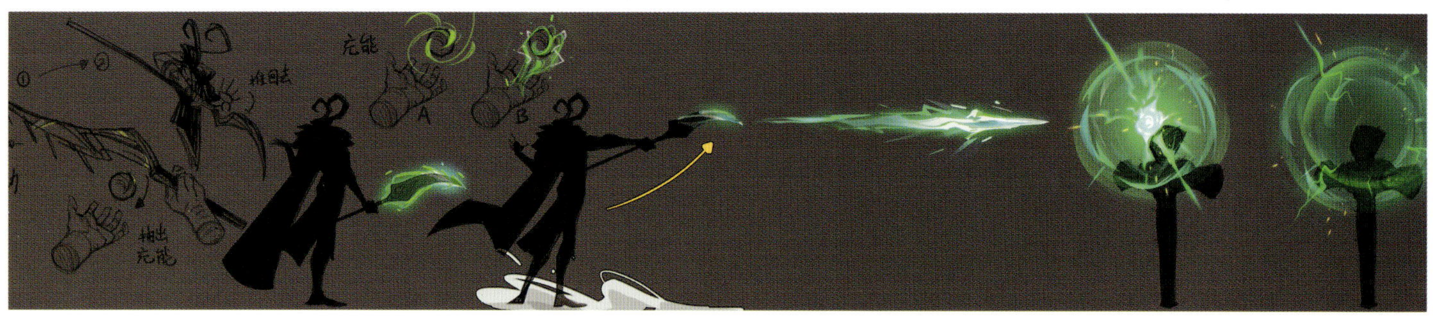

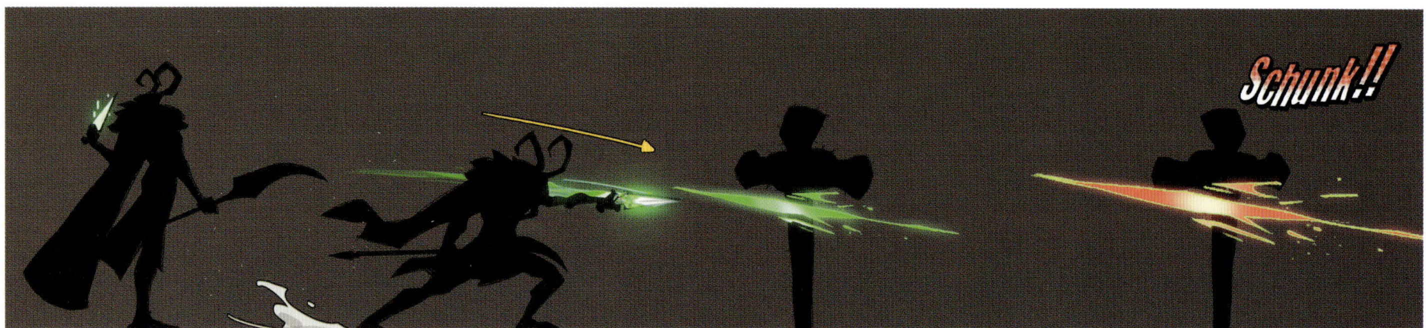

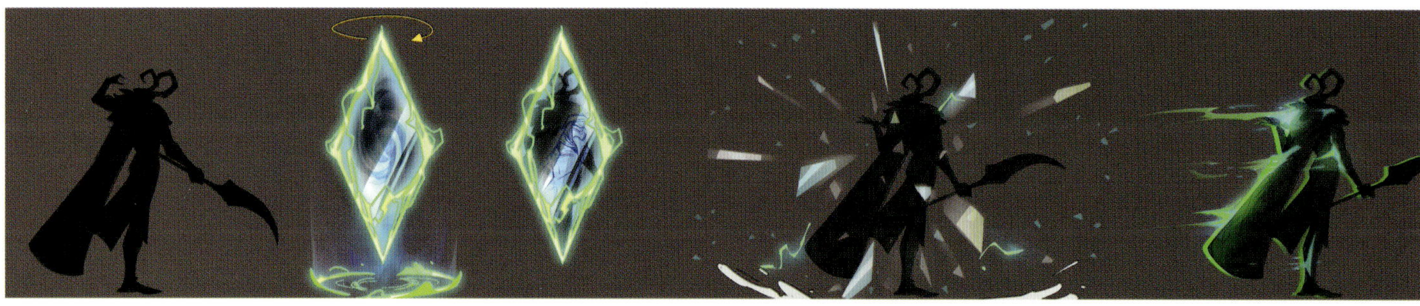

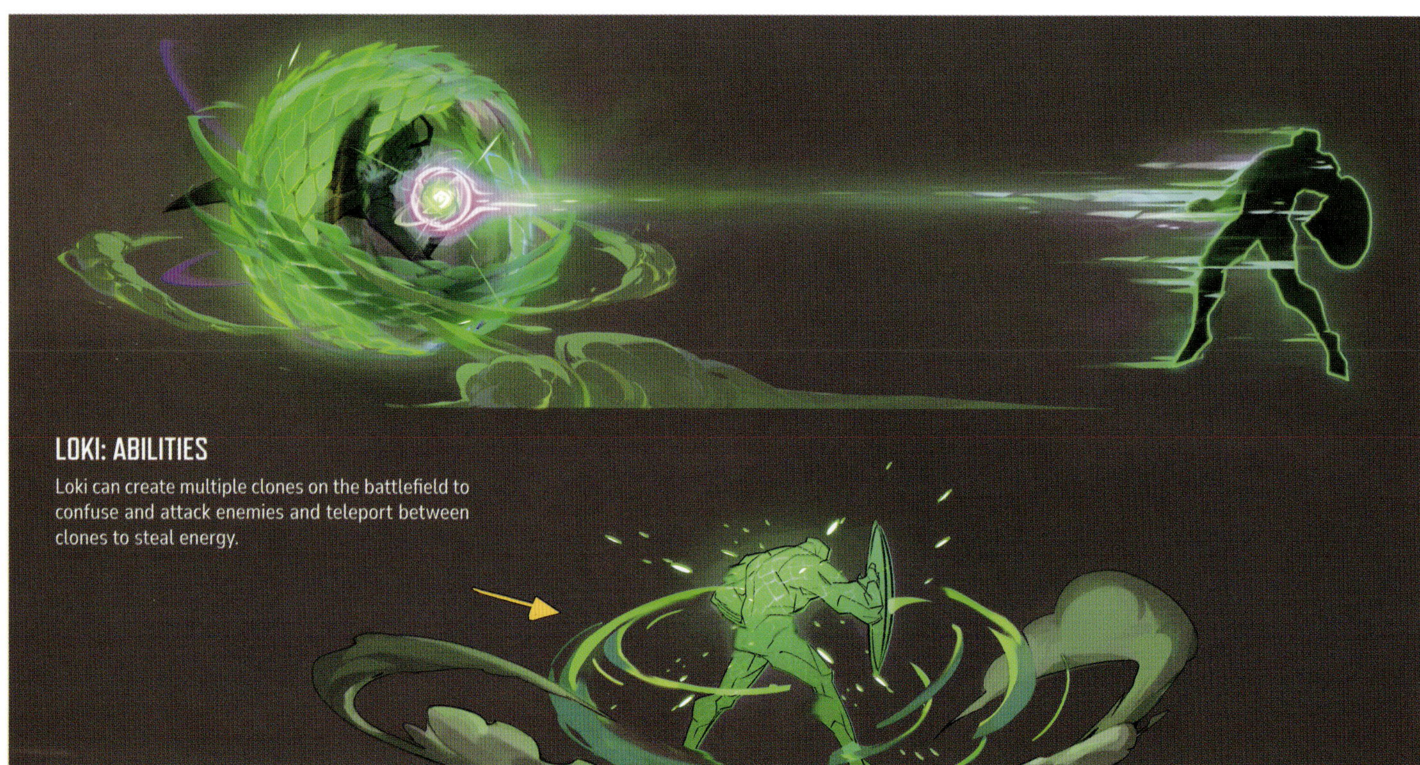

LOKI: ABILITIES

Loki can create multiple clones on the battlefield to confuse and attack enemies and teleport between clones to steal energy.

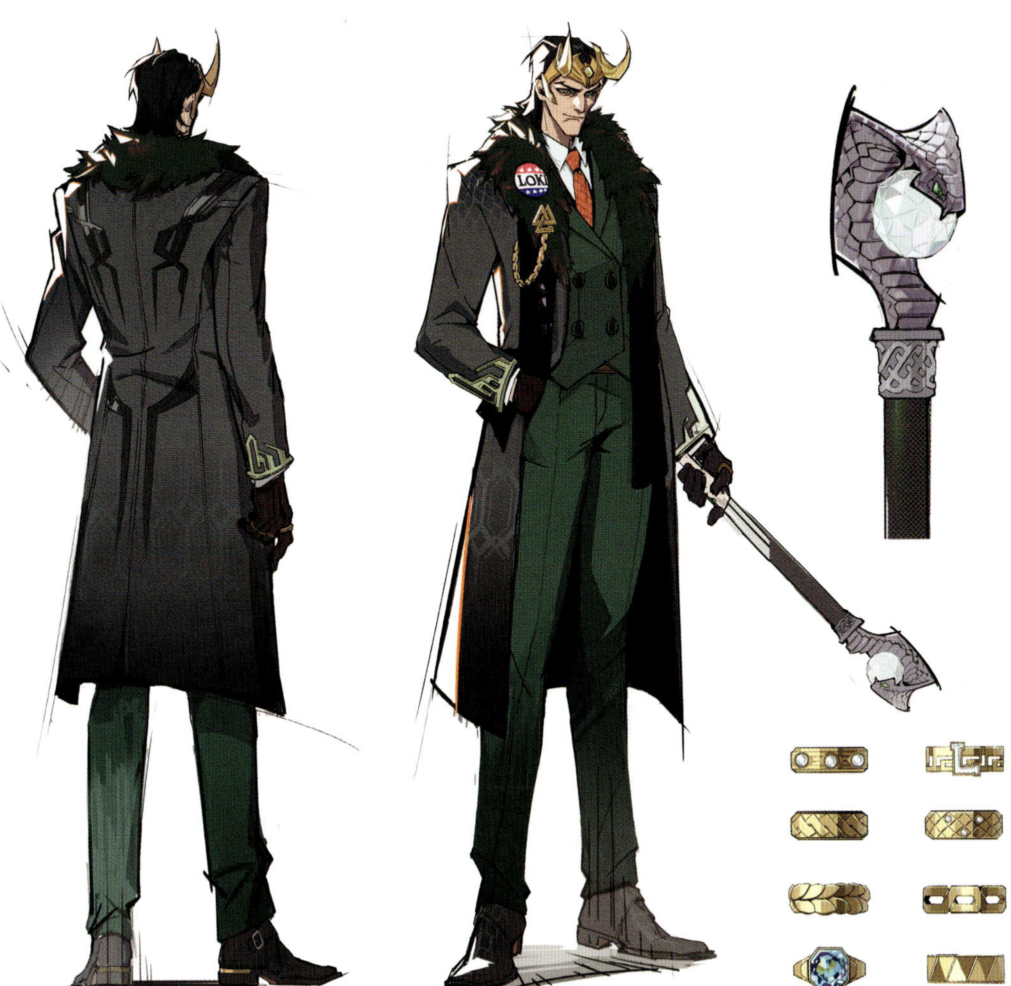

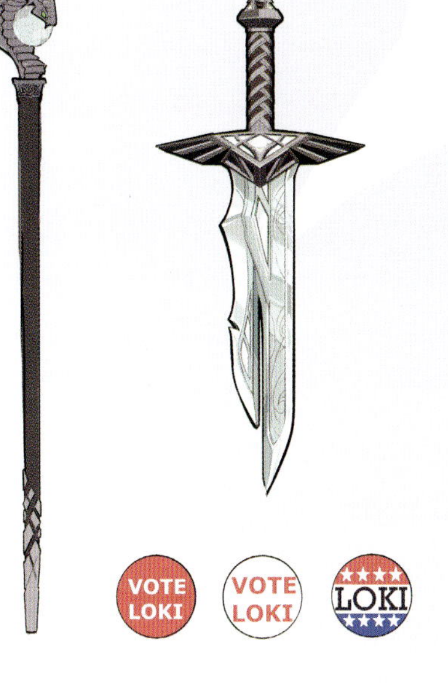

Loki, currently running for senator, makes an appearance at the Hellfire Gala clad in a black, green, and white suit blending formal and tuxedo styles, leaving everyone uncertain about his formal invitation.

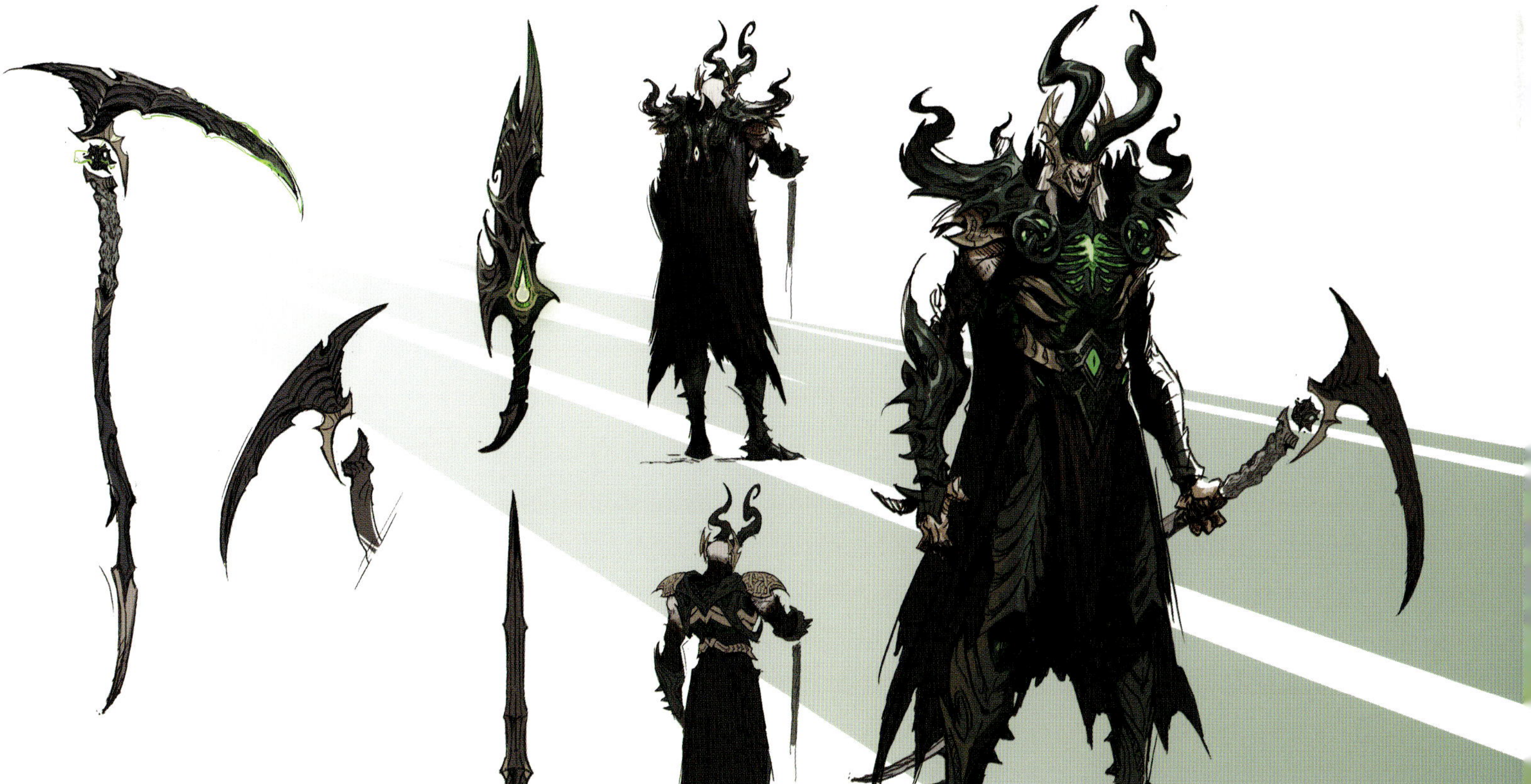

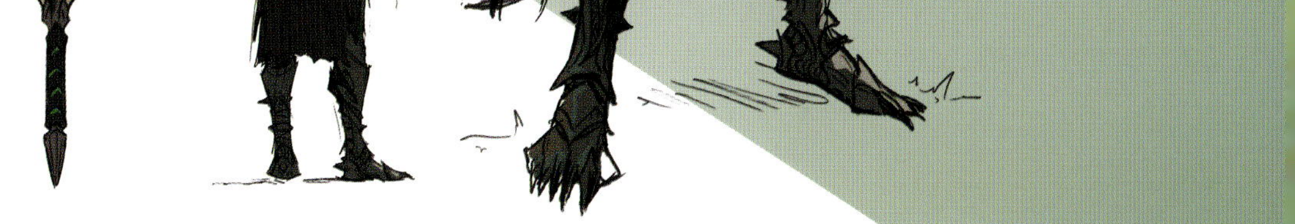

LOKI: COSMETIC VARIETY

Surrounded by the symbiote, Loki merges his will, giving rise to a black-and-green enchanted armor exuding an aura of devastation and dread.

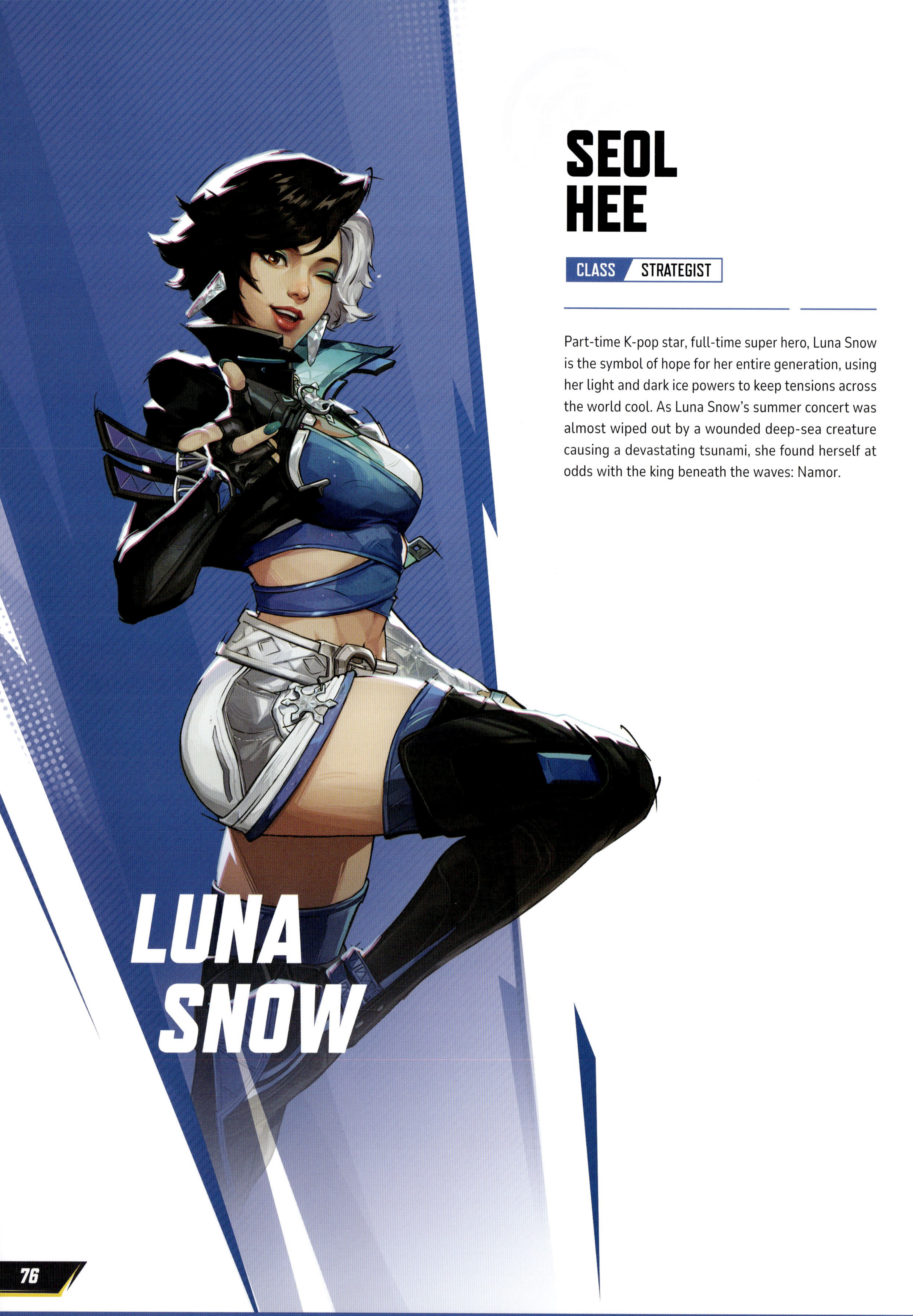

SEOL HEE

CLASS STRATEGIST

Part-time K-pop star, full-time super hero, Luna Snow is the symbol of hope for her entire generation, using her light and dark ice powers to keep tensions across the world cool. As Luna Snow's summer concert was almost wiped out by a wounded deep-sea creature causing a devastating tsunami, she found herself at odds with the king beneath the waves: Namor.

Luna Snow dazzles with her light and dark ice performance. The battlefield is her stage, as Seol Hee and her teammates meticulously craft their grand finale to put on a show and claim victory!

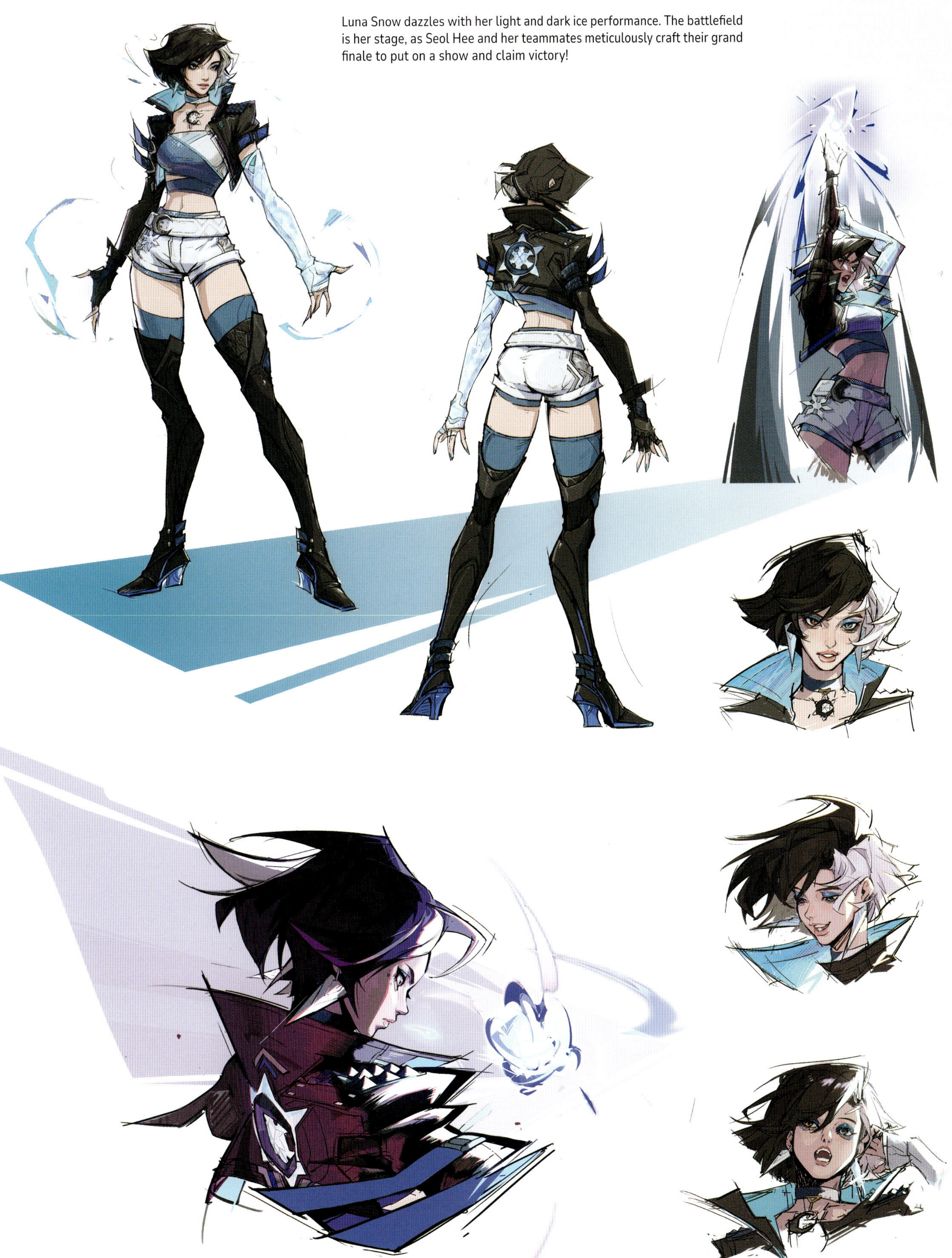

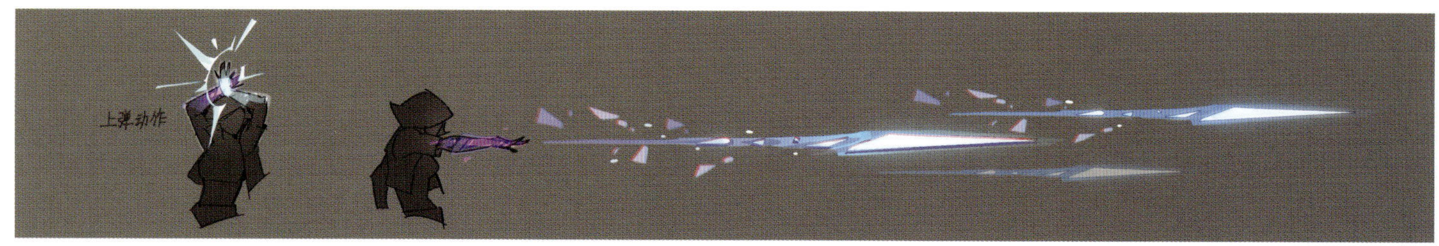

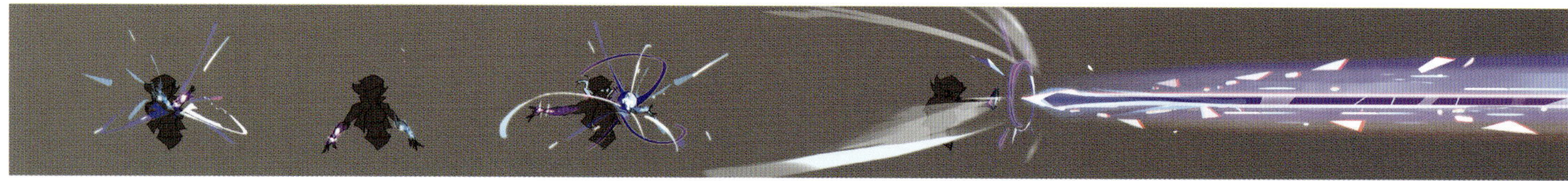

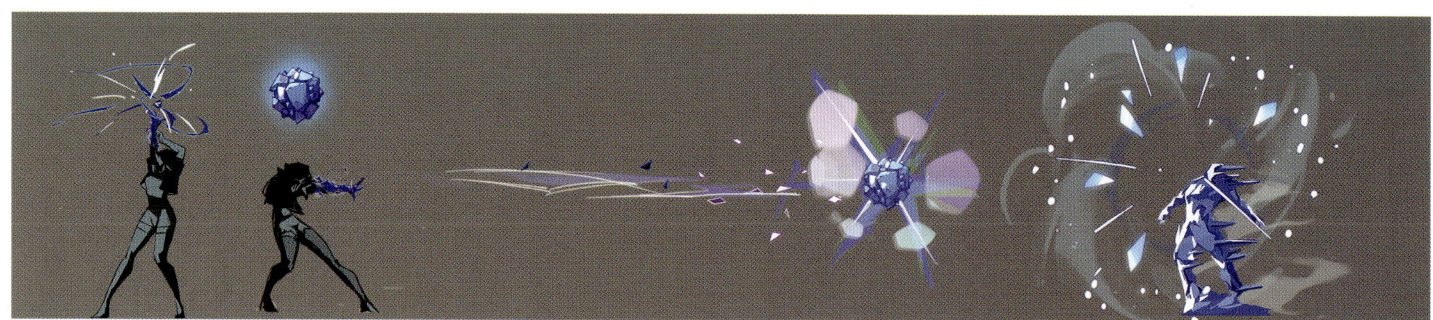

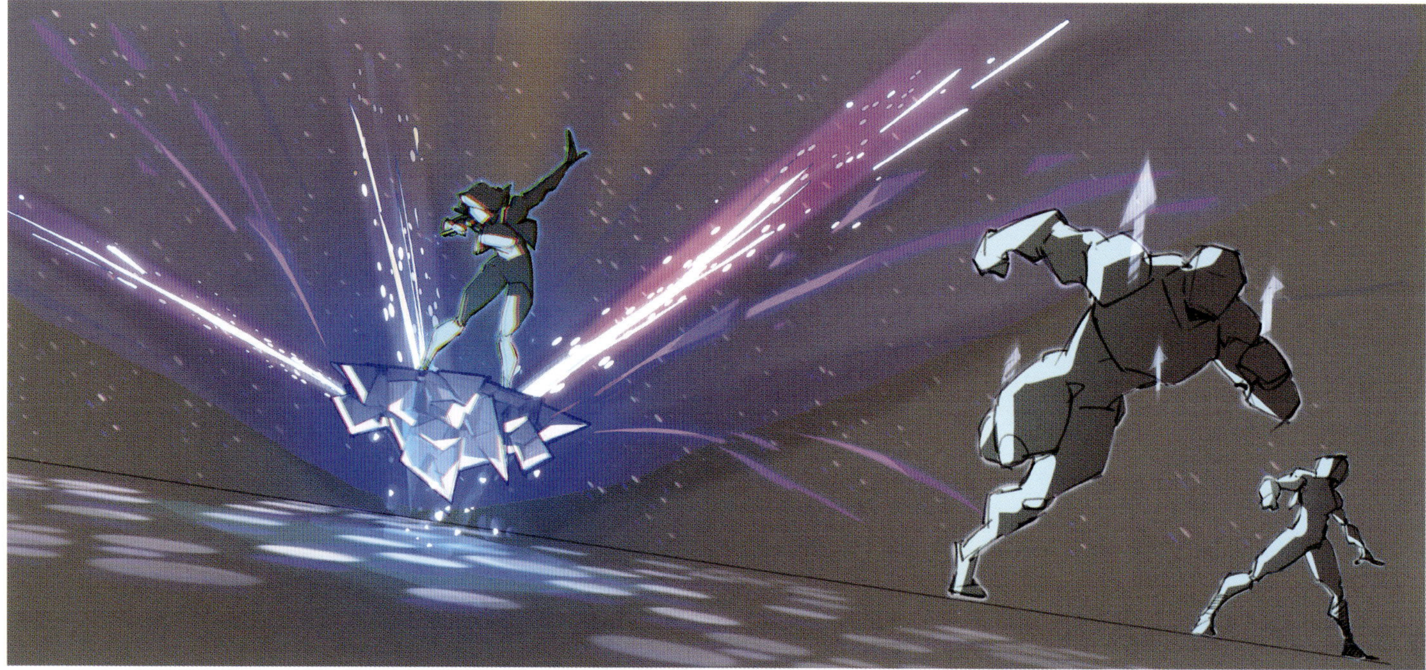

LUNA SNOW: ABILITIES

Luna Snow claims the spotlight on the battlefield, utilizing high-speed skating, ice control over enemies, and her potent recovery light ice, positioning her as the central figure leading the team's charge.

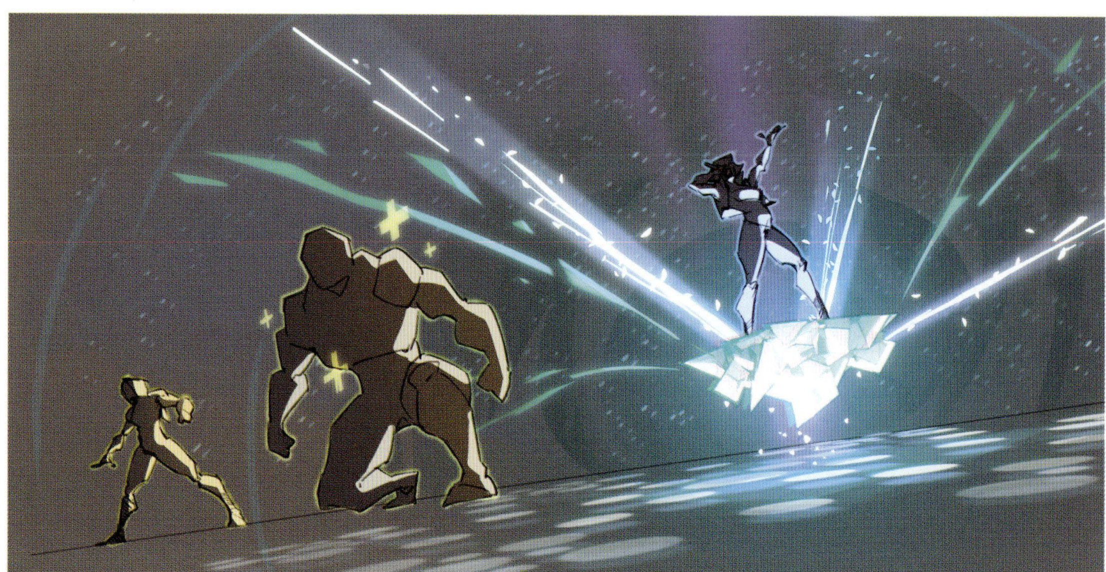

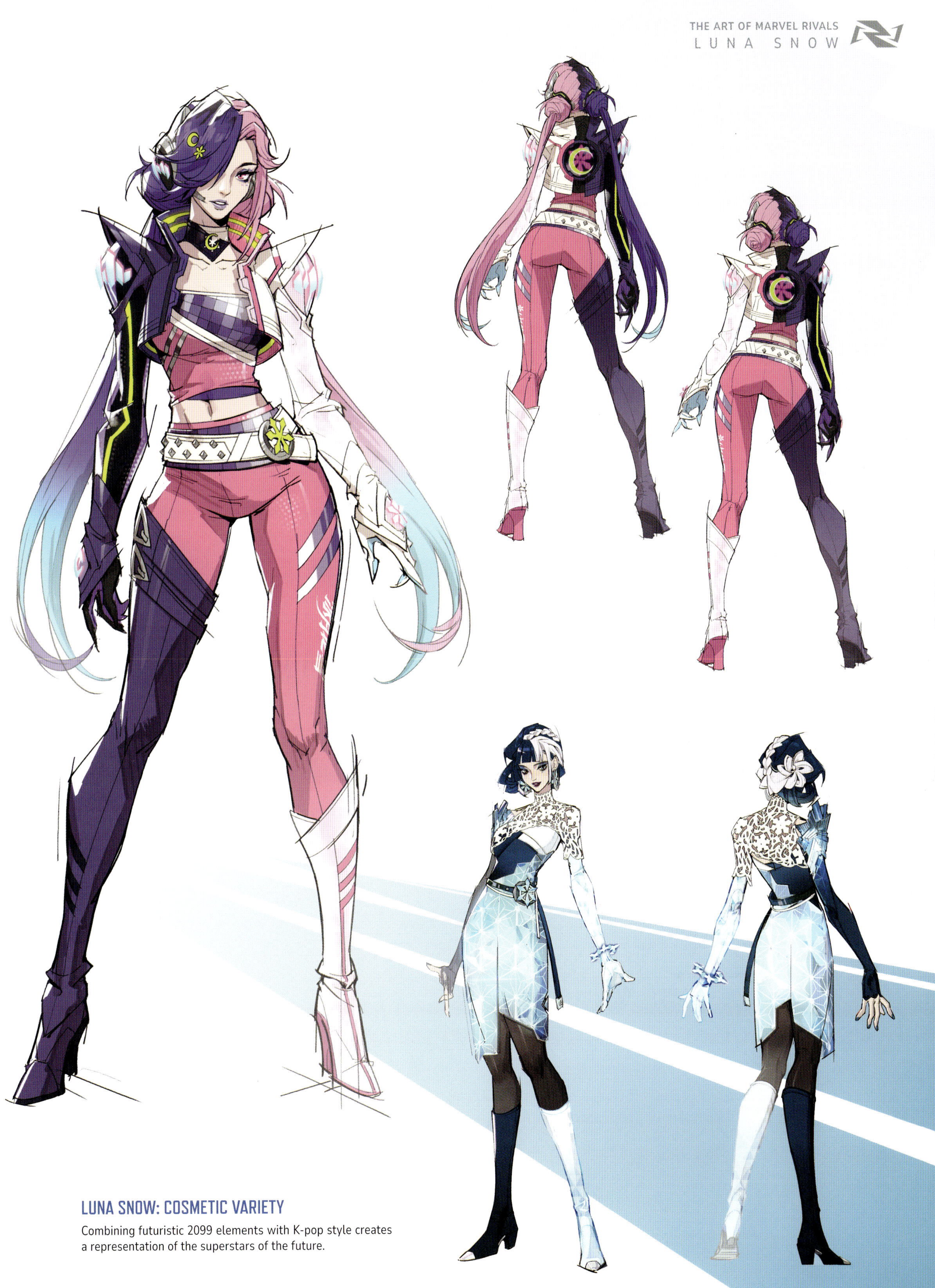

LUNA SNOW: COSMETIC VARIETY

Combining futuristic 2099 elements with K-pop style creates a representation of the superstars of the future.

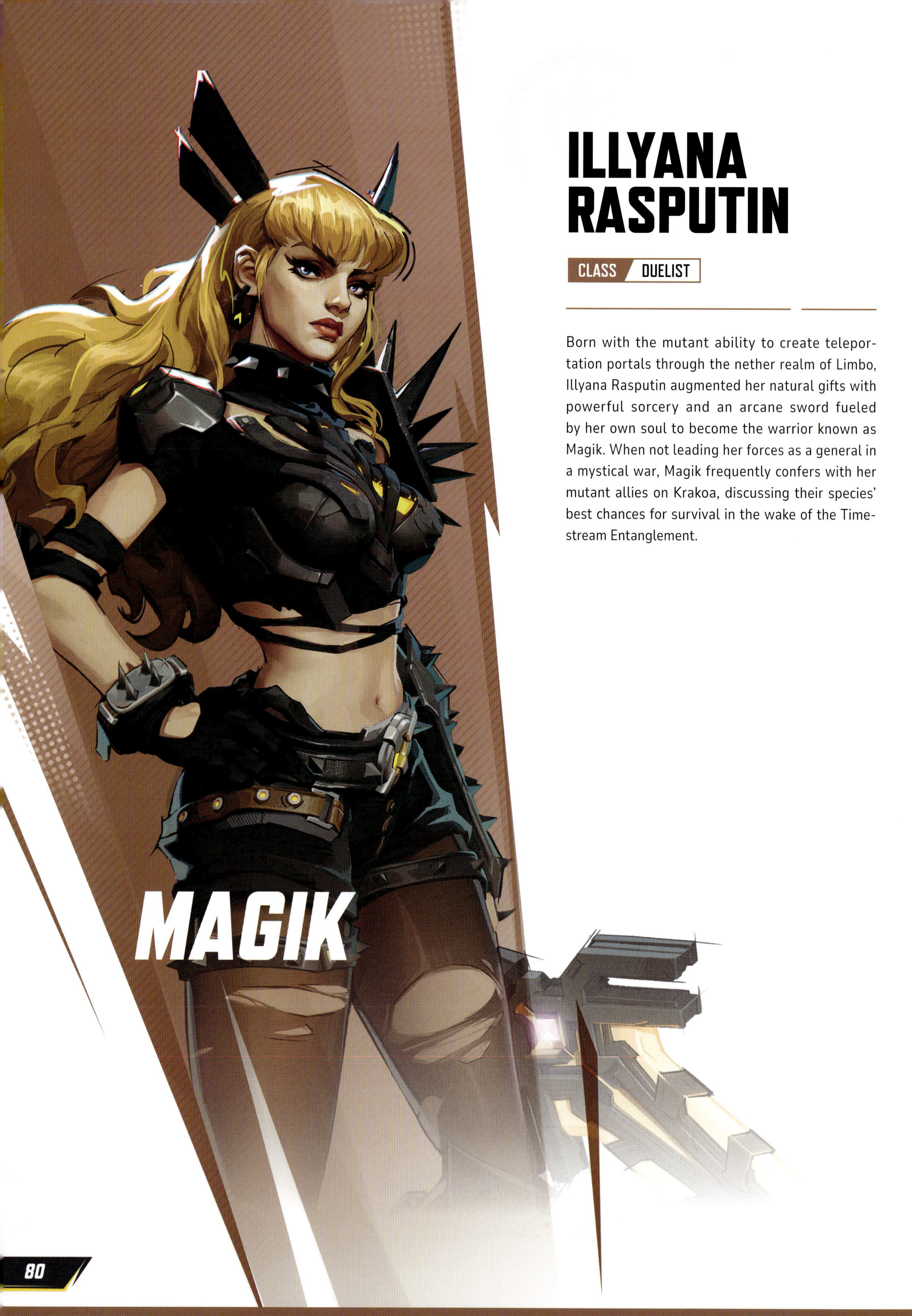

ILLYANA RASPUTIN

CLASS / DUELIST

Born with the mutant ability to create teleportation portals through the nether realm of Limbo, Illyana Rasputin augmented her natural gifts with powerful sorcery and an arcane sword fueled by her own soul to become the warrior known as Magik. When not leading her forces as a general in a mystical war, Magik frequently confers with her mutant allies on Krakoa, discussing their species' best chances for survival in the wake of the Timestream Entanglement.

The Queen of Limbo may have an abrasive personality, but Magik never shies away from a battle for her X-Men family. She embodies the daring and rebellious spirit of youth with the addition of demonic terror.

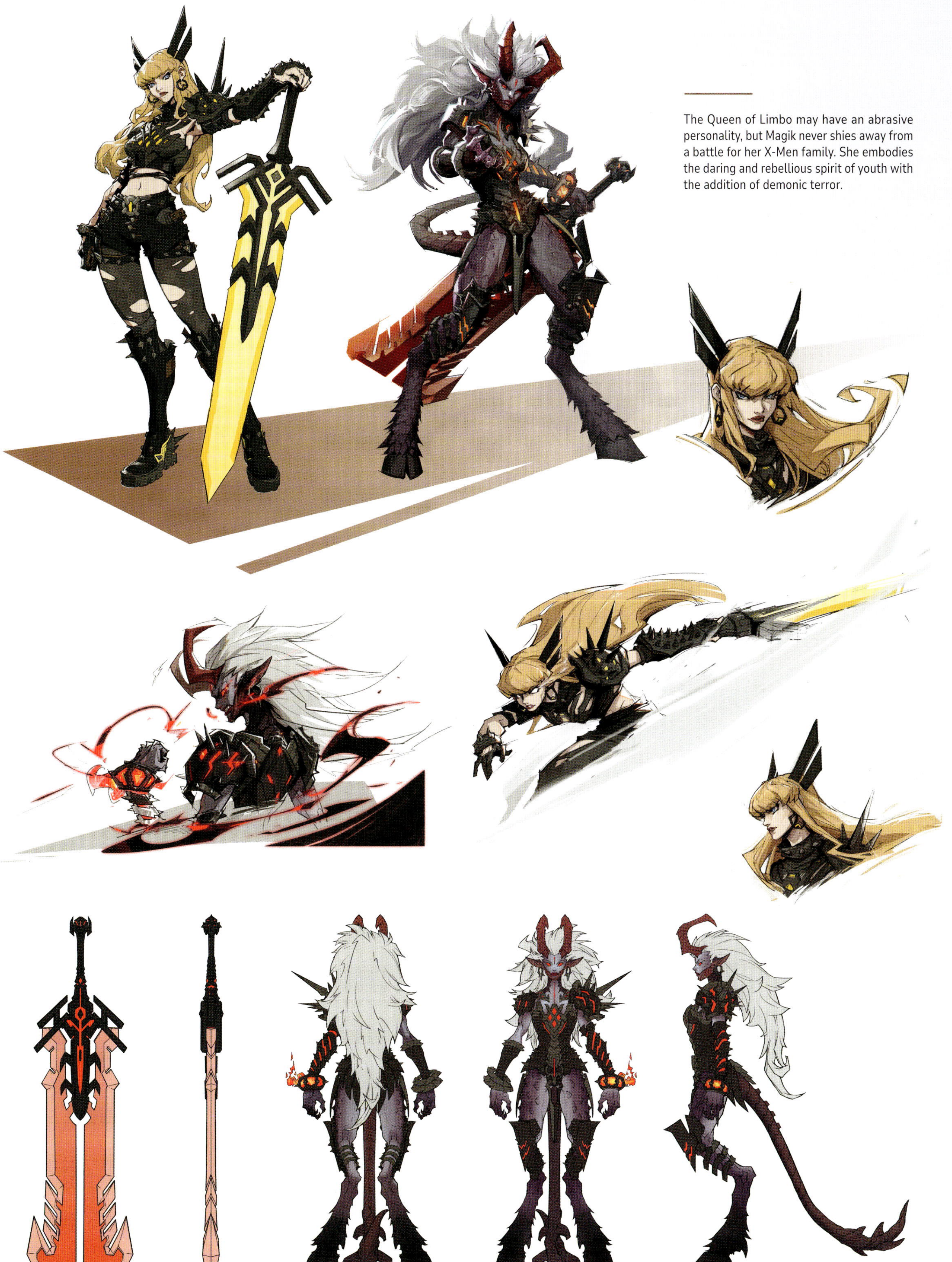

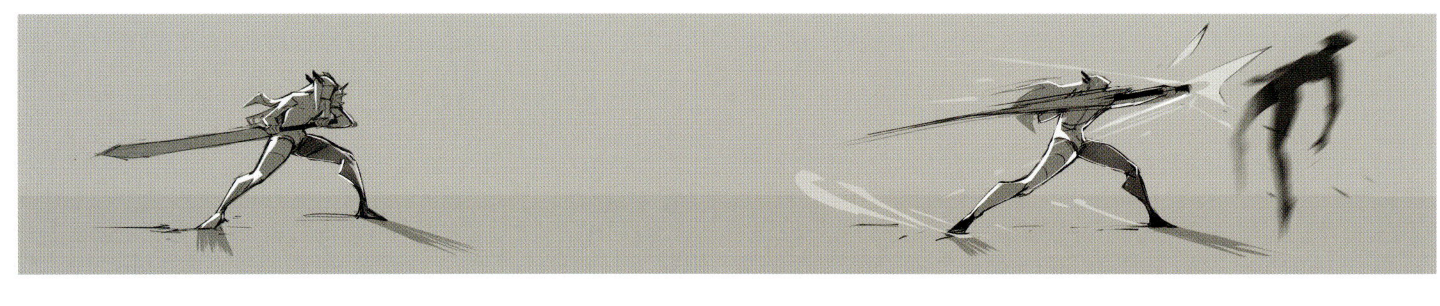

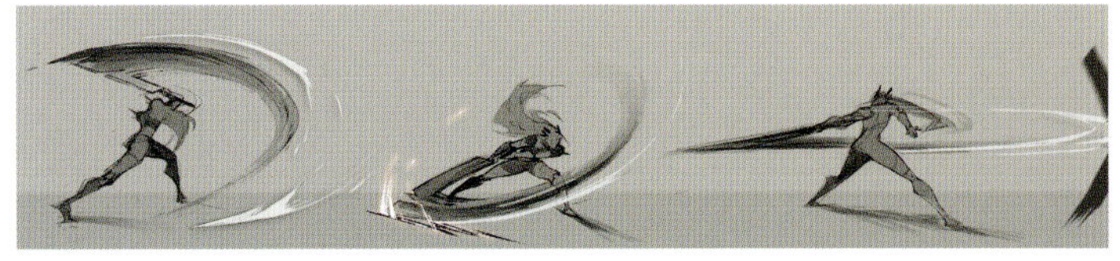

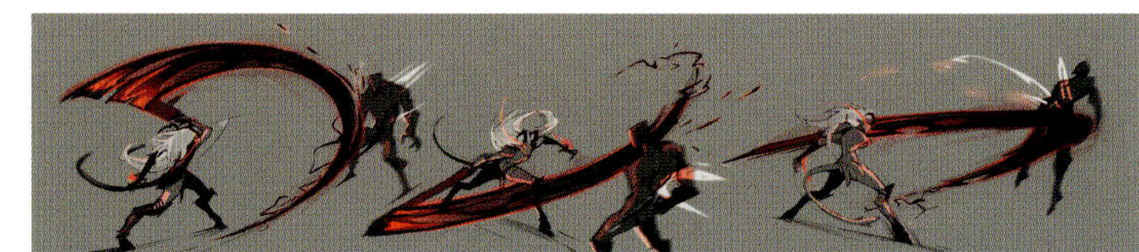

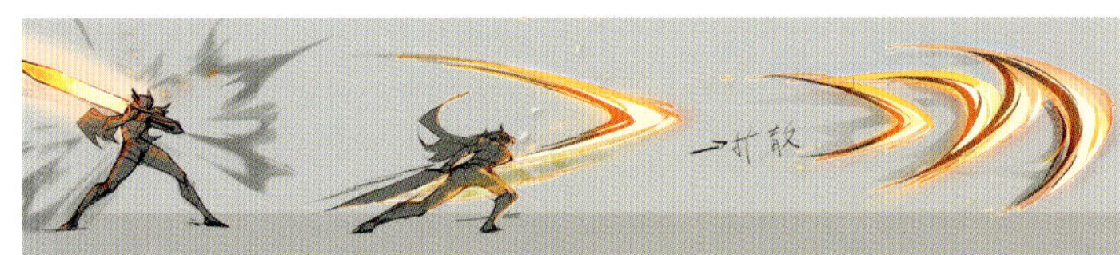

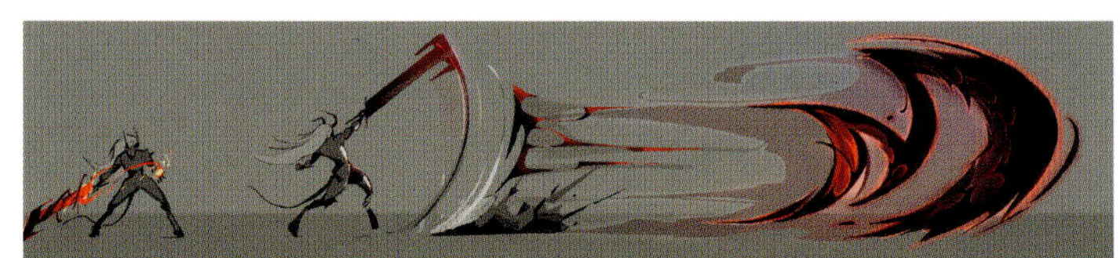

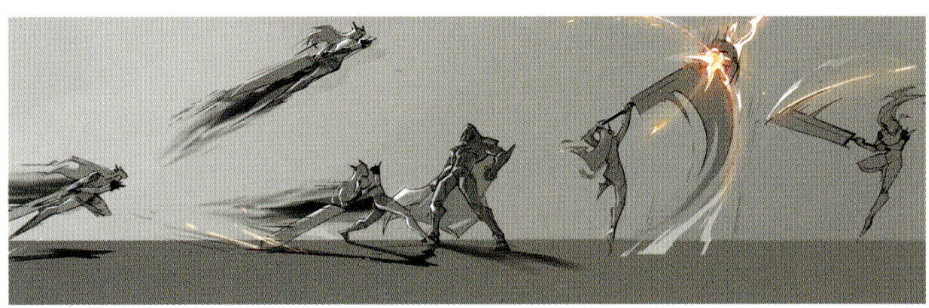

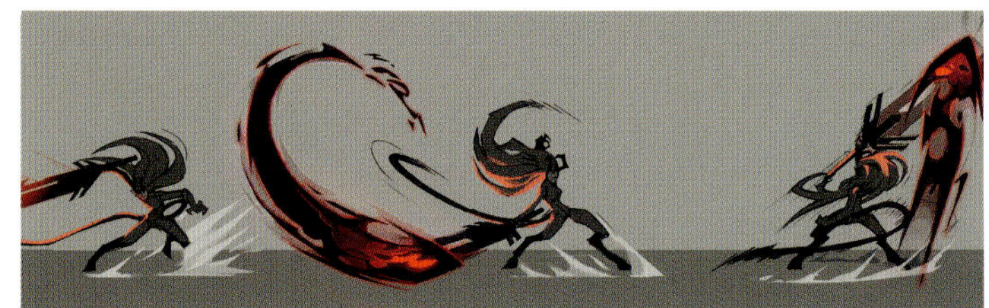

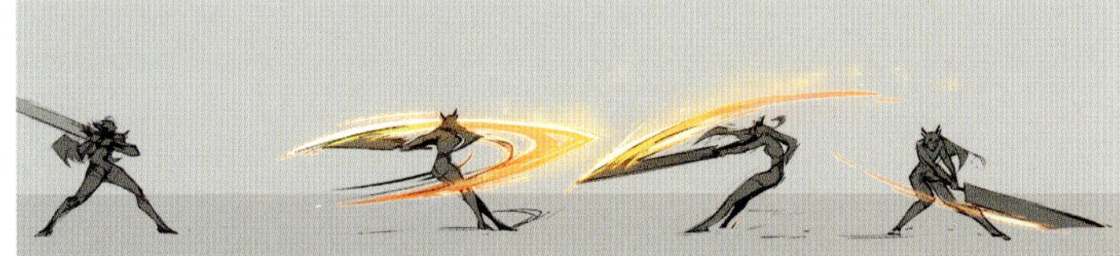

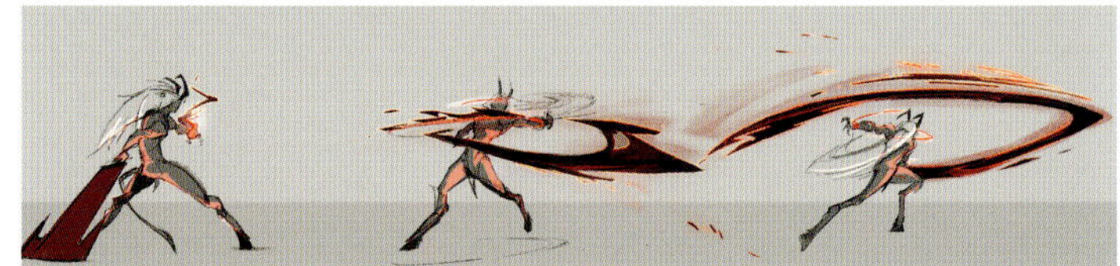

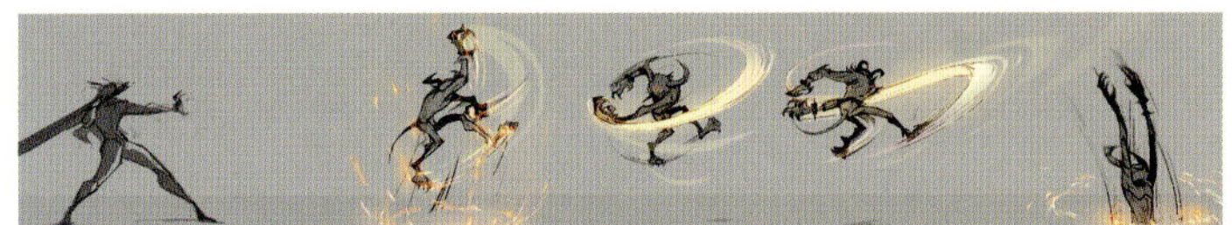

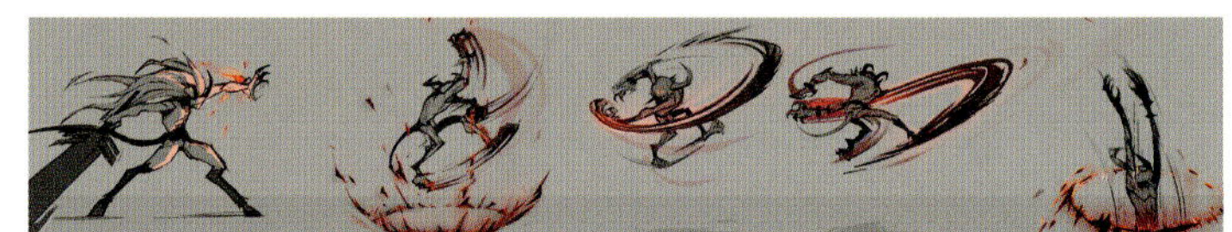

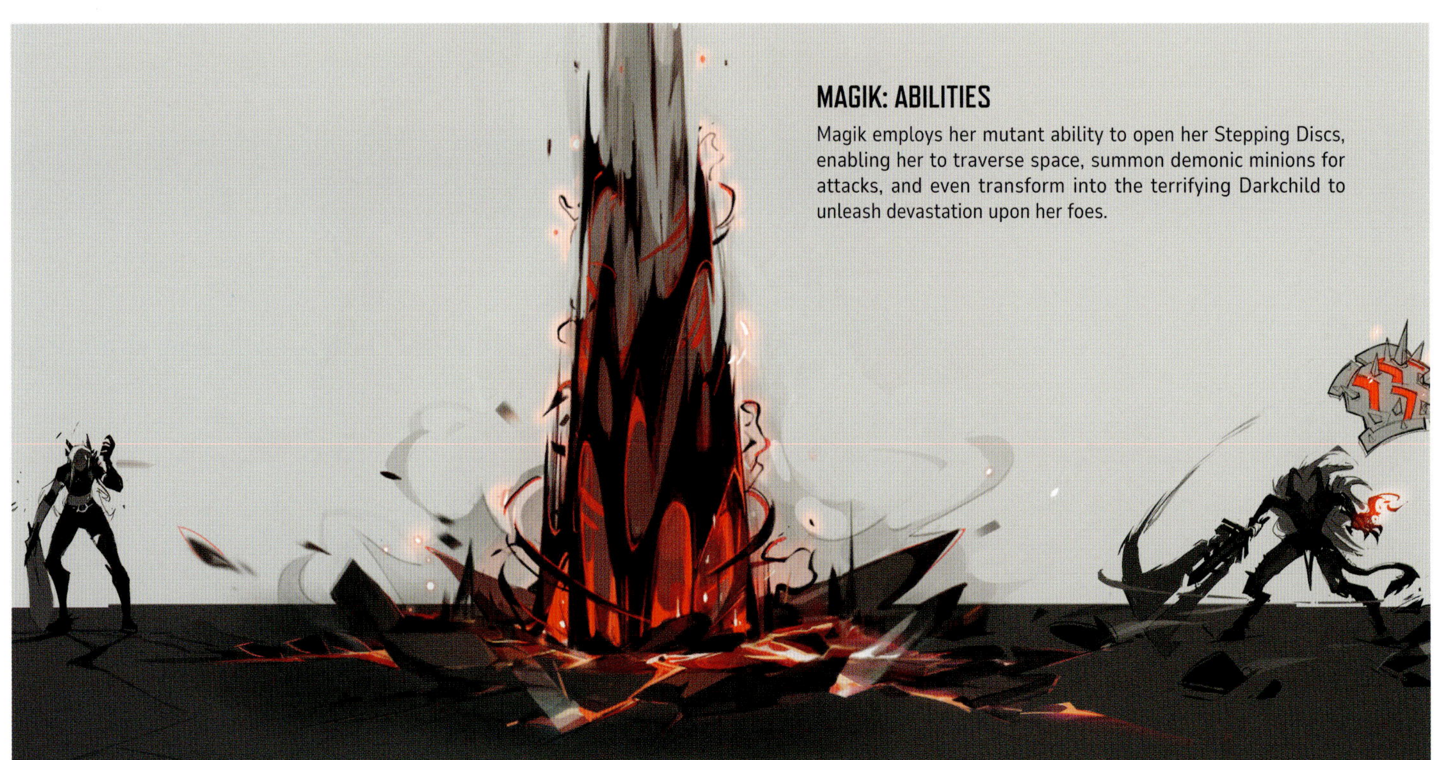

MAGIK: ABILITIES

Magik employs her mutant ability to open her Stepping Discs, enabling her to traverse space, summon demonic minions for attacks, and even transform into the terrifying Darkchild to unleash devastation upon her foes.

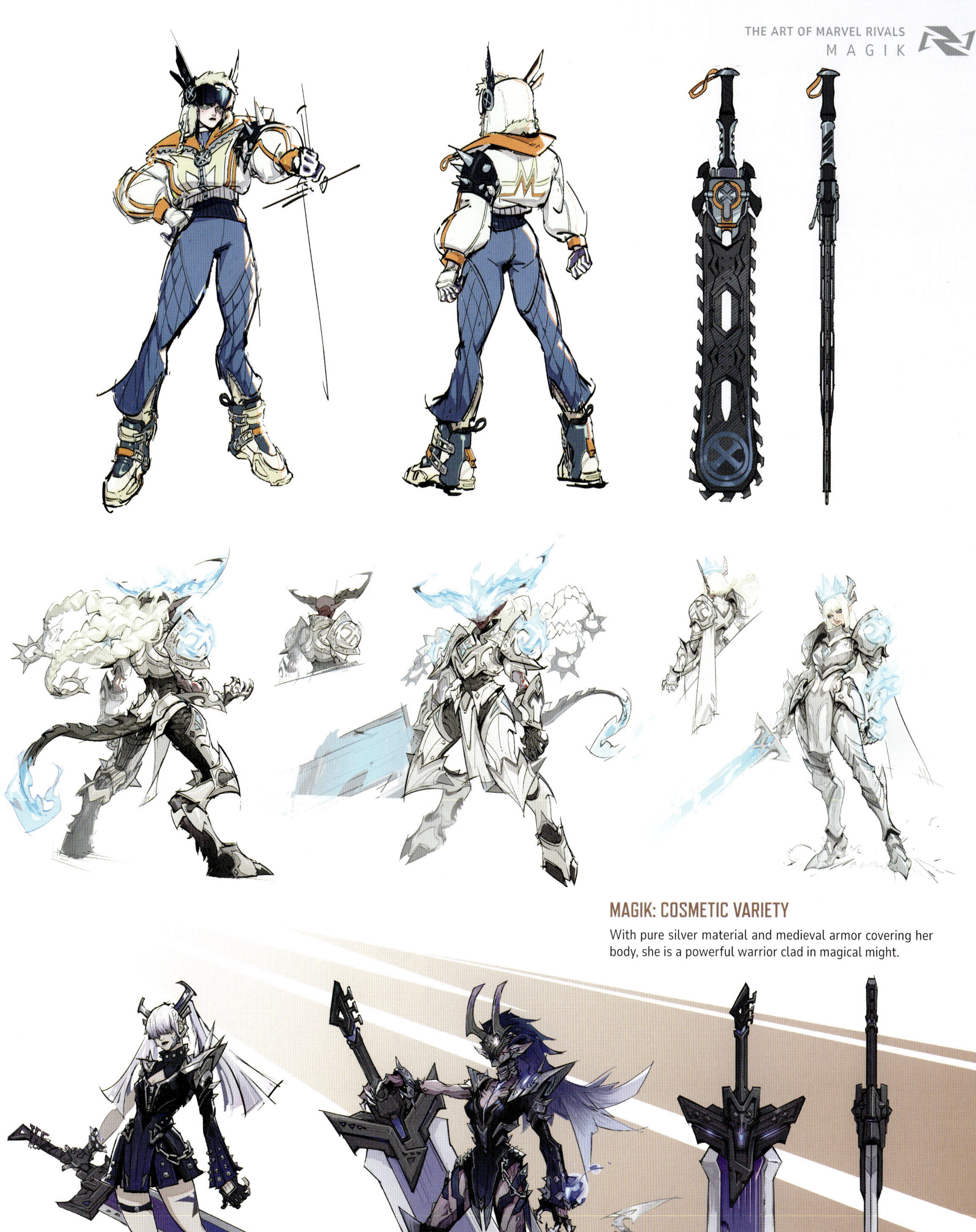

MAGIK: COSMETIC VARIETY

With pure silver material and medieval armor covering her body, she is a powerful warrior clad in magical might.

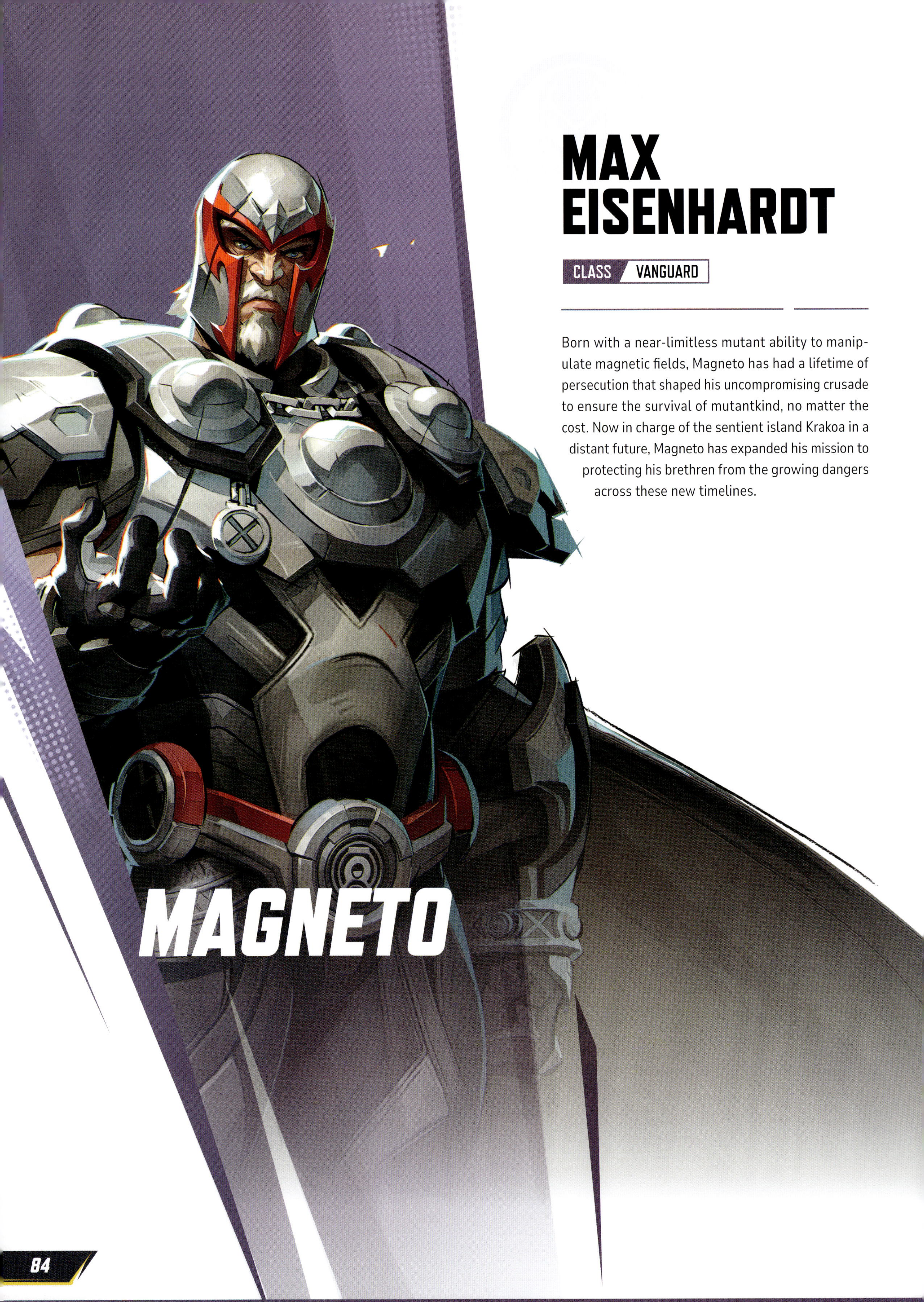

MAX EISENHARDT

CLASS / VANGUARD

Born with a near-limitless mutant ability to manipulate magnetic fields, Magneto has had a lifetime of persecution that shaped his uncompromising crusade to ensure the survival of mutantkind, no matter the cost. Now in charge of the sentient island Krakoa in a distant future, Magneto has expanded his mission to protecting his brethren from the growing dangers across these new timelines.

From Max Eisenhardt to Erik Lehnsherr, Magneto has faced tribulations that have shaped him into a figure as unyielding as steel. His adversities have honed his strength, transforming metal into a keen blade and an unyielding shield.

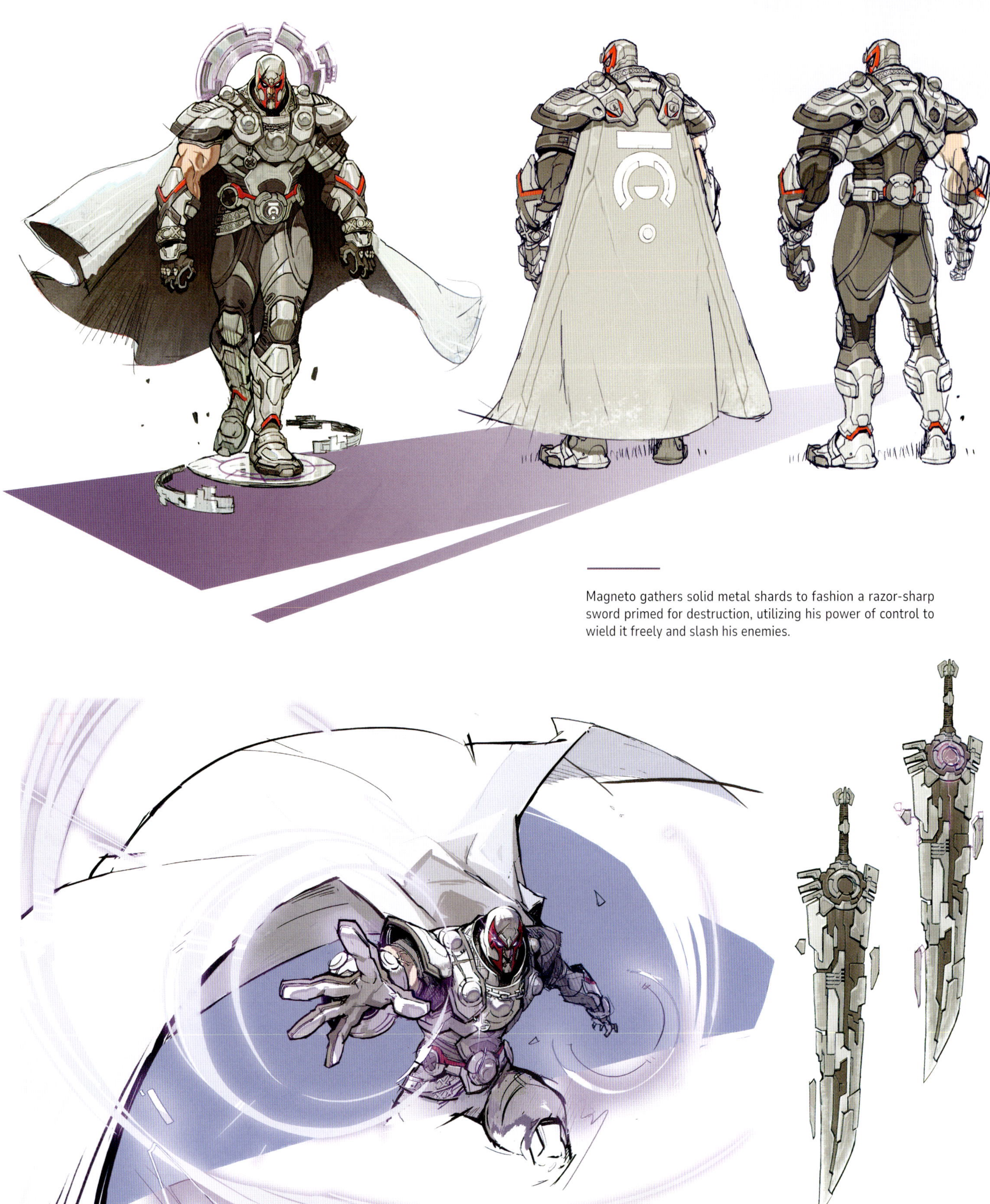

Magneto gathers solid metal shards to fashion a razor-sharp sword primed for destruction, utilizing his power of control to wield it freely and slash his enemies.

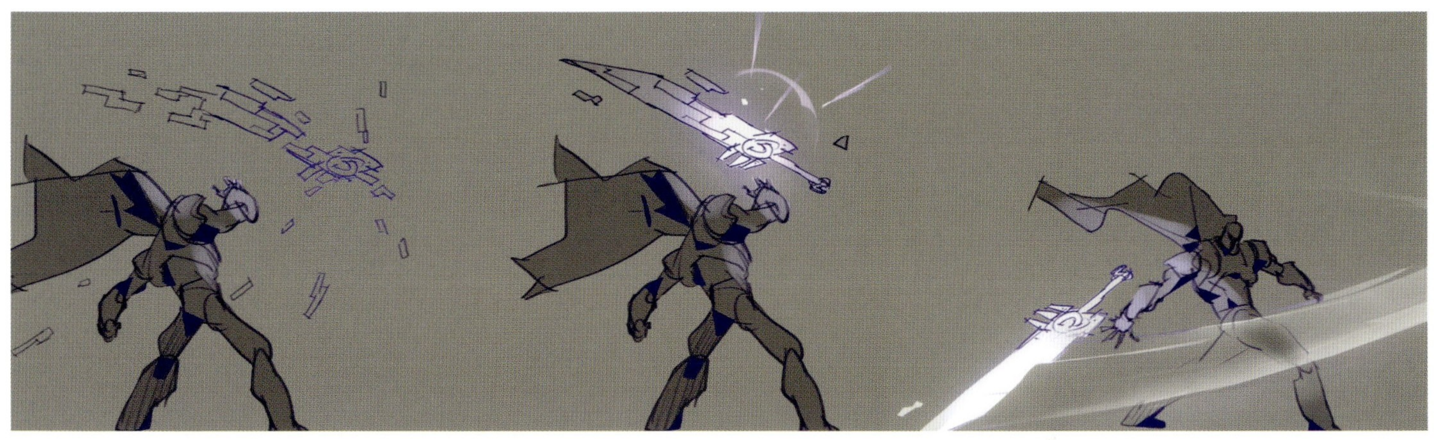

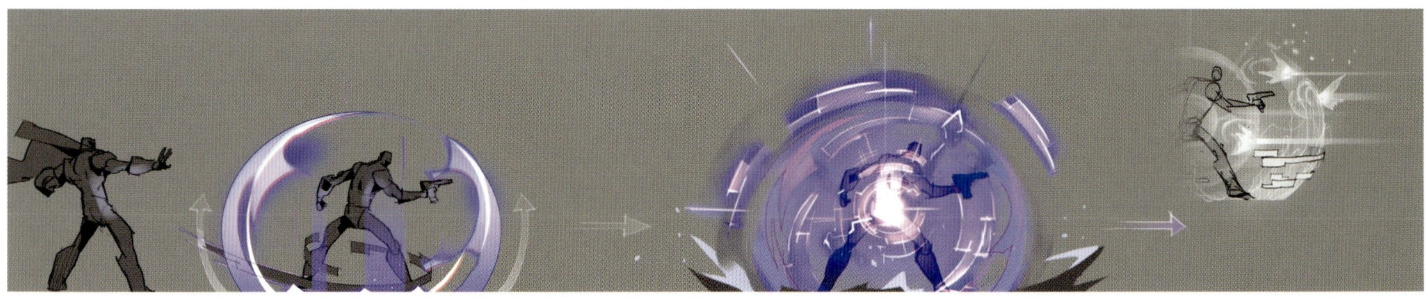

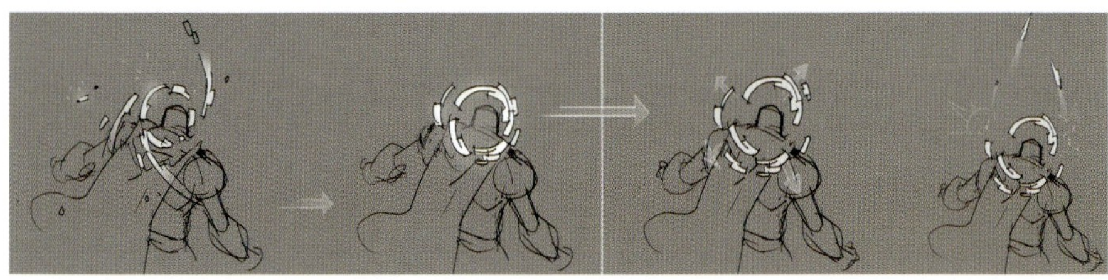

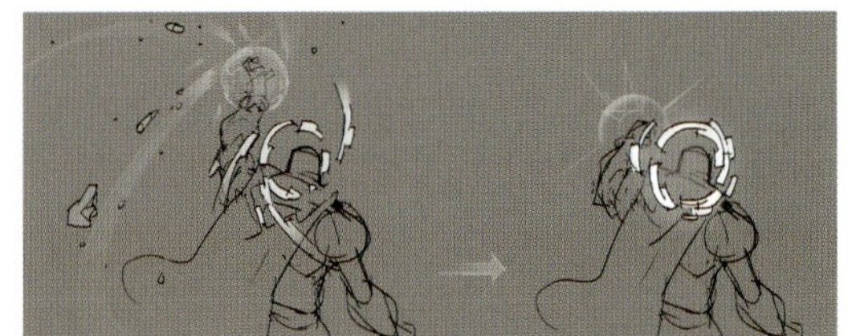

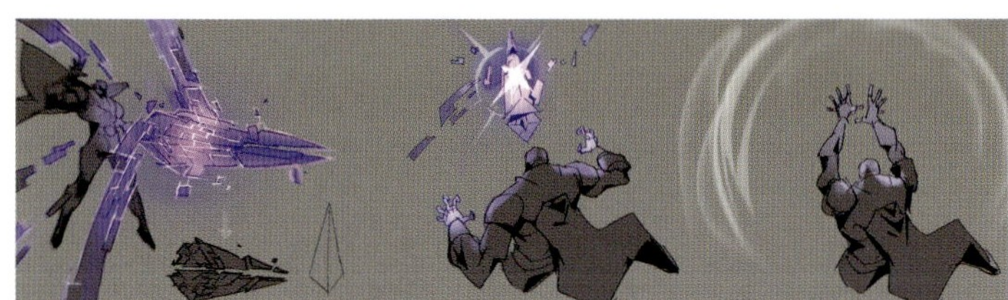

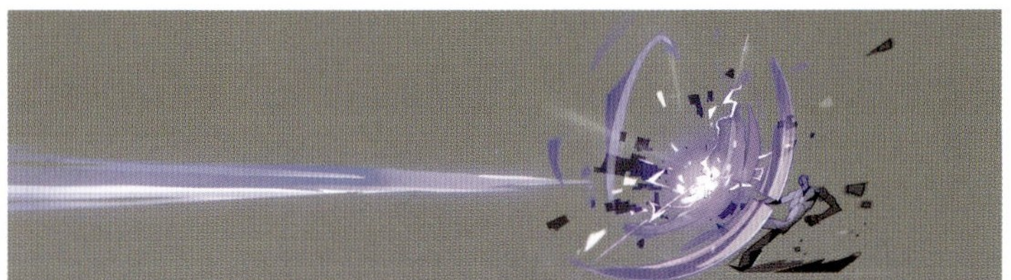

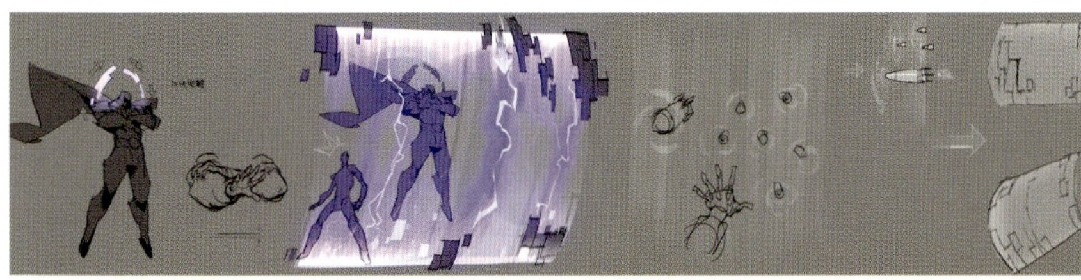

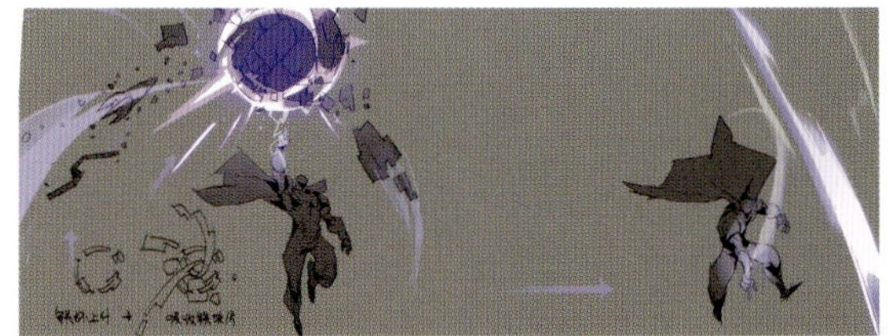

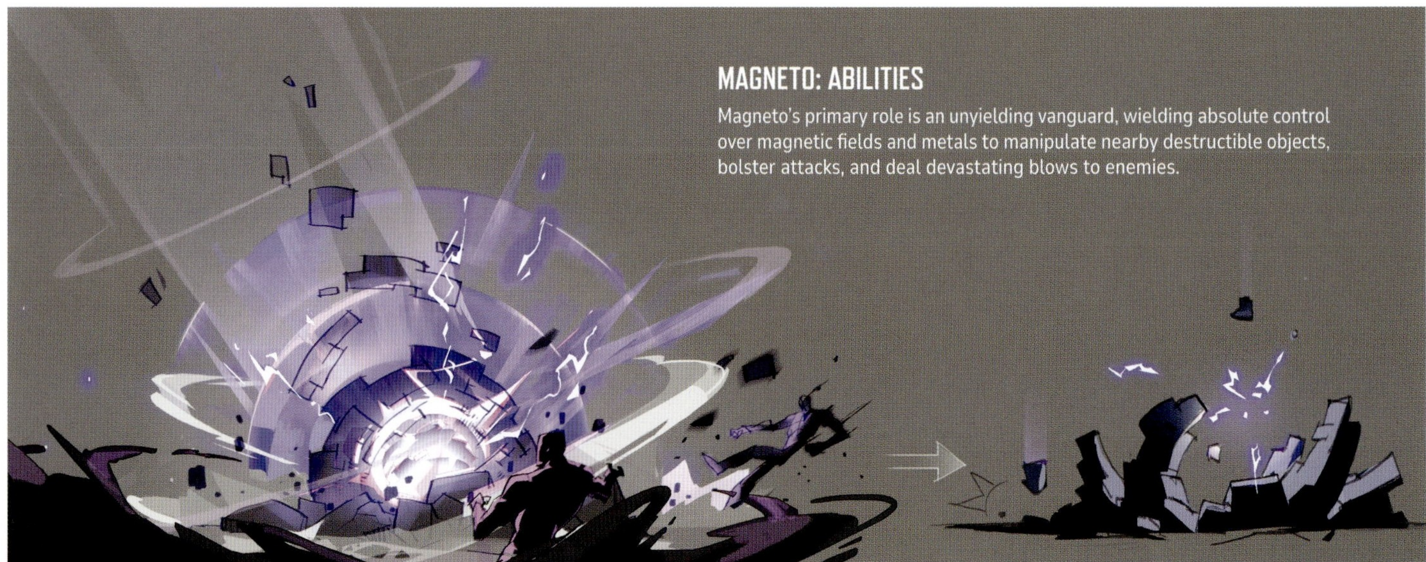

MAGNETO: ABILITIES

Magneto's primary role is an unyielding vanguard, wielding absolute control over magnetic fields and metals to manipulate nearby destructible objects, bolster attacks, and deal devastating blows to enemies.

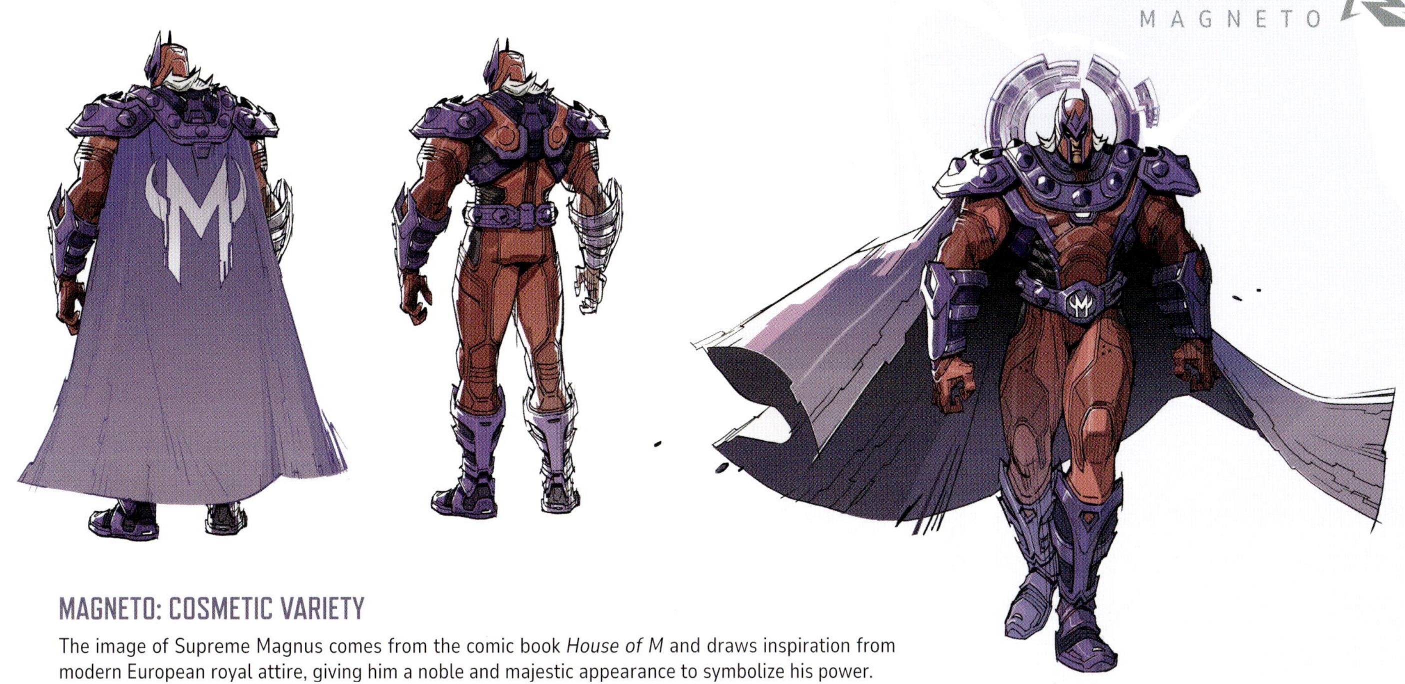

MAGNETO: COSMETIC VARIETY

The image of Supreme Magnus comes from the comic book *House of M* and draws inspiration from modern European royal attire, giving him a noble and majestic appearance to symbolize his power.

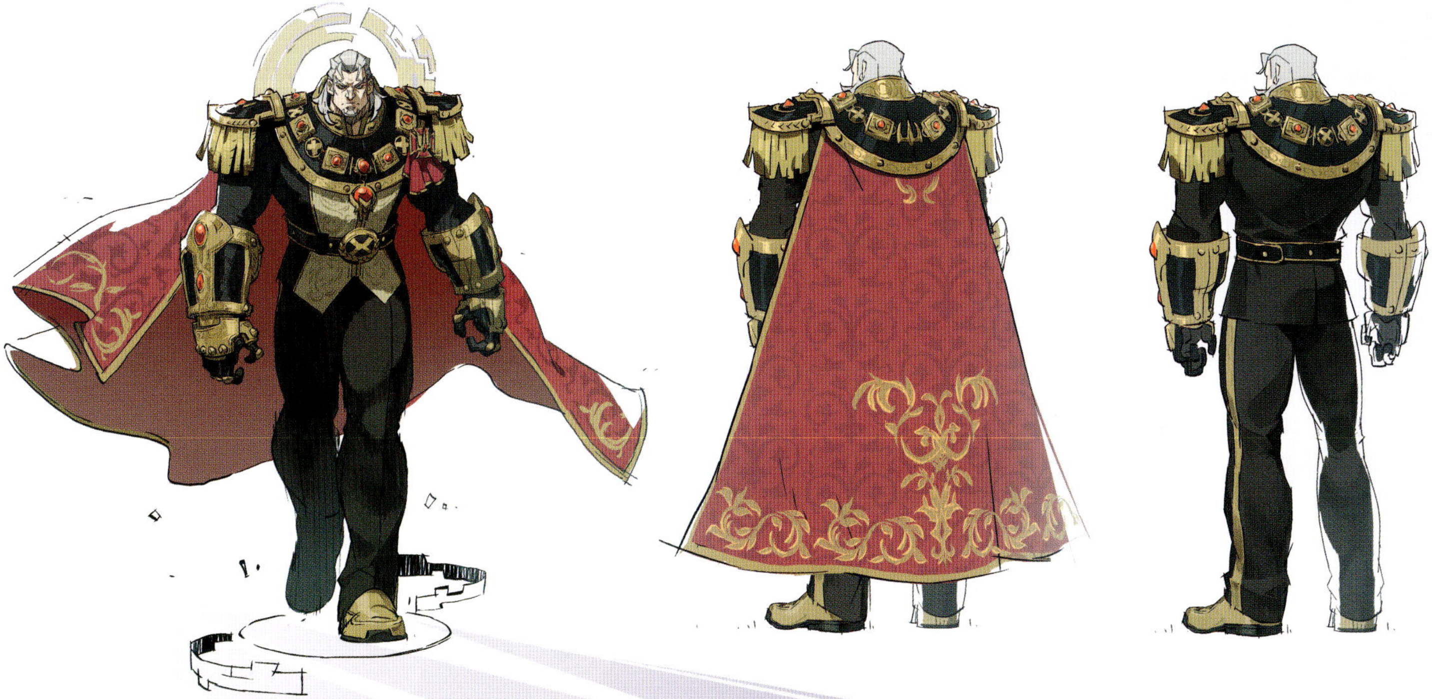

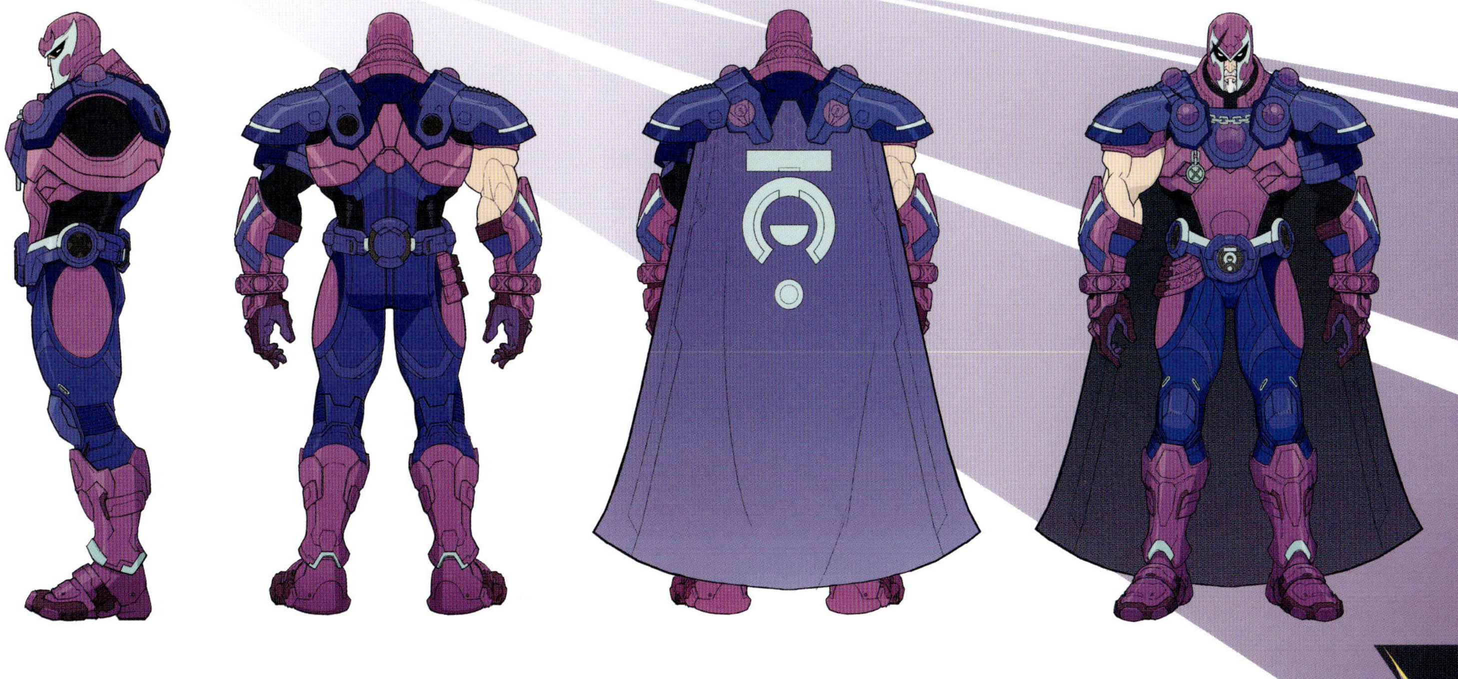

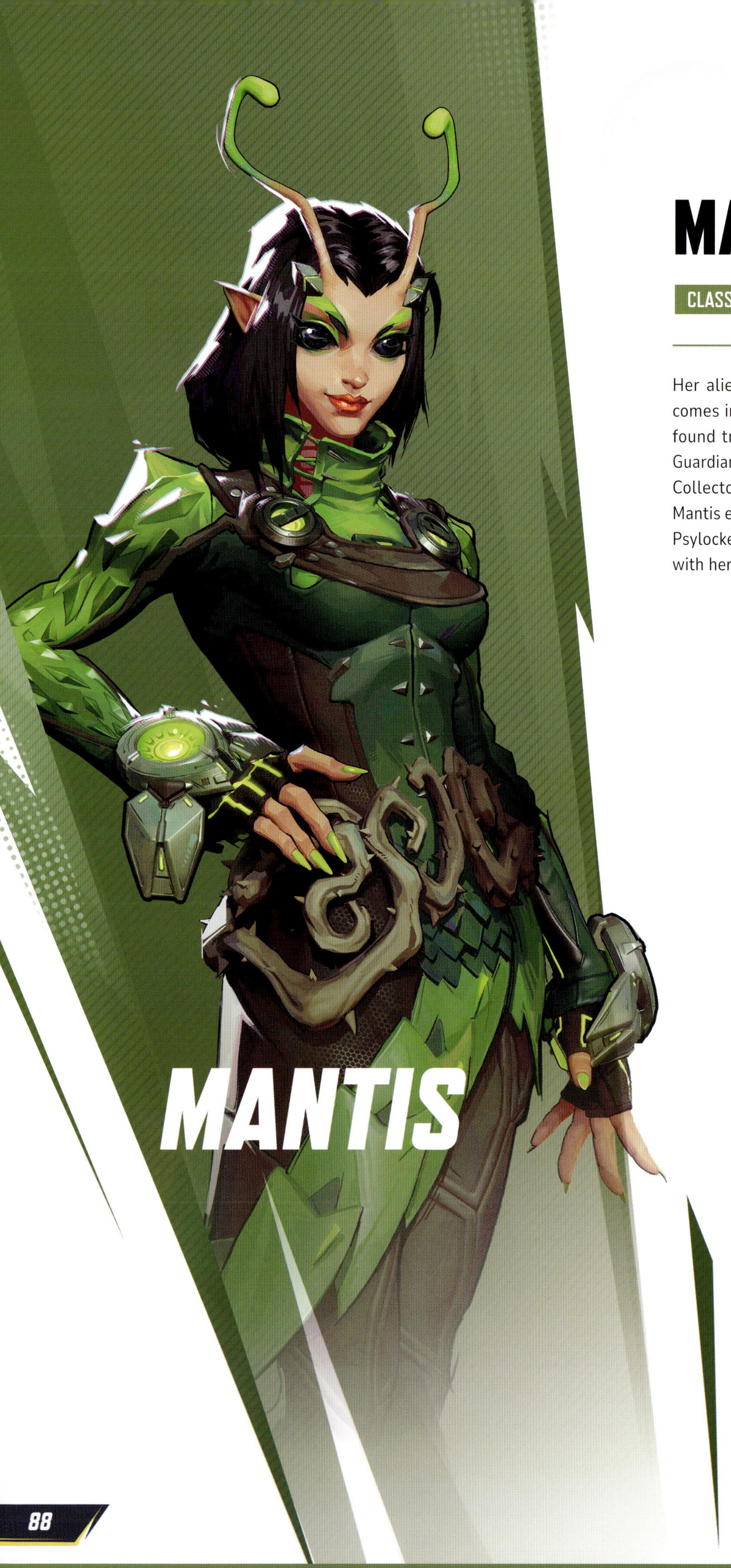

MANTIS

CLASS STRATEGIST

Her alien ability to alter the emotions of others comes in handy on the battlefield, but Mantis has found true happiness for herself with her fellow Guardians of the Galaxy. After being captured by the Collector and put on display at his theme park, Mantis escaped with the help of her fellow captives, Psylocke and Jeff, and began her journey to reunite with her team and found family.

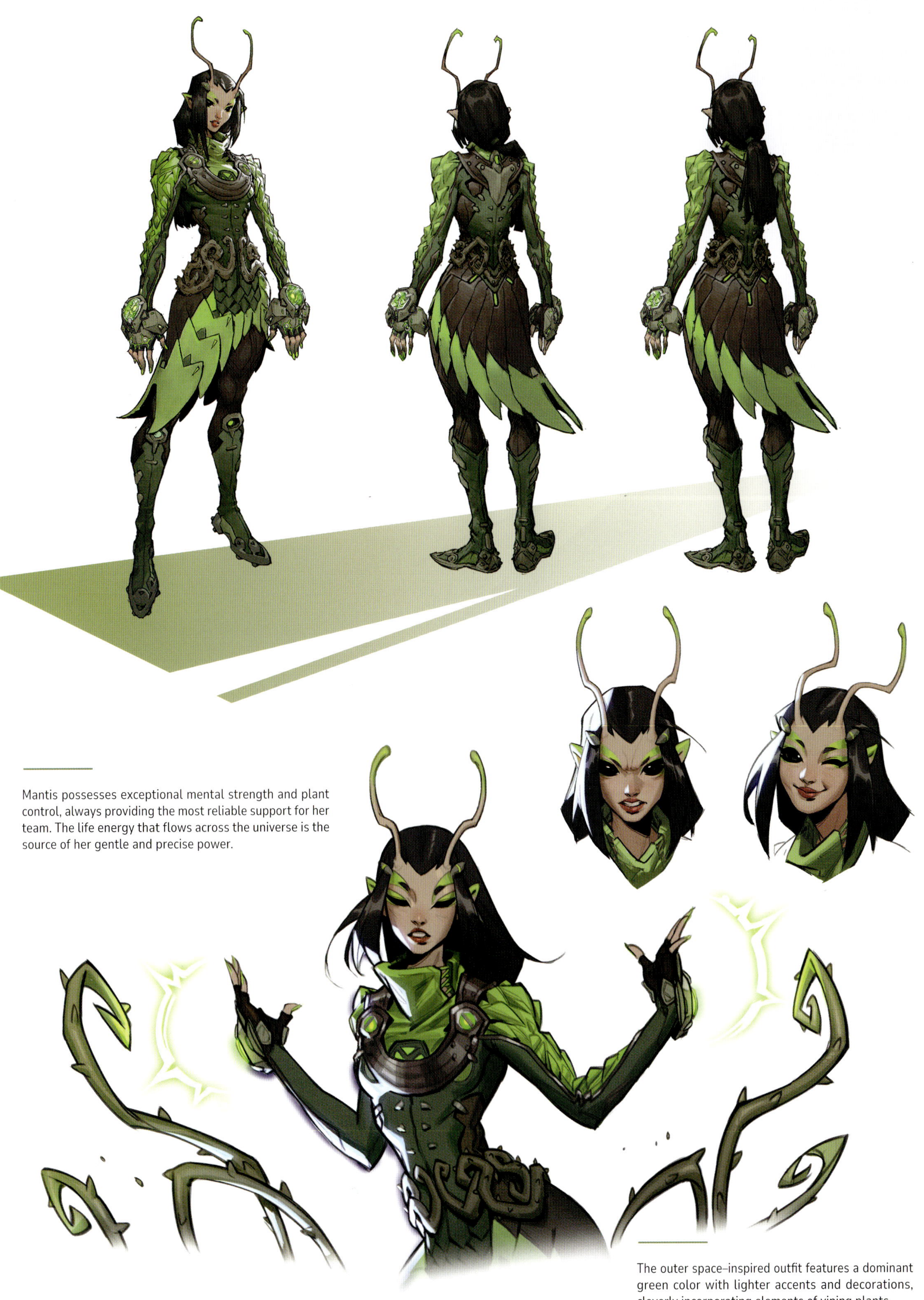

Mantis possesses exceptional mental strength and plant control, always providing the most reliable support for her team. The life energy that flows across the universe is the source of her gentle and precise power.

The outer space-inspired outfit features a dominant green color with lighter accents and decorations, cleverly incorporating elements of vining plants.

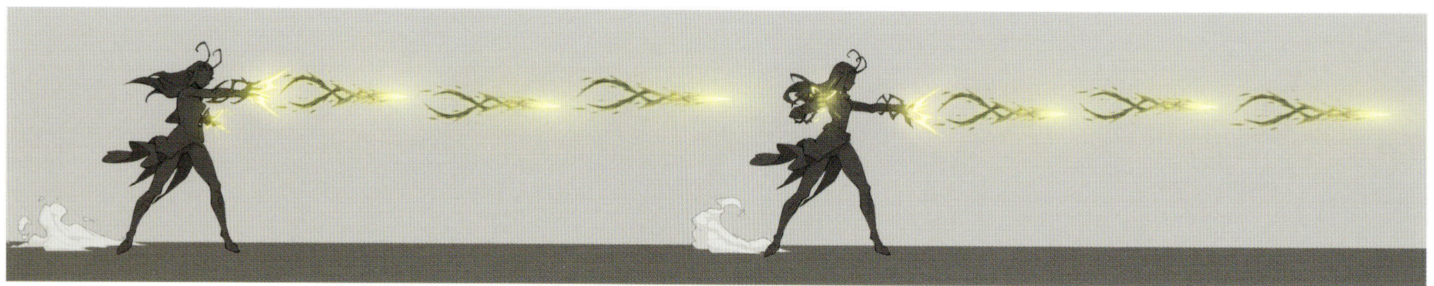

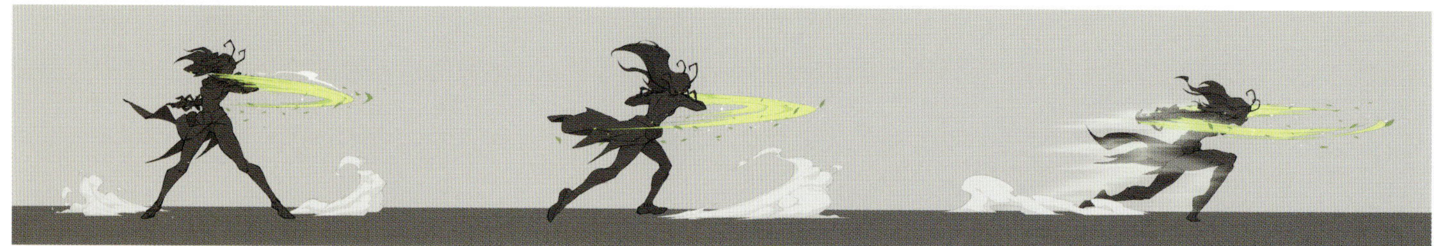

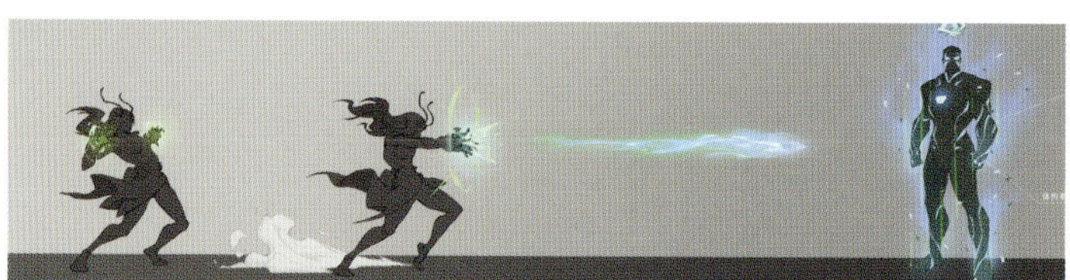

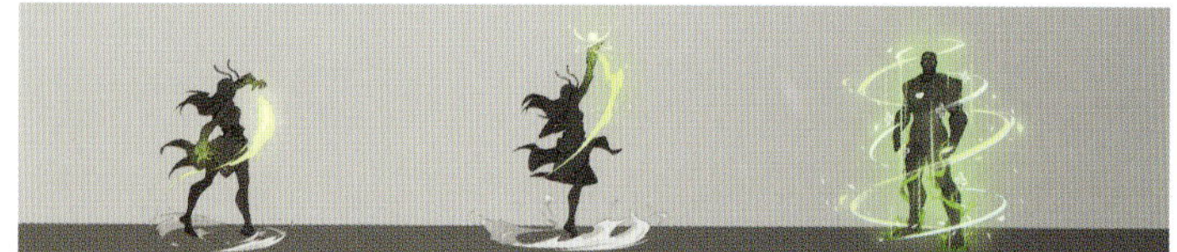

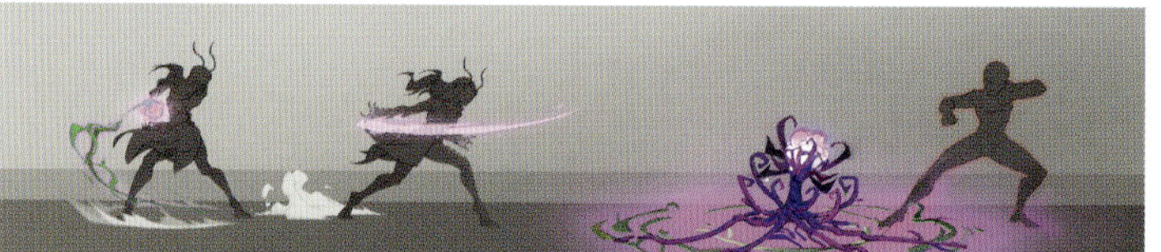

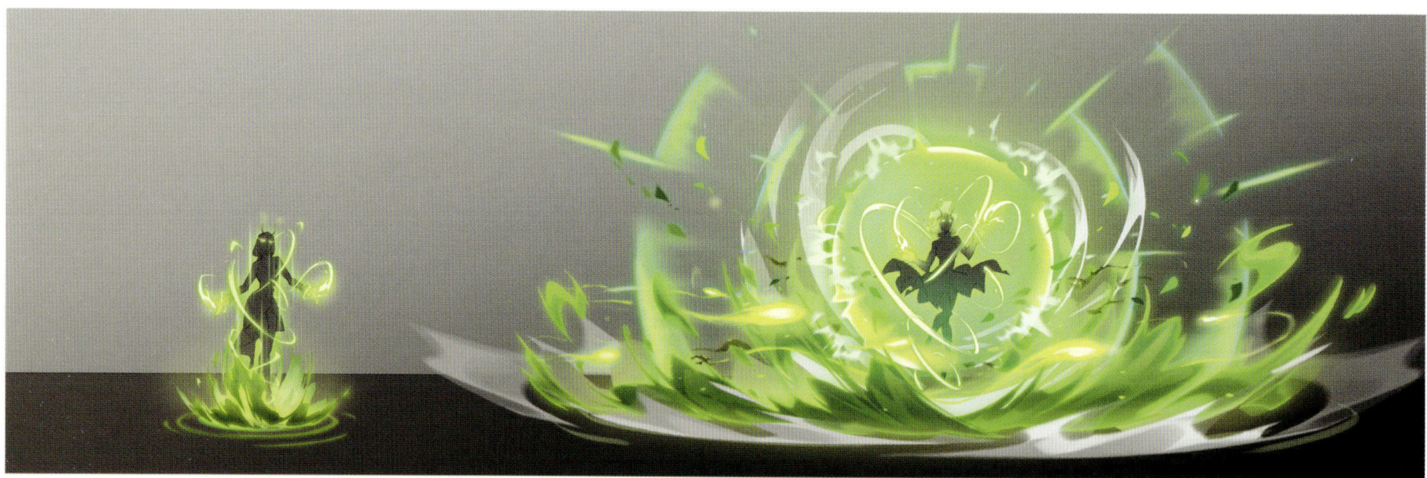

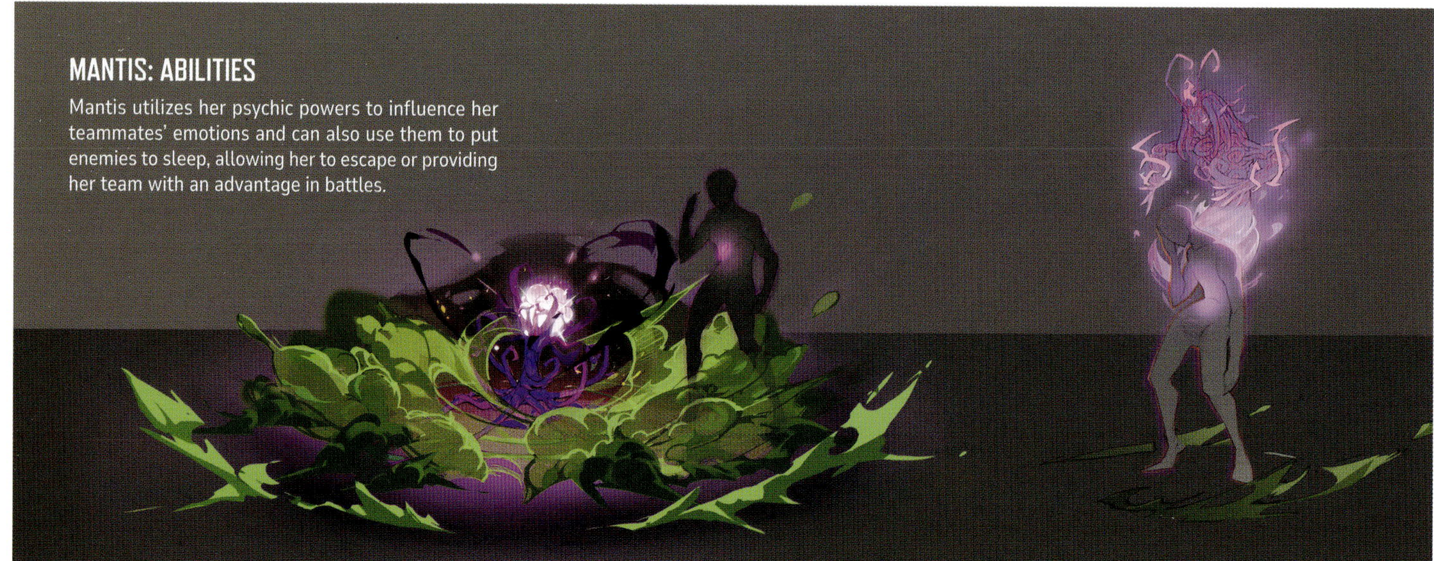

MANTIS: ABILITIES

Mantis utilizes her psychic powers to influence her teammates' emotions and can also use them to put enemies to sleep, allowing her to escape or providing her team with an advantage in battles.

MANTIS: COSMETIC VARIETY

The combination of a cheongsam, boxing gloves, and an immortal dragon embodies Mantis with the spirit of K'un-Lun, although it's a challenge to depict an entire Chinese dragon across her costume.

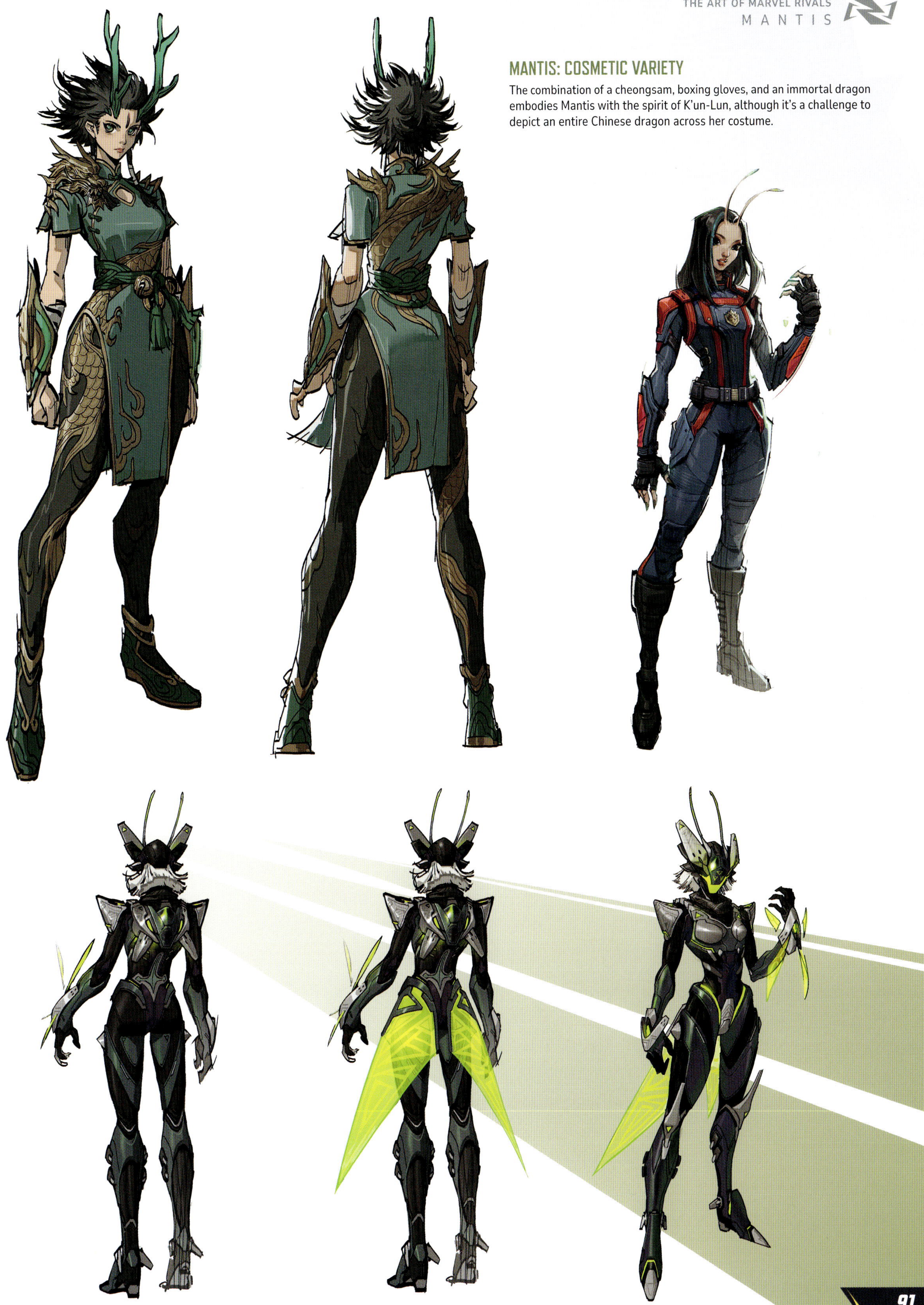

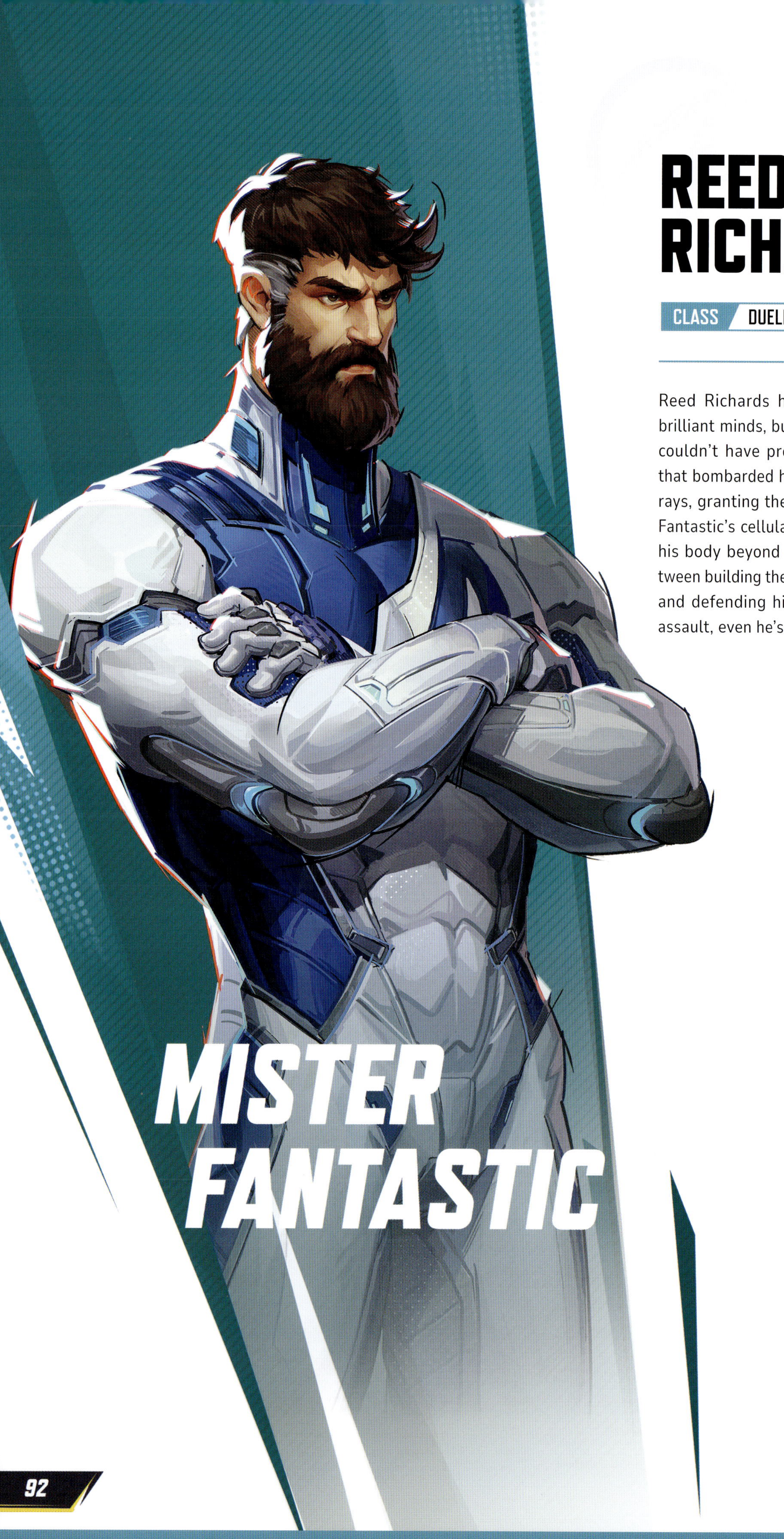

REED RICHARDS

CLASS / DUELIST

Reed Richards has one of the universe's most brilliant minds, but even a genius of his magnitude couldn't have predicted the interstellar incident that bombarded his friends and family with cosmic rays, granting them extraordinary abilities. Mister Fantastic's cellular elasticity allows him to stretch his body beyond all physical boundaries, but between building the Timestream Reintegration Device and defending his city from Dracula's relentless assault, even he's reaching his limit.

Mister Fantastic wears a special suit made from unstable molecules, designed to follow his body and stretch with him. The suit's chest displays the number 4 to represent the Fantastic Four.

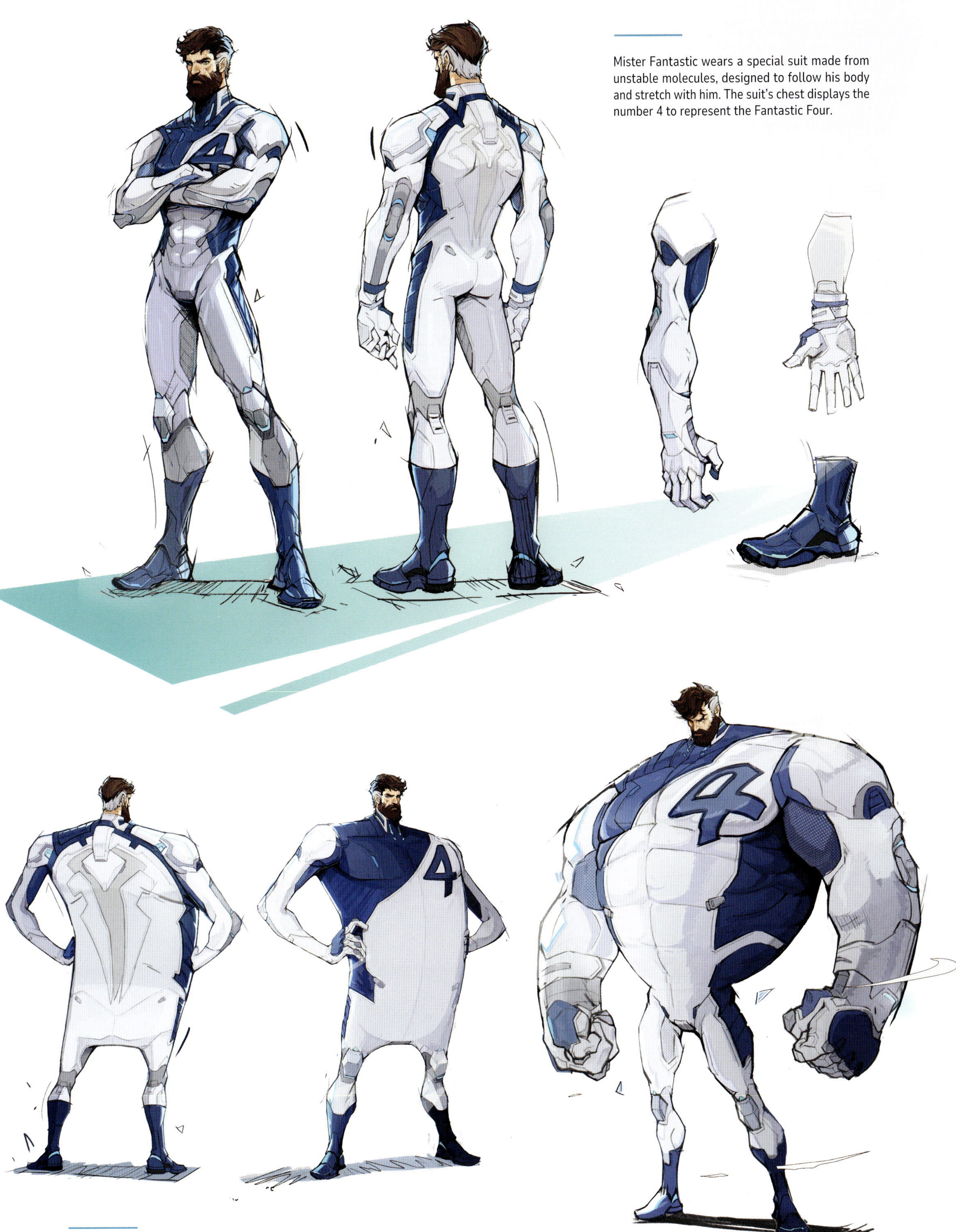

The suit features patterns of luminous materials arranged in a specific order to enhance the visual effect of transformation and extension.

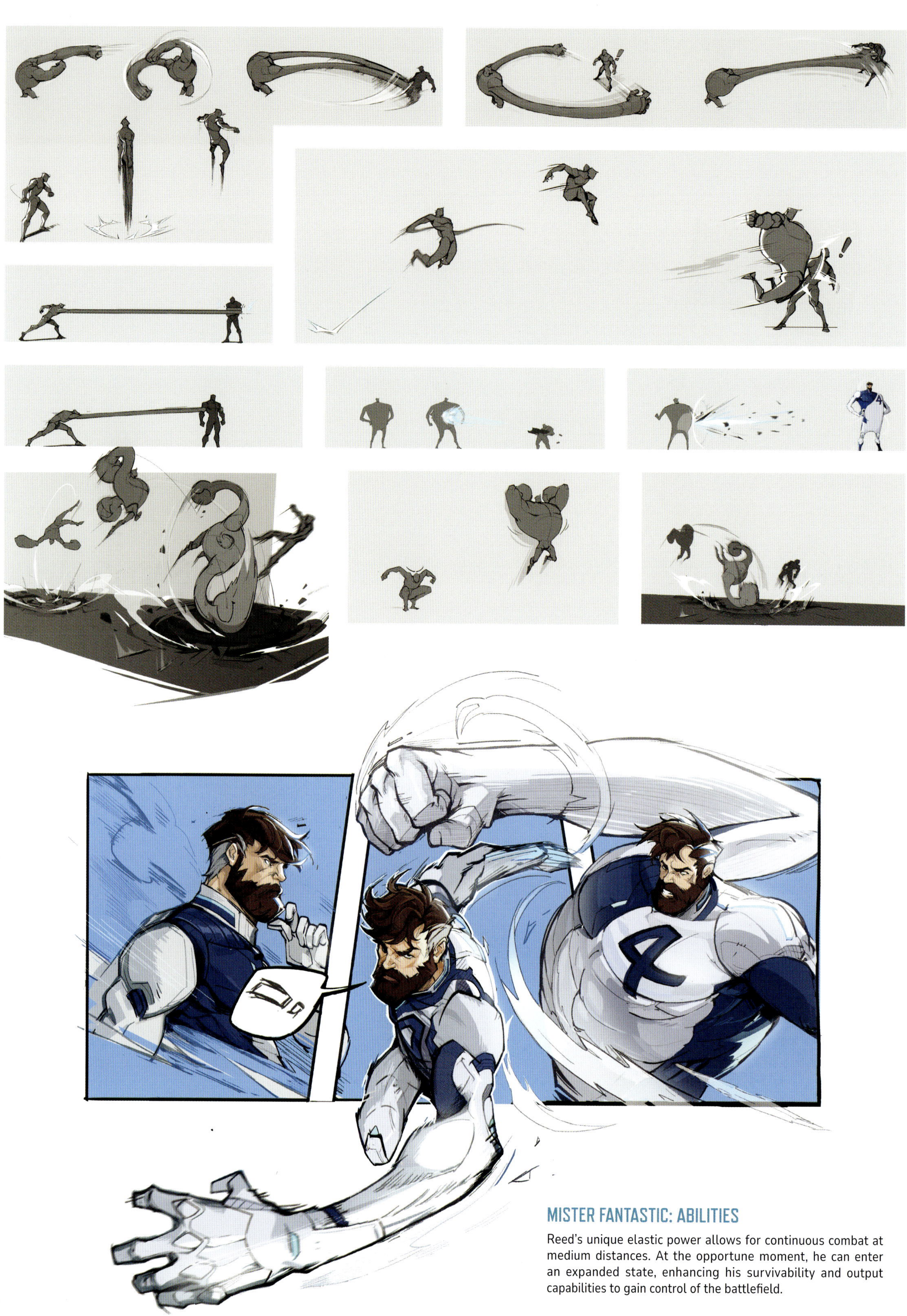

MISTER FANTASTIC: ABILITIES

Reed's unique elastic power allows for continuous combat at medium distances. At the opportune moment, he can enter an expanded state, enhancing his survivability and output capabilities to gain control of the battlefield.

MISTER FANTASTIC: COSMETIC VARIETY

The Maker costume comes from the Reed Richards of the Ultimate Universe. It showcases a futuristic sci-fi concept complete with an elaborate helmet signifying this terrifying version of the scientist.

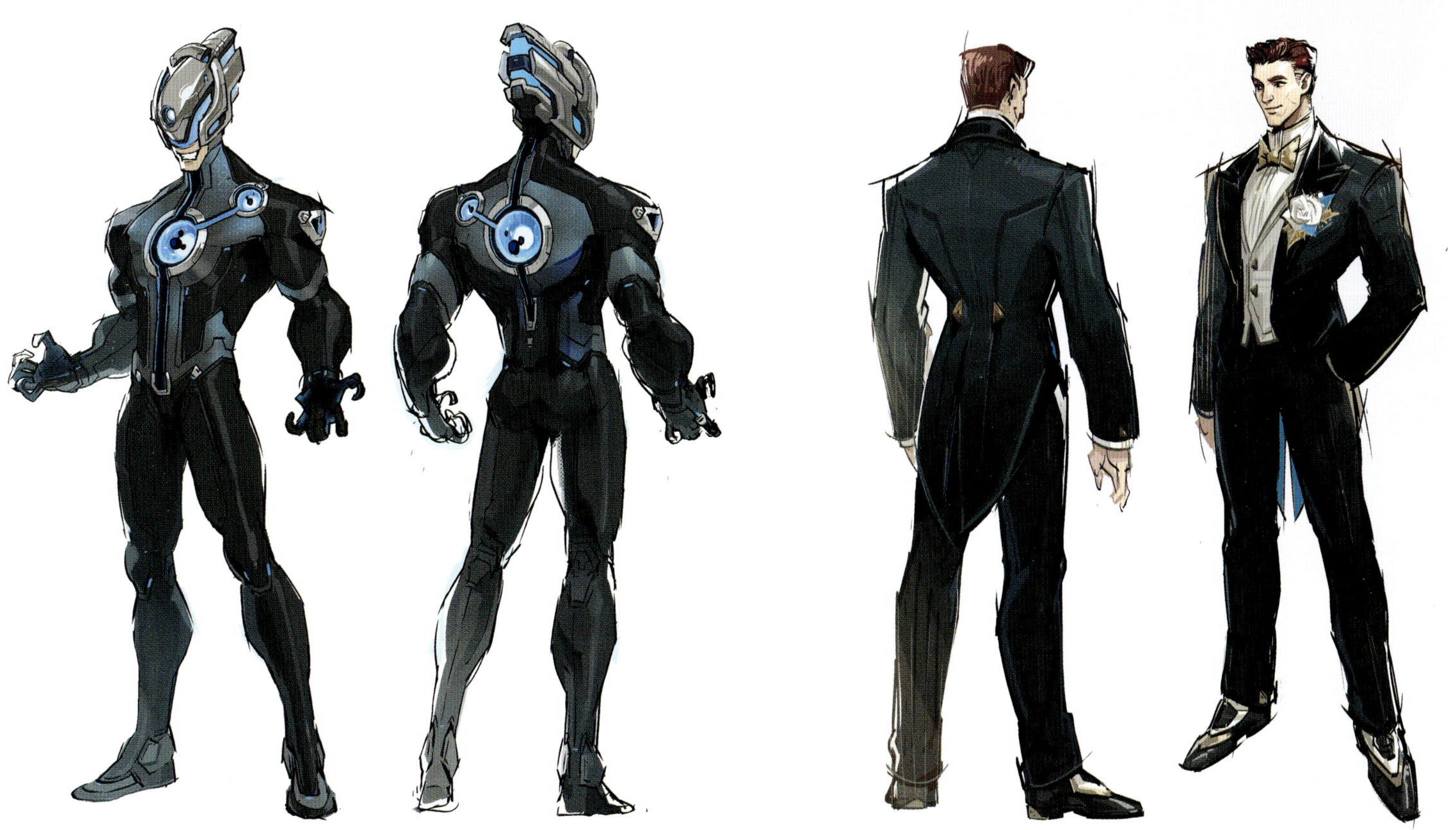

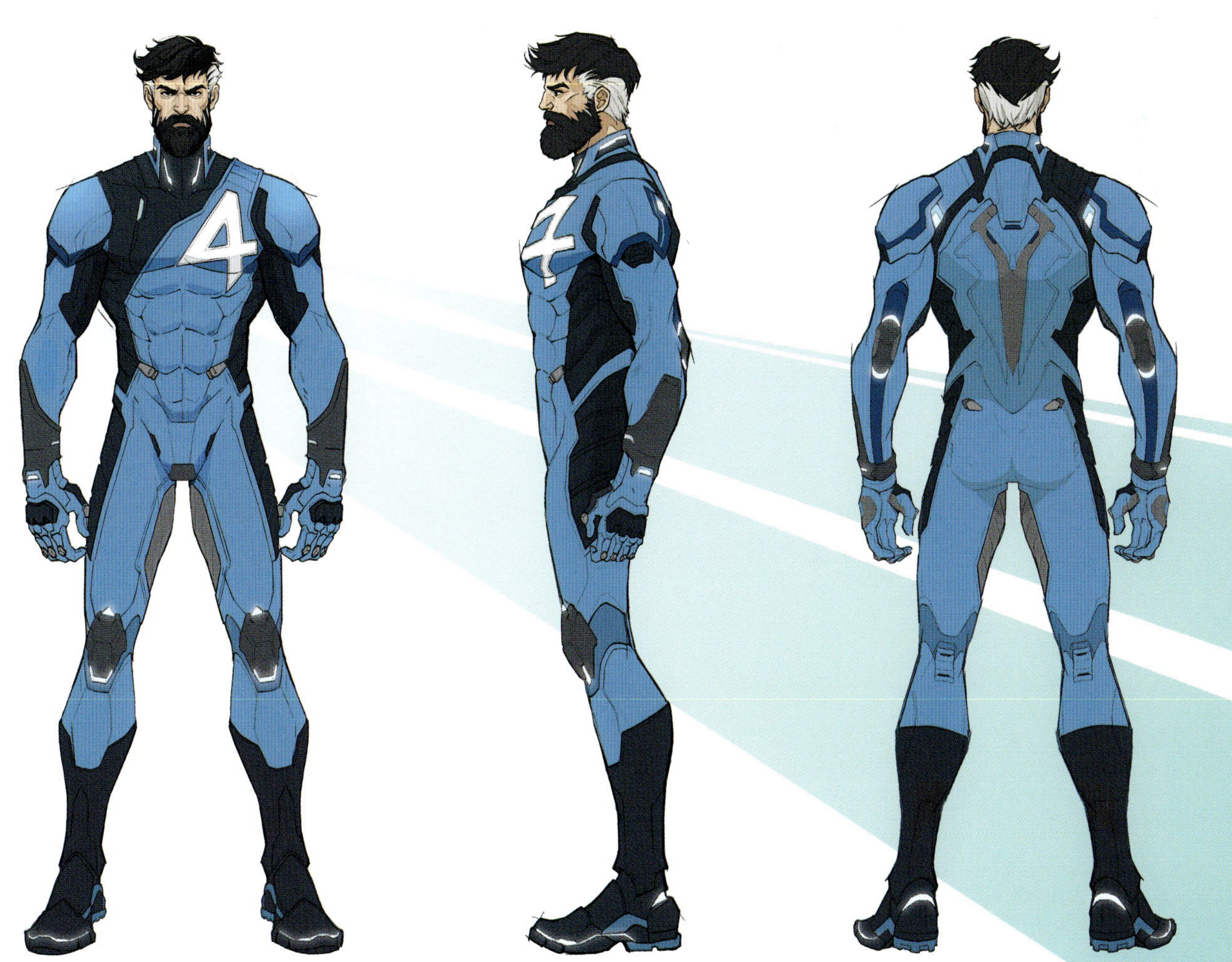

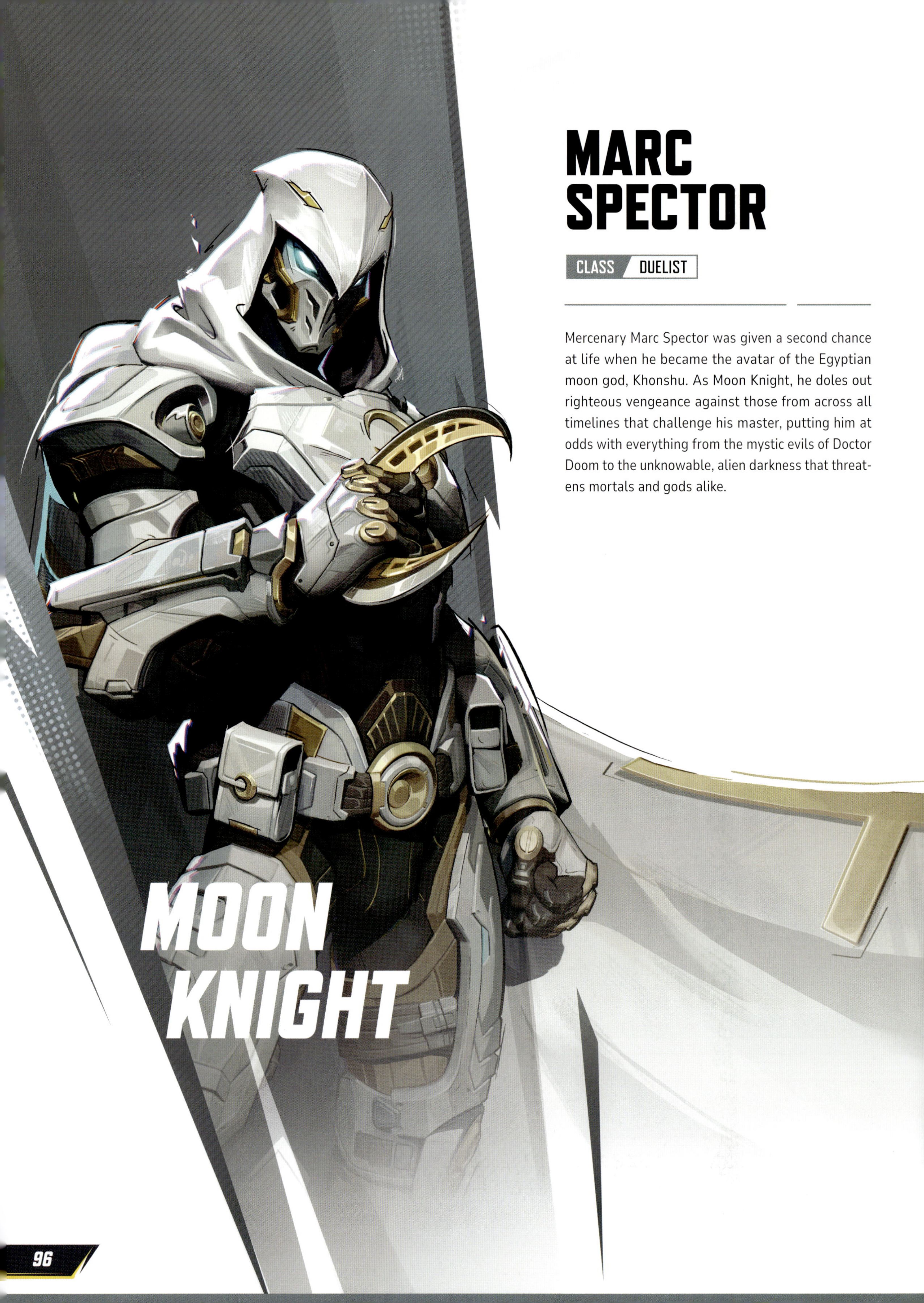

MARC SPECTOR

CLASS / DUELIST

Mercenary Marc Spector was given a second chance at life when he became the avatar of the Egyptian moon god, Khonshu. As Moon Knight, he doles out righteous vengeance against those from across all timelines that challenge his master, putting him at odds with everything from the mystic evils of Doctor Doom to the unknowable, alien darkness that threatens mortals and gods alike.

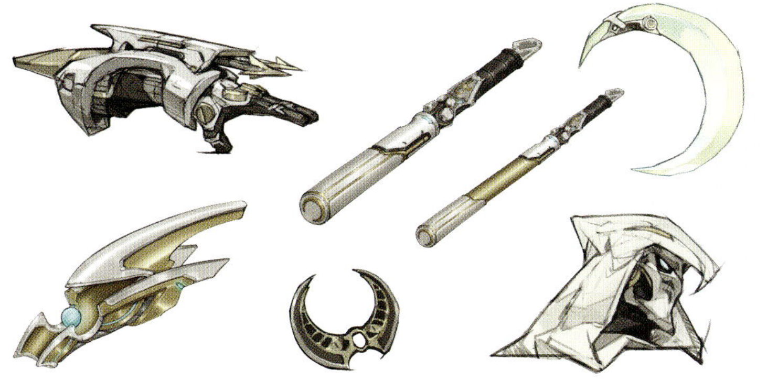

Marc Spector has a body strengthened by Khonshu, the God of the Moon. He wears Egyptian-style armor enhanced by mystic power and brandishes crescent darts and double batons as weapons.

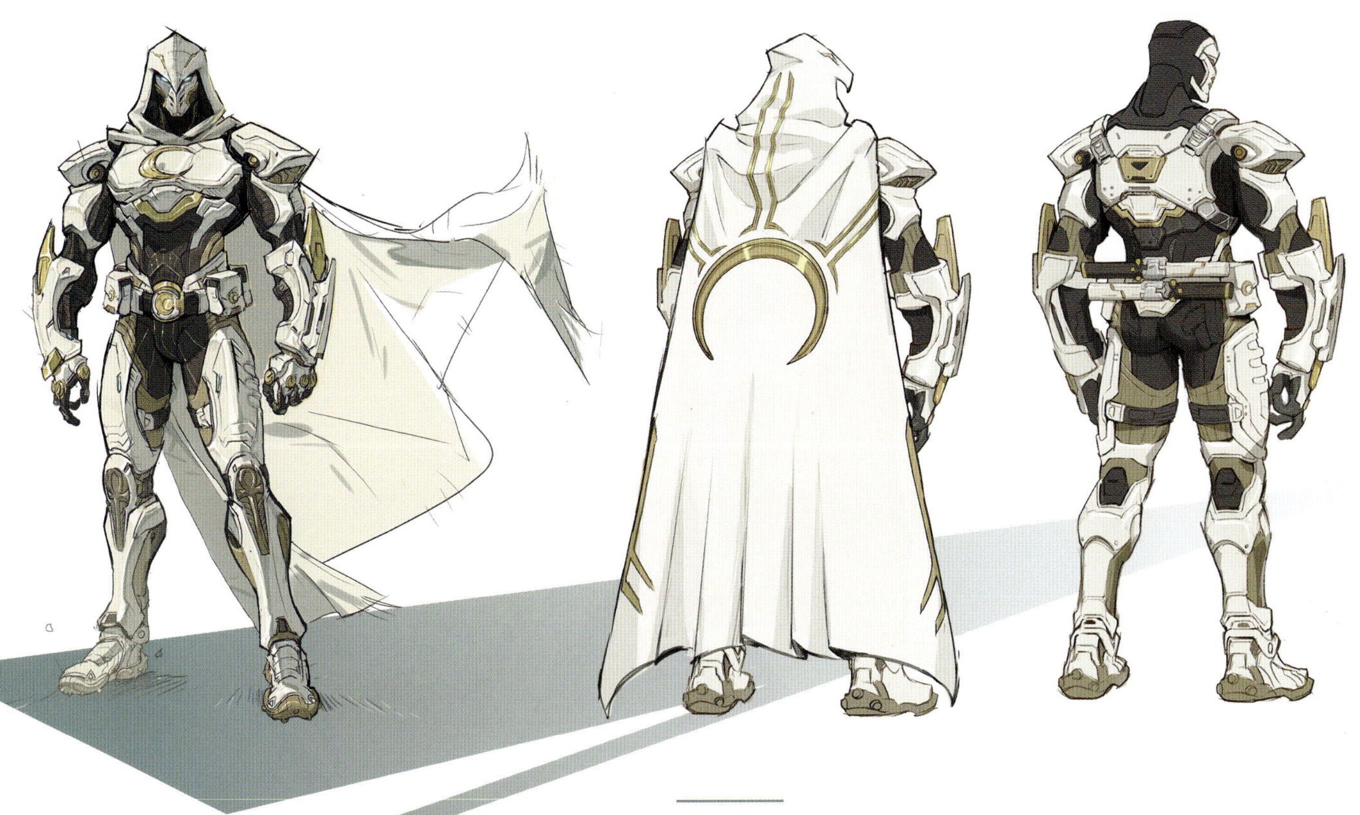

As the emissary of the ancient Egyptian God of Vengeance, Moon Knight glides through the sky, his white costume evoking the bright moonlight piercing the night.

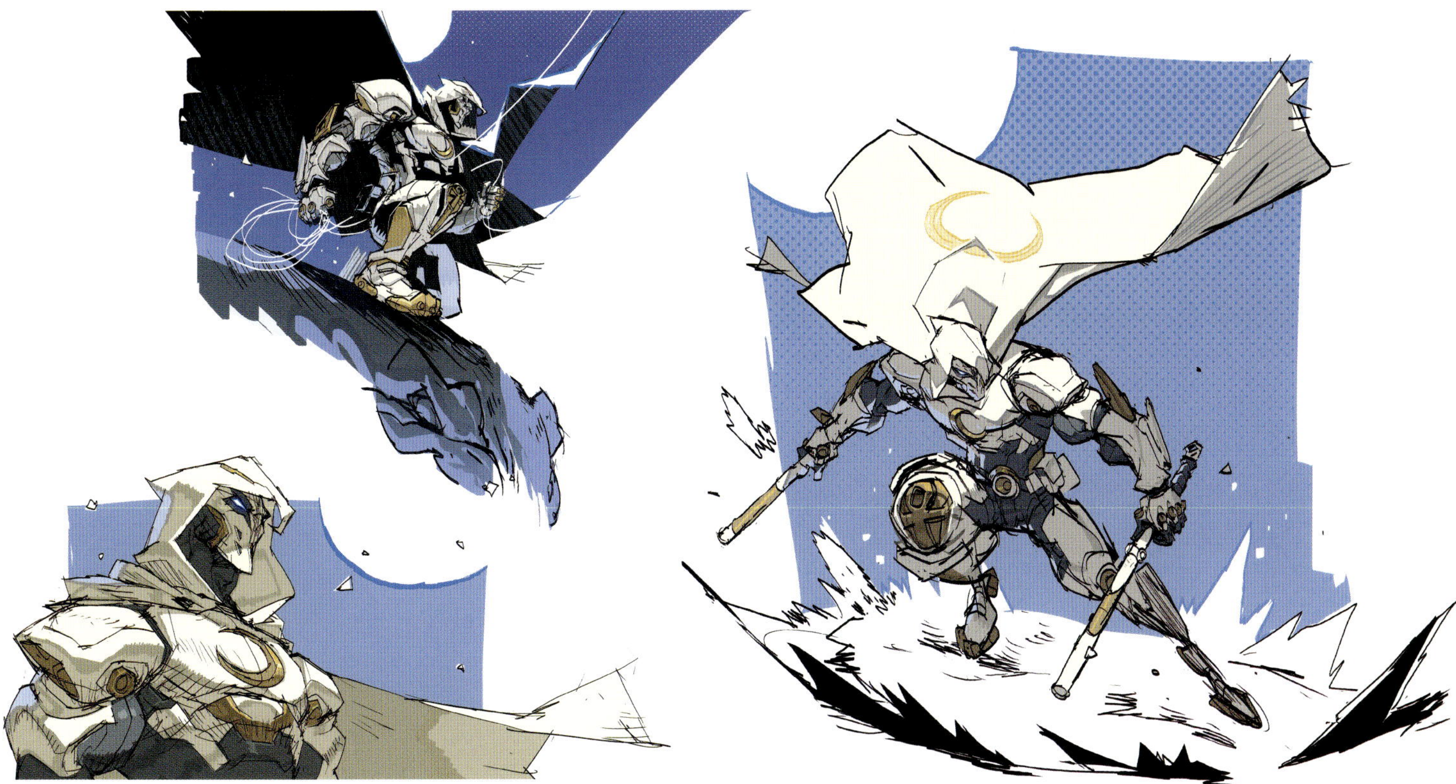

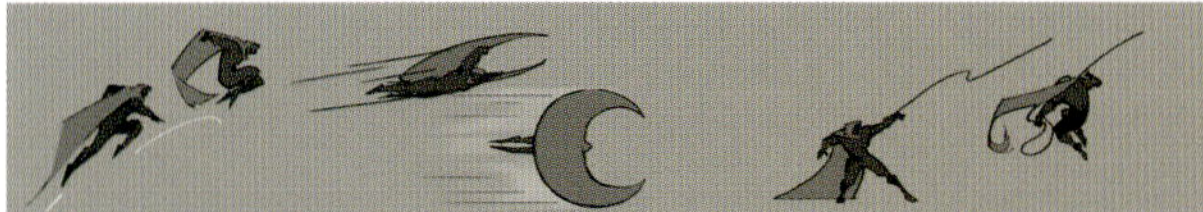

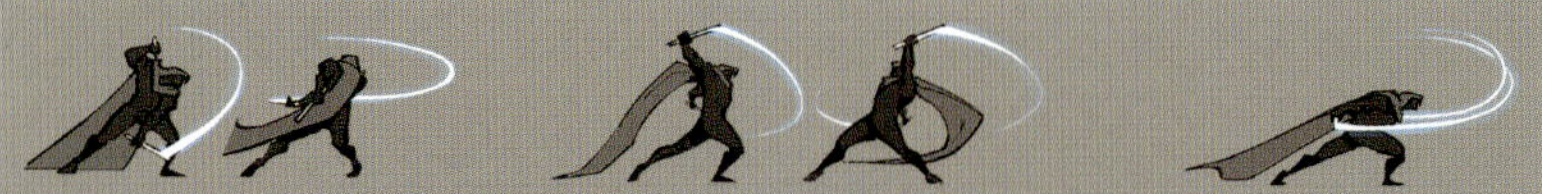

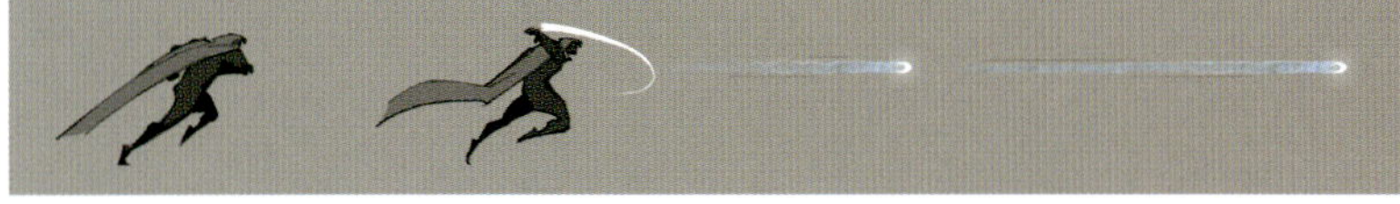

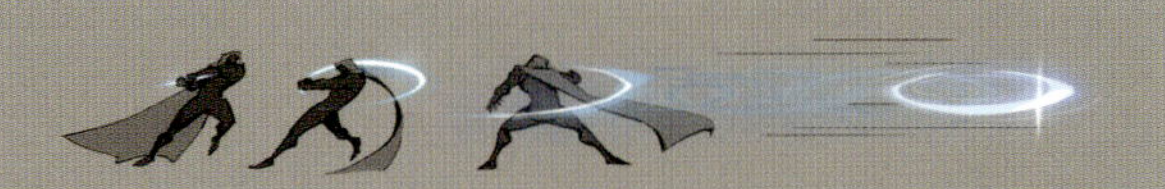

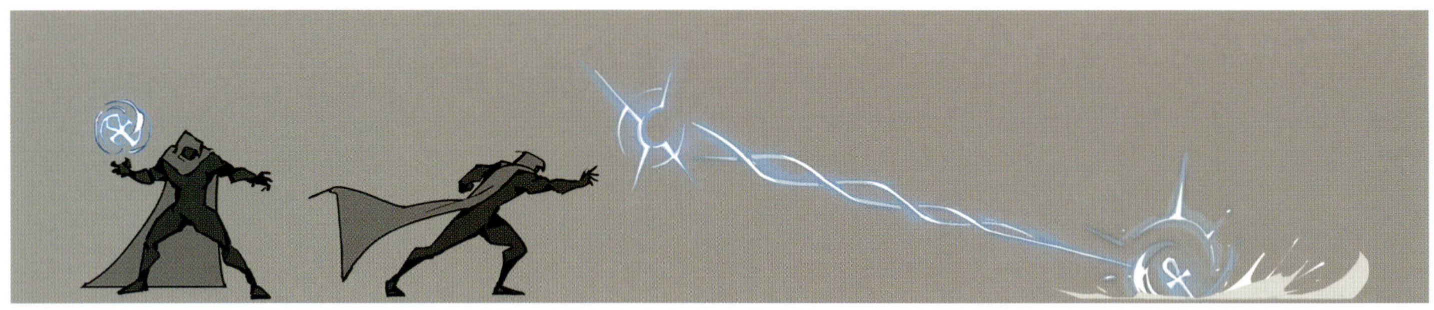

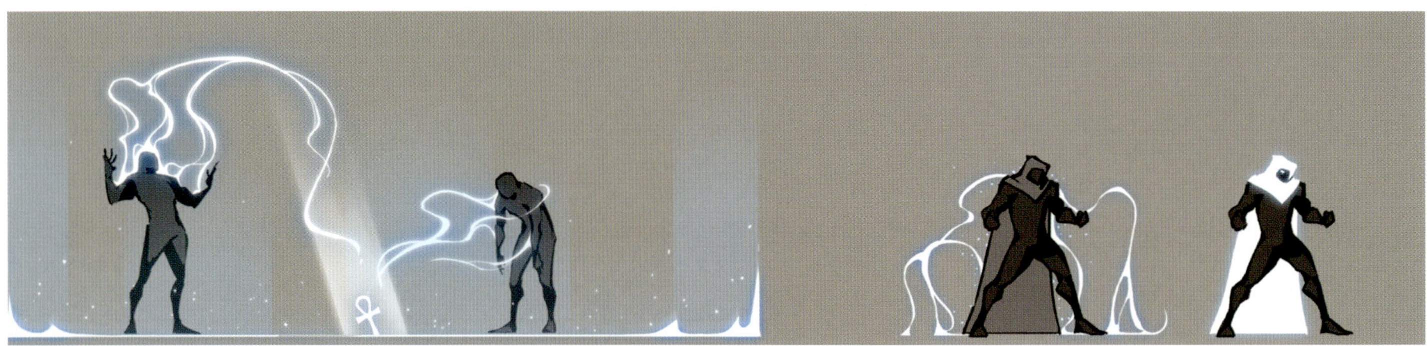

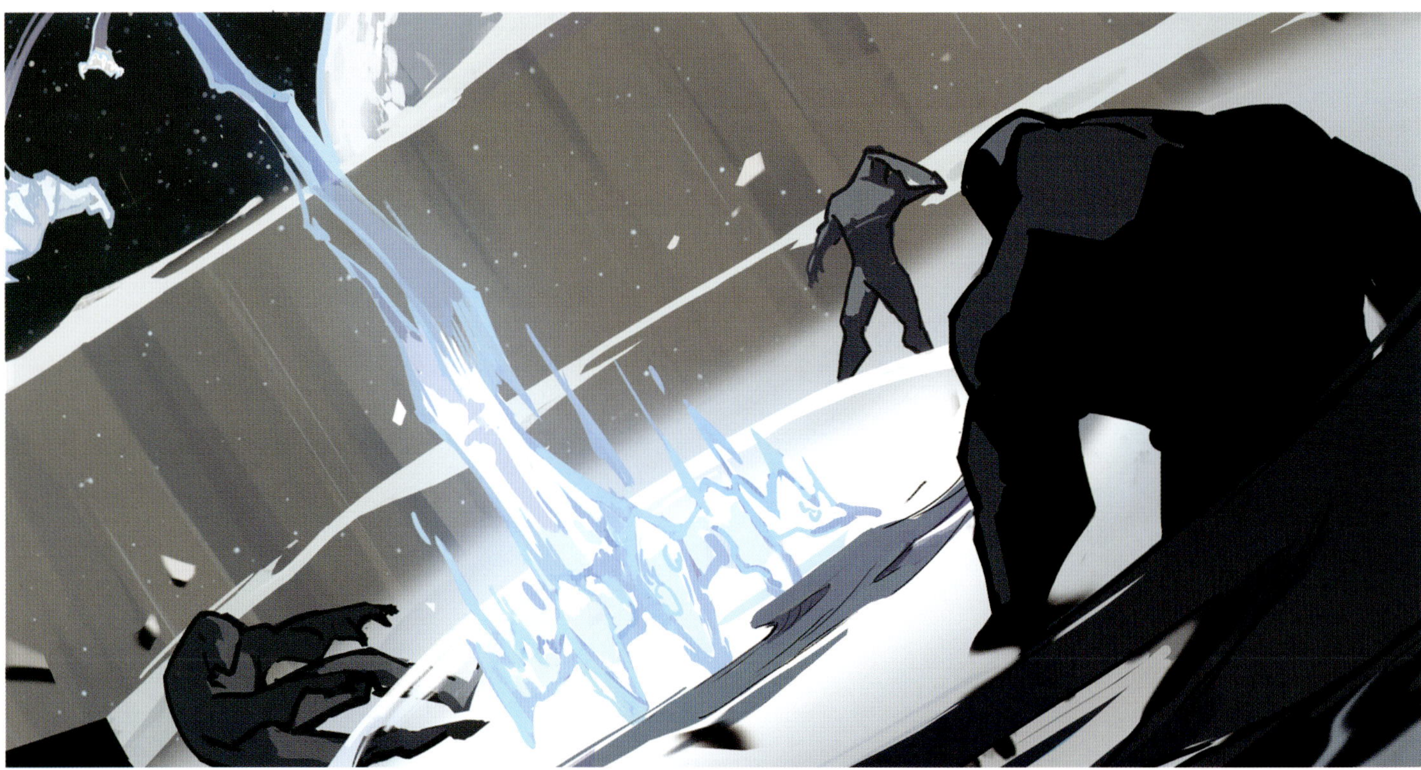

MOON KNIGHT: ABILITIES

Moon Knight utilizes ancient ankhs to disrupt his enemies while employing his crescent dart and moon blade for damage. He also has a grappling hook and gliding cape for maneuvering, enabling him to find strategic attack positions on the battlefield.

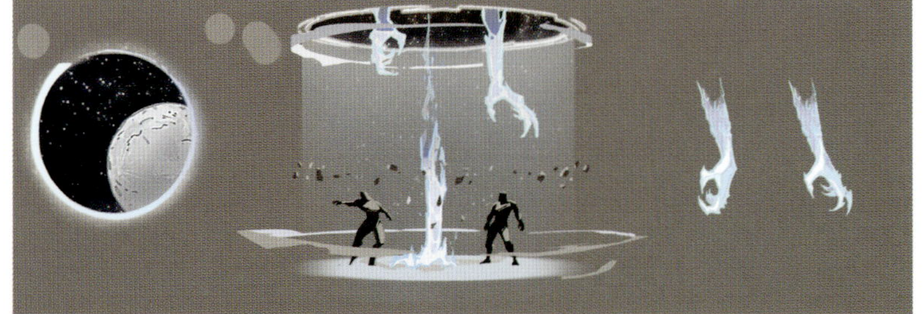

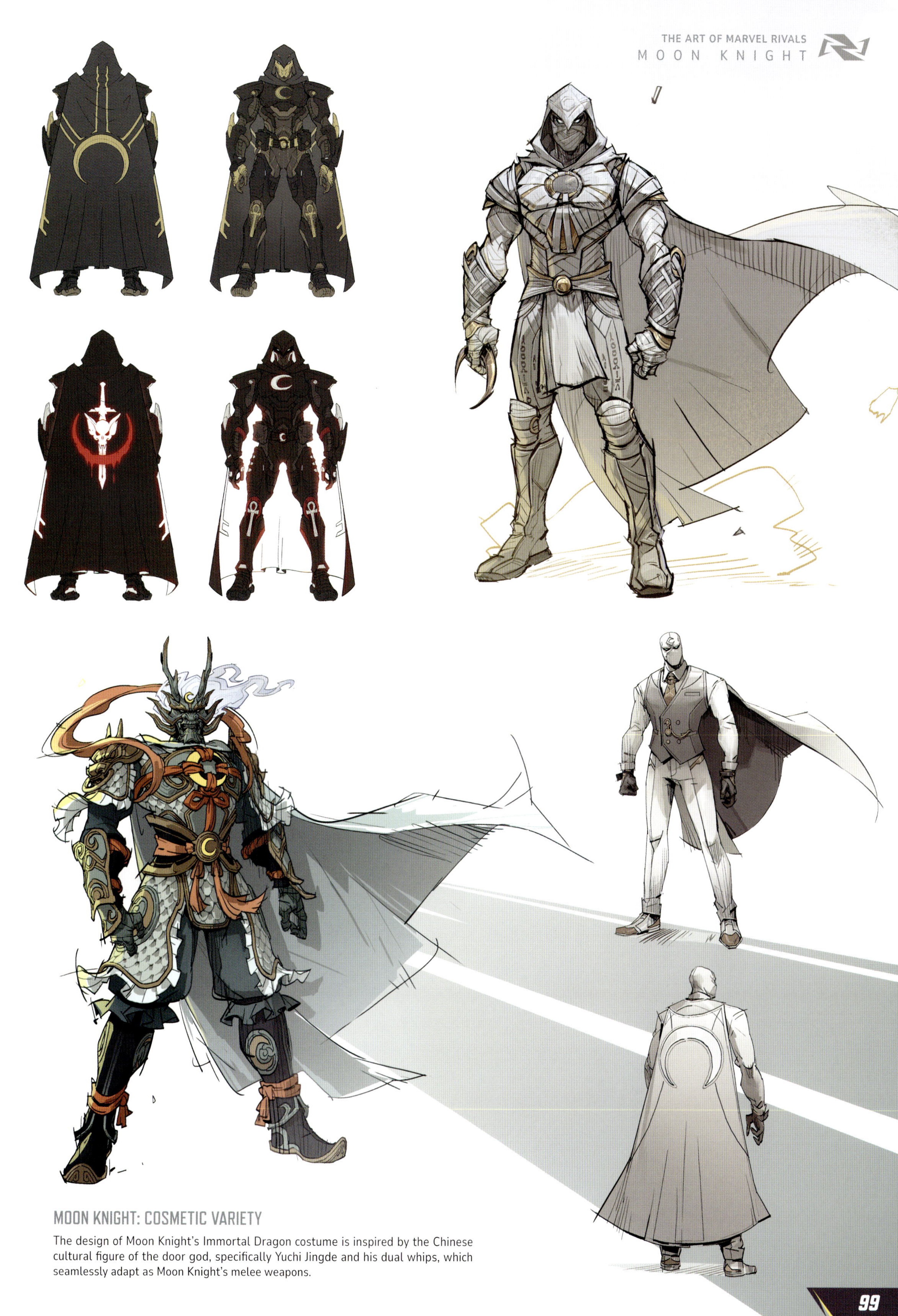

MOON KNIGHT: COSMETIC VARIETY

The design of Moon Knight's Immortal Dragon costume is inspired by the Chinese cultural figure of the door god, specifically Yuchi Jingde and his dual whips, which seamlessly adapt as Moon Knight's melee weapons.

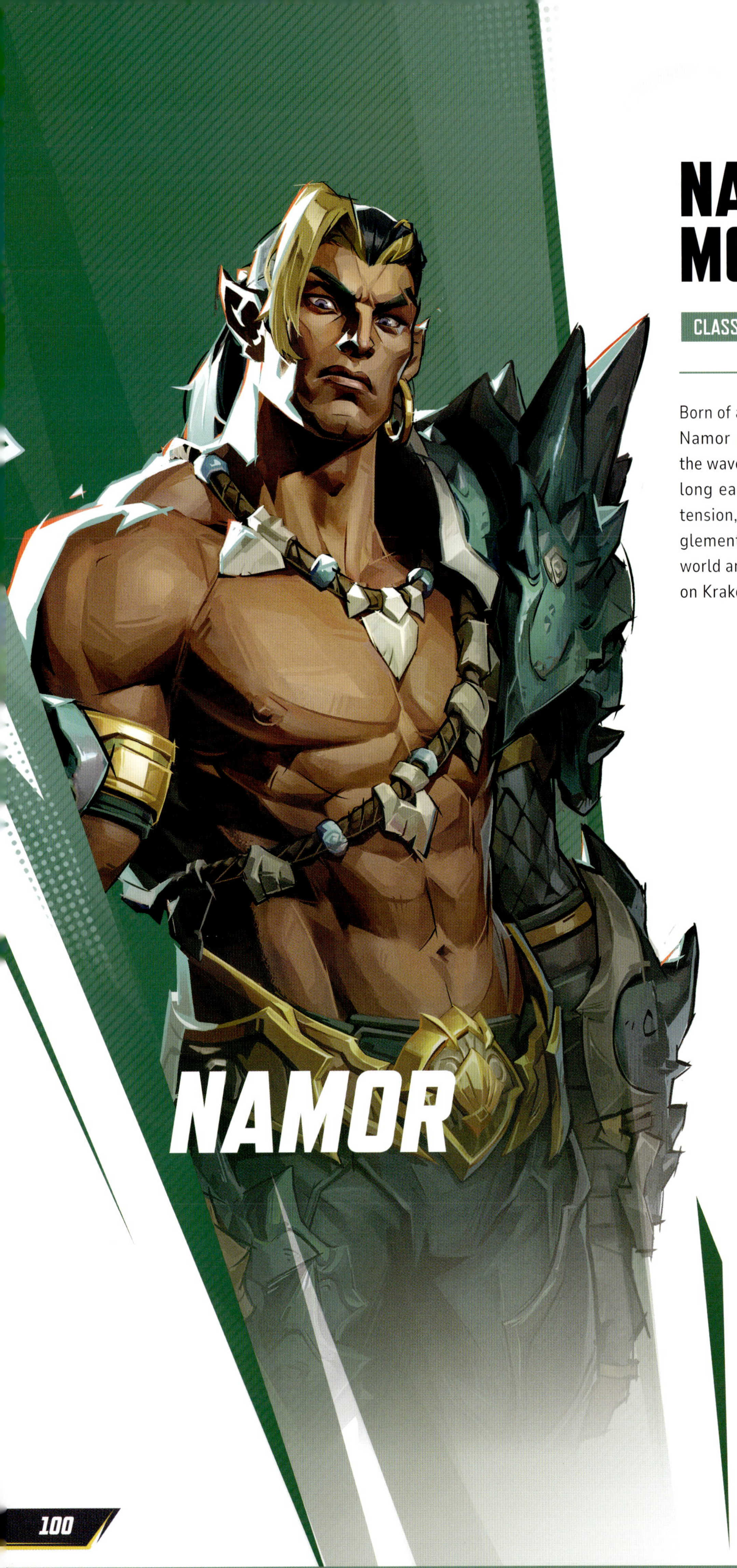

NAMOR MCKENZIE

CLASS DUELIST

Born of a union between a human and an Atlantean, Namor proudly rules those who dwell beneath the waves, while those who live on the surface have long earned his ire. After decades of simmering tension, Namor has finally decided that the Entanglement is the right time to strike at the surface world and asks his mutant allies living in the future on Krakoa to aid him.

Namor the Sub-Mariner strides through the waves, using the Horn of Proteus to summon fierce sea creatures to battle. His trident pierces the battlefield as deep-sea destruction looms on the horizon!

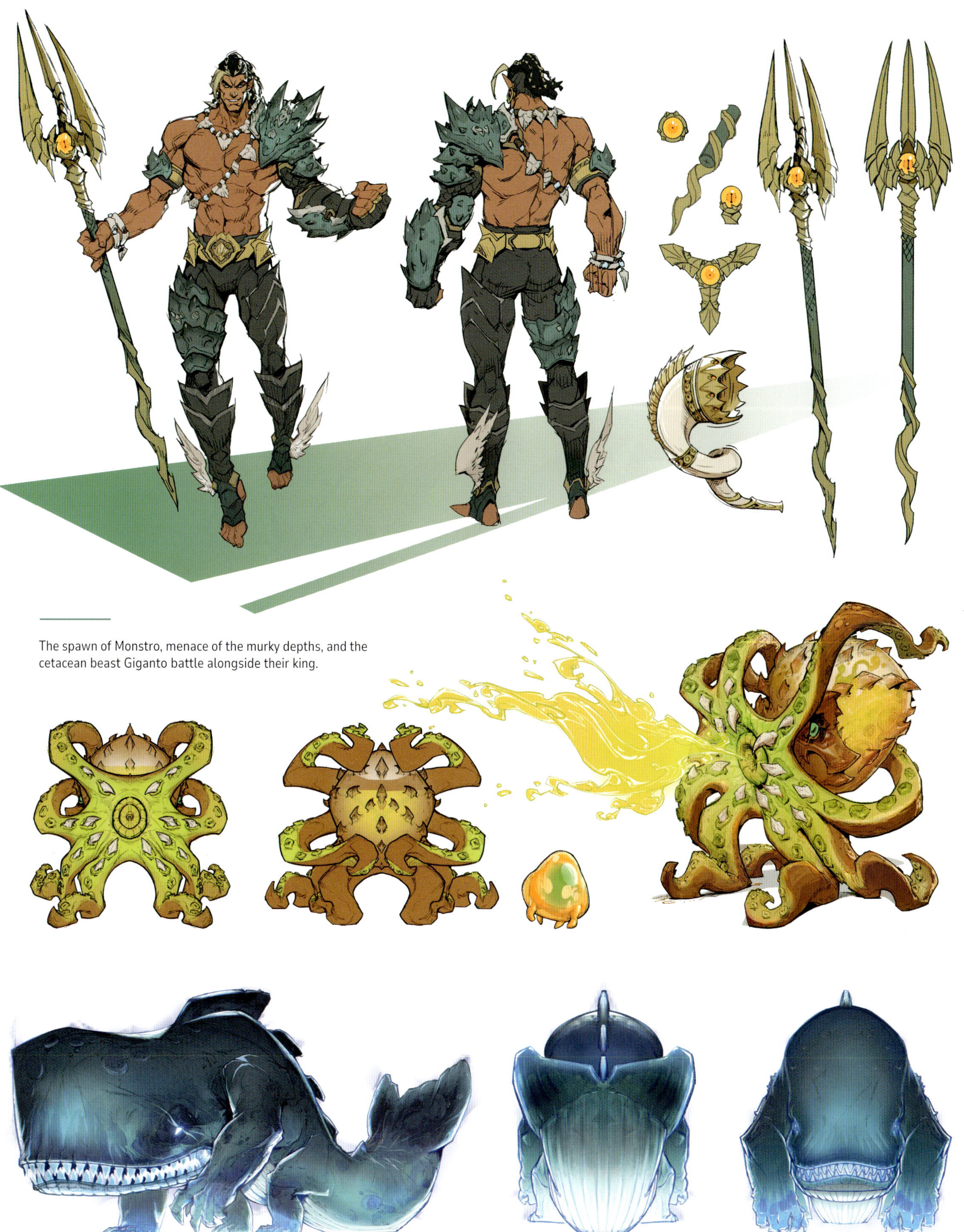

The spawn of Monstro, menace of the murky depths, and the cetacean beast Giganto battle alongside their king.

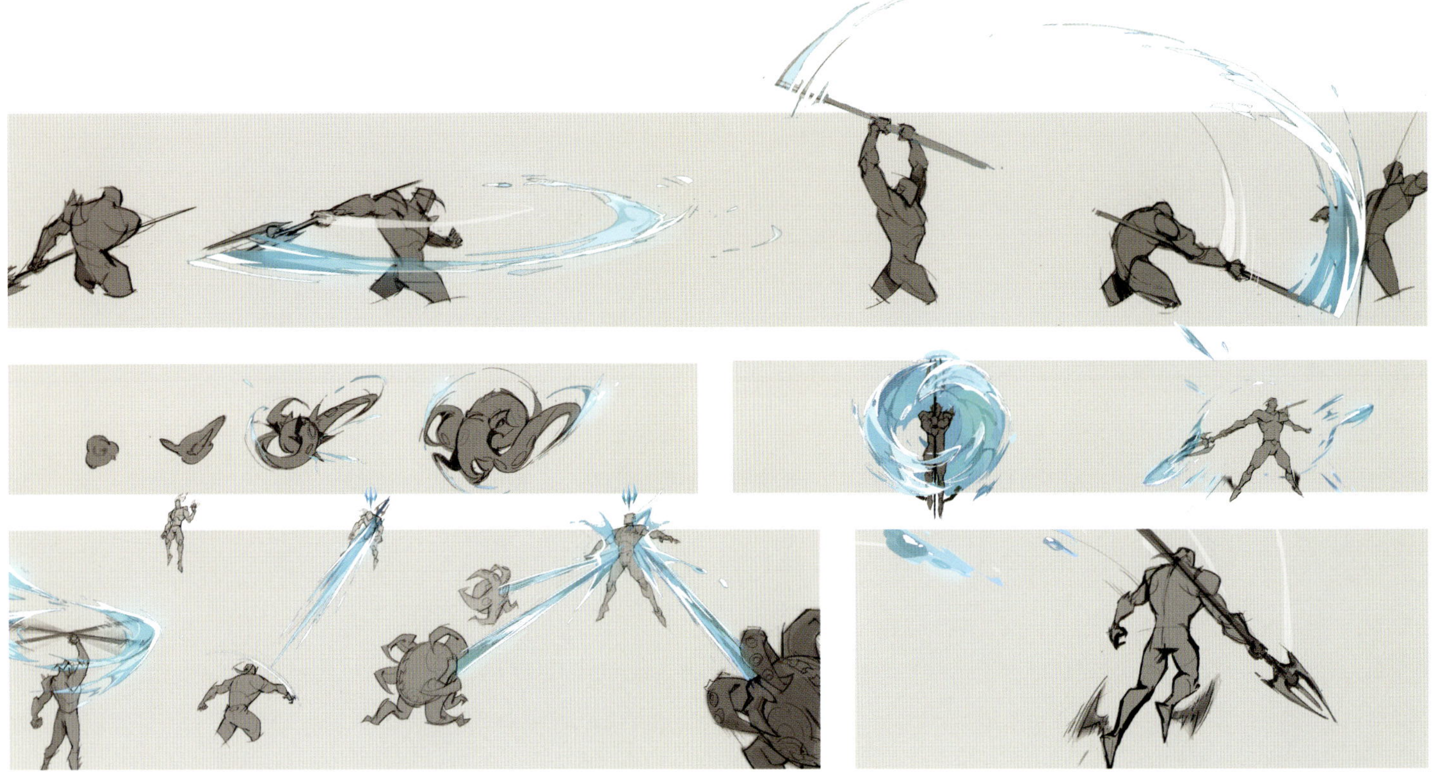

NAMOR: ABILITIES

Namor can summon sea creatures to the battlefield and command them, coordinating powerful strikes that can completely shatter the enemy's defenses!

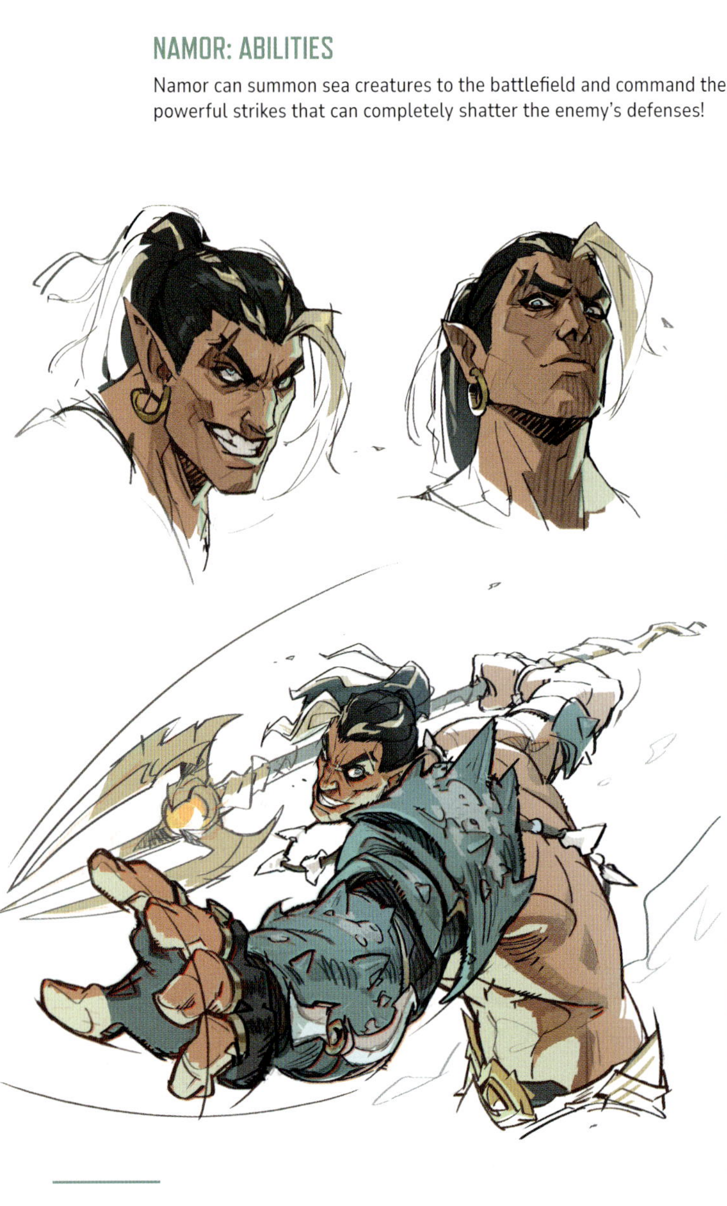

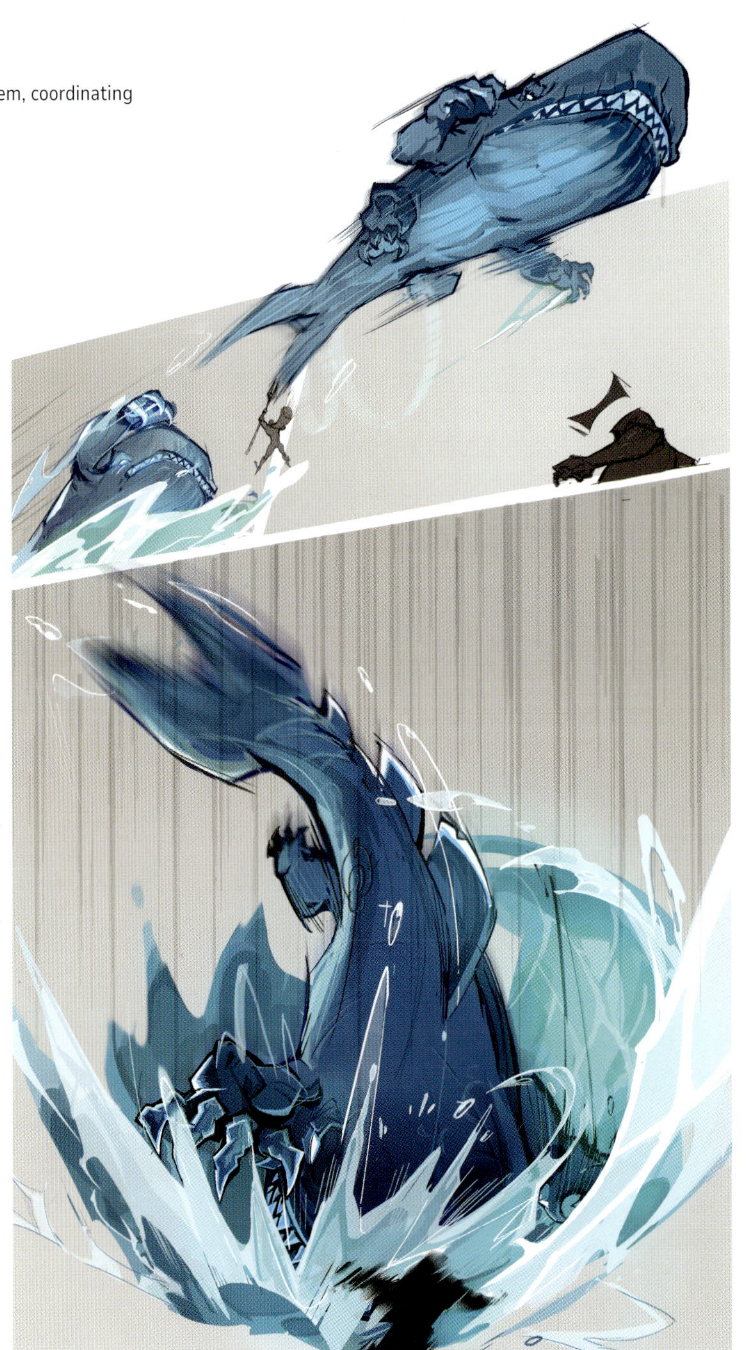

Namor summons the powerful whale-like monster Giganto from the deep by blowing the Horn of Proteus. With its indestructible and devastating power, Giganto will annihilate any enemies that dare to stand in Namor's way!

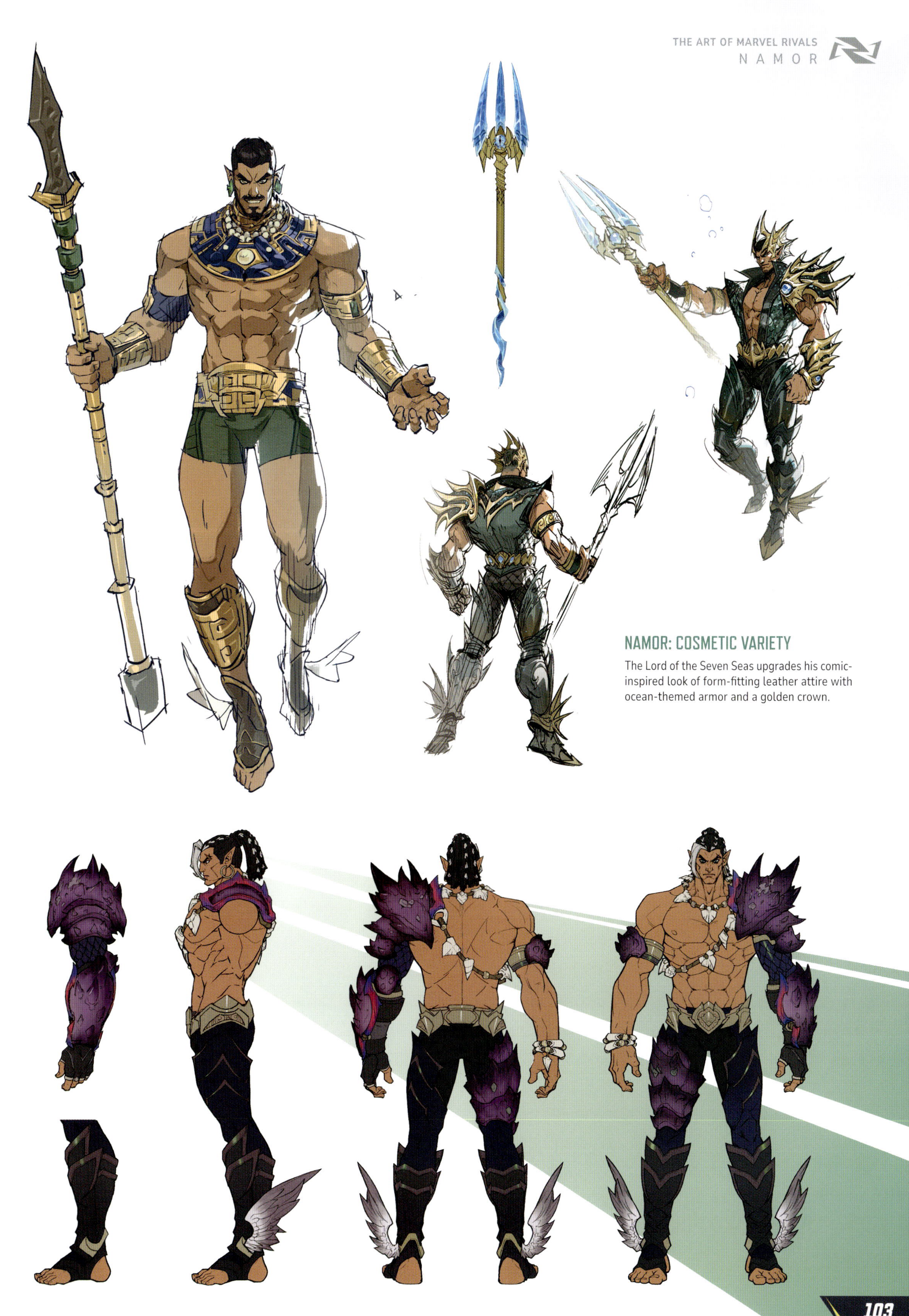

NAMOR: COSMETIC VARIETY

The Lord of the Seven Seas upgrades his comic-inspired look of form-fitting leather attire with ocean-themed armor and a golden crown.

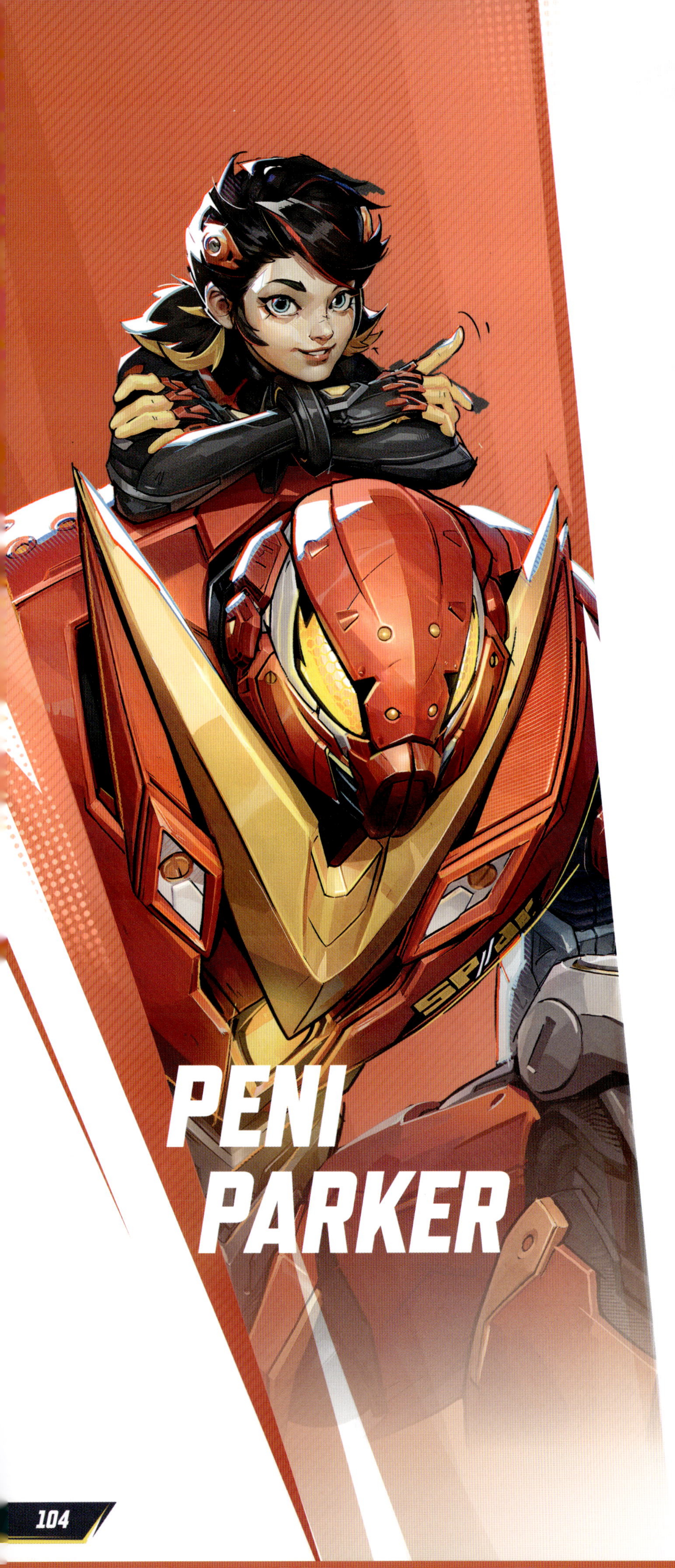

PENI PARKER

CLASS / VANGUARD

After her father's death, Peni Parker allowed herself to be bitten by an irradiated arachnid to form a psychic bond between them and control the experimental mech suit known as SP//dr. After the Timestream Entangle-ment, while Peni and SP//dr keep the people of Tokyo 2099 safe, they have found their mission is bigger than ever, and the duo devote themselves to the protection of the Web of Life and Destiny and the countless realities it connects.

Young Peni Parker stands bravely on the frontlines, protecting the Web of Life and Destiny. As a genius pilot, she and her extraordinary Spider-Mech are a powerful duo on any battlefield!

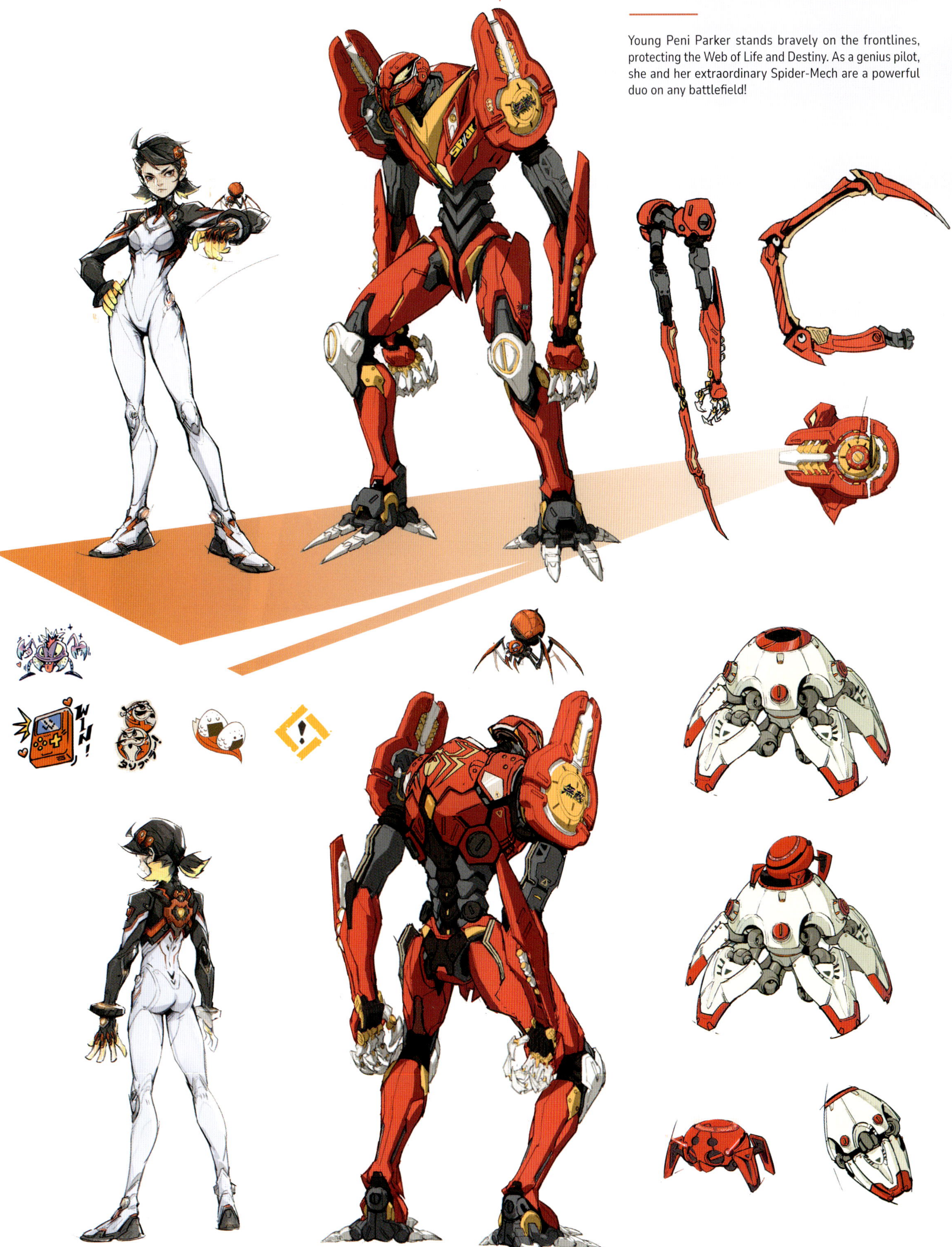

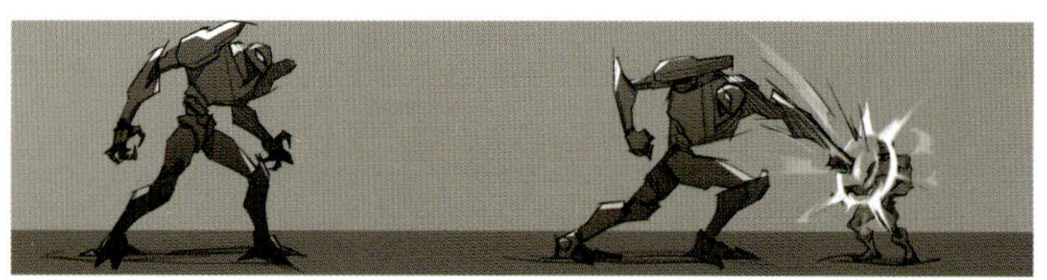
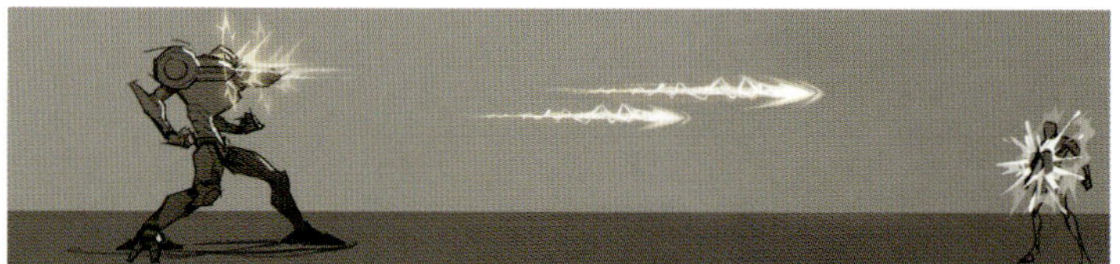
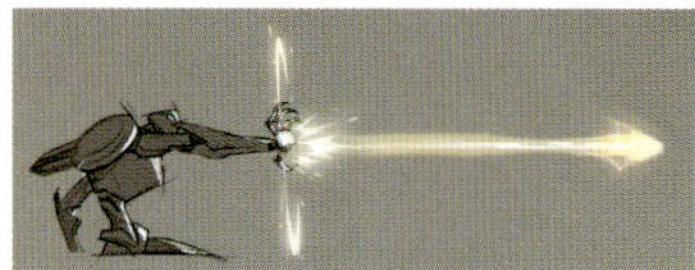
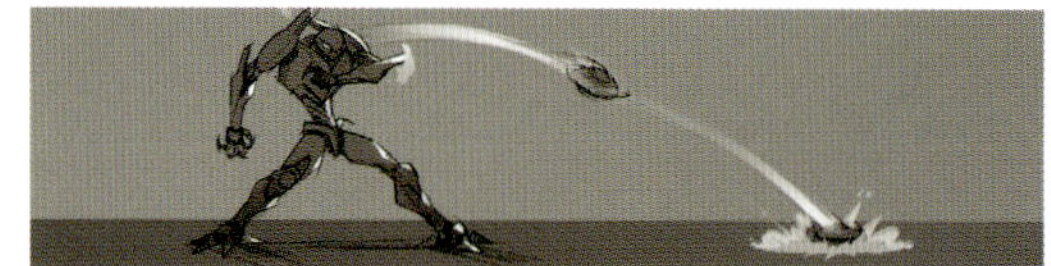
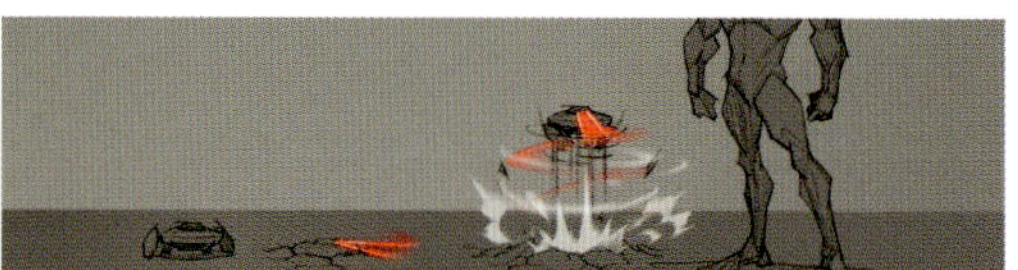
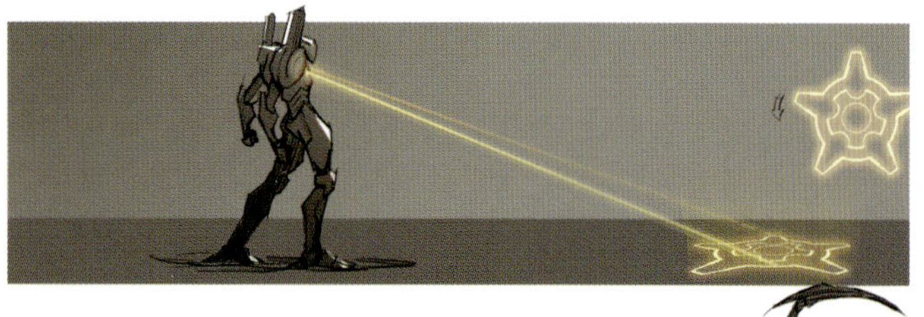
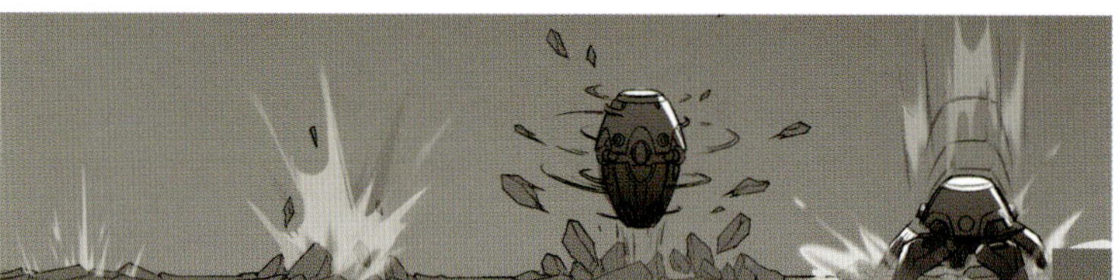
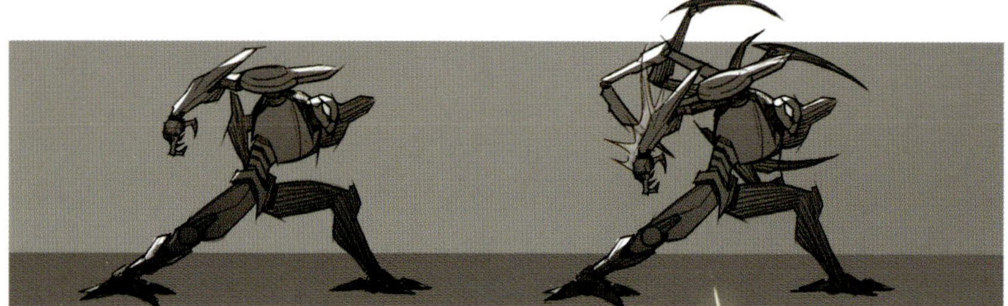
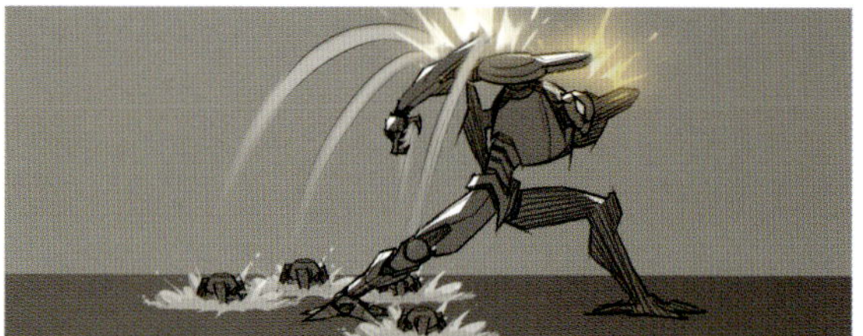
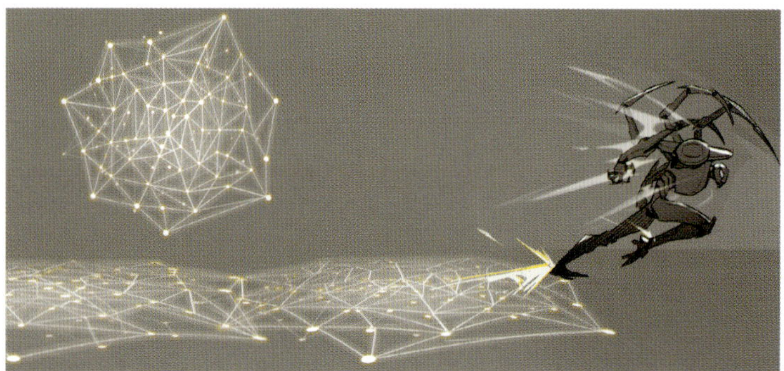
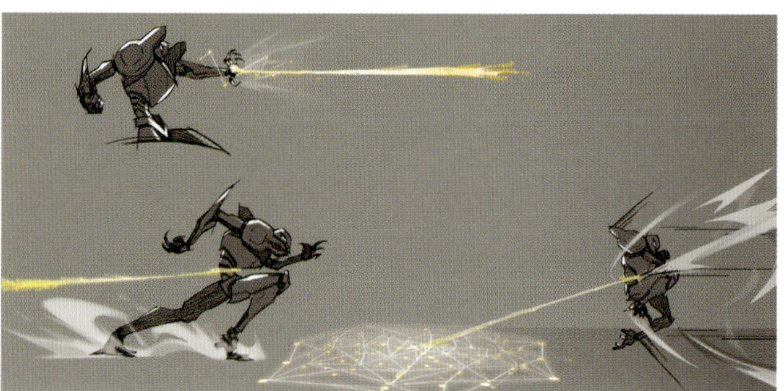

PENI PARKER: ABILITIES

Peni can expertly control the SP//dr in battle, as the mech is equipped with various high-tech devices and weapons, providing her with formidable combat capabilities.

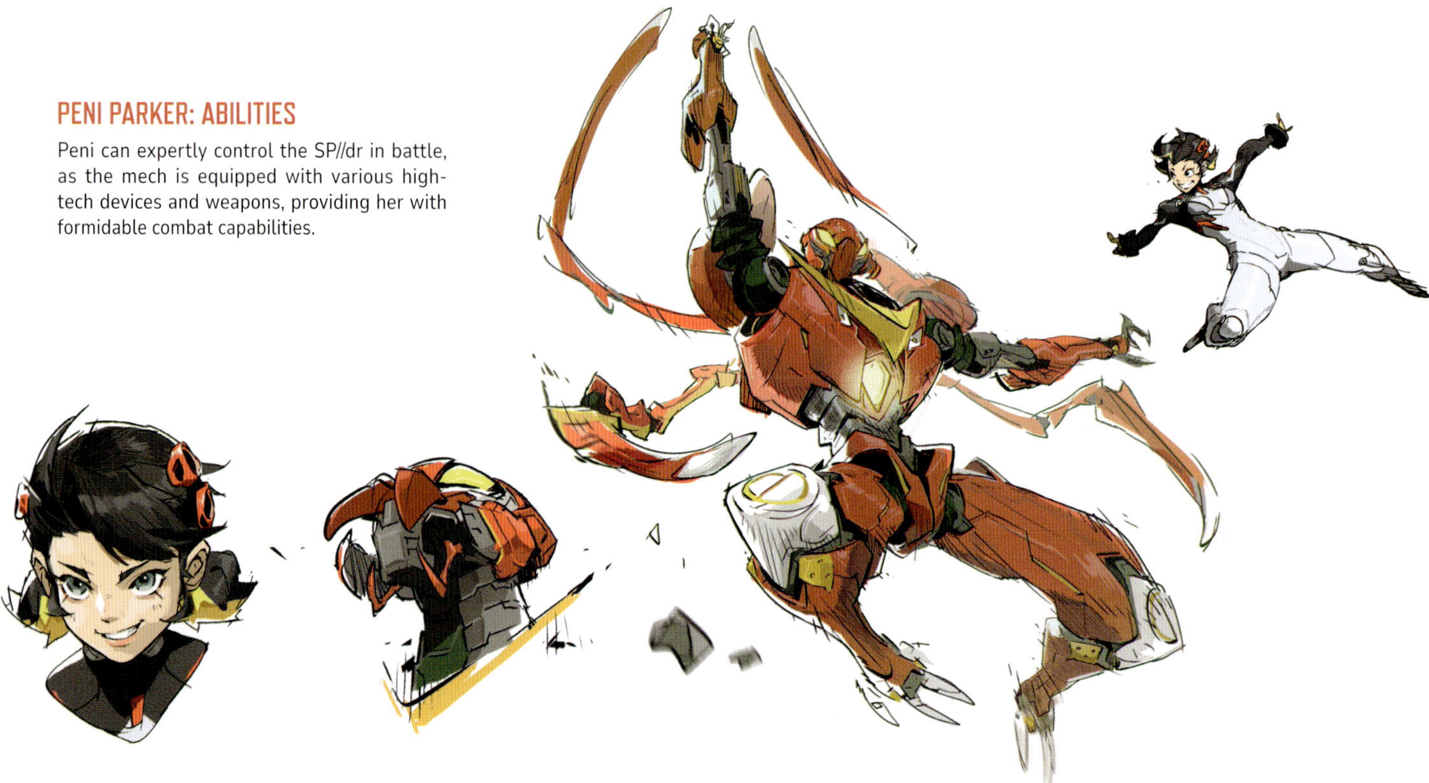

PENI PARKER: COSMETIC VARIETY

In addition to basic color changes, we've added traditional Japanese patterns to the SP//dr mech and Peni's outfit. The cool blue-and-white color scheme promises a unique mech-piloting experience.

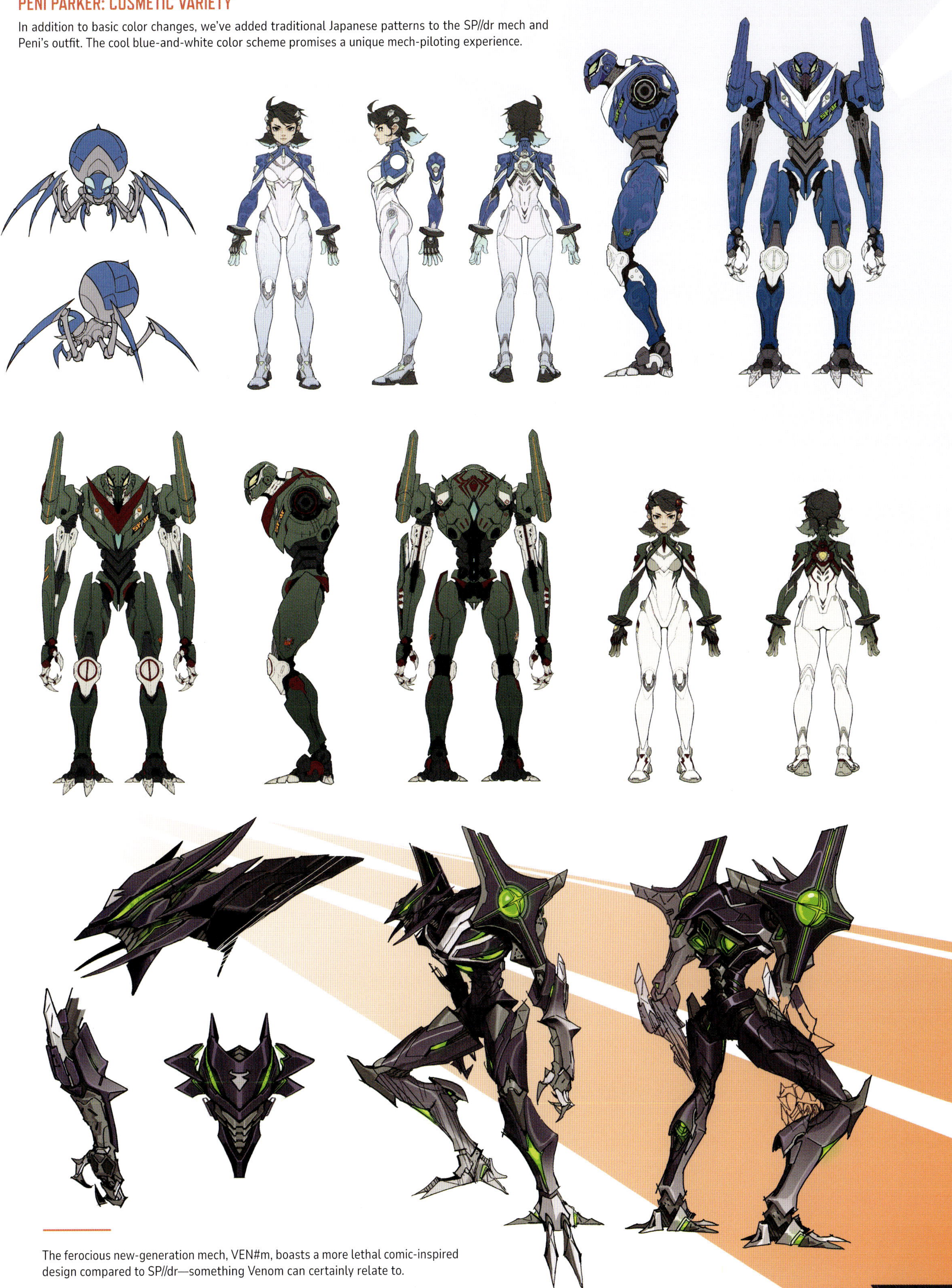

The ferocious new-generation mech, VEN#m, boasts a more lethal comic-inspired design compared to SP//dr—something Venom can certainly relate to.

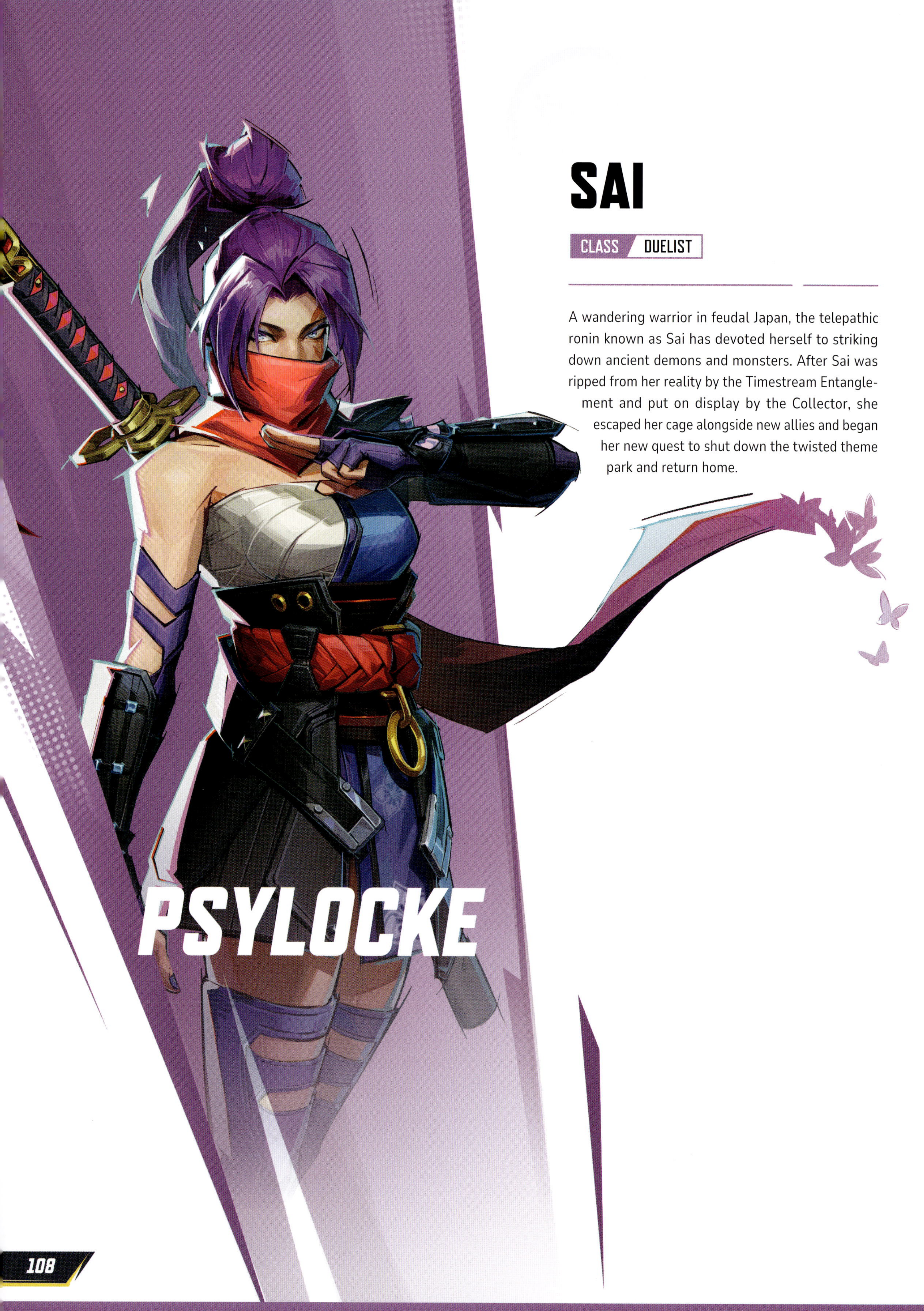

SAI

CLASS / DUELIST

A wandering warrior in feudal Japan, the telepathic ronin known as Sai has devoted herself to striking down ancient demons and monsters. After Sai was ripped from her reality by the Timestream Entanglement and put on display by the Collector, she escaped her cage alongside new allies and began her new quest to shut down the twisted theme park and return home.

Inspired by the adventurous Sai, created by Peach Momoko, Psylocke is an assassin who wields psionic weapons, blending traditional ninja movements with mutant modernity.

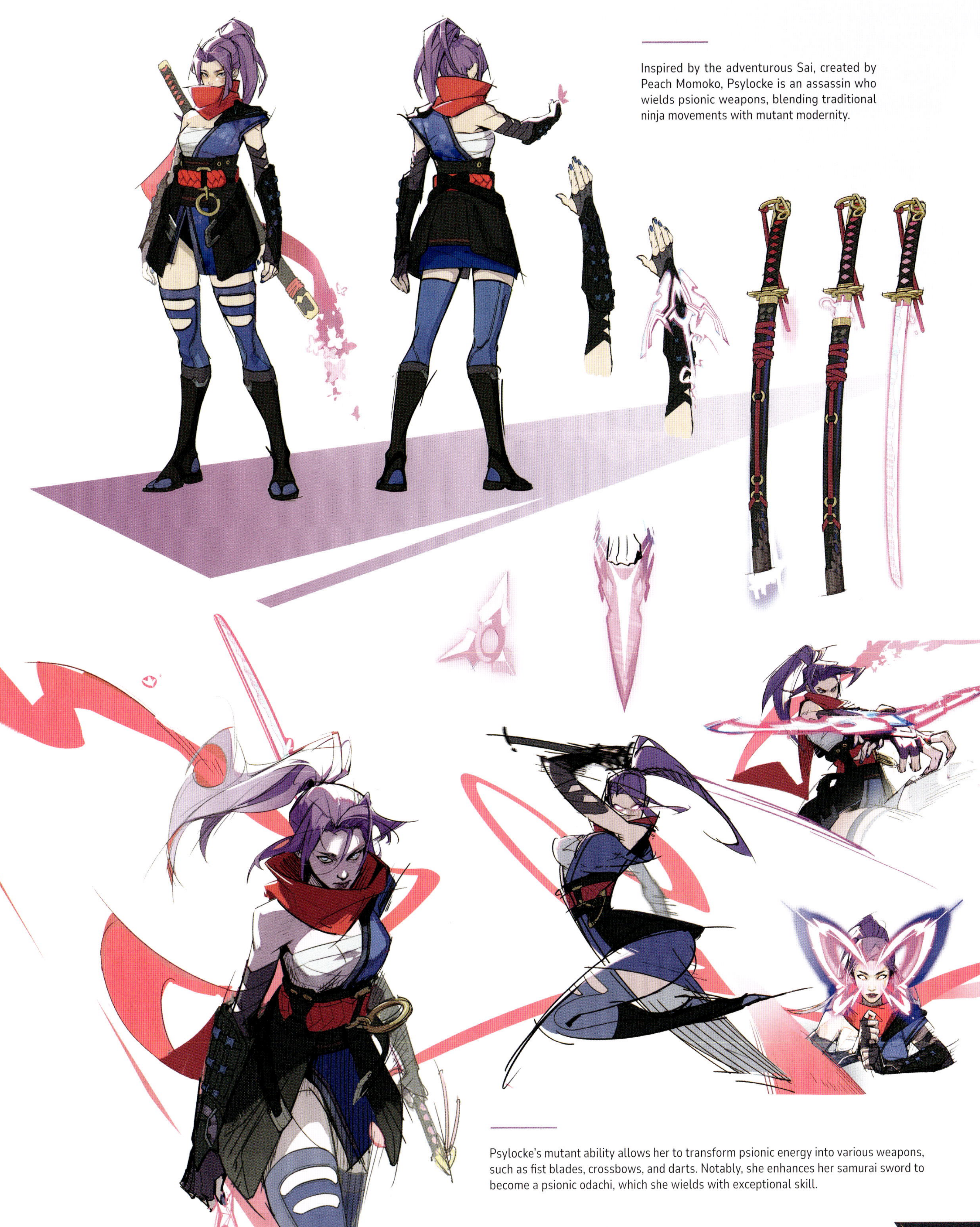

Psylocke's mutant ability allows her to transform psionic energy into various weapons, such as fist blades, crossbows, and darts. Notably, she enhances her samurai sword to become a psionic odachi, which she wields with exceptional skill.

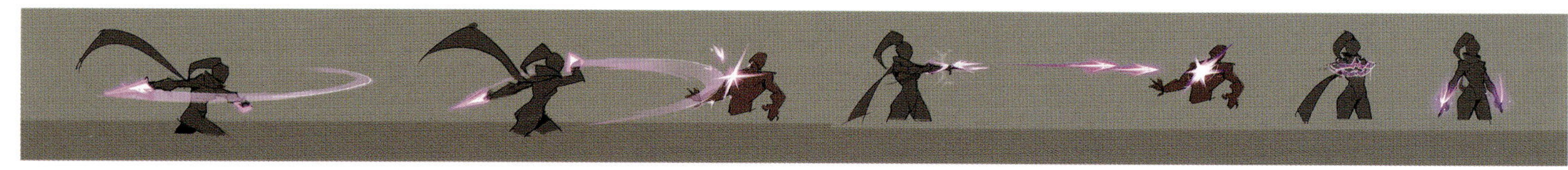

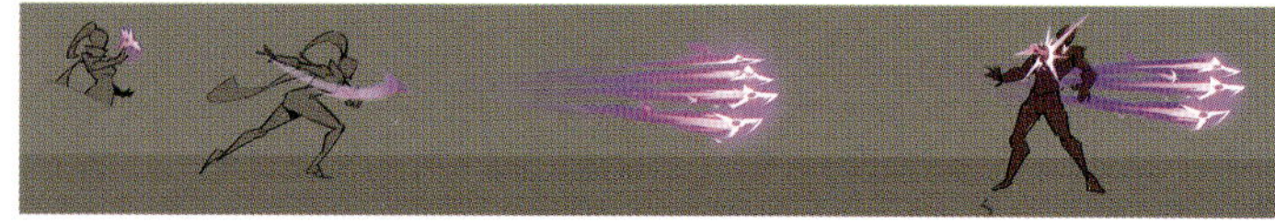

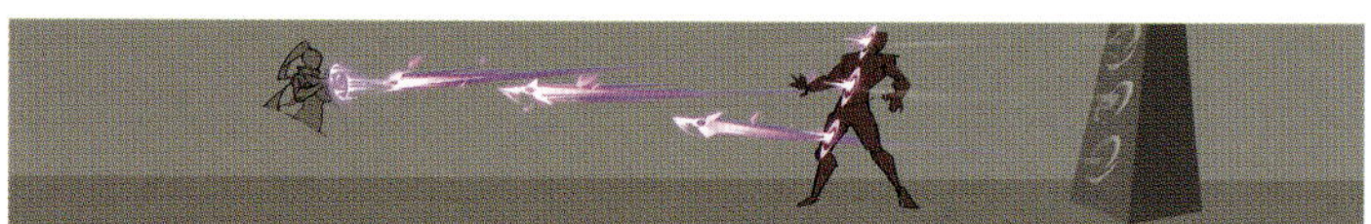

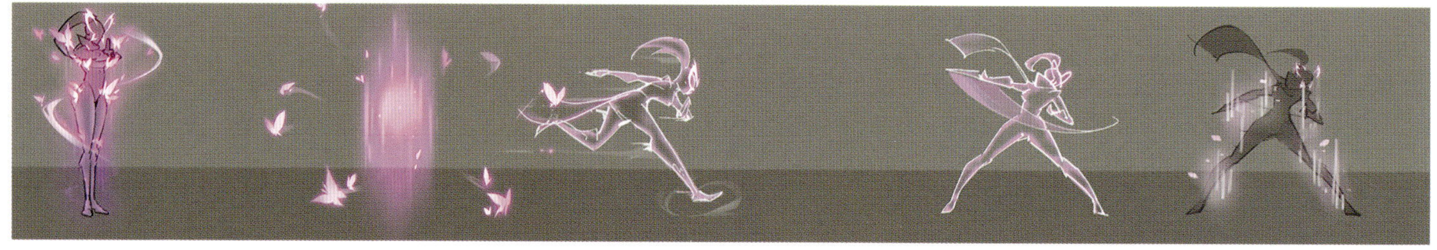

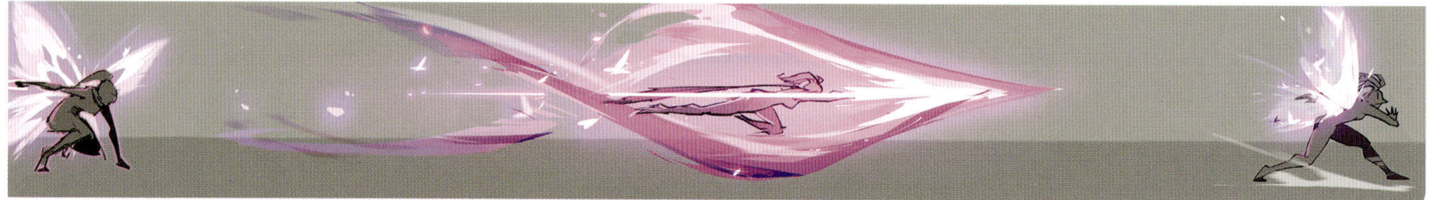

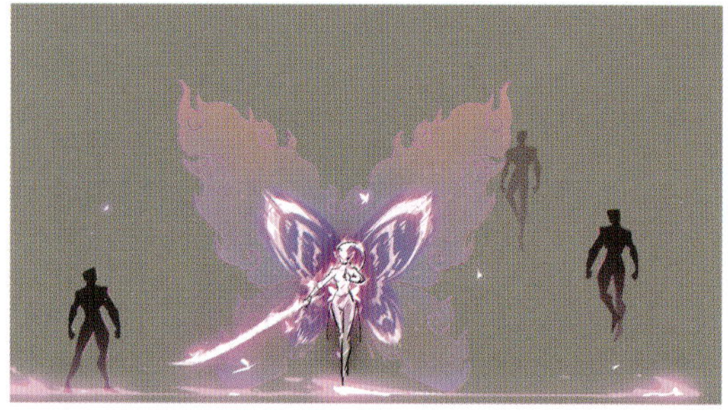

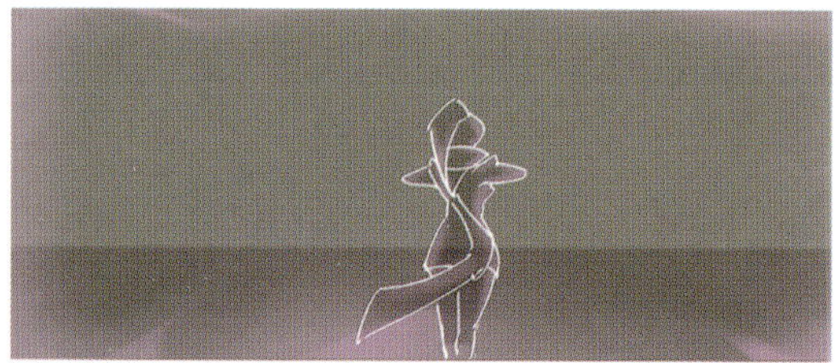

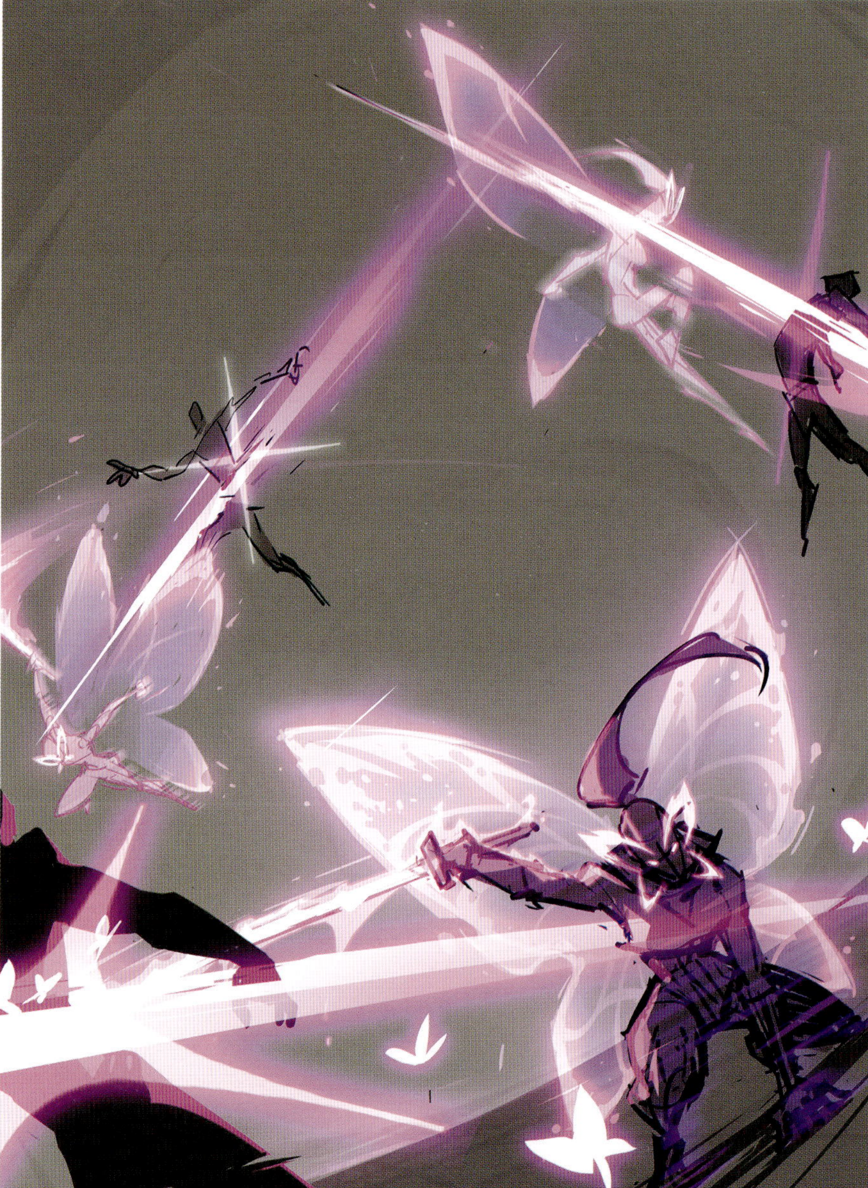

PSYLOCKE: ABILITIES

Psylocke possesses the ability to materialize her psychic powers, crafting an array of psionic weapons to equip herself for combat, which enables her to navigate and engage in diverse and challenging combat environments with ease.

PSYLOCKE: COSMETIC VARIETY

We added a variety of butterfly patterns to the classic comic costume of Psylocke for our game to give her some personalized embellishments and enhance the traditional bodysuit.

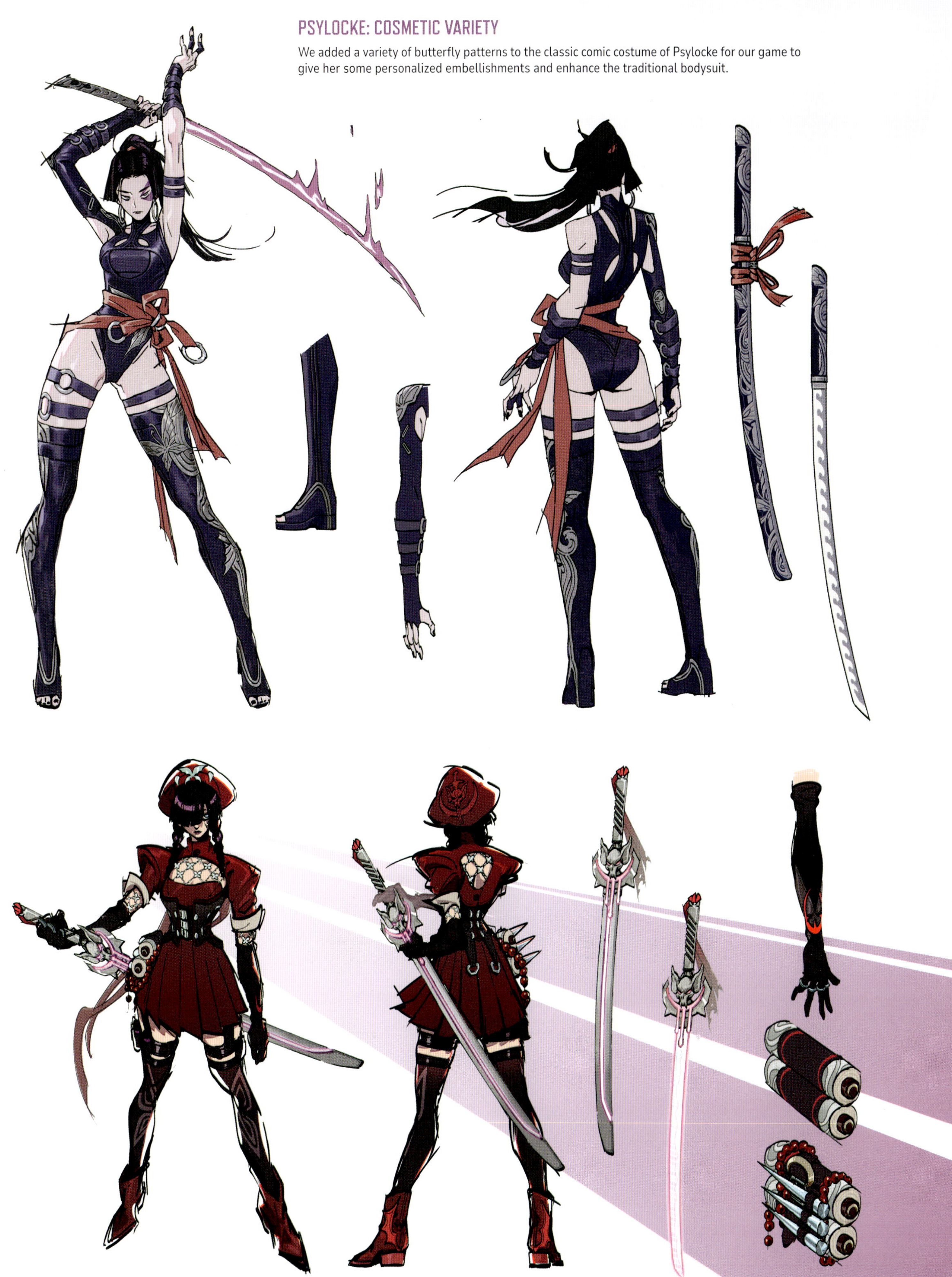

FRANK CASTLE

CLASS / DUELIST

Caught in the crossfire of a mob hit that killed his family, Frank Castle took the law into his own hands as the Punisher, clinging to life through sheer force of will and his unquenchable thirst for vengeance. Unwilling to let more innocents suffer at the hands of criminals, the Punisher has continued his war into the world of 2099 thanks to an experimental serum that vastly extended his lifespan, putting him at odds with Alchemax, Public Eye, and innumerable other futuristic forces.

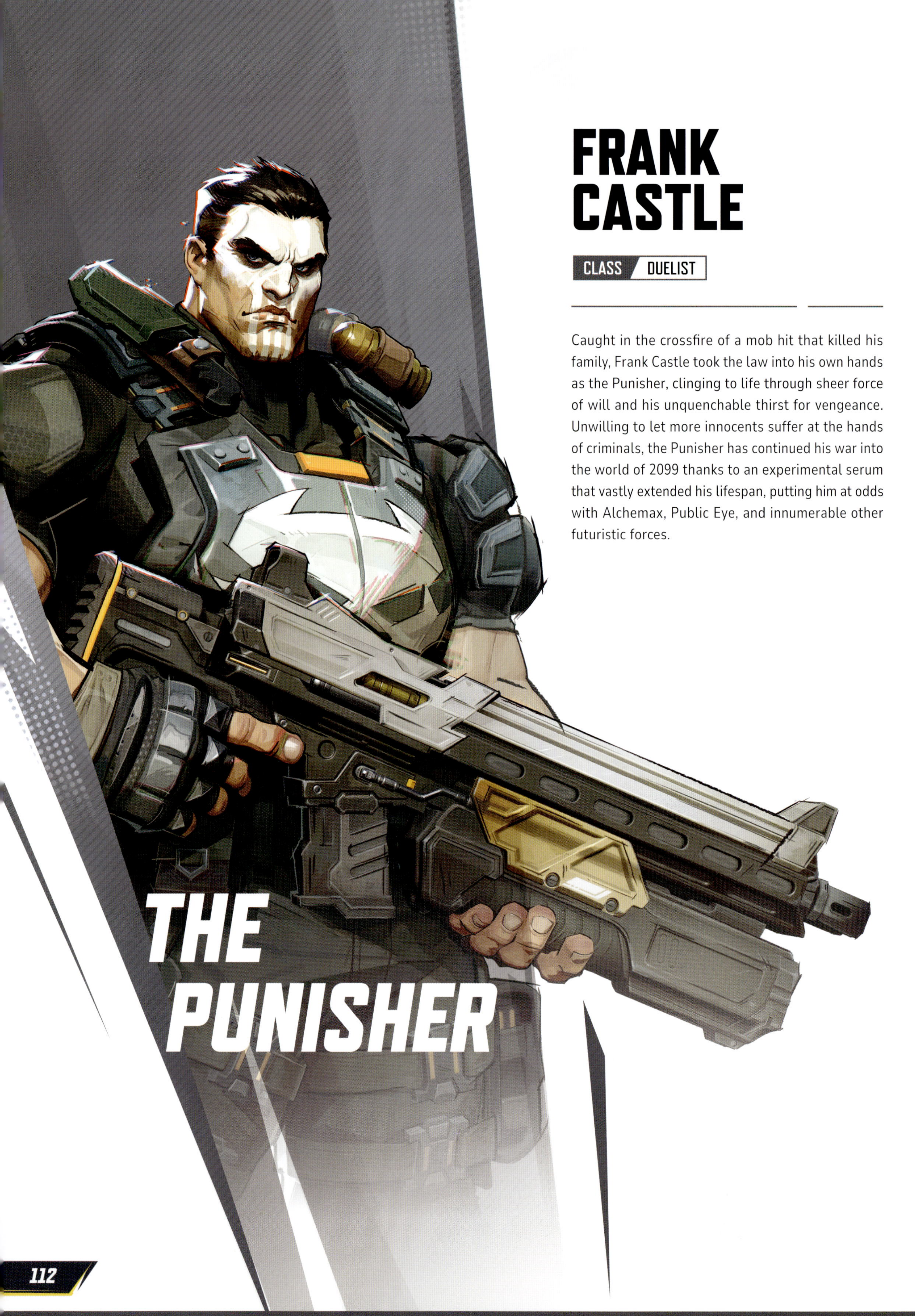

As the Punisher, Frank Castle skillfully wields various weapons, standing unwavering on the battlefield against countless super-powered foes until the last bullet is spent!

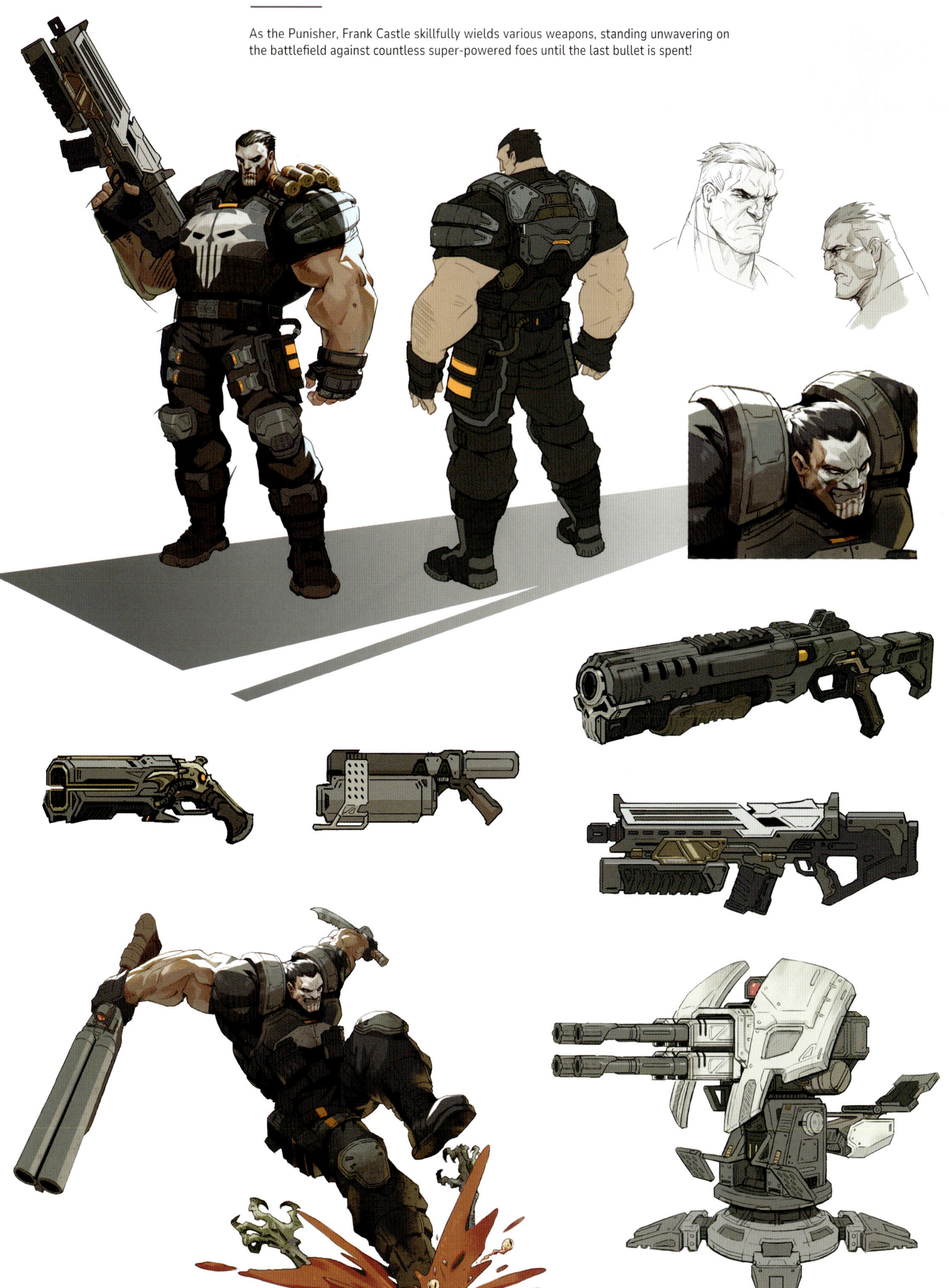

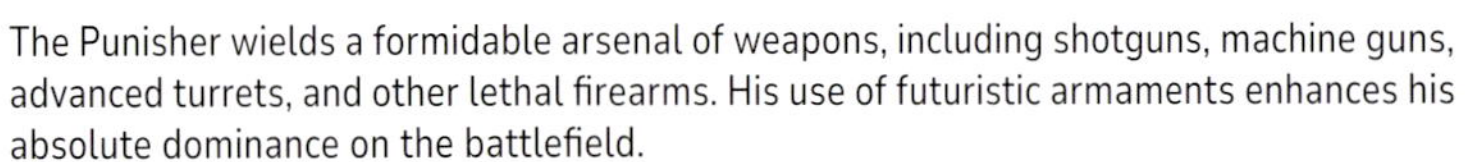

PUNISHER: ABILITIES

The Punisher wields a formidable arsenal of weapons, including shotguns, machine guns, advanced turrets, and other lethal firearms. His use of futuristic armaments enhances his absolute dominance on the battlefield.

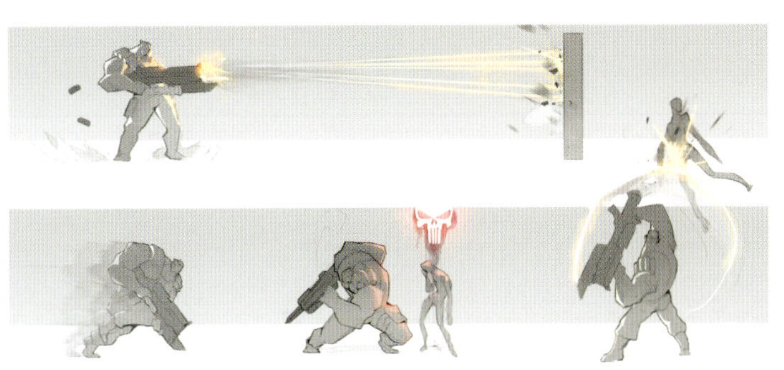

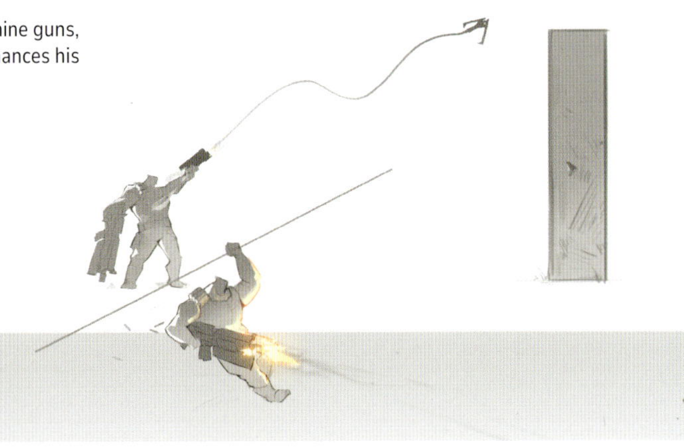

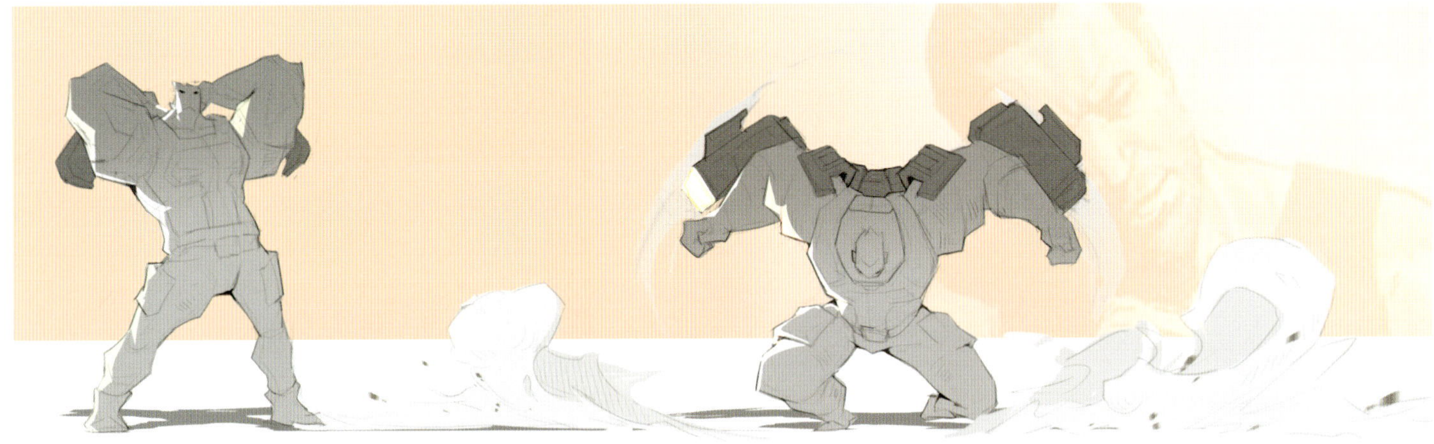

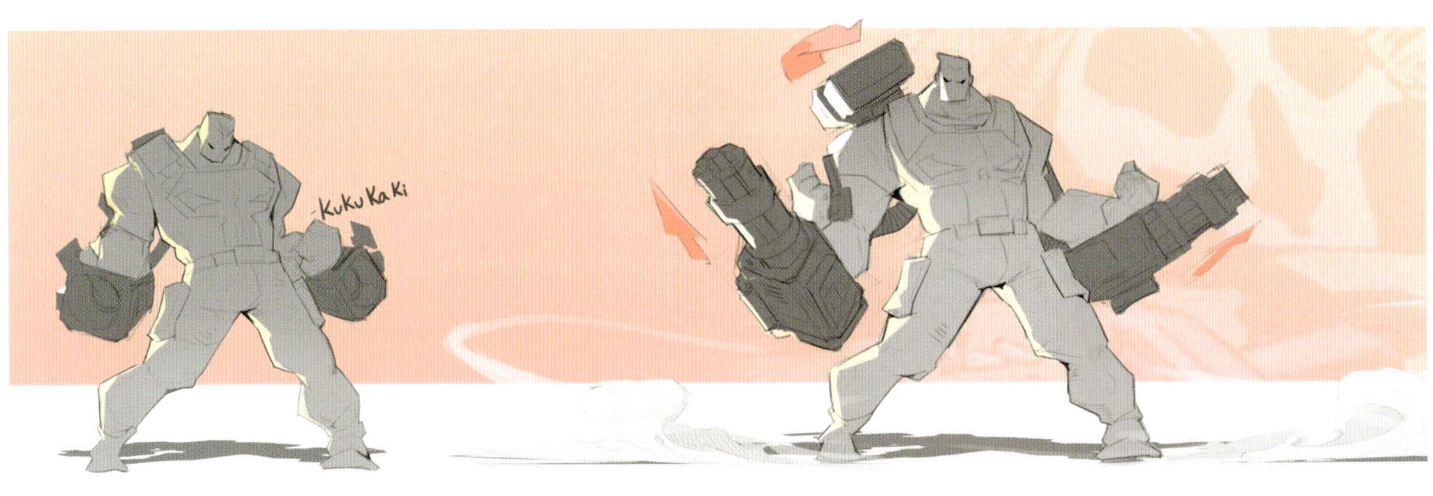

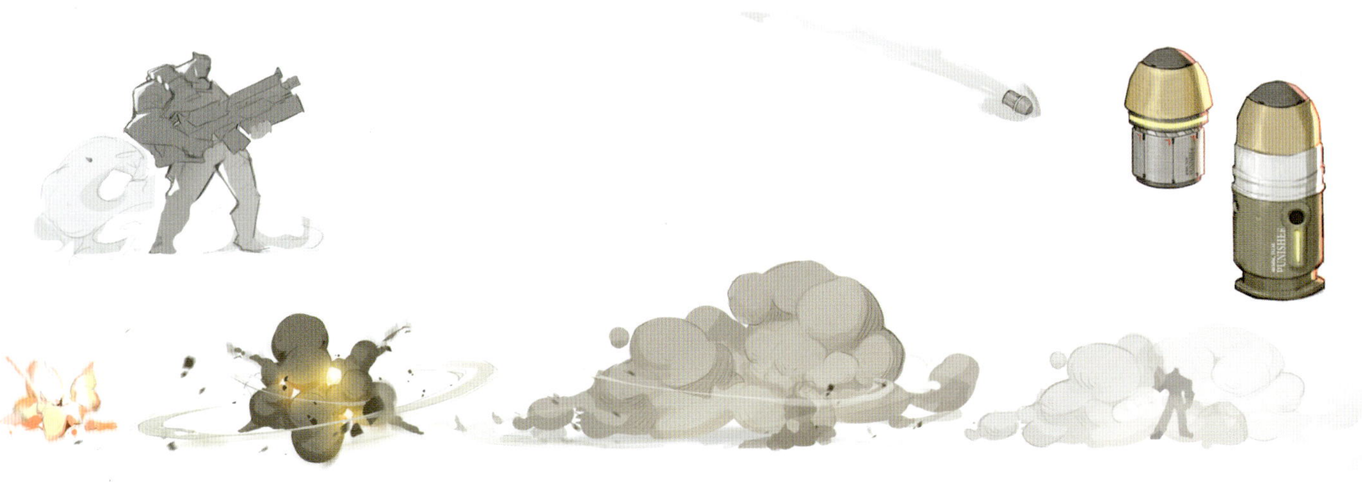

PUNISHER: COSMETIC VARIETY

The Punisher of the *Thunderbolts* era dons a dark uniform; the skull on his chest shines in a bright red, equipping him with a more menacing ghostly visage.

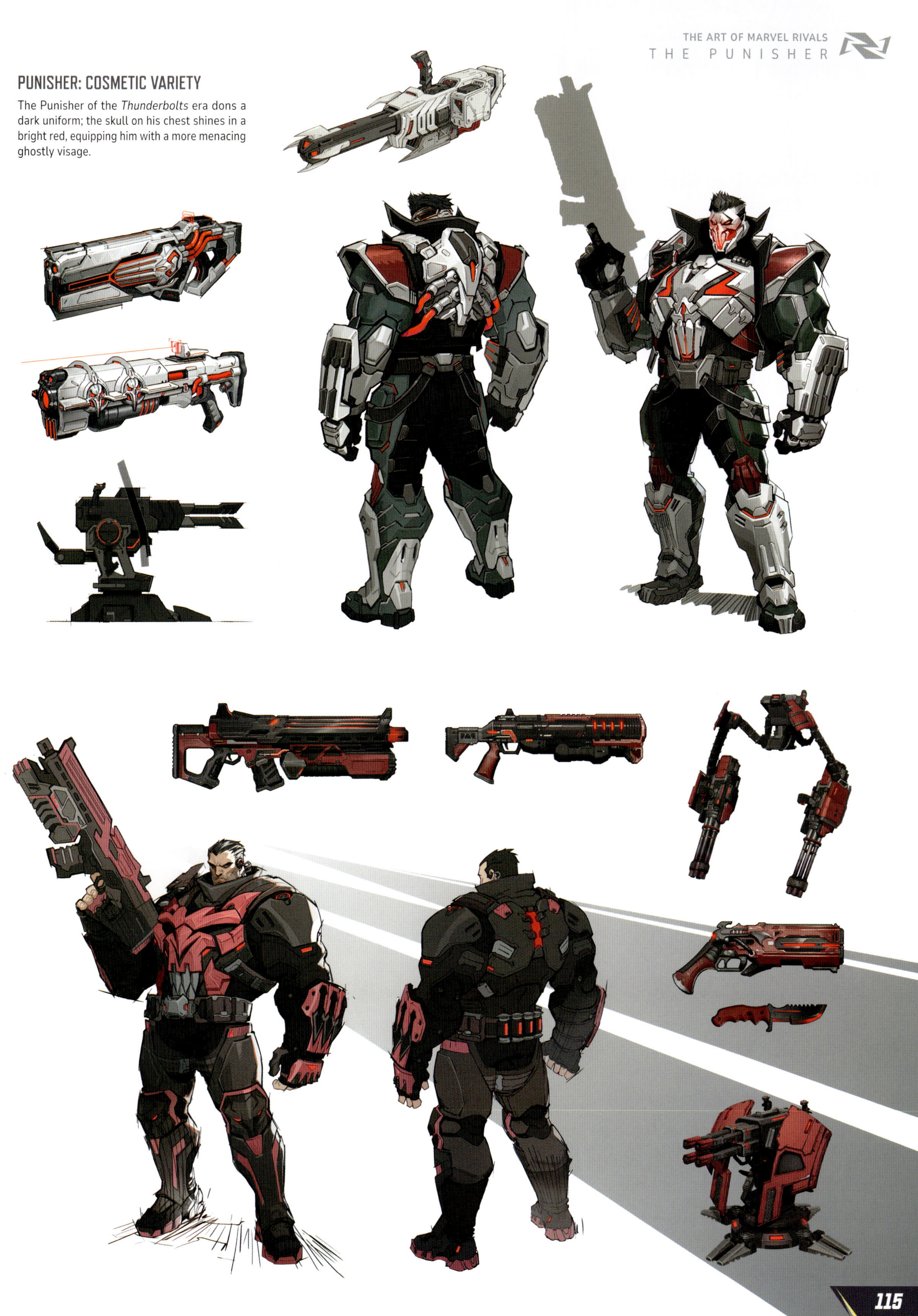

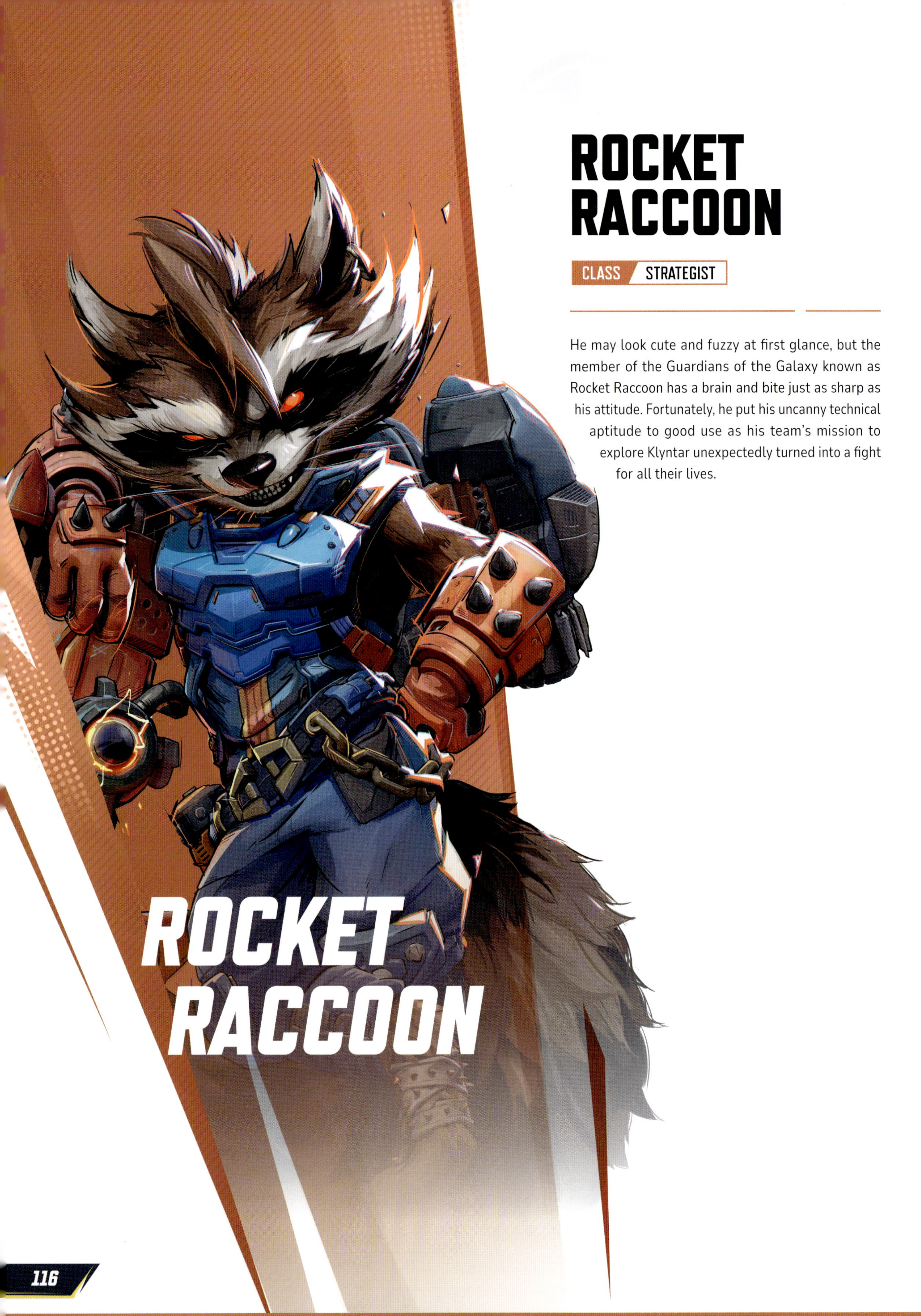

ROCKET RACCOON

CLASS / STRATEGIST

He may look cute and fuzzy at first glance, but the member of the Guardians of the Galaxy known as Rocket Raccoon has a brain and bite just as sharp as his attitude. Fortunately, he put his uncanny technical aptitude to good use as his team's mission to explore Klyntar unexpectedly turned into a fight for all their lives.

Rocket Raccoon is a genius engineer and tactical expert as well as someone with a colorful way with words. Using space technology to assist teammates and shred enemies, he makes sure everyone remembers to never underestimate a raccoon!

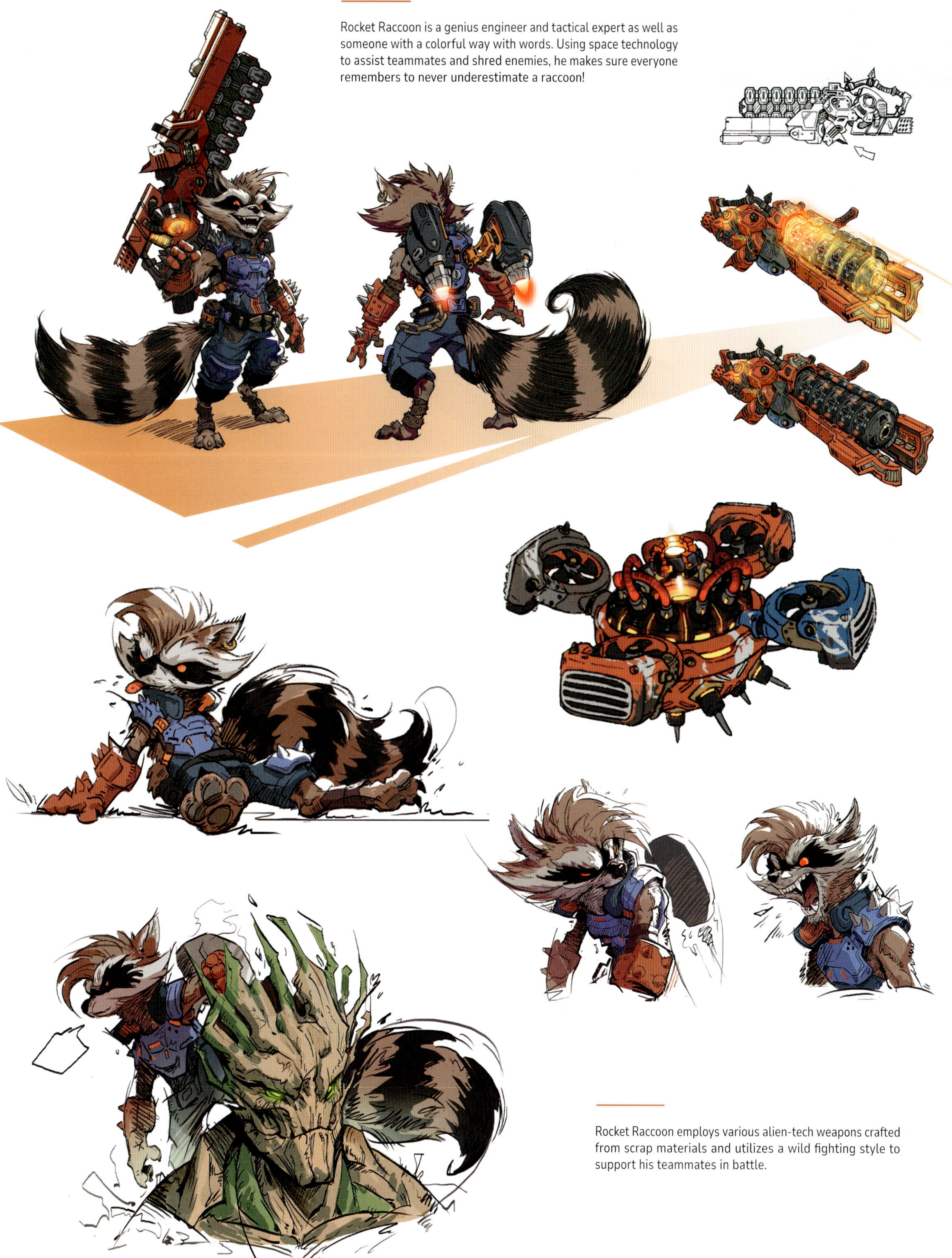

Rocket Raccoon employs various alien-tech weapons crafted from scrap materials and utilizes a wild fighting style to support his teammates in battle.

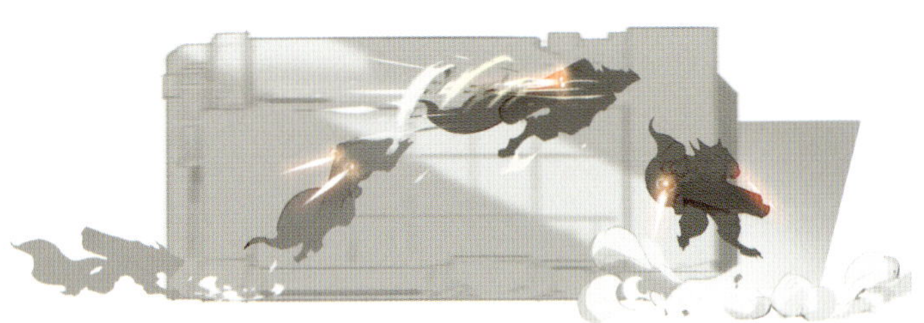
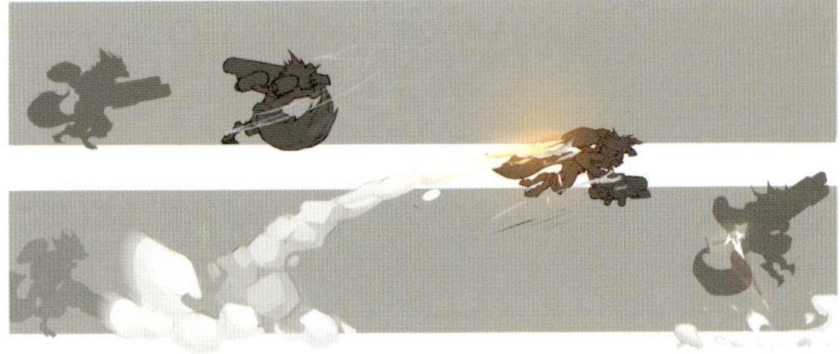

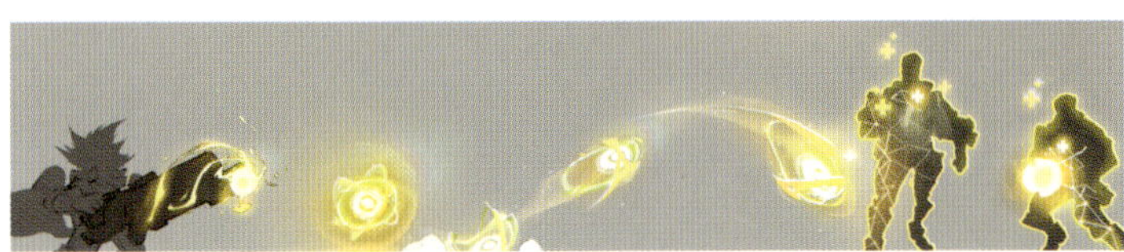

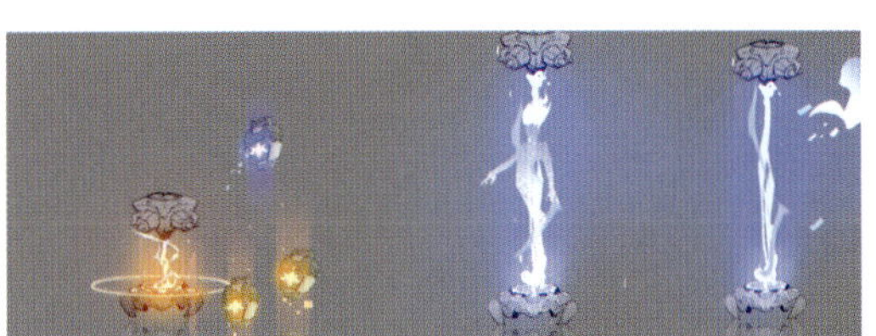
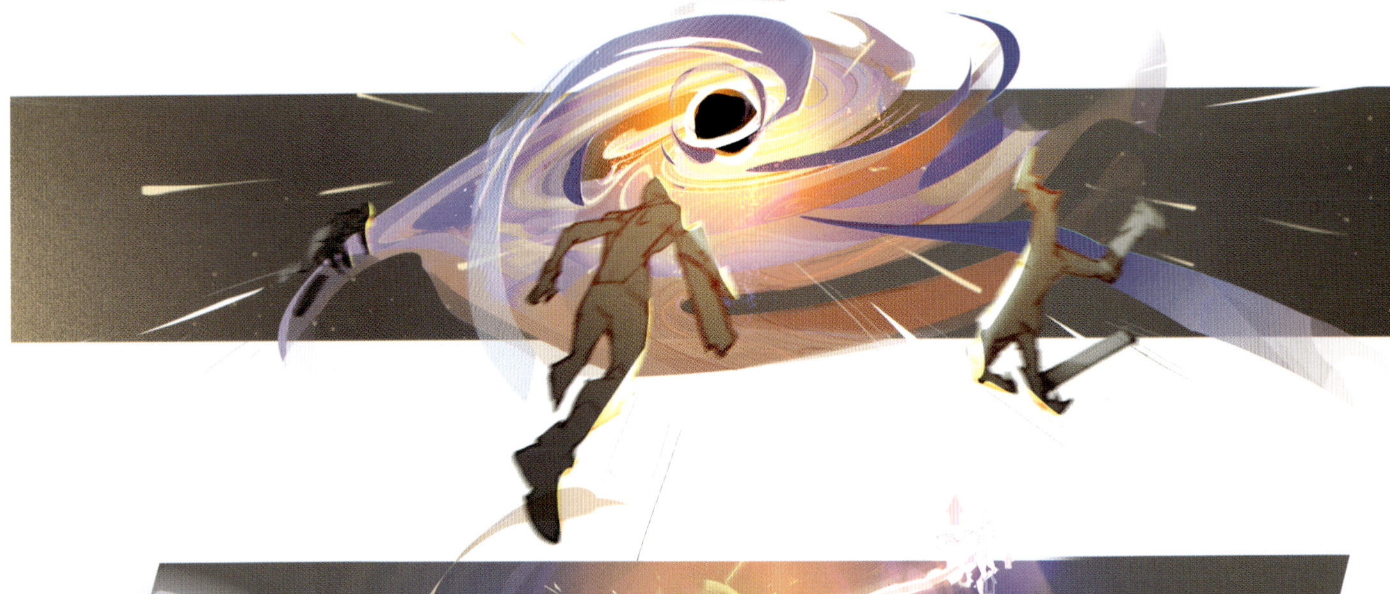
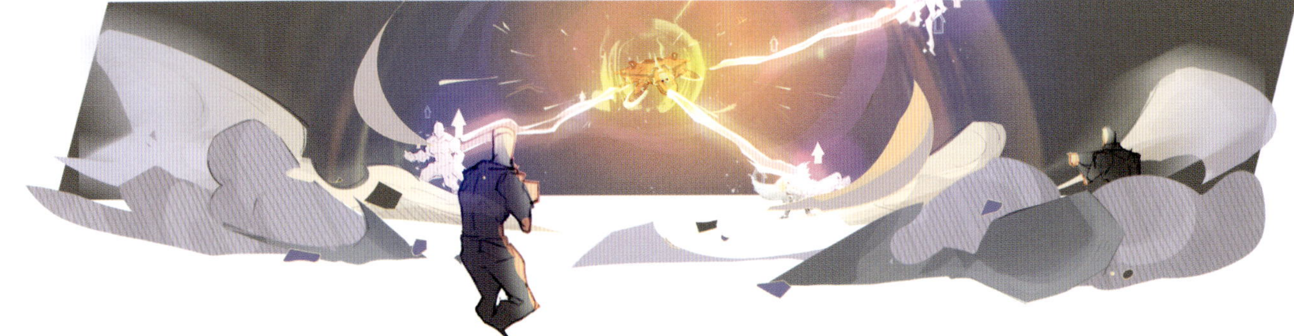

ROCKET RACCOON: ABILITIES

This Guardian of the Galaxy offers stable and dependable support for teammates. With his expertise in space technology, he swiftly maneuvers through parkour on the battlefield, delivering a familiar yet invigorating experience for players.

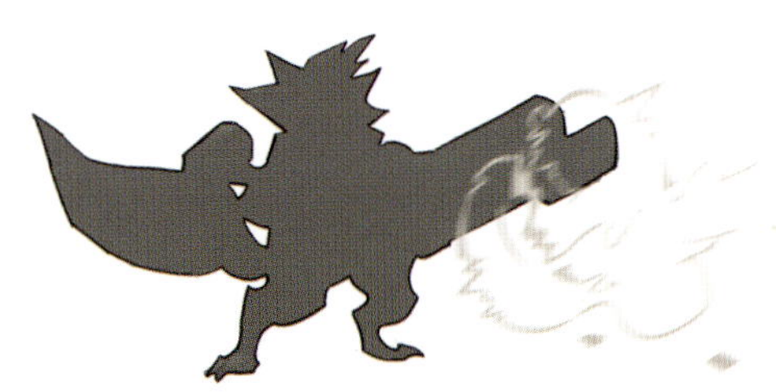
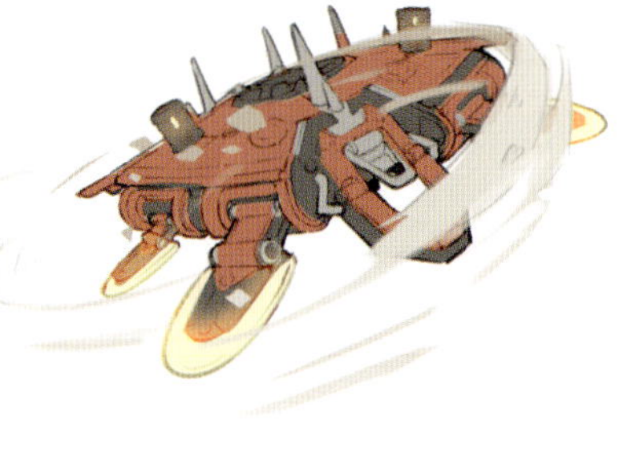

ROCKET RACCOON: COSMETIC VARIETY

The cowboy hat and steam jetpack exemplify a completely original 1872-inspired costume accentuated by his wild flaming-red fur.

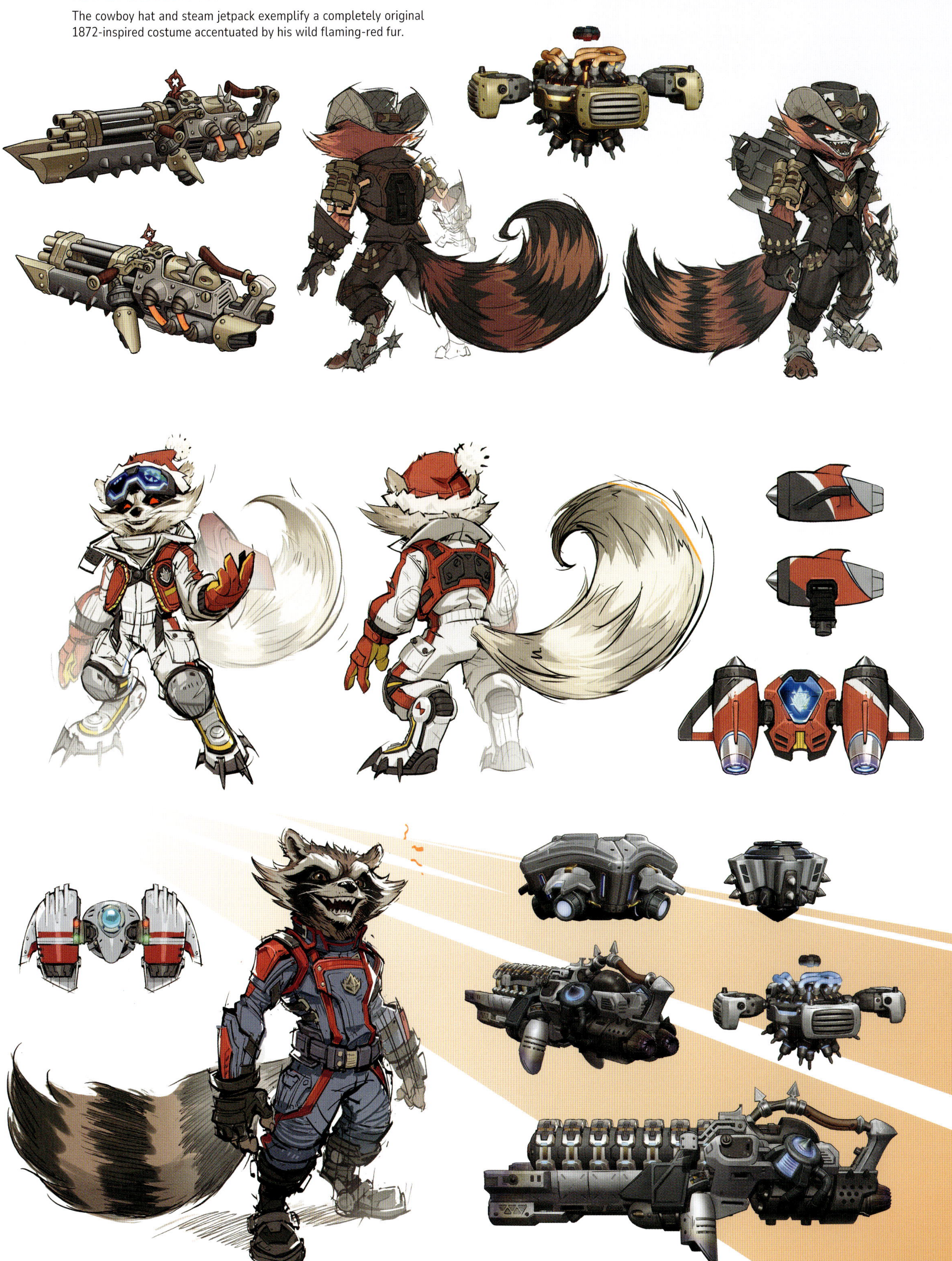

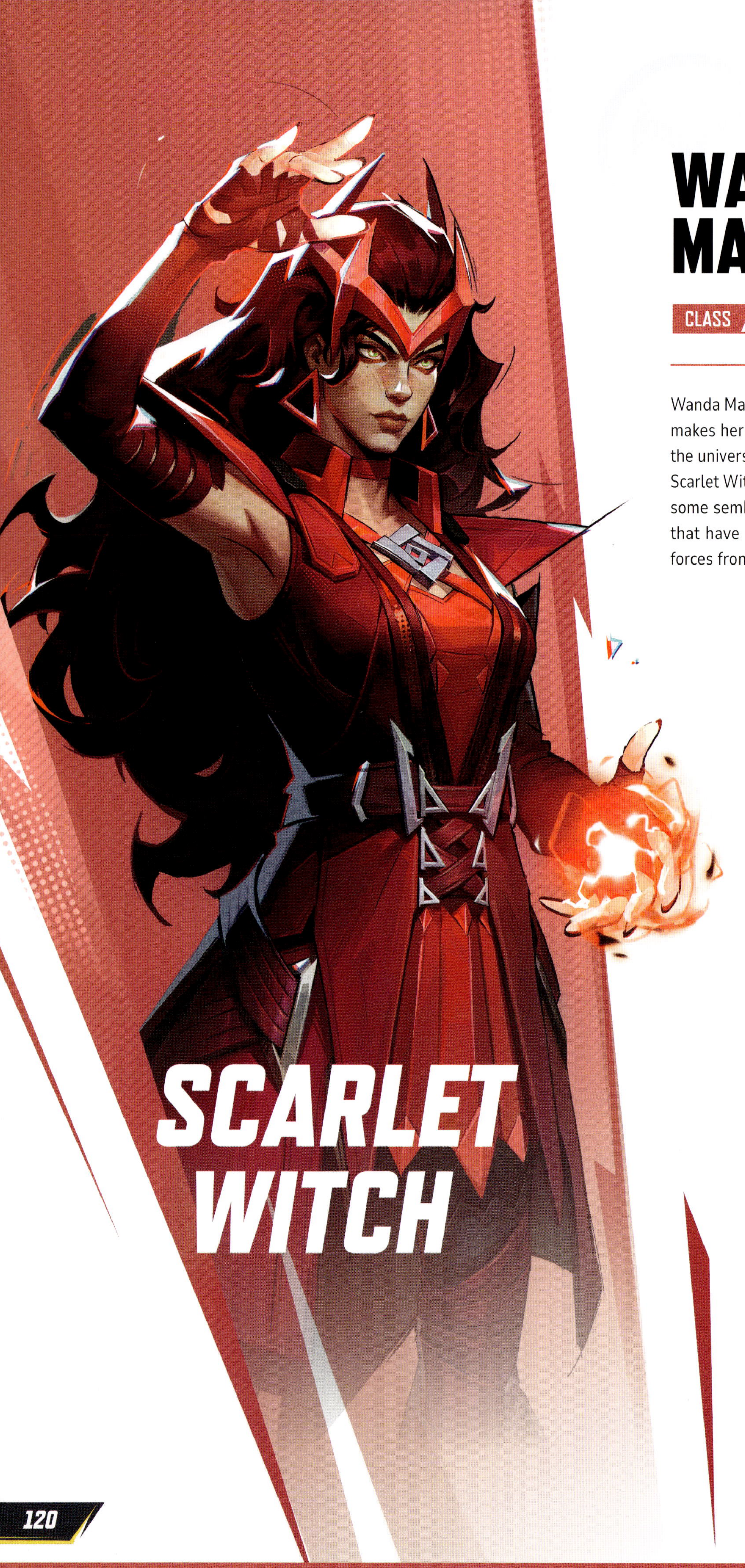

WANDA MAXIMOFF

CLASS / DUELIST

Wanda Maximoff's ability to manipulate chaos magic makes her one of the most powerful living beings in the universe. As the Sorcerer Supreme of her reality, Scarlet Witch seeks to harness that chaos and restore some semblance of order to these disparate worlds that have been brought to the brink of collapse by forces from across all time.

We explored a blend of comic design with a light gothic Romani style, depicting the tall, beautiful, and powerful Scarlet Witch as a mysterious figure who controls chaos energy and magic at her will!

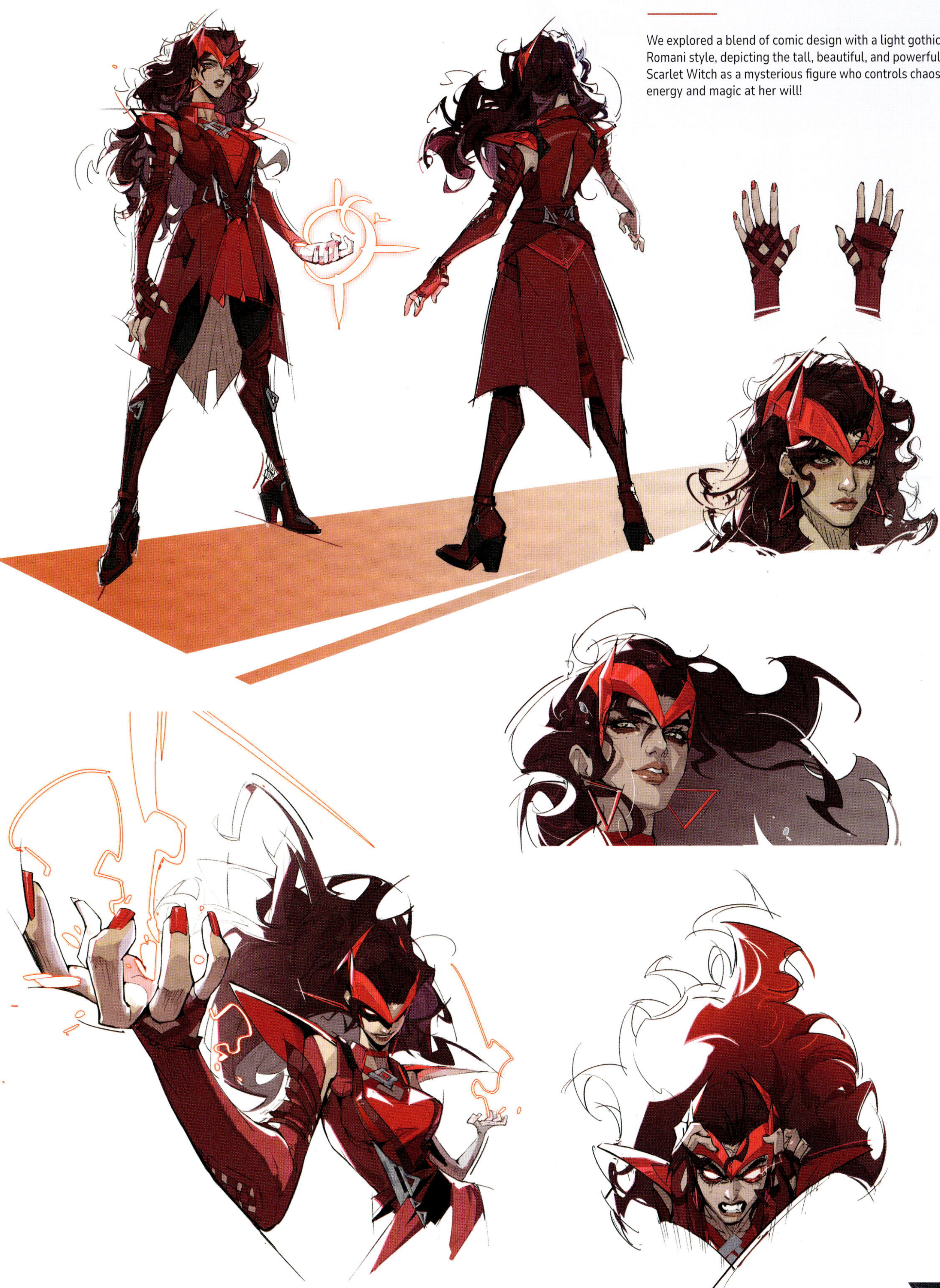

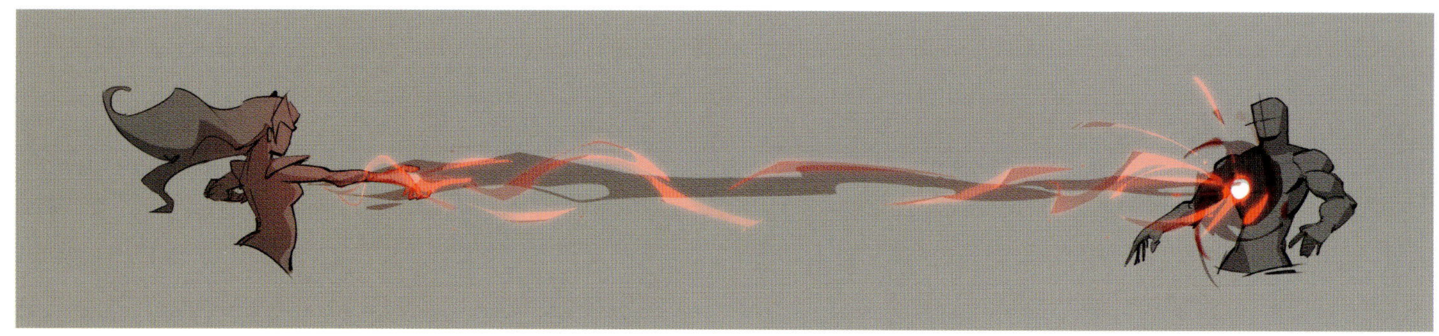

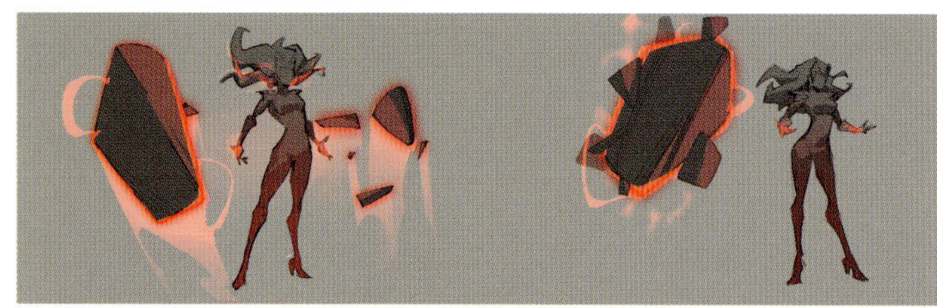

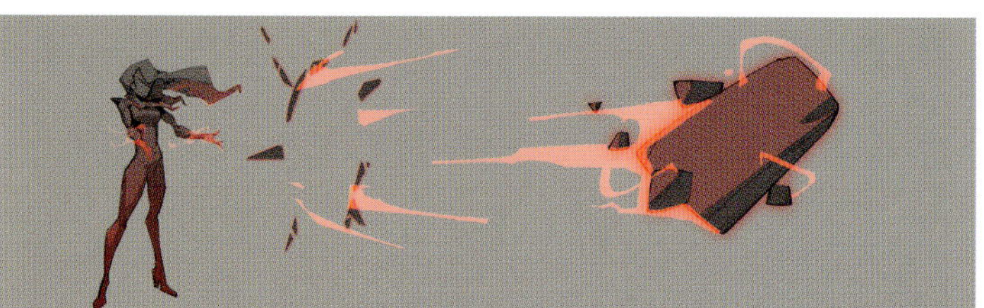

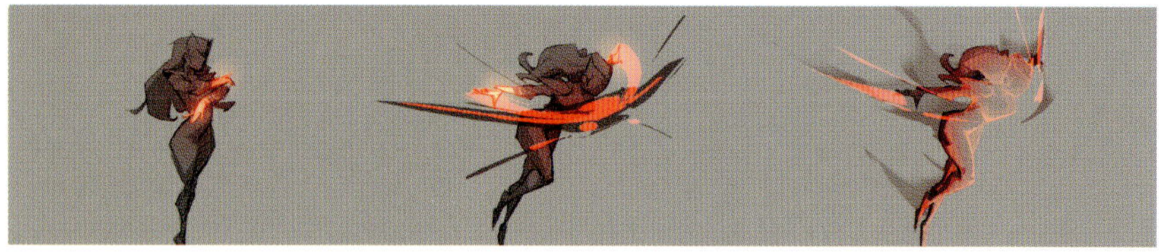

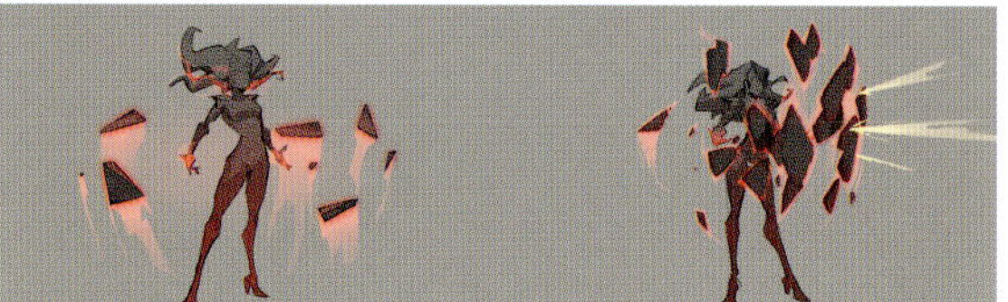

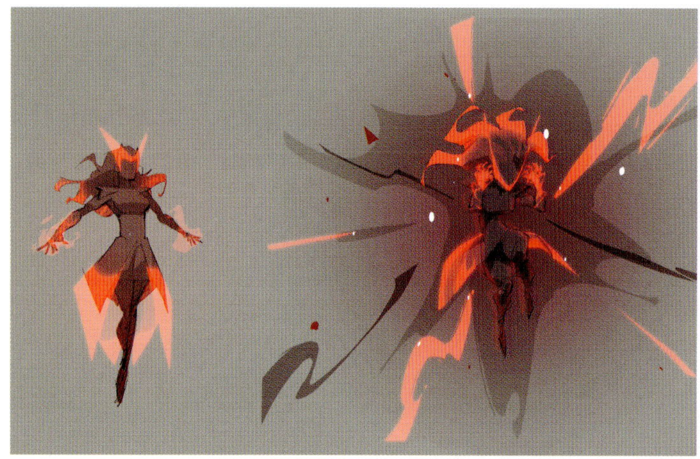

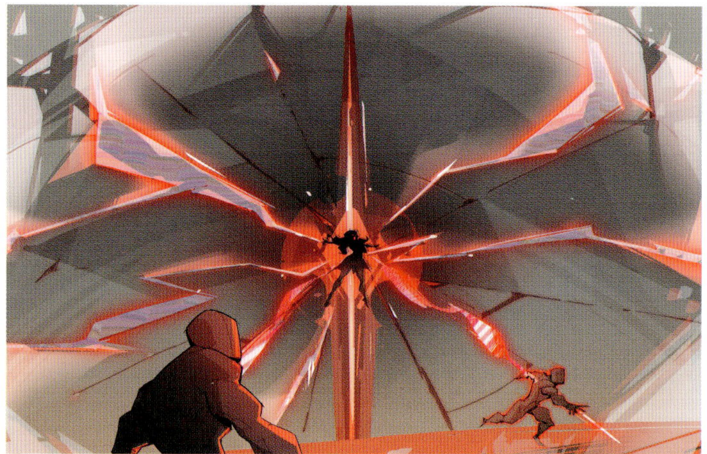

SCARLET WITCH: ABILITIES

Wanda Maximoff can employ chaos magic to absorb and convert the life force of her enemies. Once chaos magic is unleashed, Scarlet Witch's formidable destructive power can completely erase her foes.

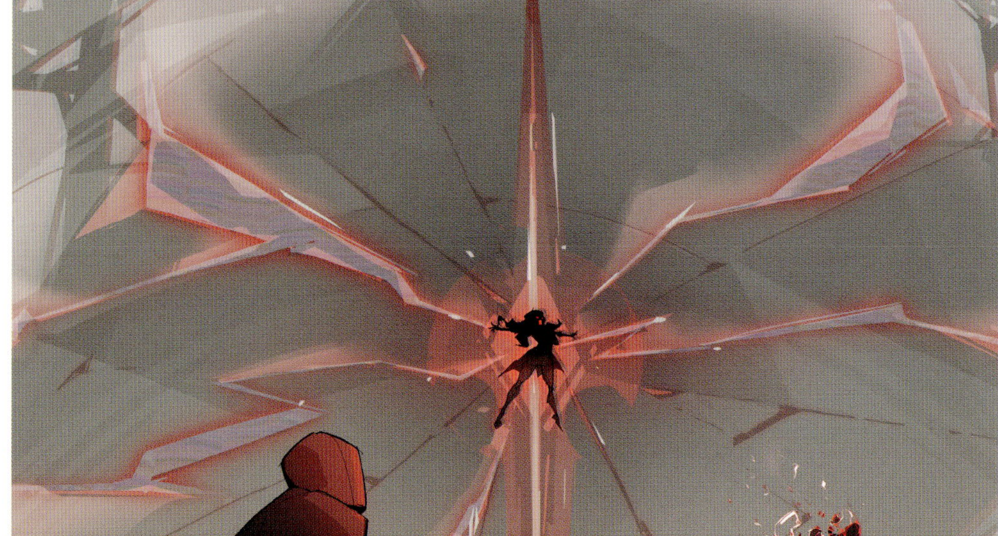

SCARLET WITCH: COSMETIC VARIETY

The gold accessories cascading from her neck to her waist embellish the overall gown. Meanwhile, the starry effects on her hair, boots, and skirt further enhance the witch's mysterious aura.

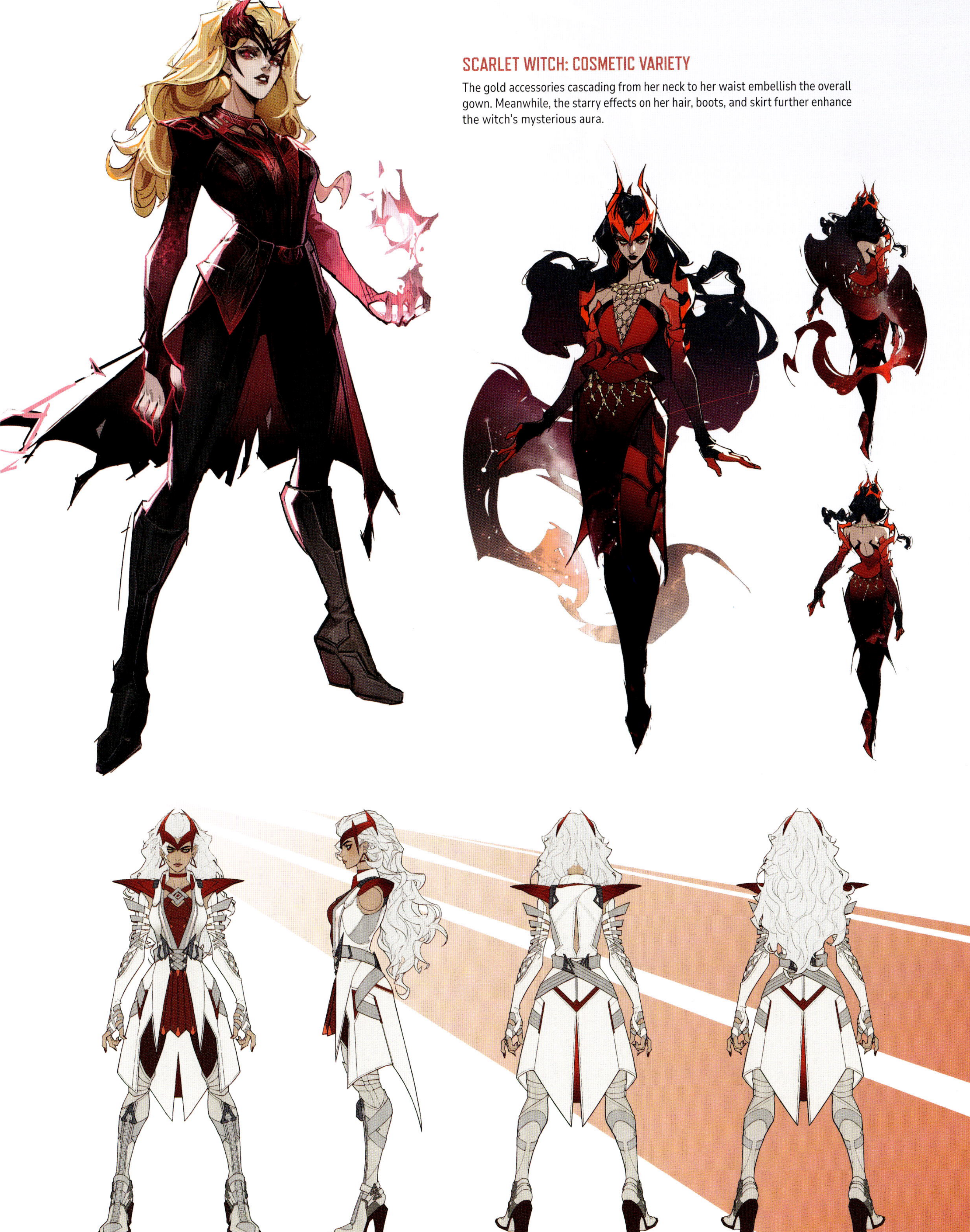

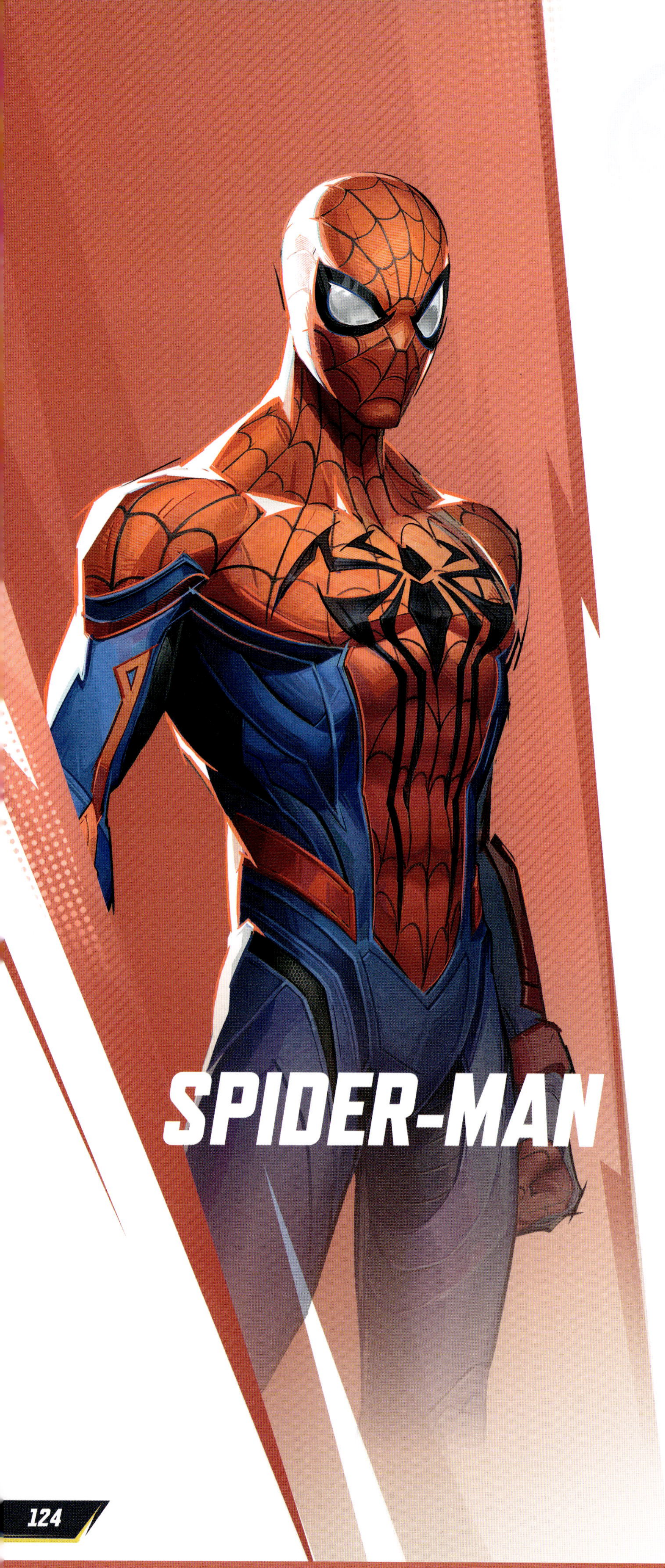

PETER PARKER

CLASS / DUELIST

Bitten by a radioactive spider, young Peter Parker gained the ability to cling to almost any surface, a "spider-sense" that warns him of danger, and the proportional speed, strength, and agility of an arachnid. Now with responsibilities split across all of time, the wall-crawling wonder known as Spider-Man strives to rally New York's heroes to fight against Dracula, all while protecting the Web of Life and Destiny with his fellow Web-Warriors in Tokyo 2099.

The friendly neighborhood Spider-Man, Peter Parker, can swing freely on the battlefield using his webbing. Enemies facing him must beware of his unexpected movement and the beatdown that follows!

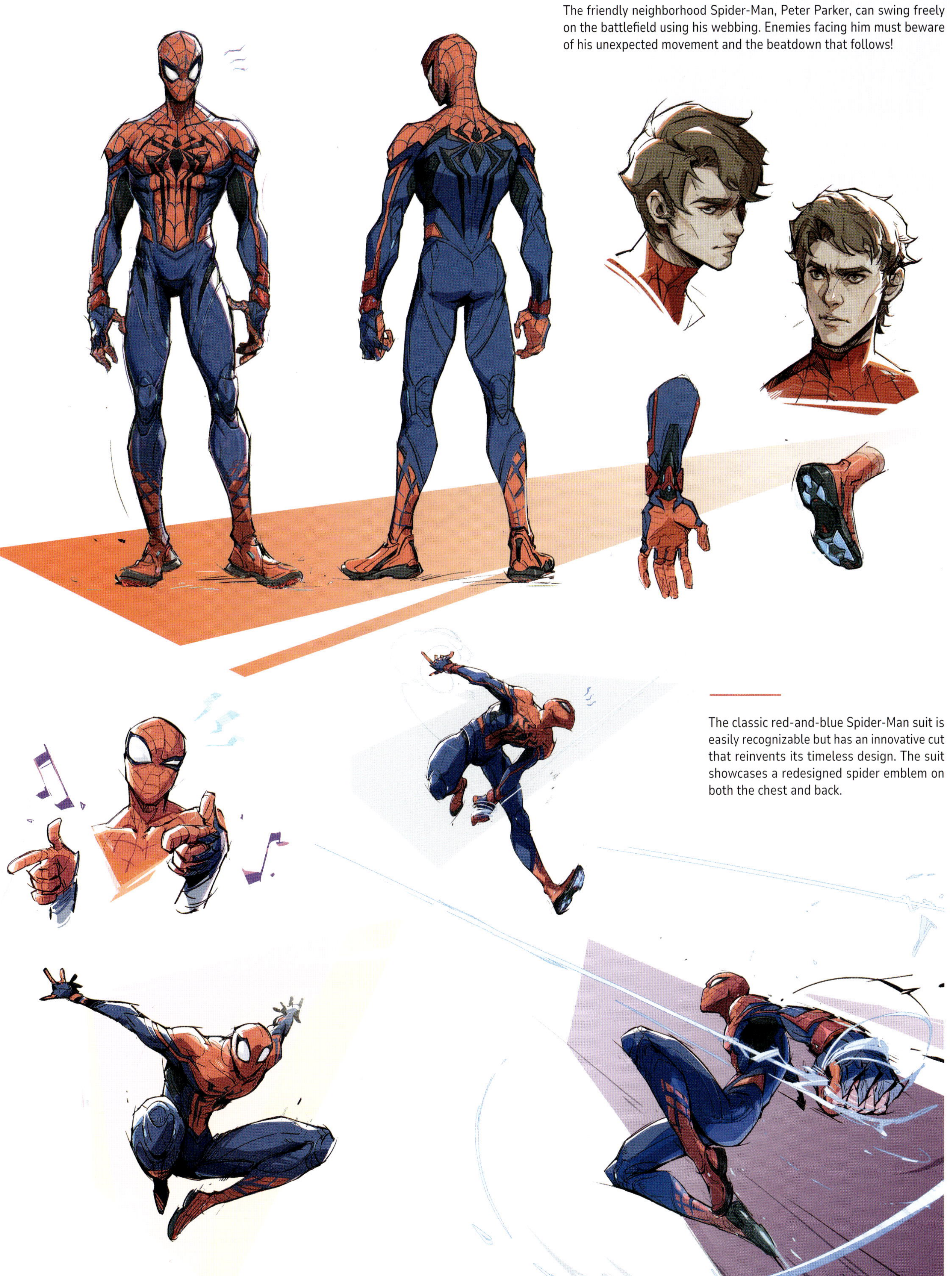

The classic red-and-blue Spider-Man suit is easily recognizable but has an innovative cut that reinvents its timeless design. The suit showcases a redesigned spider emblem on both the chest and back.

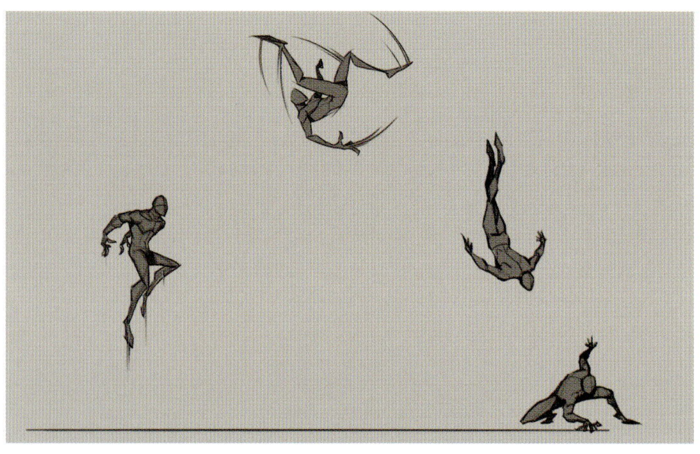

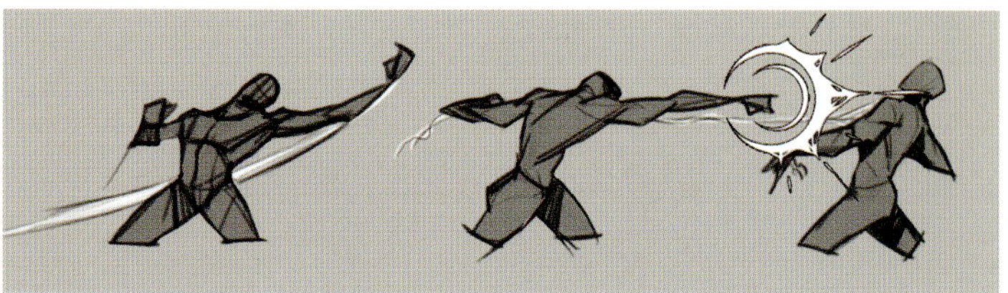

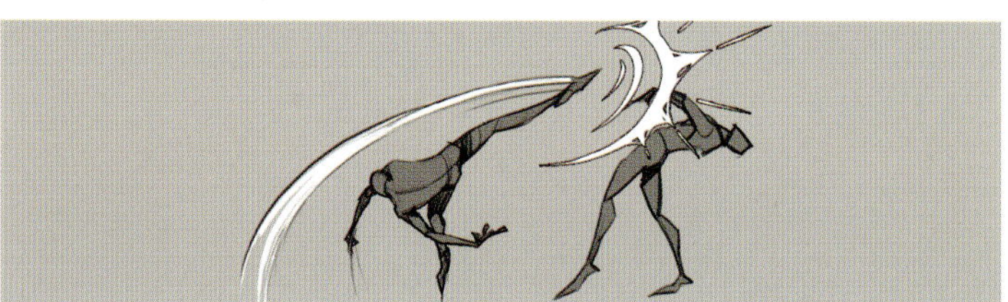

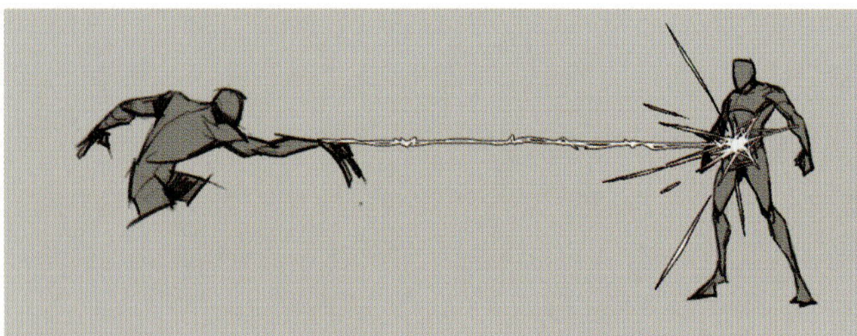

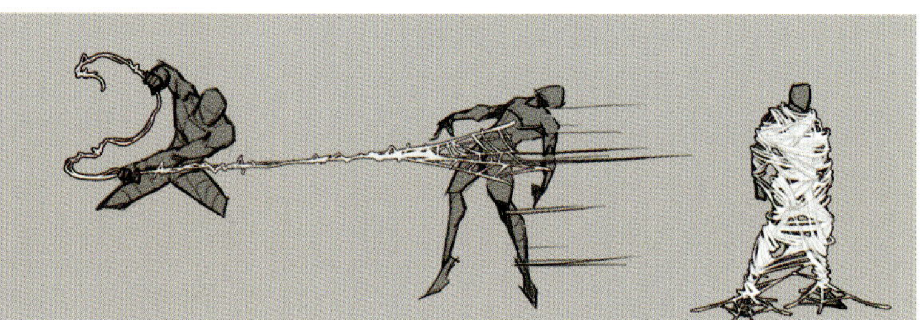

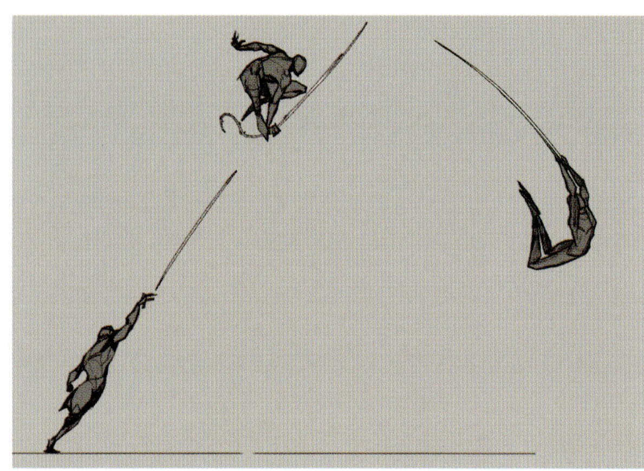

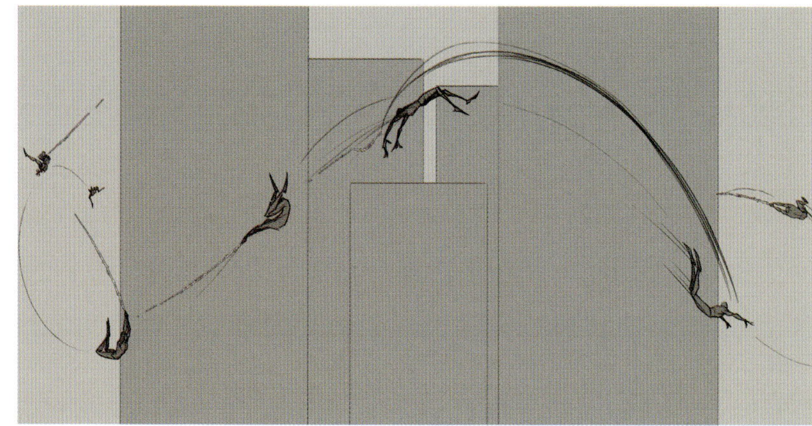

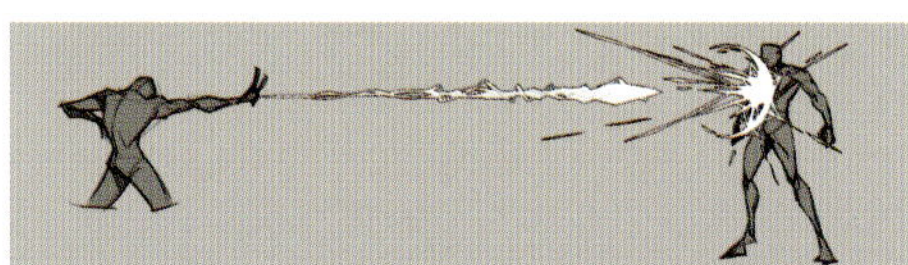

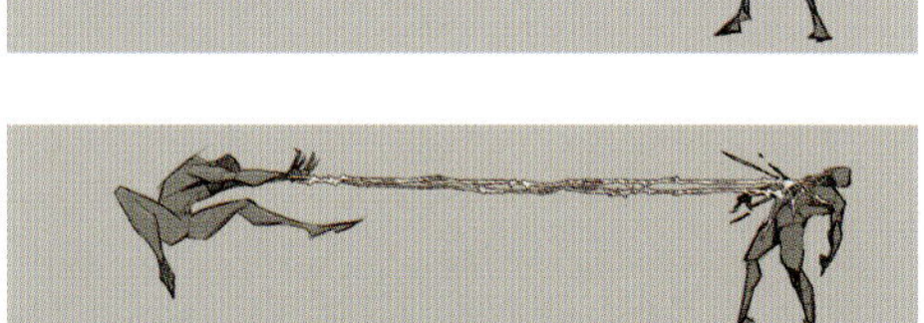

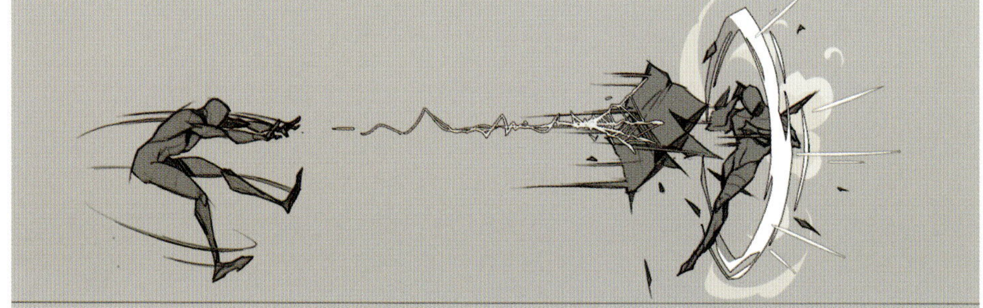

SPIDER-MAN: ABILITIES

Peter Parker employs web-shooters to swing between high-rise buildings in any environment, utilizing these spiderwebs for acrobatic melee attacks combined with potent spiderweb blasts to render his enemies helpless.

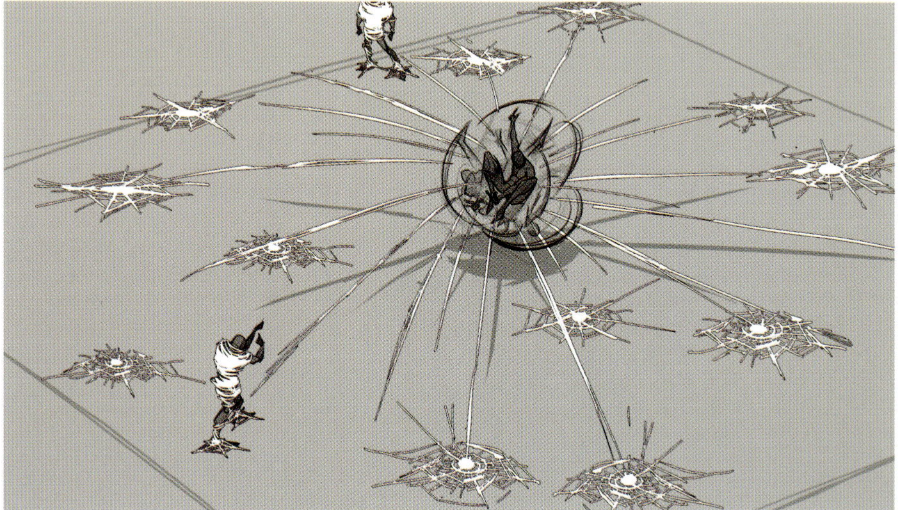

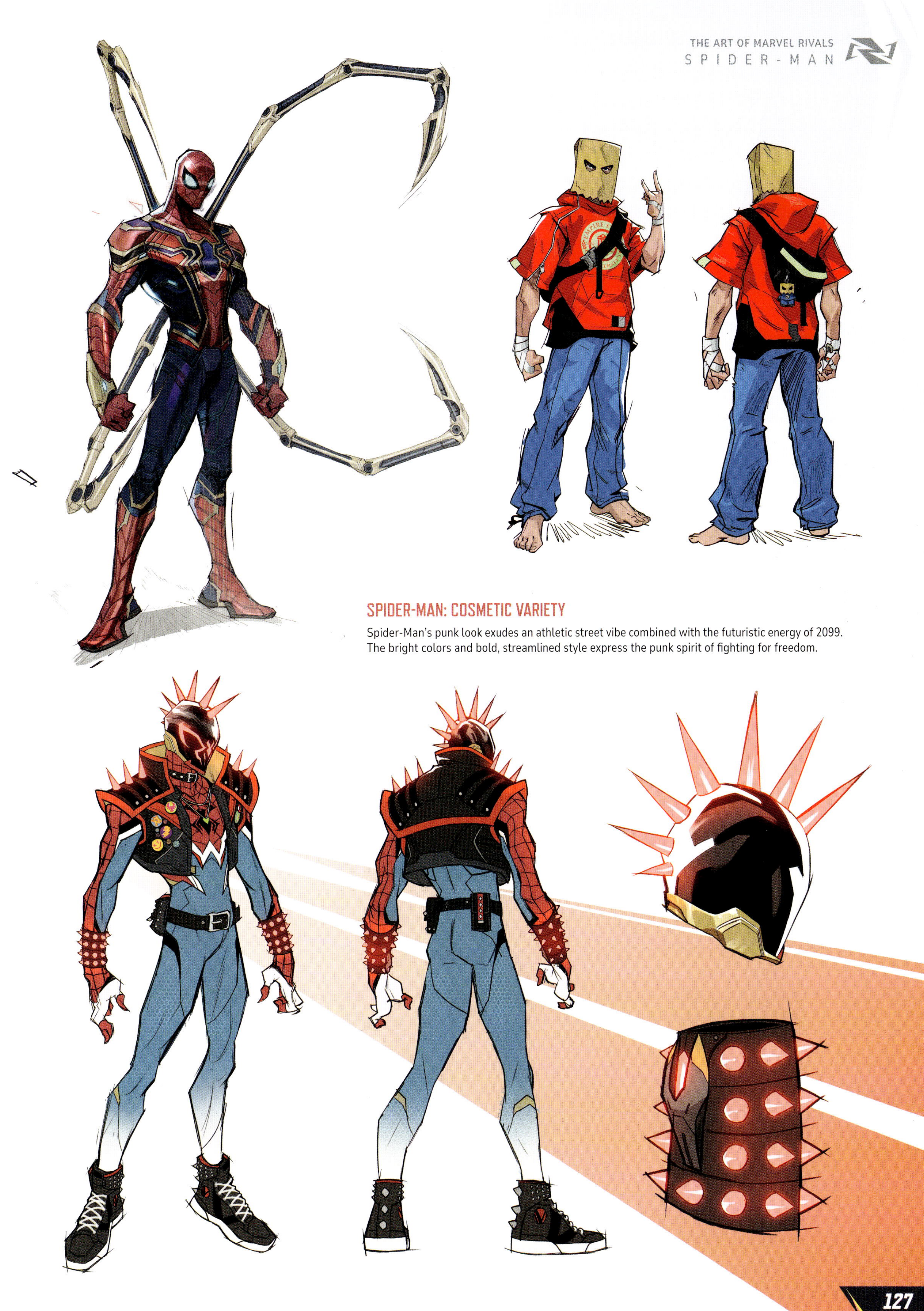

SPIDER-MAN: COSMETIC VARIETY

Spider-Man's punk look exudes an athletic street vibe combined with the futuristic energy of 2099. The bright colors and bold, streamlined style express the punk spirit of fighting for freedom.

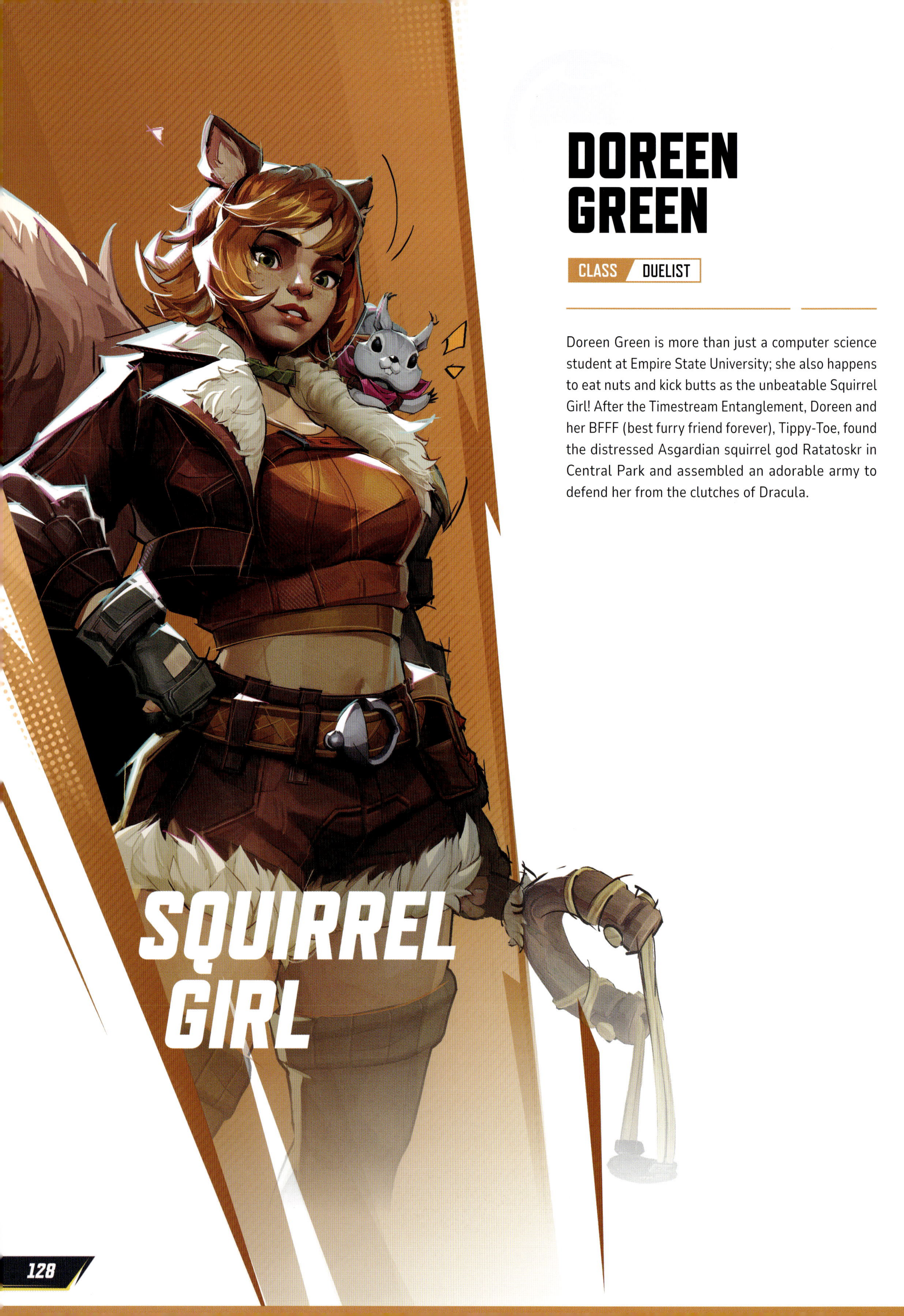

DOREEN GREEN

CLASS / DUELIST

Doreen Green is more than just a computer science student at Empire State University; she also happens to eat nuts and kick butts as the unbeatable Squirrel Girl! After the Timestream Entanglement, Doreen and her BFFF (best furry friend forever), Tippy-Toe, found the distressed Asgardian squirrel god Ratatoskr in Central Park and assembled an adorable army to defend her from the clutches of Dracula.

With the power of an ordinary squirrel, Doreen Green effortlessly defeats seemingly invincible enemies in unexpected ways. Those who underestimate her and her furry friends inevitably become the latest to face defeat by the "Unbeatable Squirrel Girl."

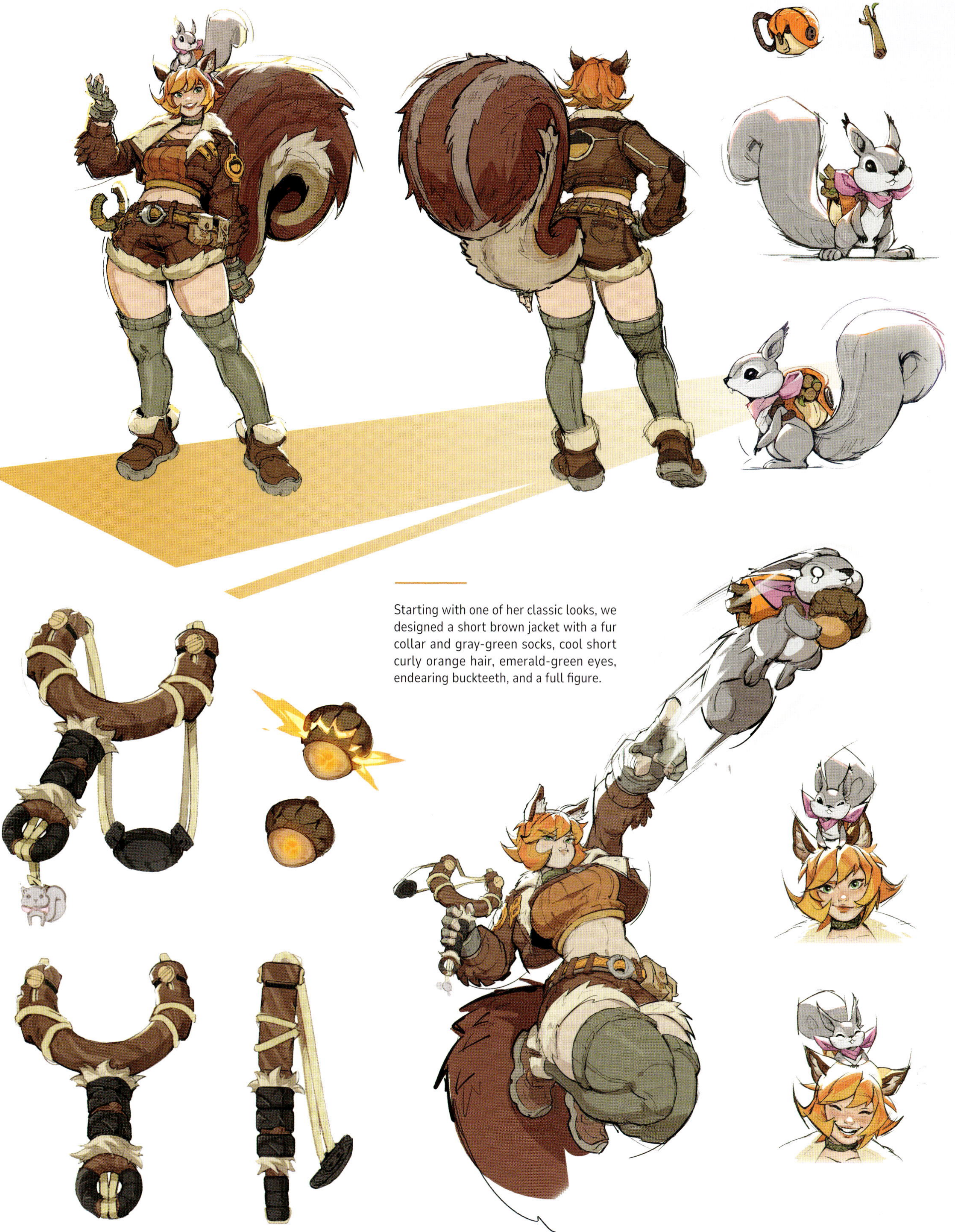

Starting with one of her classic looks, we designed a short brown jacket with a fur collar and gray-green socks, cool short curly orange hair, emerald-green eyes, endearing buckteeth, and a full figure.

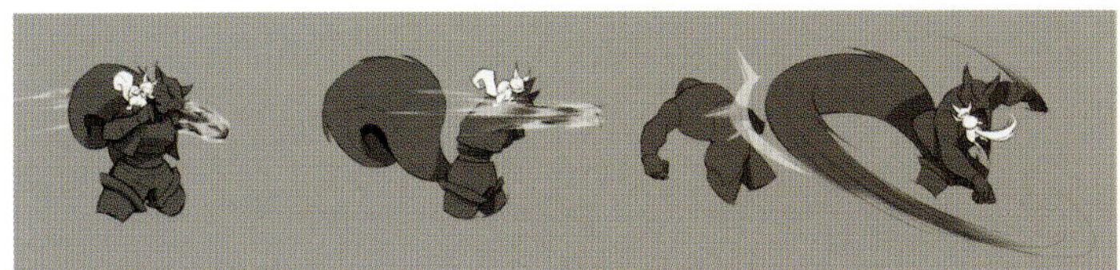
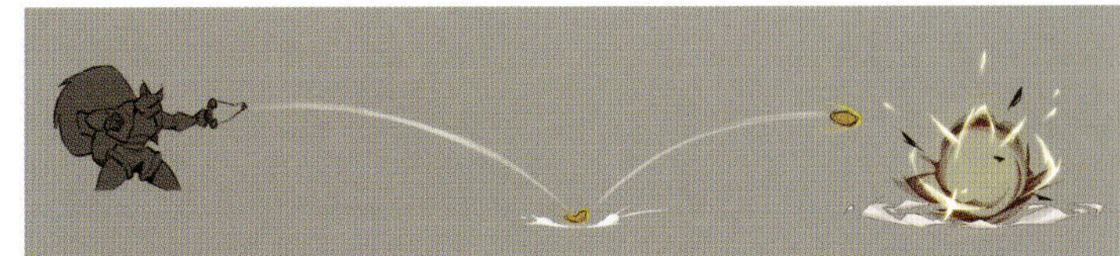
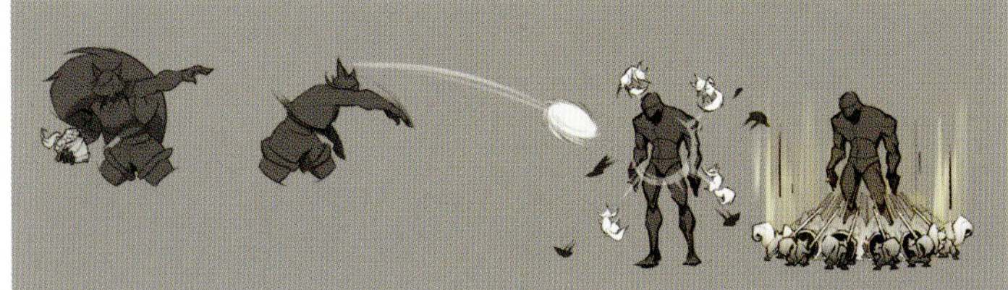
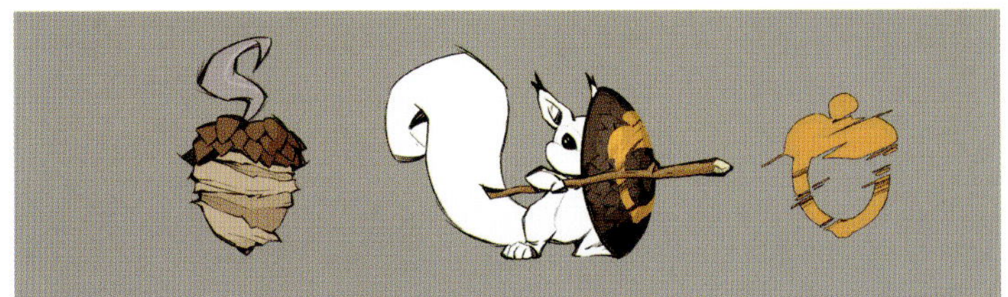
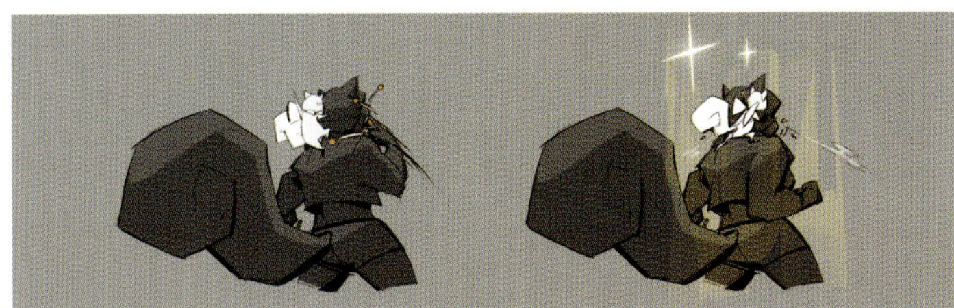
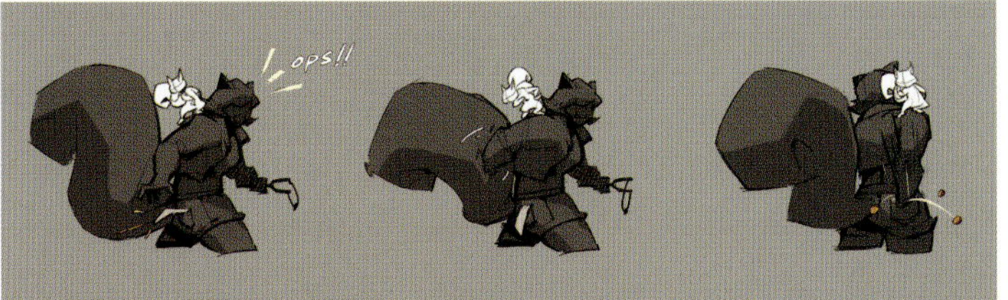

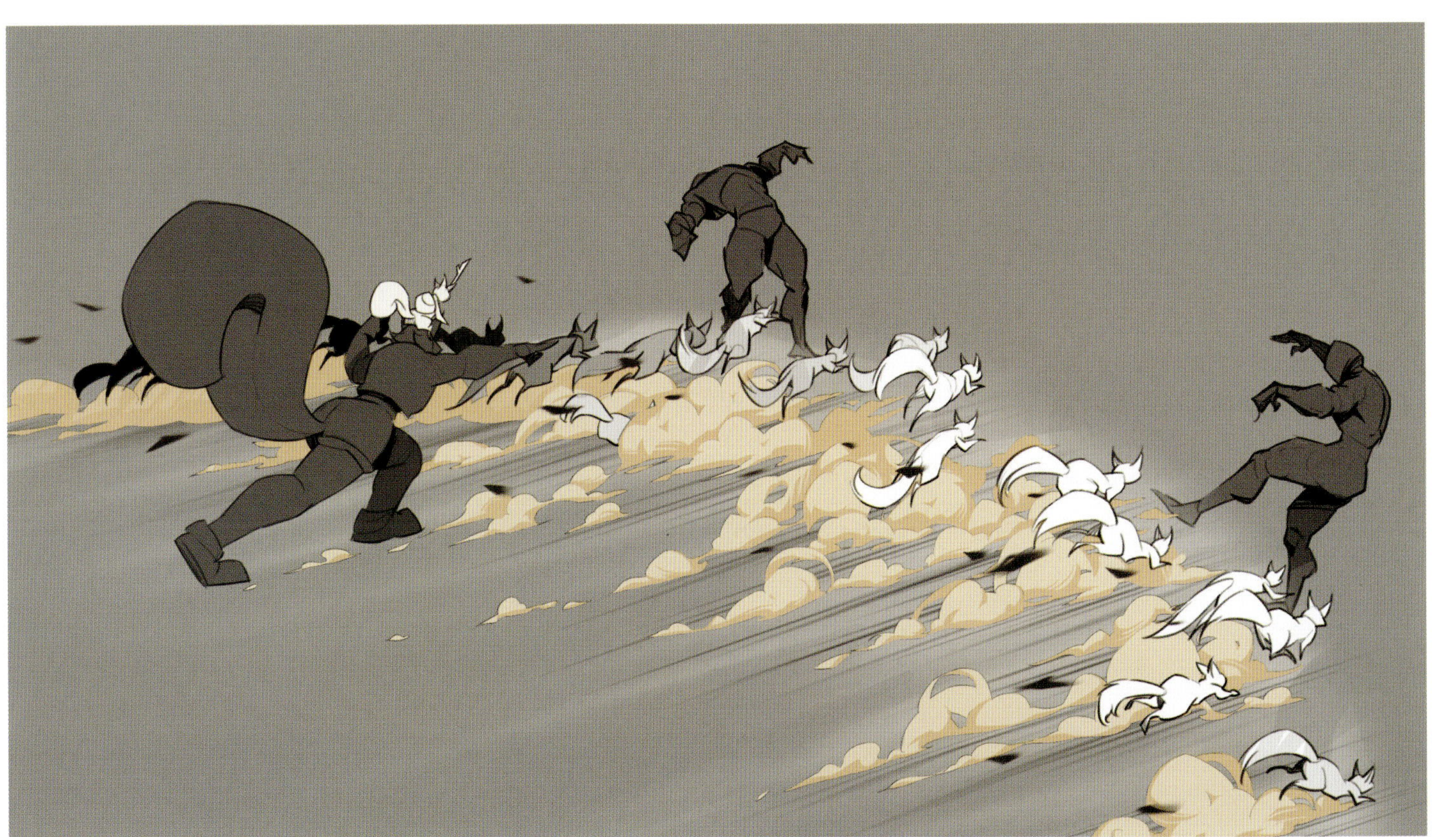

SQUIRREL GIRL: ABILITIES

Squirrel Girl's attack and action modes mimic a squirrel's behavior. She can continuously suppress enemies with long-range firepower, and her ultimate move involves commanding an army of squirrels to crush the enemy.

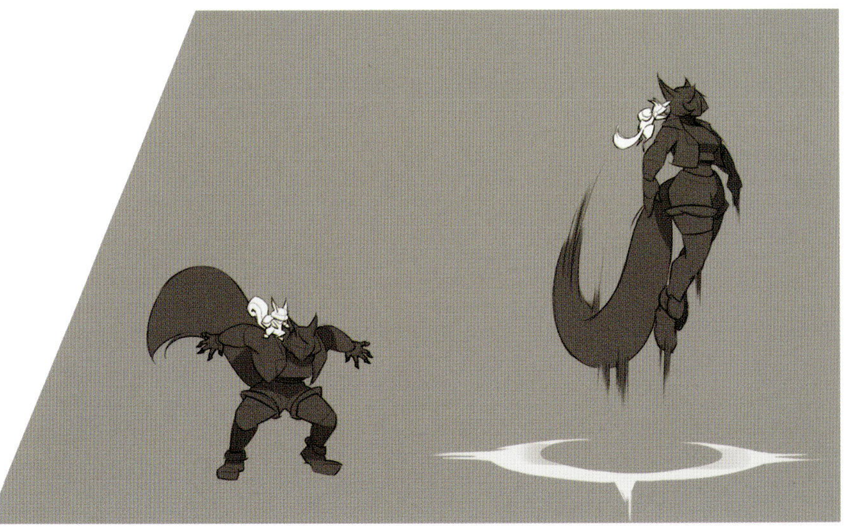

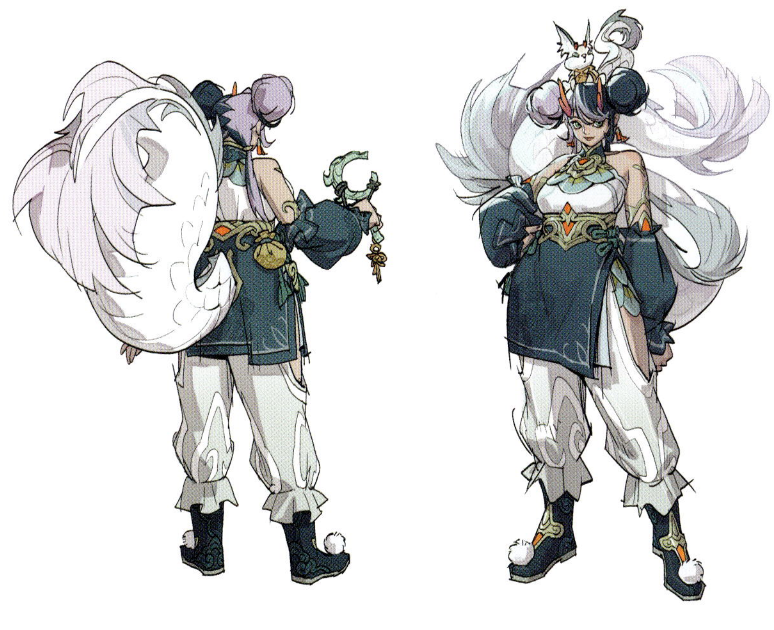

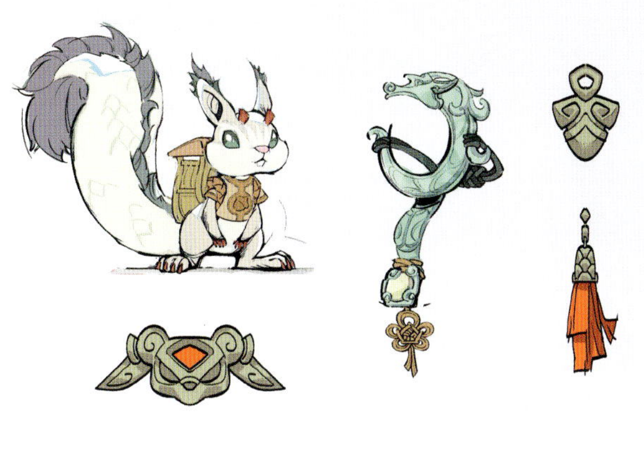

SQUIRREL GIRL: COSMETIC VARIETY

The Urban Hunter costume, inspired by American street style from the 1950s, features an aviator jacket, a polka dot scarf, cat-eye sunglasses, and bright red lips, giving her a fashionable retro appearance.

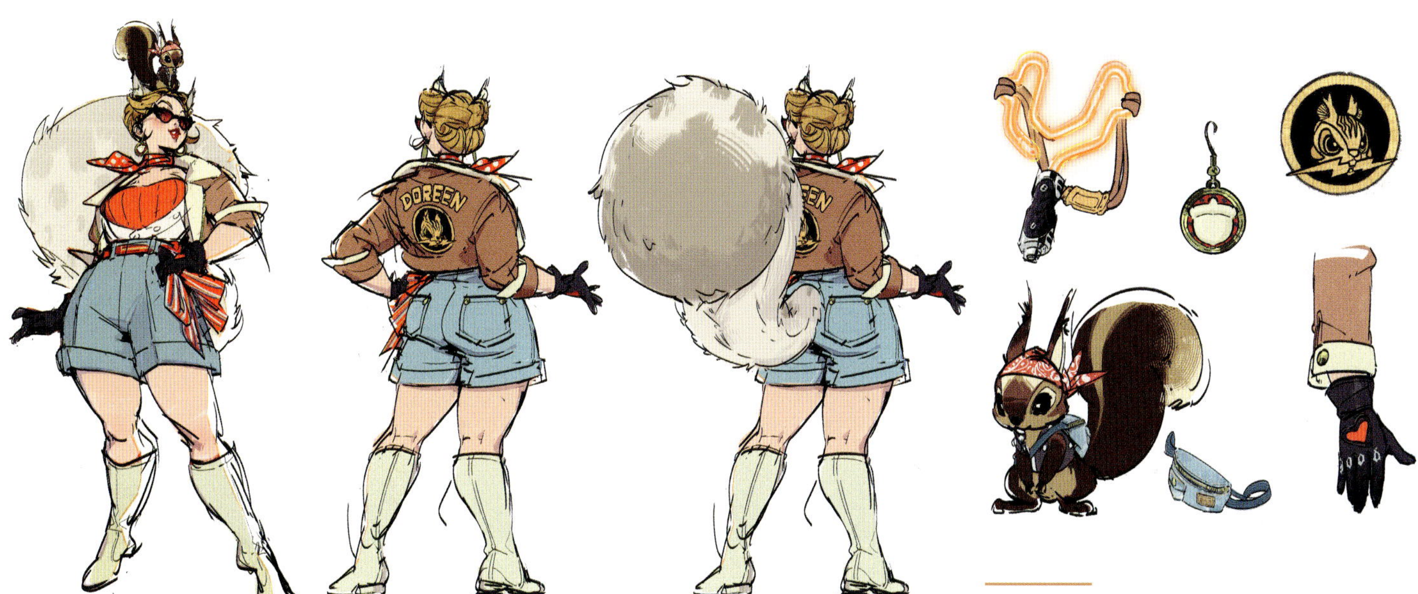

The Acorn Punk design, predominantly black with bright rose red, incorporates the characteristic acorn and features a distinctive spiked, highlighted tail that accentuates its punk and street style.

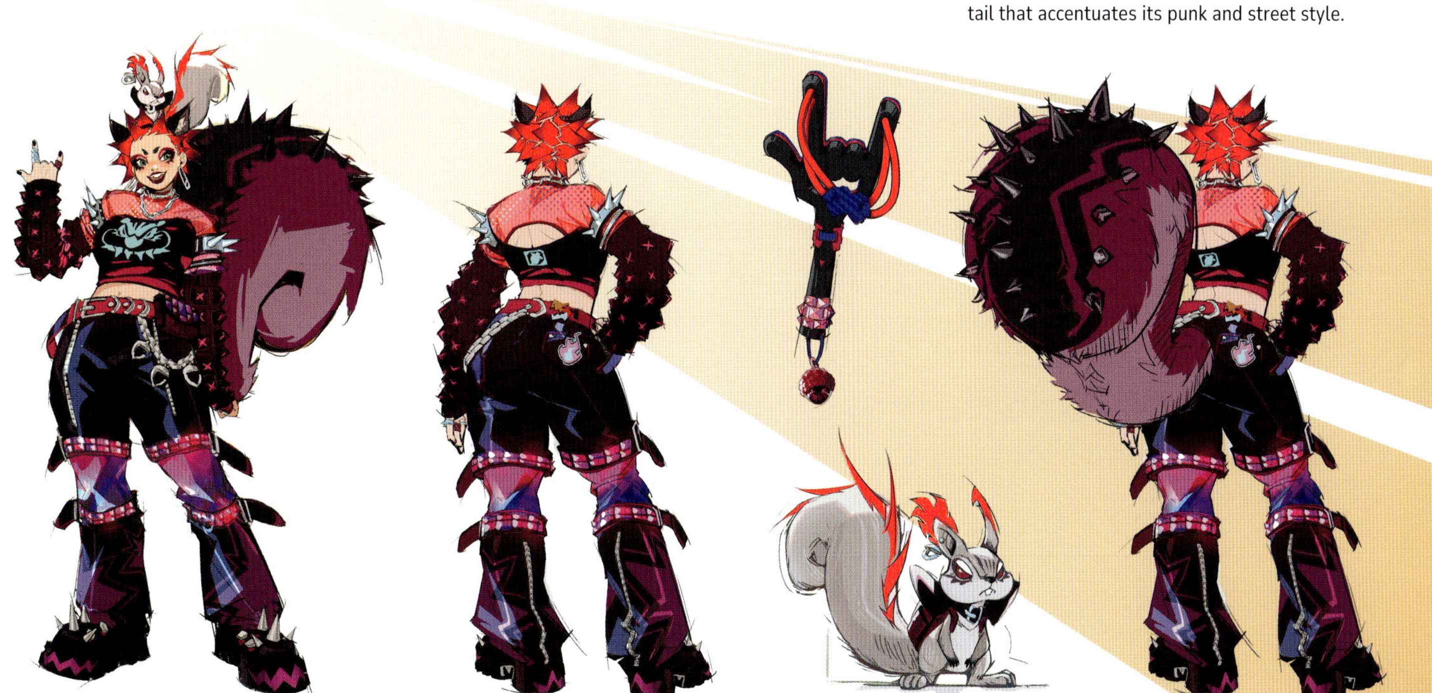

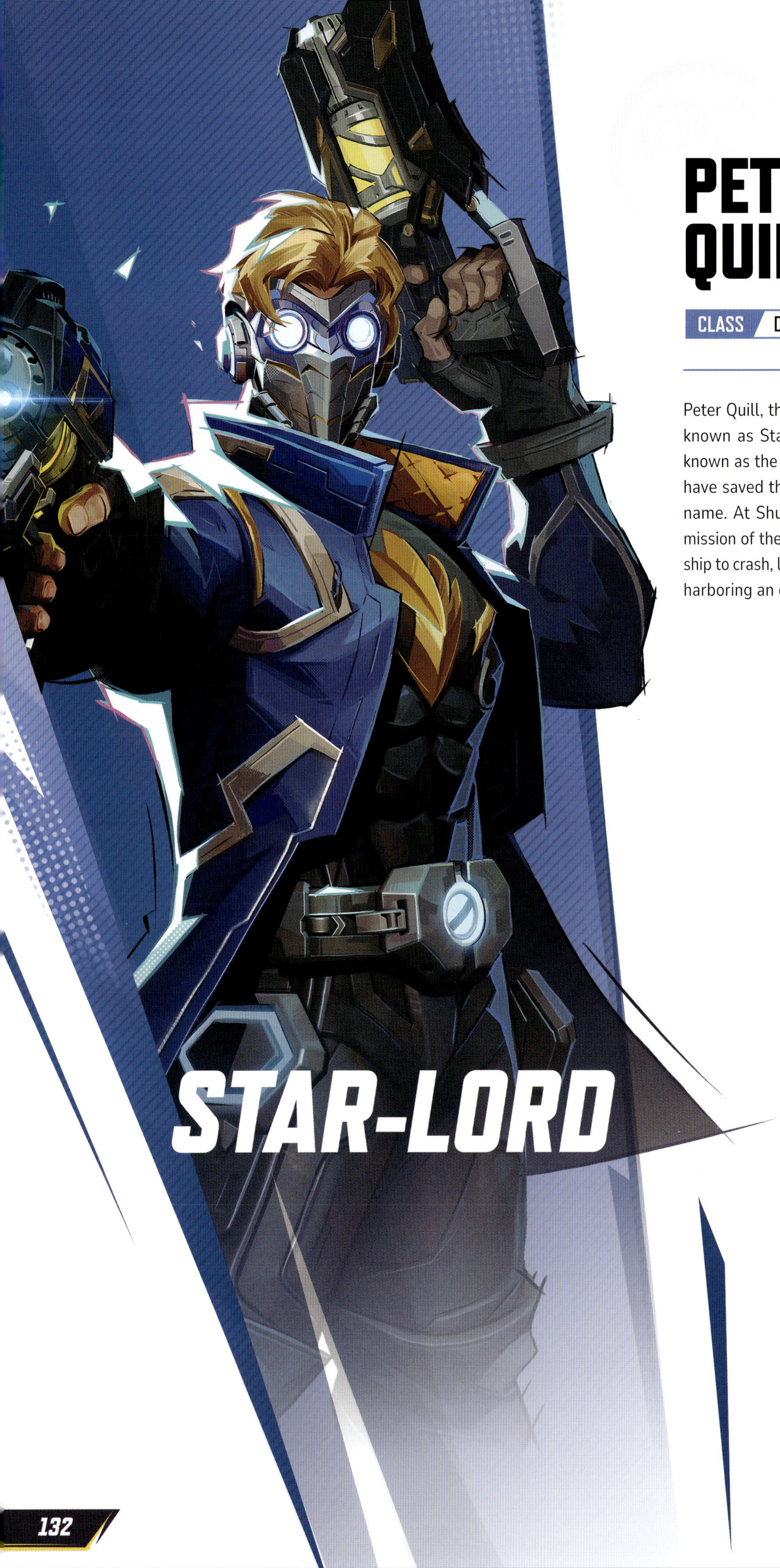

PETER QUILL

CLASS / DUELIST

Peter Quill, the legendary captain and space outlaw known as Star-Lord, leads the spacefaring heroes known as the Guardians of the Galaxy, who together have saved the universe enough times to earn their name. At Shuri's request, Star-Lord led a scouting mission of the symbiote planet, Klyntar, only for their ship to crash, leaving them stranded on a hostile world harboring an evil capable of total annihilation.

Star-Lord is a carefree, adventure-loving space pirate whose unique genes and extensive cosmic experiences have honed his exceptional combat skills.

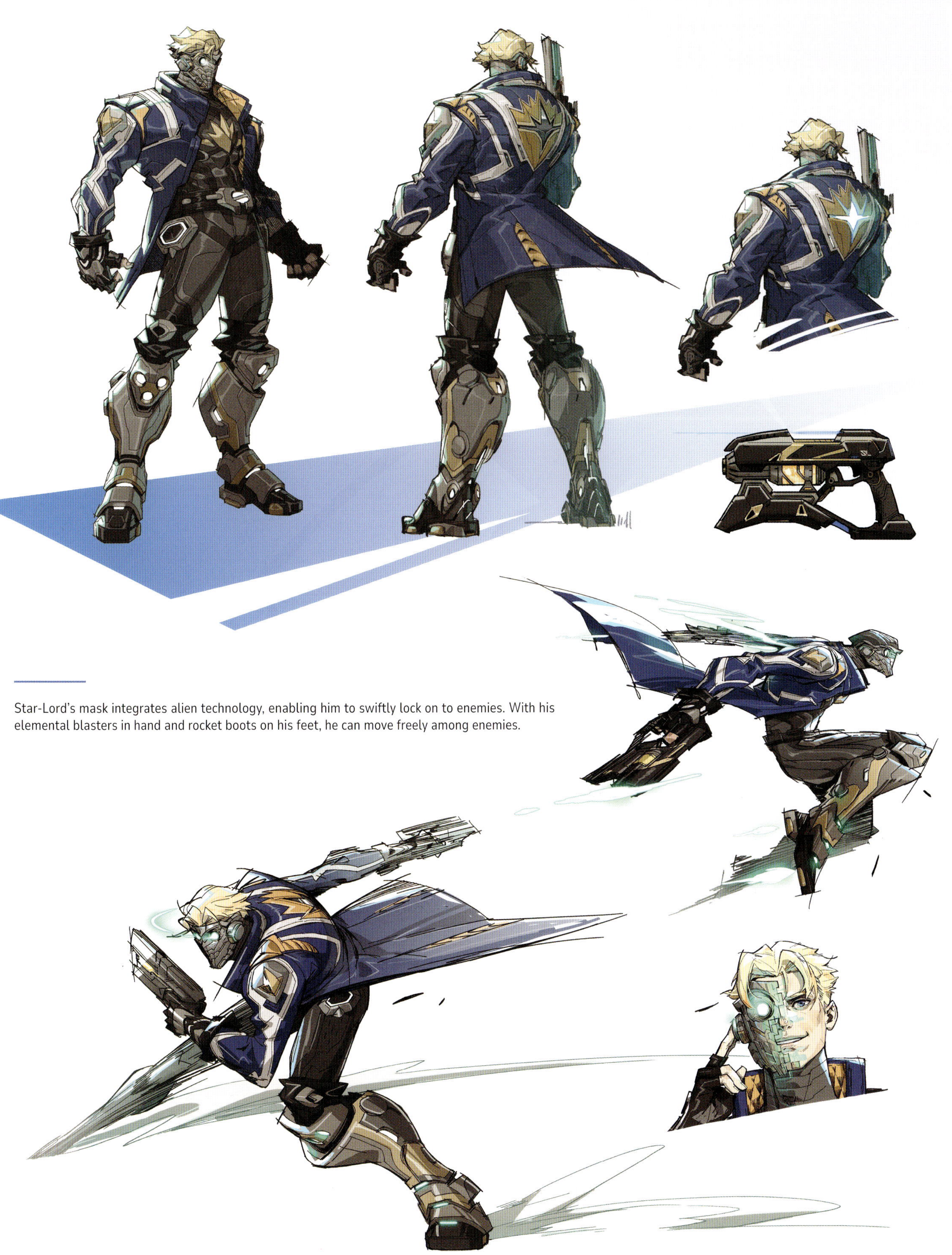

Star-Lord's mask integrates alien technology, enabling him to swiftly lock on to enemies. With his elemental blasters in hand and rocket boots on his feet, he can move freely among enemies.

STAR-LORD: ABILITIES

Star-Lord's agility allows him to swiftly enter or exit the battlefield, continuously harassing enemies. His ultimate skill can unleash unpredictable, lethal shots at the enemy.

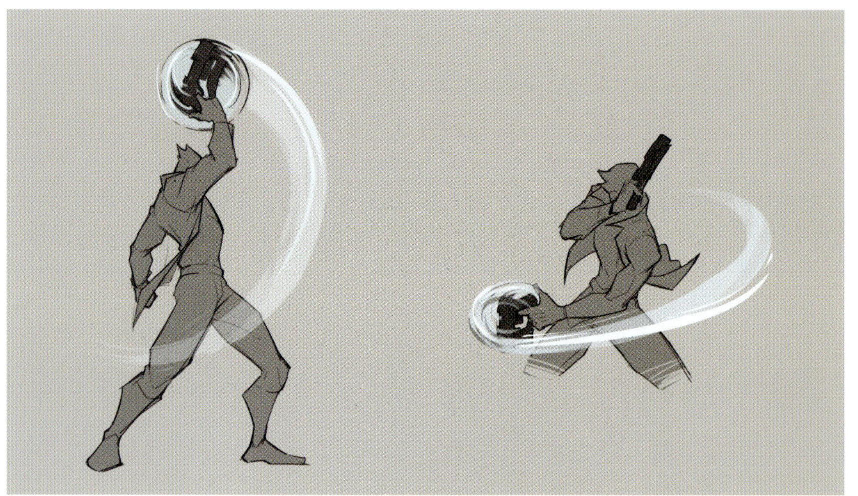

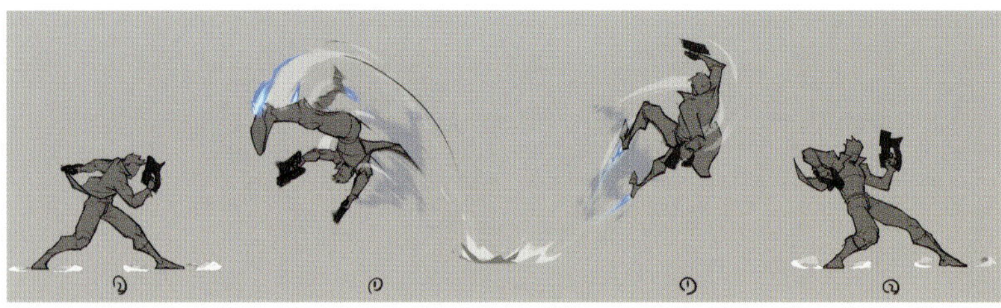

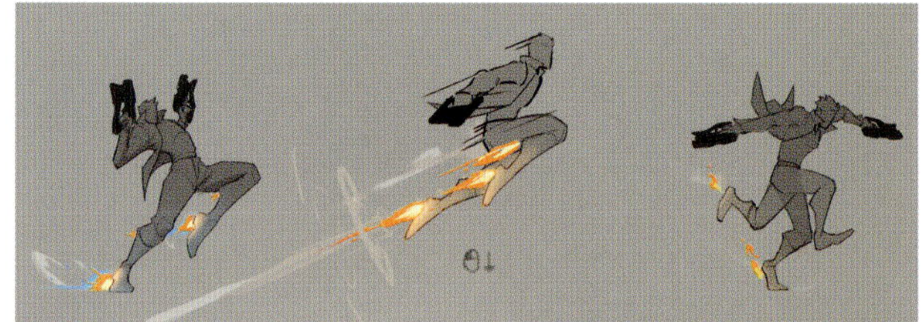

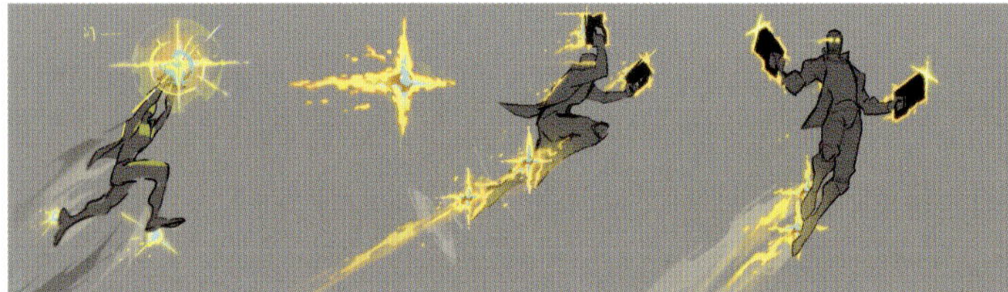

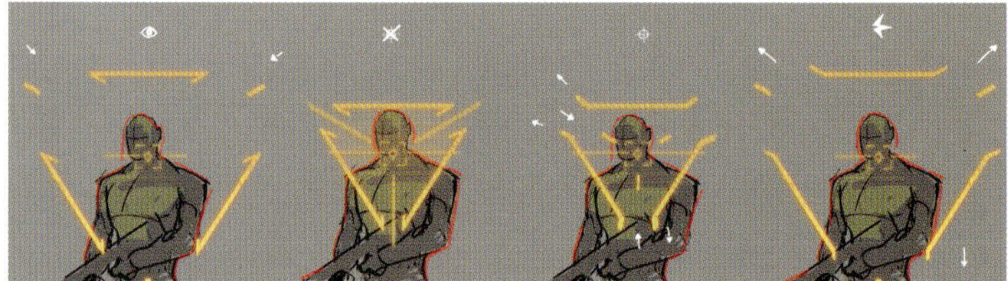

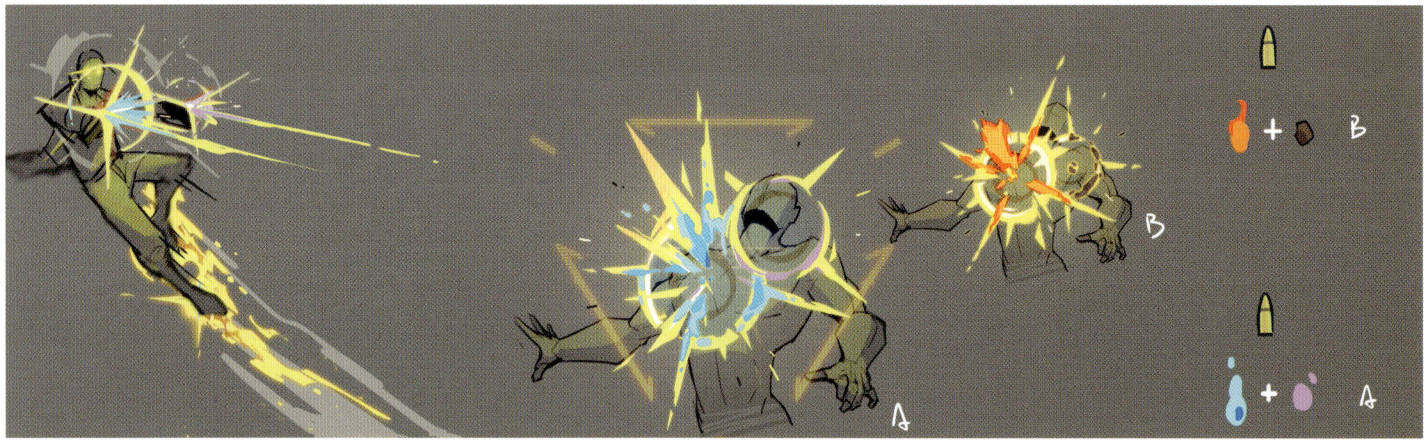

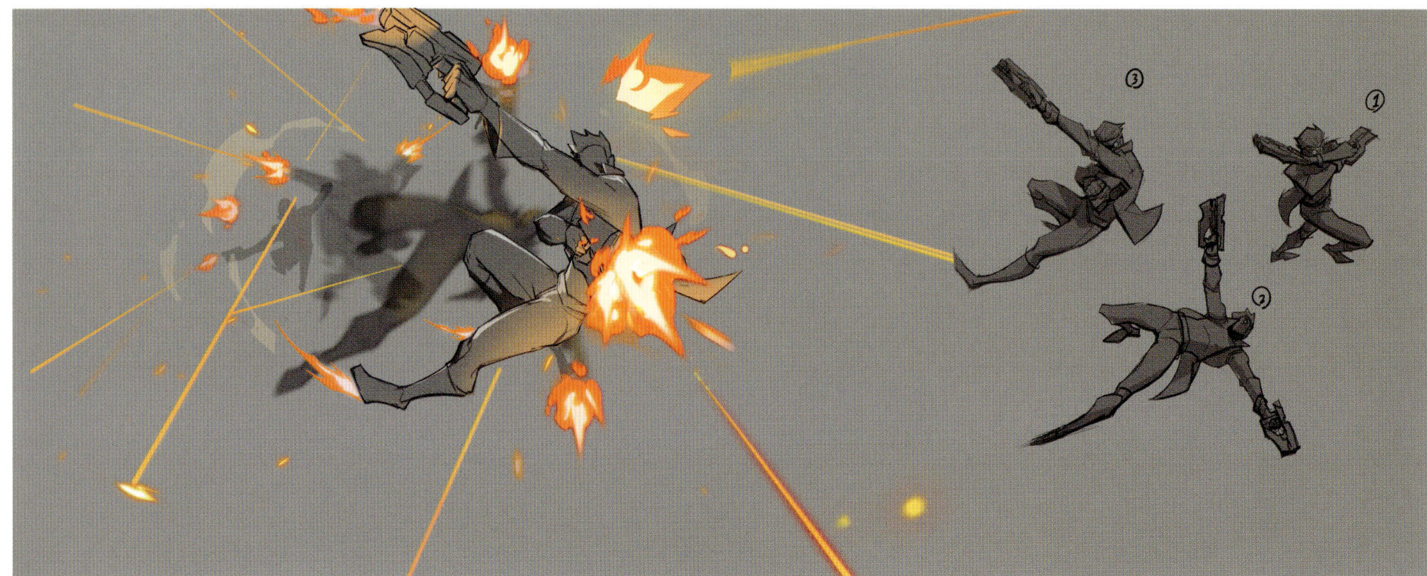

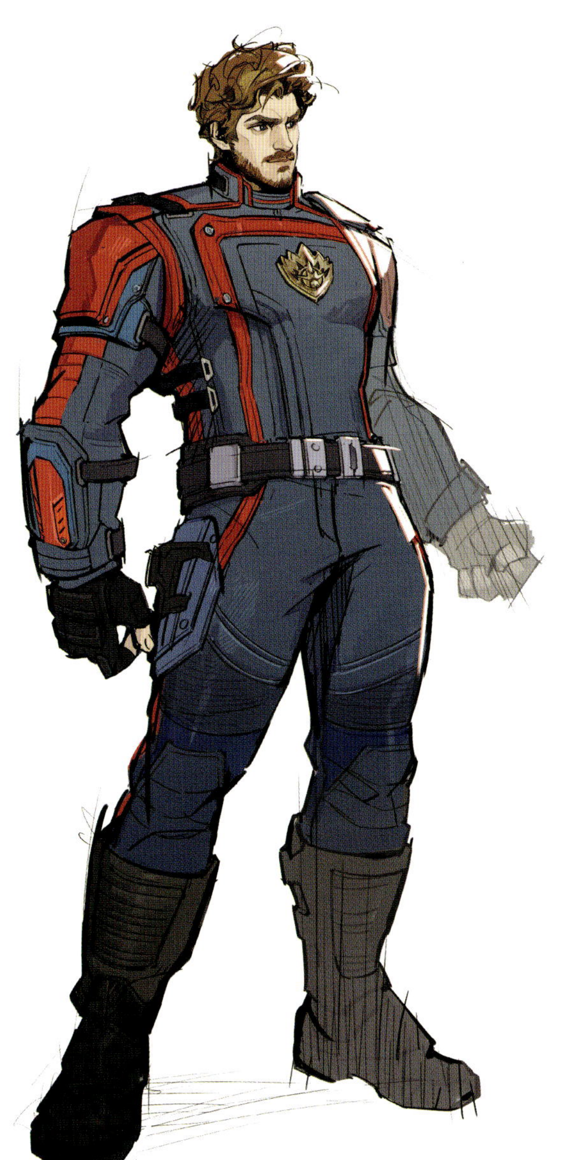

STAR-LORD: COSMETIC VARIETY

Star-Lord, as the Master of the Sun, commands cosmic consciousness. He can manipulate matter and energy, enabling his elemental gun to absorb all energy, infinitely enhancing his abilities.

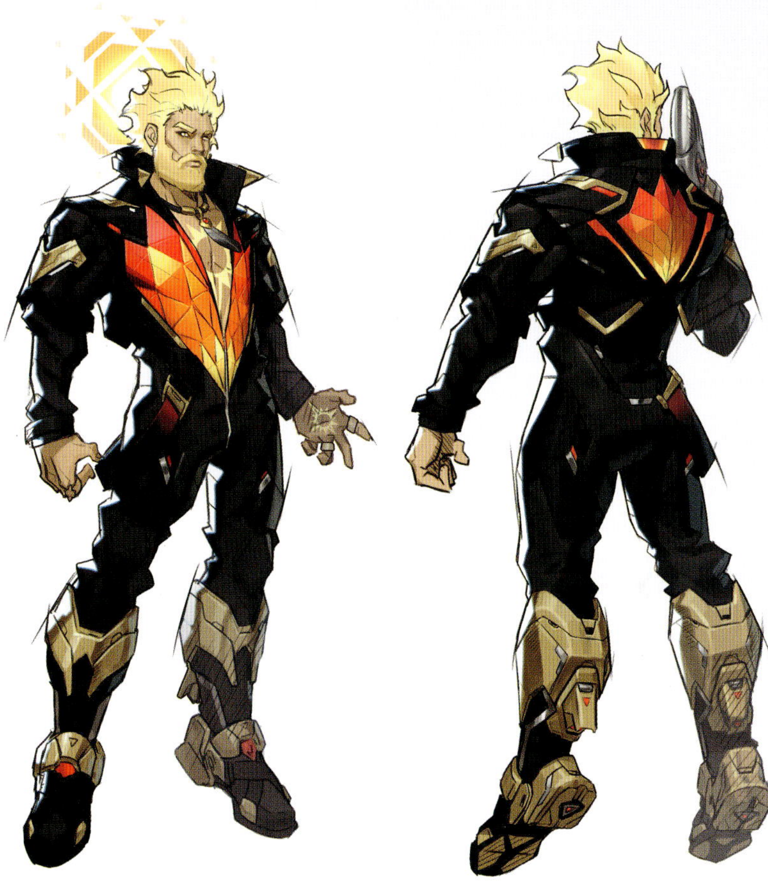

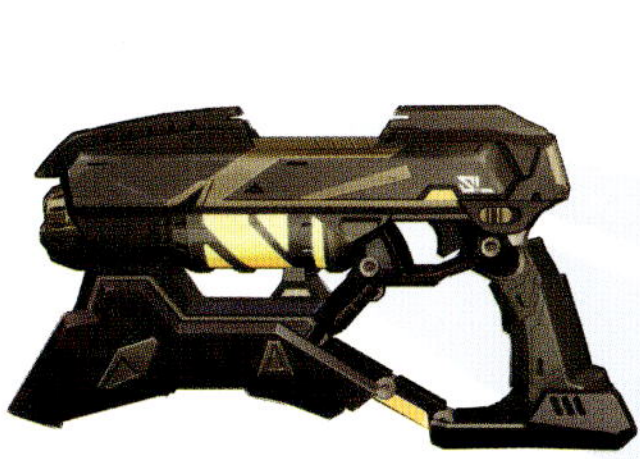

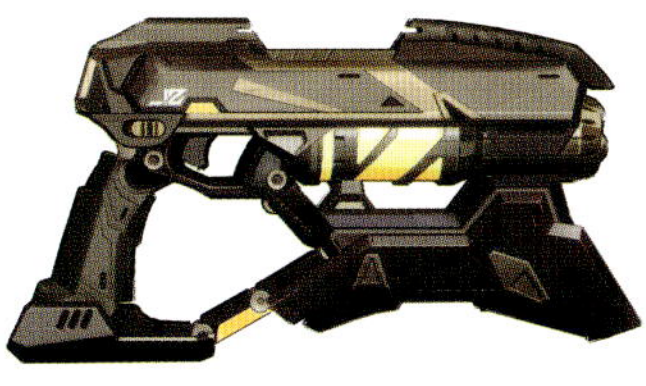

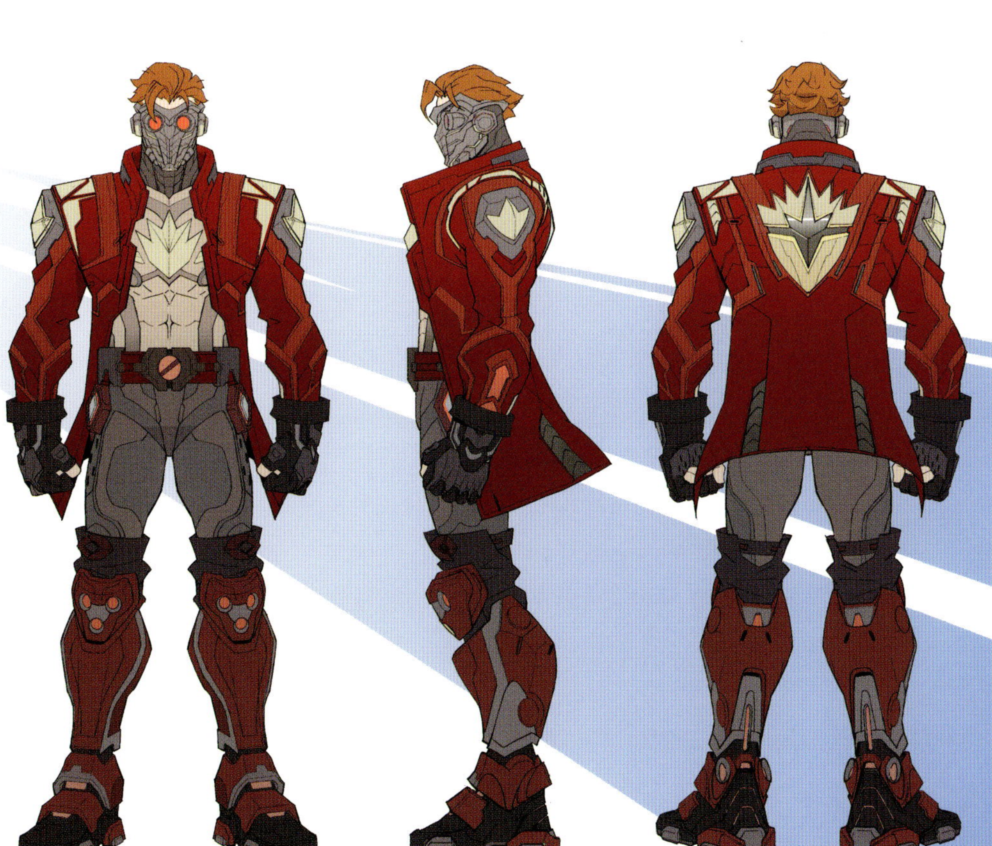

The design restores the classic comic version of Star-Lord with a striking red color palette.

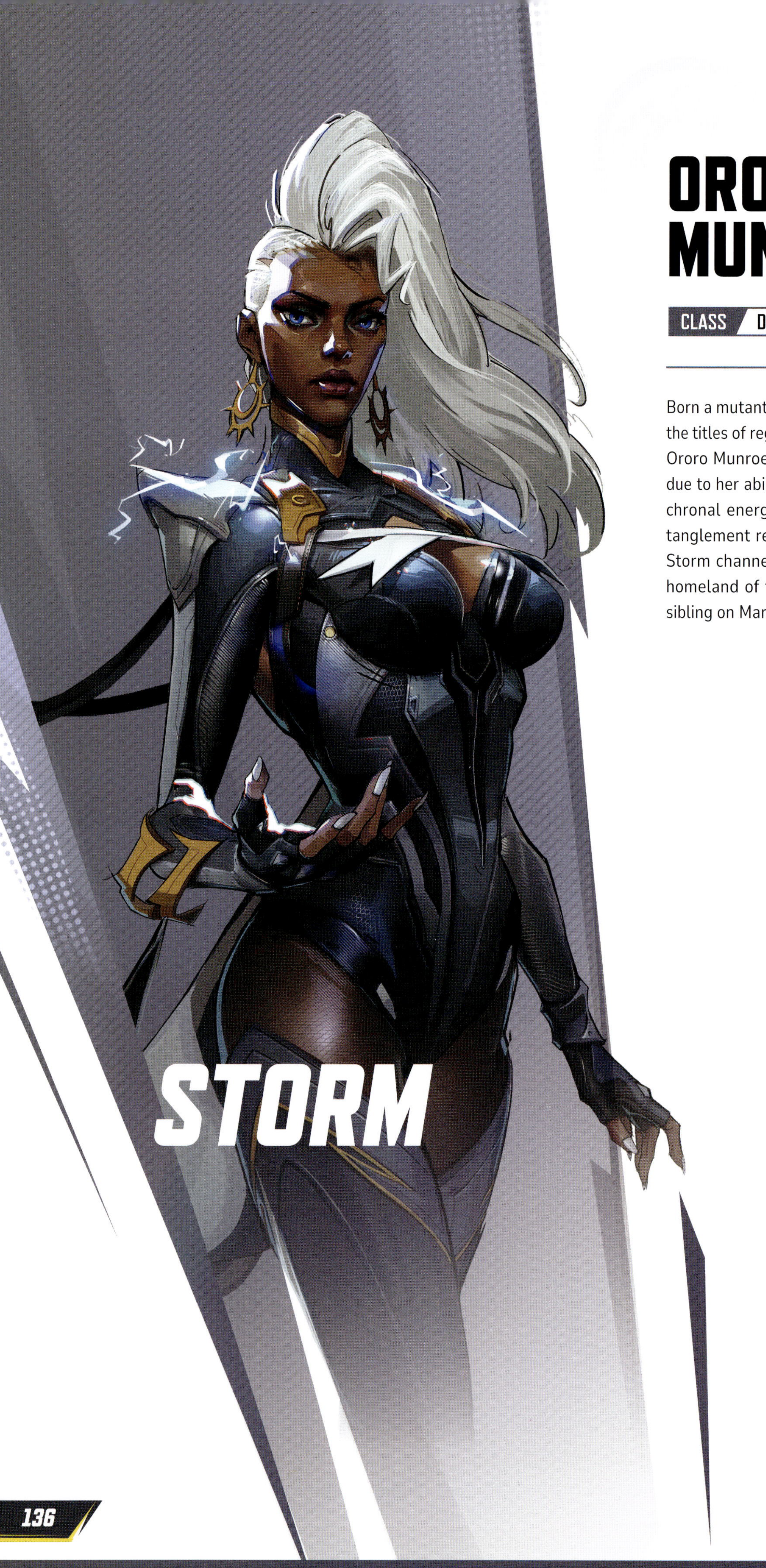

ORORO MUNROE

CLASS DUELIST

Born a mutant, worshiped as a goddess, and earning the titles of regent of Sol and the protector of Arakko, Ororo Munroe became the X-Man known as Storm due to her ability to manipulate the weather. As the chronal energy generated by the Timestream Entanglement resulted in violent temporal tempests, Storm channeled her powers to stabilize both her homeland of the sentient island of Krakoa and its sibling on Mars.

Ororo Munroe possesses omega-level mutant abilities, making her a formidable force on the battlefield. Storm embodies the weather itself, commanding wind, rain, and lightning at her will!

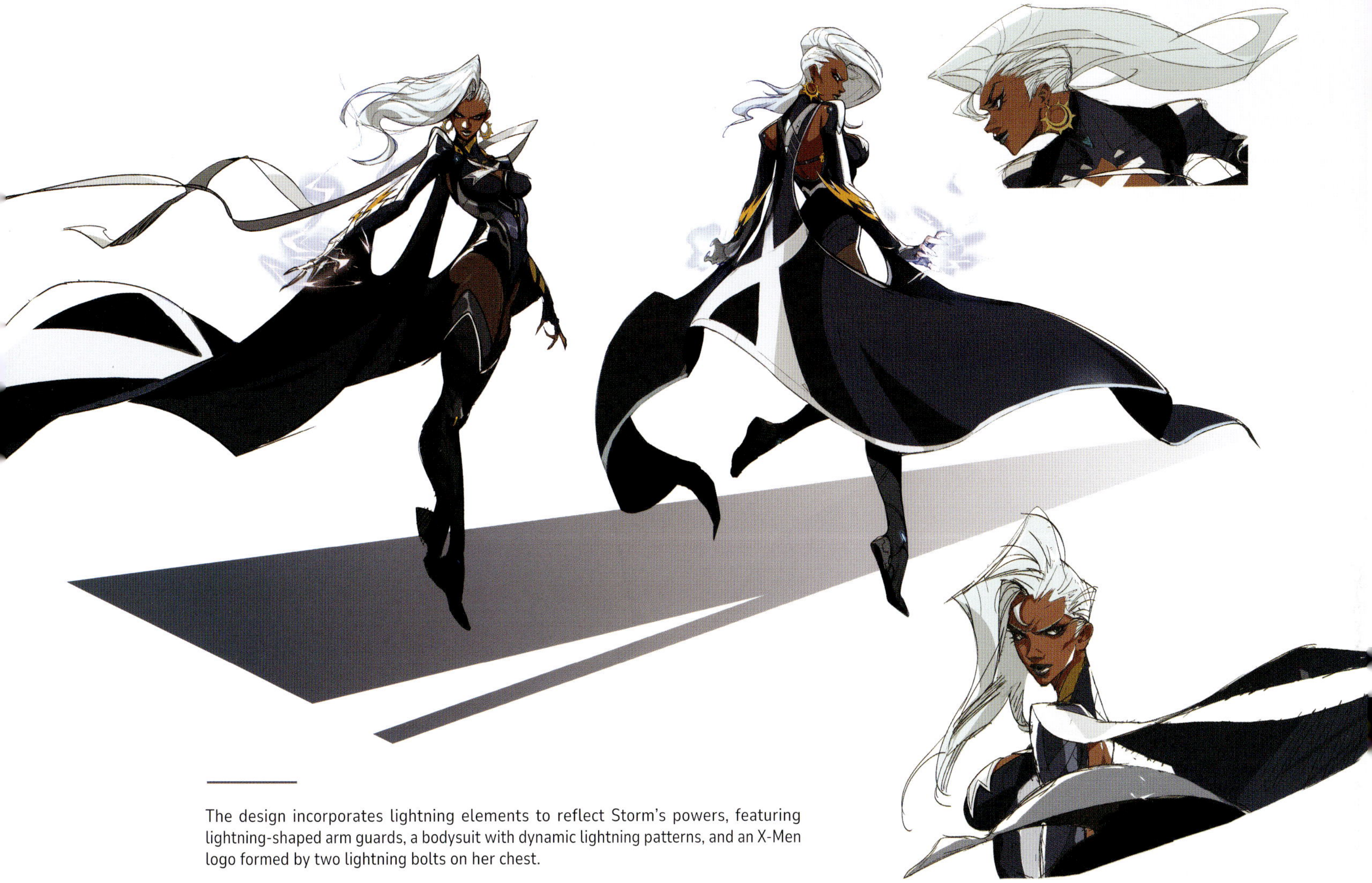

The design incorporates lightning elements to reflect Storm's powers, featuring lightning-shaped arm guards, a bodysuit with dynamic lightning patterns, and an X-Men logo formed by two lightning bolts on her chest.

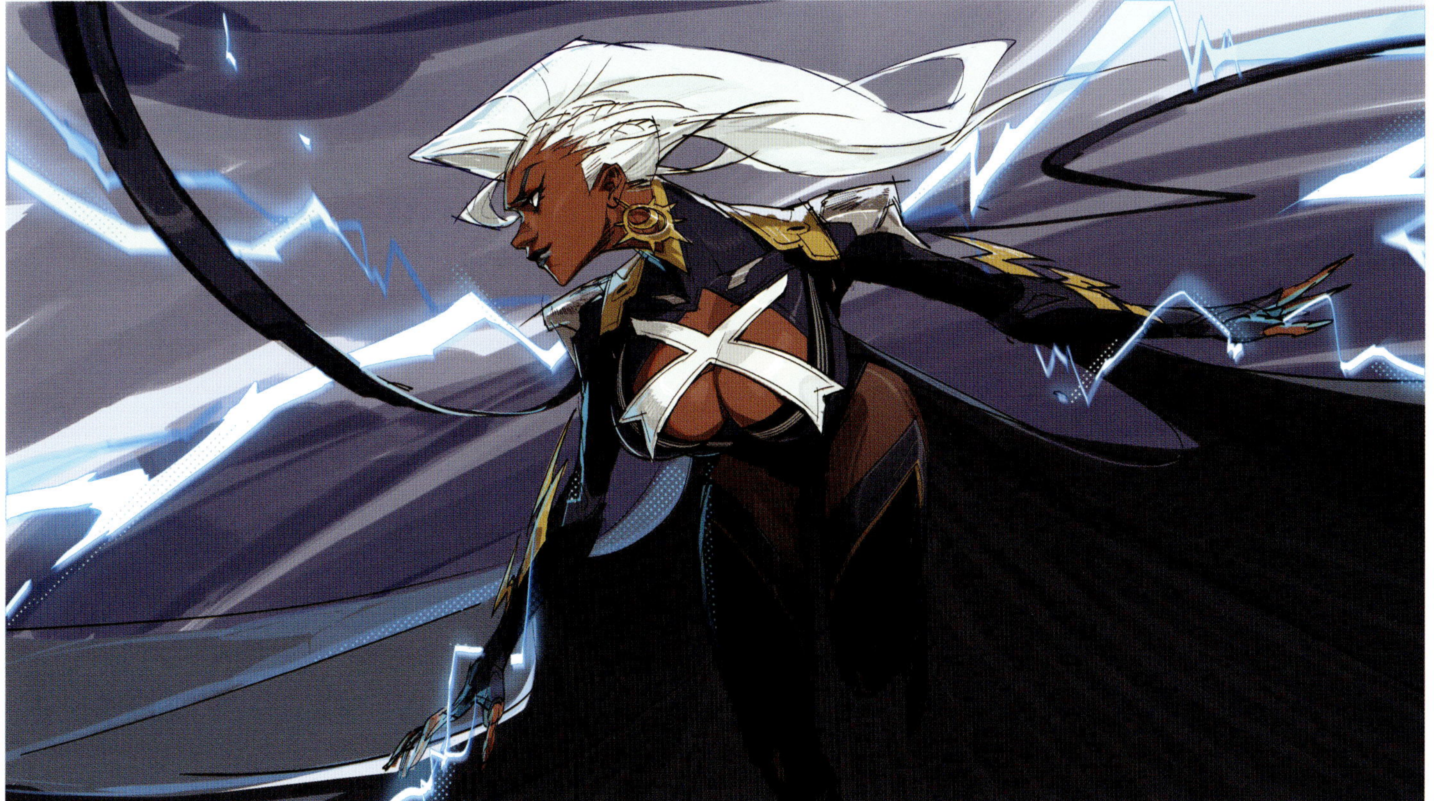

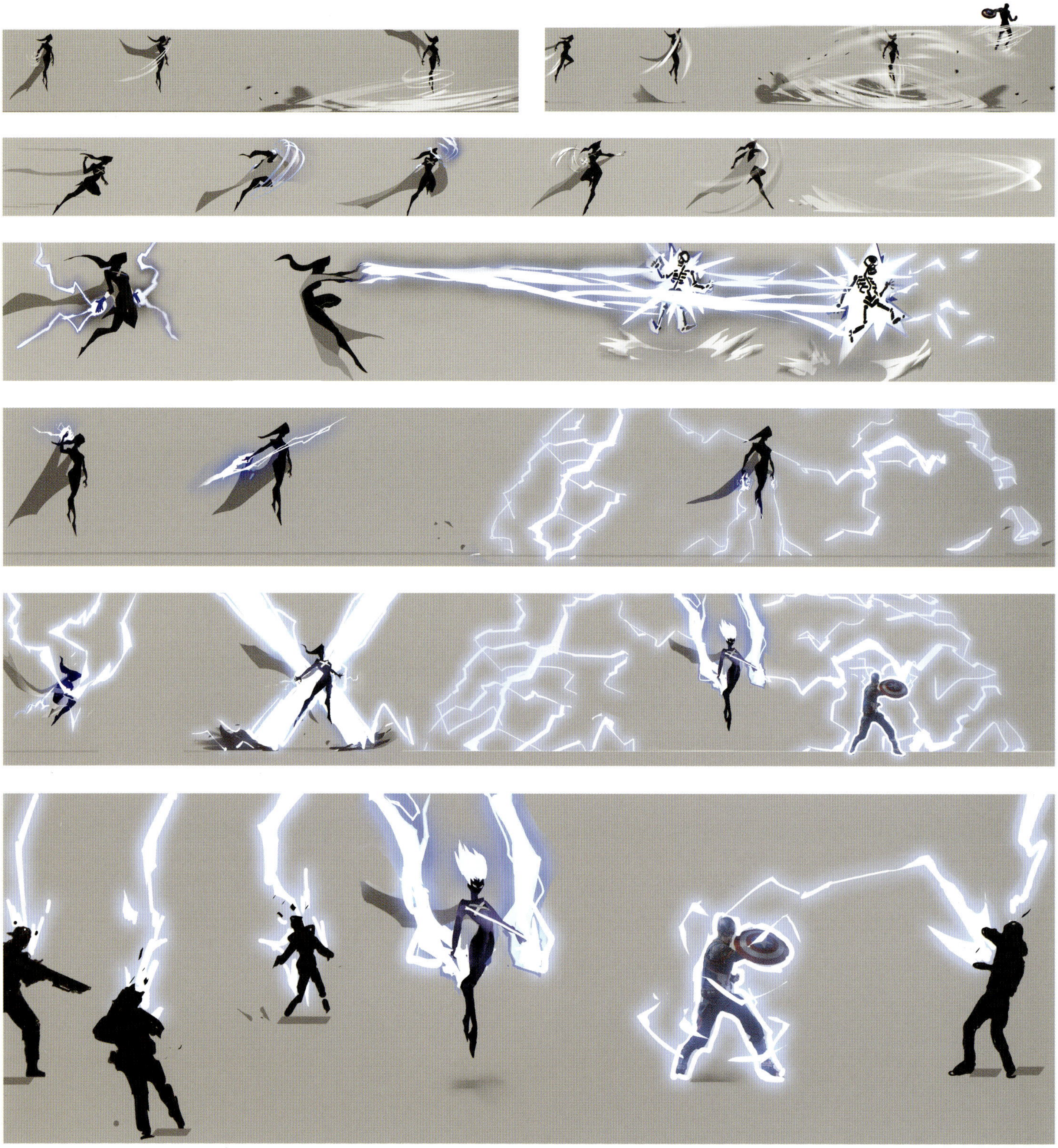

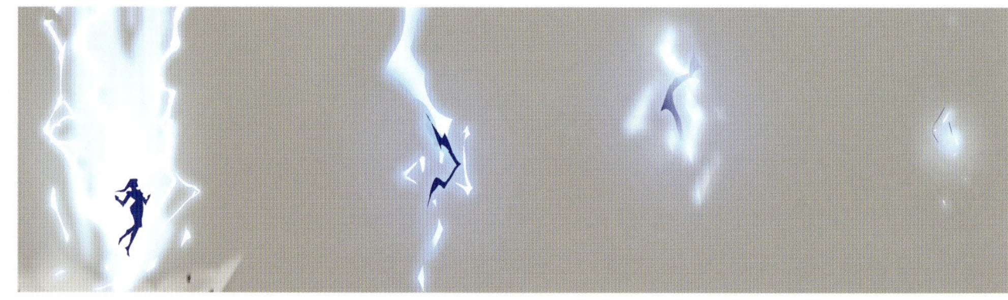

STORM: ABILITIES

Storm flies in the air, employing wind blade attacks and manipulating the weather to help teammates. Her ultimate skill transforms her into a devastating Omega Hurricane.

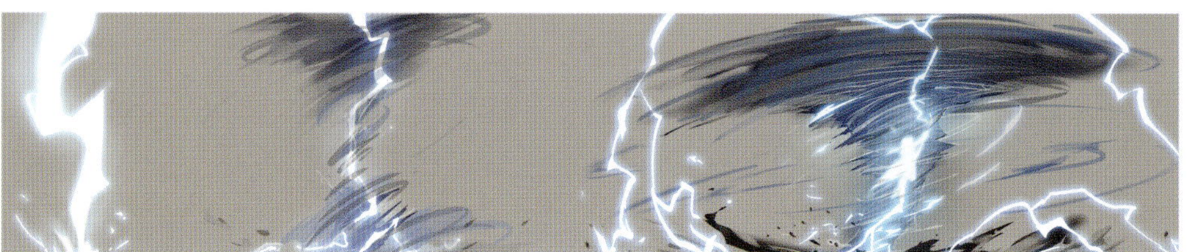

STORM: COSMETIC VARIETY

Storm's classic comic punk look features a primarily black palette, with intricate accessories, exaggerated cuts, and heavy makeup, all showcasing her commitment to individuality and independent spirit.

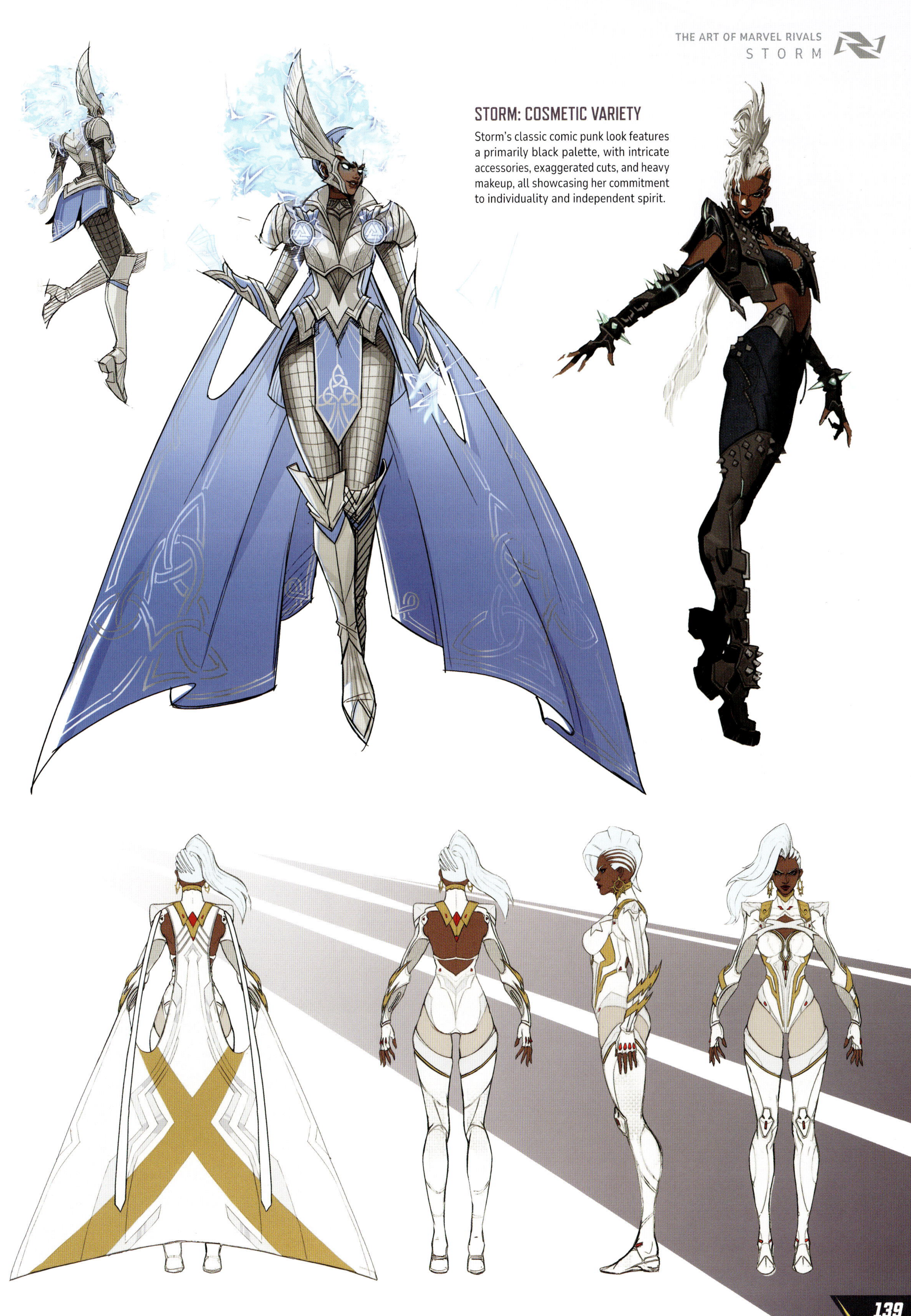

BENJAMIN "BEN" GRIMM

CLASS / VANGUARD

When Benjamin Grimm signed up to pilot an experimental spacecraft for his pal Reed Richards, he never imagined he'd return from the flight transformed into a creature known simply as the Thing. Even though cosmic rays turned his skin into a rocky, impenetrable exterior, Ben's heart of gold keeps him unwavering in the battle to protect New York City from the monsters plaguing it.

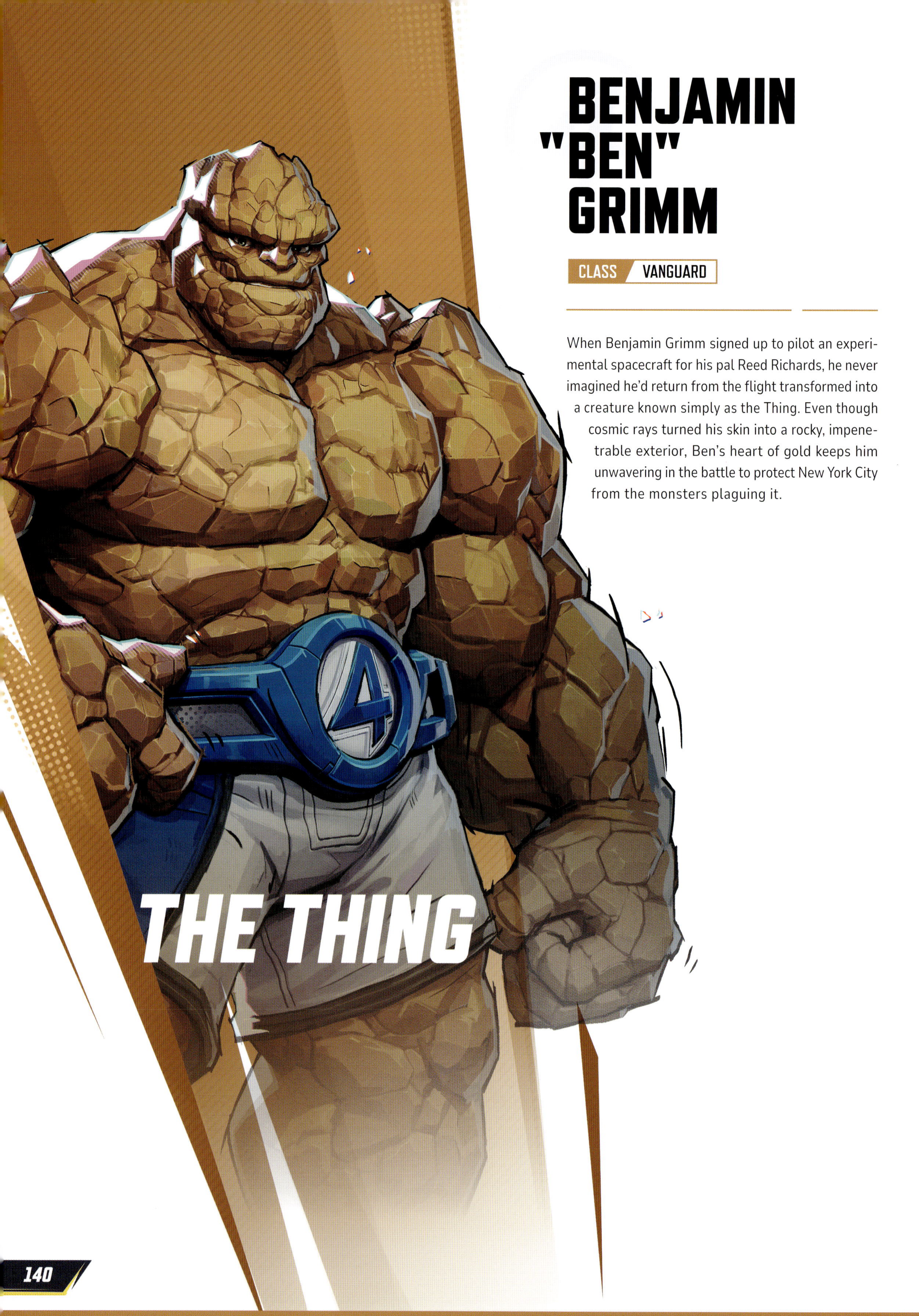

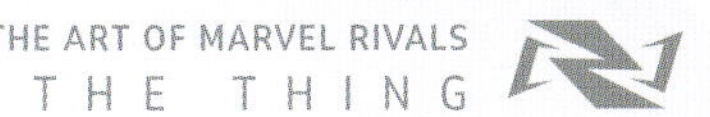

Undoubtedly, the Thing is the unbreakable heart of his team. He stands at the forefront as solid as a rock, ready to take a swing at anyone that threatens his allies.

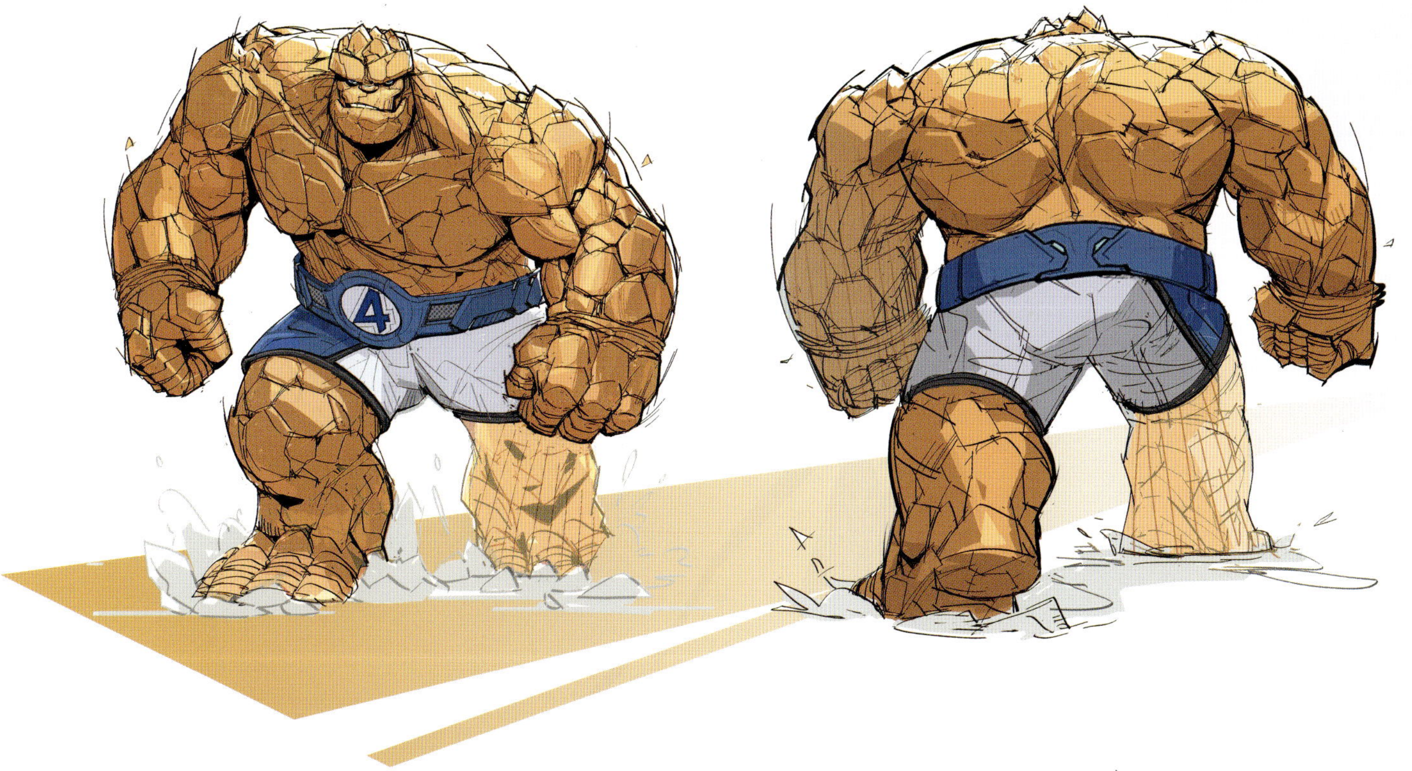

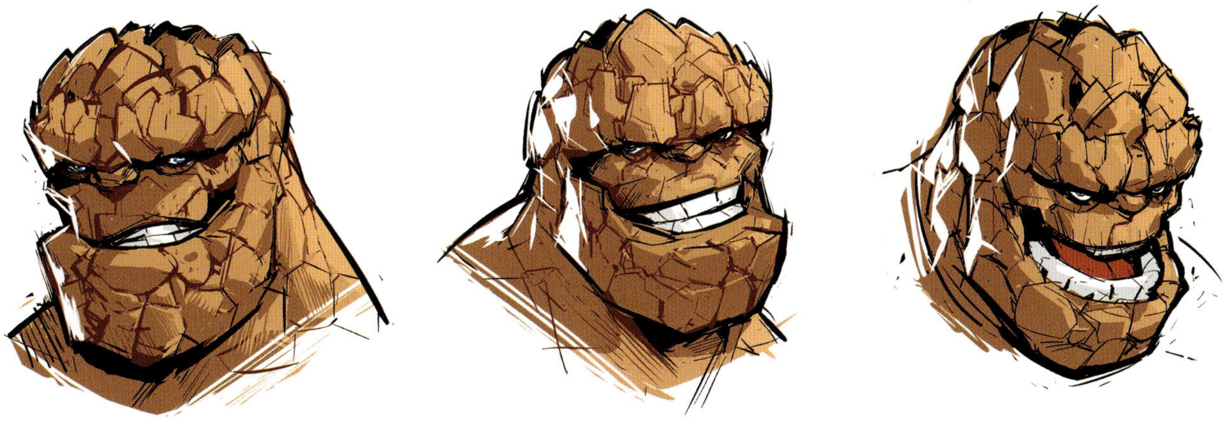

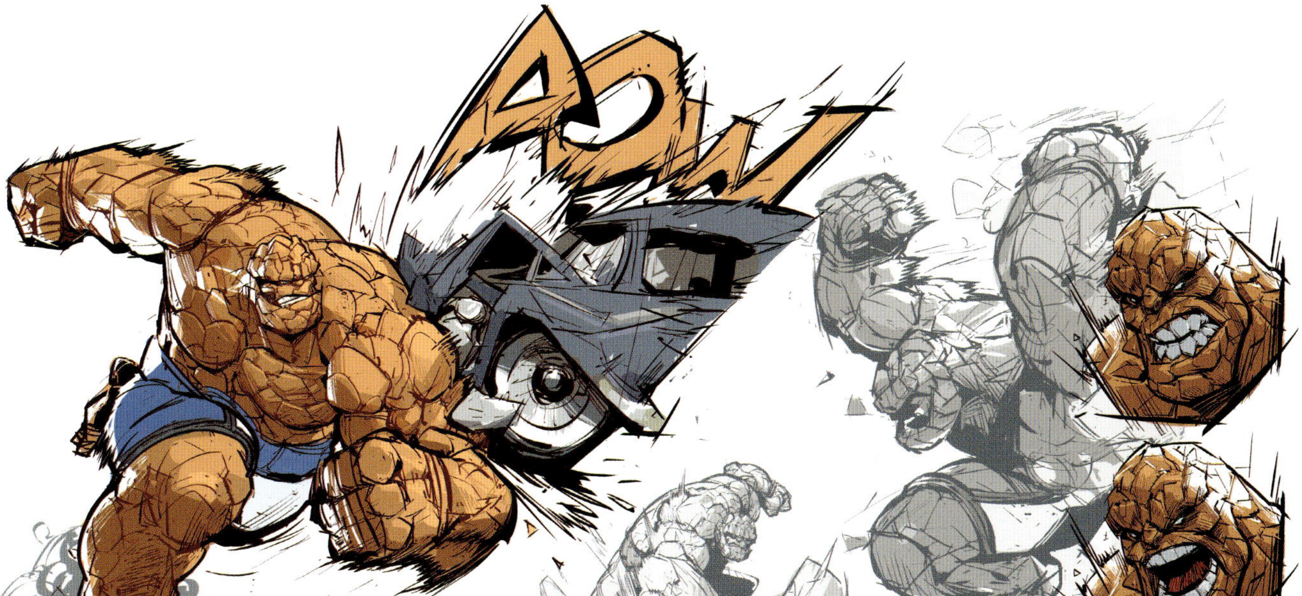

THE THING: ABILITIES

The Thing employs a unique boxing style and can jump to shield his teammates. His ultimate skill offers strong control, allowing him to knock enemies away and stun them.

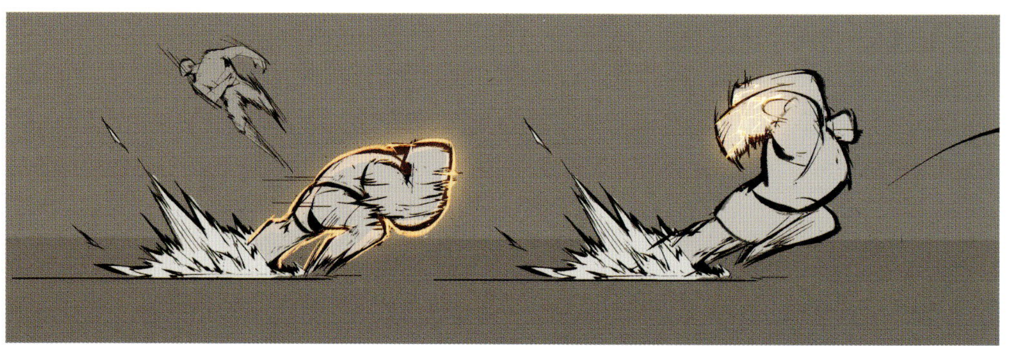

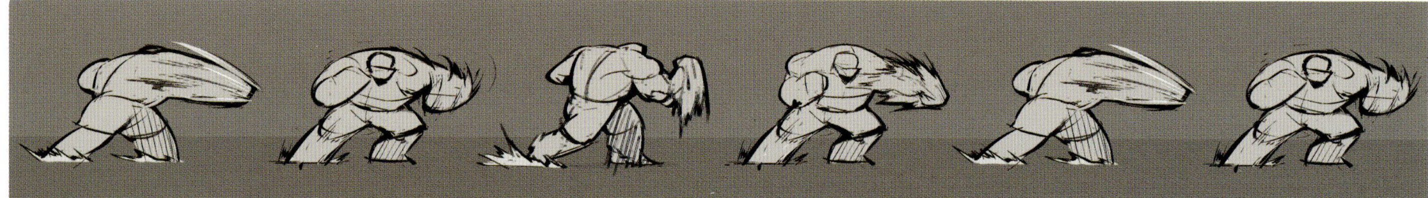

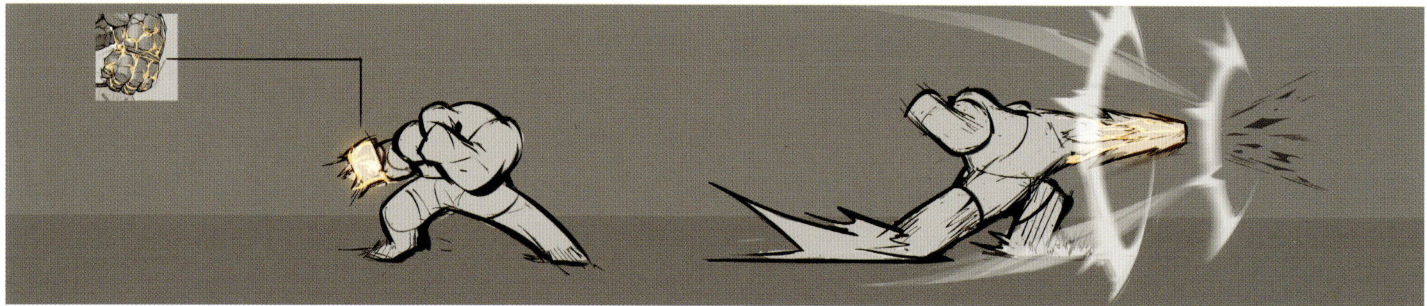

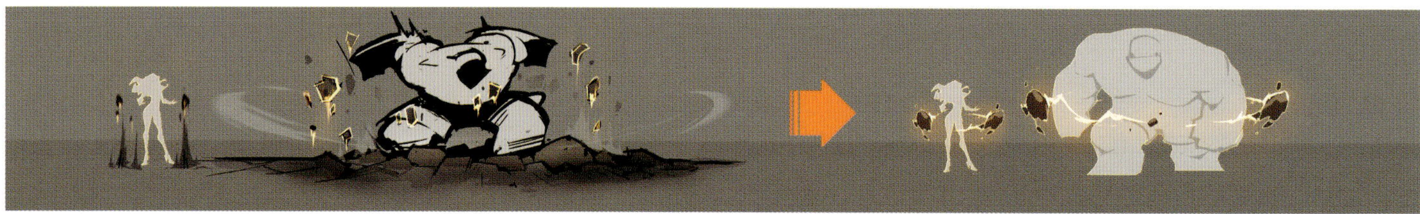

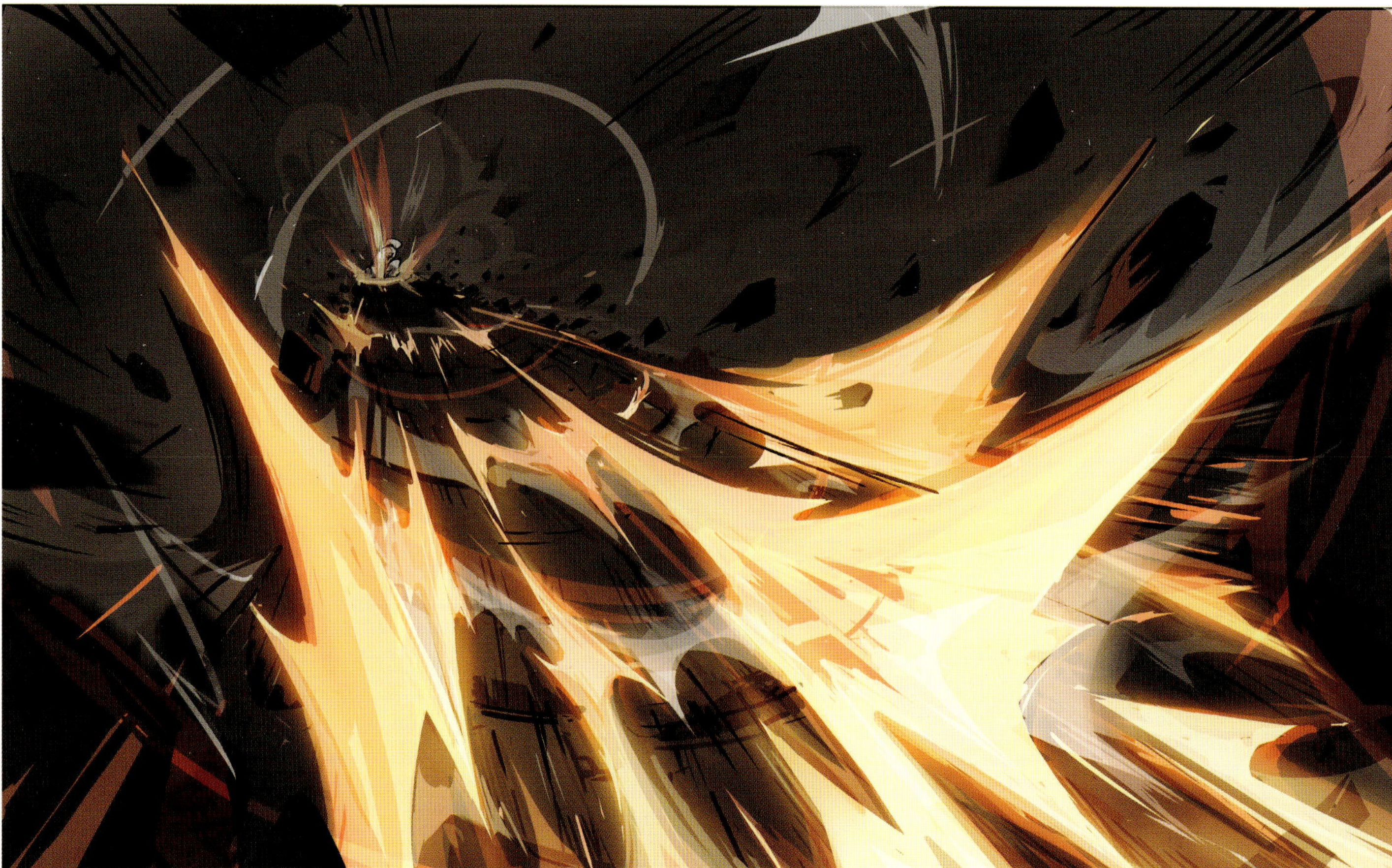

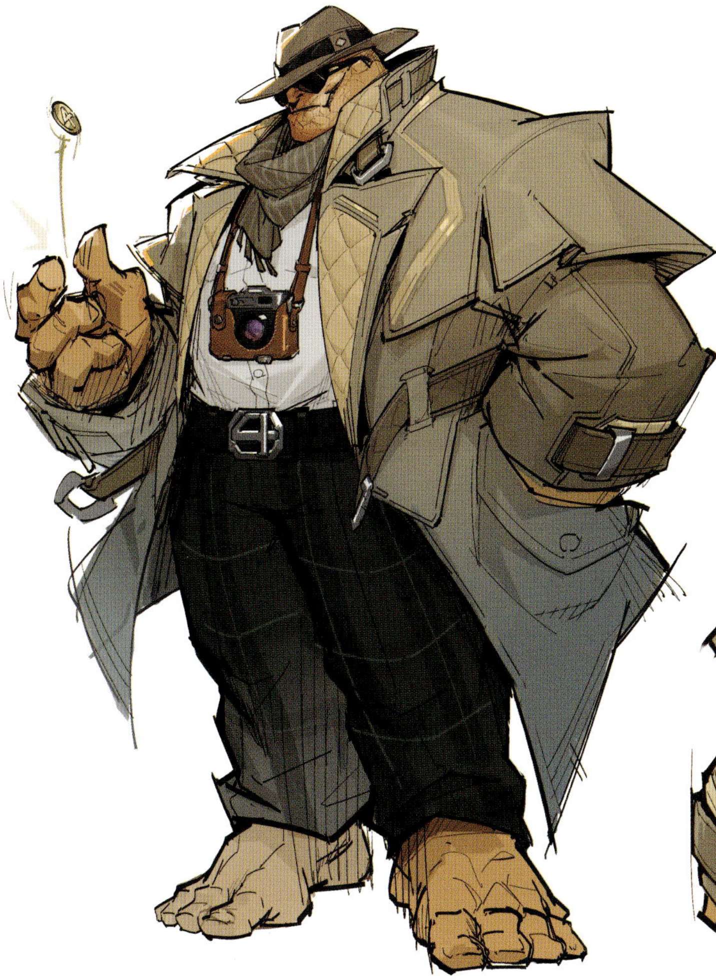

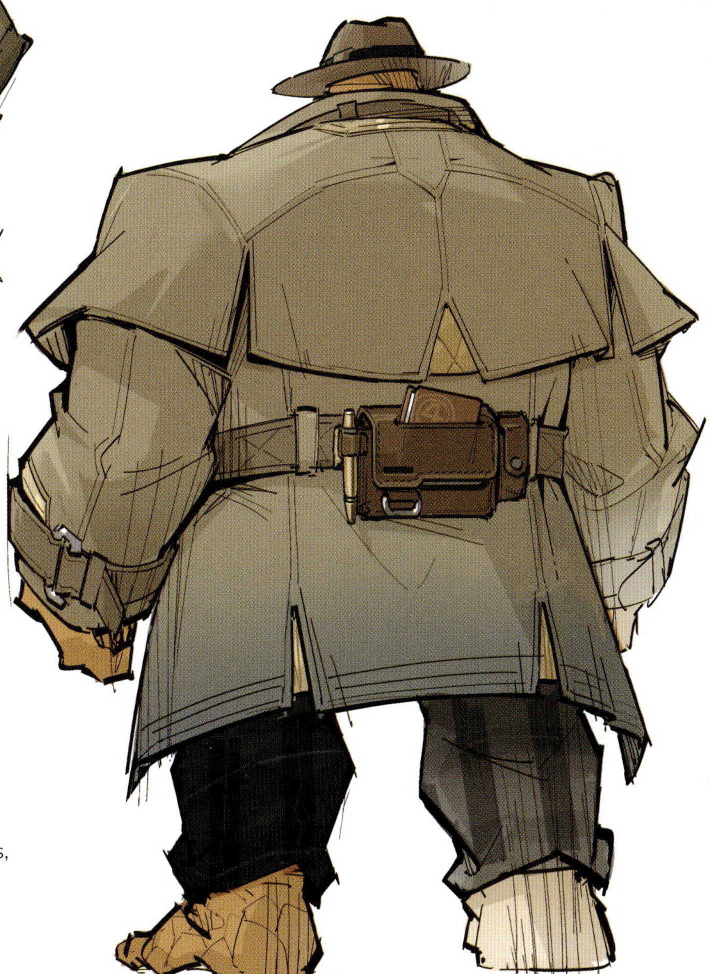

THE THING: COSMETIC VARIETY

The Thing disguises himself to avoid being noticed or judged by others, wearing a loose trench coat and hat to move around the city incognito.

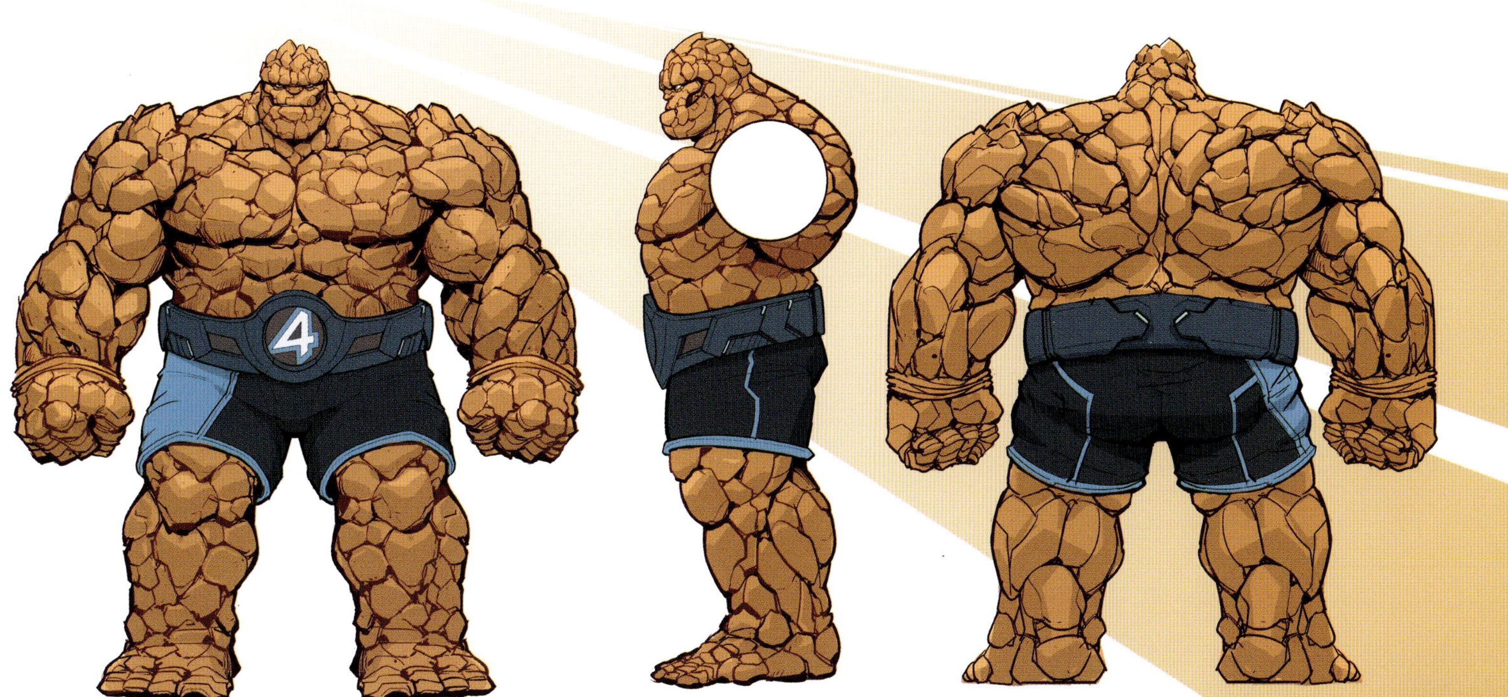

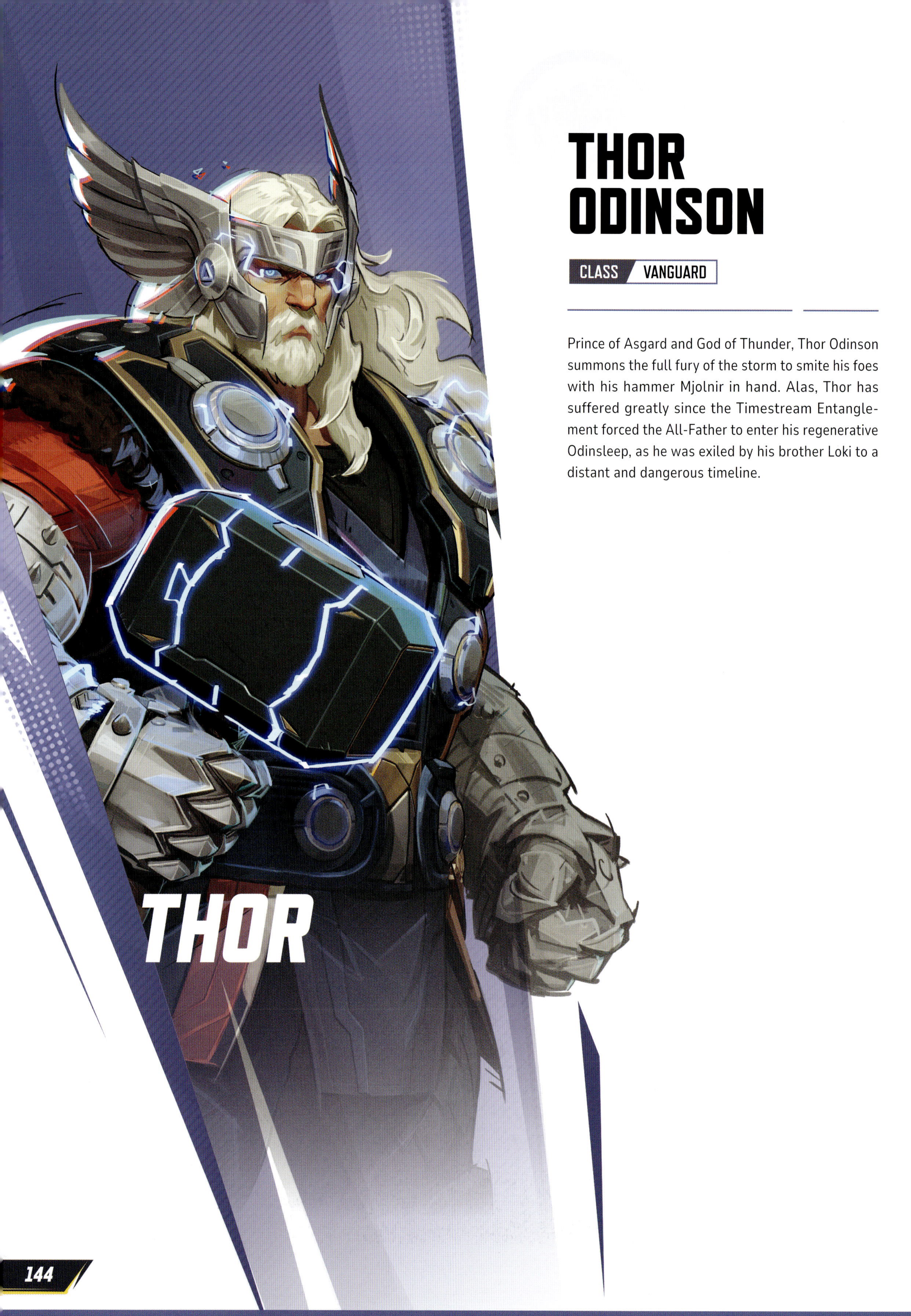

THOR ODINSON

CLASS VANGUARD

Prince of Asgard and God of Thunder, Thor Odinson summons the full fury of the storm to smite his foes with his hammer Mjolnir in hand. Alas, Thor has suffered greatly since the Timestream Entanglement forced the All-Father to enter his regenerative Odinsleep, as he was exiled by his brother Loki to a distant and dangerous timeline.

As the son of Odin, Thor wields divine power to summon lightning and unleash fury on his enemies. With his powerful hammer, Mjolnir, he commands the battlefield!

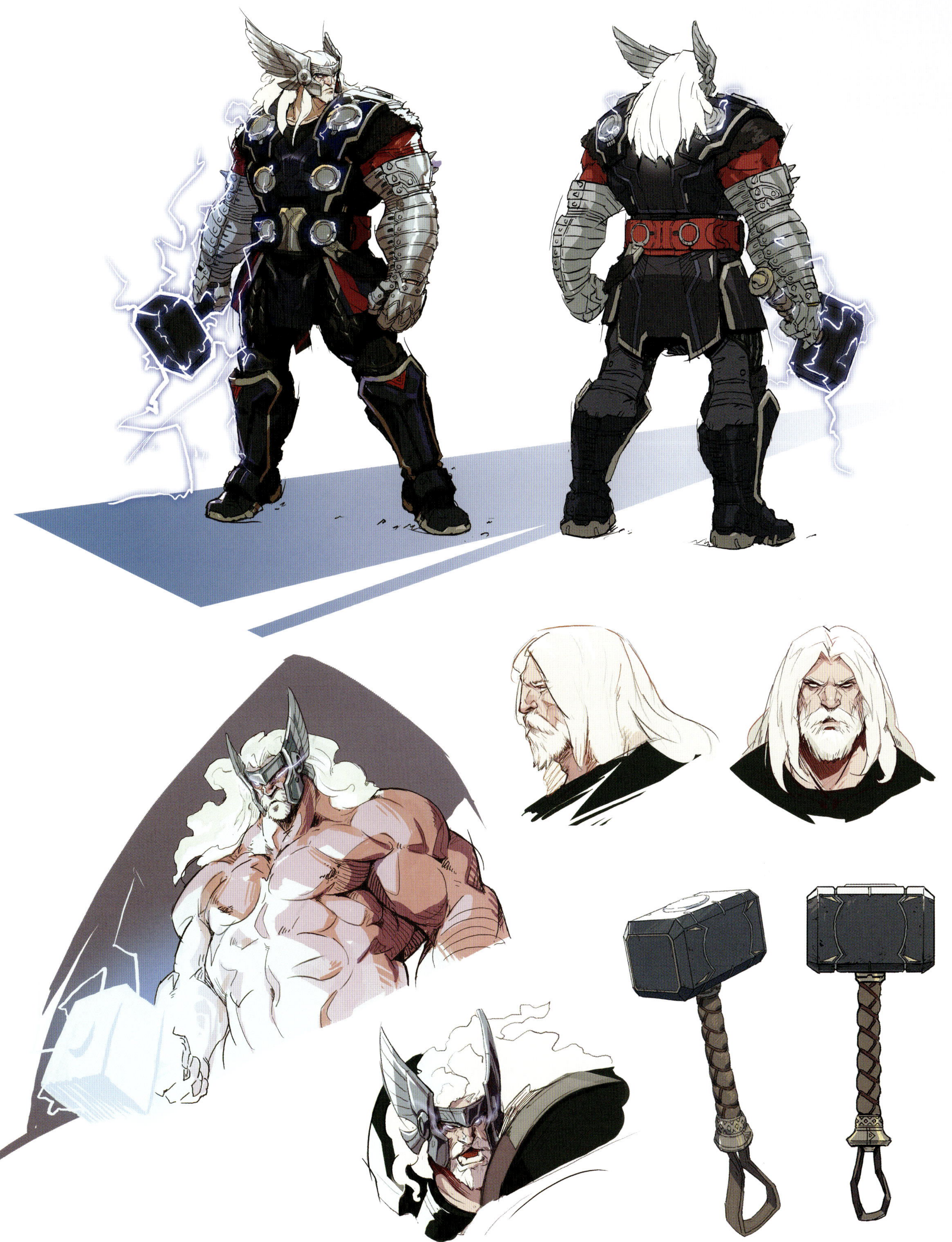

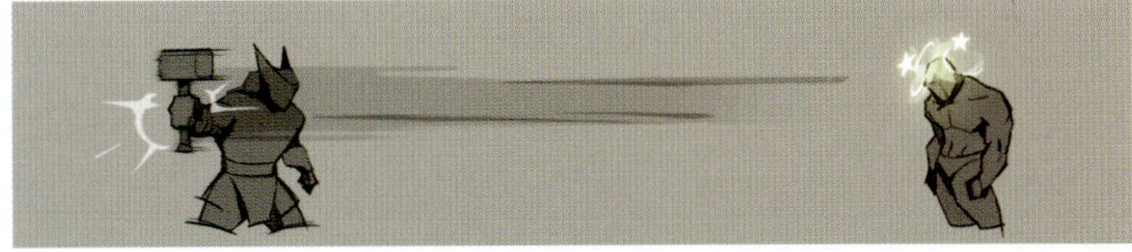
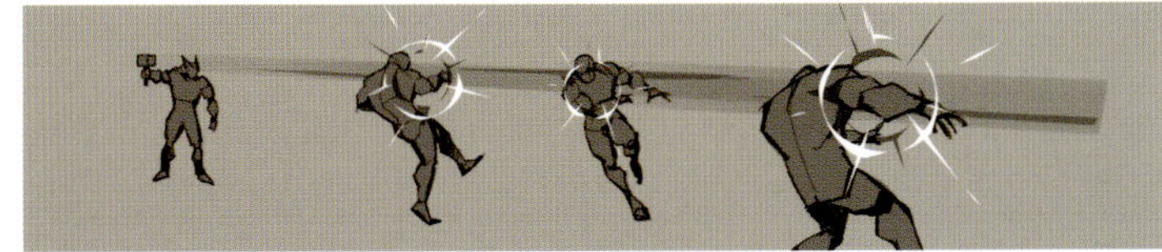
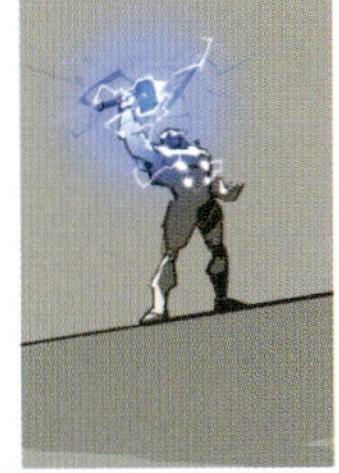
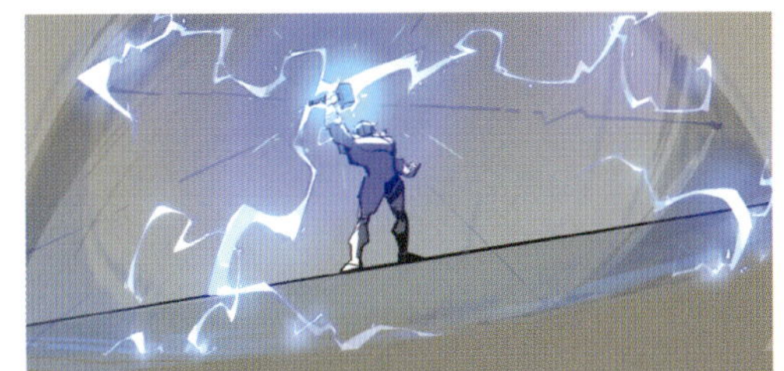
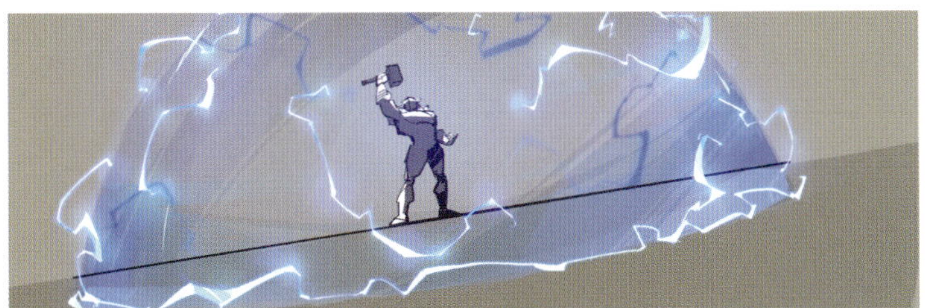
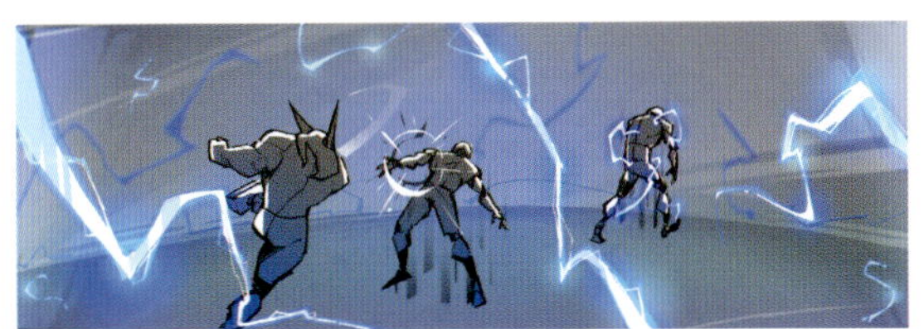
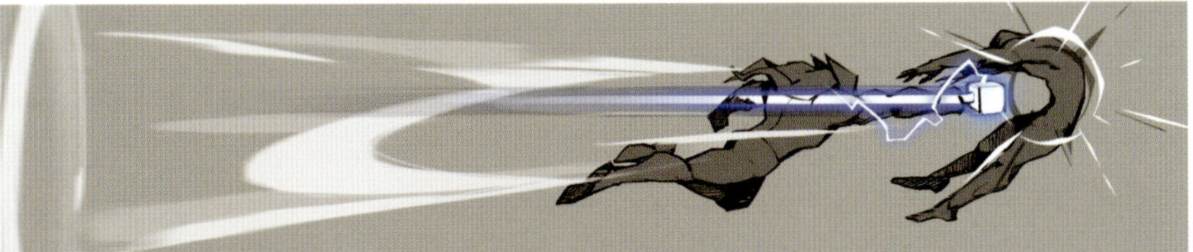
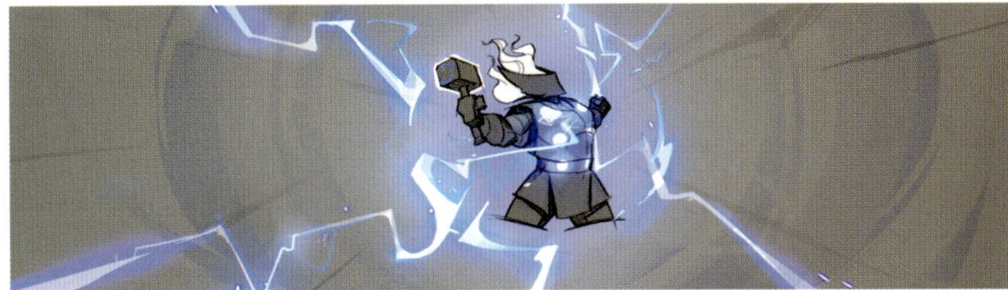
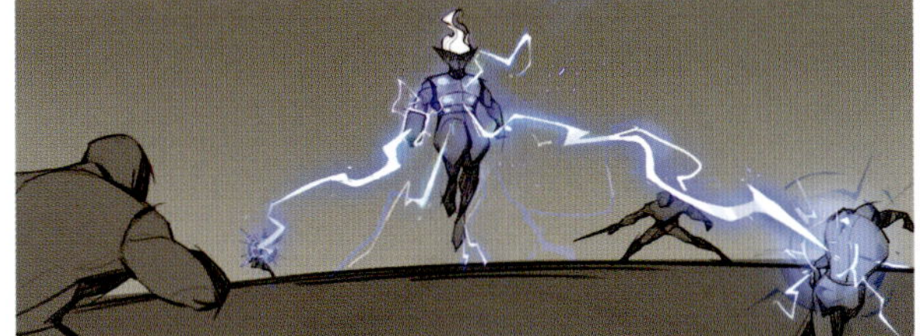
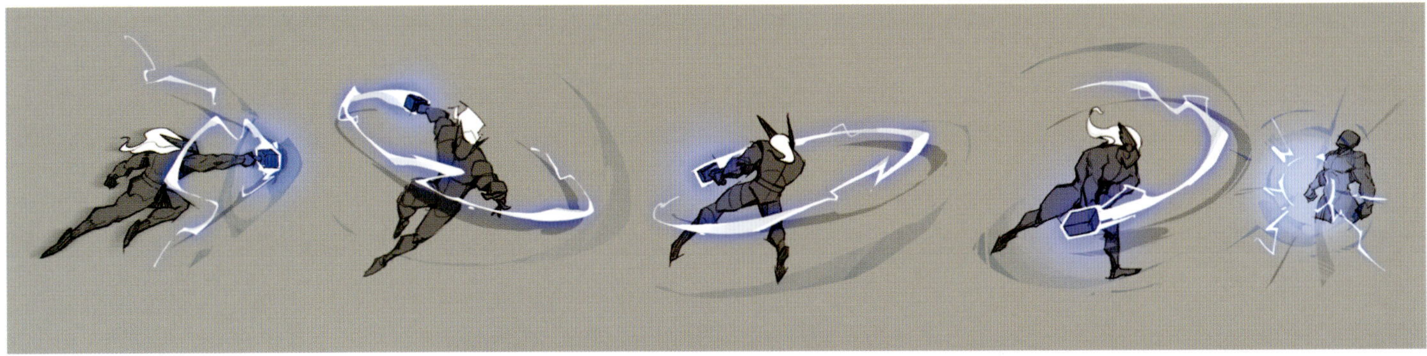

THOR: ABILITIES

Thor swings his hammer in close combat and can also use thunder to release arc lightning for ranged attacks. His ultimate skill, God of Thunder, unleashes the wrath of Asgard, leaving enemies collapsed.

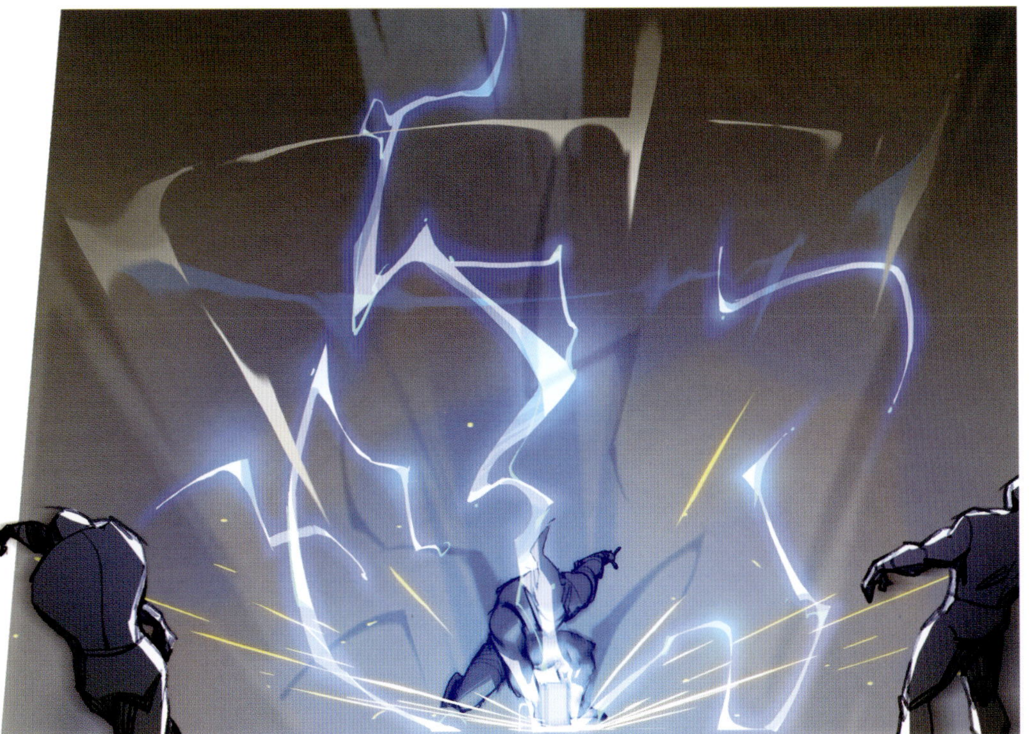

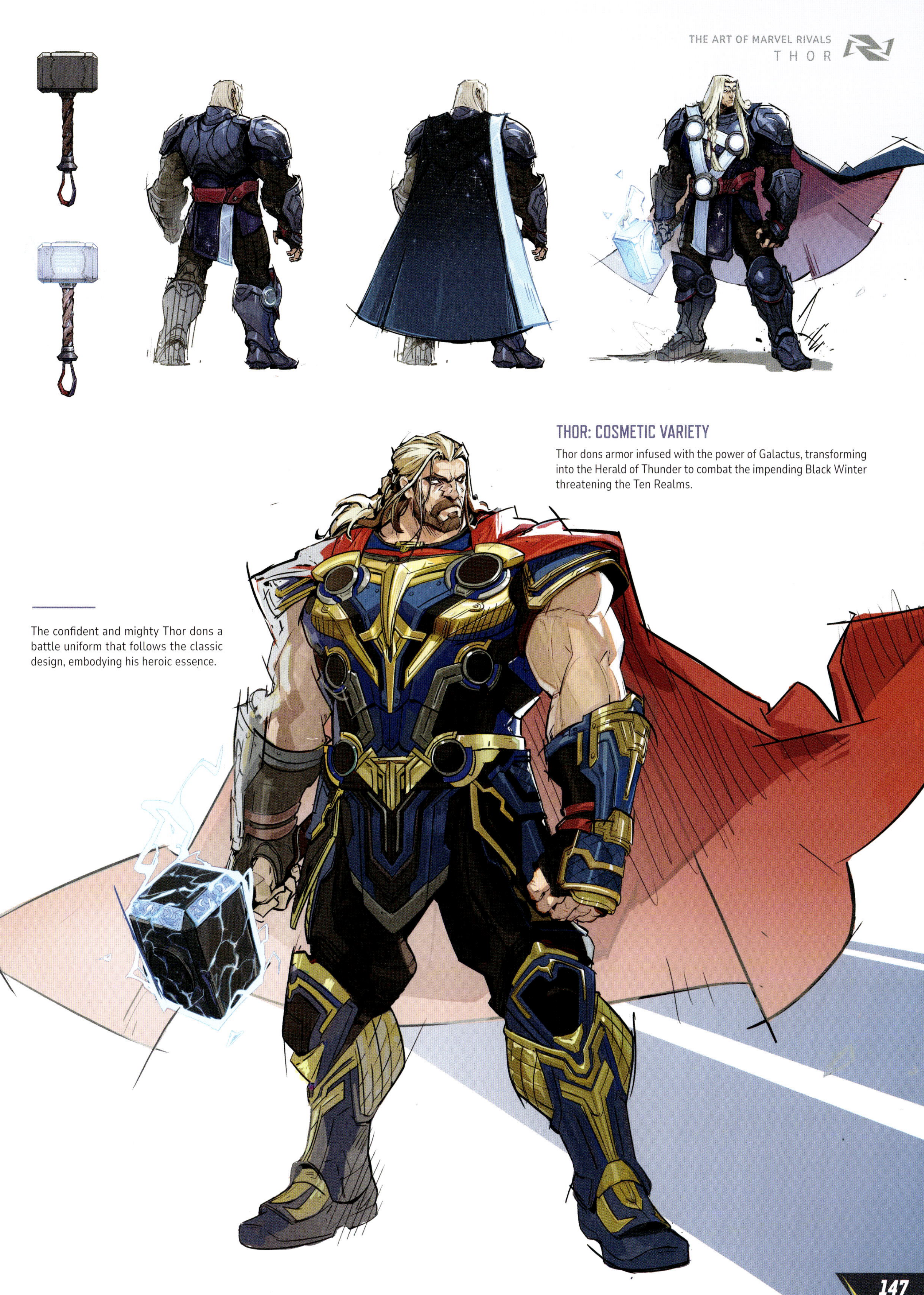

THOR: COSMETIC VARIETY

Thor dons armor infused with the power of Galactus, transforming into the Herald of Thunder to combat the impending Black Winter threatening the Ten Realms.

The confident and mighty Thor dons a battle uniform that follows the classic design, embodying his heroic essence.

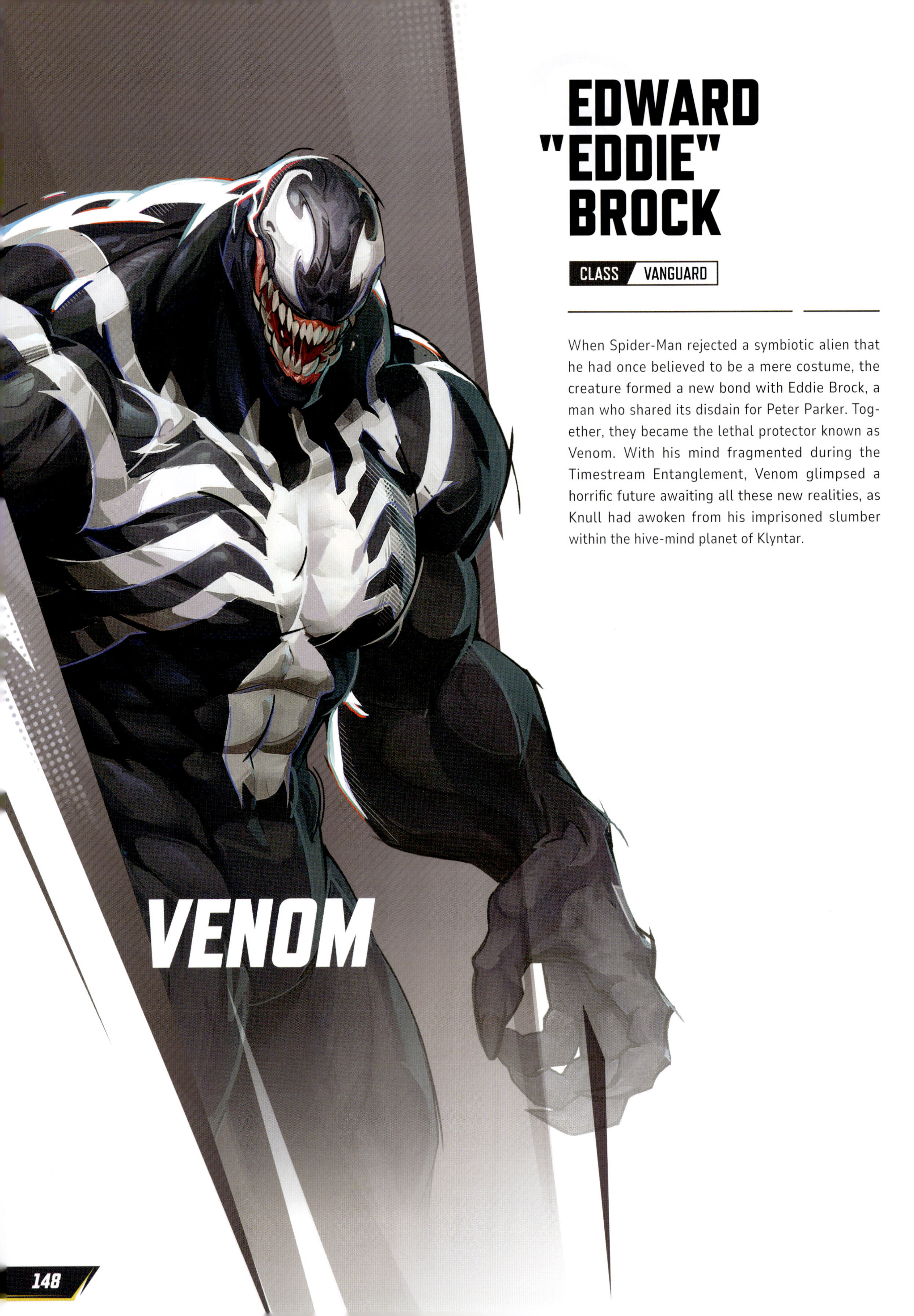

EDWARD "EDDIE" BROCK

CLASS VANGUARD

When Spider-Man rejected a symbiotic alien that he had once believed to be a mere costume, the creature formed a new bond with Eddie Brock, a man who shared its disdain for Peter Parker. Together, they became the lethal protector known as Venom. With his mind fragmented during the Timestream Entanglement, Venom glimpsed a horrific future awaiting all these new realities, as Knull had awoken from his imprisoned slumber within the hive-mind planet of Klyntar.

The symbiote's form, merged with Eddie Brock, can unleash a relentless flurry of tentacles at any moment. Enemies ensnared by Venom have no choice but to surrender to this alien predator.

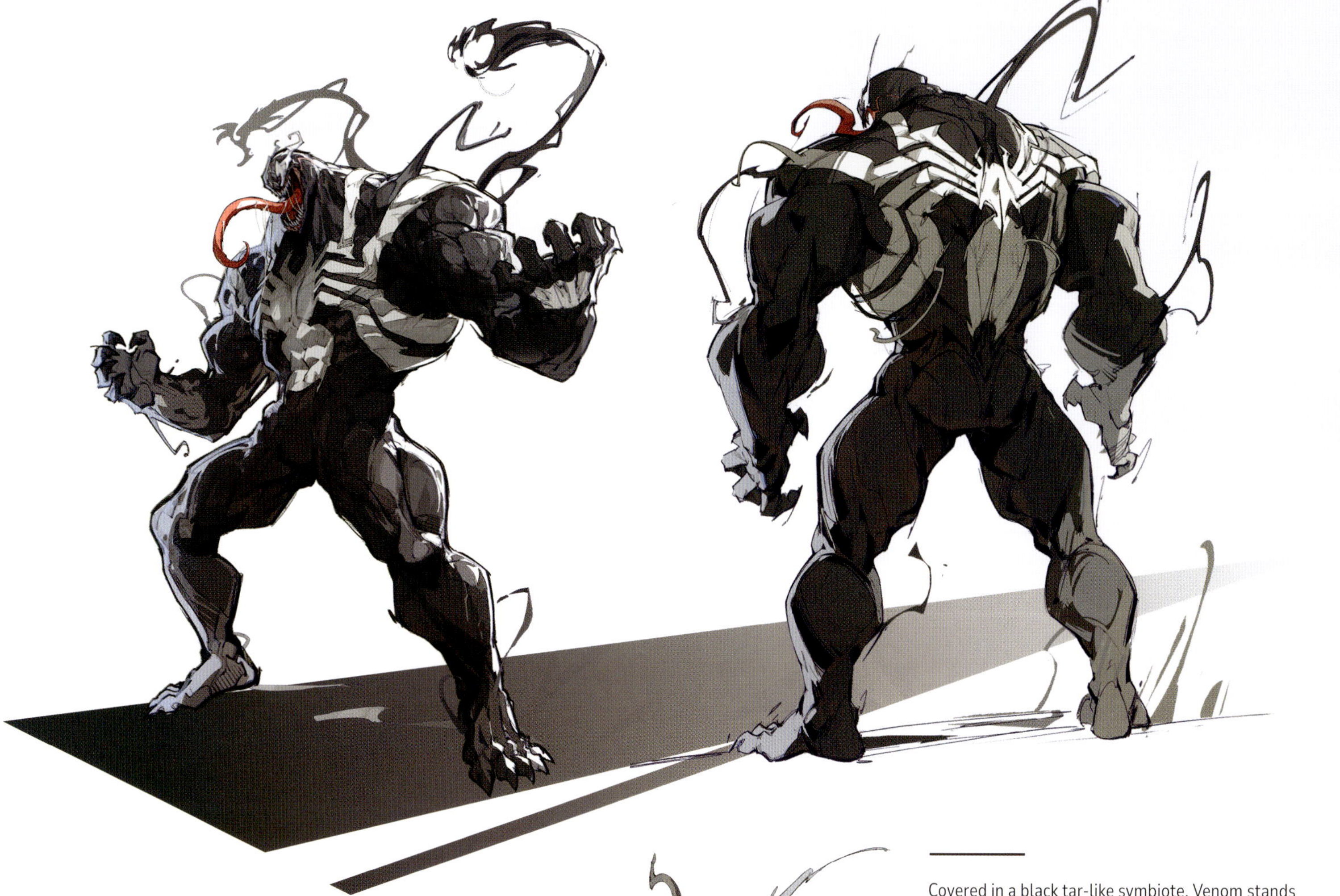

Covered in a black tar-like symbiote, Venom stands over eight feet tall and features a white winged spider logo on the chest and a white rectangular web-launching area on the back of the hands.

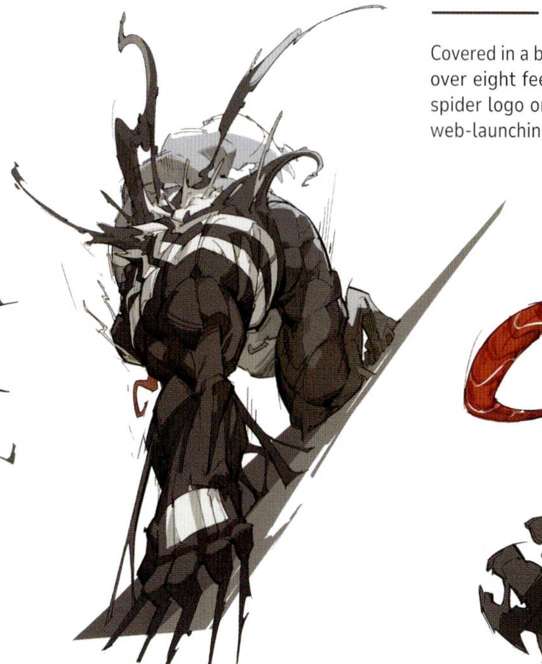

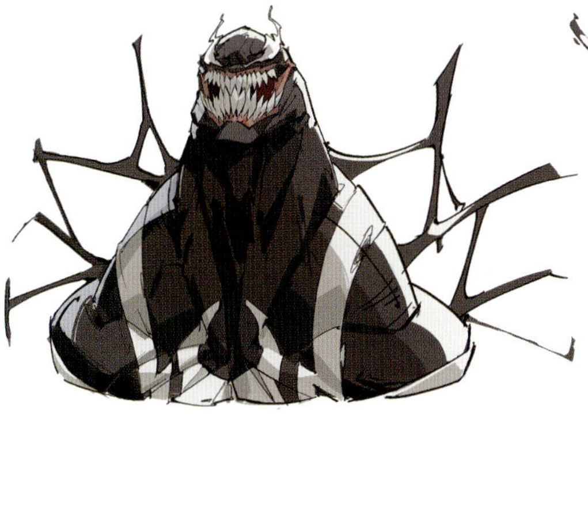

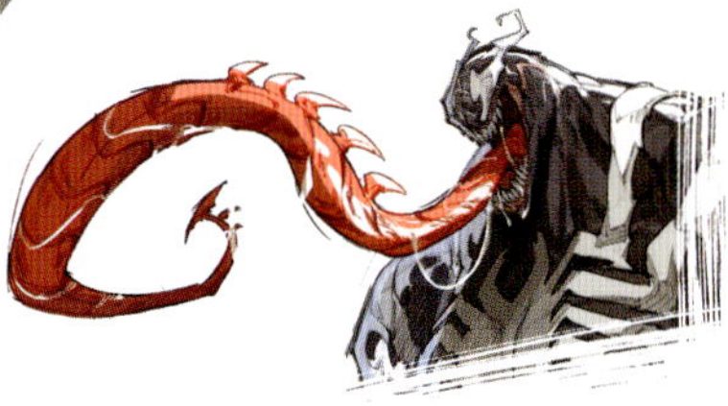

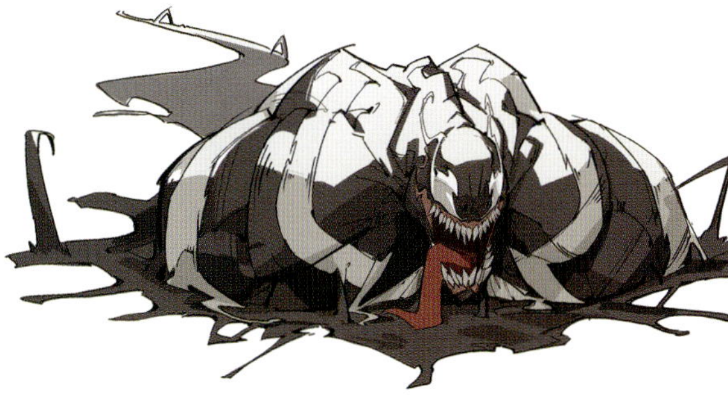

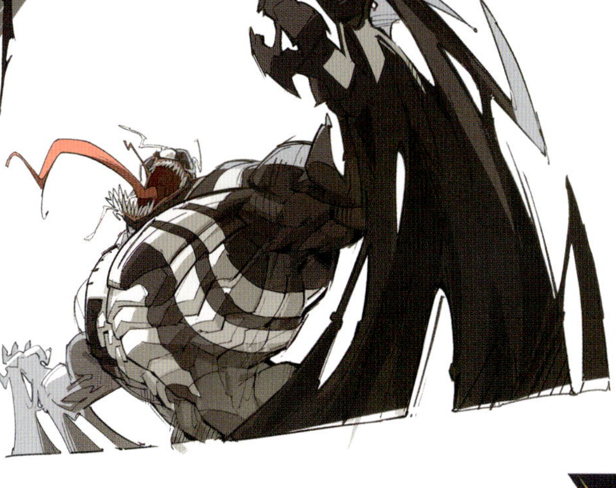

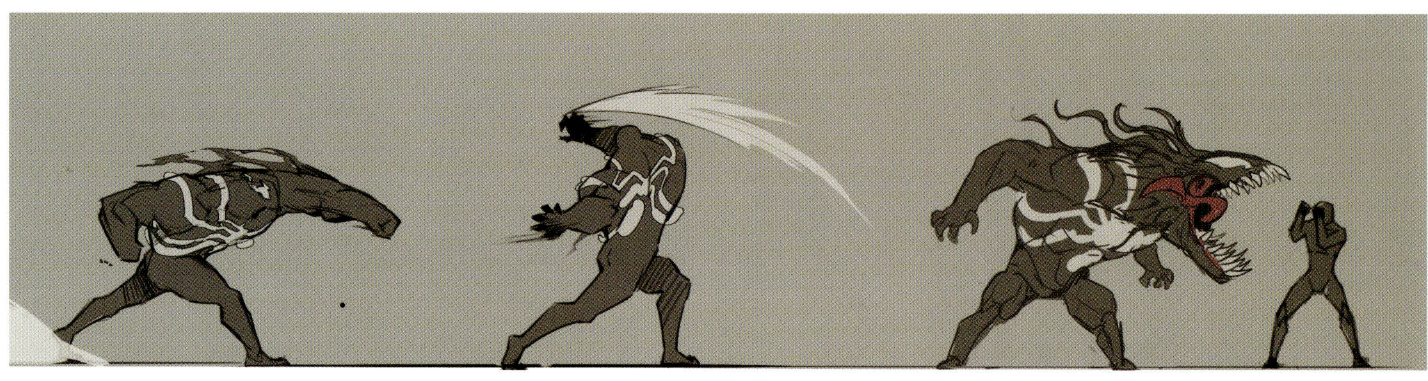

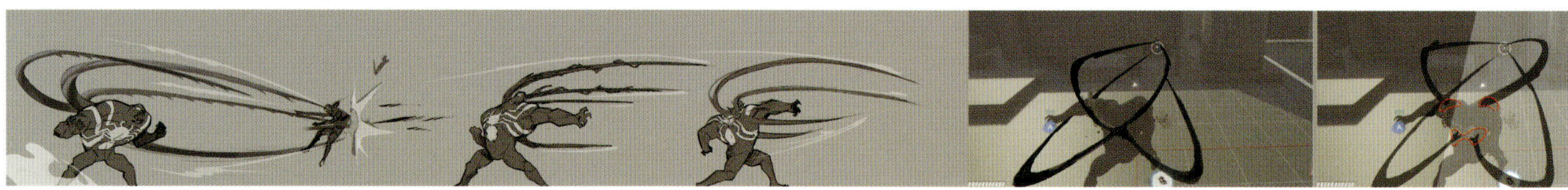

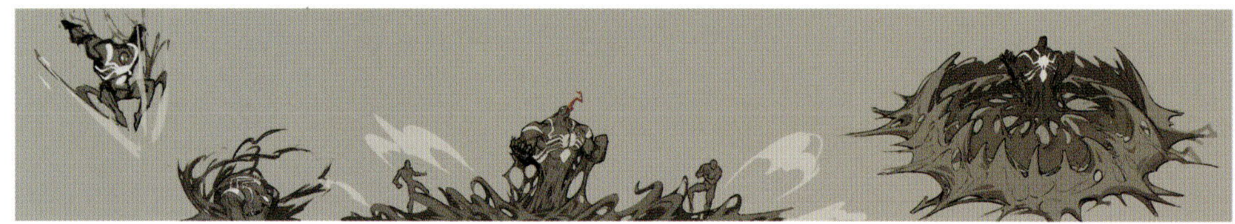

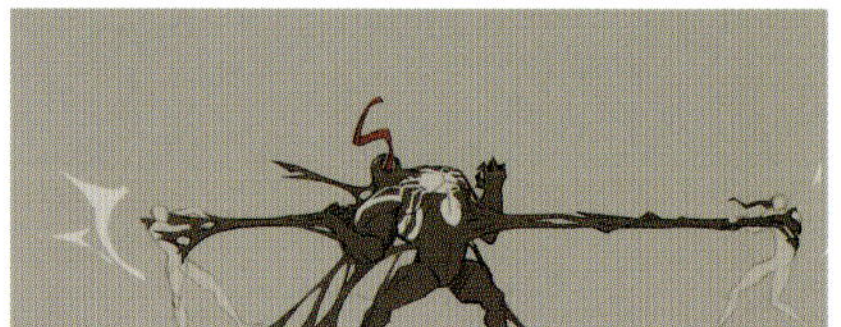

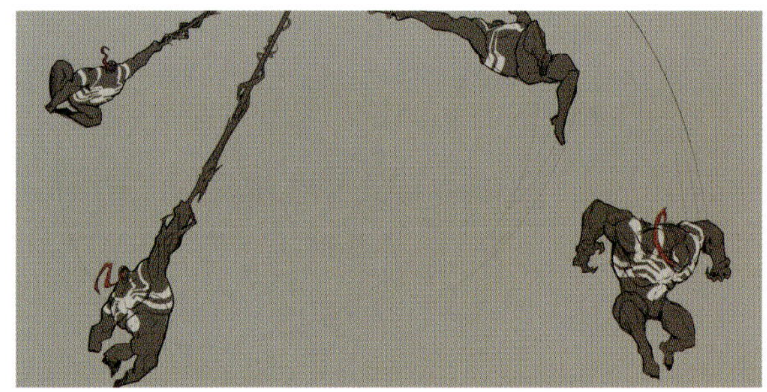

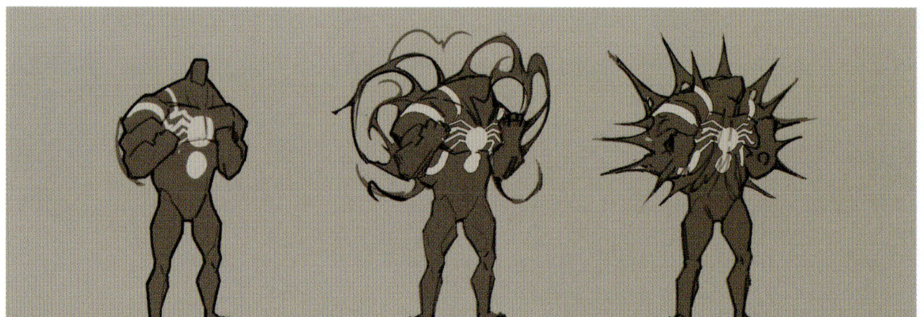

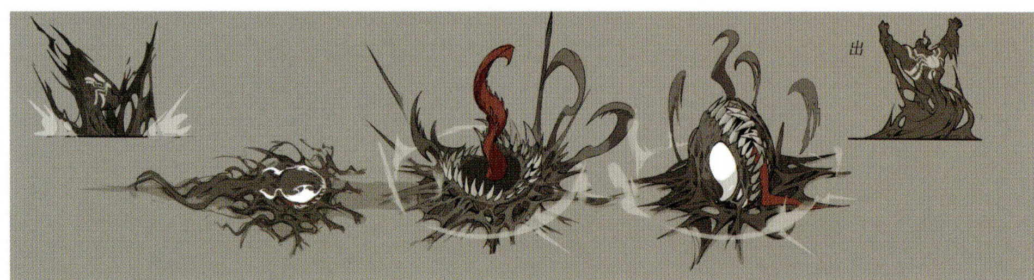

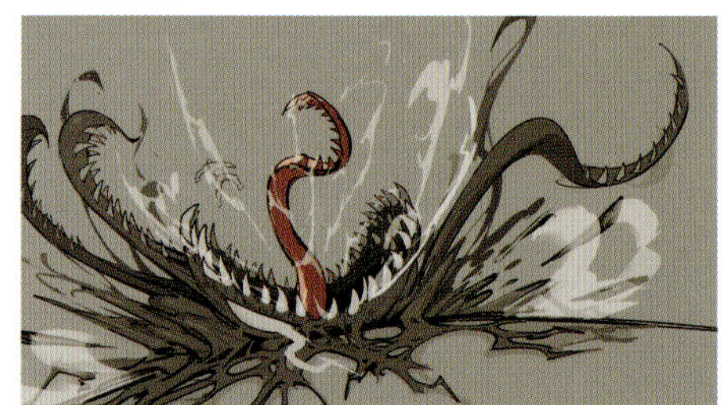

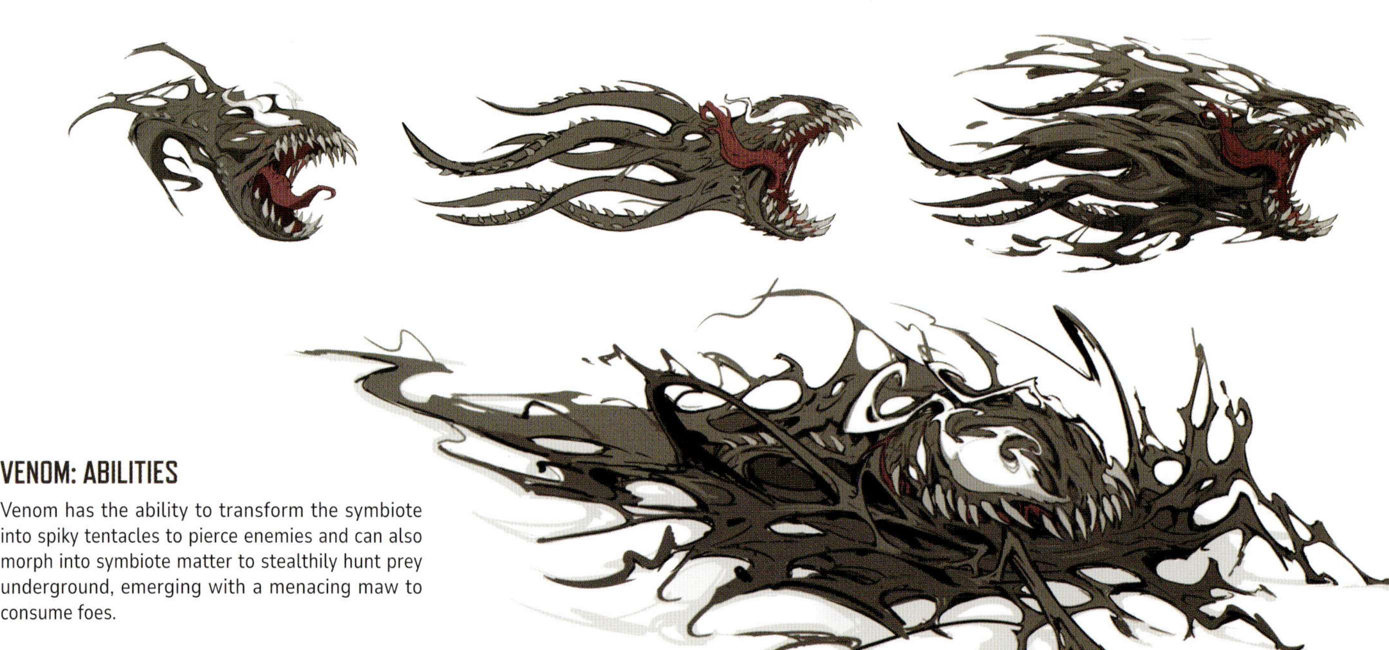

VENOM: ABILITIES

Venom has the ability to transform the symbiote into spiky tentacles to pierce enemies and can also morph into symbiote matter to stealthily hunt prey underground, emerging with a menacing maw to consume foes.

VENOM: COSMETIC VARIETY

In a winter holiday environment, Eddie and Venom are drawn to the icy surroundings. Venom merges with Eddie's white blood cells, resulting in a translucent body and the formation of sharp, icy spikes.

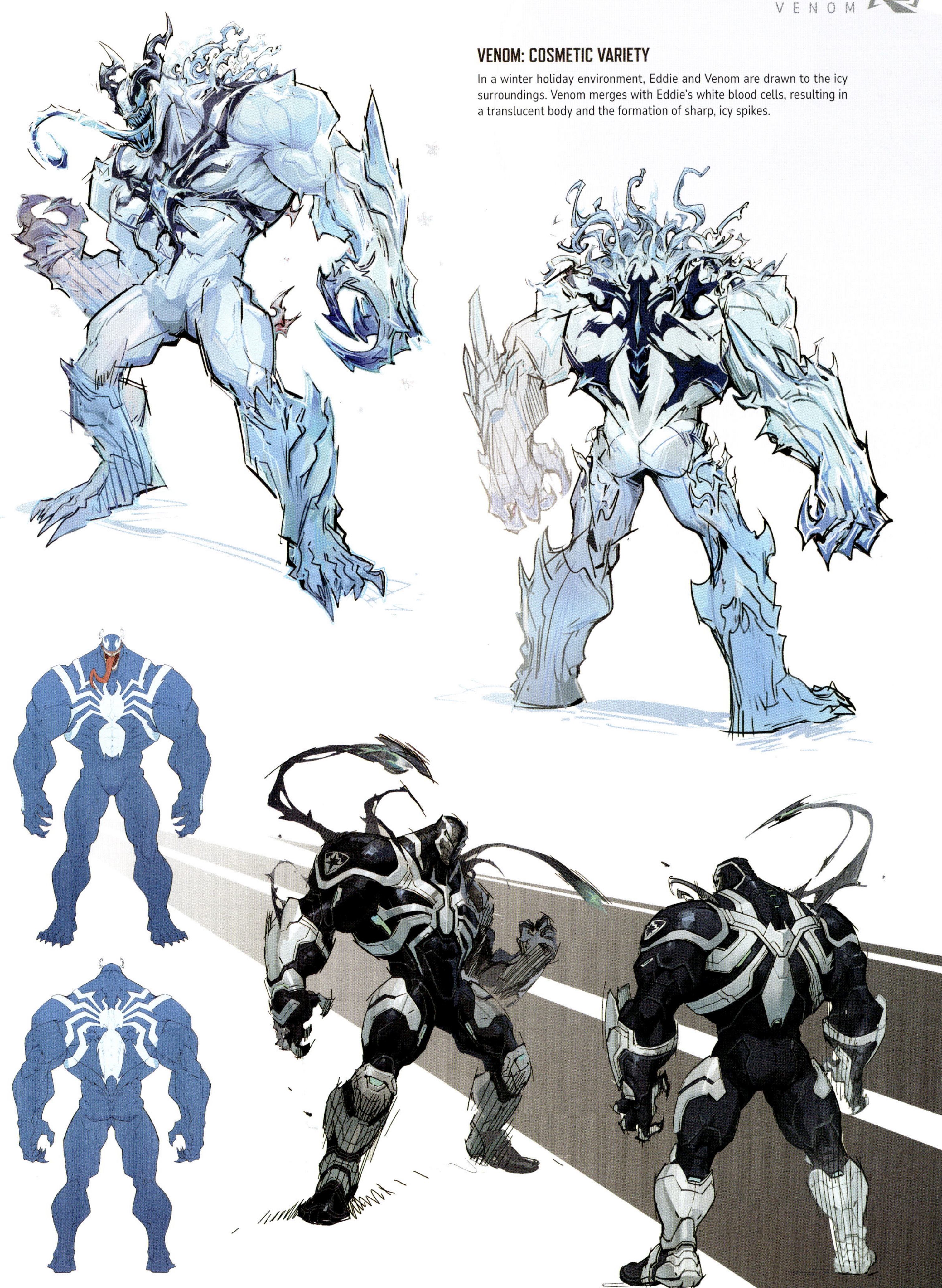

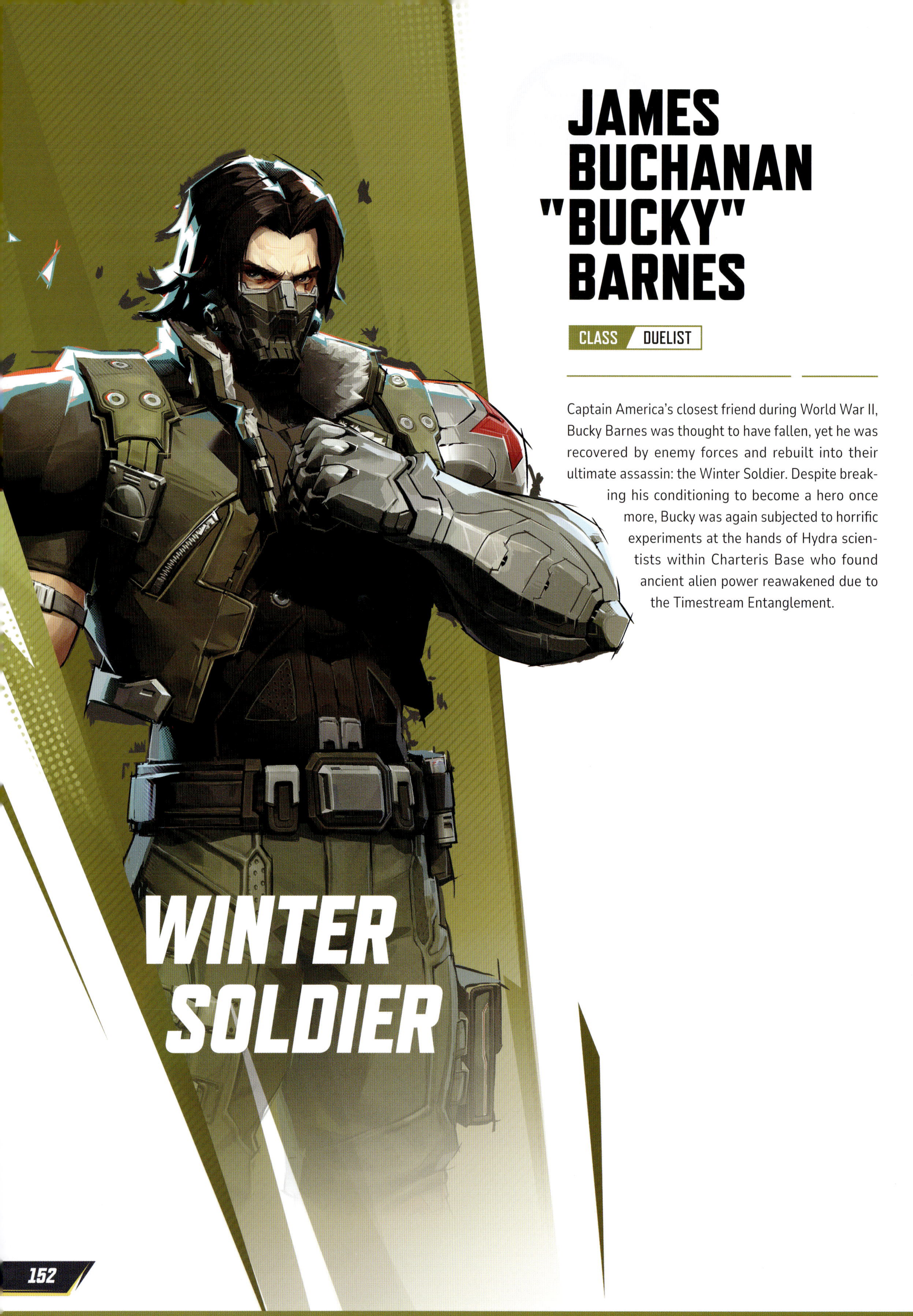

JAMES BUCHANAN "BUCKY" BARNES

CLASS / DUELIST

Captain America's closest friend during World War II, Bucky Barnes was thought to have fallen, yet he was recovered by enemy forces and rebuilt into their ultimate assassin: the Winter Soldier. Despite breaking his conditioning to become a hero once more, Bucky was again subjected to horrific experiments at the hands of Hydra scientists within Charteris Base who found ancient alien power reawakened due to the Timestream Entanglement.

Despite the brainwashing from horrific experiments, Bucky Barnes remains true to himself. He is always ready to use his ruthless skills as the Winter Soldier to do what's right, transforming his mechanical arm to deliver powerful, earth-shattering blows!

Under the combined influence of Hive corruption and Hydra's advanced technology, Winter Soldier's mechanical arms can morph into multiple mechanical tentacles in the ultimate skill.

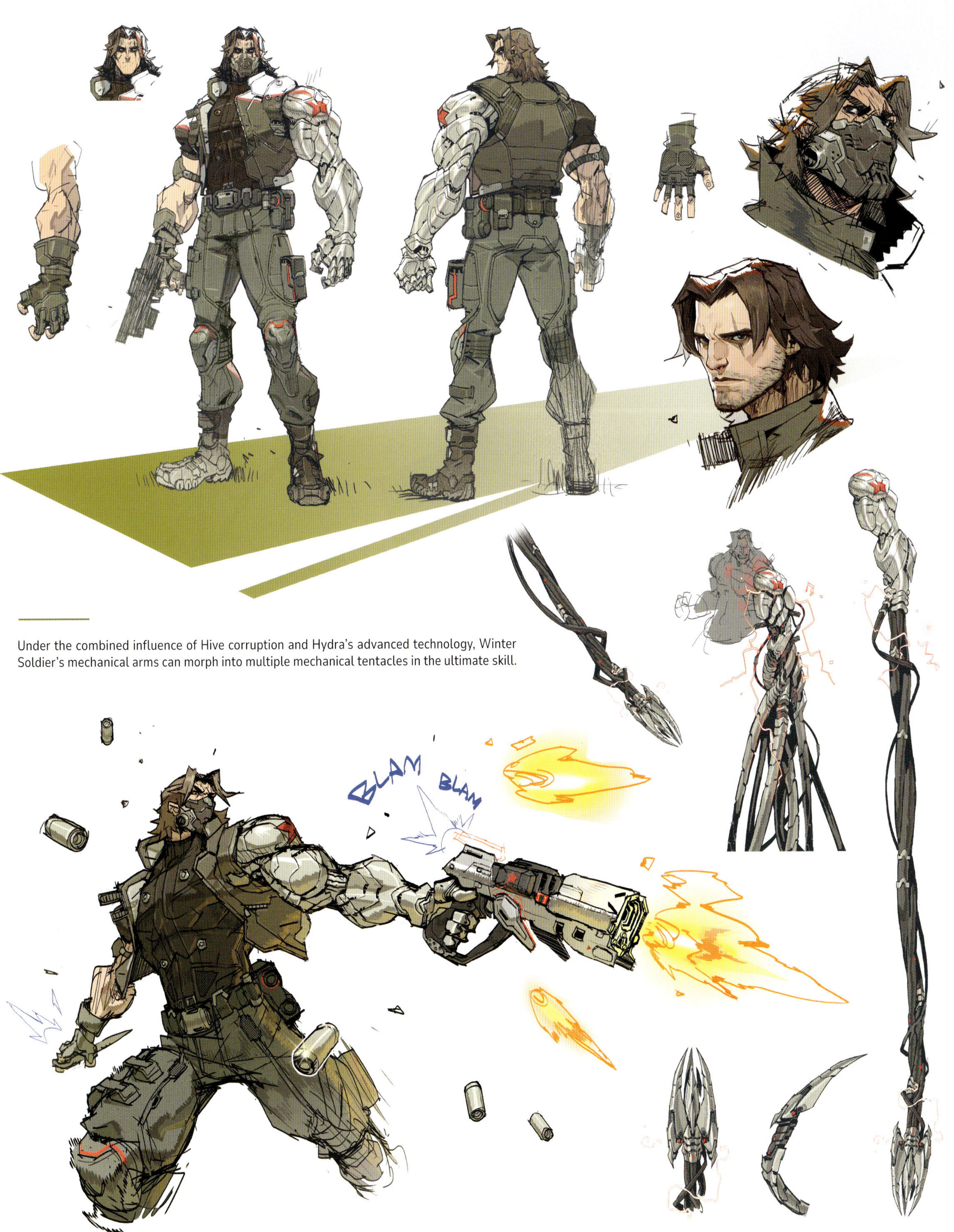

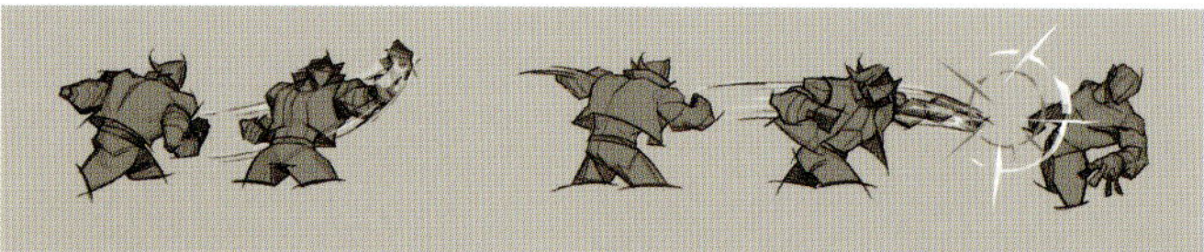

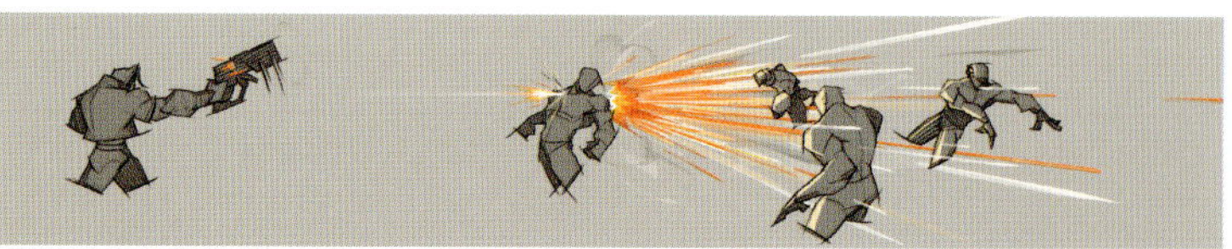

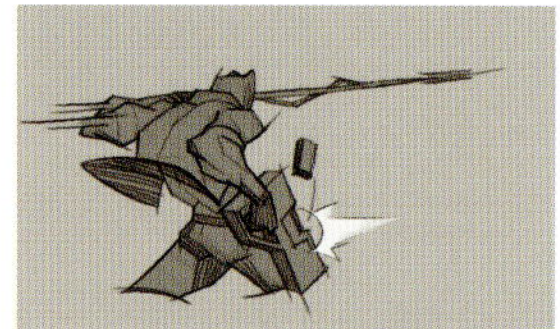

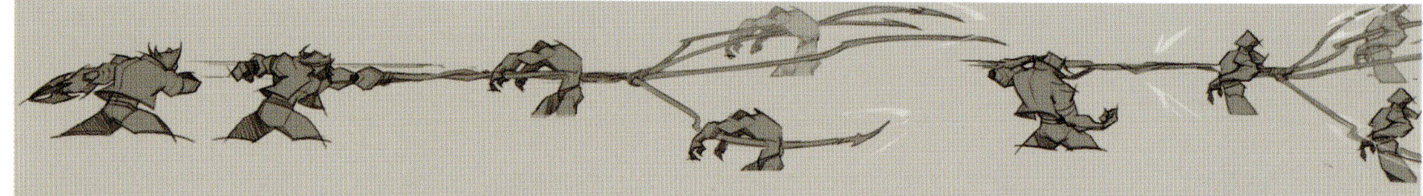

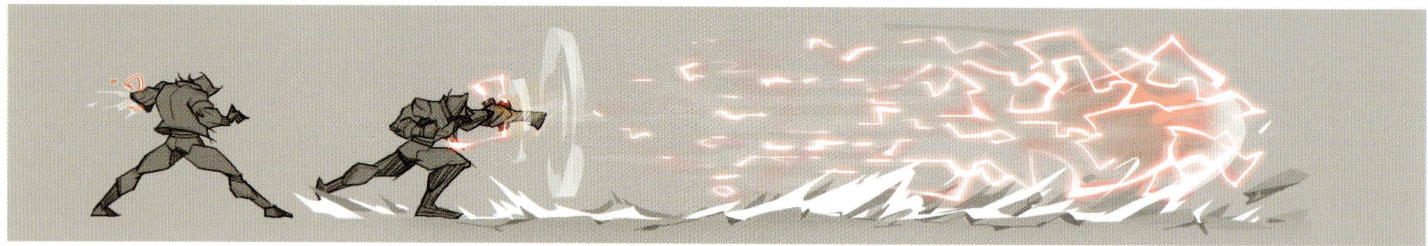

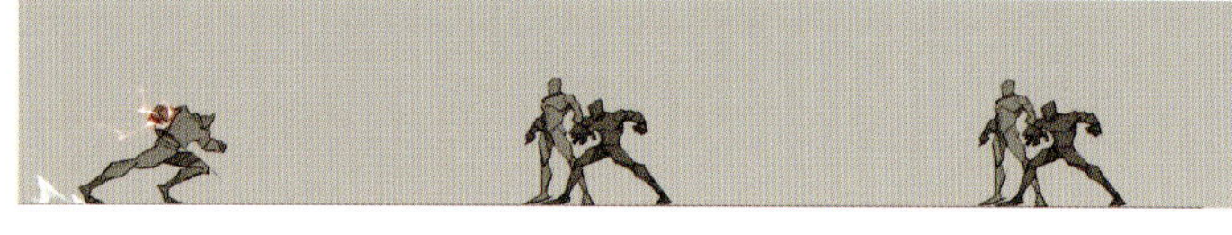

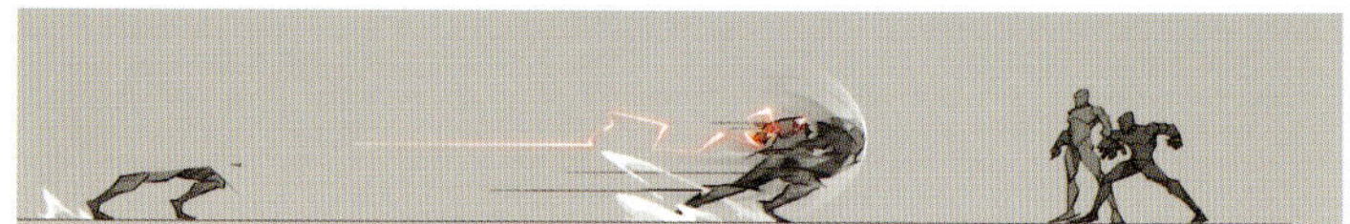

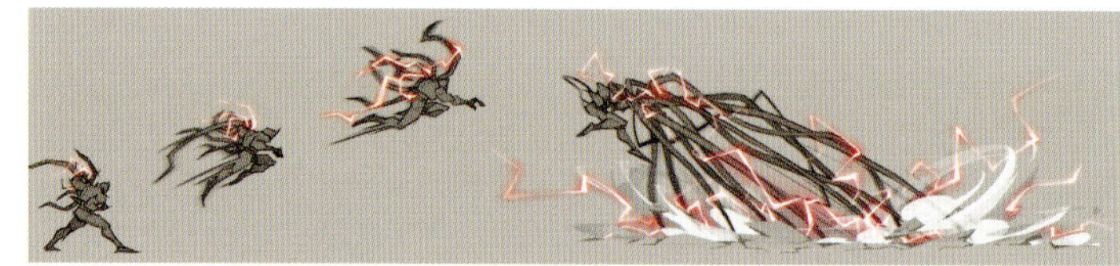

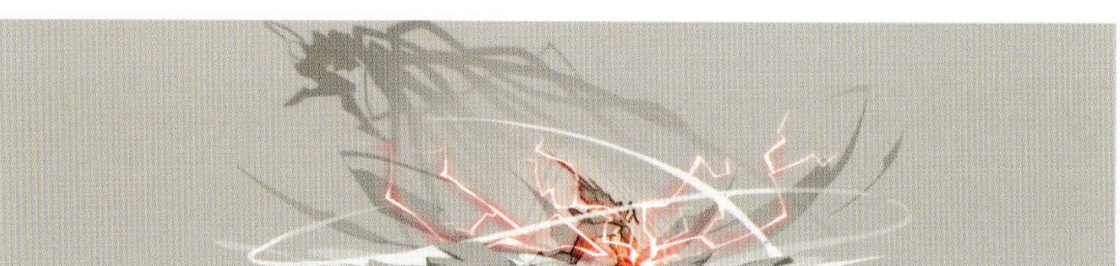

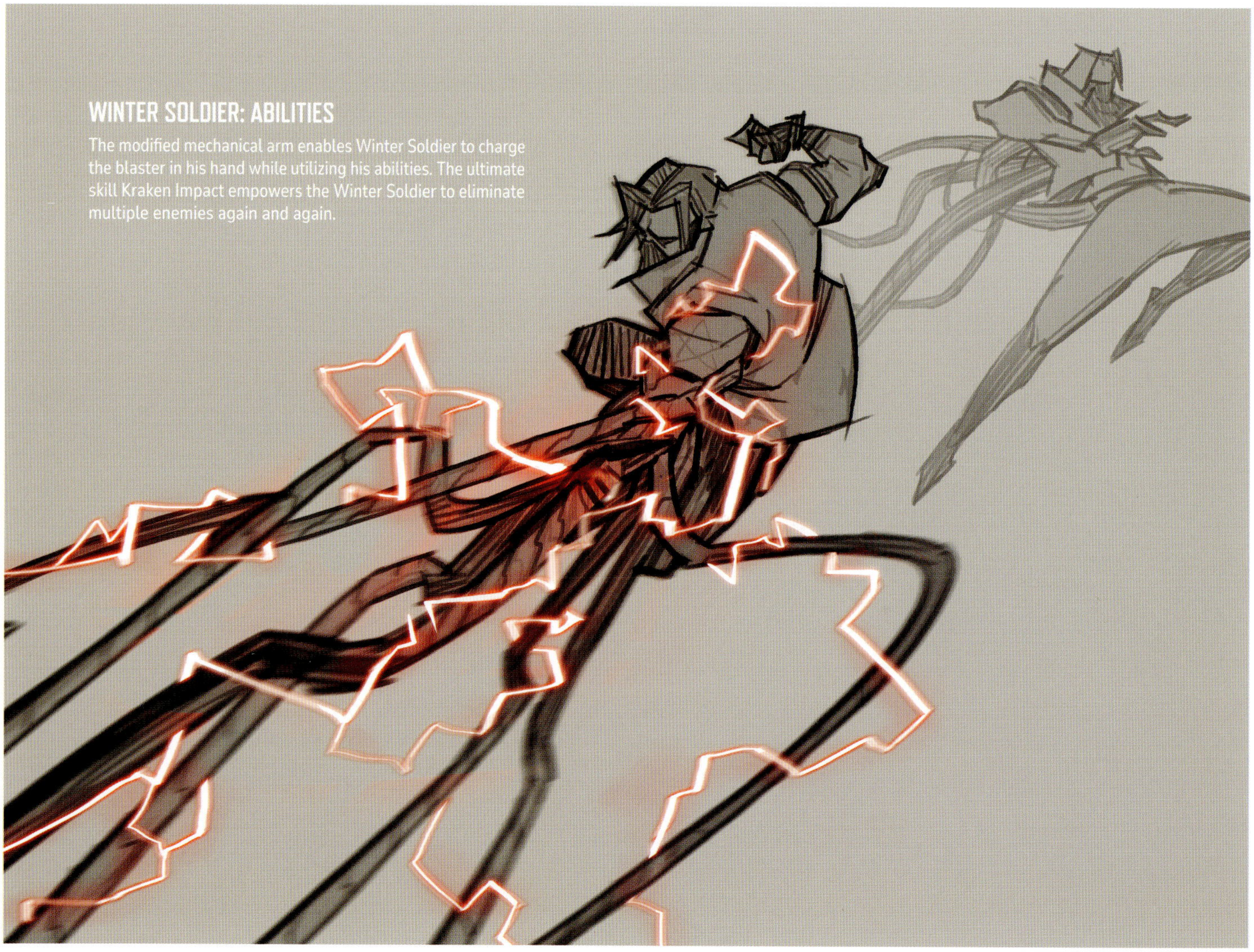

WINTER SOLDIER: ABILITIES

The modified mechanical arm enables Winter Soldier to charge the blaster in his hand while utilizing his abilities. The ultimate skill Kraken Impact empowers the Winter Soldier to eliminate multiple enemies again and again.

WINTER SOLDIER: COSMETIC VARIETY

Adorned in a black-and-red combat suit made of leather and soft armor, the trailblazer of change stands prepared to disrupt the game of manipulating global events.

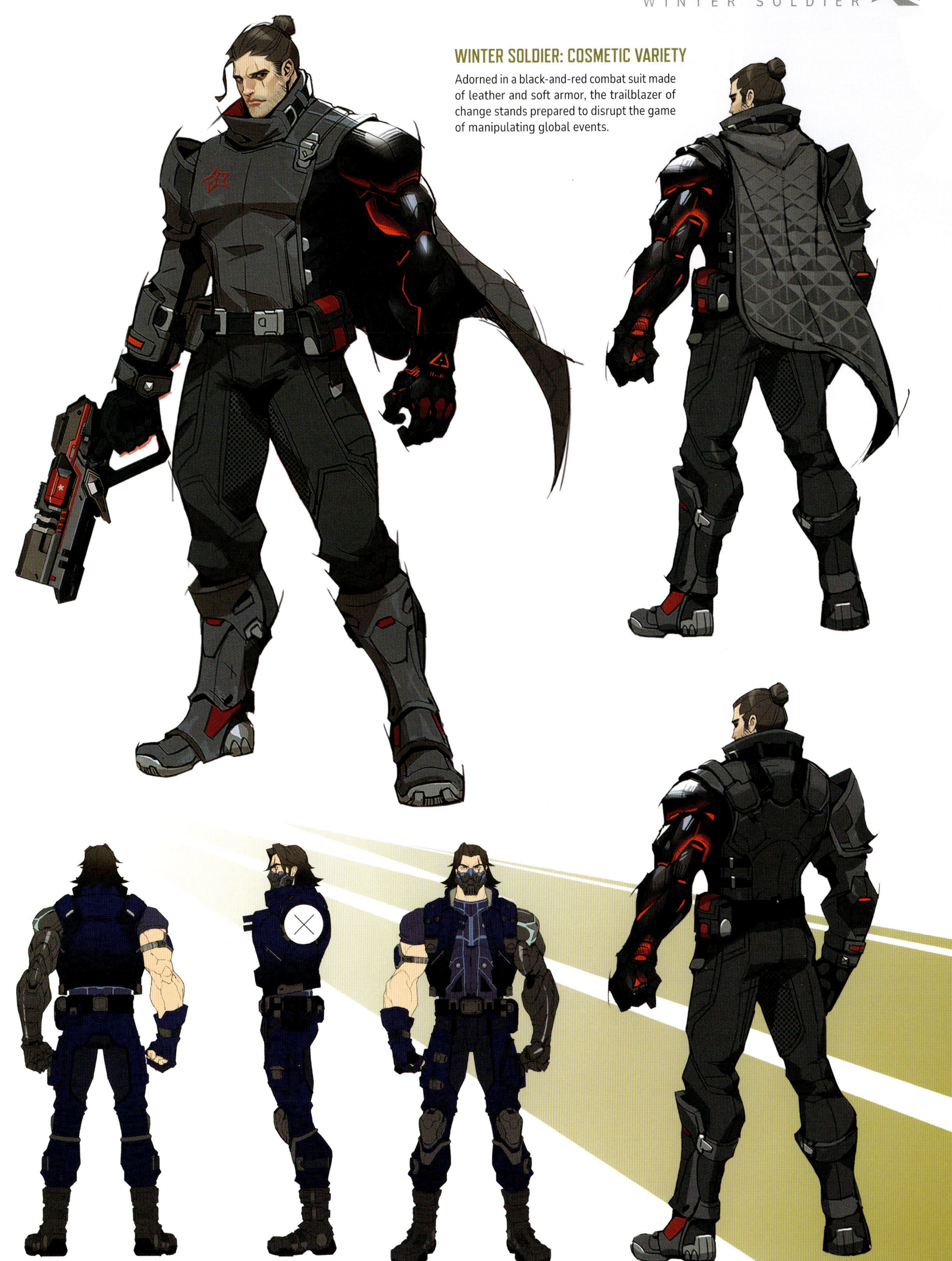

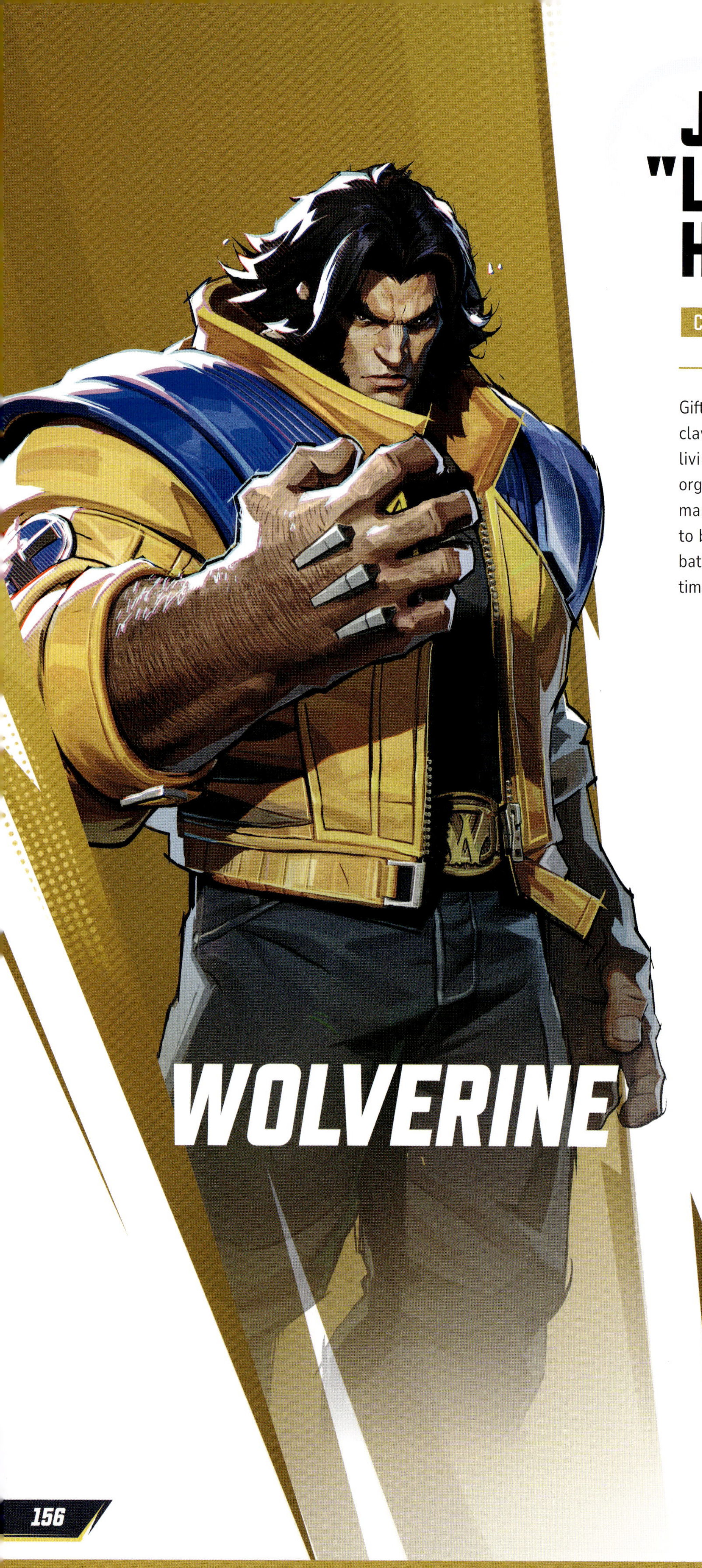

JAMES "LOGAN" HOWLETT

CLASS / DUELIST

Gifted with a powerful healing factor and razor-sharp claws, the mutant called Logan was turned into a living weapon when the clandestine government organization Weapon X bonded indestructible Adamantium to his skeleton. Now, Wolverine has proven to be more than a killing machine, finding ways to battle Doom 2099 while guiding mutants from across time to safety on Krakoa.

Thanks to his powerful mutant healing ability and berserk nature, Logan fearlessly battles his enemies. Wolverine is determined to tear apart any obstacles in his path, and he strikes fiercely with his indestructible Adamantium claws!

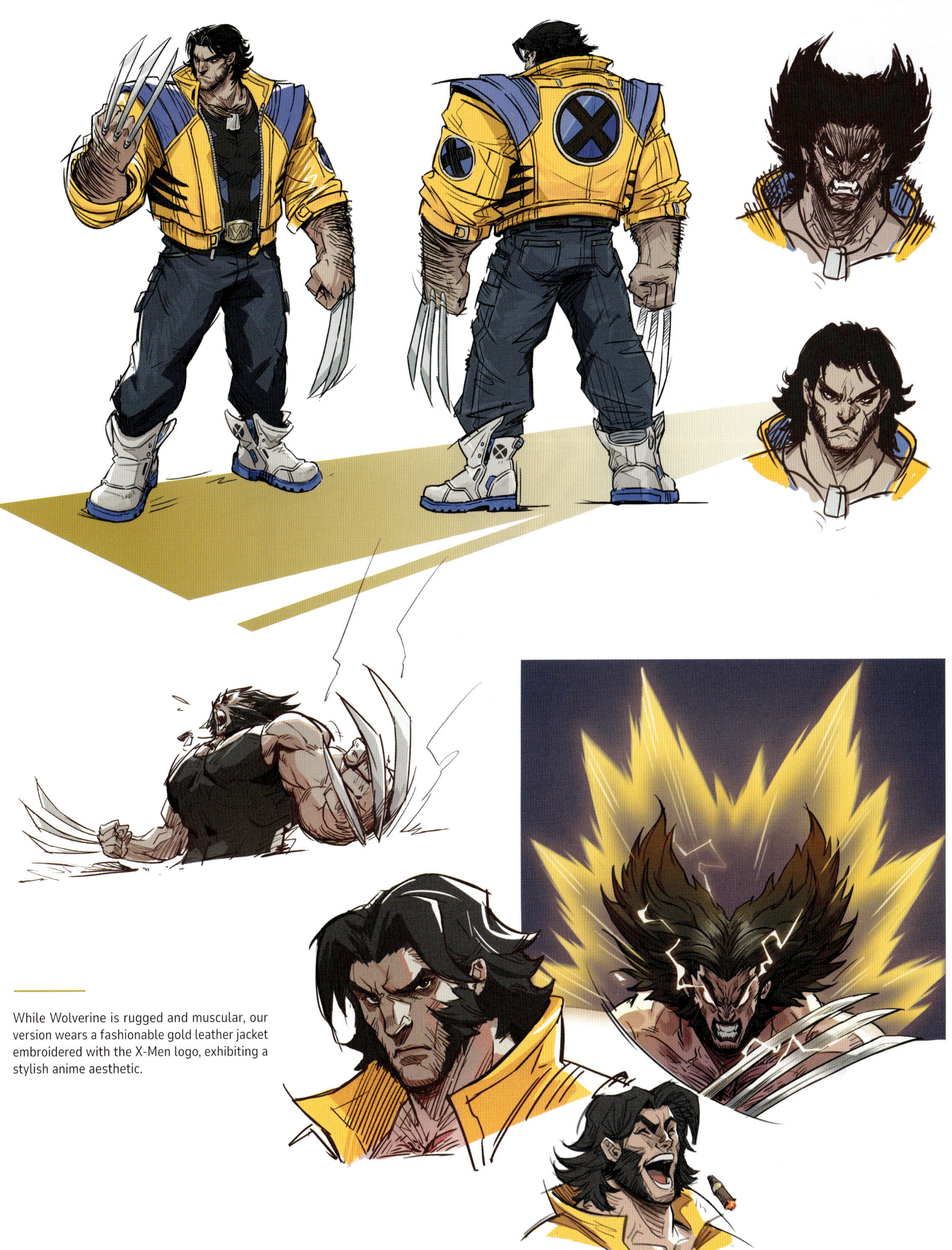

While Wolverine is rugged and muscular, our version wears a fashionable gold leather jacket embroidered with the X-Men logo, exhibiting a stylish anime aesthetic.

WOLVERINE: ABILITIES

Wolverine utilizes his Adamantium claws to shred through the enemy in front of him. His Undying Animal and Regenerative Healing Factor enable him to charge into battle, enduring pain and persisting in combat.

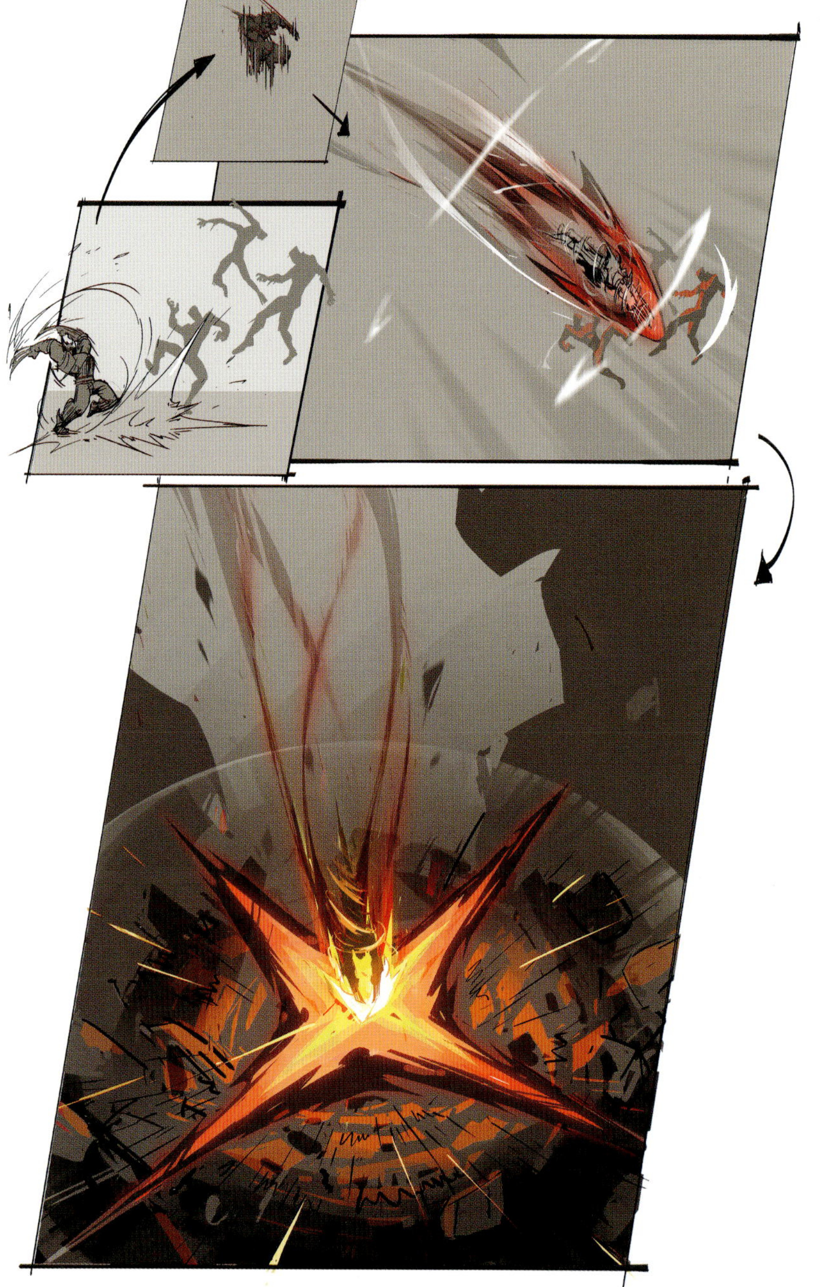

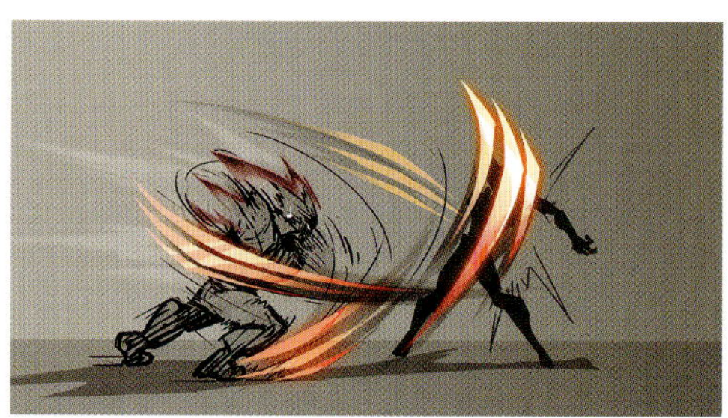

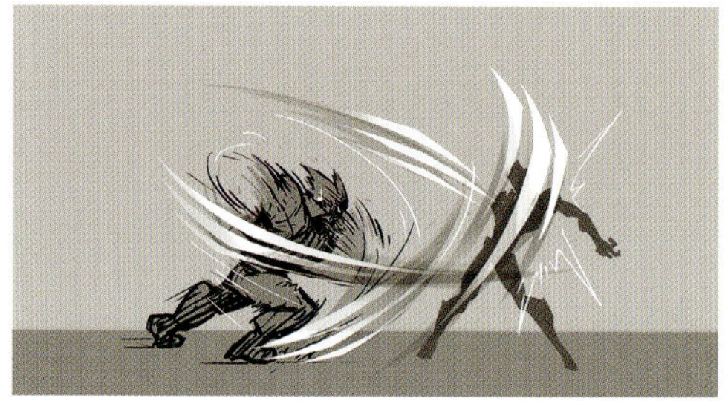

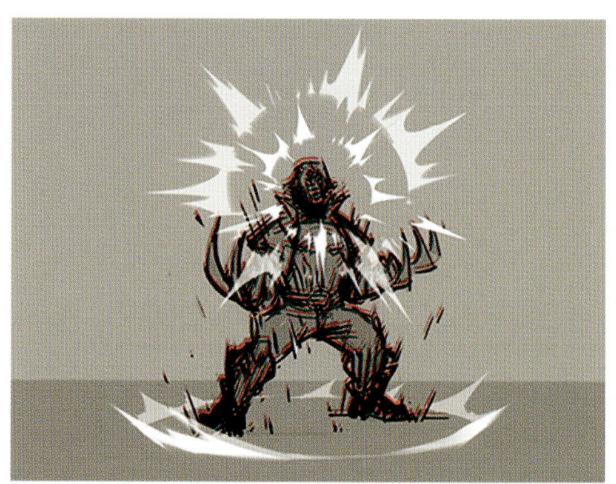

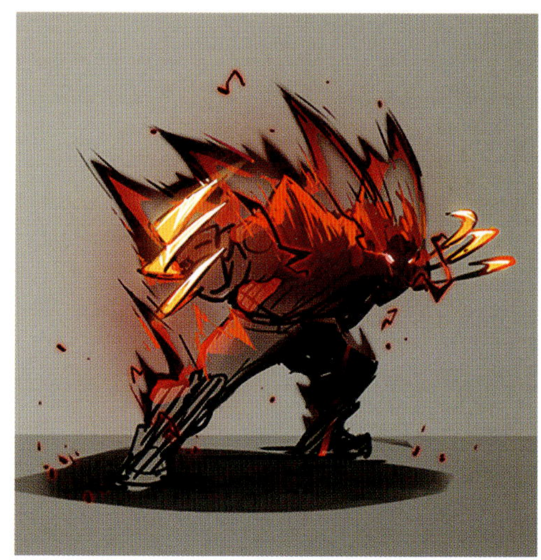

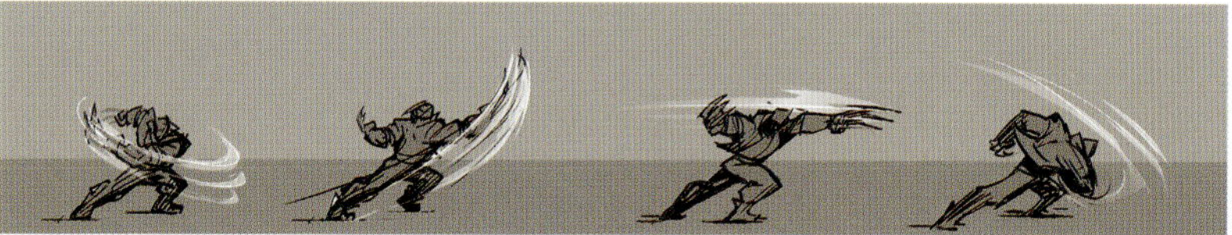

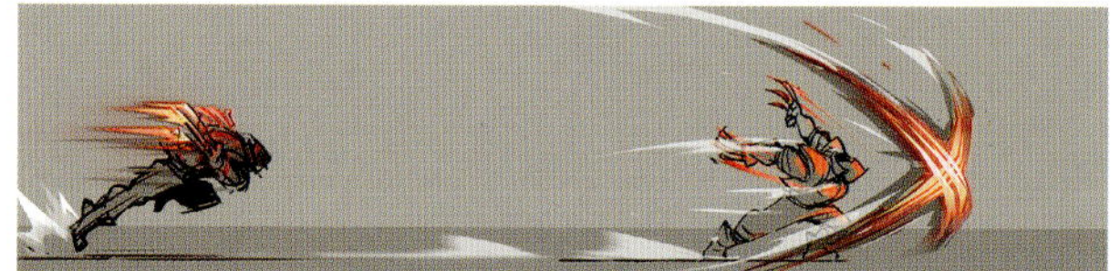

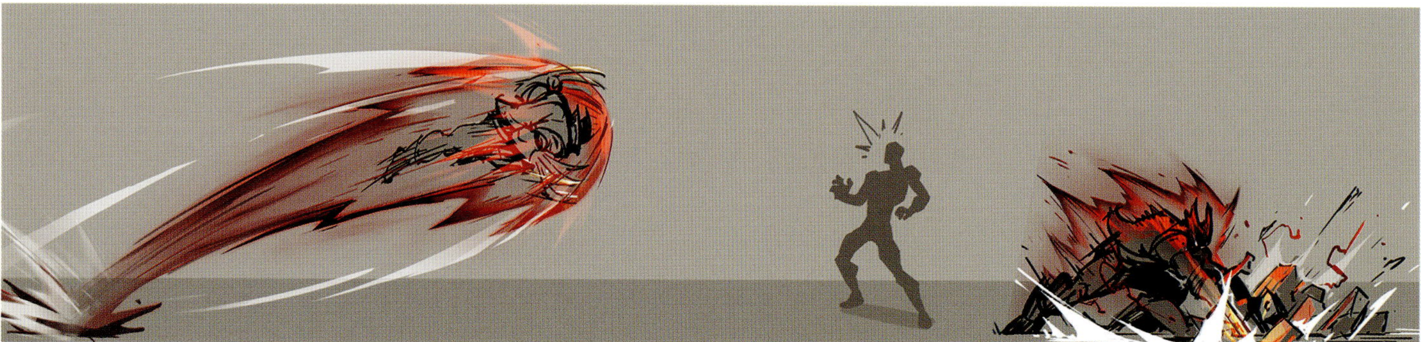

WOLVERINE: COSMETIC VARIETY

In the battle against Dracula, a group of heroes tapped into the mysterious power of Blood Chronovium to enhance their battle against the dark. Wolverine's Blood Berserker costume evokes this gothic flair as he hunts the creatures of the night.

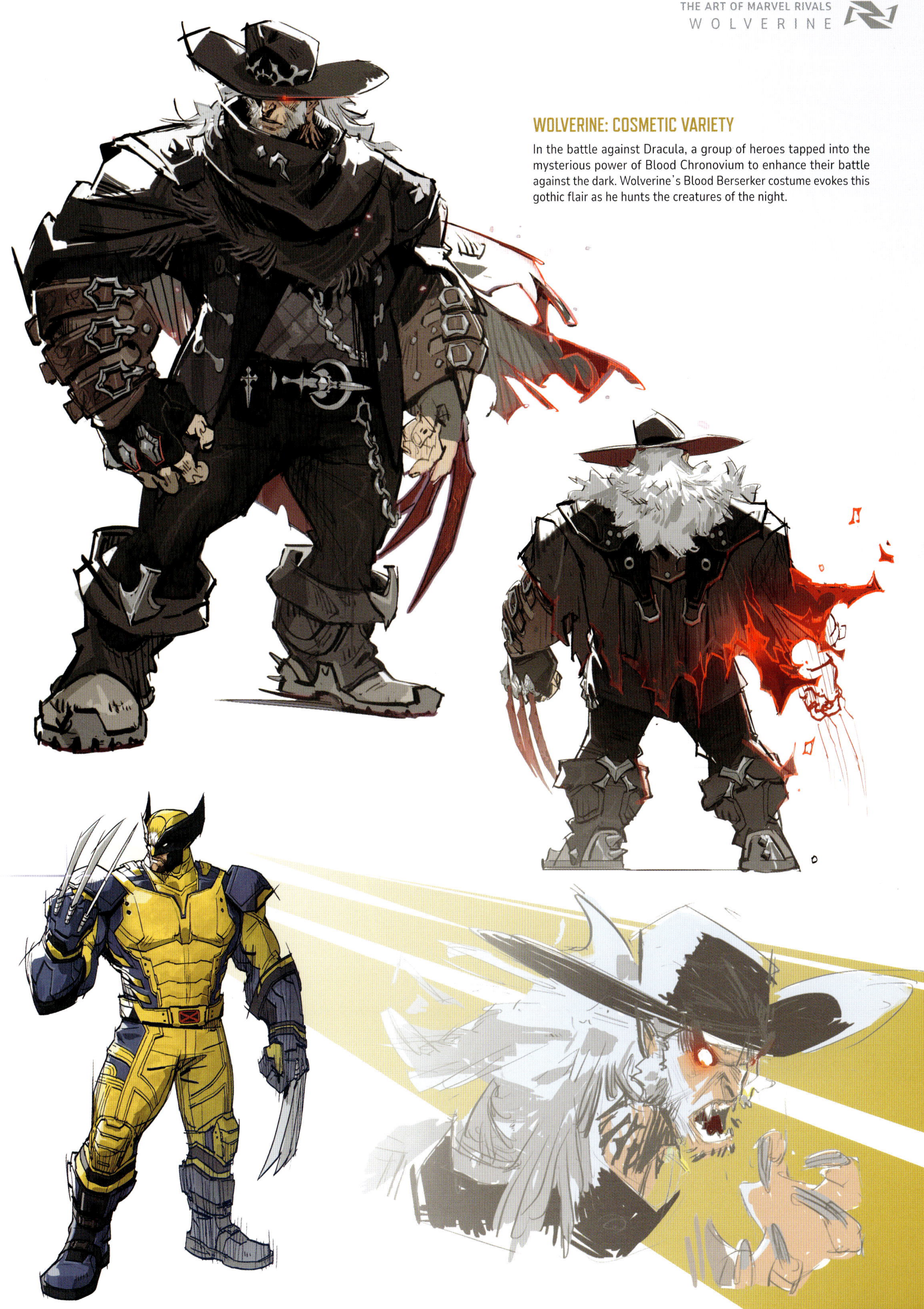

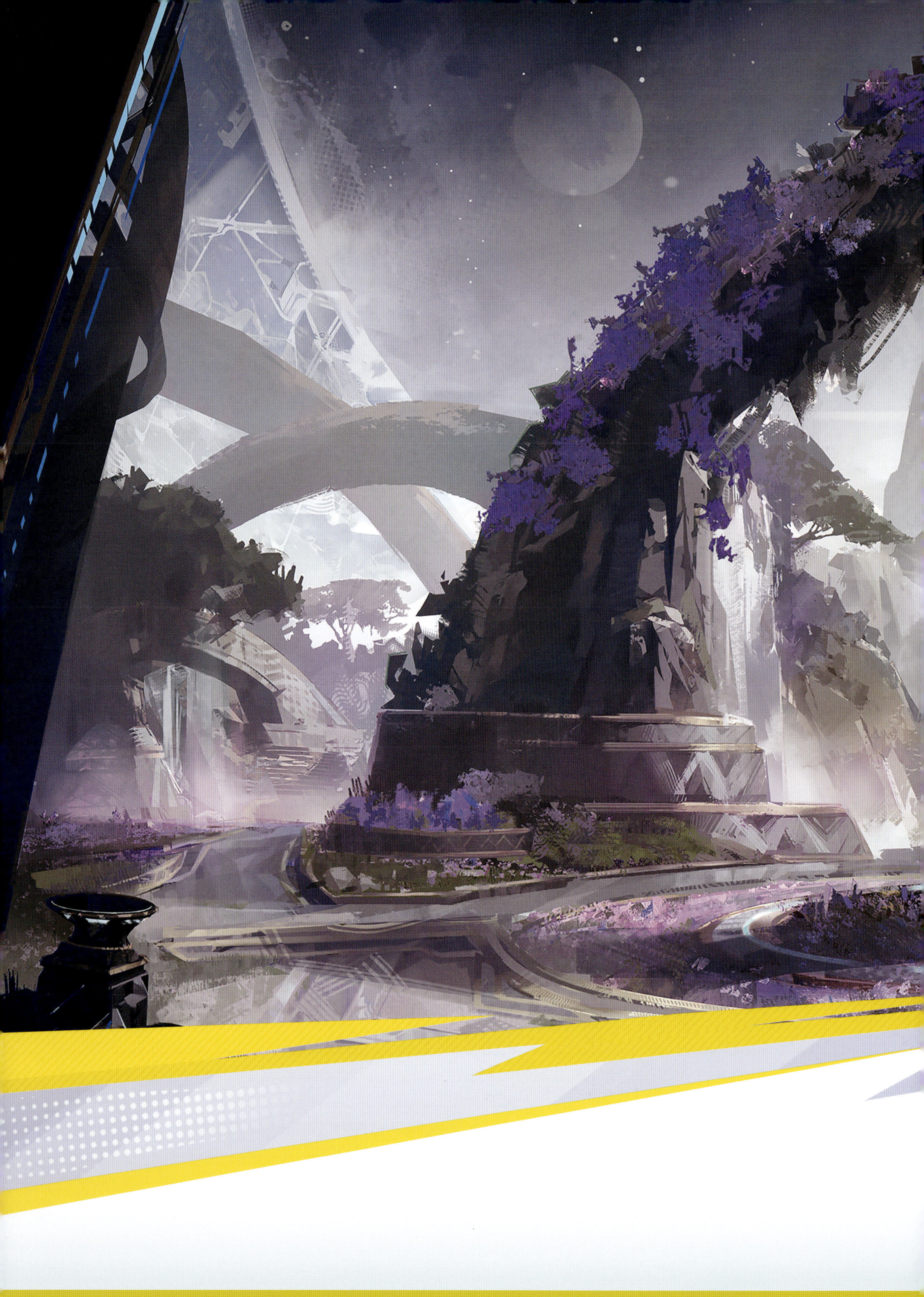

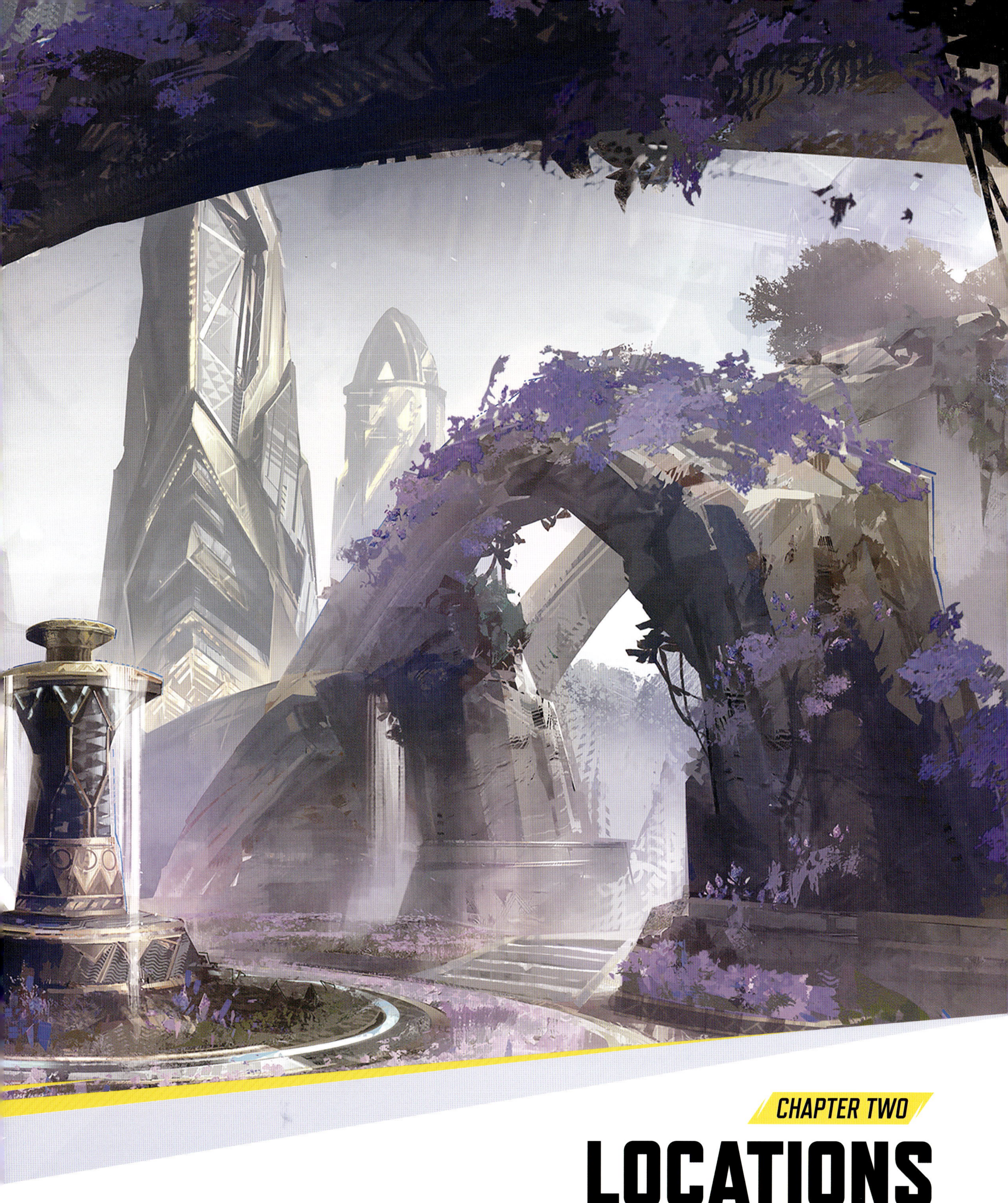

CHAPTER TWO

LOCATIONS

The Timestream Entanglement, the impetus of the *Marvel Rivals* story, created innumerable new worlds. Our task was to bring them to life as battlegrounds for the many heroes and villains of the Marvel Multiverse. From futuristic cities to divine realms, from Earth to the stars, we want everyone to see the beauty of the new Chronoverses.

YGGSGARD

YGGDRASILL PATH

Beneath the sky-covering canopy of the World Tree, Yggdrasill, lies the golden glory of Asgard, realm of the gods, now overgrown with roots and flora. However, the throne-seizing scheme of Loki, God of Mischief, threatens the everlasting prosperity of this kingdom, now fused into Yggsgard and all of the Ten Realms.

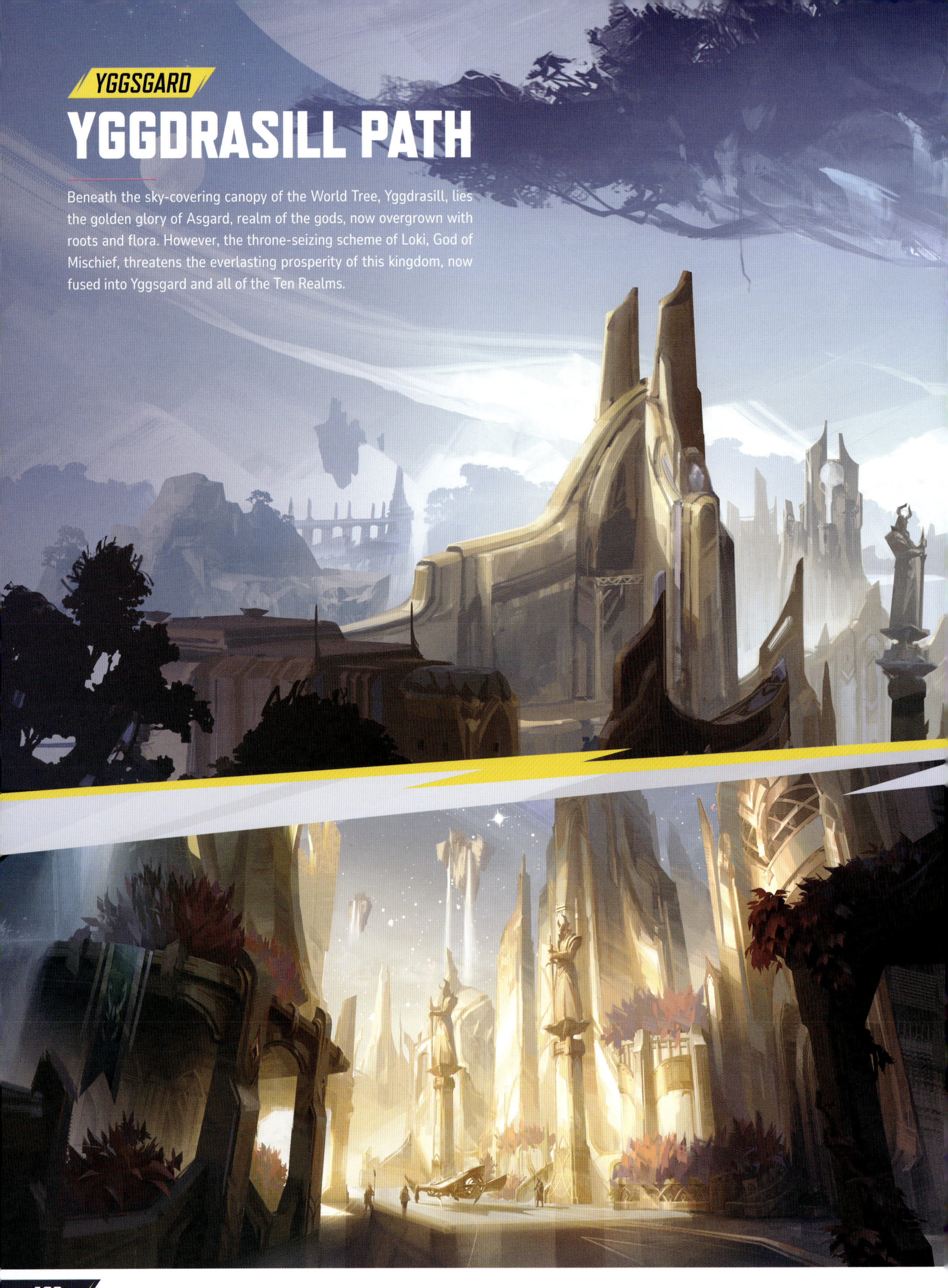

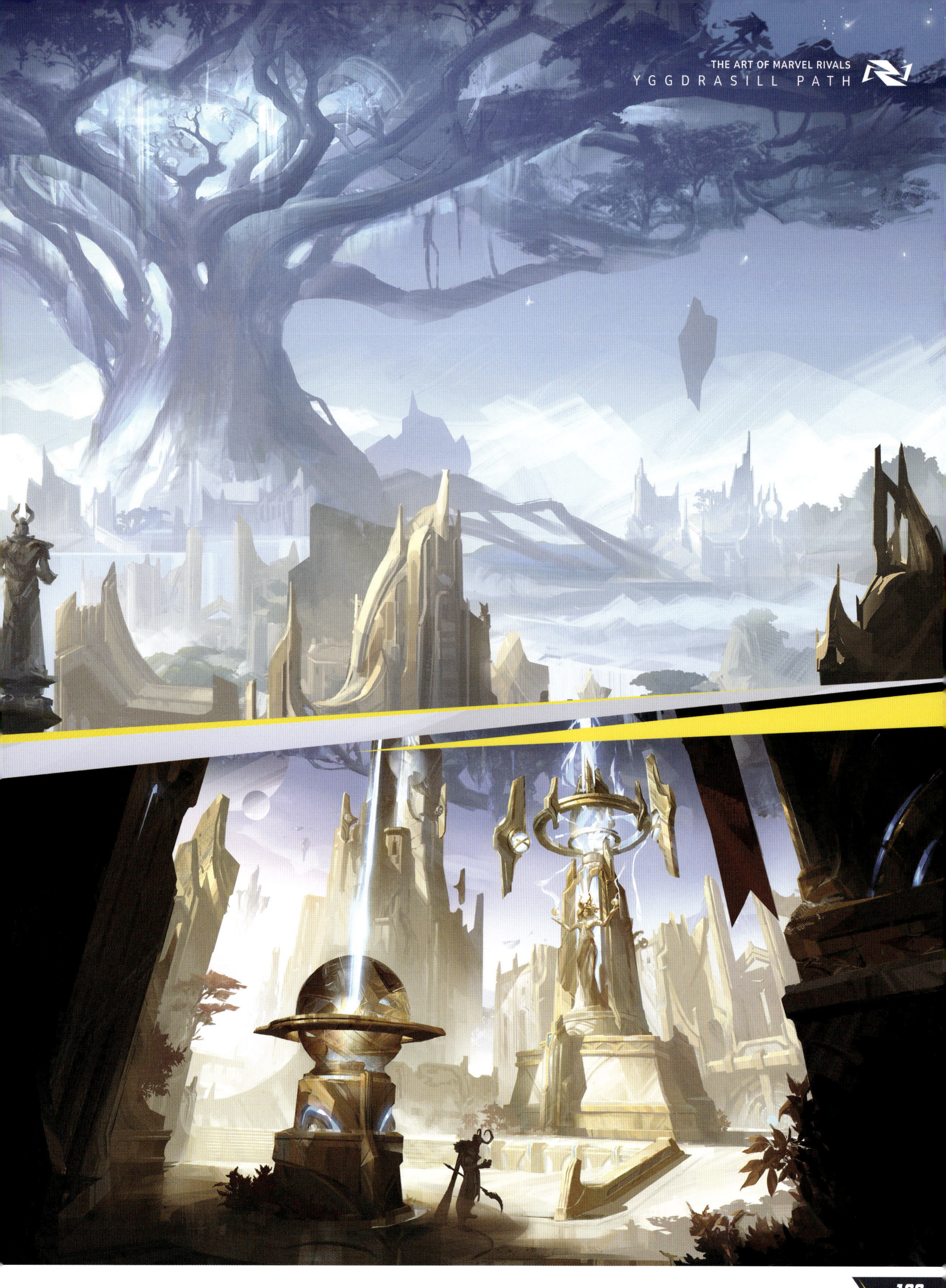

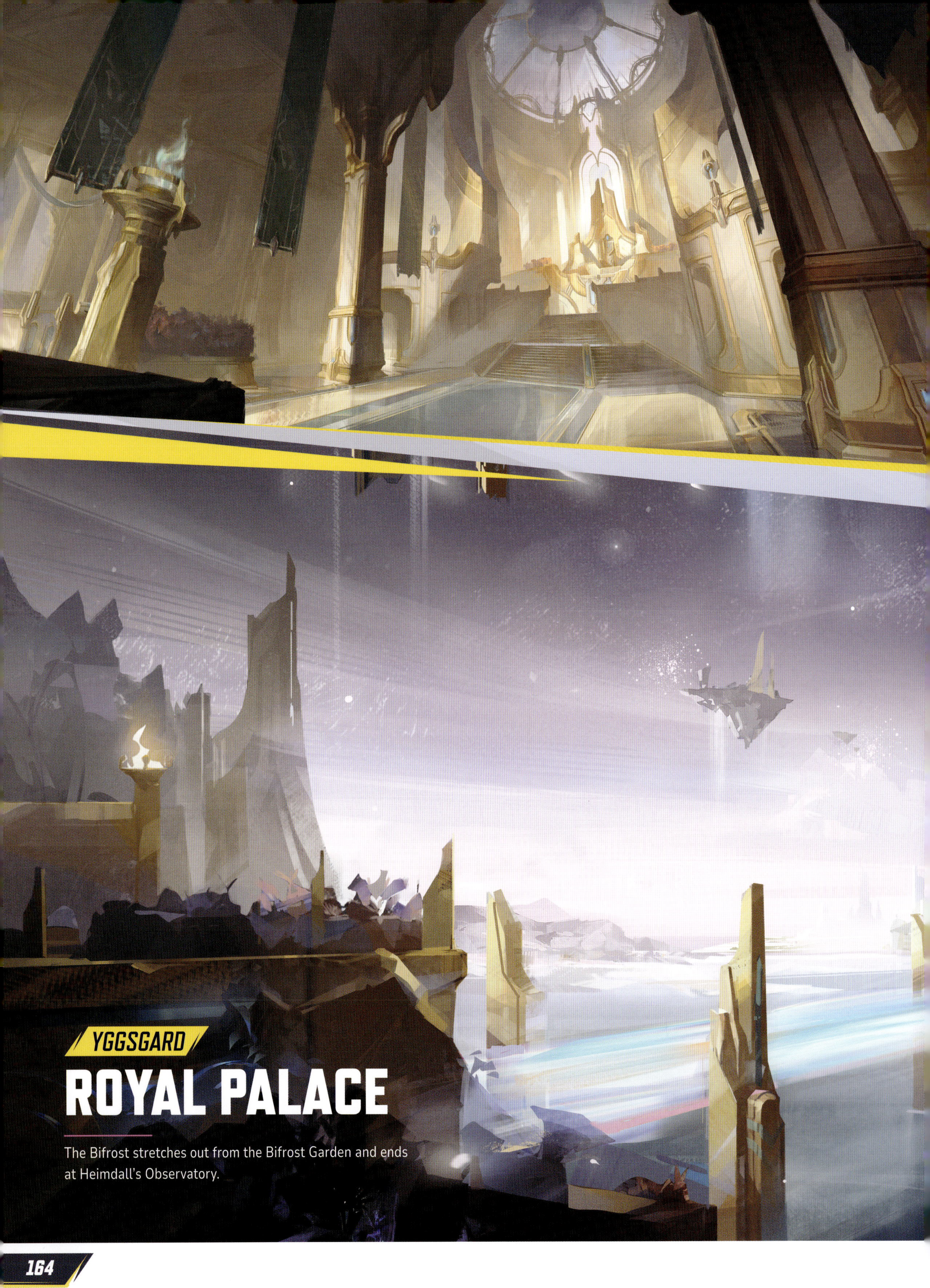

YGGSGARD

ROYAL PALACE

The Bifrost stretches out from the Bifrost Garden and ends at Heimdall's Observatory.

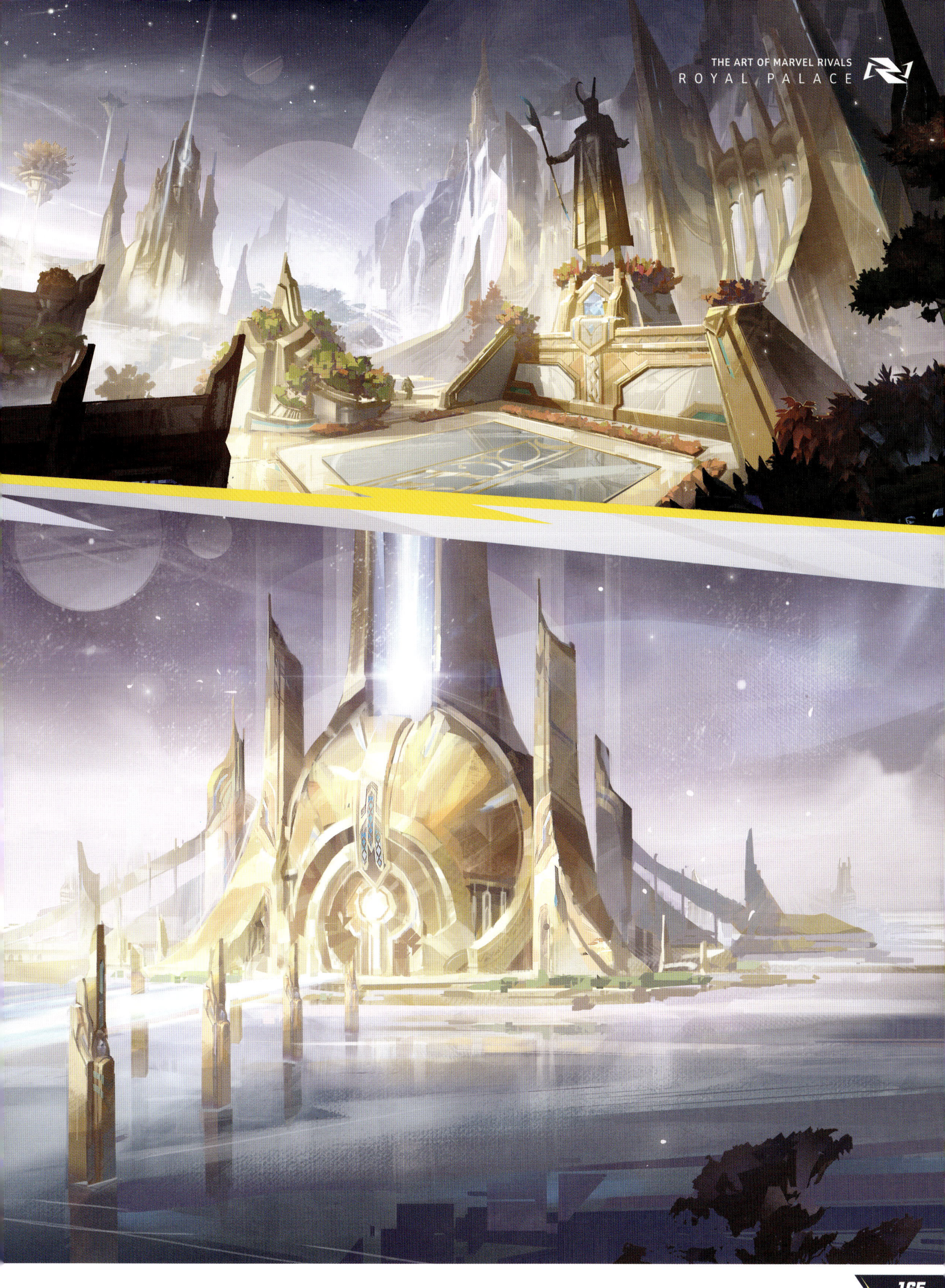

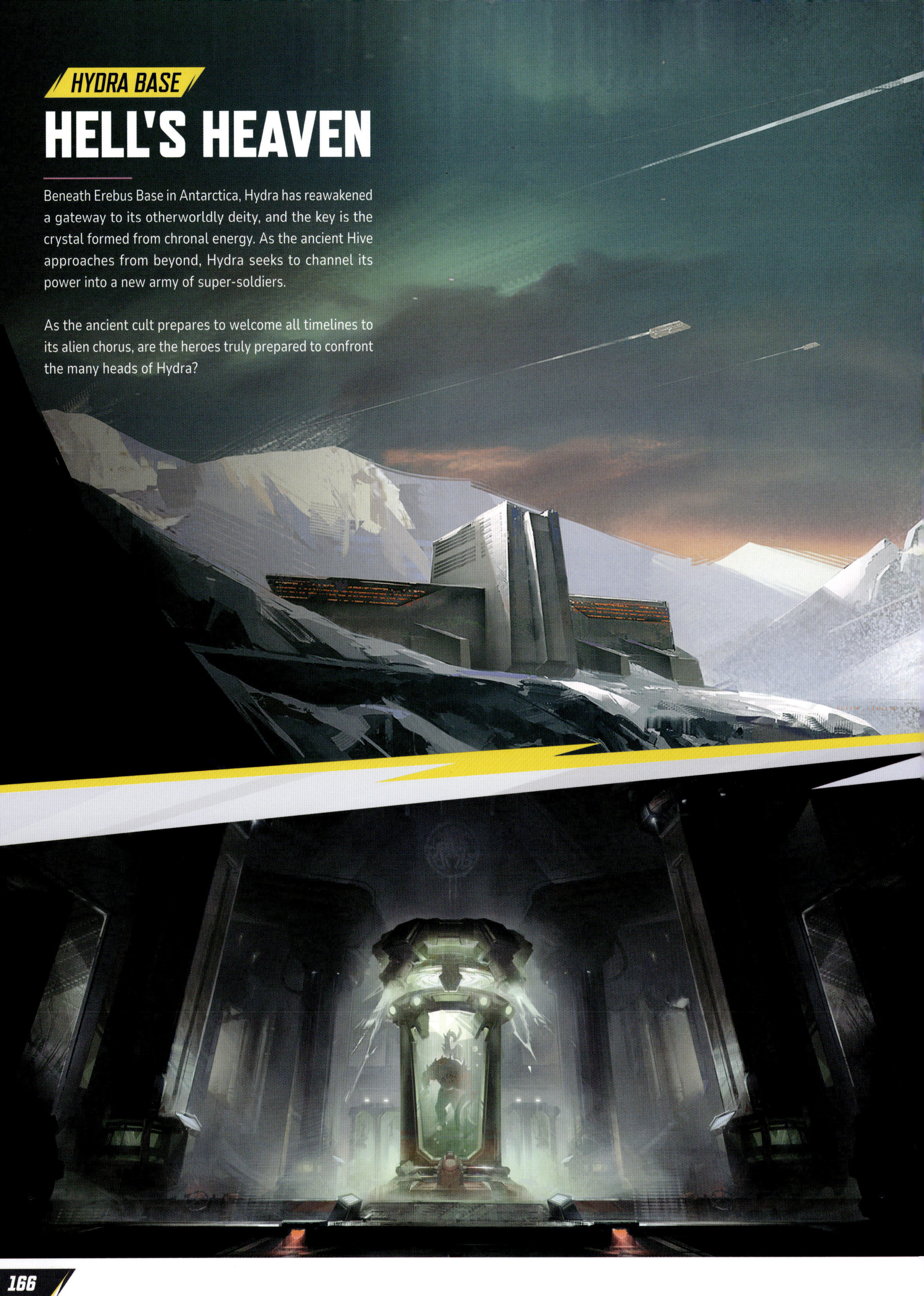

HYDRA BASE

HELL'S HEAVEN

Beneath Erebus Base in Antarctica, Hydra has reawakened a gateway to its otherworldly deity, and the key is the crystal formed from chronal energy. As the ancient Hive approaches from beyond, Hydra seeks to channel its power into a new army of super-soldiers.

As the ancient cult prepares to welcome all timelines to its alien chorus, are the heroes truly prepared to confront the many heads of Hydra?

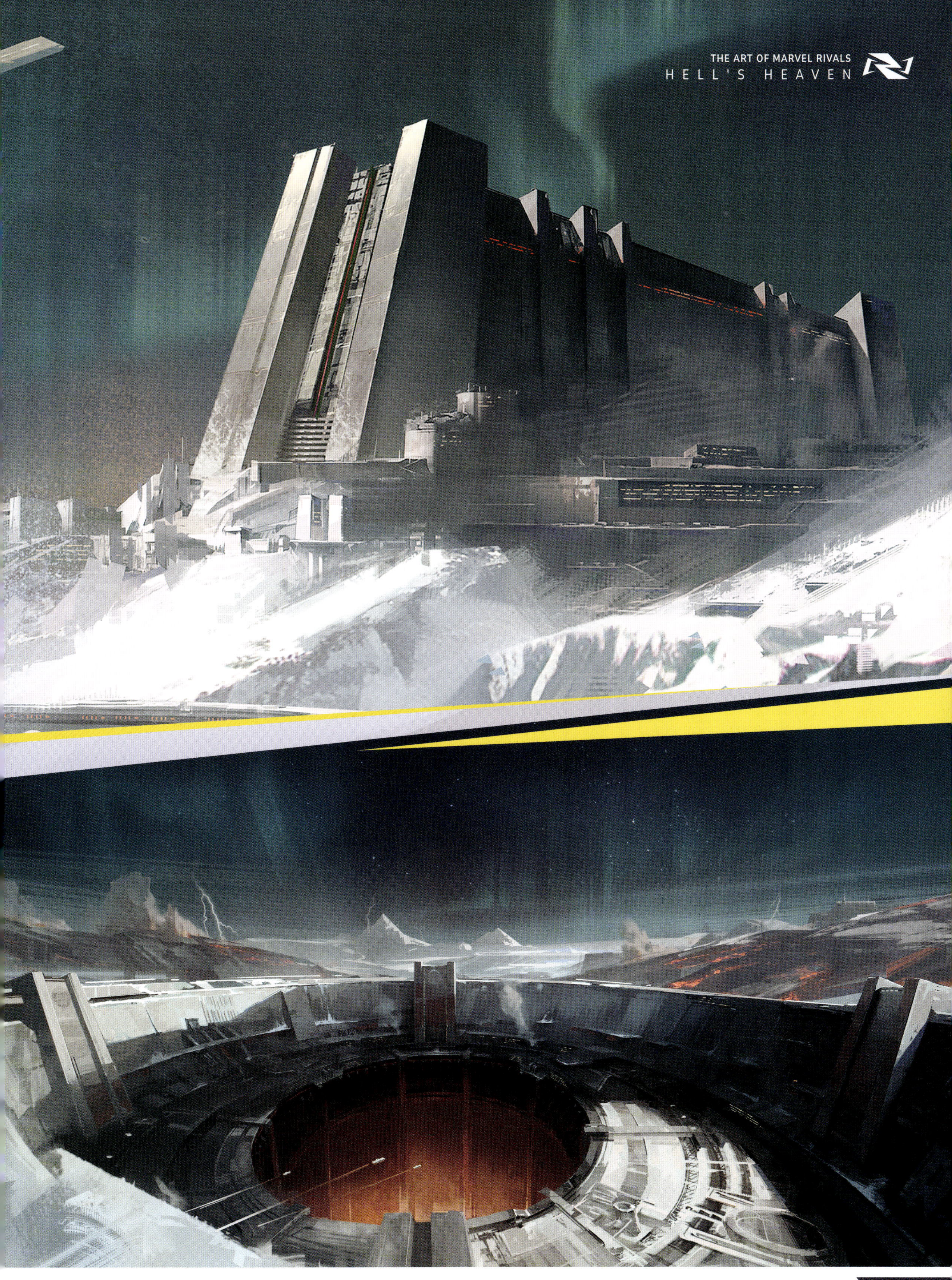

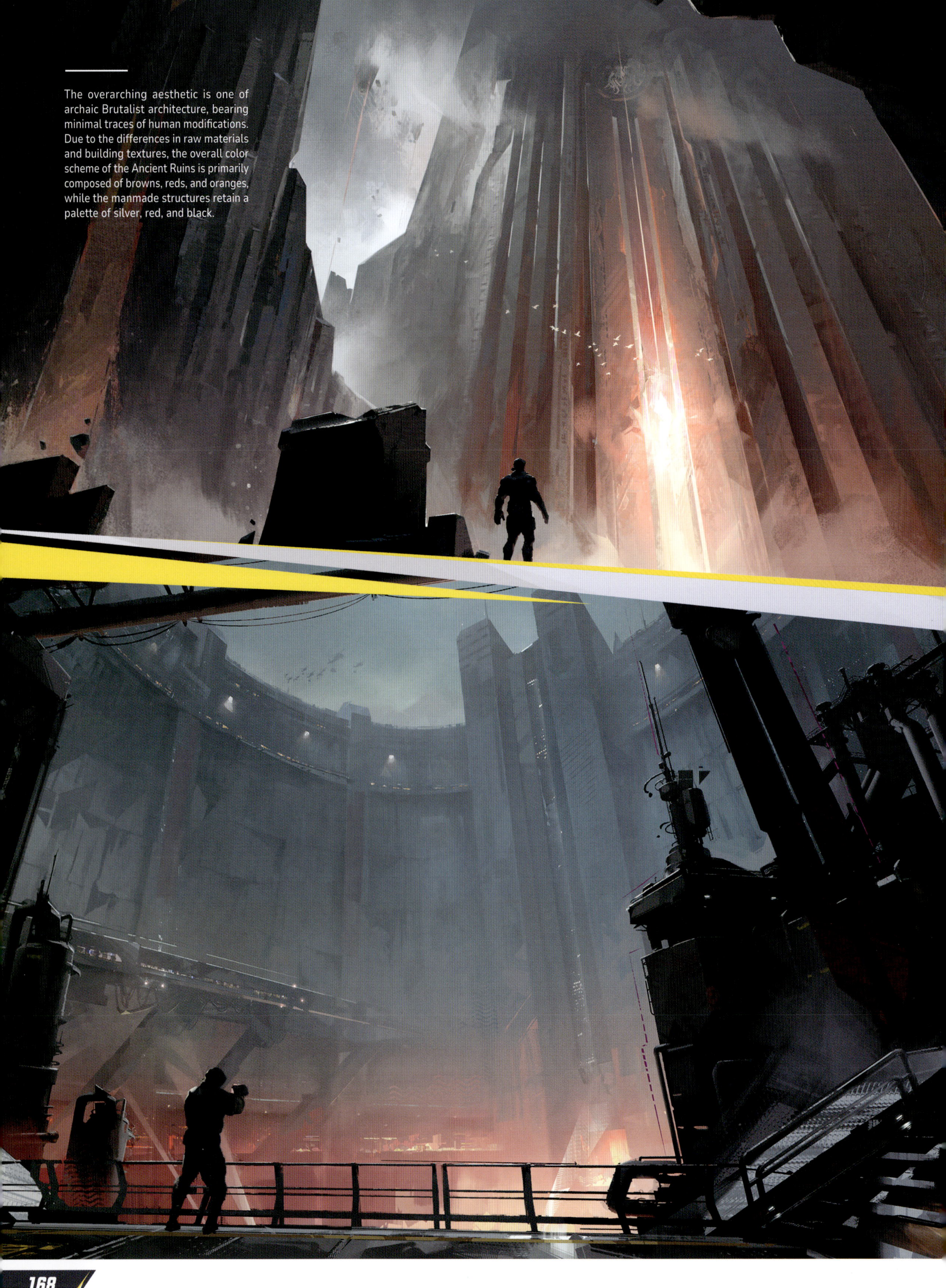

The overarching aesthetic is one of archaic Brutalist architecture, bearing minimal traces of human modifications. Due to the differences in raw materials and building textures, the overall color scheme of the Ancient Ruins is primarily composed of browns, reds, and oranges, while the manmade structures retain a palette of silver, red, and black.

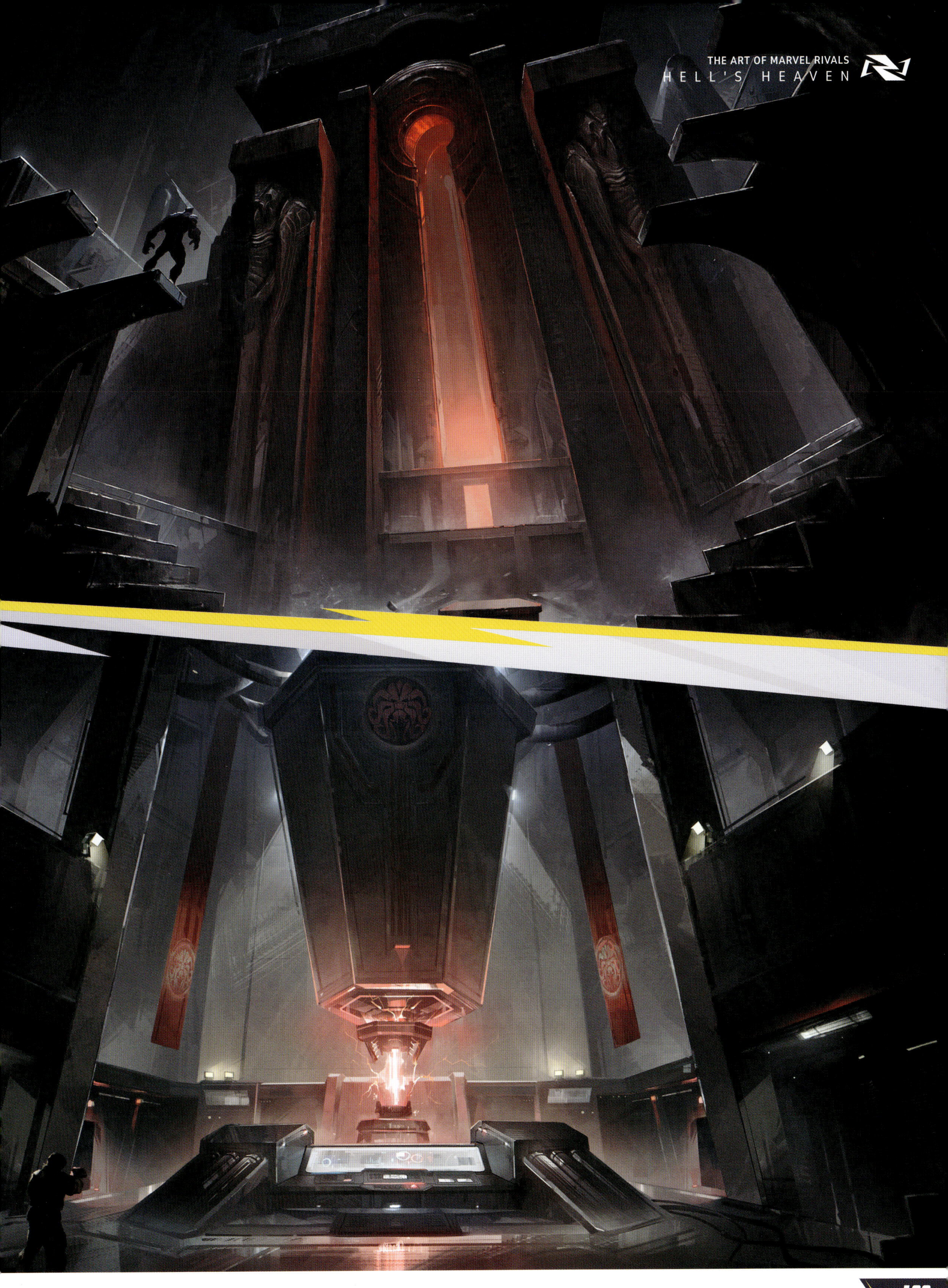

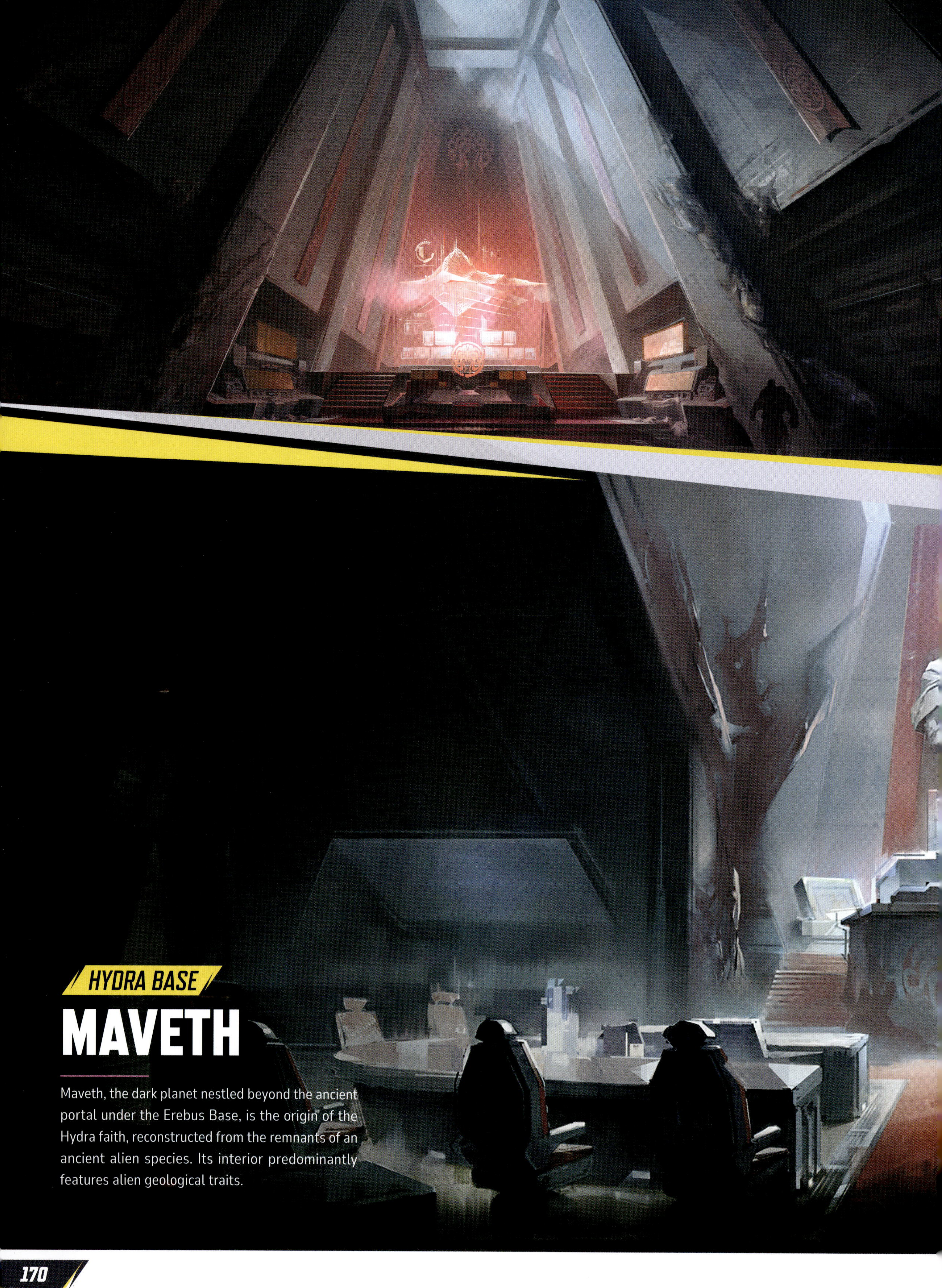

HYDRA BASE

MAVETH

Maveth, the dark planet nestled beyond the ancient portal under the Erebus Base, is the origin of the Hydra faith, reconstructed from the remnants of an ancient alien species. Its interior predominantly features alien geological traits.

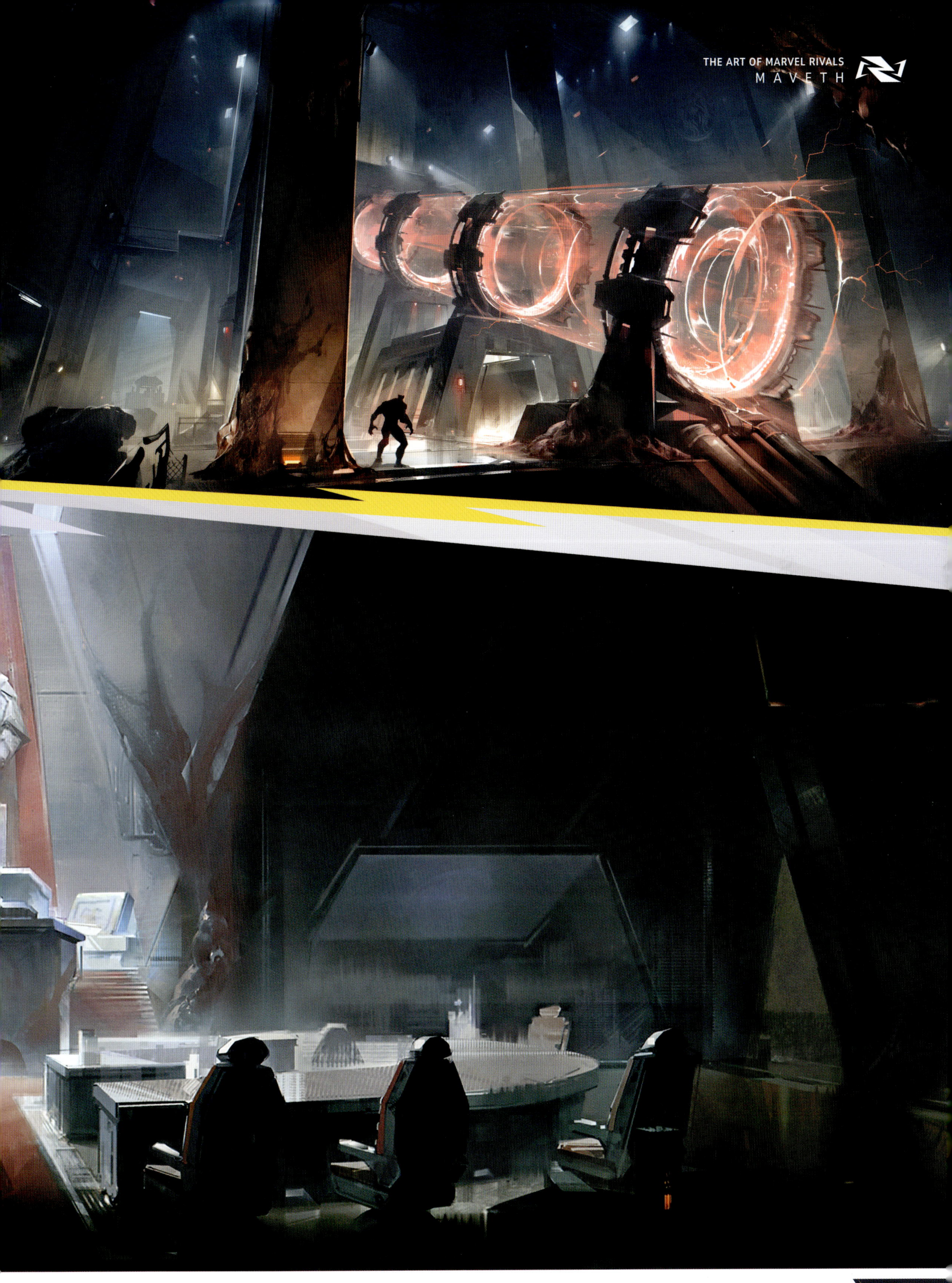

Influenced by alien energies, certain areas here exist in ways that defy the logic of our world.

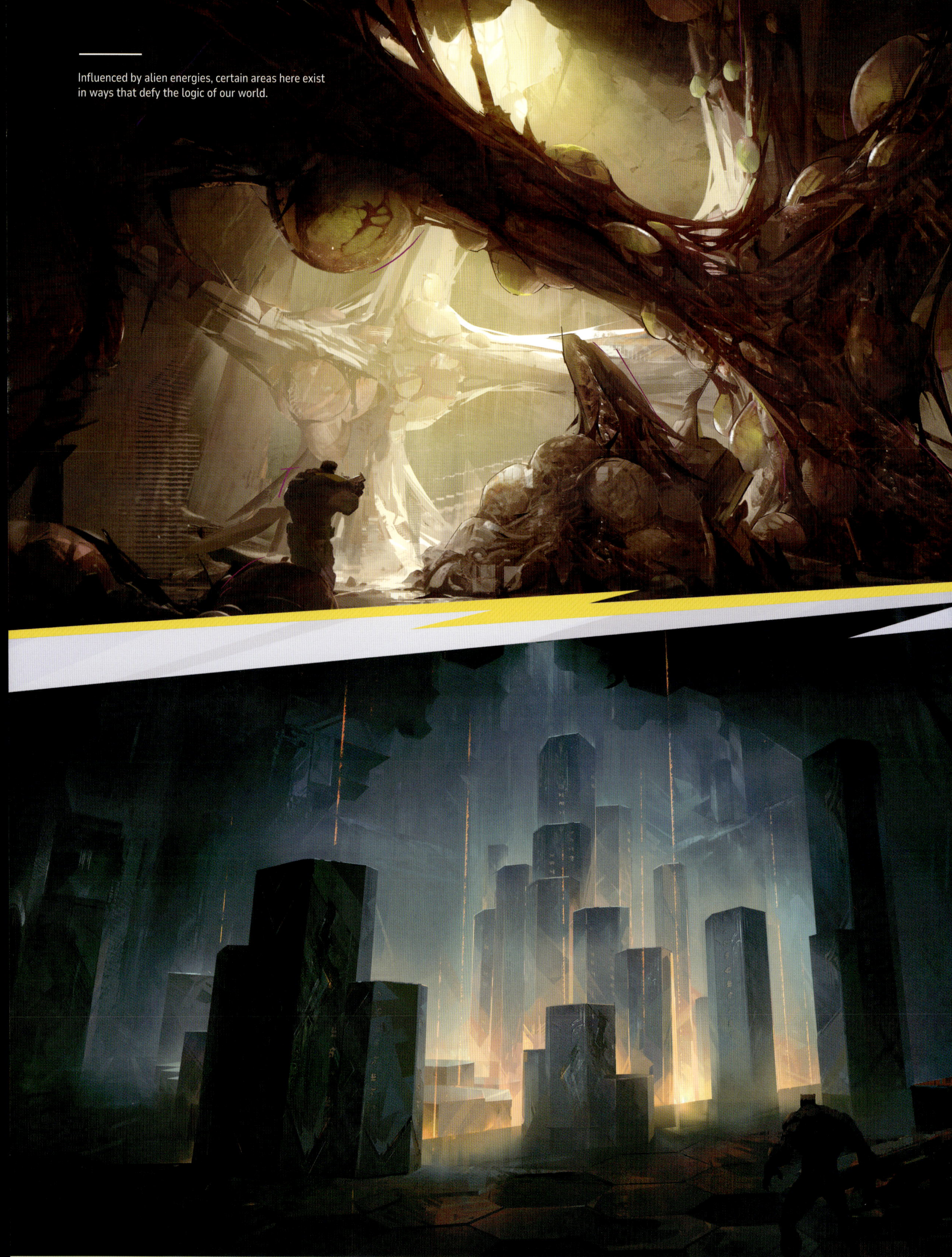

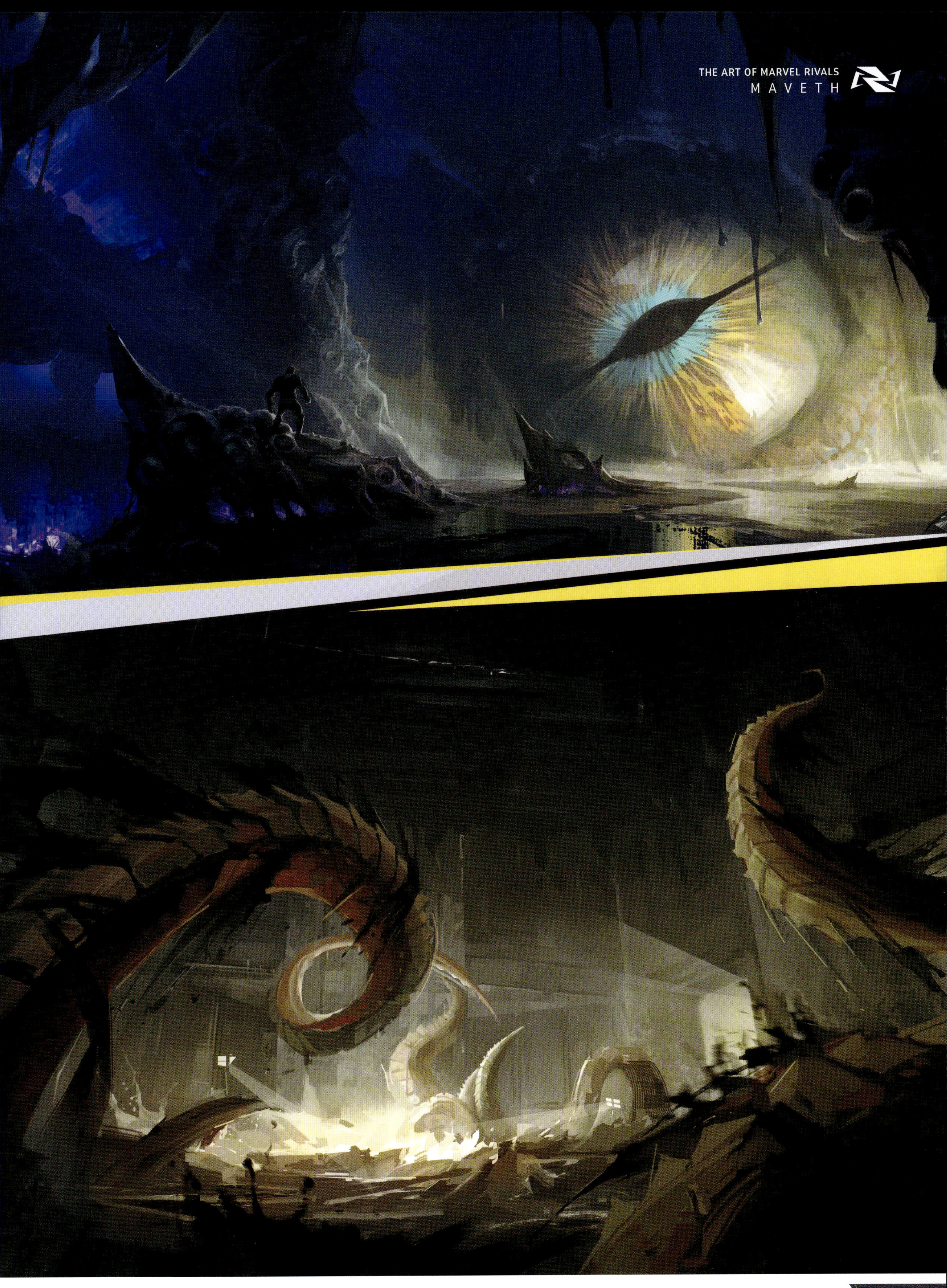

TOKYO 2099

SHIN-SHIBUYA

This is a future where cherry blossoms and neon lights dance together in the sky, a world where utopias and dystopias coexist. The Tokyo of 2099 still carries all those beautiful traditions despite finding itself under the new order formed by megacorps . . .

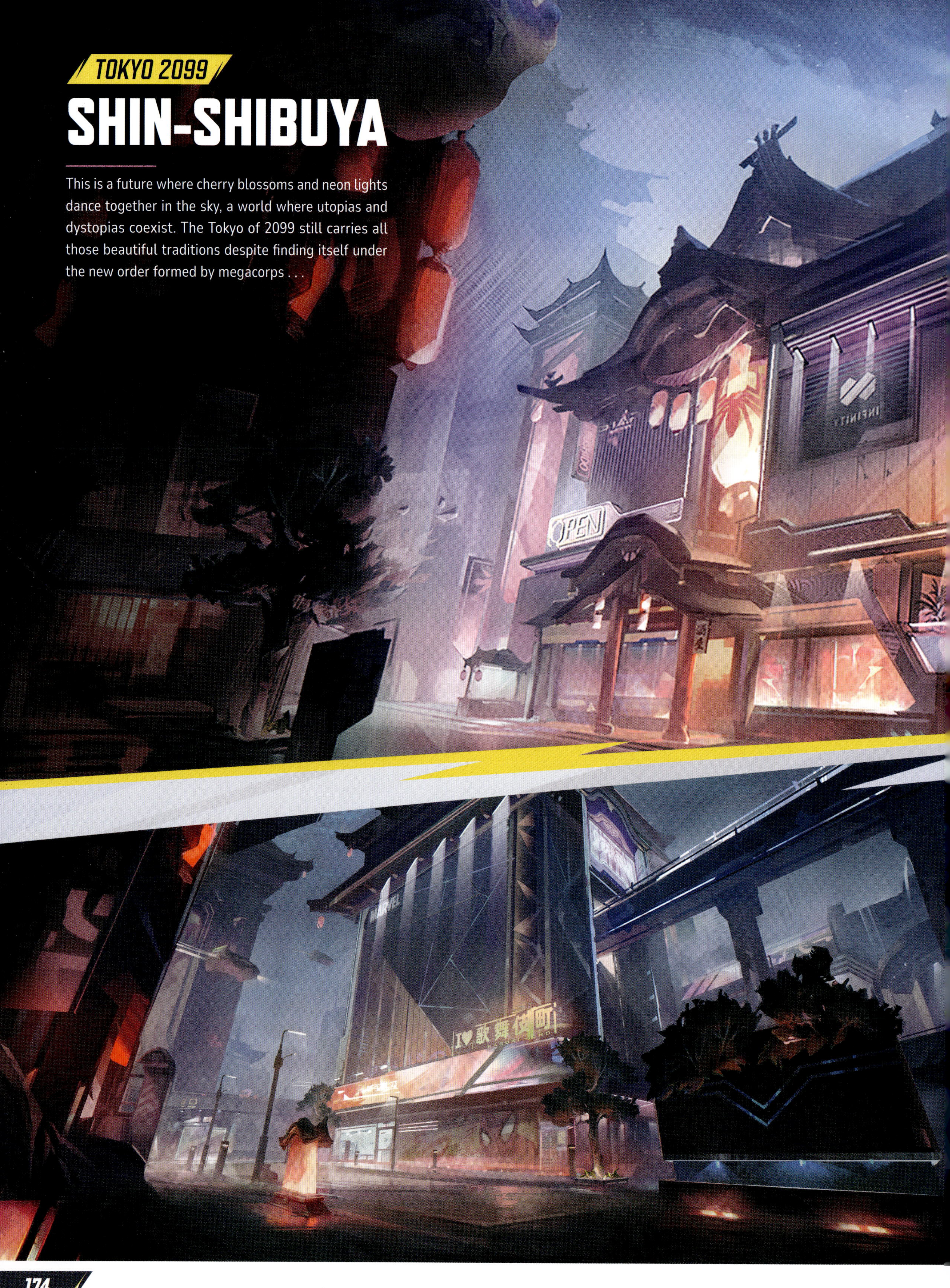

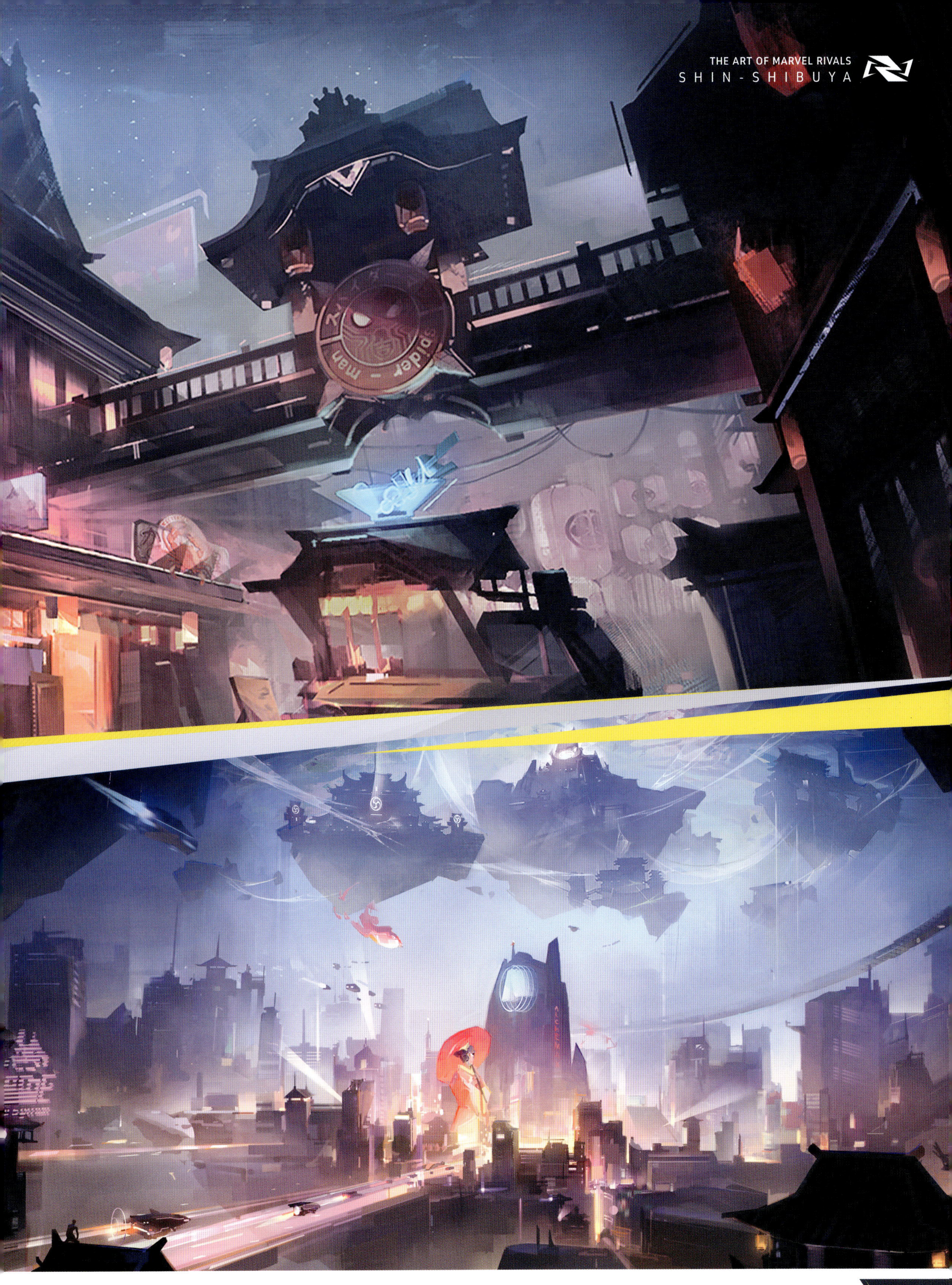
spider - man

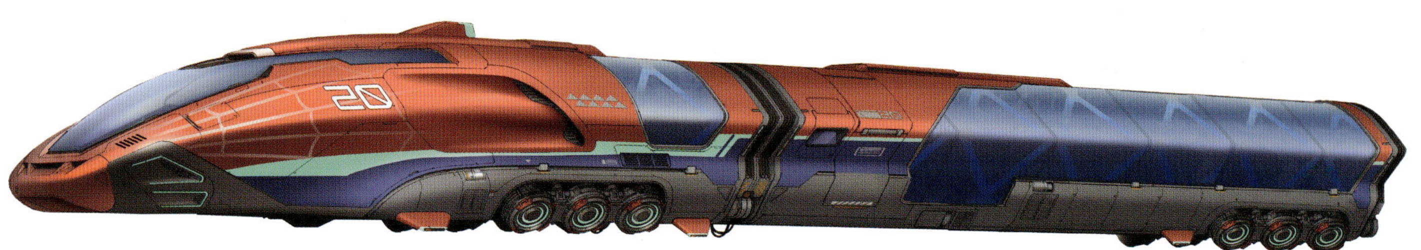

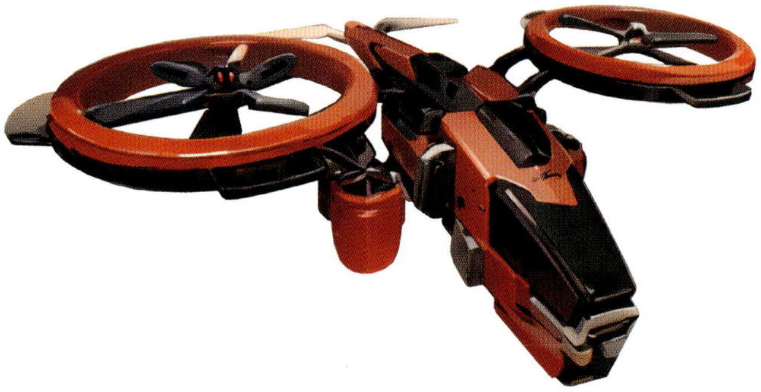

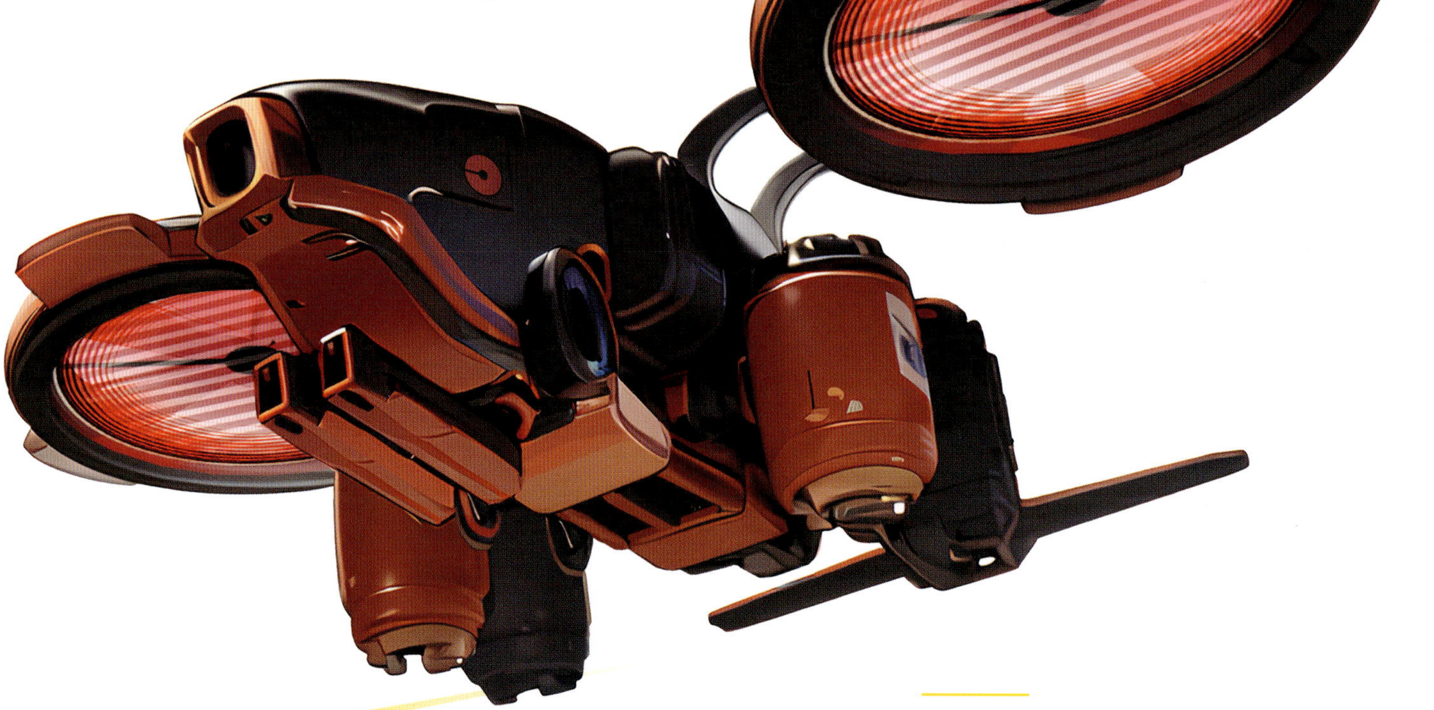

The mechanical devices scattered throughout the Tokyo 2099 map prominently incorporate Spider-Man's iconic color scheme.

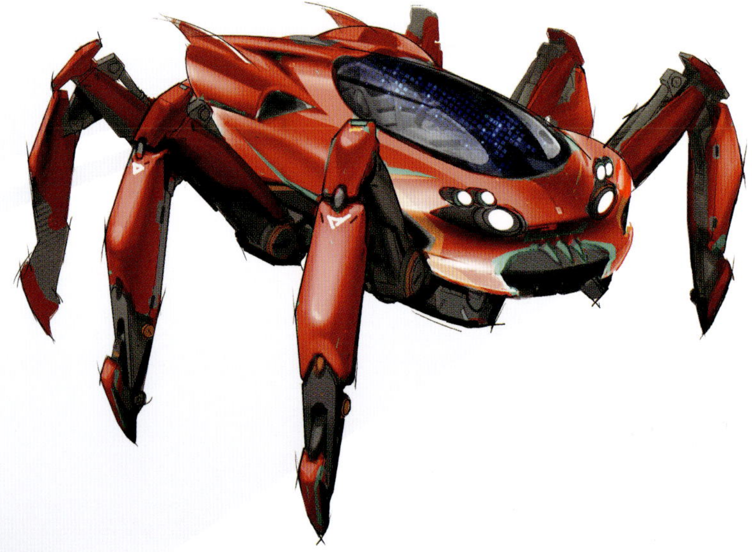

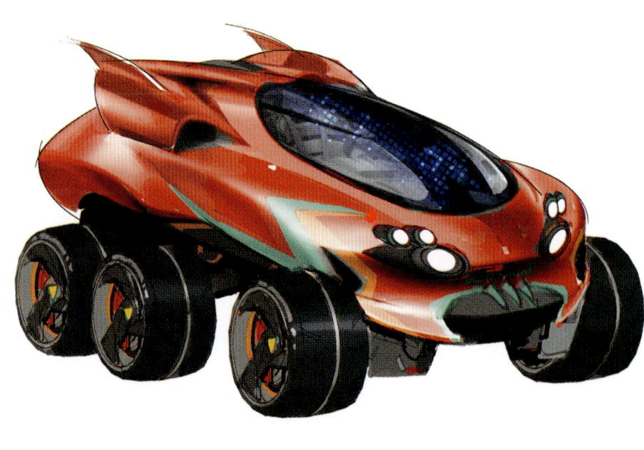

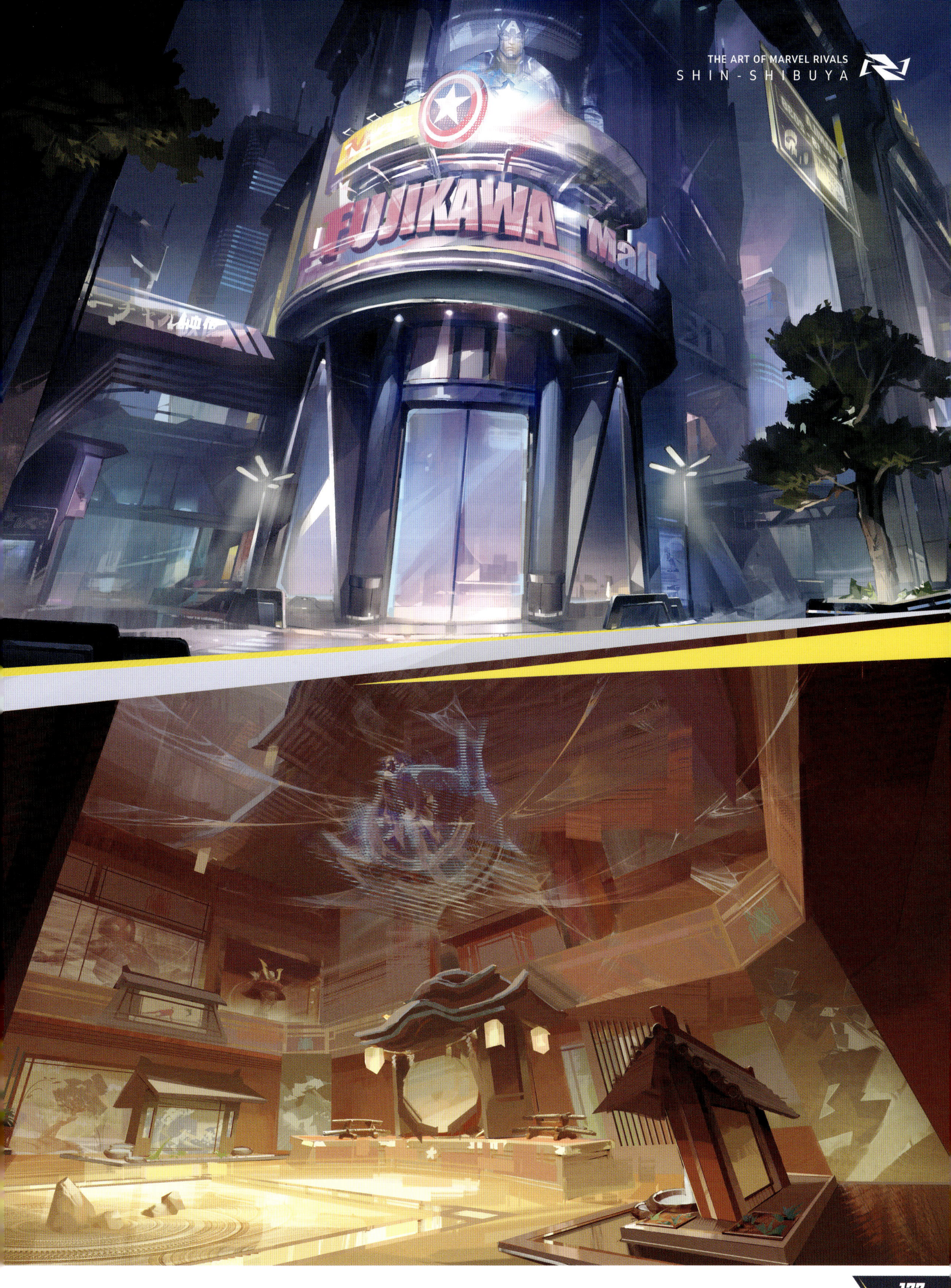
FUJIKAWA Mall

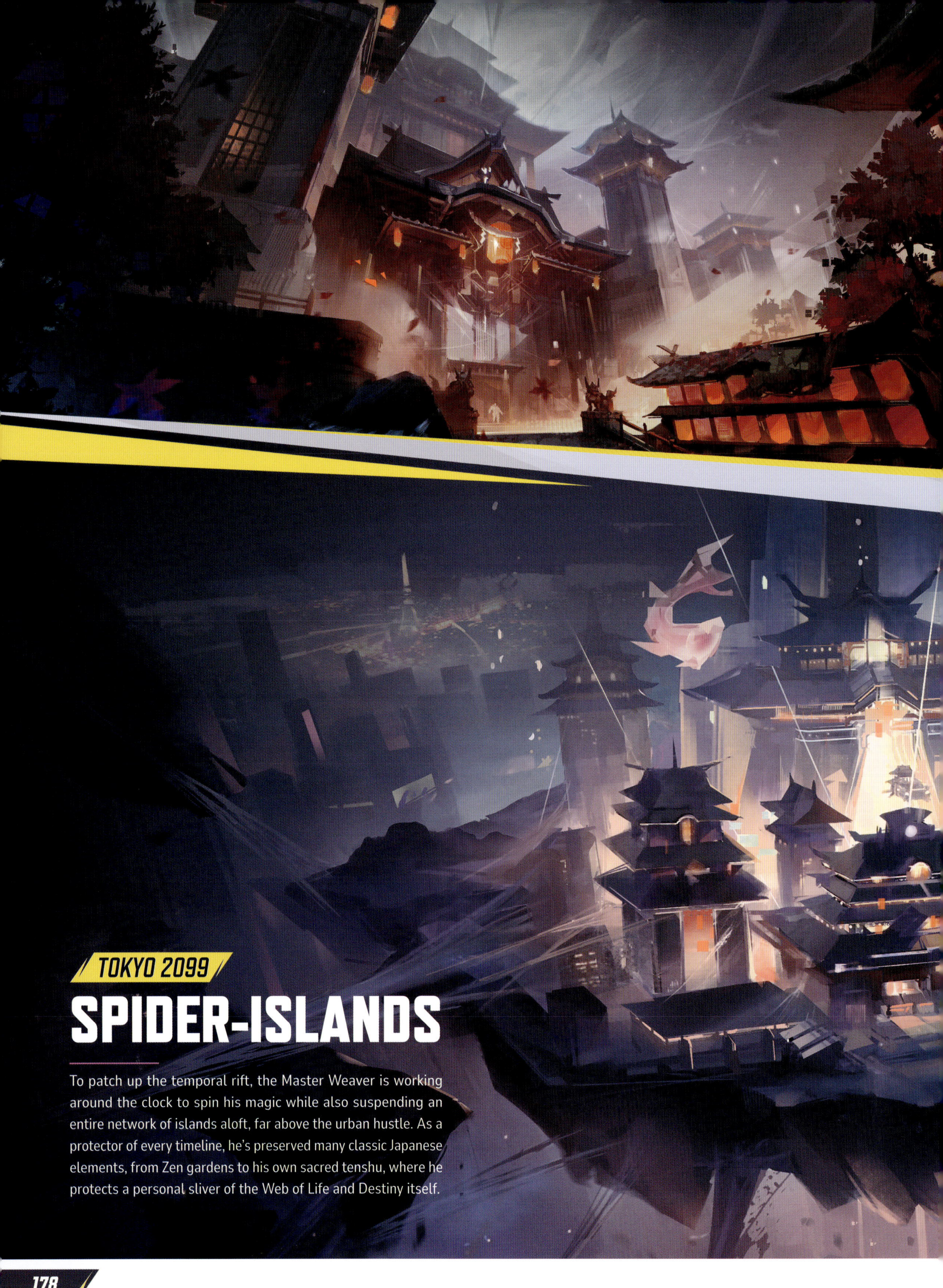

TOKYO 2099

SPIDER-ISLANDS

To patch up the temporal rift, the Master Weaver is working around the clock to spin his magic while also suspending an entire network of islands aloft, far above the urban hustle. As a protector of every timeline, he's preserved many classic Japanese elements, from Zen gardens to his own sacred tenshu, where he protects a personal sliver of the Web of Life and Destiny itself.

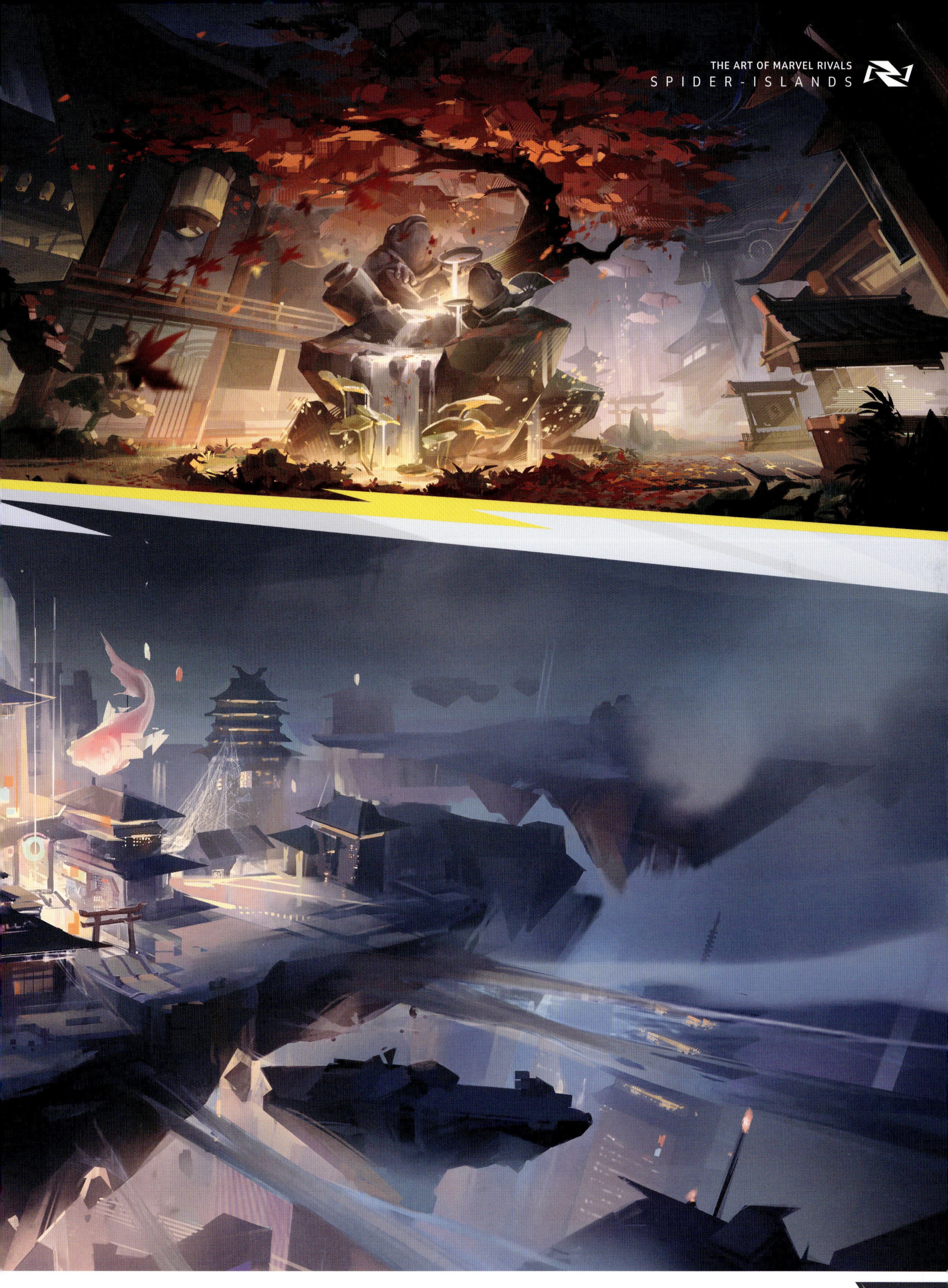

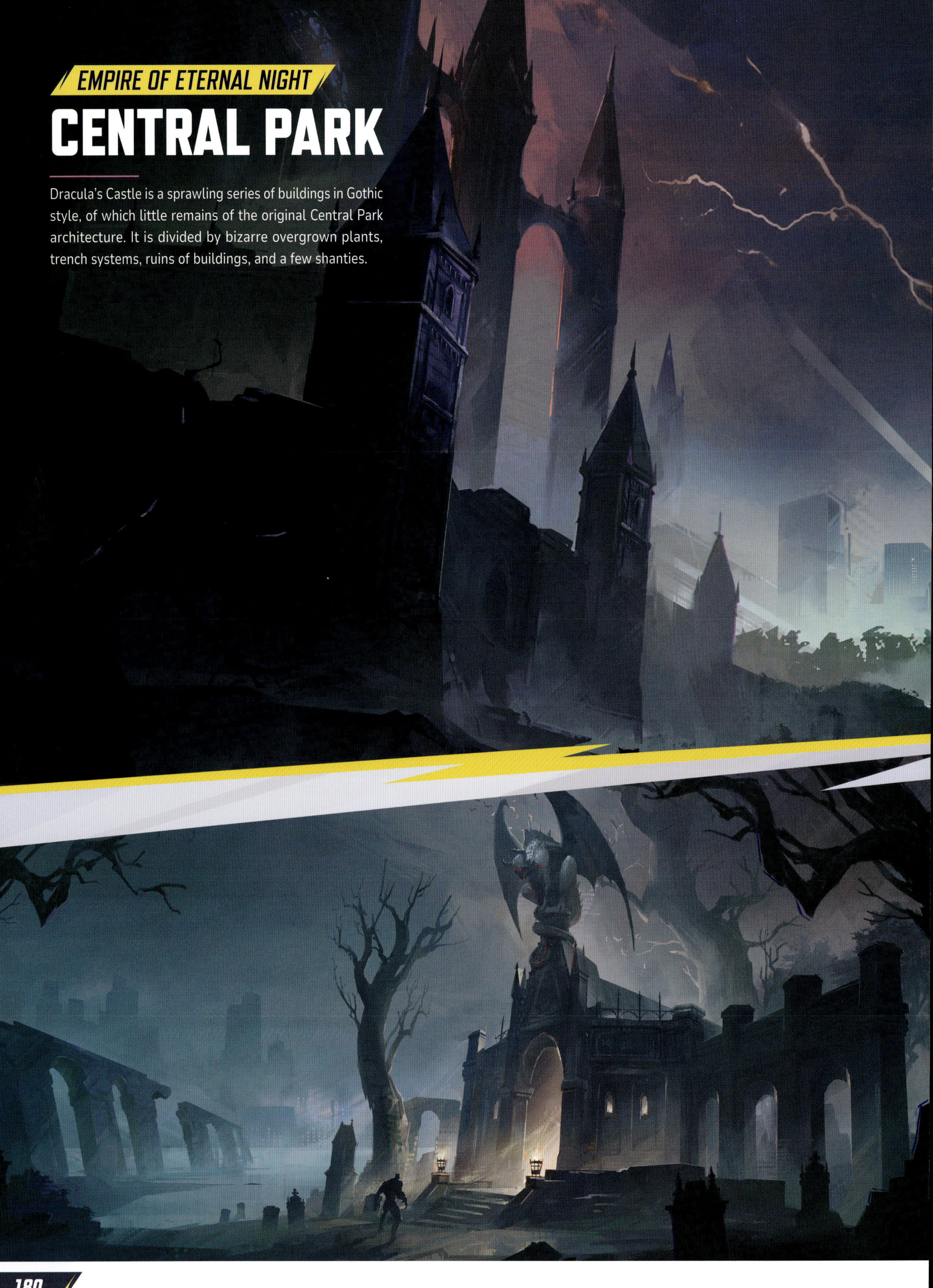

EMPIRE OF ETERNAL NIGHT

CENTRAL PARK

Dracula's Castle is a sprawling series of buildings in Gothic style, of which little remains of the original Central Park architecture. It is divided by bizarre overgrown plants, trench systems, ruins of buildings, and a few shanties.

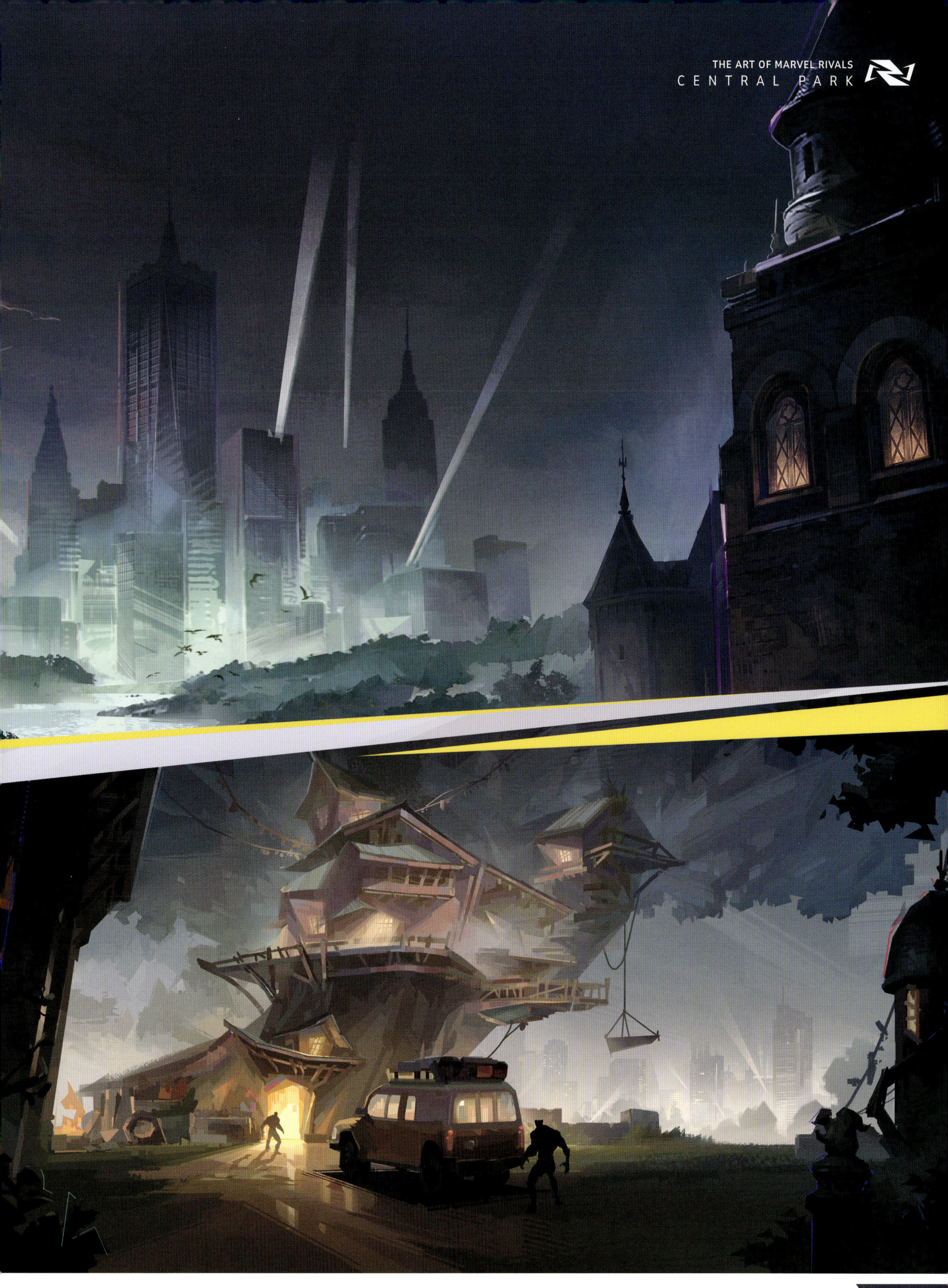

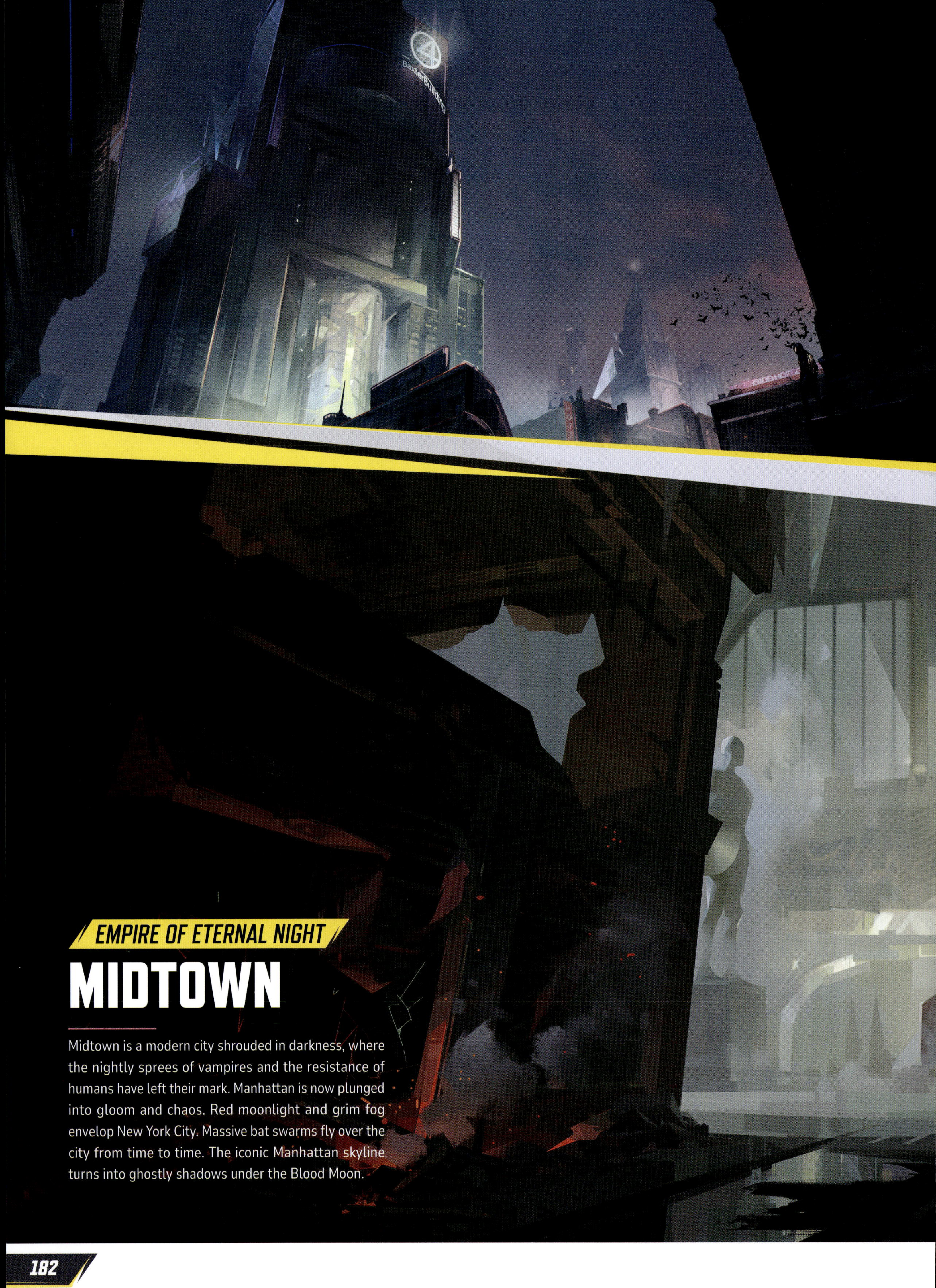

EMPIRE OF ETERNAL NIGHT

MIDTOWN

Midtown is a modern city shrouded in darkness, where the nightly sprees of vampires and the resistance of humans have left their mark. Manhattan is now plunged into gloom and chaos. Red moonlight and grim fog envelop New York City. Massive bat swarms fly over the city from time to time. The iconic Manhattan skyline turns into ghostly shadows under the Blood Moon.

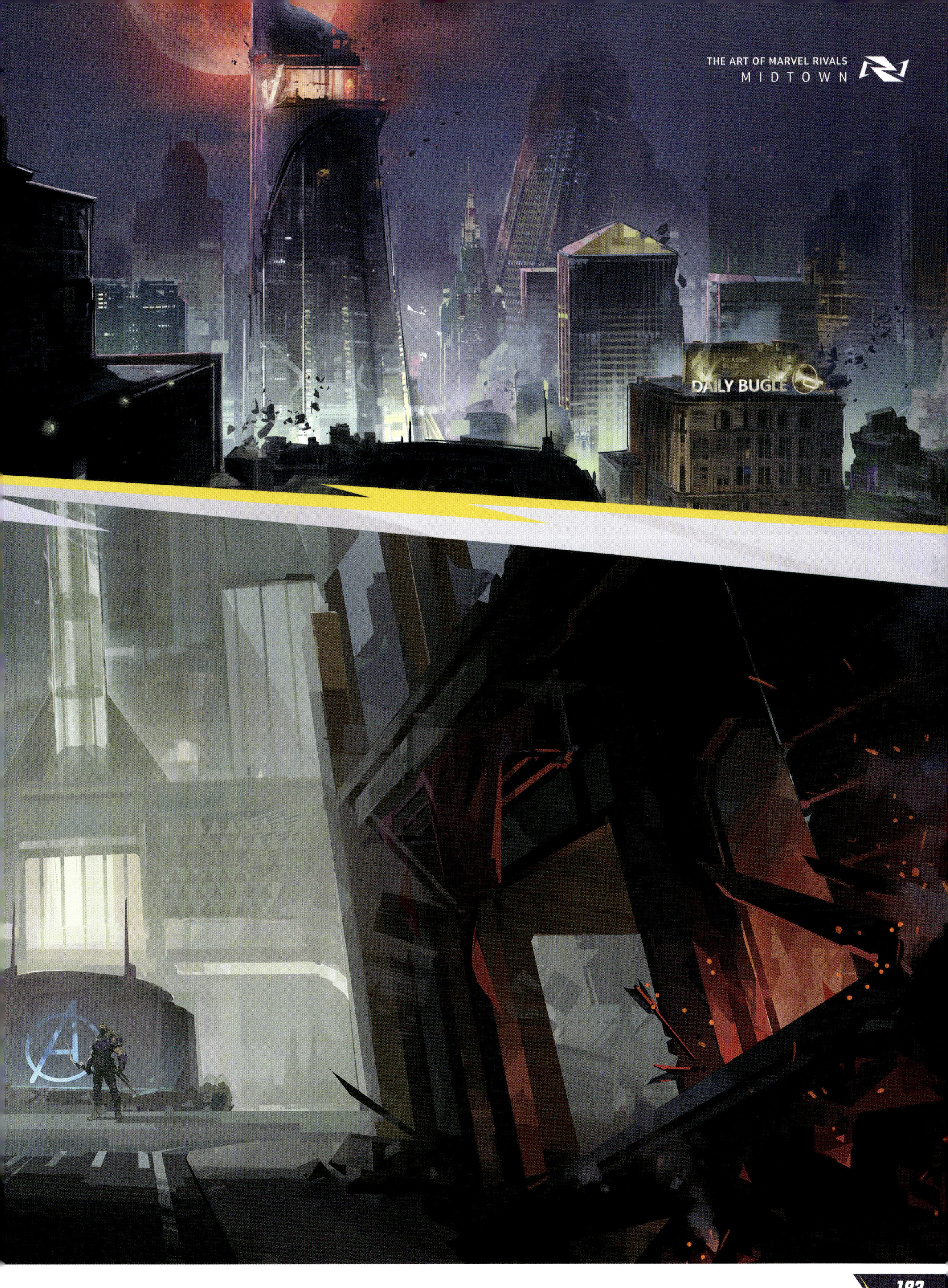
CLASSIC
BLUE
DAILY BUGLE

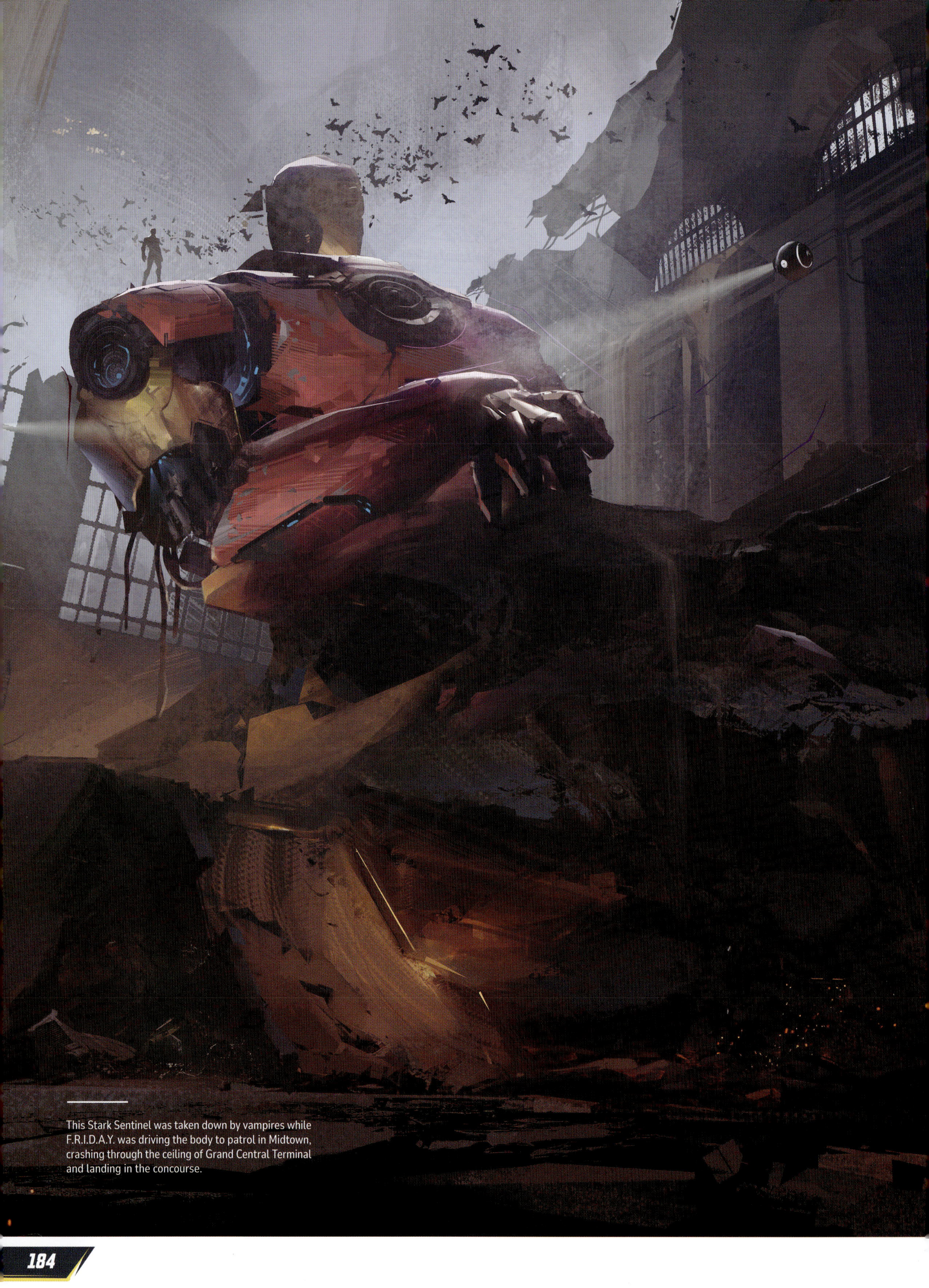

This Stark Sentinel was taken down by vampires while F.R.I.D.A.Y. was driving the body to patrol in Midtown, crashing through the ceiling of Grand Central Terminal and landing in the concourse.

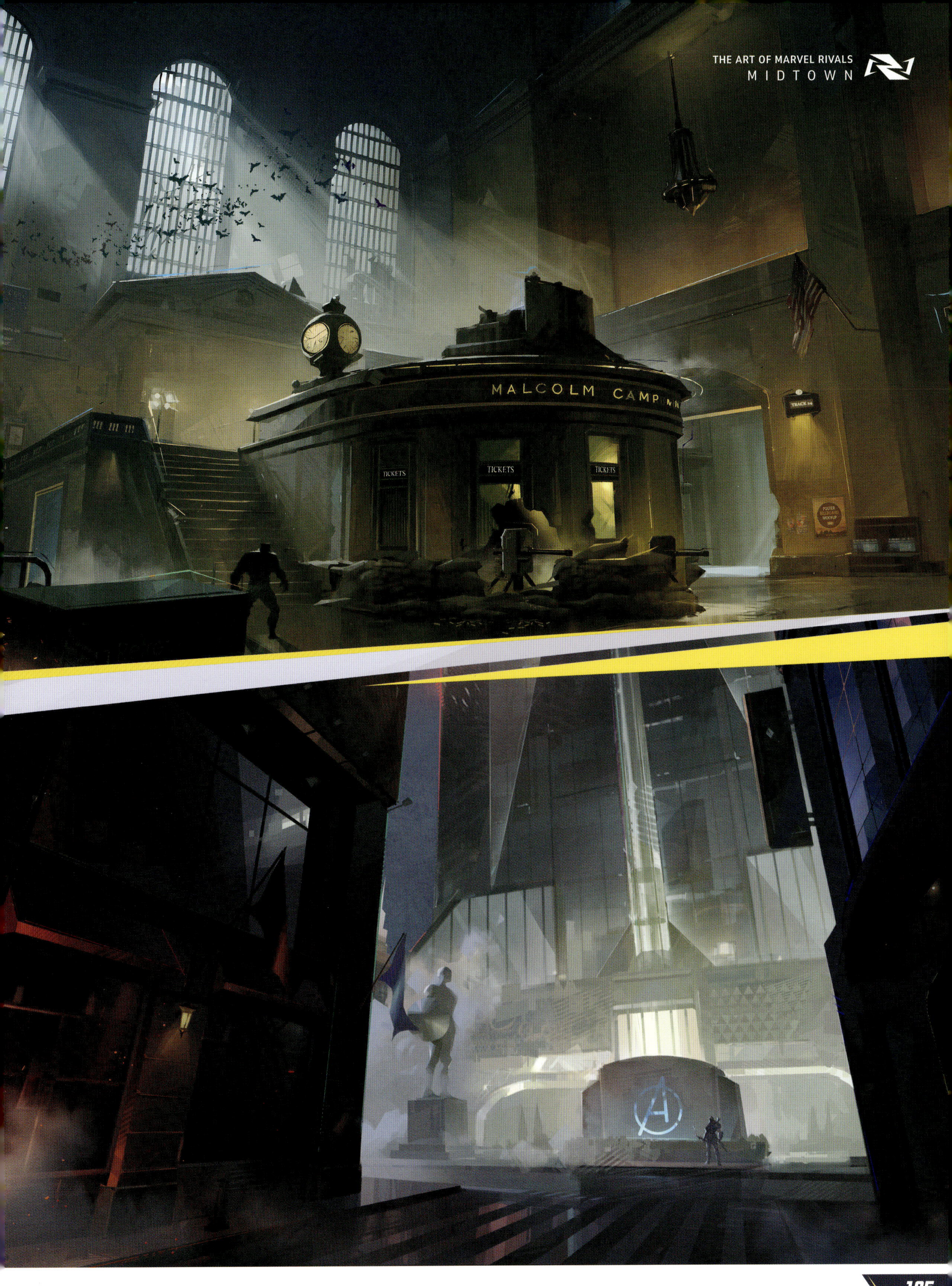
MALCOLM CAMP
TICKETS
TICKETS
TICKETS

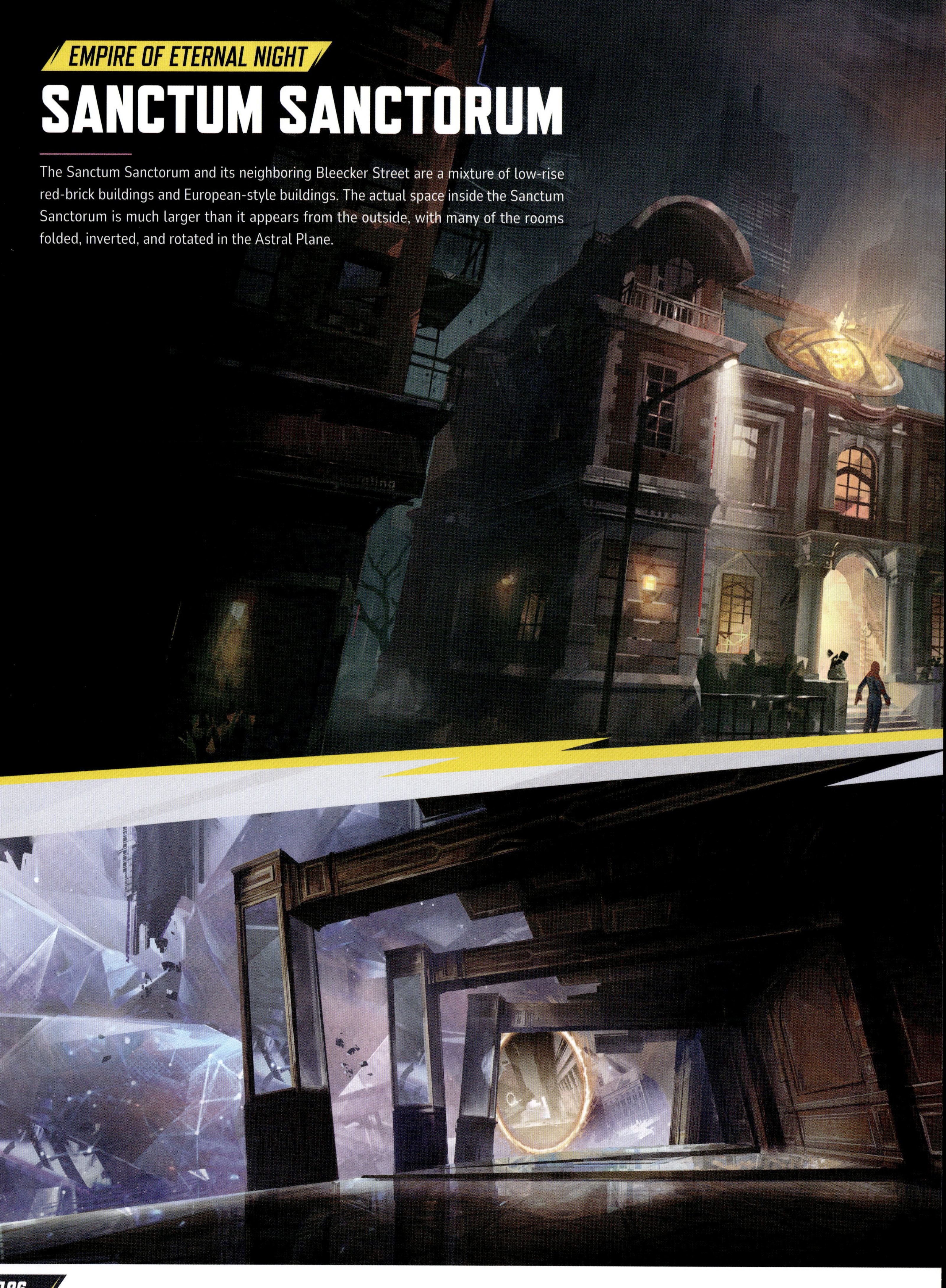

EMPIRE OF ETERNAL NIGHT

SANCTUM SANCTORUM

The Sanctum Sanctorum and its neighboring Bleecker Street are a mixture of low-rise red-brick buildings and European-style buildings. The actual space inside the Sanctum Sanctorum is much larger than it appears from the outside, with many of the rooms folded, inverted, and rotated in the Astral Plane.

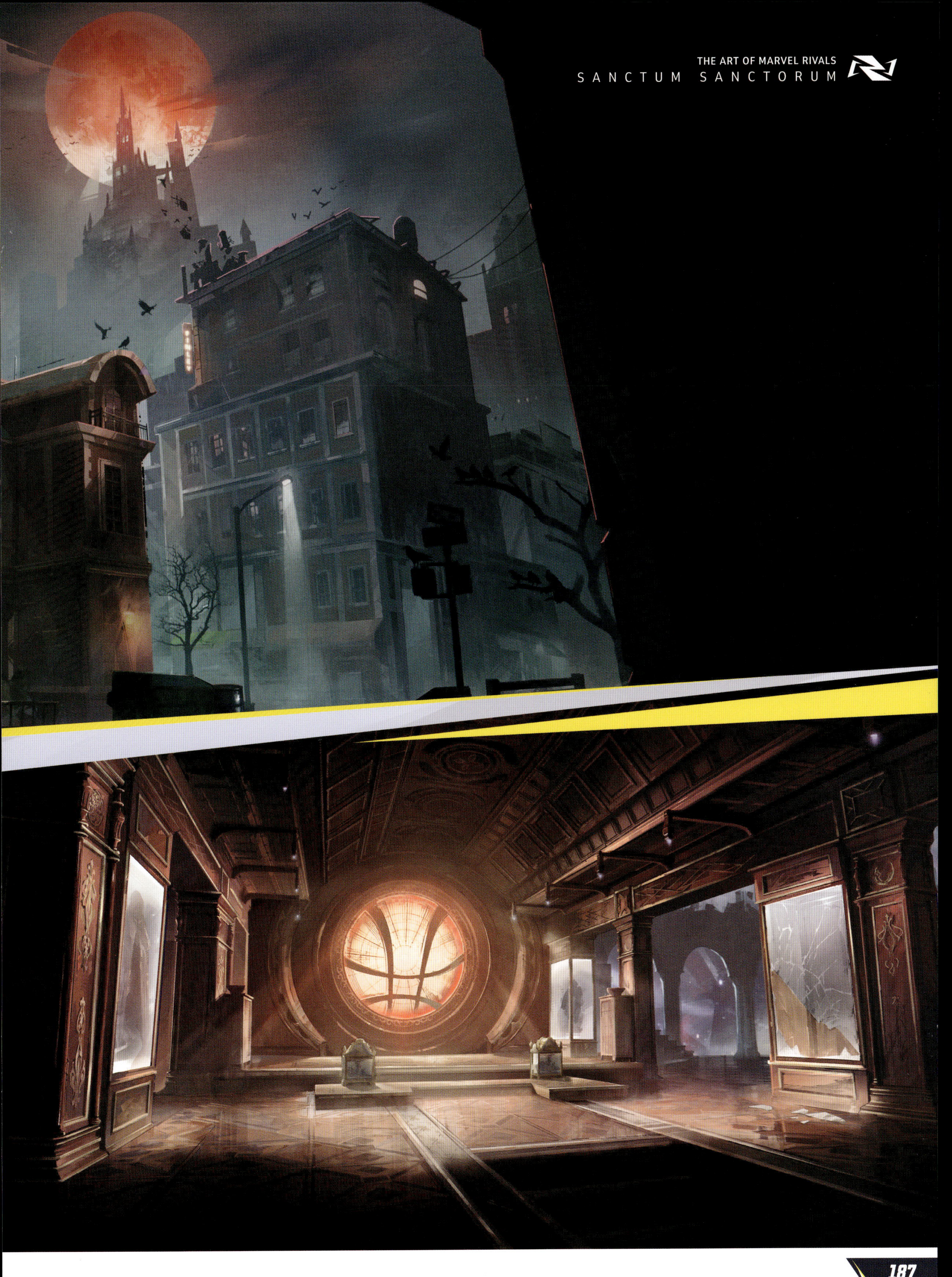

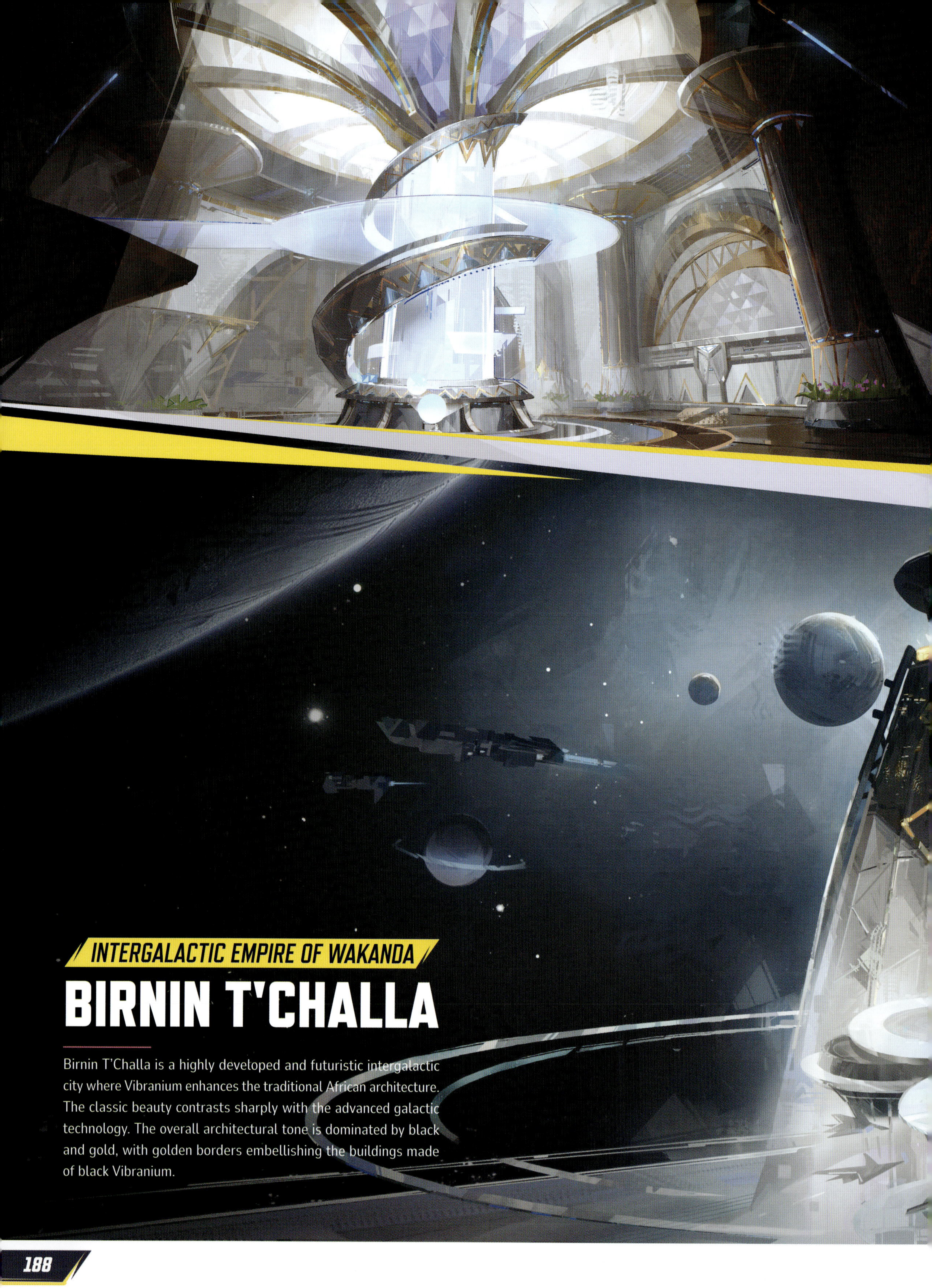

INTERGALACTIC EMPIRE OF WAKANDA

BIRNIN T'CHALLA

Birnin T'Challa is a highly developed and futuristic intergalactic city where Vibranium enhances the traditional African architecture. The classic beauty contrasts sharply with the advanced galactic technology. The overall architectural tone is dominated by black and gold, with golden borders embellishing the buildings made of black Vibranium.

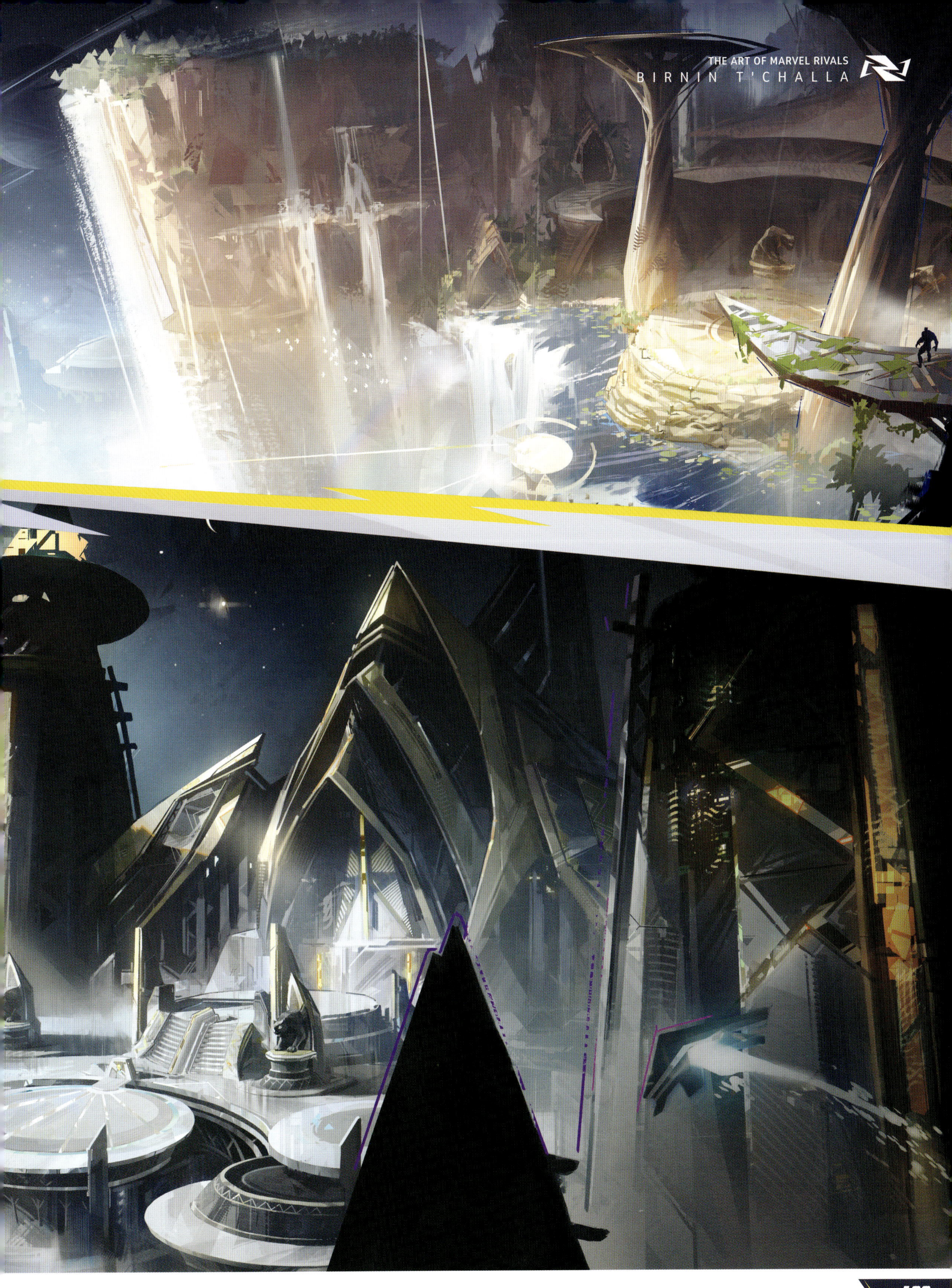

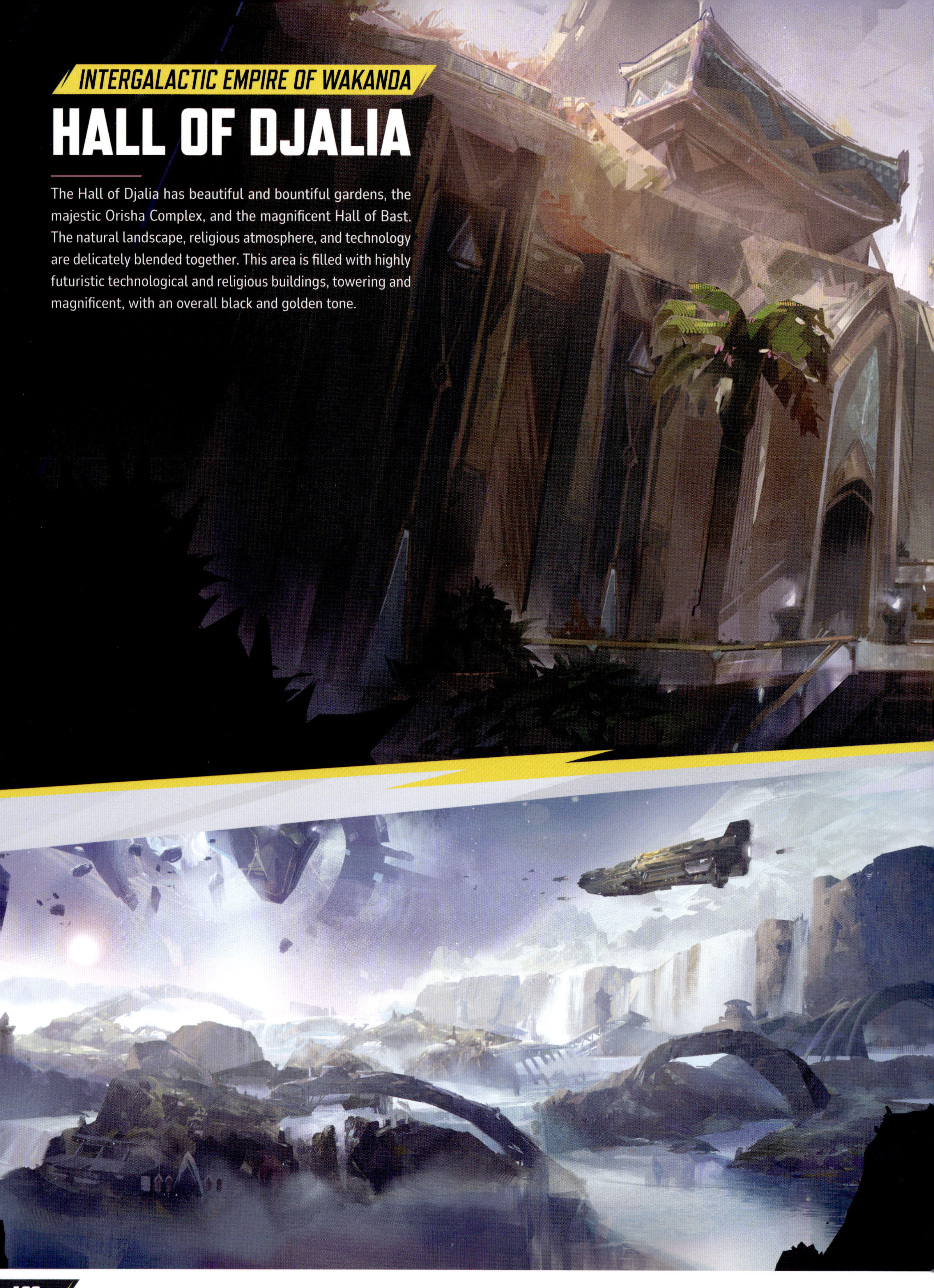

INTERGALACTIC EMPIRE OF WAKANDA

HALL OF DJALIA

The Hall of Djalia has beautiful and bountiful gardens, the majestic Orisha Complex, and the magnificent Hall of Bast. The natural landscape, religious atmosphere, and technology are delicately blended together. This area is filled with highly futuristic technological and religious buildings, towering and magnificent, with an overall black and golden tone.

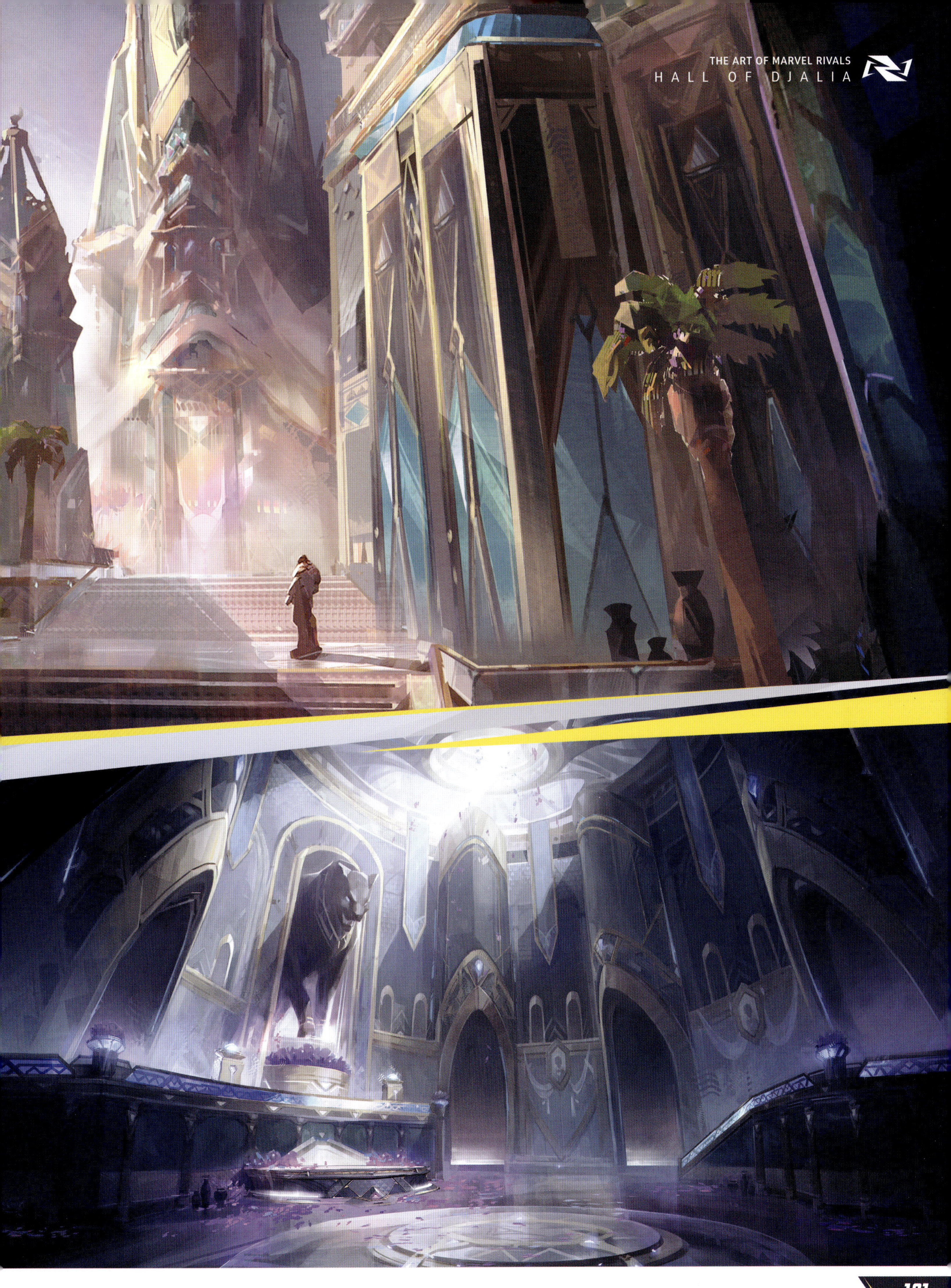

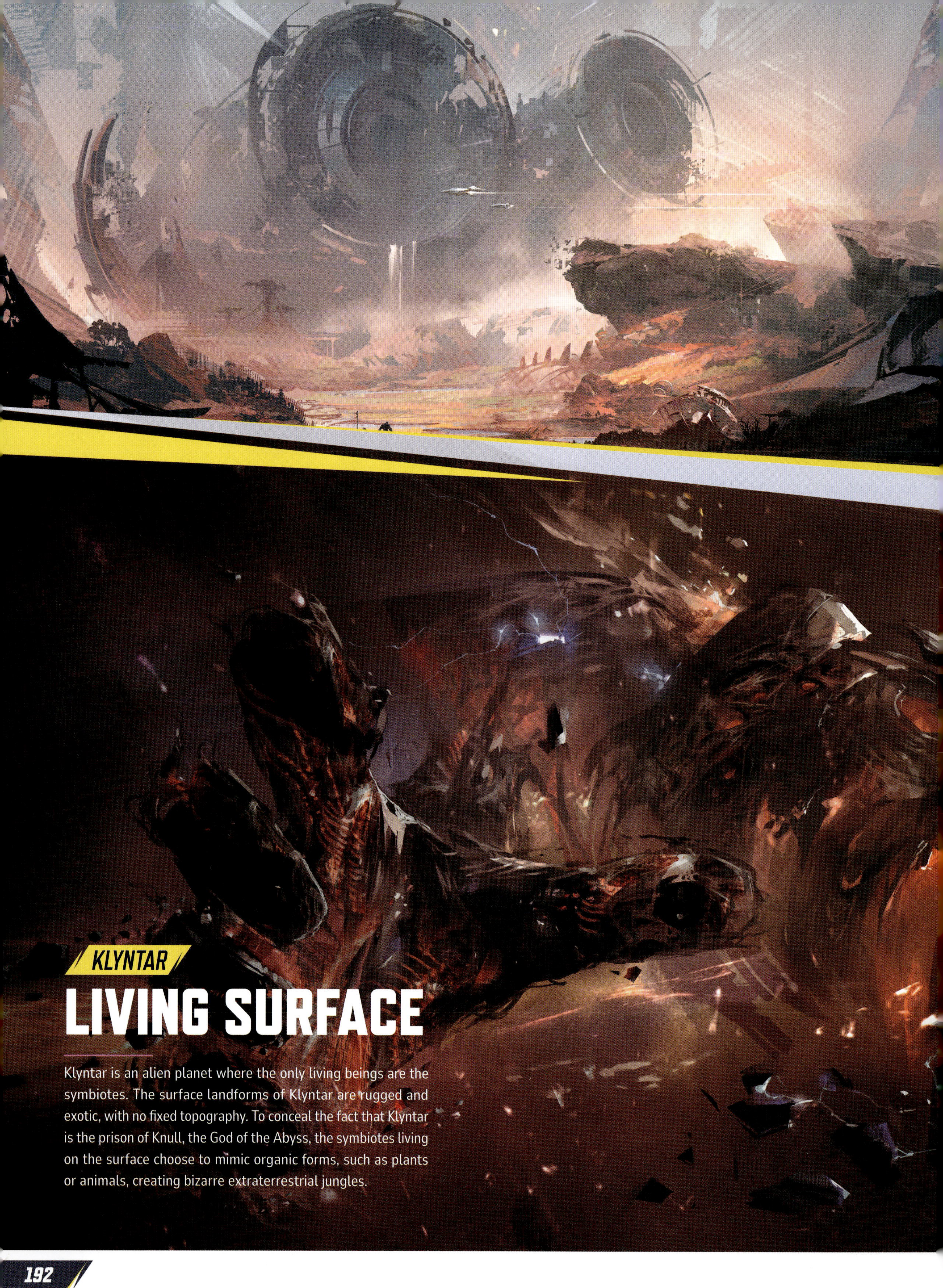

KLYNTAR

LIVING SURFACE

Klyntar is an alien planet where the only living beings are the symbiotes. The surface landforms of Klyntar are rugged and exotic, with no fixed topography. To conceal the fact that Klyntar is the prison of Knull, the God of the Abyss, the symbiotes living on the surface choose to mimic organic forms, such as plants or animals, creating bizarre extraterrestrial jungles.

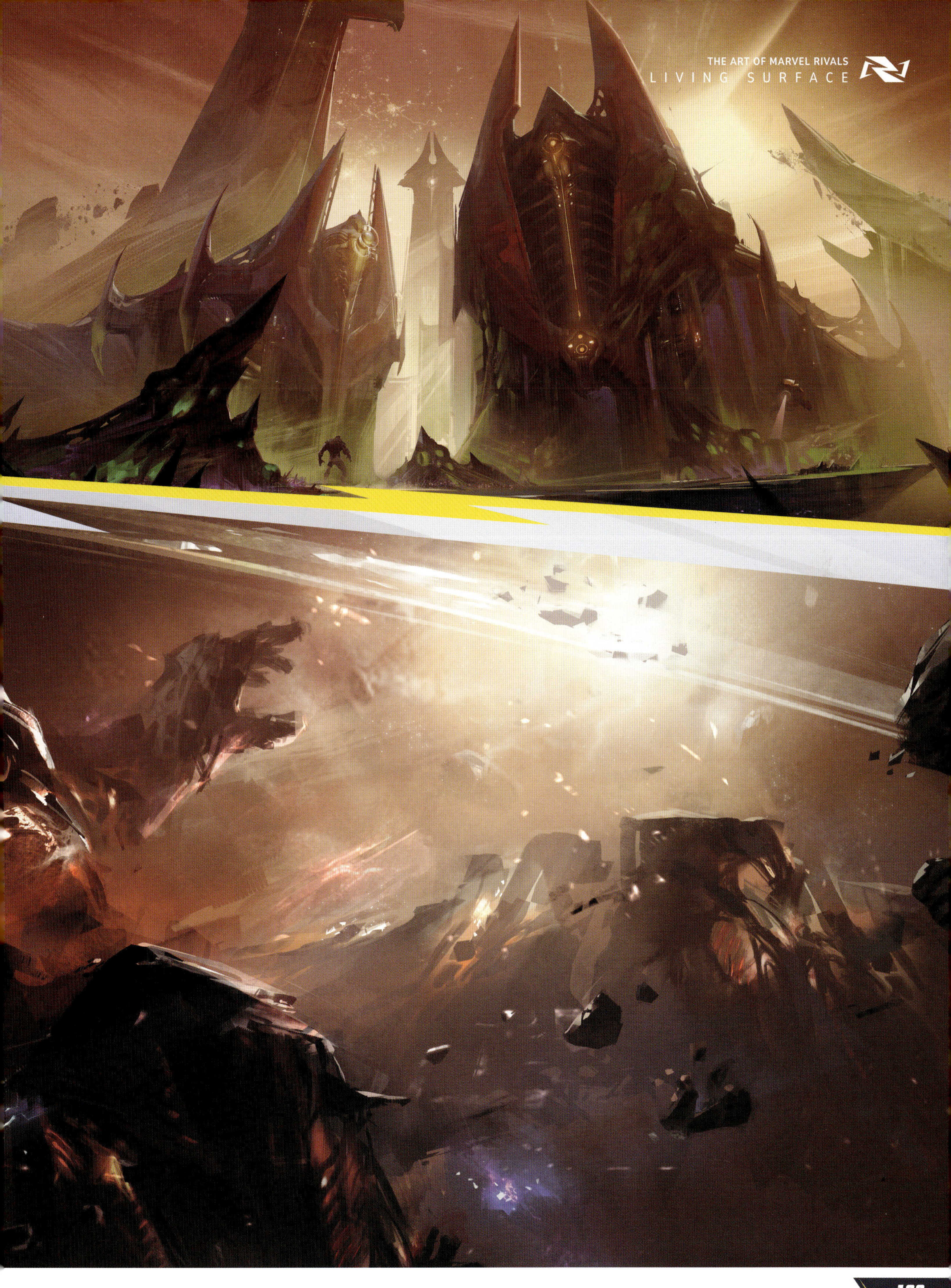

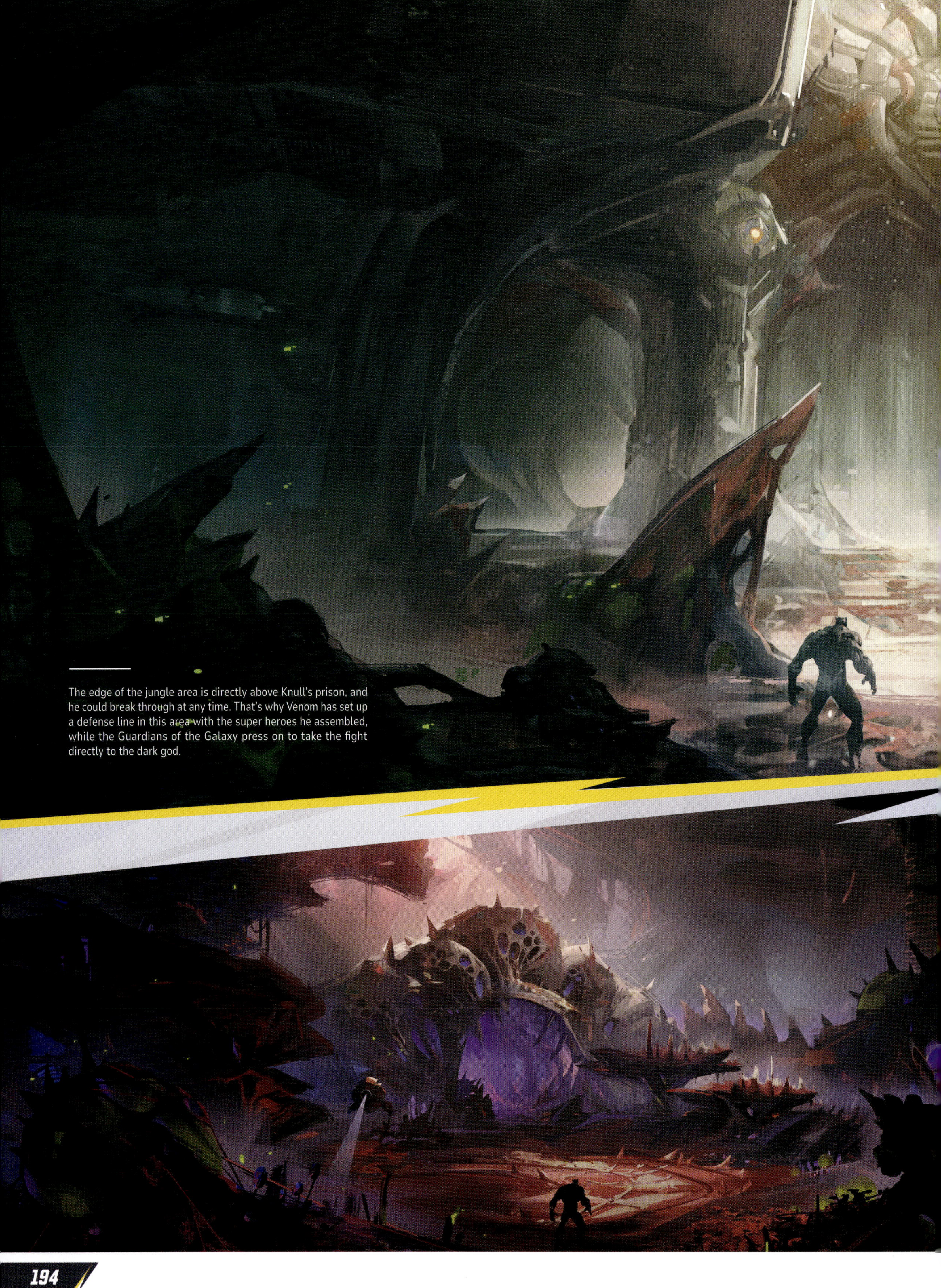

The edge of the jungle area is directly above Knull's prison, and he could break through at any time. That's why Venom has set up a defense line in this area with the super heroes he assembled, while the Guardians of the Galaxy press on to take the fight directly to the dark god.

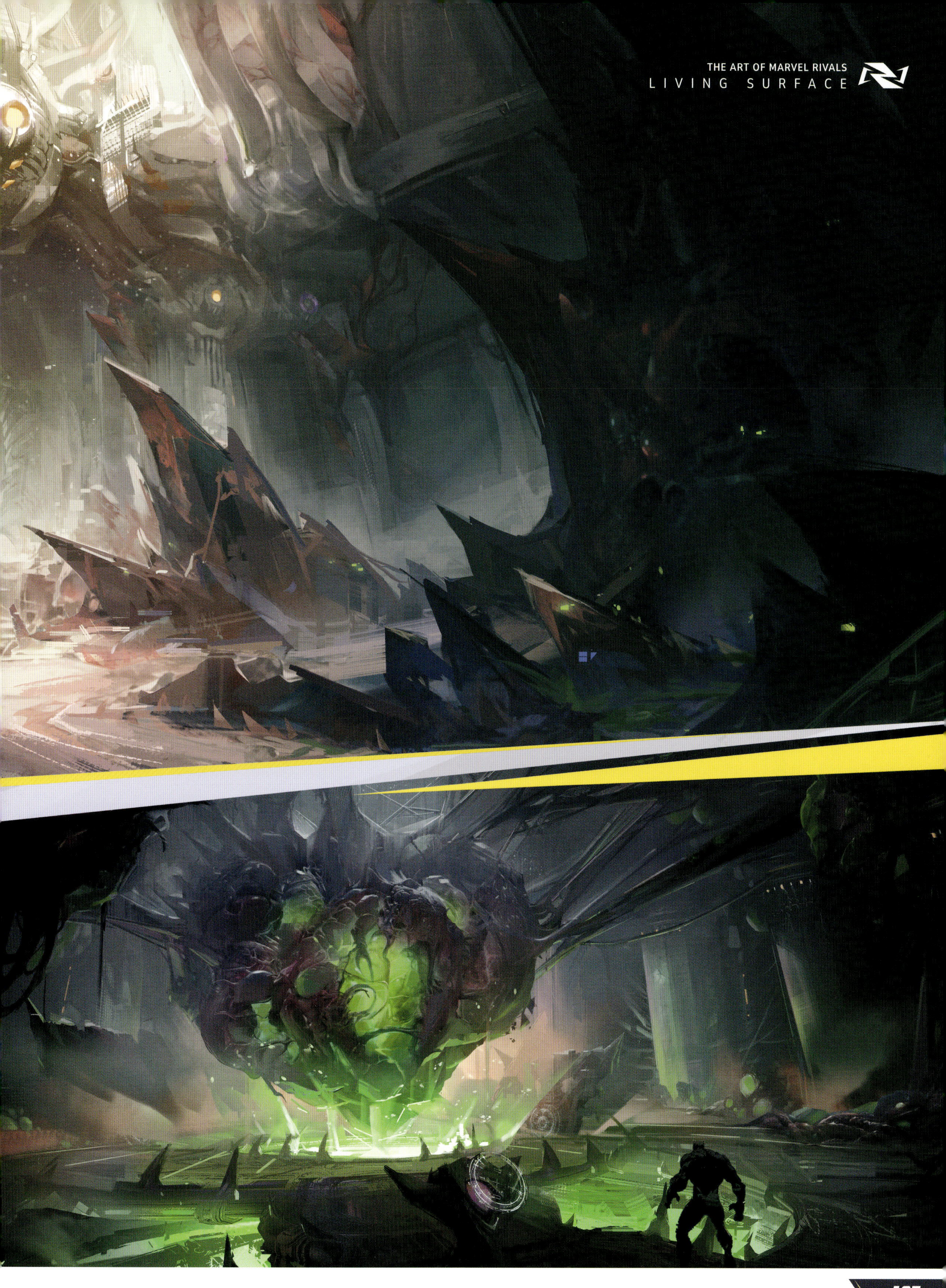

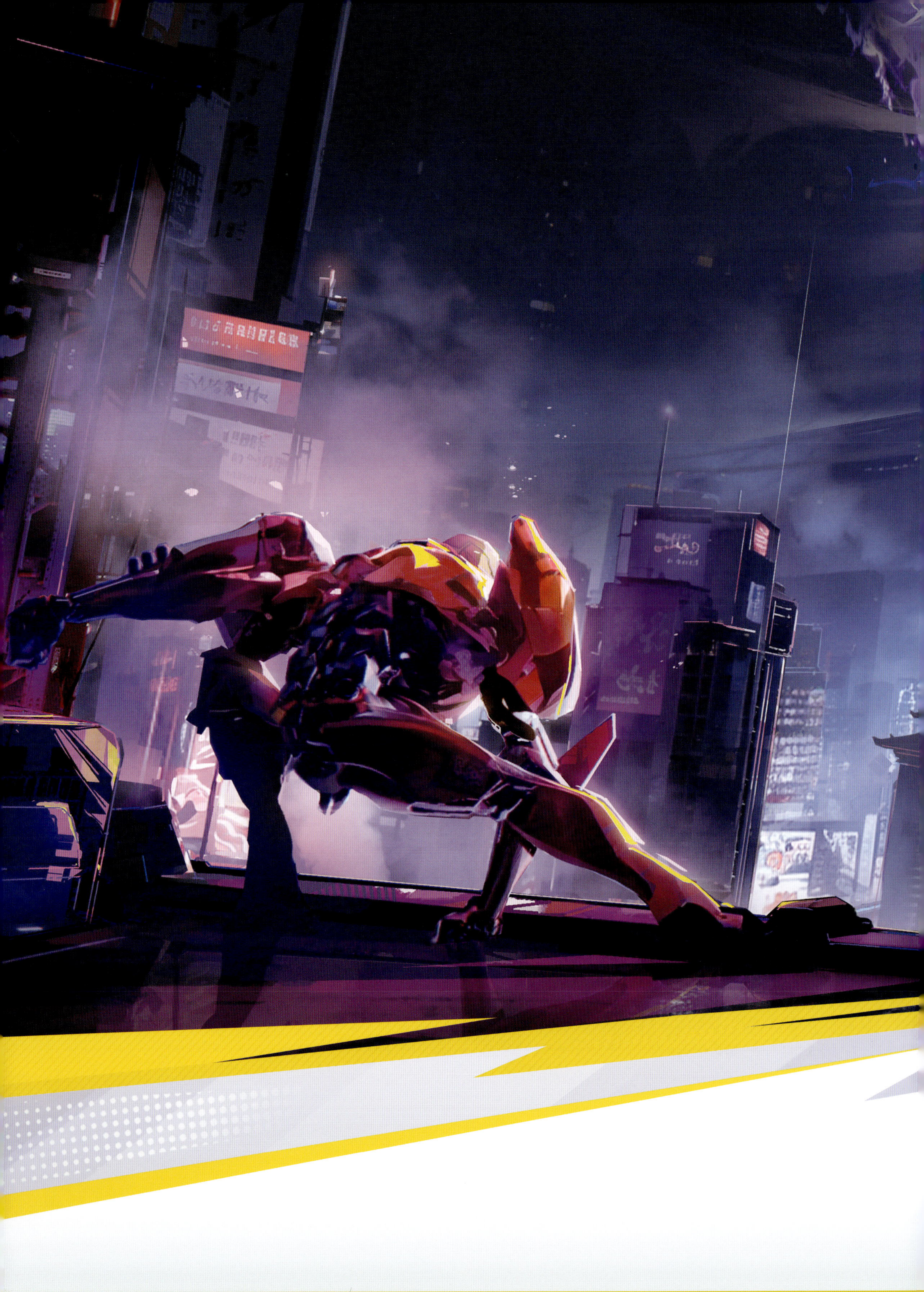

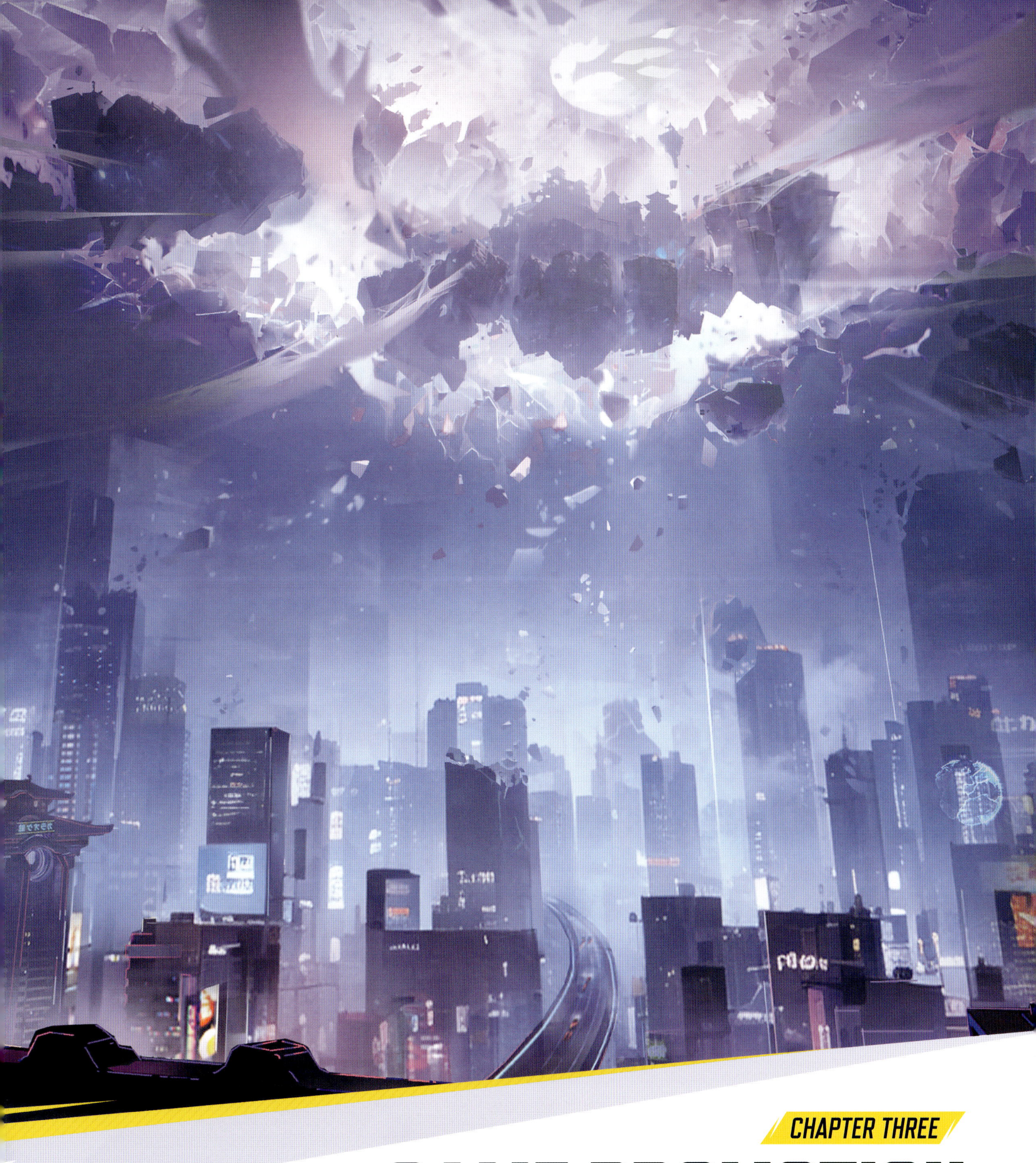

CHAPTER THREE

GAME PROMOTION

With all these maps rich in story and details, we realized that static presentations of information were not enough—they needed to be woven into the very fabric of the animation. This led us to develop our cinematic trailer and in-game cutscenes.

NARRATIVE PROLOGUE

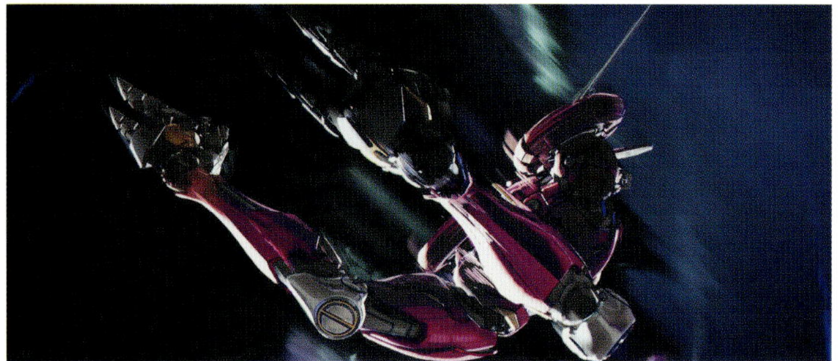

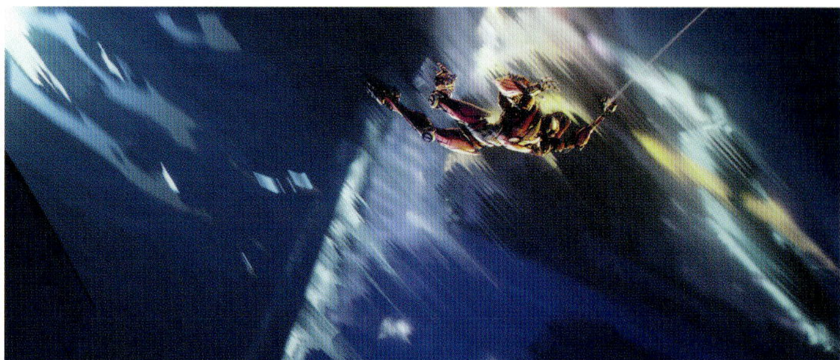

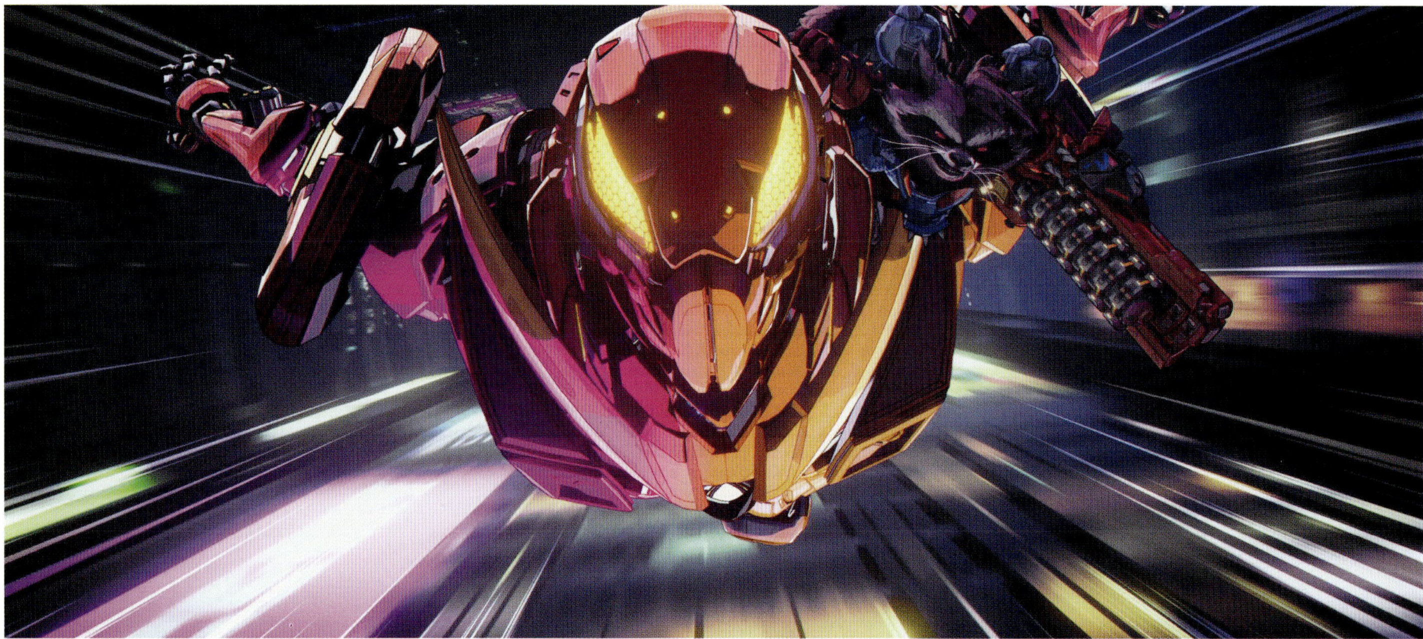

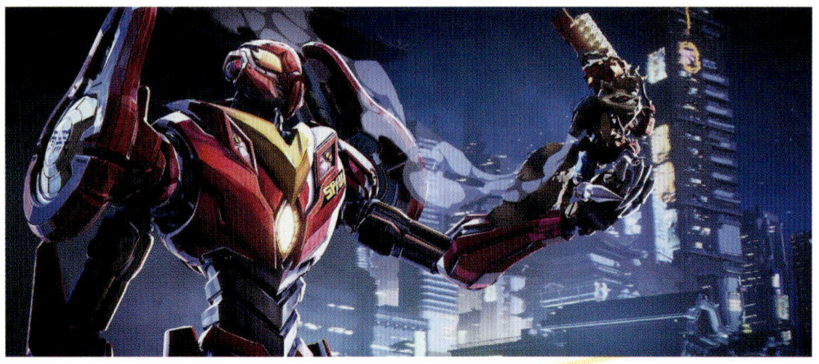

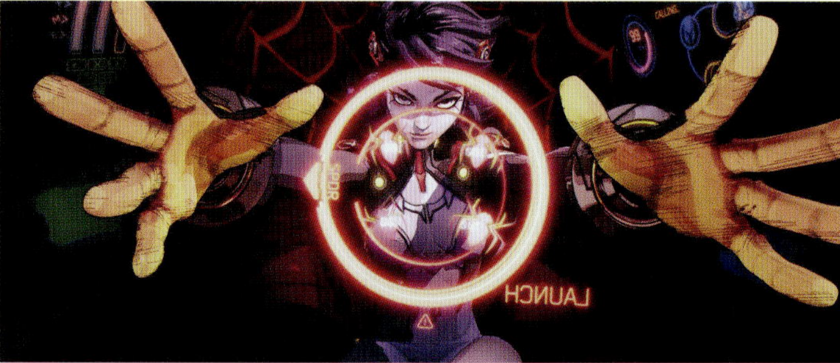

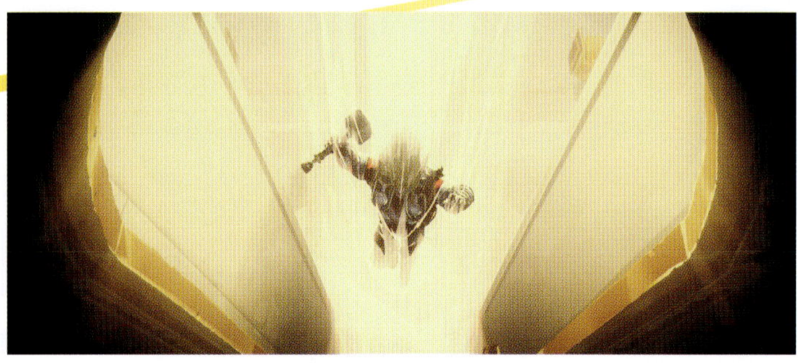

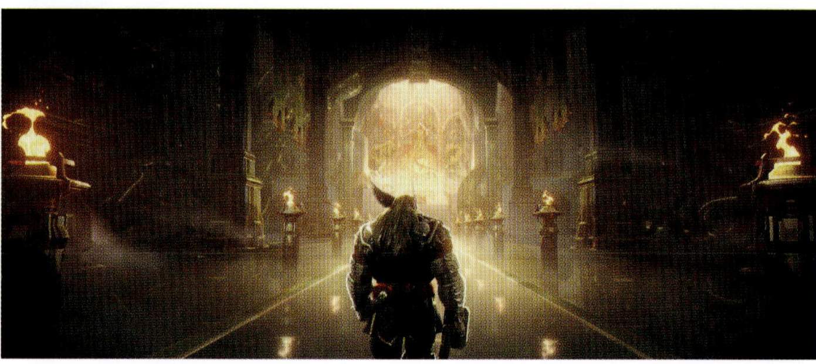

In *Marvel Rivals*, Peni Parker and Thor come from two different timelines, each facing different threats. Before the Timestream Entanglement, Peni is scouting the streets of Tokyo in the year 2099, tracking the whereabouts of Doom 2099, unaware that a second Doom is about to emerge. Meanwhile, Thor returns from a distant exile, determined to teach his disobedient brother a lesson he won't soon forget.

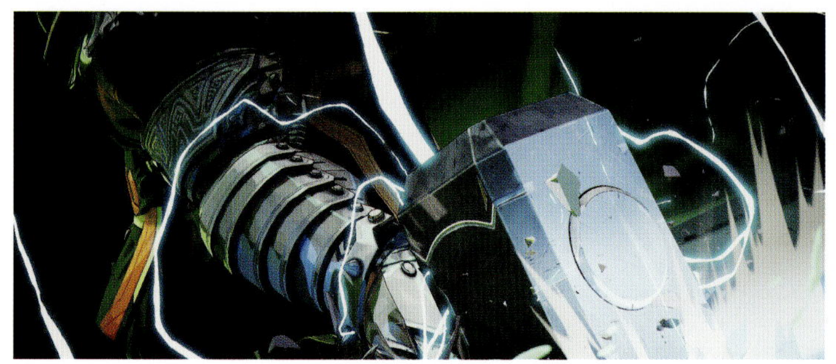

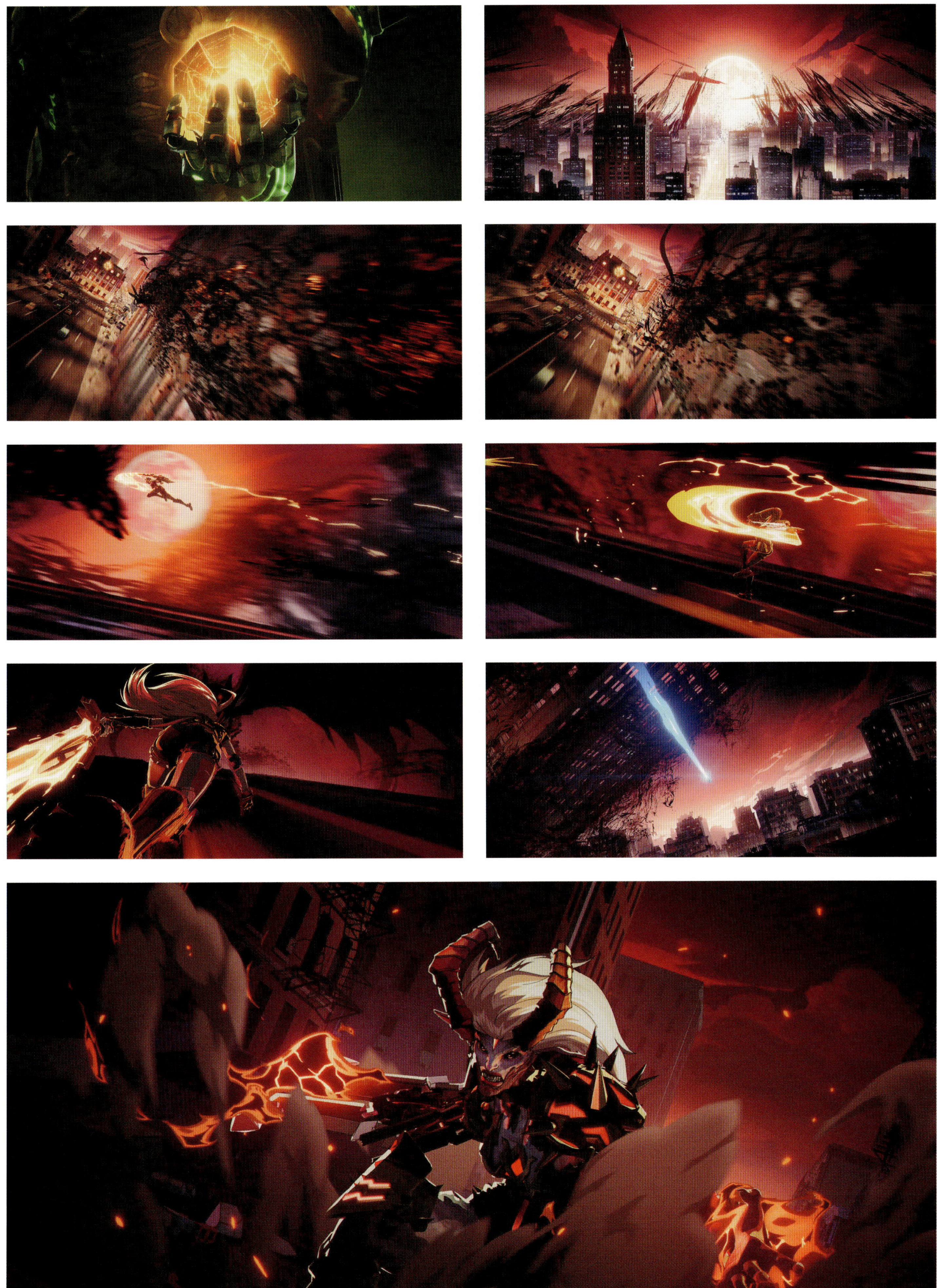

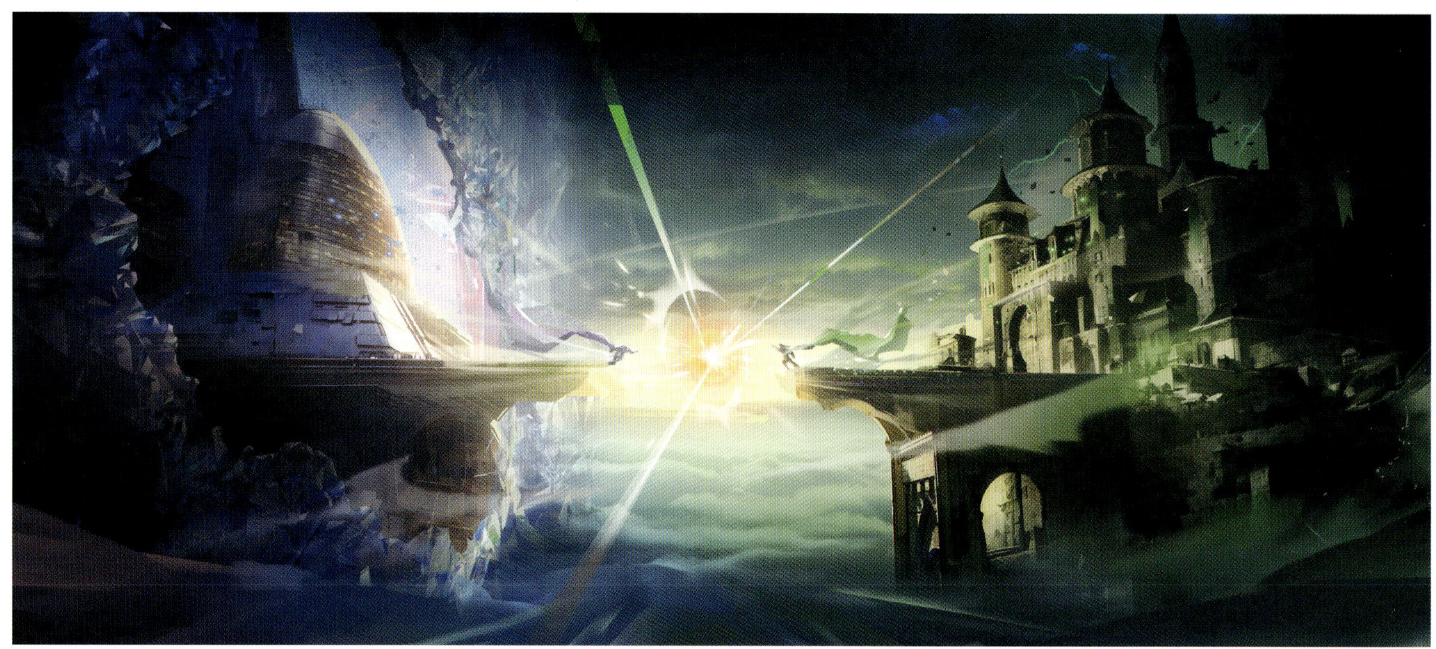

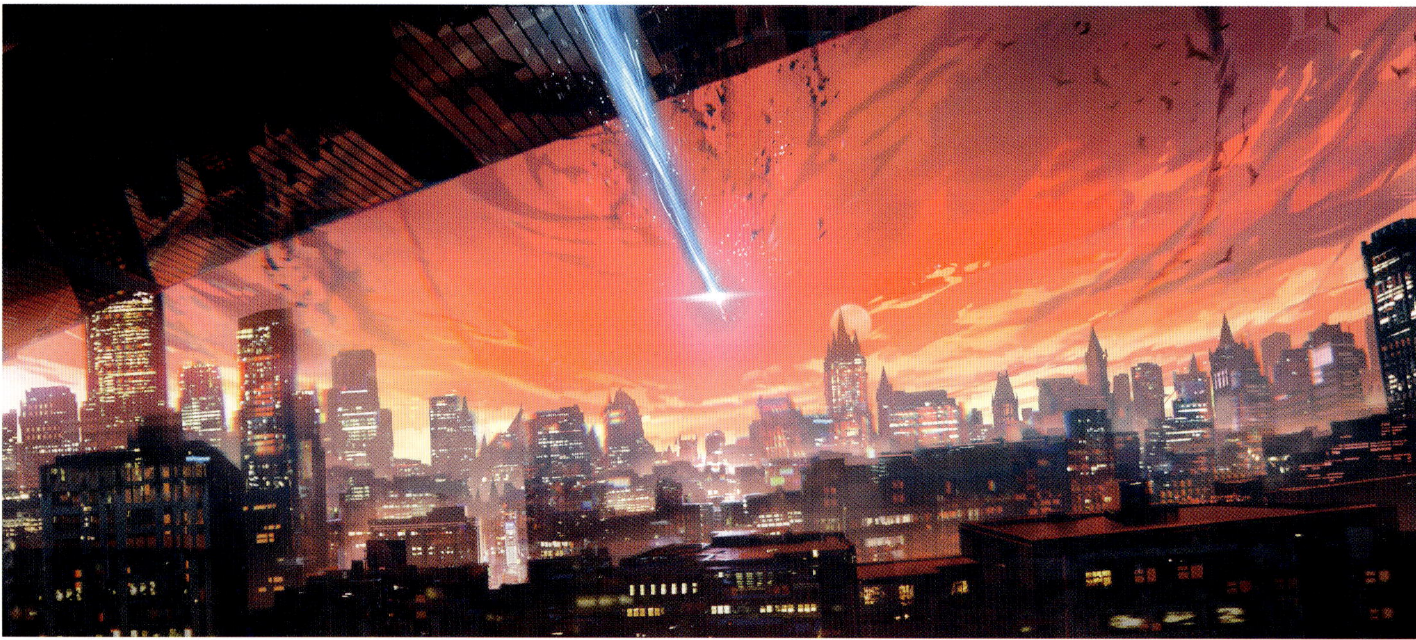

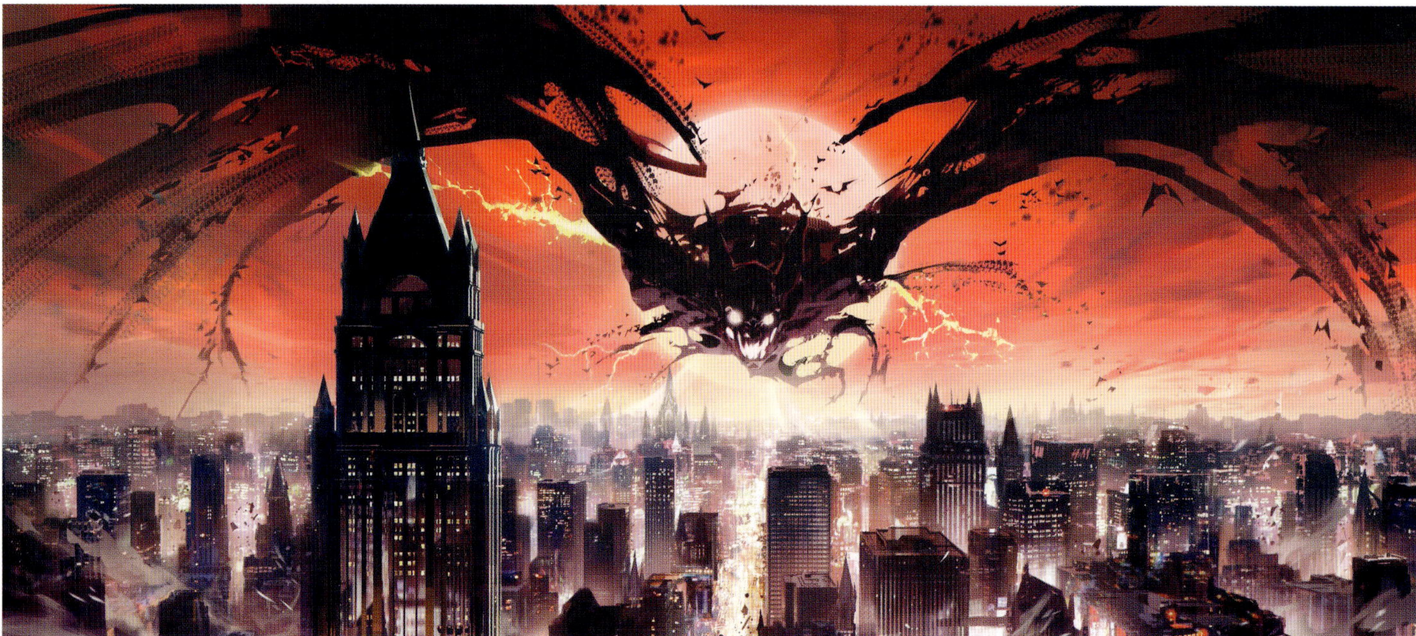

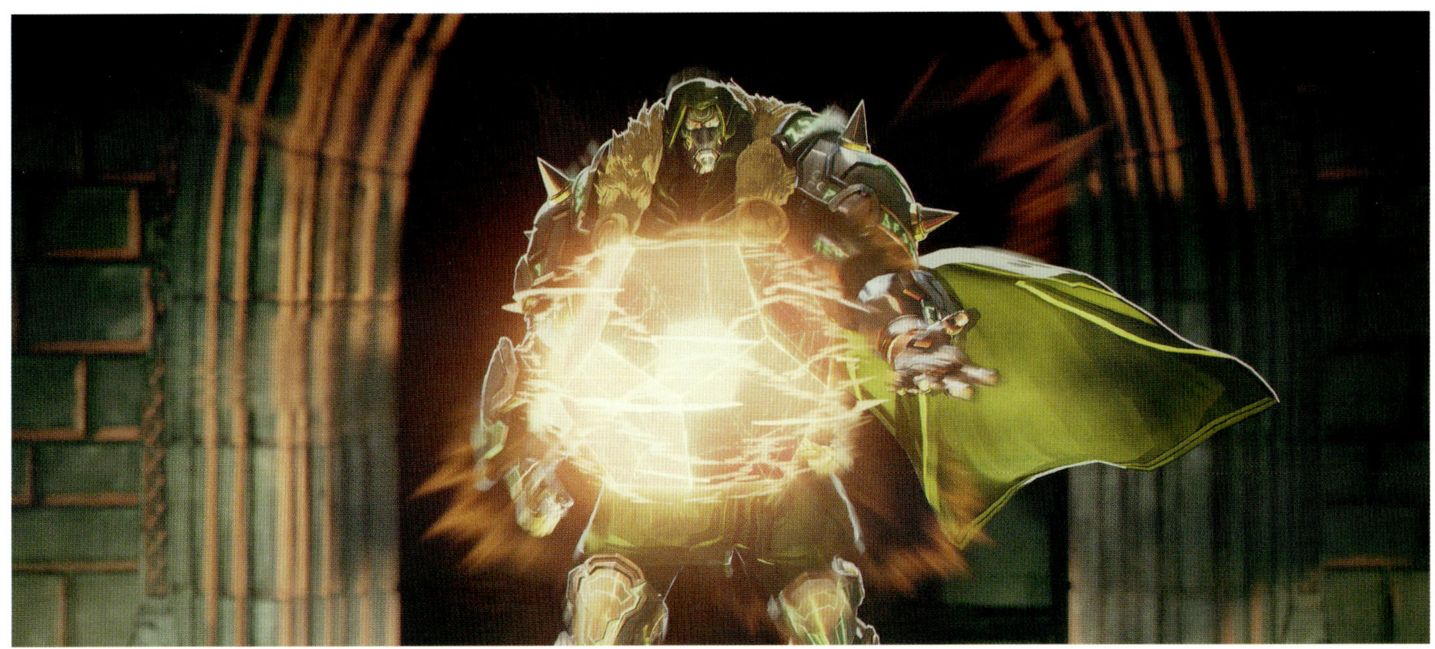

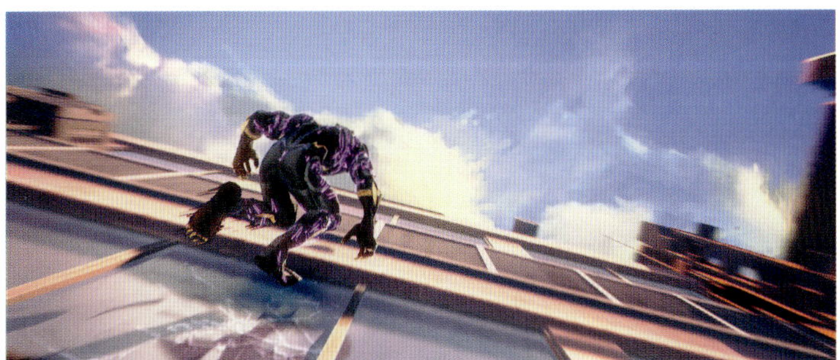

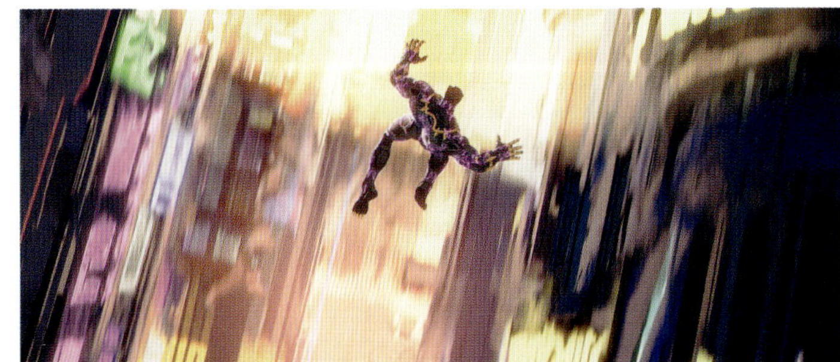

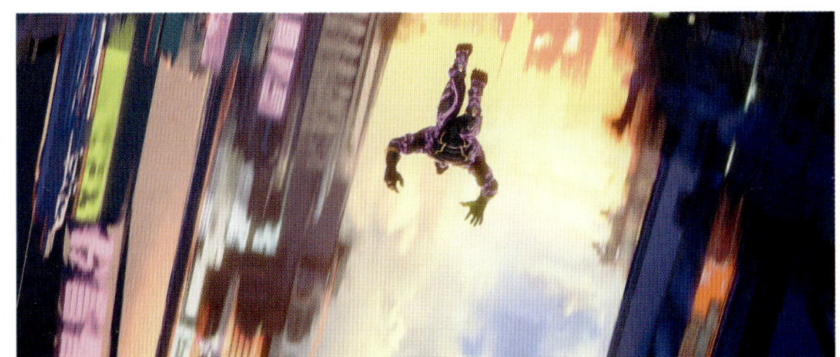

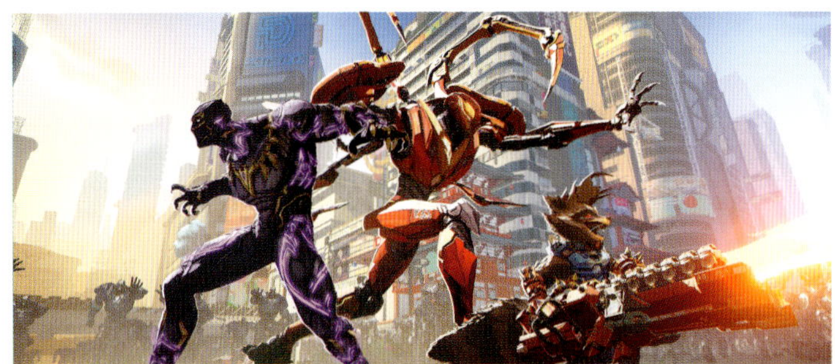

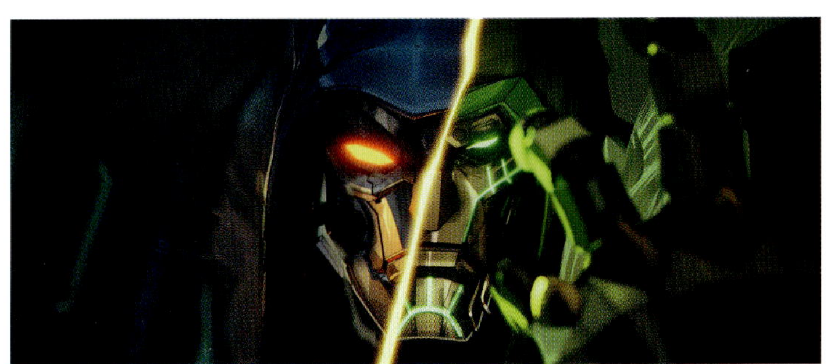

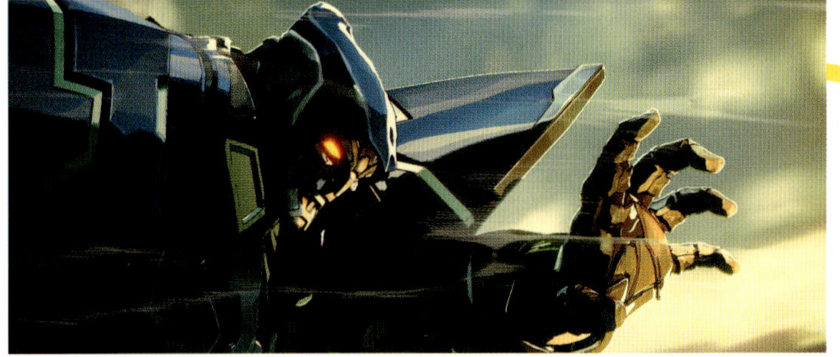

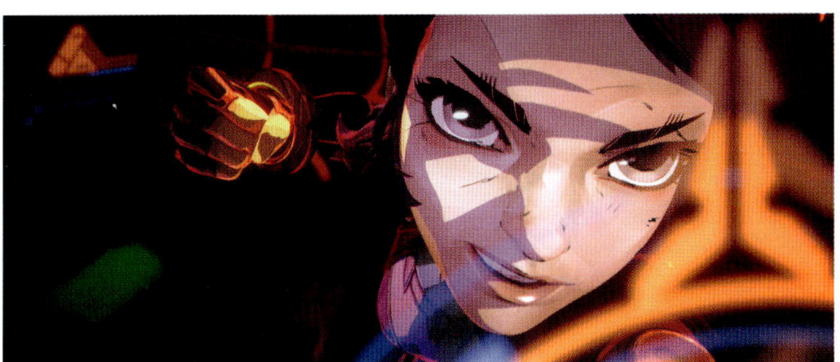

Ever wonder why Black Panther and Magneto swoop in to aid Rocket and Peni during their clash with Doombots in Tokyo 2099? If you keep your eyes peeled, you'll catch that Peni had already signaled for backup right at the start with a flick on the holographic panel.

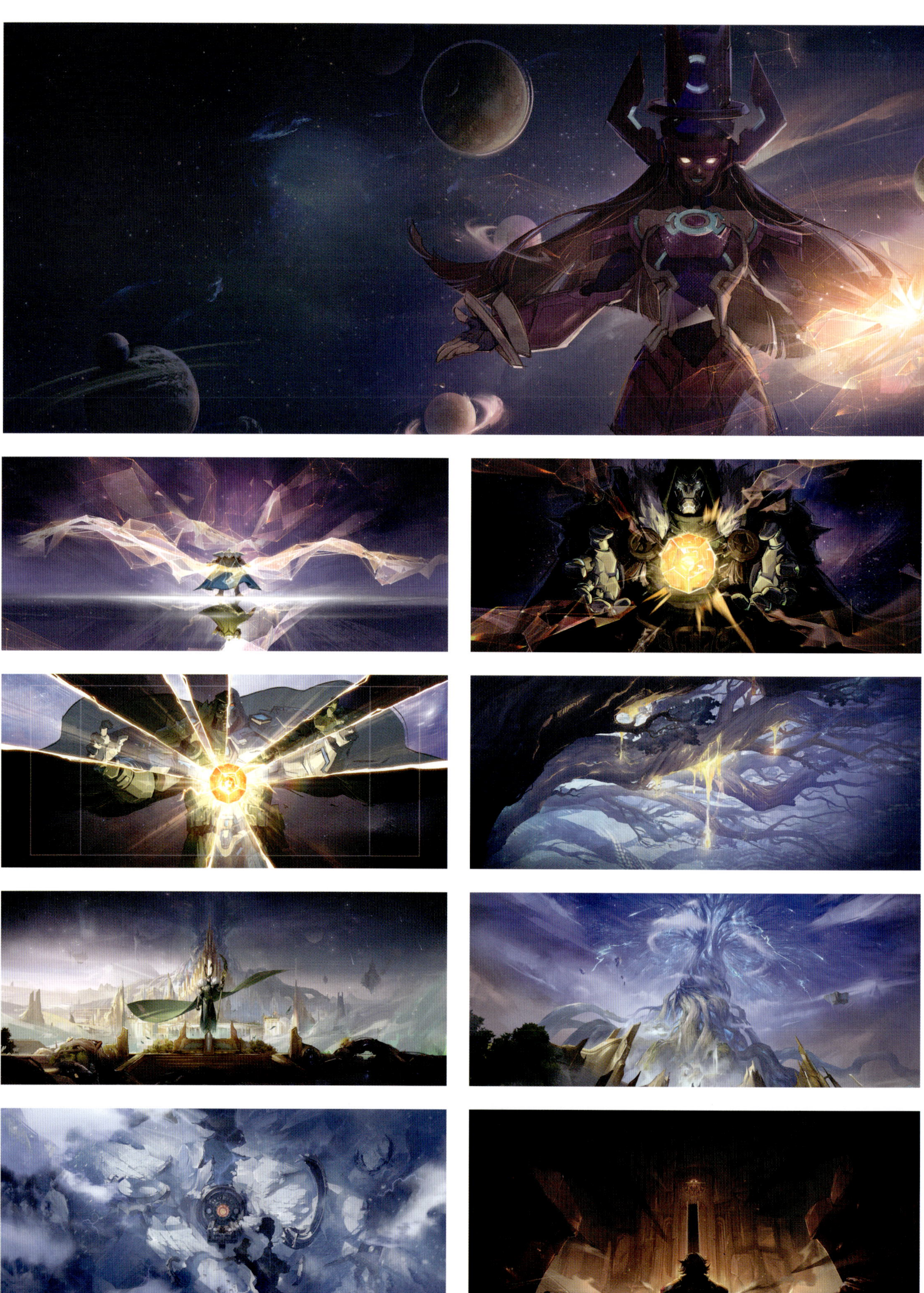

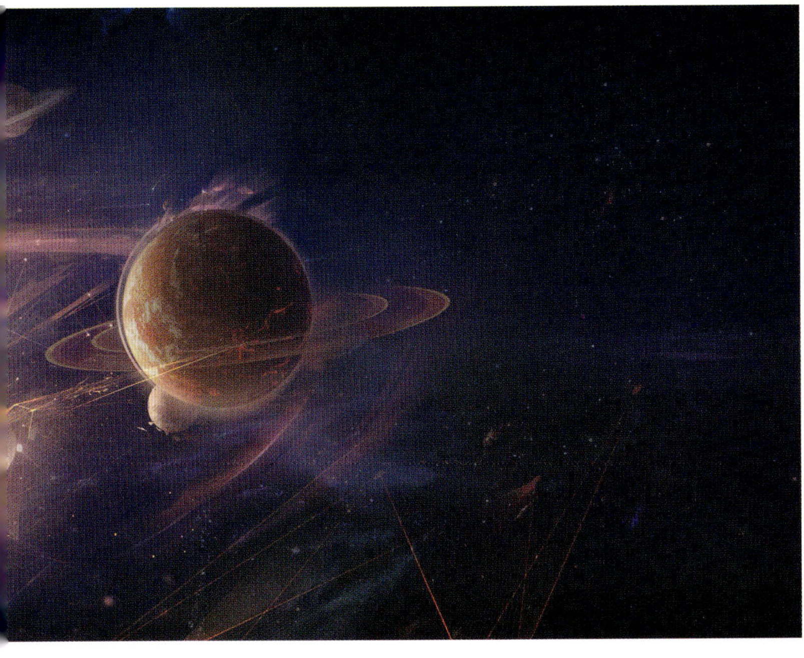

The trailer for Season 0 delves into how the Timestream Entanglement happened and the far-reaching consequences it has had. It reveals the stories behind all the maps of Season 0, all tied together through dynamic illustrations, with the narration of Galacta, the daughter of Galactus.

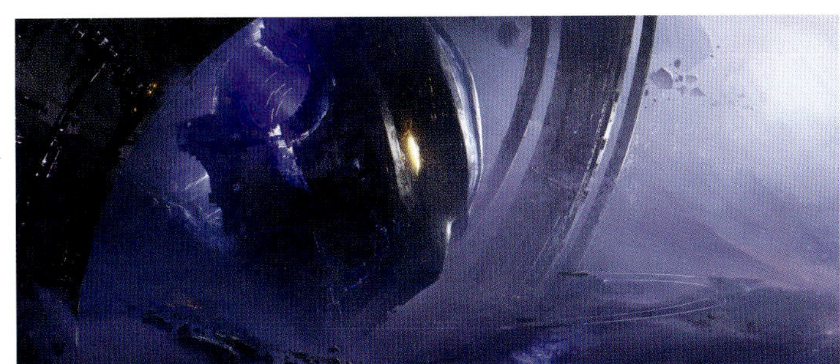

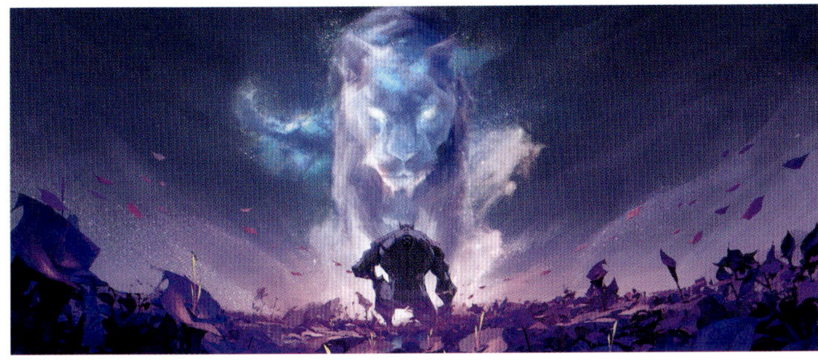

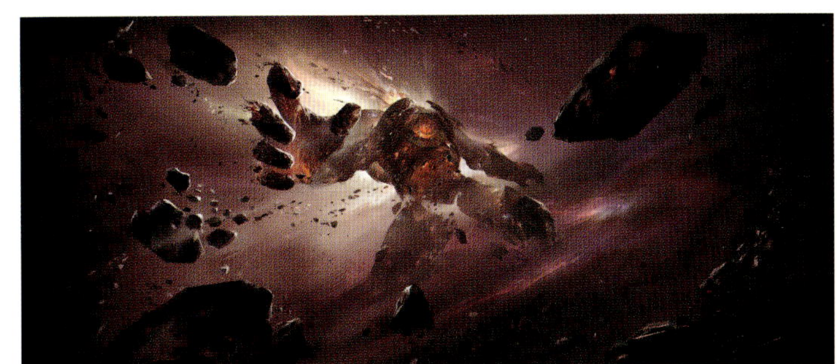

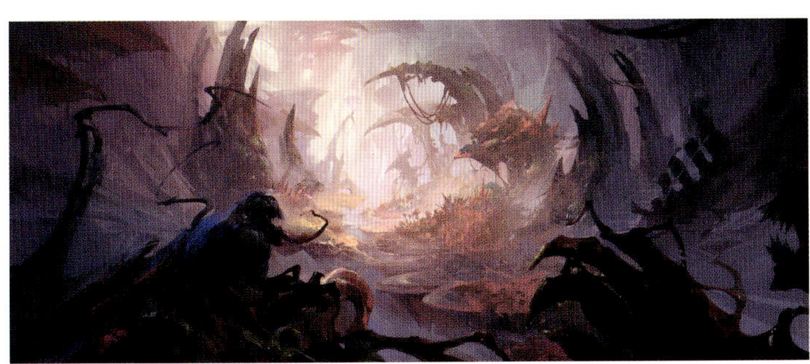

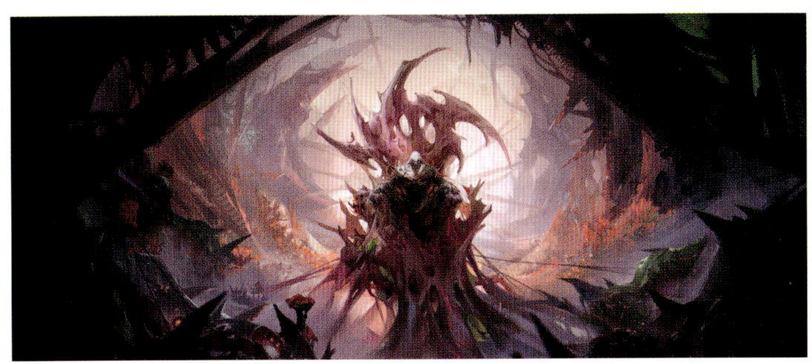

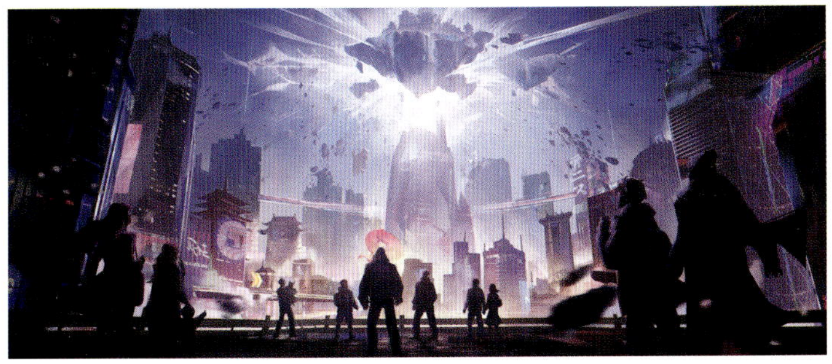

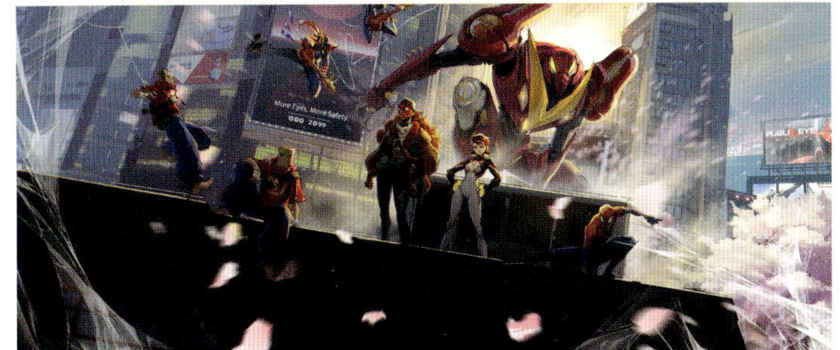

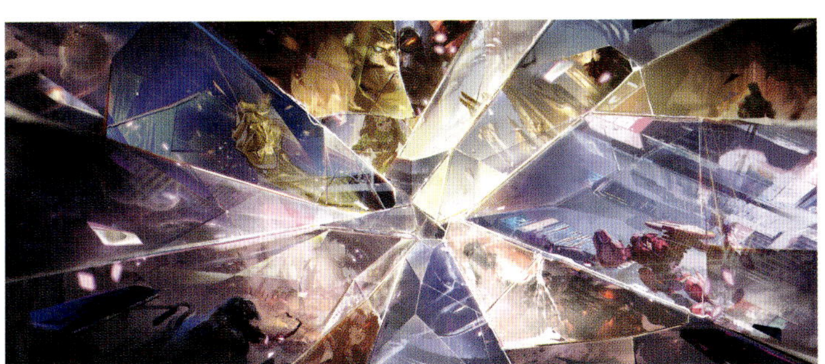

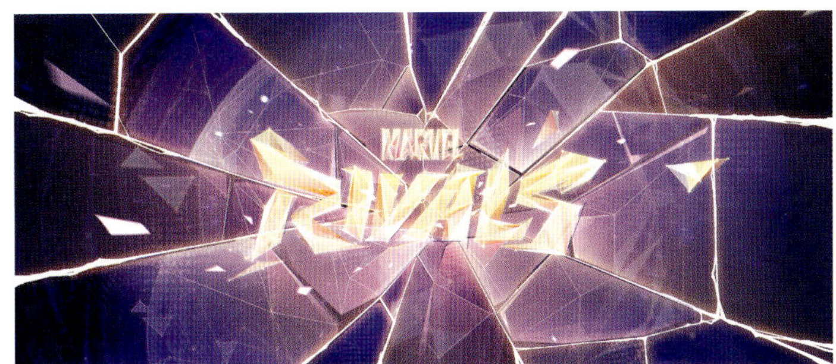

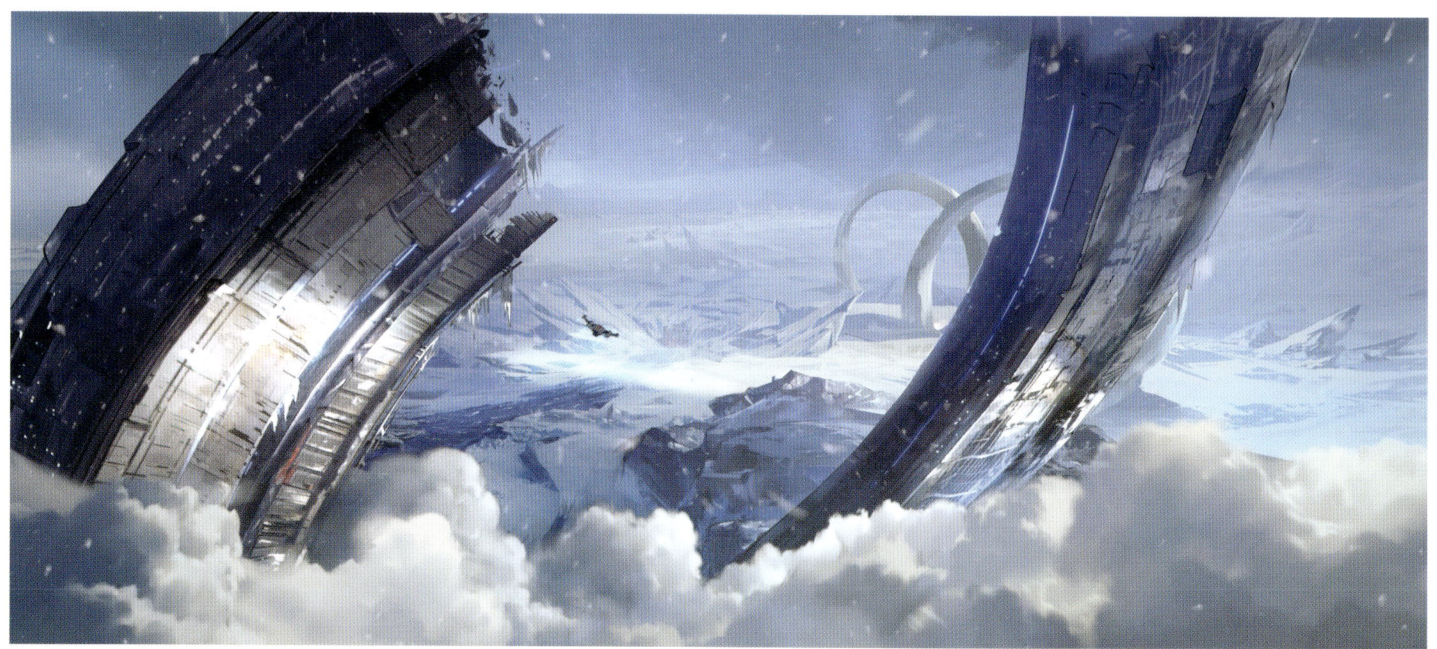

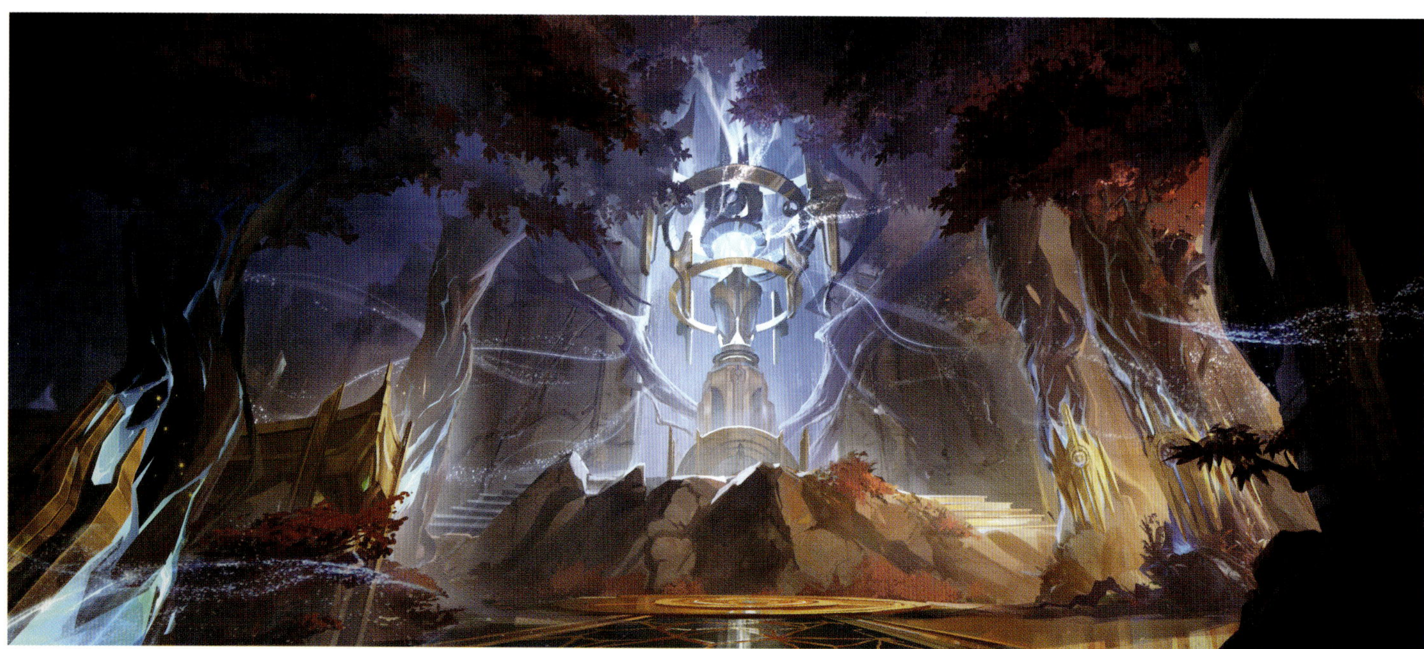

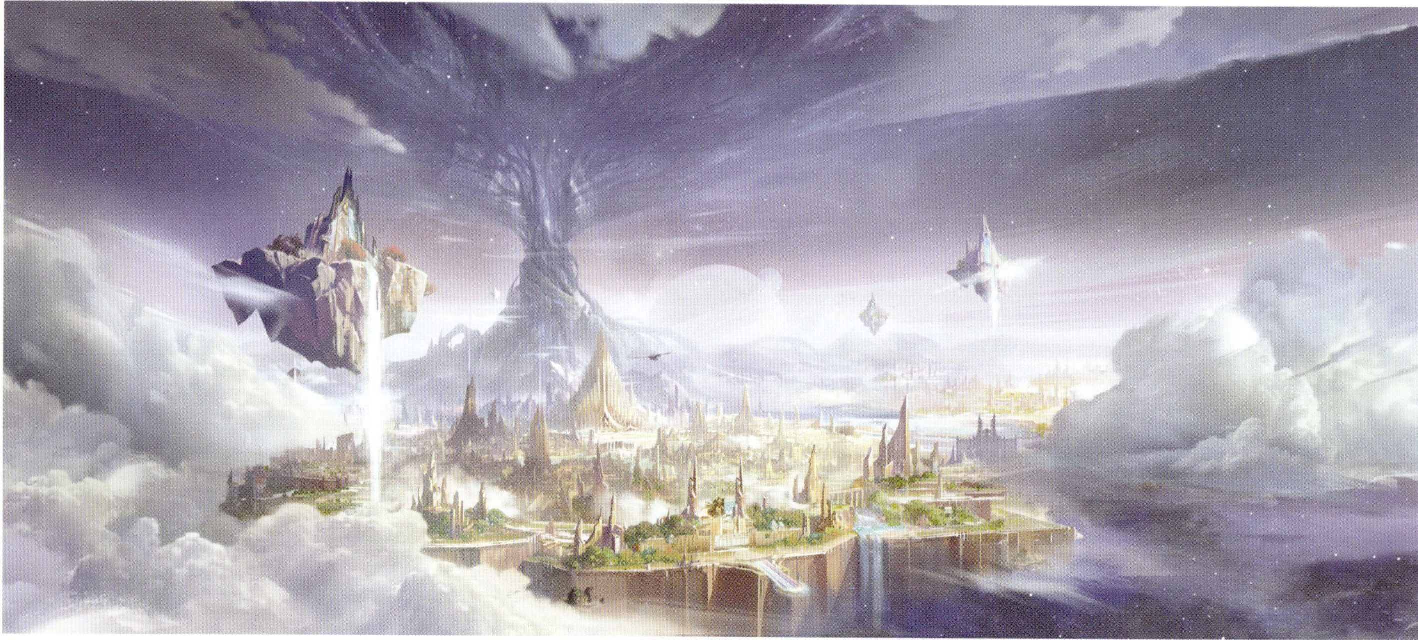

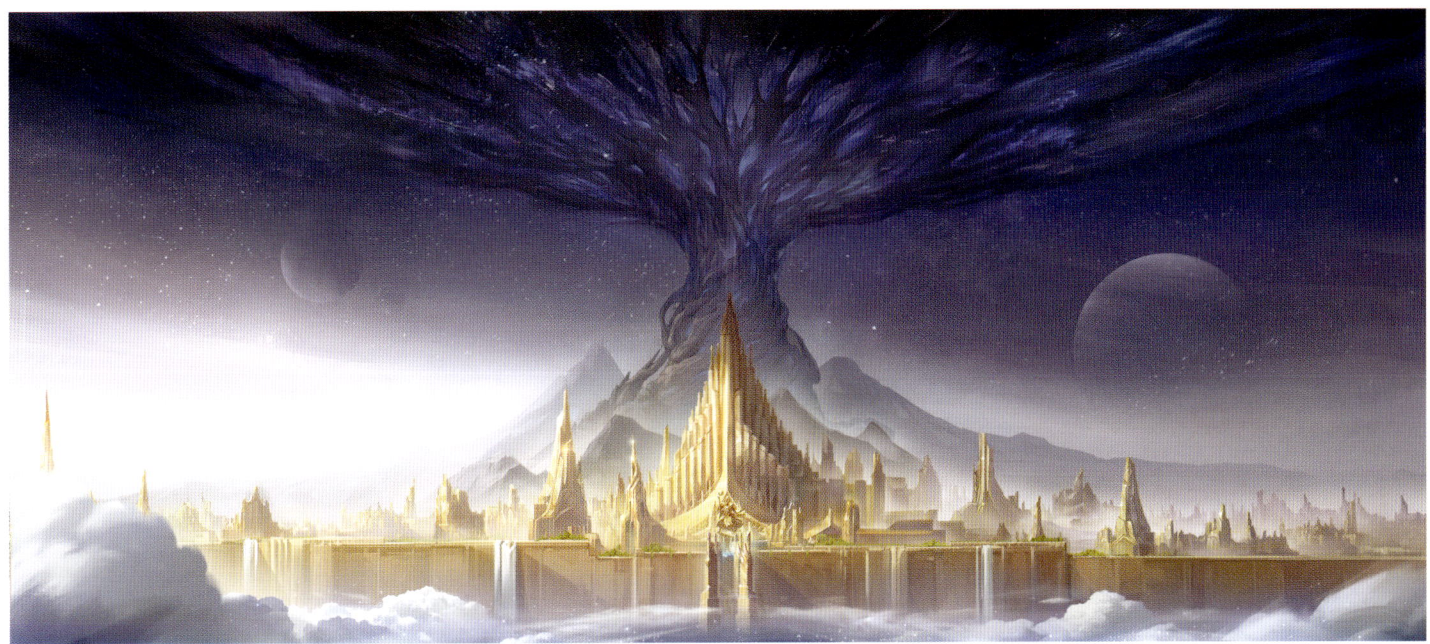

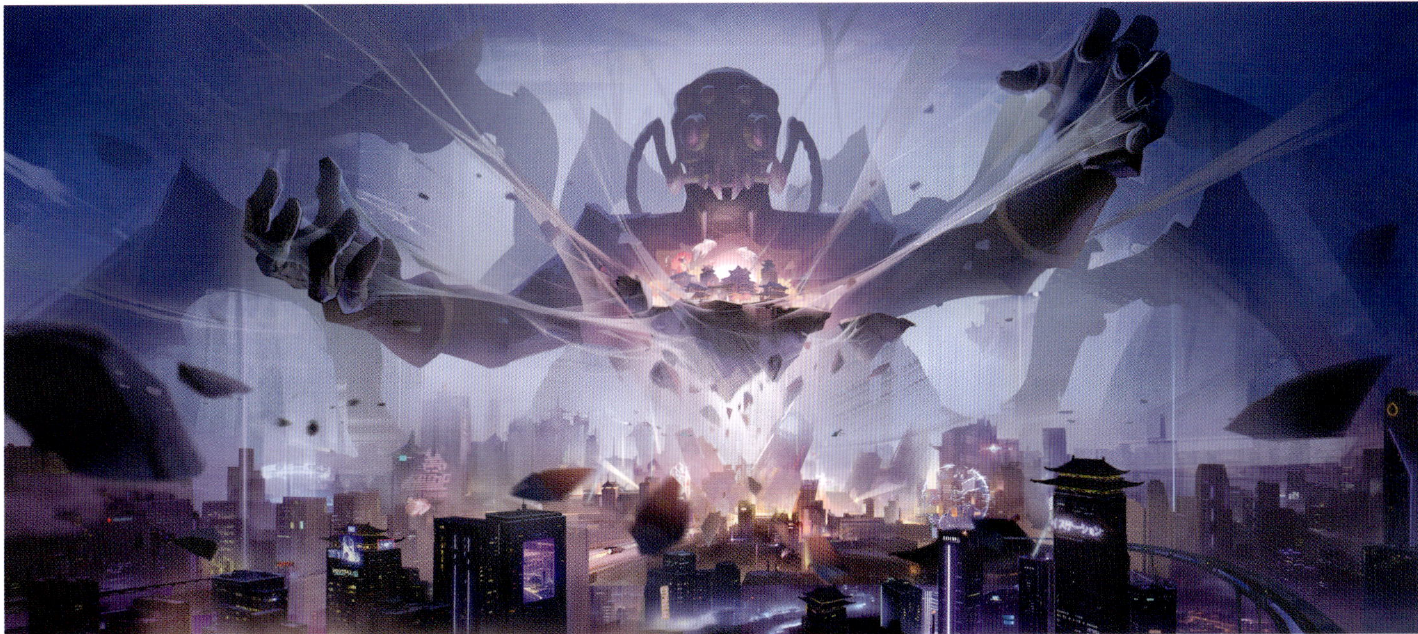

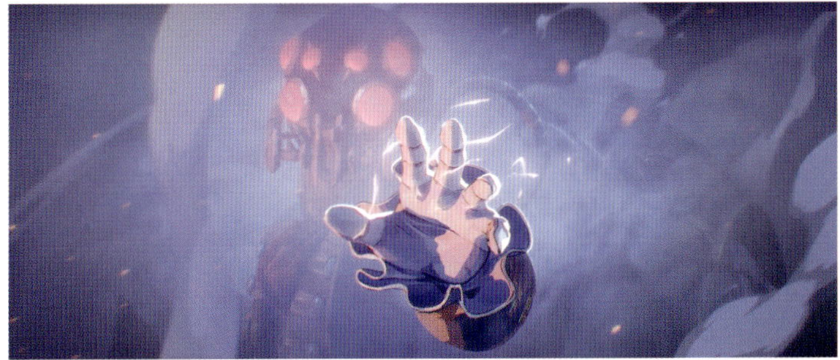

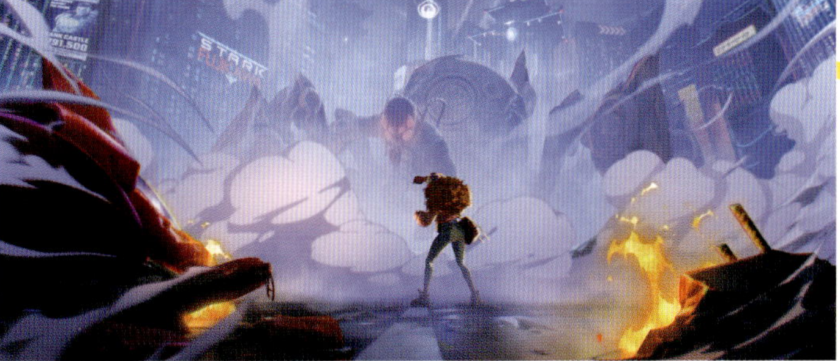

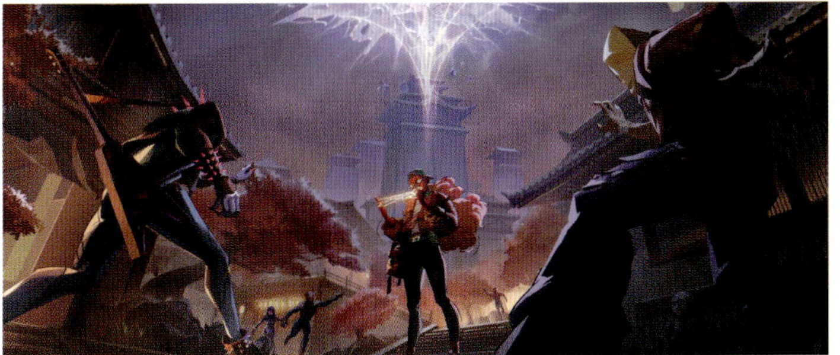

The loading animations for different maps narrate their background stories, assigning distinct missions and objectives to both sides of players. For instance, the loading animation for Yggsgard depicts Loki extracting the sap from Yggdrasill, while the loading animation of Tokyo 2099 showcases how the Master Weaver expelled his argumentative apprentice, Spider-Zero.

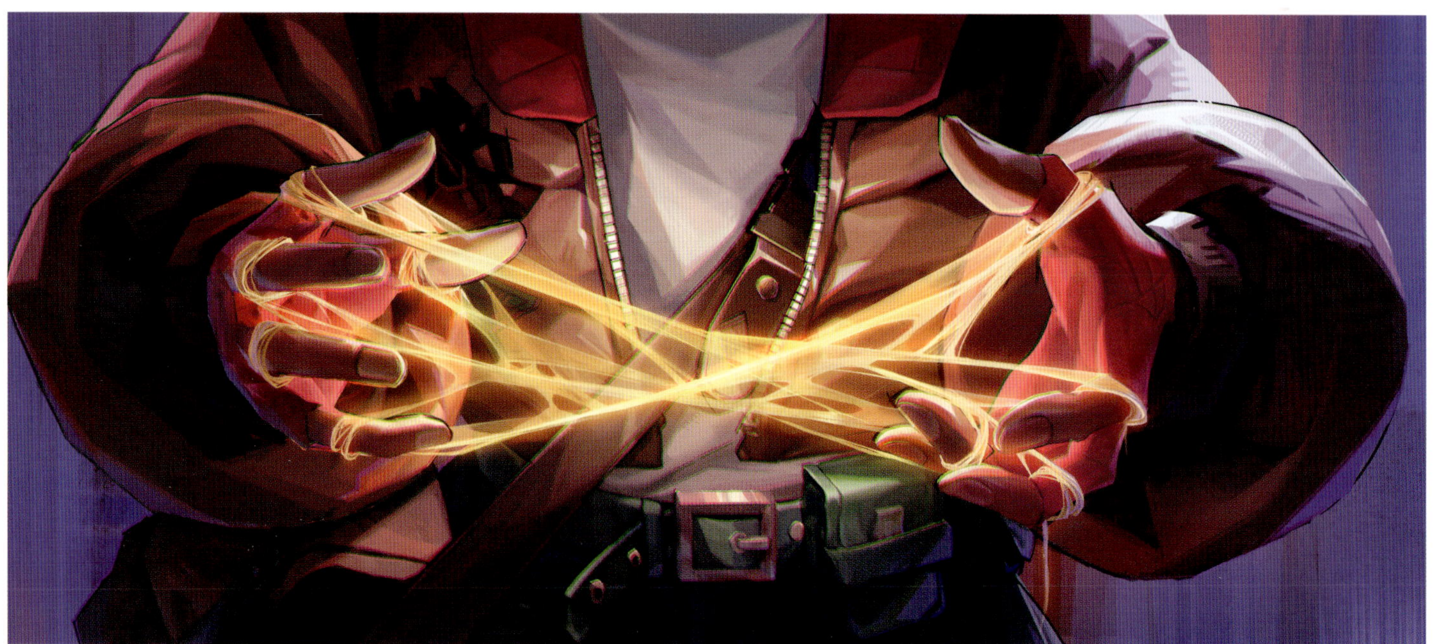

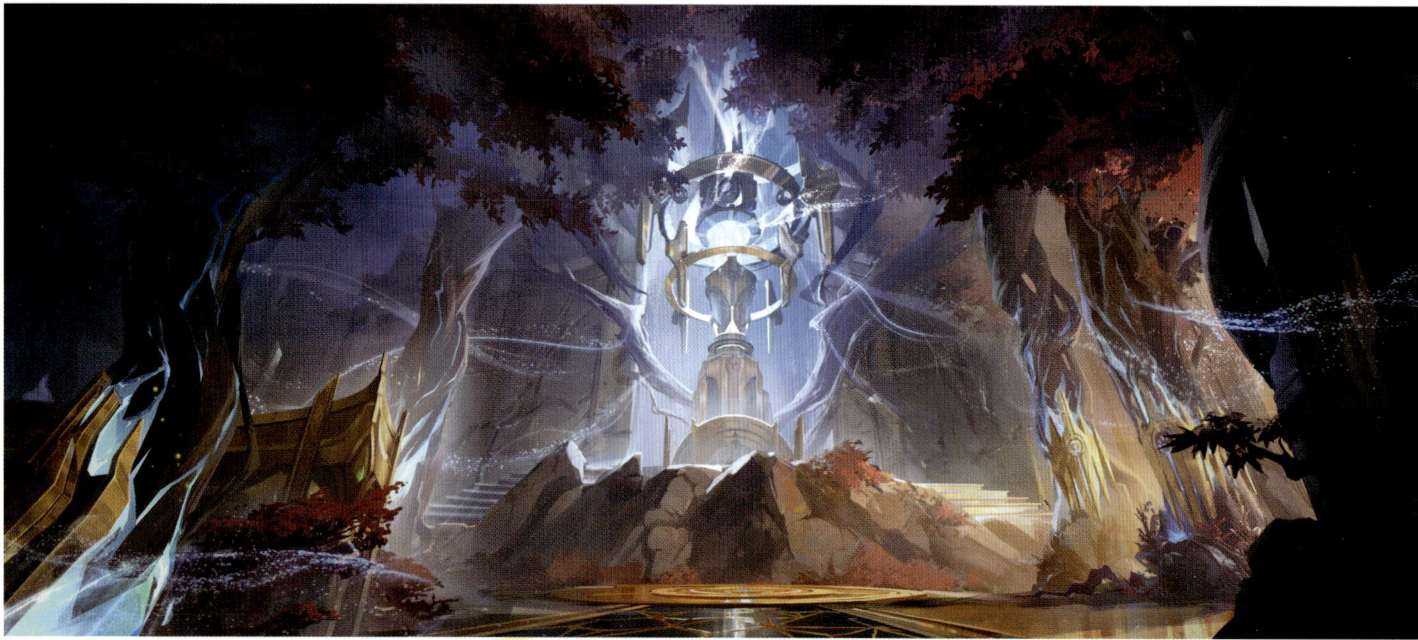

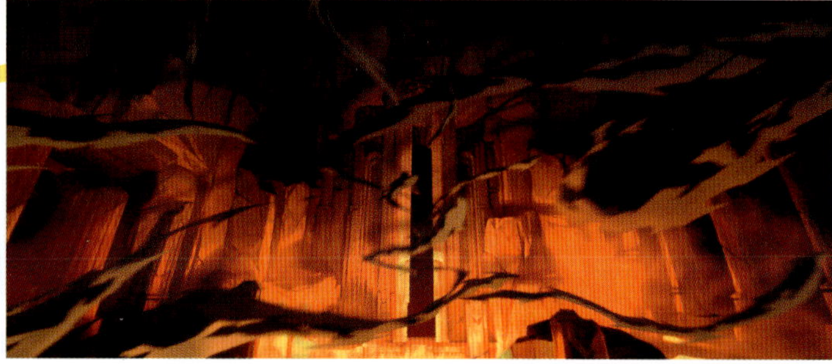

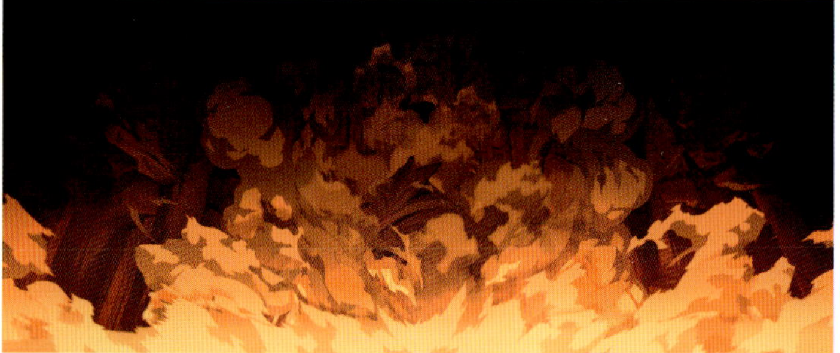

The ending animations for different maps showcase the impact or conclusion of the story following the players' victory. As a result, each map typically has two ending animations. Perhaps one victory allows Loki to firmly secure his throne, while another enables Spider-Zero to successfully return to Spider-Islands. Yet the next victory could just as easily twist everything in the opposite direction.

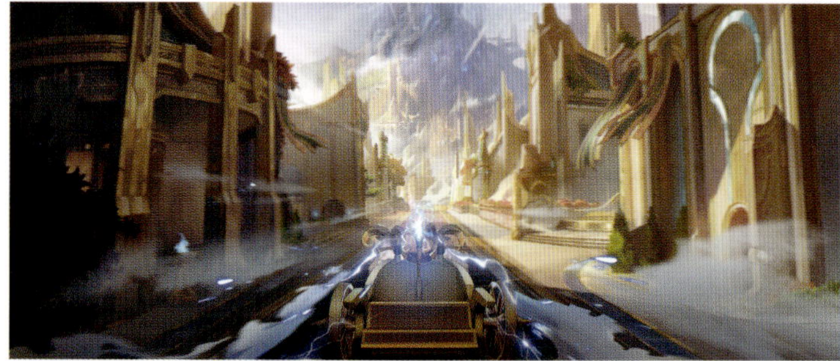

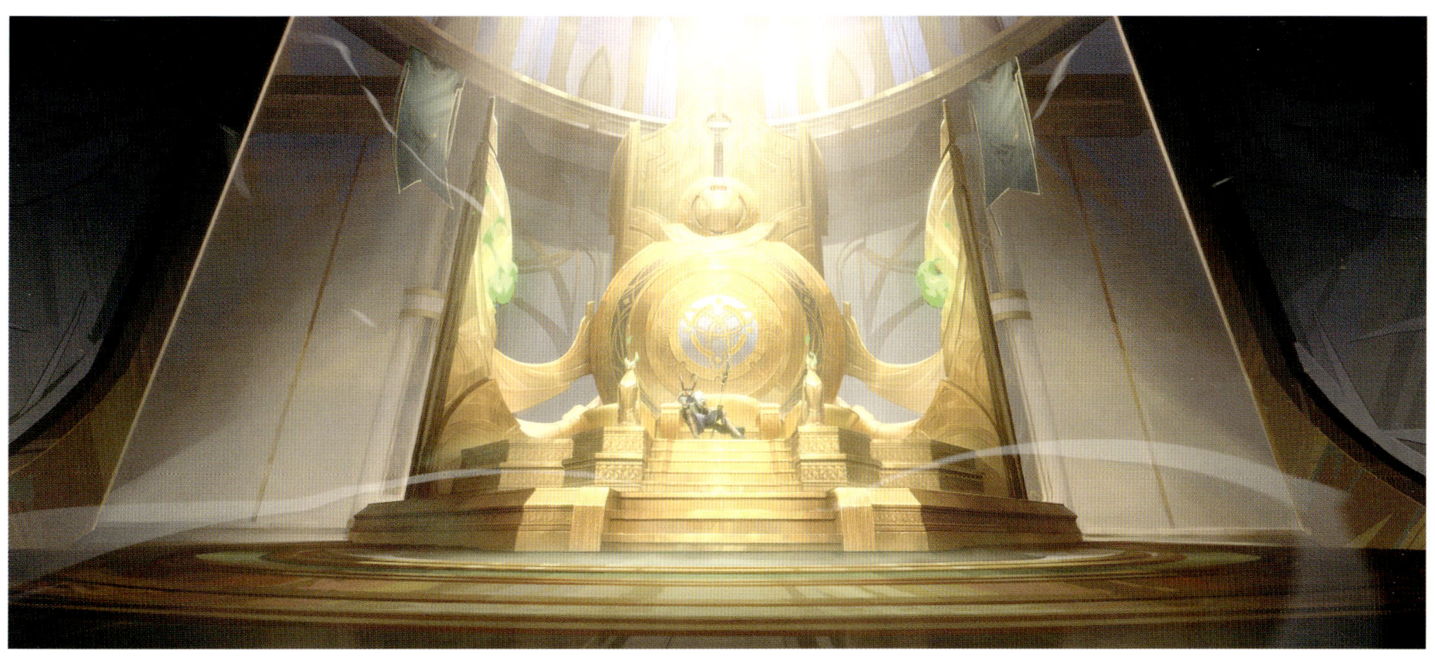

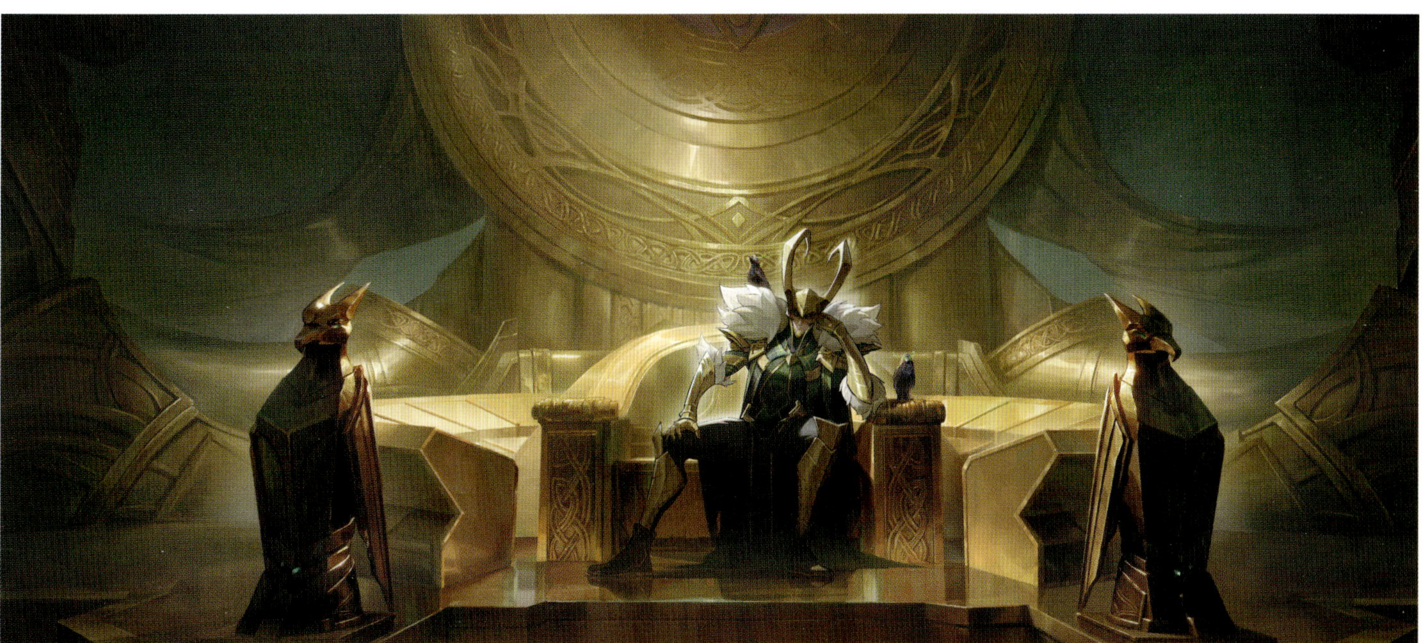

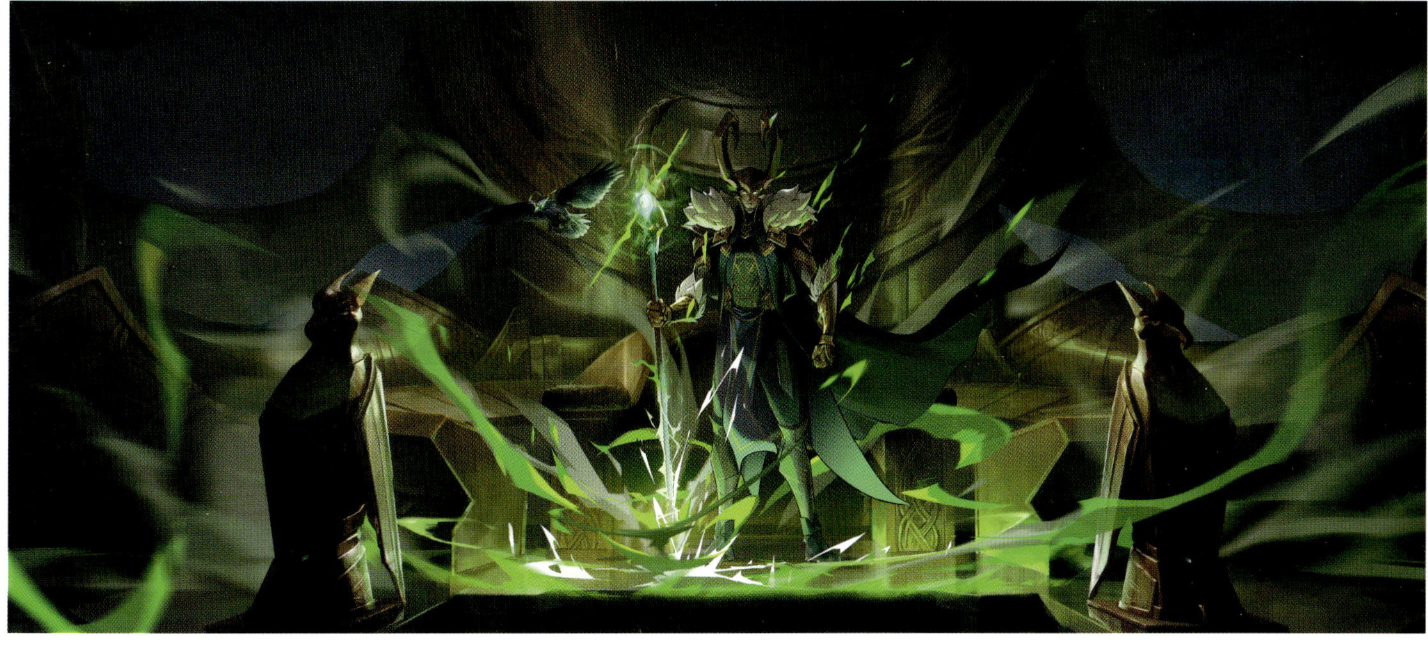

STORYBOARDS

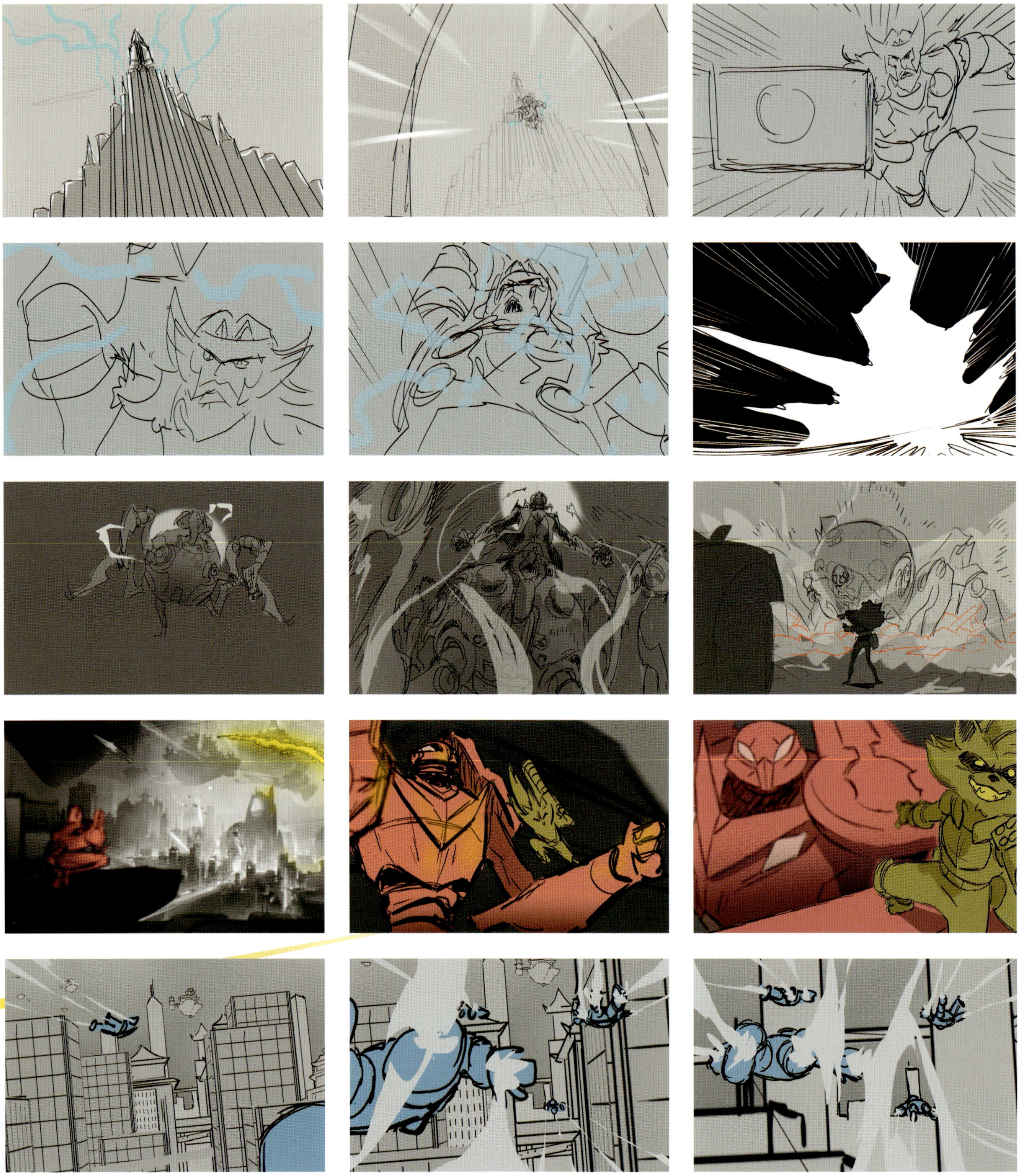

Although the storyboarding phase is often the time when our team finds it hardest to reach a consensus, the biggest advantage of sketches lies in the fact that any simple stroke or modification can give birth to a great shot in the final production. These are just some of many attempts we've made. Some are preserved in the finished product, while others remain as ideas for alternative universes.

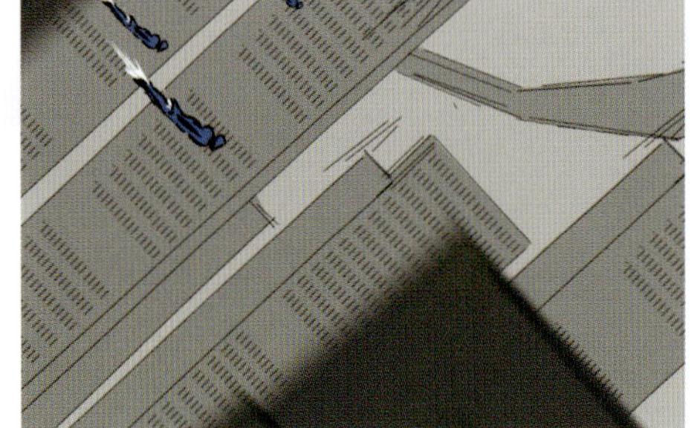

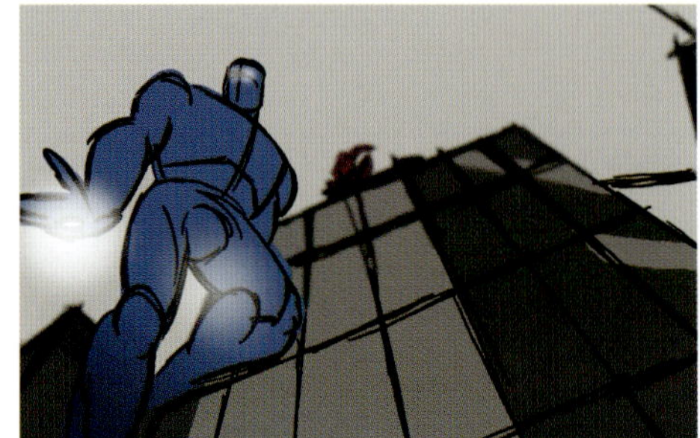